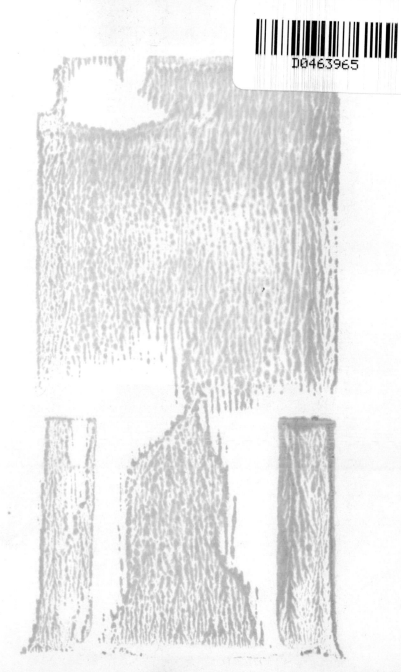

THE
MILLSTÄTTER EXODUS

The destruction of Pharaoh and the Egyptians. (Detail from Cod. lat. 13002, reproduced by courtesy of Bayerische Staatsbibliothek, Munich.)

THE
MILLSTÄTTER
EXODUS

A CRUSADING EPIC

BY

D. H. GREEN 1922.

Fellow of Trinity College and
Professor of Modern Languages in the
University of Cambridge

CAMBRIDGE
AT THE UNIVERSITY PRESS
1966

PUBLISHED BY
THE SYNDICS OF THE CAMBRIDGE UNIVERSITY PRESS
Bentley House, 200 Euston Road, London, N.W. 1
American Branch: 32 East 57th Street, New York, N.Y. 10022

©

CAMBRIDGE UNIVERSITY PRESS
1966

Printed in Great Britain at the University Printing House, Cambridge
(Brooke Crutchley, University Printer)

LIBRARY OF CONGRESS CATALOGUE
CARD NUMBER: 66–17059

CONTENTS

PREFACE

I TRUST it is not a bad omen that this book should need to be introduced with an apology for the inaccuracy of its subtitle. Had it been written in French it would have been easy to say, succinctly and adequately, *Une épopée des précroisades*. English lacks a suitable noun corresponding to *précroisades* so that, rather than fall back on a long-winded circumlocution, I have risked talking of the *Millstätter Exodus* as if it were indeed a fully fledged crusading epic. My reasons for thinking that it belongs instead to the immediate prehistory of this genre in German literature are given in the concluding chapter.

Because of its preparatory function the *Millstätter Exodus* therefore belongs only indirectly to the history of crusading literature. Wentzlaff-Eggebert, in his *Kreuzzugsdichtung des Mittelalters*, has devoted his attention mainly to works which belong explicitly to the genre, allowing no more than a few pages to such *Vorformen* as *Ezzos Gesang* and *Summa Theologiae*. The present work attempts to show that the *Millstätter Exodus* could with greater justification have been included amongst these *Vorformen* and thereby to demonstrate a fact too often ignored in Wentzlaff-Eggebert's survey: that the term crusading literature should include not merely works with an explicitly crusading theme, but also literature indirectly influenced by the crusades or whose crusading theme is no more than implicit.

It is a pleasure to record my warm thanks to colleagues who have helped in the writing of this book: Dr C. R. Dodwell, Mr E. P. M. Dronke and Dr R. A. Wisbey. Each has read either the whole manuscript or large parts of it. Only the author knows just how much he has profited from their stimulating and friendly criticism.

D. H. G.

Trinity College
Cambridge
May, 1966

ABBREVIATIONS

AfU	*Archiv für Urkundenforschung.*
AuCh	*Antike und Christentum.*
BBSIA	*Bulletin bibliographique de la Société Internationale Arthurienne.*
BJRL	*Bulletin of the John Rylands Library.*
CB	*Carmina Burana.*
GBA	*Gazette des Beaux-Arts.*
HJb	*Historisches Jahrbuch.*
HTR	*Harvard Theological Review.*
HZMTLG	*Handelingen van de Zuidnederlandse Maatschappij voor Taal- en Letterkunde en Geschiedenis.*
LG	*Literaturgeschichte* (further details will be found in the Bibliography under the author's name).
MA	*Medium Aevum.*
MF	*Minnesangs Frühling*, ed. C. von Kraus (Leipzig, 1944).
MGH	*Monumenta Germaniae Historica* (with the conventional abbreviations for the various sections).
MHG	Middle High German.
MLN	*Modern Language Notes.*
MPG	J. P. Migne, *Patrologiae cursus completus. Series Graeca.*
MPh	*Modern Philology.*
MPL	J. P. Migne, *Patrologiae cursus completus. Series Latina.*
MSD	K. Müllenhoff and W. Scherer, *Denkmäler deutscher Poesie und Prosa aus dem 8.–12. Jahrhundert*, 3rd ed. (Berlin, 1892).
NS	*Neuere Sprachen.*
OE	Old English.
OHG	Old High German.

ix

Abbreviations

ON	Old Norse.
OS	Old Saxon.
PBB	*Paul und Braunes Beiträge.* (H) stands for Halle and (T) for Tübingen.
R	*Romania.*
RHC	*Recueil des Historiens des croisades. Historiens occidentaux des croisades.*
RHR	*Revue de l'histoire des religions.*
WaG	*Welt als Geschichte.*
WuS	*Wörter und Sachen.*
WW	*Wirkendes Wort.*
ZAW	*Zeitschrift für alttestamentliche Wissenschaft.*
ZfdA	*Zeitschrift für deutsches Altertum.*
ZfdPh	*Zeitschrift für deutsche Philologie.*
ZRPh	*Zeitschrift für romanische Philologie.*

1   A Virtue defeating a Vice. (A wall-painting in the crypt at Tavant, reproduced by courtesy of Archives Photographiques, Paris.)

2 The destruction of Pharaoh and the Egyptians. (A ceiling-painting at Saint-Savin-sur-Gartempe, reproduced by courtesy of Archives Photographiques, Paris.)

3 The Vices. (From Cod. lat. 13002, reproduced by courtesy of
Bayerische Staatsbibliothek, Munich.)

4 The capture of Jerusalem. (Ms. fr. 352, f. 62, reproduced by courtesy of Bibliothèque Nationale, Paris.)

I

THE PROBLEM

ODERN scholarship in Germany has shown little sympathy with the genre of the biblical epic or with its
representative examples. Whatever attention Milton
may have attracted in England it cannot be said that his German
counterparts, or even his predecessors in Christian Latin literature, have succeeded in arousing enthusiasm for their artistic
virtues, even though their historical importance may be unchallenged. An extreme position has been adopted by E. R.
Curtius.[1] He is convinced of the incompatibility of the Christian
message of the Bible with the formal requirements of the classical
epic: any attempt to combine the two must lead to a loss of
authority in the biblical account as well as to its linguistic and
formal falsification. Curtius therefore regards the very attempt to
write a biblical epic as an indefensible compromise and the result
as a hybrid product. What for Otfrid had been the justification
of his undertaking to compose the *Evangelienbuch*—the wish to
clothe the truth of the biblical story in the only adequate form
known to him, that of classical literature[2]—is for Curtius the very
proof of his aesthetic failure. Whether they accept Curtius's
uncompromising rejection of the whole genre or not, most modern
readers would be likely to agree with him in the case of Otfrid
and regard this work,[3] however important its position in ninth-
century literature in Germany and however pervasive its influence

---

[1] *Europäische Literatur und lateinisches Mittelalter*, p. 459.
[2] See H. Rupp, *WW*, VII, 334 ff. In his description of the virtues of Christian
Latin literature (I, 1, 1 ff.) Otfrid reaches a peak in his remark:

> 29 *Ouh selbun buah frono   irreinont sie so scono;*
> *thar lisist scona gilust   ana theheiniga akust.*

[3] Cf. de Boor's choice of words (*LG*, I, 79—although in a context which seeks
to defend Otfrid from some of his critics!): 'weitschweifig, lehrhaft, schwer-
fällig', 'nicht Dichter von innerer Berufung'.

on other works, as an aesthetic failure. Nor would the situation, I suspect, be very different in so late a case as Klopstock. Yet the shortcomings of Otfrid are not enough to lead us to reject the genre in which he worked as mistaken in conception. Thus, Carolingian literature possesses, in addition to Otfrid, the impressive example of the Old Saxon *Heliand*, the aesthetic qualities of which have for long been more readily acknowledged than in the case of its Frankish counterpart.[1] In Old English literature, too, literary merits cannot be denied to a number of its biblical epics and, in any case, the artistry of a biblical epic tradition which, when applied to a secular theme, can produce some of the passages of *Beowulf* cannot be so devoid of aesthetic value as Curtius maintains. It is for reasons such as these that two contributions to this problem are particularly helpful in qualifying the force of Curtius's judgement. The first is a recent essay by Max Wehrli on 'Sacra Poesis: Bibelepik als europäische Tradition',[2] an illuminating survey of the genre which does much towards its rehabilitation. The second contribution, S. Beyschlag's *Habilitationsschrift* on the *Wiener Genesis*,[3] concerns us more nearly since the particular work he has interpreted antedates the *Millstätter Exodus*[4] by probably no more than sixty years. We

[1] E.g. A. Heusler, *ZfdA*, LVII, 45 ('Den Heliand als schöpferische Eindeutschung des biblischen Inhalts hat man oft unverständig überschätzt: seine Sprach- und Versgewalt kann man kaum überschätzen. Dieser Sachse ist einer der größten Stilmeister germanischer Zunge; "Stil" im Sinne einer kennzeichnenden, den ganzen Körper durchdringenden Formung'); G. Berron, *Studien zum Heliand als Kunstwerk*, p. 91 ('Der Heliandstil ist ein Spätstil, aber er ist ein Kunststil'). A recent analysis of the formal achievements of the Saxon author has been offered by J. Rathofer, *Der Heliand. Theologischer Sinn als tektonische Form.*

[2] In the Festschrift for F. Maurer, pp. 262 ff.

[3] *Die Wiener Genesis. Idee, Stoff und Form.* Beyschlag's concluding judgement on the achievement of the author of the *Wiener Genesis* (p. 128: 'sie ist Kunst in einem eigentlichsten Sinn als Formung: gegebenen Stoff in eine gegebene, doch lebendig-wandlungsfähige und schmiegsame Form zu gießen') is enough to show the difference between his attitude and that of Curtius.

[4] The edition which I have employed throughout is that by E. Kossmann. I have consistently refrained from collating Kossmann's edition with that of J. Diemer, *Genesis und Exodus nach der Milstäter Handschrift*, pp. 119 ff. (Vienna, 1862). To have done this on one occasion would have led me inevitably to editing the text afresh, and this was not my intention. I understand that this task has in fact been done by E. Papp, a pupil of W. Schröder at Marburg. In what follows

2

The problem

may therefore expect to learn something from the differences and similarities between these two biblical epics, both written towards the beginning of MHG literature as were the *Heliand* and the *Evangelienbuch* at the beginning of the written tradition in German literature. Beyschlag's double task (to evaluate the formal expansion of the *Wiener Genesis* to epic proportions and the connection between this and the changes in subject-matter) is the same as that which faces us in our analysis of the *Millstätter Exodus*.

Our starting-point for any discussion of the epic form of the *Millstätter Exodus* must be the observation made by Beyschlag on the earlier epic.[1] He sees in the *Wiener Genesis* an encounter with antiquity (in the double form of the two sources postulated for the German work: the Old Testament and Alcimus Avitus, a late representative of the Virgilian technique) which occurs at the start of the epic tradition in MHG literature and which may therefore help to explain its development up to the classics of courtly literature. Beyschlag also makes the point that with works later than the *Wiener Genesis*, for example the *Alexanderlied*, the epic tradition is already so far developed that any formal analysis is much more complex because of the probability of a variety of different influences. This is undoubtedly correct for most of the vernacular epics composed between the *Wiener Genesis* and the beginning of courtly literature, yet I question whether it is applicable to the *Millstätter Exodus*. The later author, whilst dependent on the Old Testament book as his source, is not known to have made direct use of any other work, whether a theological commentary[2] or the work of Alcimus

I use the forms Exodus (with a capital letter) to denote the biblical book, exodus (without a capital) to refer to the event from the history of Israel on which the biblical account is based and (*Millstätter*) *Exodus* (in italics) to designate the German poetic version. My use of such terms as 'the Millstatt epic' or 'the Millstatt author' is not meant to express any view as to the origin of the unknown author of our work. I make use of these terms merely because of their convenient brevity.

[1] *Die Wiener Genesis*, p. 3.

[2] I do not of course wish to deny that the German author was acquainted with theological commentaries on Exodus, but only to question whether he made *direct* use of them in composing his work. On this point I agree with Kossmann, *Die altdeutsche Exodus*, pp. 30 f.

Avitus which Beyschlag also suggests in passing[1] as a possible source for the *Exodus* as well as for the *Genesis*. In other words, the relationship between the *Exodus*, the second biblical epic in MHG literature, and its source appears to be even simpler than with the *Genesis*. It is this fact, together with the important consideration stressed by Beyschlag, that the *Exodus* is chronologically the next epic after the *Genesis* to allow of a direct comparison with its source,[2] which makes it so important to subject the *Millstätter Exodus* to that kind of analysis which Beyschlag employed so fruitfully for the earlier work. Such an analysis, and especially the similarities and differences between these first two biblical epics which it could suggest, might tell us more about the earliest development of the MHG epic.

If the epic expansion achieved by the Millstatt author is more thoroughgoing than that which Beyschlag has demonstrated for the author of the *Wiener Genesis*, the explanation is likely to be that the convention of the biblical epic became more firmly established in Germany between 1060 and 1120, even if this tradition did not immediately become so binding that works on the smaller scale were thereby excluded altogether.[3] To this extent we may agree with Beyschlag that the conditions which explain the epic form of the *Millstätter Exodus*, because they presuppose the force of the tradition which had been inaugurated two generations before, are already more complex than those in which the *Wiener Genesis* was composed. On the other hand, there are other factors which may explain the greater thoroughness with which the Millstatt author achieves epic proportions for his work and which make his task less complex than that which confronted the earlier author. He chose only the biblical account as his source and ignored the secondary sources which

---

[1] *WW*, v, 9 f. On my reasons for questioning the influence of Avitus on the *Millstätter Exodus* see p. 293, n. 2.

[2] How difficult it is even to determine the sources of a work such as the *Annolied*, for example, quite apart from any attempt to assess the originality of the German author by a comparison of his work with these sources, has recently been shown by D. Knab, *Das Annolied. Probleme seiner literarischen Einordnung.*

[3] Cf. the *Ältere Judith*, for example, or *Drei Jünglinge im Feuerofen*.

4

The problem

Beyschlag has emphasised for the author of the *Wiener Genesis* (Alcimus Avitus and the liturgical hymn). Furthermore, by concentrating on only one portion of the biblical book (the first fifteen chapters of Exodus, so that the account of what happened after the passage of the Red Sea is not treated) he made sure that his theme was now self-contained to an extent quite unrealised by the author of the *Wiener Genesis* with his essentially more detailed depiction of patriarchal history. This streamlining of his subject-matter by the Millstatt author serves therefore to compensate for the fact that, since he wrote at a time when the epic tradition in MHG literature had already begun, his historical position is necessarily more complex than that of the earlier author. It is thanks to this compensation that we may hope to avoid the greater complexities to which Beyschlag has drawn attention in the case of later epics and thereby to learn something of the Millstatt author's formal intentions and methods by a direct comparison of his work with his biblical source.

The formal aspect of our task (the analysis of the way in which our author achieves epic expansion of his biblical material) is therefore made easier for us than it was for Beyschlag in the case of the *Wiener Genesis* because the later author contents himself simply with his biblical source, but the same is by no means true of the second aspect, the interpretation of the subject-matter and of the author's intentions in choosing this particular theme. Here difficulties are caused precisely by the author's aesthetic tact in providing no more than indirect hints to his audience how they are to understand the significance of the biblical events, even though a final comment by him at the close of the narrative[1] makes it quite obvious that he intended an allegorical interpretation. In other words, we have to reject the idea that the Millstatt author is no more than a translator of the biblical Exodus into rhymed couplets, whose intentions were however restricted to the unambitious desire simply to render the Vulgate text into the vernacular[2]

---

[1] V. 3297. On the significance of this passage see below, pp. 119 f.

[2] Although vv. 18 ff. indicate that this was the author's intention, my point is that this was far from being his only intention.

5

for the benefit of his audience. His poetic task resembled that of the exegete to the extent that he had to extract the religious truth from the events narrated in his source and to make this truth apparent in his version[1]—it is this which the poet makes clear in his comment at the end of his narrative and we do him less than justice if we reject the possibility that he had the ability to achieve this. At the same time, his task as an epic poet differed from that of the exegete in that the religious truth he was concerned to make apparent in his work was far better left to speak for itself, to be implicit in the events described, rather than be explicitly underlined with a directness which may well be suited to the exegete, but which is too pointed for poetic statement. If we have learnt to appreciate such allusiveness as part of the tact shown by the authors of the courtly period[2] I see no reason why we should not entertain the same possibility in the case of an earlier clerical author who was certainly acquainted with the allegorical possibilities of his Exodus theme.

It is therefore his tact in exploiting these possibilities which creates difficulties in interpreting the *Millstätter Exodus* and in reconstructing its author's intentions. The problem is to decide which alternative is to be accepted in interpreting the work allegorically—or, indeed, to decide whether these alternatives

[1] On the similarity between the poet's task (in the case of Chrétien's *Erec*) and that of the exegete, cf. W. A. Nitze, *R*, XLIV, 14 ff., and also *BBSIA*, V, 78 ('Here we have the principle of Biblical exegesis or expansion taken over from the monastic schools and applied to secular literature. Consciously the poet gives the *matiere* of his story a *sensus* or meaning—a procedure already employed in the Thebes and Troy stories, and culminating in the four interpretations, literal, allegorical, moral, and anagogical, that were later given to the *Divina Commedia*').

[2] Cf. F. Ohly, *ZfdA*, LXXXIX, 19 ('Ist die Kenntnis der Methode spiritueller Worterhellung für die Bibeldichtung des Mittelalters unentbehrlich, so kann sie mit aller Vorsicht und dem nötigen Sinn für Dichterisches auch für die weltliche Dichtung fruchtbar gemacht werden'); E. Köhler, *Trobadorlyrik und höfischer Roman*, p. 16 ('Die höfische Dichtung hatte das Prinzip der geistlichen Schriftauslegung in den Dienst eines autonom-ständischen Menschenbildes gestellt, das die Geschichte einschließlich der Antike nach dem eigenen Wunschbild interpretierte'); Max Wehrli in the Festschrift for F. Maurer, p. 265 ('Es dürfte eines der wichtigsten Probleme der heutigen Erforschung mittelalterlicher Dichtung sein, ob und wieweit sich auch die weltliche Dichtung des Mittelalters nach diesen Methoden einer vielfältigen Exegese gerichtet hat').

The problem

are mutually exclusive and, if not, what their relationship is to one another. This problem is inseparable from that of medieval allegory in general, from the tradition of a fourfold meaning to be found in the Bible. As an example (referring not to the exodus itself, but to Jerusalem, the ultimate, positive goal of the exodus) we may take the theoretical definition of the four ways of interpreting the term Jerusalem given by Guibertus of Nogent in his *Quo Ordine Sermo fieri debeat*:

Quatuor sunt regulae Scripturarum, quibus quasi quibusdam rotis volvitur omnis sacra pagina: hoc est historia, quae res gestas loquitur; allegoria, in qua ex alio aliud intelligitur; tropologia, id est moralis locutio, in qua de moribus componendis ordinandisque tractatur; anagoge, spiritualis scilicet intellectus, per quem de summis et coelestibus tractaturi ad superiora ducimur. Verbi gratia Hierusalem, secundum historiam civitas est quaedam; secundum allegoriam, sanctam Ecclesiam significans; secundum tropologiam, id est moralitatem, anima fidelis cuiuslibet qui ad visionem pacis aeternae anhelat; secundum anagogen, coelestium civium vitam, qui Deum deorum facie revelata in Sion vident signat.[1]

This fourfold interpretation is not merely true of the term Jerusalem, but is equally applicable, in theory at least, to other events, objects and persons of the bible (*quibus... volvitur omnis sacra pagina*), among which we may include the exodus itself. Our task is therefore to decide which possible interpretation is implied by the Millstatt author[2] when he suggests, at the end of his work, that the events he has just narrated have a significance which far surpasses their historical importance.[3] We shall also have to inquire how the particular interpretation is suggested to his audience by the author and what importance he may have attached to it in choosing it as a basis for his vernacular version of the biblical story.

[1] *MPL*, 156, 25 D f.
[2] Or, indeed, whether there may not be an interplay between two or more interpretations.
[3] This is not meant to imply that the German author anywhere denies or minimises the importance of the literal or historical meaning of Exodus. Vv. 35 ff., where he sums up the contents of his source, are enough to refute this. See also below, pp. 128 ff.

7

The Millstätter Exodus

Two possible interpretations of the *Millstätter Exodus* may be briefly considered—not because their relevance to the work is necessarily less convincing, but rather because it is much easier to demonstrate the possibility of each of them than in the case of the interpretation advanced later. These two readings relate the events of the German epic to Christian baptism and to the Easter liturgy respectively.

The traditional equation of the passage of the Red Sea by the Israelites with Christian baptism has been demonstrated by F. J. Dölger in his article: 'Der Durchzug durch das Rote Meer als Sinnbild der christlichen Taufe'.[1] In applying Dölger's argument to the interpretation of the *Millstätter Exodus* we need not be deterred by the fact that the actual passage of the Red Sea, the only aspect of Exodus which is related to baptism, is no more than one event out of many described by the German author. The answer to this possible objection is that the passage of the Red Sea, the event which finally frees the Israelites from their bondage, is the most important event for the author: he has chosen to follow the Bible only as far as this,[2] he carefully groups his material so as to stress this scene as the climax,[3] and when he opens his work by summing up the theme he is about to relate it is significantly the Hebrews' return home from bondage which he mentions.[4] What precedes this final scene (the birth and youth of Moses, the covenant between God and Moses, the plagues of Egypt) is meant to explain it and to demonstrate in detail the power of the God whose final intervention in the Red Sea brings freedom to His people. There is therefore no real contradiction between the fact that it is only the passage of the Red Sea which is equated allegorically with baptism and the fact that the *Millstätter Exodus* contains so much more than this one event. The other events in the Millstatt work are no more than preliminaries, subordinated to the all-important happening by the Red Sea.

[1] *AuCh*, II, 63 ff. Dölger has also shown (*ibid.* pp. 70 ff.) that the same interpretation could also be given to the crossing of the Jordan, but this does not invalidate the case for the Red Sea.

[2] On the possible reasons for this decision see below, pp. 432 ff.

[3] See p. 44.   [4] Cf. vv. 35 ff.

The problem

Dölger accounts for the possibility that Christian baptism was equated with the passage of the Red Sea by suggesting two considerations. One is the obvious, tangible fact that the manner in which the baptizand stepped down into the baptistery (we have to imagine total immersion, not the sprinkling of water from a font) and emerged again on the other side could readily suggest the idea of passing through water, especially since the time of year for the baptism of new converts was commonly Easter or Pascha, the time at which the Jews celebrated their departure from Egypt.[1] Equally important is a linguistic observation made by Dölger.[2] He points out that, in accordance with the original meaning of *pascha* (the passage of the angel over the houses of the Israelites, sparing them but bringing death to the houses of the Egyptians), the Hebrew word can be translated by ὑπερβασία.[3] On the other hand, Philo of Alexandria translates it by διάβασις, in the sense of the Israelites passing over the Egyptian frontiers, and it is from this new meaning that he develops his moral interpretation: the transition from passion to the practice of virtue.[4] It is this interpretation which, according to Dölger, is taken over from the Hellenistic Jew Philo by the Alexandrian school of Christian exegetes[5] and which explains what becomes the conventional Christian interpretation of this event from Hebrew history as a prefiguration of Christian baptism. In this interpretation the moral reading equates Pharaoh with the devil and the Egyptians who accompany him as sins, washed off by the cleansing water of baptism, so that the newly baptised Christian is redeemed by the water of baptism, as the Israelites were saved by the waters of the Red Sea.

[1] *AuCh*, II, 63.
[2] *Ibid.* pp. 66 ff. See also J. Daniélou, *Sacramentum futuri*, pp. 182 f.
[3] E.g. by Flavius Josephus, *Antiquitates* II, 14, 6.
[4] Dölger cites here Philo's *De migratione Abrahami* 25, *De specialibus legibus* II, 146 and *De sacrificiis Abelis et Caini* 63.
[5] E.g. Clemens of Alexandria and Origen. It is also important for the future development of this interpretation in Western Europe that Ambrose should have here followed Philo (e.g. *De Cain et Abel* I, 8, 31: 'Pascha enim Domini transitus est a passionibus ad exercitia virtutis').

9

Echoes of this conventional interpretation of Exodus are to be found in the Millstatt work. In the first place, it can hardly be fortuitous that the German author, in a passage where he independently expands the biblical account, underlines Pharaoh's remarks on the differences between the Egyptian overlords and their Hebrew slaves by having the Egyptian ruler say of the Hebrews' rite of circumcision: *ʒe touffe wellent si daʒ haben* (v. 86). We shall later have to consider this remark,[1] but for the moment what concerns us is the fact that the author, instead of equating the Hebrews with the Christians by means of any other typological parallel between them, has specifically chosen the parallel circumcision: baptism, thereby granting himself an opportunity to refer explicitly to that Christian feature which traditional exegesis so frequently stressed in connection with the book of Exodus.

Clearly, this verse alone would not be enough to suggest that the allegorical equation of exodus with baptism was an important concern of the Millstatt author. It does, however, prepare us for a more revealing passage when God gives detailed instructions to Moses how the Jews are henceforth to celebrate the Passover, for here mention is three times made of the necessity to admit to this feast only those who are circumcised (vv. 2805, 2821 and 2829). Here two points need to be made. The first concerns the fact that Easter, as the Christian continuation of the Passover feast, was traditionally the period for the baptism of new converts,[2] so that the threefold mention of the Jewish rite of circumcision in the context of the Passover and its celebration, coupled with the equation between baptism and circumcision given so explicitly by the author at the start of his work, but tactfully removed from this vital passage, justifies us in reading these instructions on the Jewish feast as a prefiguration of the Christian festival of Easter and of its attendant baptismal rite. This is confirmed by a second point, for the German author introduces two further Christian

---

[1] See pp. 151 f.

[2] Cf. J. A. Jungmann, *The Early Liturgy*, p. 263: 'In between the lessons and the Mass, the sacraments were administered, especially Baptism, for on this night (i.e. Easter vigil) the neophytes were to rise together with Christ.'

The problem

details: the focal point of the ceremony is described as a Christian altar (v. 2824: *vrôn tiske*) and the ceremony itself is referred to explicitly as Easter (v. 2826: *die ôsteren begên*).[1] These references are enough to suggest that what is being described here is not the Jewish festival, but instead, by prefiguration, the Christian ceremony, so that the allusions to the fact that only the circumcised are to be admitted are intended to be read as applying to those who have been baptised in the Christian faith. It is this reading which, finally, explains why it is that the Millstatt author feels at liberty to devote a lengthy passage to a description of what is, on the face of it, a purely Jewish rite, for he elsewhere does not hesitate to drop biblical details which are too exclusively Jewish.[2] The explanation in this case must be, as he took pains to suggest as far back as v. 86, that his real intention was to emphasise the intimate connection between the festival of Easter and the sacrament of baptism.

To this possible interpretation of the *Millstätter Exodus* in terms of Christian baptism it could be objected that, although it might help to explain the detail of God's instructions to Moses on how the Jews are to celebrate the Passover, it does little to account for those scenes which have more obviously caught the author's attention and in which he dwells on the military splendour of the departing Israelites and of the Egyptians in pursuit. Such prolonged descriptions of knightly armies and their equipment, it might be argued, are hardly reconcilable with this typological interpretation. To meet this objection we have only to recall that the moral interpretation of Exodus by Philo of Alexandria inaugurated the Christian tradition of reading this book as a form of psychomachia, as an escape from sin to virtue, and that traces of a similar distinction between virtues (attributed to the Hebrews) and vices (shown by the Egyptians) can be detected in the German work.[3] In other words, it would be possible to defend the baptismal interpretation of the Millstatt epic by reference to the

[1] Cf. also v. 2541. On these Christian details see also pp. 152 f.
[2] See pp. 32 ff. and 138 ff.
[3] See p. 137, n. 1, pp. 169 f. and pp. 390 ff.

medieval tradition of psychomachia,[1] where the depiction of virtues and vices by painters and sculptors in medieval dress and armour would agree with the German author's knightly description of the Hebrews and Egyptians. Even though the precedent established by Prudentius is so compelling that the Virtues frequently appear as female warriors, as is the case with the painting in the crypt at Tavant,[2] where a dark red monster is transfixed by a lance wielded by a Virtue wearing a helmet, a chainmail coat and a long, ankle-length skirt, this is by no means always the practice. This is clearly shown by the psychomachia illustrations in the *Hortus Deliciarum*[3] and in the Shropshire church of Claverley,[4] where the contestants are depicted as male knights.

More important for us is the fact that a psychomachia could be illustrated not merely in terms of contemporary knighthood, but particularly with reference to the theme of the passage of the Red Sea. Here important testimony is provided by the biblical cycle in the church of Saint-Savin-sur-Gartempe whose chosen subjects, taken from the books of Genesis and Exodus, have been convincingly connected by P.-H. Michel with the theme of the psychomachia.[5] We need only dwell on the painting in which the Egyptians, following Pharaoh in his chariot, are engulfed in the Red Sea,[6] although we must recognise that his psychomachia interpretation of the other paintings in this cycle lends added weight to Michel's similar explanation of this particular scene. The drowning of Pharaoh in his chariot and of his horses dominates the centre of the scene; to the left (i.e. spatially: behind Pharaoh) are depicted Pharaoh's horsemen who are about to be

[1] On this tradition see especially A. Katzenellenbogen, *Allegories of the Virtues and Vices in Mediaeval Art*, and the contribution of H. R. Jauss ('Form und Auffassung der Allegorie in der Tradition der *Psychomachia*') to the Festschrift for W. Bulst, pp. 179 ff.

[2] See Pl. 1.

[3] See *Hortus Deliciarum. Le 'Jardin des Délices' de Herrade de Landsberg*, pl. 8.

[4] See E. W. Tristram, *English Medieval Wall Painting. The Twelfth Century*, pp. 48 f. and pls. 72 and 73.

[5] *GBA*, XL, 319 ff.   [6] See Pl. 2.

overwhelmed by the waters, so that some on the left of this group are shown looking to the left (i.e. behind them) in their wish to escape (cf. Exod. 14. 25).[1] The Israelites are not depicted in the act of crossing the sea, but instead we see to the right of Pharaoh (i.e. in front of him) a scene with the angel of the Lord, the column of fire and the Israelites following Moses who is leading them, without even a glance backwards on his part, from the bondage of Egypt and from the scene of Pharaoh's downfall.[2] In interpreting this impressive painting as a psychomachia Michel refers to St Bernard's sermon on Cant. 1. 8 ('Equitatui meo in curribus Pharaonis assimilavi te, amica mea').[3] St Bernard begins his sermon by equating the passage of the Red Sea with baptism and the drowned Egyptians with the sins washed away by baptism: 'In exitu Israel de Aegypto, geminoque illo admirabilis maris obsequio, et transitum scilicet populo dantis, et ultionem de hostibus, baptismi gratia evidenter exprimitur, salvantis homines, et crimina submergentis.'[4] Michel uses this parallel to interpret the scene at Saint-Savin as depicting in the drowning of the Egyptians not the destruction of men, but the destruction of the sins of men, of our sins—an interpretation which fits in with the underlying psychomachia theme he has established for the whole cycle. He might also have quoted from other passages in this same sermon to strengthen his case, as for example when St Bernard directly equates the liberation of the bride from the yoke of sin after the mortification of the works of the flesh with the liberation of Israel from the bondage of Egypt after the destruction of Pharaoh's chariots.[5] The comparison of the bride with a

[1] This scene is reproduced in H. Focillon, *Peintures romanes des églises de France*, pl. 32.
[2] *Ibid.* pls. 34 and 35.
[3] *GBA*, XL, 326. The dating of the Saint-Savin cycle (c. 1100) would exclude any appeal to St Bernard's sermon as a direct source for the painter, but nonetheless his argument loses none of its force as an illustration of the manner in which this biblical episode could be understood in the twelfth century.
[4] *MPL*, 183, 977 C.
[5] *Ibid.* 978 A: 'Et primum quidem est, quod eam assimilavit equitatui suo in curribus Pharaonis, liberandoque utique a jugo peccati, mortificatis universis operibus carnis; quemadmodum ille populus liberatus est a servitute Aegypti, subversis et submersis cunctis curribus Pharaonis.'

13

The Millstätter Exodus

whole army serving the Lord is justified by reference to her virtues, constituting a psychomachia in their conflict with the foe: 'Nec miraberis unam animam equitatus multitudini similatam, si advertas quantae in ipsa una, quae tamen sancta anima sit, virtutum acies habeantur; quanta in affectionibus ordinatio, quanta in moribus disciplina, quanta in orationibus armatura, quantum in actionibus robur, quantus in zelo terror, quanta denique ipsi cum hoste conflictuum assiduitas, numerositas triumphorum.'[1] The military terms employed by St Bernard to describe the virtues of the bride, explicitly seen in the context of the passage of the Red Sea, may be compared with the military scenes of the Millstatt epic, whose author uses contemporary knightly vocabulary as readily as the psychomachia illustrators depict their conflicts in terms of contemporary armour and weapons. Finally, when St Bernard emphasises that the tyrant Pharaoh, still in his own day, pursues Israel in its departure from Egypt (...*in his etiam his diebus exeuntem Israel de Aegypto insequitur*[2]—he refers, of course, typologically to Christendom as the new Israel), he is doing no more than the Millstatt author in pointing out that the psychomachia interpretation of Exodus or baptism reveals a conflict which is timeless and that the military confrontation described in Exodus has lost none of its relevance for the present day.[3]

A final example of the manner in which a twelfth-century psychomachia could be conceived in military and contemporary terms and as the truth conveyed by the passage of the Red Sea is provided by a scene from a pair of twin Regensburg miniatures of about 1165.[4] The two pictures are each divided into six compartments, every one of which (apart from those entitled *Filia*

---

[1] *MPL*, 183, 978 D.

[2] *Ibid.* 981 B.

[3] On this aspect of the Millstatt work see below, pp. 123 ff.

[4] The scene in question is given in the frontispiece and the miniature from which it is taken in Pl. 3. For a discussion of the miniature see A. Boeckler, *Die Regensburg–Prüfeninger Buchmalerei des XII. und XIII. Jahrhunderts*, pp. 24 ff., and A. Katzenellenbogen, *Allegories of the Virtues and Vices in Mediaeval Art*, p. 57. The miniature with the complementary virtues is reproduced in both these works (fig. 16 and fig. 55 respectively).

The problem

Babilonis and *Filia Syon* respectively) illustrates a particular sin or virtue by reference to an episode from Old Testament history (in one case from classical history: the imprisonment of Croesus). In each compartment a personified vice or virtue is depicted and named so that the meaning of the scene may be more readily grasped. To illustrate the sin of *potentia* (violence: it is opposed to the virtue of *mansuetudo*) the artist has depicted the scene of the destruction of Pharaoh's chariots (explicitly named as such), showing his followers in knightly helmets and chainmail and equipped with contemporary shields. It is true that this particular illustration has no reference to baptism, but I draw attention to this example only to show that a twelfth-century German artist, like the Millstatt author, could readily interpret this scene as a psychomachia and conceive it in military, i.e. knightly terms. If the Millstatt author further suggests the parallel between this scene and baptism as a psychomachia he by no means stands alone in this, as we have seen. Likewise, even though the similarity between the Regensburg miniaturist and the Millstatt author would have been closer if the artist had agreed with the poet in seeing in this scene not an illustration of *potentia*, but an example of *ubirmuot* or *ruom* (instead he takes the suicide of Saul, I Sam. 31. 4, as an illustration of *gloria* and the hanging of Haman, Est. 7. 10, as a case of *honoris appetentia*), my point is not so much that the artist and the poet agree in details as rather that they both describe this scene from Exodus in terms of a psychomachia in which not all sins are represented by the Egyptians, but one sin in particular. Why the Millstatt author should have chosen *ubirmuot* or *ruom* as the sin of which the Egyptians were guilty in this scene will later engage our attention,[1] but for the moment we may observe that there are contemporary parallels for his interpretation of the passage of the Red Sea as a military, even knightly psychomachia and for the close connection which he suggests between this and Christian baptism.

The second possible allegorical interpretation of the *Millstätter Exodus* concerns the close connection between the events of

[1] See below, pp. 169 f.

The Millstätter Exodus

Exodus and the Easter liturgy.[1] That such a connection should exist is explained by their common concern with the historical fact of the redemption achieved by Christ since, as we shall see, the Old Testament Exodus was frequently interpreted typologically as a prefiguration of the salvation of mankind by Christ and it is this same historical event which is commemorated in the liturgy of the period preceding Easter.[2] Furthermore, as J. Daniélou has made amply clear,[3] it was already the case that certain books of the New Testament not merely establish a parallel between Moses and Christ, but even present the life of Christ in terms of the new exodus announced by the prophets.[4] If the connection between exodus and Christ is established so early as this, there is little reason to be surprised at the frequency of the allusions to Exodus in the liturgy of the days in which Christ's liberation of His people is celebrated.

These paschal references to Exodus fall into a number of distinct groups.[5] The most important concerns the equation of

[1] I am indebted to E. P. M. Dronke and to R. A. Wisbey for first drawing my attention to the possibilities of this interpretation.

[2] See also J. A. Jungmann, *The Early Liturgy*, p. 25 : 'Even in the Old Testament, Easter was the feast par excellence; it was the feast commemorating the liberation from Egypt and the journey to the promised land. God so directed events in the history of salvation that the Redemption of the world by our Lord in the New Testament was seen as the fulfilment of what was prefigured in the Old Testament even to the days on which it occurred. There, liberation from the slavery of Pharaoh; here, liberation from the slavery of Satan; there, setting out to the promised land; here, the opening up of the eternal kingdom of God.'

[3] *Sacramentum futuri*, pp. 135 ff. See also G. Hebert, *When Israel came out of Egypt*, pp. 112 ff.

[4] See below, p. 112, n. 3.

[5] It goes without saying that the liturgical references to Exodus which may be regarded as relevant to the Millstatt author's conception of his theme are all to be found in the liturgy of Good Friday and of Holy Saturday before the twelfth century. To establish this I have mainly followed J. W. Tyrer, *Historical Survey of Holy Week, its Services and Ceremonial*, but also L. Eisenhofer, *Grundriß der Liturgik des römischen Ritus* (5th edn, ed. J. Lechner). For the passages I have adduced from the liturgy of Good Friday the evidence is as follows. Although the ninth-century *Ordo Romanus primus* does not specify what the two *lectiones* were, the agreement of all documents of the Roman rite of whatever age makes it almost certain that the second of these was in fact Exod. 12. 1 ff. (Tyrer, *op. cit.* p. 120). The inclusion of the Passion from Joh. 18. 1 ff. is already to be found in the *Ordo Romanus primus* (Tyrer, *op. cit.* p. 120). On the *Improperia* Eisenhofer

16

the paschal lamb (Exod. 12. 1 ff.) with Christ, an equation which lies at the heart of most interpretations of the crucifixion as a fulfilment of Old Testament prophecies. Thus the liturgy of Good Friday includes as its second *lectio* the passage from Exodus (12. 1–11) where the commemoration of the Hebrews' delivery from Egypt by means of the yearly sacrifice of the paschal lamb is enjoined upon the Jews by God. Later in the service, where the Passion is recited, it is the text of Joh. 18. 1– 19. 42 which is given with its reference, when mentioning that Christ's bones were not broken on the cross (Joh. 19. 33), to the injunction contained in Exod. 12. 46 (Joh. 19. 36: 'Facta sunt enim haec, ut Scriptura impleretur: Os non comminuetis ex eo'). The liturgy of Holy Saturday likewise provides two allusions to the paschal lamb: the blessing of the paschal candle contains a reference, brief in itself but significant in its context,[1] to Christ as the true Lamb with whose blood the door-posts of the faithful are consecrated ('Haec sunt enim festa paschalia, in quibus verus ille Agnus occiditur, cujus sanguine postes fidelium consecrantur'), and in the ninth *lectio* the same passage from Exodus on the paschal lamb is given as in the second *lectio* for Good Friday.

A second theme in the liturgy of these two days is that of liberation, where the rescue of the Hebrews is seen in connection with the redemption of mankind by Christ. This is a theme which plays an important part in the liturgy of Good Friday, where the

says (p. 133) that traces of them are to be found in the seventh century, but that they appear in tenth-century France and a little later in the Roman liturgy. For Holy Saturday the evidence is equally clear. Already in Gallican sacramentaries of about 700 (from which it spread to the Roman rite and to most of the Western rites) the blessing of the paschal candle consists of three parts, of which the last is the blessing proper (Tyrer, *op. cit.* pp. 151 f.). In the twelve *lectiones* used in the liturgy of Holy Saturday the employment of Exod. 12. 1 ff. is attested as early as the Gelasian sacramentary of the early eighth century (Tyrer, *op. cit.* p. 158, who also says, p. 159, that the sequence of lessons, canticles and collects is of considerable antiquity, occurring in MSS of the latter half of the eighth century). On the *Praefatio* of the vigil mass no more need be said than what Tyrer (p. 169) says of this mass at large: that it shows hardly any change from the eighth century to the present day.

[1] This passage is followed by the *haec nox* references which are discussed below, pp. 19 f.

17

The Millstätter Exodus

Improperia dwell at length on the contrast between the assistance rendered to Israel by God and the scorn which they in turn have shown Christ. Here the important point for us is that, apart from two quite general references to God's favours shown to Israel ('Ego quidem plantavi te vineam meam speciosissimam' and 'Ego te exaltavi magna virtute'), all the passages illustrating God's unfailing assistance refer to events from Exodus. It is God who led His people out of Egypt ('Quia eduxi te de terra Aegypti'), who led them through the desert, who fed them with manna and guided them into the Promised Land ('Quia eduxi te per desertum quadraginta annis, et manna cibavi te, et introduxi te in terram satis bonam'), who struck the firstborn of Egypt for their sake ('Ego propter te flagellavi Aegyptum cum primogenitis suis'), who led them out of Egypt and drowned Pharaoh in the Red Sea ('Ego eduxi te de Aegypto, demerso Pharaone in Mare Rubrum'), who opened the sea for them ('Ego ante te aperui mare'), who went before them in the column of cloud ('Ego ante te praeivi in columna nubis'), who fed them with manna ('Ego te pavi manna per desertum'), who gave them water from the rock ('Ego te potavi aqua salutis de petra'), who struck the kings of Canaan for their sake ('Ego propter te Chananaeorum reges percussi') and who gave them kingship over their lands ('Ego dedi tibi sceptrum regale'). In each case God's act of assistance is contrasted with the fact of the crucifixion or with a detail from the process of crucifixion in which the Jews show their scorn for God, so that the parallel which is here established is not merely one of contrast (between God's constant loyalty and the Jews' ingratitude), but also a typological parallel between the events of Exodus and those of the crucifixion. Against this the liturgy of Holy Saturday contains, in the blessing of the candle, only one indirect reference to the redemption of exodus, where the sacrifice of the Son is seen as made for the liberation of the slave ('O inaestimabilis dilectio caritatis: ut servum redimeres, Filium tradidisti!'). Here the slave signifies the fact of Israel's bondage in Egypt (Exod. 1. 14), but also man's bondage to sin; the sacrifice is likewise that of the paschal lamb or of Christ, each of which

18

The problem

is the means through which redemption is brought to Israel or to mankind respectively.

A last group of references to Exodus occurs only in the liturgy of Holy Saturday, but is emphatic enough to impart a particular note of urgency to the form of this service. Each of these references stresses the fact that it was *on this night* that redemption was accomplished and that the decisive event in the liturgical year is so soon to be commemorated. We have already considered the reference in the blessing of the candle to the fact that it is today that the true Lamb is sacrificed ('Haec sunt enim festa paschalia...'),[1] but this is followed emphatically by a fourfold repetition stressing the importance of this night. It is on this night that God led our fathers out of Egypt and through the sea ('Haec nox est, in qua primum patres nostros, filios Israel, eductos de Aegypto, Mare Rubrum sicco vestigio transire fecisti'), that the darkness of sin was driven away by the brilliance of the column of fire ('Haec igitur nox est, quae peccatorum tenebras columnae illuminatione purgavit'), that all who believe in Christ are removed from the darkness of sin and given back to grace ('Haec nox est, quae hodie per universum mundum in Christo credentes, a vitiis saeculi, et caligine peccatorum segregatos, reddit gratiae, sociat sanctitati') and that Christ victoriously defeated death ('Haec nox est, in qua, destructis vinculis mortis, Christus ab inferis victor ascendit'). By the conjunction of the first two of these parallel passages (stressing the redemption achieved in the exodus) with the second two (where Christ's conquest over sin and death is praised) greater emphasis is implicitly given to the close connection between the liberation of the Jews in their exodus and the salvation of mankind in Christ's victory. Soon after this passage the blessing of the candle is concluded by a passage which once more stresses the blessedness of this night (*O vere beata nox...*), which praises its ability to drive away sins and to wash away guilt (*fugat scelera, culpas lavat*— as in the baptismal interpretation of Exodus) and its capacity, not merely to restore peace, but also to bring low the powerful

[1] See p. 17.

The Millstätter Exodus

(...*et curvat imperia*—as with Pharaoh). When, after the blessing, the candles are lit this night is once more praised for the robbing of the Egyptians and the enriching of the Hebrews ('O vere beata nox, quae exspoliavit Aegyptios, ditavit Hebraeos!'), a typological reference to Christ's descent into hell and to His liberation of the patriarchs. Finally, in the *Praefatio* of the vigil mass for Holy Saturday the importance of praising God on this occasion is stressed by a concluding reference to the paschal lamb ('Te quidem, Domine, omni tempore, sed in hac potissimum nocte gloriosius praedicare, cum Pascha nostrum immolatus est Christus. Ipse enim verus est Agnus...'). Each one of these *haec nox* references thus derives its force from the constant parallelism between the events of the Jewish exodus and those of the crucifixion and redemption.[1]

Yet to demonstrate that the liturgy of Good Friday and Holy Saturday had an influence on the Millstatt author in the composition of his work it would not be sufficient to show the relevance of the biblical Exodus to the liturgy, for one would also have to show direct traces of the liturgical conception of Exodus in the German work. The cases where this can be done may well be few but, as with the equation of Exodus with baptism, they are significant. When Pharaoh reacts to Moses' first request for permission to lead the Israelites out of Egypt by angrily ordering their slave-labour to be intensified, the author says of the Hebrews

[1] Welcome confirmation is provided by the OE *Exodus*. This poem has been convincingly interpreted with reference to the Easter liturgy (see J. W. Bright, *MLN*, xxvii, 97 ff. and also C. W. Kennedy, *The Earliest English Poetry*, pp. 178 f.: 'The Old English poem must be considered, in some sense, a *carmen paschale* growing out of one of the most significant ceremonials of the Christian year'). This gives added significance to the pointed time-reference in v. 47 of the English poem (*Dæg wæs mære*), which has been interpreted with reference to Exod. 12. 14, 42 and 13. 3, as well as to the employment of Ps. 117. 24 in the gradual on the first six days of the Easter period (see also p. 413, n. 2). The OE poem therefore gives convincing support to the paschal interpretation of the MHG epic.

Another kind of reference in the liturgy of Holy Saturday, of less importance than the other groups, consists of the two psychomachia allusions towards the beginning of the service: 'et adjuva nos contra ignita tela inimici, et illustra gratia caelesti' and also 'expulsa diabolicae fraudis nequitia, virtus tuae majestatis assistat'.

20

The problem

(vv. 1091 ff.): 'si îlten dare gâhen | dâ si die boten sâhen, | die got gesant hête | der verdammôten diete, | diu dâ was in sorgen | den abent unde den morgen. | si hêten weinôt unde wuoft, | chlagennes alzoges genuoch.' The interpretation of this passage must turn on the metaphysical (not simply secular) function of the verb *verdammôn*,[1] for the employment of this particular verb in this context shows that, behind the literal meaning that the Hebrews had been condemned to slavery by the tyrant Pharaoh, the author wished to suggest the image of those who had been condemned to a place where there is wailing and gnashing of teeth and from which only Christ could redeem them by the new exodus foretold by the prophets. The author is therefore describing not merely the fate of the Hebrews in Egypt, but also that of the patriarchs, released from hell by the victorious descent of Christ. Since it is precisely on this plane that the liturgy of Holy Saturday employs its Exodus references we may assume a direct connection between the liturgy and the vernacular epic. A similar conclusion is suggested by the manner in which the Millstatt author refers to the Hebrews' spoliation of Egypt on their departure by means of the verb (*be*)*roubôn* (vv. 683, 2749, 3000). If we are to associate this choice of verb with the occurrence of *exspoliare* in the liturgy of Holy Saturday when the candles are lit,[2] rather than with the biblical *spoliare*,[3] then this

[1] *Trübners Deutsches Wörterbuch* (s.v.) suggests that the word was borrowed from Latin after the Second Sound-Shift, probably as part of the missionary activity of the eighth century, because there existed no need to take over this word in its purely secular meaning. This predominantly metaphysical meaning of the word (also implied by the absence of the term from K. F. Freudenthal's survey of legal terminology, including the concept *judicare*, in *Arnulfingisch-karolingische Rechtswörter*) is suggested by Otfrid's usage of the term (to mean religious damnation, whether literally or in terms of a parable—see J. Kelle, *Glossar der Sprache Otfrids*, s.v.) and by Notker's similar employment of the noun *ferdamnunga* (see E. H. Sehrt and W. K. Legner, *Notker-Wortschatz*, s.v.). When, however, Notker once uses *ferdamnôn* of Pilate's condemnation of Christ, just as does Otfrid on one occasion only (iv, 23, 9), this is probably as a means of heightening the impression of the injury done to Christ's majesty, rather than an example of secular employment of this verb.

[2] 'O vere beata nox, quae exspoliavit Aegyptios, ditavit Hebraeos!'

[3] This verb occurs in Exod. 3. 22 and 12. 36, corresponding to vv. 683 and 2749 of the German work respectively. V. 3000 has no literal counterpart in the bible.

can only be justified by a characteristic of the German author which will occupy us later: he is at pains to expunge from his account any suggestion which the biblical version may still imply that the Hebrews acted in any way deceitfully in their dealings with the Egyptians.[1] If, despite this marked tendency to remotivate the biblical account on this score, he nonetheless retains this one case of the Hebrews robbing the Egyptians it is likely to be because of the force of the liturgical example with its typological suggestion that this detail is a prefiguration of Christ descending into hell, winning the souls of the patriarchs from the devil and granting them access to paradise.[2]

Another suggestion of liturgical influence occurs at the conclusion of the *Millstätter Exodus* where, after the hymn of thanks sung by the Israelites for their deliverance and after the passage in which the author retrospectively informs his audience of the need for an allegorical interpretation, he employs three significant time-references in describing his poetic activity. He thanks the Holy Ghost, to whom he had appealed at the start of his work for inspiration (vv. 21 ff.), for granting his request *in disen stunden* (v. 3306); he praises the Holy Ghost for the way in which the Israelite host *nû ist chomen durch daʒ mere* (v. 3313); and he shows his gratitude for being enabled to describe in German *die vroude sîner liute | an disem tage hiute* (vv. 3311 f.). These three passages, especially v. 3312, all stress the present time or the particular day when the poem was recited—a fact which is especially significant if we recall the function of the *haec nox* references in the liturgy of Holy Saturday and if we interpret the words *die*

---

[1] See below, pp. 182 ff.

[2] The same attitude informs the passage in *Eʒʒos Gesang* (vv. 299 ff.) dealing with Christ's victorious descent into hell. Christ is here described as taking what was legally His (v. 302), i.e. the souls of the patriarchs awaiting Him there, but the subsequent double reference to this same action (v. 308: 'der zevuorte im sîn geroube al. | er nam imo duo elliu sînu vaz') makes it clear that the paschal event is here being interpreted in connection with its prefiguration in the events of Exodus. *Geroube* thus corresponds to (*ex*)*spoliare* and although, as Waag suggests (p. xviii), *vaʒ* may be a reference to Marc. 3. 27 ('Nemo potest vasa fortis ingressus in domum diripere, nisi prius fortem alliget') its primary function is to illuminate Exod. 12. 35 ('et petierunt ab Aegyptiis vasa argentea et aurea').

The problem

vroude sîner liute | *an disem tage hiute* as an allusion to the concept of *paschale gaudium*. This suggestion that the German work was originally designed for an Easter reading and that it was conceived as having a role to play within the liturgical year would be confirmed by the passage which we have already considered in the context of the baptismal interpretation and in which, against the author's usual tendency to omit specifically Jewish details, a description is given of the manner in which the rite of the Passover is to be celebrated.[1] It now becomes evident that these details are retained in the Millstatt work because they are not simply to be understood literally with reference to the Jewish rite, but also typologically as a prefiguration of the Christian celebration of Easter, so that the author's employment of such terms as *vrôn tisk* and especially *die ôsteren begên*[2] is by no means so naïve as might appear. These allusions make it clear, but with extreme tact (so that the possibility of other readings, including the literal, is nowhere excluded), that the liturgical celebration of Easter, and therewith the particular manner in which the events of Exodus are conceived in the liturgy of these two crucial days, has had a vital part to play in helping the Millstatt author to formulate his thoughts about the events he has chosen to narrate.

I am not convinced, however, that this paschal interpretation of the *Millstätter Exodus* (even if it were to be combined with the baptismal interpretation which we first considered)[3] accounts for the whole of the German epic or for enough of the detailed changes introduced by the German author for us to be able to accept it as a total interpretation. I am prepared to concede, in other words, that these two interpretations can explain certain aspects, even important aspects, of the Millstatt work, but would maintain that a more thoroughgoing explanation can be achieved by yet a third approach. By this I mean an approach which interprets the events of Exodus, as narrated by the German author in about 1120, in the light of the contemporary crusading

[1] Vv. 2787 ff.   [2] V. 2824 and v. 2826.
[3] On the possibility of combining these two readings see below, pp. 377 ff.

23

movement. It can be shown that this crusading interpretation can be reconciled with the two interpretations we have up to now considered,[1] but that, unlike them, it can also provide a satisfactory explanation of such features of the Millstatt work as its military atmosphere (where, despite occasional suggestions that the Israelite warriors were not guilty of the *ubirmuot* of the Egyptians, there is no hint that these military scenes are to be understood *only* metaphorically, i.e. *exclusively* as a psychomachia) and the presence of feudal elements in a work addressed explicitly to a feudal audience. These are features for which it would be difficult to provide a complete explanation in the baptismal or the liturgical interpretation, and it is this consideration, together with the fact that the particular advantages of these two interpretations do not have to be sacrificed if we accept the crusading theory, which has led me to regard the crusading theory as central to any understanding of the *Millstätter Exodus* and to dwell on it in such detail.

An interpretation of the Millstatt work in the light of the crusades will have to answer the question how it was possible for the first fifteen chapters of the biblical book to suggest the theme of Christian warfare. Such a conception of this part of Exodus may seem foreign to us today, but was certainly not strange to medieval thought. To illustrate this we need do no more than consider two complementary examples—one occurring towards the start of the tradition of a Christian war waged on behalf of God against the pagans and the other from the late sixteenth century, when medieval thought is already used in the new context of the Age of Absolutism—where the book of Exodus is employed to illustrate and interpret warfare between Christians and pagans.

The first example concerns the account of the battle of the Milvian Bridge between Constantine and Maxentius given by Eusebius of Caesarea in his *Vita Constantini*[2] (with a closely similar version by the same author in his *Historia ecclesiastica*).[3] This decisive event for any Christian interpretation of history

[1] See below, pp. 377 ff.　　　[2] I, 38.　　　[3] IX, 9.

and for the life of Constantine himself (whom Christian historiography could not fail to regard as occupying a special position
in Christian history, comparable only to that of Moses in the
history of Israel) is set by Eusebius in conscious parallel with the
passage of the Red Sea. This choice of image was suggested to
him by the obvious fact that Constantine, fighting under the sign
of the Christian labarum, was granted victory against the pagan
Maxentius and that his position, established by this success, as the
first Christian emperor lent itself to a comparison with that of
Moses as the proclaimer of God's covenant with Israel, but also
by the particular detail that both pagan leaders, Maxentius as well
as Pharaoh, were defeated in the waters of a river (or sea). It is
for this reason that Eusebius in his account explicitly quotes
Exod. 15. 4 and 5 at the point where the defeat of Pharaoh and
his followers by drowning is compared with the fate which overtook the foes of the new Moses:

ὥσπερ γοῦν ἐπ' αὐτοῦ ποτε Μωϋσέως (καὶ) τοῦ θεοσεβοῦς ῾Εβραίων
γένους 'ἅρματα Φαραὼ καὶ τὴν δύναμιν αὐτοῦ ἔρριψεν εἰς θάλασσαν
καὶ ἐπιλέκτους ἀναβάτας τριστάτας κατεπόντισεν ἐν ἐρυθρᾷ', κατὰ
ταῦτα δὴ καὶ Μαξέντιος οἵ τ' ἀμφ' αὐτὸν ὁπλῖται καὶ δορυφόροι
'ἔδυσαν εἰς βυθὸν ὡσεὶ λίθος', ὁπηνίκα νῶτα δοὺς τῇ ἐκ θεοῦ μετὰ
Κωνσταντίνου δυνάμει τὸν πρὸ τῆς πορείας διῄει ποταμόν, ὃν αὐτὸς
σκάφεσι ζεύξας καὶ εὖ μάλα γεφυρώσας μηχανὴν ὀλέθρου καθ' ἑαυτοῦ
συνεπήξατο, ὧδέ πη ἑλεῖν τὸν τῷ θεῷ φίλον ἐλπίσας.[1]

It is for the same reason that Eusebius also quotes from Exod. 15. 10[2]
and that he closes his account by inserting the verses 15. 1 and 2[3]
with which Moses begins his song of praise and thanksgiving to
the God who has brought His people into safety and freedom
and annihilated their foes.

It is this same scene from Exodus which, in its dramatic vividness, has attracted the attention of a sixteenth-century author.
The later author is Fernando de Herrera who in his *Canción en
alabança de la divina Magestad por la vitoria del señor don Juan*[4]

[1] 1, 38 (p. 25, 5 ff.).
[2] 1, 38 (p. 25, 23). Exod. 15. 11 is also quoted (p. 26, 1 f.).
[3] 1, 38 (p. 25, 27 ff.).
[4] I am grateful to Professor E. M. Wilson for drawing my attention to this
poem.

25

celebrates the Christian victory over the Turks at the battle of Lepanto, so that once again it is the particular association of a war between Christians and pagans with the fact of a battle at sea which has suggested the relevance of the passage of the Red Sea by the Israelites. However, Herrera is far from restricting his Old Testament allusions to the book of Exodus alone. He provides his poem with a significant resonance by establishing parallels between Hebrew history and the Christian present in his recurrent allusions to books of the Old Testament such as Judges, Kings, Isaiah, Jeremiah, Ezechiel, Amos, Maccabees[1] and, especially, the Psalms.[2] If, amongst these allusions concerned above all with points of detail, we can also include a passing reference to Exodus as well,[3] this is hardly sufficient as a demonstration that it was this book in particular which, as in the account of Eusebius, informed the Spanish poet's conception of his theme. This demonstration is provided, however, by the emphatic manner in which the poem begins with a sustained allusion to the opening of the hymn of thanksgiving sung by Moses after the destruction of the Egyptians and also utilised by Eusebius in his account of Constantine's victory. Herrera's opening words (v. 1 : *Cantemos al Señor*) thus echo the beginning of Moses' hymn (Exod. 15. 1 : *Cantemus Domino*), but this parallel, however revealing, is only a prelude to the lengthier allusion which follows:

> 5   Tú rompiste las fuerças y la dura
>   frente de Faraón, feroz guerrero.

---

[1] Jud. 5. 7 is quoted in v. 103 and 5. 8 in v. 106. IV Reg. 19. 23 occurs in v. 16, Is. 2. 11 ff. in vv. 141 ff. and 23. 14 in v. 181, Jer. 1. 18 in v. 57, Ezech. 26. 17 in v. 176, Amos 8. 10 in v. 42 and Mach. 1. 18 in v. 12.

[2] Ps. 16. 12 is reflected in v. 111, Ps. 17. 35 in v. 117, Ps. 51. 8 in v. 63 and Ps. 83. 14 in v. 131. Allusions to Ps. 78 occur frequently in one passage (78. 4 = v. 69; 78. 9 = v. 71; 78. 10 = vv. 70 f.), and also to Ps. 82 (82. 3 = v. 81; 82. 5 = v. 83; 82. 7 f. = v. 91; cf. also the reference to Ps. 82. 14–17 in vv. 123 ff.). The reference in vv. 69 f. ('¿Dónde | el Dios destos está ? ¿de quién se esconde?') to Ps. 78. 10 (*Ubi est Deus eorum*) is of particular interest to any crusading interpretation of the German *Exodus*, since it was precisely this passage from the Psalms which was used by St Bernard as a means of kindling enthusiasm for the crusades (Letter 467, *MPL*, 182, 672C; *De Consideratione*, *MPL*, 182, 742C; *De laude novae militiae*, *MPL*, 182, 925A).

[3] V. 121 thus reflects Exod. 15. 15.

26

The problem

Sus escogidos príncipes cubrieron
los abissos del mar, y decendieron
qual piedra en el profundo; y tu ira luego
los tragó, como arista seca el fuego.

These verses, significant for their critical position at the start of
the poem and because they describe the whole of the poet's theme
(the battle and its victorious outcome), rather than only a detailed
aspect of it, similarly echo the start of the Exodus hymn: vv. 5 f.
make explicit the parallel between the present and the event from
the Hebrew past, vv. 7–9 recall Exod. 15. 4 f. and vv. 9 f. depend
upon Exod. 15. 7. In other words, this passage, both by its position and its length, establishes from the beginning a clear parallel
between the battle of Lepanto and the events by the Red Sea.
It therefore ensures that, however frequent the allusions to other
books of the Old Testament in this poem, it is this event from
Exodus which was employed by Herrera, as it had been by
Eusebius, to give meaning to his theme.

If the book of Exodus could therefore be used both at the start
and at the end of the Middle Ages to support the idea of a Christian
war waged against the pagans, we need feel little surprise that
a similar view was possible in the twelfth century. Nor need
we feel surprised that this century should regard the book of
Exodus not merely in the general terms of a holy war waged
against pagan enemies, but in the particular context of the crusades, the special form of holy war which preoccupied this century. This possibility is demonstrated for us by *CB* 47,[1] a
crusading poem written between the capture of Jerusalem by
Saladin in 1187 and the start of the third crusade. Quite apart
from the allusion to the Lamentations of Jeremiah (1. 1) in
stanza 1, vv. 7 f. and the reference to martyrdom (stanza 3,
vv. 11 f.),[2] the importance of this poem for us lies in the way in
which the poet criticises the slowness with which efforts are made
to win back the Holy Land from Saladin. He describes Palestine

[1] *Carmina Burana*, I, 92 and II, 97 ff.
[2] See below, p. 410, on the relevance of this Old Testament book to the
crusading theme and pp. 317 ff. on crusading martyrdom.

The Millstätter Exodus

as groaning under the same yoke (stanza 2, v. 7: 'iam regalis |
in luto et latere | elaborat tellus') as that under which the Israelites
suffered in Egypt (cf. Exod. 1. 14: 'ad amaritudinem perducebant
vitam eorum operibus duris luti et lateris') and as bemoaning the
dilatoriness of Moses (stanza 2, v. 9: 'plorat | Moysen fatiscere').
This last allusion is clearly a reference to the doubts which first
assail Moses when the Lord informs him of his divine task
(cf. Exod. 3. 11 and 13),[1] but is also, within the crusading context
of this poem, an implied criticism of the slowness which potential
crusaders are showing in bringing deliverance to the Holy Land.
Much of the force of this poem therefore derives from the association of Exodus with the crusades which the author can so much
take for granted that he has no need to make it at all explicit.
If this was possible for a Latin author writing at some time between the second and third crusades I see no reason to deny it in
the case of a vernacular poet active between the first and second
crusades. Such an equation of Exodus with the particular type of
holy war known to his own day is fully understandable in the
case of the Millstatt author, for it is one of his most obvious
characteristics to minimise the distance separating the Hebrews
of the Old Testament from the society of his own day and to
stress more the timeless relevance of patriarchal history to the
Christian present.[2]

An interpretation of the *Millstätter Exodus* by reference to the
crusades is no novelty, however, since it has been suggested
before by J. Schwietering and L. Wolff.[3] The justification of the

[1] See also below, pp. 350 f.
[2] See below, pp. 123 ff.
[3] Cf. J. Schwietering, *LG*, 69 f. ('Nicht auf mittelalterlich ritterliche Kostü-
mierung der Ägypter und Juden als solche kommt es an, sondern darauf, daß
Juden und Ägypter als Kreuzfahrer und Sarazenen, als Christen und Heiden, als
Gottes- und Teufelsstreiter in ihrem unablässigen Kampf um das irdische Gottes-
reich gesehen werden, daß der Untergang der Ägypter als alttestamentliche
Verheißung auf die Gegenwart gedeutet wird, als Gewähr für geschichtliche
Sendung, für endlichen Sieg mittelalterlicher Kreuzfahrer über die Heiden') and
L. Wolff, *LG*, 159 ('Der Kreuzzugsgedanke als der innere Quell des Lebens,
der sich freilich im herben Stil der Frühzeit nur in andeutender Verhüllung zeigt,
hilft zur Vereinigung des Religösen und des Weltlichen und trägt zur Anerken-
nung der kämpferischen Ideale bei').

present attempt must be, first, the fact that this suggestion of Schwietering and Wolff has not found universal acceptance[1] and therefore deserves a detailed investigation and, secondly, the fact that these two scholars both made their suggestion very much in passing and had no opportunity to develop it. The question still remains open, therefore, and if any attempt to answer it can throw further light on the problem of Christian warfare in the twelfth century and on the possible contributions of the crusading ideal to the rise of a knightly class newly conscious of its position and duties in twelfth-century society, then this will further justify detailed analysis of the *Millstätter Exodus* in the light of this suggestion. I repeat, though, that a crusading analysis of this work need not exclude the possibility that the baptismal and paschal readings also have a contribution to make to any total interpretation. How these three readings may be reconciled with one another must be considered in the concluding chapter.

[1] On these divergent views see below, pp. 296 ff.

II

OMISSIONS AND EXPANSION

THE author of the *Millstätter Exodus* leaves us in no doubt as to the origin of his theme: it is his purpose, he says in the opening lines, to tell his audience 'ettewaz von den buochen | da wir inne sculen suochen | des himelisken chuniges êre' (vv. 3 ff.) and to this end he will have to translate a Latin text into the vernacular (vv. 18 ff.). A Latin text of religious content need not of itself suggest a biblical source, but the author subsequently tells us that his source was the book of Exodus (vv. 35 f.). Even so, a biblical source still need not be the Vulgate itself, as has been made clear by Kossmann's discussion of the passages where the German poem and the Vulgate differ factually.[1] These discrepancies are, however, few in number (Kossmann established only eleven), small in scope and concerned only with details of no significance for the narrative. Nor is the probability that the author used the biblical account as his source much weakened by the suggestion that he may also have employed a commentary. He certainly knew traditional interpretations of Exodus,[2] but he rarely subjects his text to an exegetical analysis and instead, with considerable aesthetic tact, he allows the import of the story to emerge from his narrative.[3] We may therefore agree with Kossmann that what appears to derive from a commentary is more likely to be an addition of the author himself or a reflection of his own general religious training.[4]

The conclusion that the Millstatt author used the biblical Exodus as his source is relevant to the method of our inquiry: it means that our problem is simpler than that which confronted Beyschlag in his analysis of the *Wiener Genesis*. The fact that this earlier work was dependent not merely on the Bible, but also on

[1] *Die altdeutsche Exodus*, pp. 24 ff. [2] See pp. 109 f.
[3] See pp. 108 ff. [4] *Die altdeutsche Exodus*, pp. 30 f.

Omissions and expansion

Alcimus Avitus and the liturgical hymn, meant that Beyschlag's task in determining the artistic individuality of his author was much more complex. In our case this variety of sources does not exist, or has not been established,[1] so that we may hope to assess our author's personality by a direct comparison of his work with the biblical account,[2] by an analysis of what he has decided to omit and of what he has added. He closely follows his source in the outlines of his narrative, but has retained the liberty of changing the emphasis in certain episodes so that a consideration of these changes may tell us much about his artistic intentions. It may well be true that the author's self-discipline in avoiding exegesis imposed certain limitations upon him, but these restrictions, far from depriving him of all liberty, acted as a challenge to his artistry.

We may determine the epic form of the *Exodus* by following Beyschlag's method with the *Wiener Genesis*[3] and by considering those cases where the author has contracted his source and those where he has expanded and enriched what he found in Exodus. To apply Beyschlag's method to the later work may therefore clarify the relationship between these two epics, the first biblical works of epic proportions in MHG literature, and tell us whether they both stand in the same line of development towards the large-scale epic or whether this development was encouraged by different factors at different times. Beyschlag has shown that the *Genesis* is characterised by a twofold technique, since it includes numerous sections where the narrative form is markedly more compact and concise than in the source, but other sections where the pace is more leisurely, fuller details are given and a true epic

---

[1] Beyschlag has recently argued (*WW*, v, 9 f.) that the author of the *Millstätter Exodus*, like the author of the *Wiener Genesis*, used Alcimus Avitus as an additional source. I am prepared to accept this as theoretically possible, but I do not believe that Beyschlag's comments are enough to establish this (see below, p. 293, n. 2).

[2] In what follows I have compared the Millstatt text with the Vulgate version of Exodus. This is justified as long as we remain ignorant of the precise bible version used by the German author and in view of the restricted number of discrepancies established by Kossmann (*op. cit.* pp. 24 ff.).

[3] *Die Wiener Genesis*, pp. 63 ff.

form is achieved. Beyschlag also makes it clear that epic expansion generally occurs in the *Genesis* where the author wishes to elaborate the relevance of his Old Testament story to the conditions of his own day, but that the more compact form predominates whenever this is not attempted.[1] We do not encounter such a formal dualism in the *Exodus*, whose proportions and tempo are more consistently epic, but Beyschlag's theory of a direct relationship between epic expansion and the author's attitude to his subject-matter (in his case, relevance of the Old Testament world to the medieval present) suggests a parallel in the case of the *Exodus*. Here too it is a constant concern of the author to demonstrate the relevance of these events from Hebrew history to the present condition of his audience,[2] so that we cannot afford to ignore the possibility that what Beyschlag has shown for the earlier epic may also be true of its successor. I propose to consider first the small number of omissions from his source for which the Millstatt author is responsible, and then to devote the rest of this chapter and the two following chapters to different aspects of the expansion and enrichment of biblical material which is so much more characteristic of his style.[3]

The evidence for omissions from the author's source falls into four groups. The most obvious is the deliberate exclusion of details which characterise the action as an event from Jewish history which befell the Hebrews in a particular period. How this exclusion of historical details serves the author's intentions will occupy us later;[4] for the moment we must simply record these omissions as forming a coherent group. In place of the chronicle introduction of the biblical account (1. 1 ff.) with its list of Israelite names the German author avoids all Jewish particularity by giving no names of the children of Israel (vv. 43 ff.)

[1] *Die Wiener Genesis*, p. 64: 'die epische Ausweitung fällt zum größten Teil mit dem Ausbau der Gegenwartsbezogenheit zusammen, mit der Einbeziehung der heimischen Welt.'

[2] See pp. 123 ff.

[3] Reasons of space make an exhaustive treatment of these problems impossible. For a more detailed discussion of omissions, expansion and characterisation in the *Millstätter Exodus* see my forthcoming articles in *MA*.

[4] See pp. 124 ff.

—he has thus excised most of those too particular details which formed an obstacle to any thorough assimilation of Hebrew history to the medieval present.[1] The same is true of the other cases where lists of Hebrew names are passed over in the German text. Where the Bible sometimes mentions God's compact with Israel by referring to the patriarchs Abraham, Isaac and Jacob (3. 15; 3. 16; 6. 3; 6. 8) the *Exodus* either omits this reference altogether (as in the last two passages) or designates the patriarchs anonymously as the ancestors of Moses (v. 606). By contrast, two other biblical references to them by name (3. 6; 4. 5) are retained by the German author (vv. 497 ff. and 725 ff.), although this exception is only apparent since there are positive reasons why the author should have here retained the explicit reference.[2] Something similar is probably true of the omission of the Canaanite place-names mentioned in 13. 5 (cf. vv. 2855 f.) by contrast with their retention on an earlier occasion (cf. 3. 8 and vv. 525 ff.), for here too particular reasons explain this choice.[3] Apart from these examples the cases where a biblical detail is omitted because of its Hebrew particularity (i.e. its resistance to assimilation to the medieval present) are few and unimportant. For example, the excuse twice advanced by Moses for his inability to act as the mouthpiece of God (6. 12 and 6. 30: *incircumcisus labiis*) is omitted because of its patently Jewish imagery: on the first occasion the whole question of Moses is dropped, but on the second it is rendered innocuously by v. 1194: *ich nechan nicht reden.* In 9. 26 the place-name Gessen is omitted (cf. vv. 1905 f.), presumably because of its biblical particularity, although local details are retained elsewhere when they can be made to serve other intentions of the author.[4] Despite his doubts

---

[1] Similarly, the long biblical list (6. 14–27) is contracted to a succinct and undifferentiated remark (vv. 1169–72).

[2] See pp. 140 ff.

[3] See pp. 142 ff.

[4] *Egyptinlant* is retained, for example, because of its traditional allegorical significance as the place of bondage not merely of the Hebrews, but of all human beings to whom this life represents an exile from the bliss of Paradise (see pp. 119 f.). Particular Egyptian place-names occur in any frequency only towards the end of the work (e.g. *Ramassê* 2753; *Sôchôt* 2753, 2769, 2957; *Bêthan* 2960; *Jayrôt* 2975,

about too Jewish an atmosphere the German author was therefore occasionally ready to retain a Hebrew detail if it could be employed to serve another purpose.

The second group of omissions in the German epic reflects the author's wish for an economy in the means by which he narrates the action. This might appear to contradict any trace of epic expansiveness, although it is possible to attribute it to the author's wish for clarity of action and his awareness of the difficulty of reconciling this with any profusion of epic detail. The German author prunes down the biblical action by largely concentrating it upon two protagonists, Moses and Pharaoh, and by minimising the role of others. The Jews provide resonance for Moses (Aaron has become little more than an instrument of Moses' authority), whilst the Egyptians are seen more often as victims of Pharaoh's arrogance than as fellow criminals. Kossmann[1] rightly contrasts the biblical remark that both Pharaoh and his followers hardened their hearts (14. 5) with the German author's reference to Pharaoh alone (vv. 2990 ff.), but other examples are present.[2] Another type of contraction occurs when the twofold rhythm of a biblical scene (e.g. 7. 15–19, God's prophecy or command, followed by 7. 20, its human execution) is replaced by a single rhythm in the vernacular. In the corresponding scene the Millstatt author therefore omits the prophecy apart from two short oblique references, the one a comment of the narrator (v. 1214) and the other attributed as direct speech to Moses and Aaron (v. 1224). Instead, he concentrates his attention on the performance of the miracle itself (vv. 1235 ff.), so that the two episodes of the biblical scene have been contracted to one. God's prophecy is not described at all explicitly, but only obliquely, so that if He has not been excluded from the scene entirely it is true that the human actors dominate this scene much

3089; *Magdalôn* 2977; *Belsephôn* 2977, 3091). Their function here is to indicate tangibly the various stages of the Israelites' journey, to illustrate their exodus from the land of bondage.

[1] *Die altdeutsche Exodus*, p. 78.
[2] Cf. 1. 6 and v. 61; 4. 16 and vv. 813–16; 7. 10 and vv. 1212 f.; 8. 29 and vv. 1569 ff.

more obviously than in the Bible. This same technique is also used to particular effect by the German author in his characterisation of Pharaoh. Where the Bible frequently gives God's promise to cause Pharaoh to react in a preordained way to Moses' request (e.g. 14. 4) and then describes in similar terms how this promise was kept (14. 8), the German author in every case passes over God's promise.[1] The result is a contraction of the action, but also a gain in narrative directness as well as the ability to depict the story more convincingly in terms of human activity. This contraction for the sake of narrative effectiveness is not confined to Pharaoh's actions, however. The Bible also frequently describes Moses' deeds not as actions undertaken independently by him, but rather in execution of commands issued by God (e.g. 8. 1), so that once more the human execution is phrased in terms which recall God's command (e.g. 9. 22 and 23). Again the Millstatt author concentrates on the human action and ignores God's words to Moses (vv. 1867 ff.), not merely in this scene but elsewhere in the epic.[2] If he departs from this practice on only two occasions, this is probably because of other, more powerful considerations.[3]

[1] The standard biblical phrases for God's promise (14. 4: *Et indurabo cor ejus*...) and its fulfilment (14. 8: *Induravitque Dominus cor Pharaonis*...) are regularly omitted from the German epic—thus 7. 3 and 7. 13 f. (as well as 7. 22) are missing in the Millstatt version of this scene (vv. 1211 ff.), even though some indirect hints of what the source had stated explicitly are still to be detected (e.g. vv. 1214, 1224, 1262). The fulfilment of God's promise is omitted regularly, no matter whether it is seen in explicit terms of God's control of Pharaoh's actions (as 14. 8 above; cf. also 9. 12; 10. 20; 10. 27; 11. 10) or more obliquely as a suggestion that Pharaoh hardened his heart as the Lord had ordained ('ingravavit cor suum...sicut praeceperat Dominus': 8. 15; 9. 35). On two occasions only does the German version retain a similar phrase (v. 849 — 4. 21 and v. 660 is a free rendering of 3. 19), but even here any direct reference to God as the cause is avoided.

[2] Cf. 8. 1 and vv. 1313 f.; 10. 12 f. and vv. 2151 ff.

[3] The twofold rhythm of 9. 8 + 9. 10 is reflected in vv. 1725 f., but since this expression of the Israelite leaders' joyful obedience immediately follows the closing lines of God's speech in which the refractoriness of the Egyptians is emphasised (vv. 1723 f.) it is probably the contrast between God's people and His opponents (elsewhere expressed in terms of humility, vv. 2927 f., and arrogance, v. 3038—see p. 169) which has led the German author to retain this feature. On the second exception (10. 21 f. and vv. 2263, 2279) see p. 175.

The Millstätter Exodus

A third class of omissions arises from the Millstatt author's avoidance of repetitions which only slow down the action or blur its outlines. In the Bible verse 3. 9 recounts how God tells Moses that He has seen the sufferings of Israel, but since this reiterates the similar idea of 3. 7 (translated in the *Exodus* by vv. 507 ff.) any repetition is avoided in the German version between vv. 534 and 535. Similarly, verse 6. 11 is not rendered into German after v. 1166—apparently because it is itself a repetition, compounded of 5. 23 and 5. 1, both of which had earlier been translated in the vernacular version (vv. 1119 f. + 1122 and vv. 947 ff.). This dislike of repetitiveness is also the likely explanation of the Millstatt author's most striking omission: his conflation of the third and fourth of the plagues of Egypt. In the source the third plague was of *sciniphes* and the fourth of *muscae*, but the German text makes of these only one plague of *hundesfliegen*, describing it with details from both the biblical plagues. This drastic step was probably taken because of the close similarity of these two plagues: they are the only ones in which similar insects play a part (only the locusts are comparable, but their attacks are described differently) and, further, this similarity linked two consecutive plagues with no helpful interval of time. Another difficulty lay in the narrative poverty of the third plague in the Bible (8. 16–20), where only one of these five verses provided the German author with promising material. Thus, v. 16 gives the Lord's command to Moses and v. 17 its execution, so that effective use could only be made of the latter; v. 18 was also unusable, as had been the case with 8. 7 of the preceding plague, either because of the repetitiveness of this detail or because it distracted attention from the main action. In v. 19 the sorcerers' warning to Pharaoh might have been welcome narrative material if it had not been dependent for its effect on a standing phrase, regularly omitted in the *Exodus*, describing God's hardening of Pharaoh's heart. Finally, v. 20 was unacceptable since it contains a divine command to Moses and a prophecy of what Pharaoh will do—both such references are regularly expunged in favour of a direct description of human activity.

Omissions and expansion

The remaining class of omissions is quite unrepresentative. It consists of a restricted number of descriptive details which are passed over in the German epic, however rich in details it may otherwise be. Where 3. 8 says *in terram bonam, et spatiosam* this second adjective is missing in vv. 518 ff.; in 4. 9 the phrase *aquam fluminis* is weakened to the simplicity of *daʒ waʒʒer* (v. 752) and the explanatory detail of 10. 6 has no counterpart in the German work. Such cases are infrequent, but they are the only examples where the Millstatt author contracts his source without any obvious reason, since all the other cases admitted of some sort of explanation: an avoidance of patently Jewish details which resisted assimilation to the medieval present, an economy of narrative action achieved by concentrating on the main actors and by showing them as acting independently, and an avoidance of repetition as blurring the outlines of the action. In other words, contraction for no clear aesthetic reason is quite uncharacteristic of the *Millstätter Exodus*: here it differs radically from the *Wiener Genesis* where, as Beyschlag has shown, contraction not merely occurs much more frequently, but even constitutes a *Grundform* from which occasional deviations are made only for special reasons. Almost the converse is true of the *Exodus*, whose author generally contracted his source material only for certain formal reasons, where any other decision (retention of the biblical motif or its expansion) would have conflicted with other aesthetic demands on his attention.

The next stage in comparing the *Exodus* with its biblical source is to consider what additions have been made by the German author. It will show us that this process of epic expansion is a much more characteristic feature of his work than was the contraction resulting from omissions. It will also make it clear that the examples of such expansion fall into three categories: minor details (where the addition concerns no more than a single verse, but sometimes also two or three); individual scenes, already suggested in the biblical account but expanded from within by the German author; and finally those scenes for which there is no real counterpart *as scenes* in the biblical Exodus, but

37

which have been so emphasised by the German author that a passing reference in the Bible has with him acquired a wholly new status as an independent unit. For the rest of this chapter we shall be concerned with the first category, whereas each of the two following chapters will be devoted to the more important evidence of the other two categories.

Expansion by interpolating minor details is a technique most open to the criticism of being little more than the result of a desperate search for a tolerable rhyme by an author of modest ability whose formal ambitions do not rise above this primitive need and who is therefore all too ready to sacrifice other aesthetic considerations. This accusation has indeed been made against the Millstatt author by his editor[1] and clearly, if Kossmann is correct here, it will make it difficult to argue that such interpolations form part of a conscious technique of epic expansion. I certainly do not wish to suggest that the Millstatt author nowhere makes use of a lame phrase because of its convenient rhyme, but in what follows I shall concentrate, in an attempt to defend our author against his editor, on those cases where this consideration of rhyme cannot be the whole explanation.

Kossmann has drawn attention to one example[2] (to which several others could be added)[3] where expansion in the German work was apparently dictated by the need to find a rhyme adequate to the verse which has just been rendered into German. In this type of passage the *a*-verses correspond to an idea expressed in the biblical source whereas the *b*-verses are additions of the German author,[4] but are inserted in such a mechanical, line-for-line manner that no harm would be done to the sense or syntax if only the *a*-verses were to be read. One example should make this clear. The biblical account of the scene where God first appears to Moses in the burning bush has it that God called Moses

[1] Kossmann, *Die altdeutsche Exodus*, p. 42, and even more harshly, p. 74.
[2] *Ibid.* p. 44.
[3] Cf. 8. 27 and vv. 1519–22; 10. 16 and vv. 2203–6; 12. 10 and vv. 2505–8; 12. 13 and vv. 2541–4.
[4] In this context, by *a*-verse I mean the first verse of a rhymed couplet and by *b*-verse the second.

by name twice and that Moses replied to this with one word
(3. 4: 'et ait: Moyses! Moyses! Qui respondit: Adsum'). The
simplicity of these two addresses is broken down in the German
version by the fact that each of these remarks is followed by
another verse to complete the couplet:

> 481   zwire in got nande,
> *wole er in bechande.*
> der ander sprach 'hie bin ich,
> *wie bechennest du mich?'*

Here vv. 481 and 483 between them adequately reproduce the
biblical source without any omission, but the *b*-verses (in italics)
have no counterpart in the source, do not disrupt the syntax and
add very little to the effectiveness of the scene, so that they could
be attributed solely to the necessities of rhyme. Such an example
by no means stands alone and the suggestion of a poet at the mercy
of formal problems to which he can find no more effective solution becomes even more insistent when we observe the same
phenomenon not simply in passages of four lines, but also in
groups of six or even eight lines.[1] Examples such as these, where
groups of two, three or four expansionary *b*-verses constitute
passages in which the concision of the biblical source is replaced
by a detailed loquacity, must strengthen the suspicion that other
passages in the *Exodus* where expansion takes place in only one
b-verse, rather than in a cluster, similarly reflect the difficulties
of an unskilled author. The rhyming of a Latin name ending in
-us with the word *sus*[2] or of the word *antwurte* with a standing
phrase like *mit ubellîchime worte*[3] is particularly suspicious, as is
the expansion of a positive statement (e.g. v. 947) by the addition
of its negative counterpart in the *b*-verse (v. 948).[4]

This kind of criticism is obviously valid at many points, yet
this still does not mean that the epic form of the whole work is to

---

[1] Cf. 10. 5 and vv. 2017–22; 11. 1 and vv. 2361–6; 12. 11 and vv. 2519–26.

[2] E.g. vv. 45 f. (cf. 1. 1), vv. 533 f.

[3] E.g. vv. 307 f., but the phrase can be varied slightly by a change of the
adjective: *sus getân* (vv. 686, 2316), *luzzel* (v. 980), *zornlîch* (v. 1066), *wârlîch*
(v. 1196) or *churzzelîch* (v. 2090; cf. 1419).

[4] For other examples see vv. 1669 f., 1799 f., 2001 f., 2375 f., 2587 f.

be explained by the rhyme difficulties encountered by its author. It is possible to indicate other features of the *Exodus* (they will concern us in the next two chapters), of greater artistic importance than the addition of single verses at intervals, which make of it a work epic in scope and conception. If epic expansion also takes place by means so skilful and well chosen as these then we must do the author the justice of believing that this expansion was a change in form which he consciously intended and that it was not the incredible result of someone of modest talents struggling with the difficulties of rhyme. We have already seen that he was preoccupied with a number of aesthetic problems so that, as with his omissions, he was sometimes ready to accept a solution which contradicted the epic requirements of his work if it could be made subservient to his other needs. This suggests that, given his general wish for epic expansion and the pressure sometimes exerted on him by rhyme, our author may have made use of these expansionary *b*-verses to introduce other aspects important to him. In other words, we cannot be certain that these *b*-verses are inflationary material forced upon him by the needs of rhyme alone until we take into account not just the obvious fact of expansion, but what it was that was so important to the author that he made use of it in this process of expansion. It would be possible, for example, to analyse some of the passages where clusters of *b*-verses represent expansionary material and to show that, whilst these *b*-verses certainly solve the rhyme problem, they are also there because they meet other aesthetic demands,[1] so that it oversimplifies the issue to say that expansion is forced upon the author by formal demands alone. Expansion may have been originally suggested by rhyme, but the author has skilfully utilised it to meet other, more important aesthetic needs, thereby making a virtue out of necessity and maintaining his artistic independence in the face of demands to which, in Kossmann's view, he had succumbed entirely.

This can also be shown in the case of expansion by the addition of a solitary *b*-verse. A revealing example occurs at the conclusion

[1] See my forthcoming article in *MA*.

of the description of the Egyptians' preparations for departure in pursuit of the Israelites, where the author says, just before he passes over to depicting the actual pursuit, that they set out in full force (3070: 'die hiezzen in gewinnen | alles wîges sarwât | unde huoben sich an die vart, | bogen unde scafte, | si huoben sich mit chrafte'). What concerns me here is not the fact that v. 3073 belongs syntactically and logically immediately after v. 3071, so that it may have been transposed in order to ease the rhyme position; more indicative is the parallel between vv. 3072 and 3074, for this might suggest that v. 3074, adding nothing essentially new, was a repetitive addition for the sake of rhyme. Yet I am not convinced that this parallel is merely the fortuitous result of a search for a rhyme. In the first place, the emphasis which the parallel provides rounds off the lengthy passage describing military preparations and indicates that, with the pursuit which is now about to commence, the narrative thread is being resumed. Further, v. 3074, although a syntactical parallel to v. 3072, is no mere repetition. The earlier verse says simply that the Egyptians set out and therefore anticipates the pursuit which begins in v. 3079, whereas the later verse stresses the *manner* in which they set out, i.e. as an armed host (*mit chrafte*), and therefore subsumes the military description which has been interpolated here. Between them these two lines act as a bridge between the description about to be concluded (which, despite the author's concern to convert a static description into a process, has an unavoidably static function since it delays the progress of the action)[1] and the resumption of the narrative in the following lines. To argue that v. 3074 is a repetitive line-filler is to ignore the skill with which the Millstatt author has met one of the difficulties confronting any epic author: the problem of a smooth transition from a static description of some length to the next stage in the narrative action.

Another example is provided by the words spoken by God to Moses after the passage of the Red Sea and just before the waters close upon the Egyptians. He tells Moses to stretch out his hand:

[1] On this problem see pp. 83 ff.

'ut revertantur aquae ad Aegyptios, super currus et equites eorum' (14. 26). To this there corresponds in the Millstatt epic:

> 3243 so chêret ez sich zesamene sâ
> widir, *daz ist al wâr*,
> ubir die vîant dîn:
> *der gewalt der ist mîn.*

Here we need pay no attention to the way in which (although *Aegyptii* is rendered generally by *vîant*) the terms *currus* and *equites* are omitted altogether—where the Bible had just said briefly *Et subvertit rotas curruum* (14. 25) the German author characteristically expands this military allusion (vv. 3227 ff.), so that he is now compelled to avoid repetitiveness by omitting the same image in 14. 26. Admittedly, the conventional phrase *daz ist al wâr* (v. 3244) is an addition for the sake of rhyme, but it is doubtful whether the same is true of the more important phrase *der gewalt der ist mîn* with which God closes His address. These are the last words spoken by God to Moses in the *Exodus* and as such they have a double function. First, they hark back to the words which He had spoken to Moses at their first encounter, when He had promised to redeem His people (v. 515: 'daz ich sî von Egypto | lôse mit gewalte'). We are reminded of this promise in the words spoken by God on the eve of another highlight of the action, just before the final plague of Egypt (vv. 2530, 2624), and they recur finally after the destruction of the Egyptians as a testimony that God has kept faith with His people (vv. 3280 ff.). In addition, these last words spoken by God are a conscious echo of the last ones uttered by Pharaoh, who concludes the speech in which he announces his decision to pursue the Israelites with a similar phrase (v. 3013: 'si ne mugen hinnen | mêre nieht entrinnen, | si muozen iemer hie sîn: | der gewalt ist mîn'). Since these words, like v. 3246 itself, are an addition of the Millstatt author we may regard the parallel between these two remarks of Pharaoh and of God, and the commentary on the whole action of the story which it implies, as an effect consciously intended by the author. Behind this parallel there lies the antithesis between Pharaoh's impotence, repeatedly shown in the plagues and soon to be confirmed in his destruction, and God's ability to keep faith. The antithesis implied by v. 3016 and v. 3246 is thus comparable with the author's employment of the technique of *epische Vorausdeutung*, used to illustrate the impotence of the Egyptians and the essential loyalty of God towards His chosen people.[1] In view of these essential functions of v. 3246 we may conclude that this addition, although it may help to create a rhyme, cannot be explained by this alone.

These two examples are suggestive enough to make us doubt whether expansion by means of a *b*-verse, even though it may solve the problem of rhyme, is simply the result of our author's technical embarrassment. However, any rehabilitation of the Millstatt author must proceed further and we must ask whether, amongst the many cases of such expansion, any recurrent features are to be found. If the import of the various *b*-verse additions covers a wide spread of haphazard features, making up no recognisable pattern, then it is probable that these additions are quite fortuitous, i.e. the chance product of an author who is so preoccupied with the difficulties of rhyme that he will countenance expansion without regard to any other aesthetic intentions. If, on the other hand, these additions largely fall into a number of well-defined categories they are likely to be the result of the author's conscious preoccupation with these categories (impelling him to revert to them whenever the expansionary material grants him this liberty), and not simply stopgaps inserted for the sake of the rhyme alone. There are, in fact, three such categories.

The first of these is the author's use of the traditional technique of *epische Vorausdeutung*, every example of which occurs in a *b*-verse. We shall have to revert to this problem later, but what the Millstatt author achieves by this technique is a depiction of the action as guided by the hand of God who is omniscient enough to know the outcome before the action starts (cf. vv. 514 ff.) and omnipotent enough to bring it to a successful conclusion (cf. vv. 3279 ff.). Such anticipatory formulas emphasise the power and loyalty of this God but also, by contrast, the impotence and

[1] See pp. 180 ff.

43

arrogance of Pharaoh. This technique contributes so much to an understanding of the action that any role it may also play in giving the author an easy rhyme is quite secondary. This is confirmed by what we shall later see of the formal aspects of this technique as used in the *Exodus*. For example, this formula is always employed of future events known to the narrator or to God, but never (as in other works) to suggest that one of the actors is himself aware of what the future will bring.[1] Secondly, *epische Vorausdeutung* can be effectively used to sustain tension and the interest of an audience already acquainted with the theme of the work—since the author employs other methods to achieve this end,[2] this function can safely be attributed to this formula in his work. Lastly, the frequency with which he uses this technique increases markedly towards the end of the *Exodus*, especially from the moment of the Israelites' departure. This increase serves to enhance the tension of the narrative as it approaches its climax in the final redemption of the Jews from Egypt, but it also contributes to the depiction of God's effective control of events and of the loyalty with which He accomplishes what He had originally promised Moses. In all these purposeful restrictions on the way in which he chooses to use this conventional device the Millstatt author reveals a disciplined artistry and control of his material which suggest that its employment, far from resulting from the embarrassment of a clumsy workman unable to manage the problem of rhyme, demonstrates how effective an instrument he made of it to convey to his audience how he wished his subject-matter to be understood.

A second category into which many of the *b*-verse additions of the *Exodus* fall is that of time: either in the sense that the duration of an event will be expressed where the Bible had no reference to

---

[1] Knowledge of future events can of course be attributed to Moses as a sign of his confidence in God (e.g. vv. 3147 ff.), but significantly not in the form of an *epische Vorausdeutung*.

[2] For other examples of the way in which the author repeatedly emphasises the tension of the events he is narrating see below, pp. 45, 50, 61 f., 84 and 86 f. It is clear that he is so concerned to stress this that he employs a number of quite distinct methods for this purpose whenever the situation offers him an opportunity.

this, or as an indication of the lapse of an interval of time between two events, or simply as a means of imparting temporal urgency to the event described. These time-references may well be bald and conventional, but they serve to give the narrative a greater appearance of temporal precision. We may be quite sure that this was a formal preoccupation of the author quite apart from his *b*-verse additions, since we shall see in the following chapter that he also frequently expands a biblical scene by depicting it as a process composed of various episodes related to one another in time. This method shares with the role granted to time in so many *b*-verse additions a common concern with the need to relate the various events described to one another and thereby to clarify the course of the narrative action. The author's time-references and time-distinctions may be simple and stereotyped, but at least one may say of him that he has seen their formal necessity: to articulate a work of such expanded proportions and, by providing a variety of pointers, to clarify the action of his story. To criticise him for the conventional schematism of most of these references is irrelevant to the fact that he had the insight to realise that the structure of a work of epic proportions demanded the kind of clarity which these references were able to provide. Nor is the function of his time-references confined to the formal aspect of his work alone, for the Millstatt author's treatment of his subject-matter also reveals an attitude in which the two concepts of time and timelessness undergo a strange amalgam.[1] His formal preoccupation with the need for time-references can therefore be interpreted as a reflection of this attitude towards his subject-matter.

The third category for the sake of which the German author is prepared to make use of the latitude he has won by his *b*-verse additions is the related one of space or the geographical setting in which he places the events he is narrating. If he introduces such place-references much less frequently than time-references, however, this is likely to be due to two reasons. Since the close relationship between time and timelessness (which assists the assimi-

---

[1] See pp. 122 ff.

lation of these events from Hebrew history to the situation of the twelfth century) is crucial for the author's interpretation of his subject-matter, it is understandable that he should have devoted so much attention to the formal problems of time in an epic narrative. Secondly, although the Millstatt author retains many of the biblical place-names when he begins to describe the departure from Egypt itself, nonetheless in his work as a whole he has expunged many of these place-names[1] as part of his wish to assimilate the events which took place in Egypt and by the Red Sea to the needs of the present. Even so, we shall see in the following chapter that the category of space still plays a part in his technique of breaking up a single biblical scene into its various component episodes. To this extent, although he still uses this category sparingly, he has at least taken the first step and grasped its potential importance in the art of epic narrative. His understanding of its possibilities goes beyond the formal needs of an epic narrator, however, for several of his place-references are to be understood symbolically rather than realistically. Thus the German text expands the brief biblical reference of 12. 27 ('Incurvatusque populus adoravit') into a direct hymn of praise sung by the Israelites when they learn of God's promise to assist their departure from Egypt. The words of this thanksgiving (vv. 2632 ff.) are the work of the German author alone and here we encounter a place-reference which, in addition to placing these events in some kind of setting (however indeterminate), also hints at their deeper significance (vv. 2635 f.): 'daz wir suln ze lande | von disem ellende'. The nature of this *lant* had been told to Moses by God (vv. 518 ff.) and is later interpreted by the author (vv. 3300 f.). Equally, the flight *von disem ellende* is not merely a flight from Egypt, but also an escape from bondage and the acquisition of the Jews' long-lost freedom (vv. 2637 ff.). In such a passage the category of space is not merely a device of the epic artist for articulating his narrative material, but also a means of indicating (without any of the explicitness of allegorical interpretation) his attitude toward his subject-matter.

[1] See p. 33, n. 4.

Omissions and expansion

In conclusion, a number of explanatory interpolations have been made by the German author. These are of two kinds: either passages which he has inserted for the formal reason that he wished to make clear the course of an action which, with its epic expansion and consequent detail, may otherwise have been obscure to his audience, or insertions where he explains, briefly and thus avoiding any serious dislocation of the narrative, the moral import of the events in question. An example of the first type introduces the Millstatt narrative. Where the biblical Exodus presupposes knowledge of the prehistory of the events it recounts (and can therefore simply say in 1. 5 that *Joseph autem in Aegypto erat*) the German author briefly recapitulates the events with which Genesis had concluded, converting the static remark of his source into a short account of the process (vv. 47 ff.). He also consults the needs of his audience in his expansion of 1. 9: in place of the brief statement *Ecce, populus filiorum Israel multus, et fortior nobis est* he inserts a lengthy speech (vv. 71 ff.) in which Pharaoh expatiates not on the superior strength of the Israelites, but on their strange qualities setting them apart from the Egyptians. By this the author illustrates in subjective terms the antithesis between the two peoples which is to dominate the work and which he had previously introduced (against his source) only objectively in *heidinisker diete* (v. 48) and *gotes diet* (v. 51). In the opening lines of the narrative (which had only begun in v. 43) the author has recapitulated its prehistory to his audience and explained, through the mouth of one of the actors, the emotional grounds on which the rest of his story rests.

The other type of insertion is also meant to ensure that the audience will not fail to understand the events narrated in their full import. Where, for example, the biblical account of Moses' first encounter with God describes his two attempts to evade the responsibility which God is thrusting upon him (4. 10 and 13) and God's anger on the second occasion (4. 14), the German author prefaces his translation of this last phrase with the comment: 'ze verre habet er geredet' (v. 793). This is not the moralising explicitness of a clerical author, since what this verse accom-

47

plishes is to draw attention to the reason why Moses has here offended God, an indication which is also provided by the words with which he introduces Moses' second attempt to evade responsibility (v. 787: 'Moŷses der guote | ienoh zwîvelôte'). Since *zwîvel* plays a critical role both in this scene and in the whole action of the *Millstätter Exodus*[1] the insertion of this remark is meant to draw the attention of the audience to the significance of this point, alerting them to the import of the story to which they are listening. Not expansion for its own sake, and certainly not simply expansion for the sake of rhyme, but instead a wish to make clear the course of the action and its meaning for the present is the reason for these expansions by the German author.

[1] See pp. 336 ff.

III

THE EXPANSION OF SCENES
FROM WITHIN

THE various types of expansion which we considered in the preceding chapter all had this in common: they added, at the most, certain significant details which either imparted a greater degree of vividness to the action or made its development quite unmistakable or, on the other hand, gave more weight to the author's interpretation of his subject-matter. These expansions were therefore normally nothing more than details (even when, as in vv. 2059 ff., they may add as much as twenty lines of new material), without the ability to alter the pattern of the work by introducing structural changes in particular scenes. It is this which distinguishes this type of expansion from those which we must consider in this and in the following chapter, for now we must analyse the process of epic expansion as it affected various scenes in the exodus story: first, the expansion of a scene from within by breaking it down into its constituent stages (so that not so much the one isolated event as the sequence of events is depicted) and, secondly, the virtual creation of new scenes for which there is no parallel in the biblical source.

The expansion of a scene from within by a description of its various stages is essentially the technique of an author of the large-scale epic, and not of the *Lied*, for it presupposes an unhurried leisure and a taste for detail which, whilst not obligatory in any narrative technique, certainly help the author in imparting credibility to the events he is narrating. Furthermore, the elaboration of the separate stages in what is now conceived more as a process than as a series of isolated events helps to accentuate the continuity of events (in space and in time) and thus to keep the thread of the action clear and intelligible. Whereas the author of a *Lied* concentrates on dramatic essentials and proceeds from highlight to highlight, the composer of an epic, with its greater wealth of secondary material, must welcome any device which will enable him to prevent the lines of his plot from being lost to view under the pressure of such profusion of details. Lastly, the slow depiction of a number of preparatory stages leading up to the decisive event itself will necessarily introduce a degree of concealed tension into the total scene. Since we have already had occasion to remark on this preference of the Millstatt author for tension as an epic device (e.g. *epische Vorausdeutung* and especially the mounting tension of events once the exodus has begun) we may the more readily see in this another reason why the expansion of particular scenes from within offered him aesthetic advantages.

To appreciate the significance of this technique of expansion we may best consider initially one or two examples of the converse technique, employed by the author of the *Wiener Genesis*, where a sequence of events is pruned of all inessentials and cut down to the one decisive event. This technique of the earlier author has been analysed by Beyschlag[1] and in what follows on the *Wiener Genesis* I shall base myself on his findings. His observations are relevant to our present problem, for they throw into relief the nature of the expansionary style of the *Millstätter Exodus* and the differences which exist between it and its predecessor.

A revealing example is provided by Beyschlag's analysis of the way in which the *Wiener Genesis* compresses the episode of Abraham's entry into Egypt down to the barest essentials of this scene. The departure for Egypt is described in the German work (*Genesis* 1600–3) in terms which correspond closely enough to those of the Bible (Gen. 12. 10), but contraction begins when Abraham is about to enter Egypt. Instead of the biblical placing of the following detail in place and in time (Gen. 12. 11: 'Cumque prope esset ut ingrederetur Aegyptum, dixit Sarai uxori suae: Novi quod pulchra sis mulier') the German work says quite baldly (*Genesis* 1604 f.): 'sin wib was uile scone, | er uorhte daz

[1] *Die Wiener Genesis*, pp. 64 ff.

ime dannen scade chome', so that the biblical detail of where this took place, representing a stage on Abraham's journey to Egypt, is omitted and we are instead told of this journey no more than that he simply went to Egypt (*Genesis* 1603). What is essential for the course of the action is therefore retained (the journey and Abraham's fears), but what does not contribute directly to this action (the detail that Abraham felt these fears as he approached Egypt) is discarded. The same process is repeated more drastically in what follows. The Bible reports what happens after the entry into Egypt as a series of events, conceived as forming a sequence in time: Abraham and his wife enter Egypt, the Egyptians admire her beauty, they praise it to Pharaoh and she is taken by force to Pharaoh (Gen. 12. 14 f.: 'Cum itaque ingressus esset Abram Aegyptum, viderunt Aegyptii mulierem quod esset pulchra nimis. Et nuntiaverunt principes Pharaoni, et laudaverunt eam apud illum; et sublata est mulier in domum Pharaonis'). Of all this only the one essential fact is retained in the German work: 'Ich weiz si ime si namen | si brahten si uure den chunich heren' (vv. 1610 f.), so that an incident which had been viewed in the Bible as composed of four interrelated episodes has now been compressed into the one indispensable episode. Such compression has the virtues of economy and concentration, but the modifications of the source which led to this result (whatever its own aesthetic virtues may be) are hardly reconcilable with the characteristics of an epic style.

A comparable compression of events is encountered in the description of the preparations for the sacrifice of Isaac. Here the biblical description of these preliminaries reveals an effective tension as events move up to their climax: Abraham rises one morning, saddles his ass, summons Isaac and two servants, chops wood for a burnt offering and then sets out for the place where God had ordered the sacrifice to be made (Gen. 22. 3). After a journey of three days their goal is seen in the distance (Gen. 22. 4) and Abraham orders the servants to remain behind while he and Isaac go forward alone (Gen. 22. 5). Isaac, carrying the wood for the offering, and Abraham with the fire and the sword approach the designated place (Gen. 22. 6). There follow Isaac's question as to the missing sacrificial animal and Abraham's answer (Gen. 22. 7 f.), the arrival at the place of sacrifice, the building of the altar and the placing of the wood on top of it (Gen. 22. 9). Only at this stage does Abraham bind Isaac and then raise his knife (Gen. 22. 10). The German version of these events is remarkable for its extreme concision: 'Daz chint er uie, | an den berg er gie. | er worhte sinen altare. | daz chint sprach wa der uriskinc ware. | der uater sprach daz got wole wesse | welich oppher ime geriste' (*Genesis* 1852 ff.). With these six lines the German author has now reached v. 10 of his source. What has been dropped from his account is all the circumstantial detail (the manner of the departure, the presence of two secondary figures, the chopping of wood, the length of the journey and the stages registering their approach to the distant goal); what has been retained are the essential facts alone: the journey to the site appointed by God (although it is hardly depicted as a journey, but rather as a sudden switch of the action from one place to another), the construction of the altar and, because of their direct effectiveness in revealing the heart of this scene, the exchange of words between father and son. What has been lost is the circumstantial detail of the source and the mounting tension discernible through the many preparatory stages; what has been gained is a monumental and powerful simplicity. The two styles have different advantages, but it is clear that the technique employed in the German scene, despite its own effectiveness, is not that of a large-scale epic.

A last example from the *Wiener Genesis* concerns the encounter between Abraham's servant and Rebecca at the well. The Vulgate describes this meeting at some length (seven verses) and with a wealth of detail. Rebecca is first sketched going to the well, carrying a pitcher on her shoulder (Gen. 24. 15) and then, after being praised for her beauty and virginity, going down to the well, filling her pitcher and coming up again (Gen. 24. 16). Abraham's servant then approaches her, asking for water (Gen. 24. 17), and she takes the pitcher from her shoulder and gives him water to drink (Gen. 24. 18). When he has refreshed himself she offers to give water to his camels (Gen. 24. 19) and empties her pitcher into a trough, goes once more to the well to fetch water and provides water for all his camels (Gen. 24. 20). Meanwhile, the servant stands silently, observing all she does (Gen. 24. 21). This is a scene rich in detailed activity and in allusiveness and eminently fit to be incorporated as it stands into an epic work. Instead, the German author simplifies it drastically, concentrating only on what he regards as indispensable to the needs of his plot. With him Rebecca is described simply as going to the well (*Genesis* 1948–50: the presence of maids who accompany her is part of what Beyschlag has shown to be the courtly stylisation of Old Testament conditions to be found in the *Wiener Genesis*[1] and also serves as a convincing foil to Rebecca's superior beauty). With her arrival at the well the German author compresses the series of biblical events into no more than four lines:

> 1951   Er sprach ire zů
> 'wande netrenchest du mich, urŏwa'?
> ime selben si scanchte,
> sin olbenten si ouch tranckte.

With that the essential needs of the action have been served, so that the author has no compunction in passing over the conversation between the two (he therefore retains the servant's words, 24. 17, but omits her words to him, 24. 18 and 19) and the various stages in the action, as well as Rebecca's movements to and fro (recorded in detail in the biblical version) which led up to this conclusion. Again it is improper to weigh the advantages of the one style against those of the other,[2] for each work has different ends in view and has therefore chosen the style most adequate to its particular intention.

---

[1] *Die Wiener Genesis*, p. 42.

[2] Cf. Beyschlag's comments, *Die Wiener Genesis*, p. 68: 'Das Ergebnis der Verknappung all dieser Szenen ist eine Erzählart von ungemein strenger und herber Art, von einer eigentümlichen großschrittigen Handlungsführung; keine Rede davon, daß diese dichterisch etwa unkünstlerischer wäre als die Darstellung der biblischen Genesis; sie ist nur wesentlich anders, aber in dieser ihrer eigenen Art von innerer Größe und gedrängter Kraft.'

It is, however, proper to claim that the German style is not that of the large-scale epic. Where its affinities lie has also been established by Beyschlag,[1] for he demonstrates that a style of such economy, mentioning only the barest essentials, is the traditional style of the German *Lied* as revealed, for example, in the narrative sections of *Die Hochʒeit* and of the *Lob Salomons* and also in *Die drei Jünglinge* and the *Ältere Judith* (these are the works on which Beyschlag bases his comparison with the *Wiener Genesis*, but they are, as he suggests,[2] only the latest exponents of a stylistic tradition which goes back to the *Ludwigslied*, the *Georgslied* and the *Galluslied*). Beyschlag makes it highly probable that this particular style is the fundamental style of the author of the *Wiener Genesis*[3] and that he was compelled to deviate from it and undertake formal expansion because of the very proportions of his Old Testament model and also because his need to adapt the biblical story to the conditions of the present and demonstrate their relevance to his own day forced him to dwell in more detail on those aspects of his biblical material which were susceptible to such an interpretation.[4] The formal nature of the *Wiener Genesis* is therefore a complex phenomenon (in this it may partly reflect the variety of its sources), but the fundamental form of the work is that of the *Liedepos* as opposed to the *Buchepos* or *Großerʒählung*.[5] Deviations from this form occur only when there is a particular reason, an opportunity, present in the narrative material itself, to illustrate convincingly that this Old Testament book still possessed a direct relevance to the needs of the eleventh-century audience.

It is precisely at this point that the contrast between the *Wiener Genesis* and the *Millstätter Exodus* is most striking. With the later work it is conversely the case that a particular reason has to be present for contraction of the biblical source to be undertaken. Where no such reason is to be found expansion of the

---

[1] *Die Wiener Genesis*, pp. 98 ff. [2] *Ibid.* p. 107.
[3] See especially Beyschlag, *op. cit.* p. 96.
[4] *Die Wiener Genesis*, p. 108.
[5] These terms have been used by Beyschlag in his article in *WW*, v, 6 ff.

Bible normally takes place. To illustrate the first of these two points we must return to consider briefly some of the examples in chapter II where the Millstatt author either omitted or shortened his biblical material. We saw that the frequent twofold rhythm of the biblical narrative was simplified by the German author's omission of a scene in which God instructed Moses and Aaron what to do in their next encounter with Pharaoh and by his concentration on the actions of Moses and Aaron instead. The same is true where God, instead of issuing an order to Moses, prophesies to him the situation in which he will soon find himself in his dealings with his enemies. Here again the German author excludes this divine incursion into the realm of human activity[1] and instead simply depicts, as part of his narrative, the situation in question, so that what had been represented in the Vulgate in a twofold rhythm (divine prophecy, followed by its realisation) has been compressed into a single rhythm. A similar contraction is encountered in the case of God's relationship with Pharaoh: in place of the divine promise to harden the tyrant's heart the German author depicts only what had come as the second stage of the biblical account, namely Pharaoh's hardening of heart, as part of the narrative action. All this implies a contraction of the biblical material, yet the importance of these occasional examples of contraction in the *Millstätter Exodus* is, as we saw, precisely the fact that they occur only so that another of the author's intentions may be realised. By excluding the role of God in all these biblical episodes he was enabled to depict the action of his story as unfolding constantly on the level of human activity. Even though a few blind references to Moses' obedience are retained (where in fact the author had passed over the divine injunction to which they refer) and even though on a few occasions the scene in which God instructs Moses may not be dropped, the total impression of the *Millstätter Exodus* up to the exodus itself (at which stage other considerations come into play) is

---

[1] Although the Millstatt author may exclude God from some of his scenes this does not mean, of course, that divine activity is absent from the whole work. On this see pp. 42 f.

much more unified than in the Vulgate account. The vernacular work gives more the effect of a continuous action proceeding on the one level, whereas in the Bible the action shows more discontinuity, unfolding on the human level only by fits and starts and exposed to repeated interruptions by an intervening God. In this closer approach to complete continuity on the one level of narrative the German author provides a parallel to what is also true of his employment of allegorical exegesis:[1] by restricting it to an insignificant minimum he avoids the discontinuity of the *Vorauer Bücher Mosis*, for example, with its constant changes of focus from the sphere of time and human activity to that of timelessness and the eternal truth of Christian revelation. The few cases, therefore, where the Millstatt author compresses and simplifies the twofold rhythm of the Bible are best explained as the result of a clearcut aesthetic decision. The same is true of a few other cases, quite distinct from those with this characteristic rhythm, where the German rendering is more compact than the Bible (e.g. 12. 30 f. and vv. 2675 f.; 13. 17 and vv. 2871 ff.; 15. 1 ff. and vv. 3279 ff.) because of the weakening of effect which, for different reasons in every case, a more expansive treatment would have produced.[2] In other words, a special reason everywhere explains those cases where the Millstatt work is more compact than its source, whereas with the *Wiener Genesis* the reverse is true: special reasons are here required to explain those passages where the author expands his biblical source. The biblical narrative technique (if one is justified in equating the style of Genesis with that of Exodus) consequently stands somewhere between the two German works: for the author of the *Wiener Genesis* it presents an account which is too rich and detailed for his purposes and which he therefore normally reduces to the simple proportions he has in mind, whereas for the author of the *Millstätter Exodus* it is already too economical and terse for him to be able to use it without expansion. How far this is in fact so we must now assess by analysing a number of particular examples from the work of the Millstatt author.

[1] See pp. 114 ff.   [2] See my forthcoming article in *MA*.

The expansion of scenes from within

We may start this analysis by considering a few cases where the Millstatt author's technique presents an obvious contrast to that employed by his German predecessor. One case occurs at the beginning of the narrative where Pharaoh orders his overseers to show no leniency towards the Hebrews in their task of building cities. This is expressed with relative brevity in the Bible (1. 11): 'Praeposuit itaque eis magistros operum, ut affligerent eos oneribus; aedificaverunt urbes tabernaculorum Pharaoni, Phithom et Ramesses', a verse which narrates two actions (*praeposuit* and *aedificaverunt*) and indicates in one clause Pharaoh's motives (*ut affligerent*). The German author, untrue to his normal procedure, makes no mention here of Pharaoh's intentions, presumably because he devotes such emphatic attention to the action (which he describes at some length in terms of the oppression it meant) that Pharaoh's motives were more effectively left to express themselves in his action. The vernacular author therefore narrates that Pharaoh appointed his overseers (vv. 107 f.), as in the source, but the biblical account that the Jews then built cities for him is changed in two ways. In the first place, it is no longer recounted as an event which followed Pharaoh's command, but is instead included in Pharaoh's command as part of his indirect speech, and secondly the compact verb *aedificaverunt* is now extended so as to indicate the various facets and stages of this task (vv. 109 ff.): 'er hiez sie daz sî vuoren, | die juden samenôten, | sî nâmin al gemeine | ziegel unde staine, | noch si ne getwâlten, | ê si ime zimberôten | zwô burge âne lôn'. The one action has now been divided into its two stages (the action of the overseers and the work of the Hebrew slaves), but each of these has been further subdivided into the two steps of each process: the overseers are first to leave Pharaoh's court and go to the various parts of his kingdom (*sî vuoren*) and then assemble the Hebrews (*samenôten*), whereas the slaves in their turn are first to collect their materials (*sî nâmin . . . ziegel unde staine*) and then to start their building work (*zimberôten*). The one simple verb of the source, implying nothing of the duration of its activity, has thus been extended to a description of the lengthy and complex process which this episode was in reality. Not content with this, however, the Millstatt author then reinforces this tyrannous edict of Pharaoh by showing its execution. He introduces this further expansionary passage (which has no counterpart in the Vulgate) by saying (vv. 119 f.): 'Die brobeste tâten durh nôt | daz in der hêrre gebôt.' We have already seen that it is his normal practice to omit such references, and indeed the very twofold rhythm of command + execution on which they rest, when they concern the relationship between God and Moses.[1] Here however this characteristic rhythm of the biblical account is retained, not merely so that the author may imply the tyranny of Pharaoh over his own subjects as well as over the Hebrews, but also because he is concerned to depict as emphatically as possible the slavish degradation to which the latter are exposed by this tyranny. What follows is a description of the Egyptian overseers actually riding to the different parts of the country and assembling the Jews for their menial labours (vv. 121 ff.): 'Si riten after lande | die iuden samenonde; | gotes si vergâzzen, | sine wolten sî erlâzen | scalklîcher vorhte, |dielîcher werche.' Again, as in vv. 109 ff., it is the gradual process which is described rather than any isolated event, but this time more emphatically because of the emphasis placed on the degrading tasks which await the Hebrews and on the offence against God which this implied. The concluding passage, in which the menial labour of the slaves is actually described, we shall consider later,[2] when we shall see that the German author attaches such importance to the whole of this scene because he can best hope to appeal to the sympathies of his aristocratic audience by illustrating in drastic terms the readiness of the tyrant Pharaoh to impose such slavery on the Hebrews of noble birth. This insight into the author's attitude towards his subject-matter tells us why he expanded this particular scene, but for the moment we must content ourselves with observing the manner in which he effects this expansion: by breaking down the simple verbal references of his source into various stages and by de-

---

[1] See p. 35.   [2] See pp. 77 ff. and pp. 162 f.

scribing these stages as a series of events lasting over a period of time.

Our next example shows equally that the Millstatt author's expansion of his biblical material results from the epic narrator's interest in the details of his action. In the Bible God instructs Moses and Aaron what they are to do in order to call forth the sixth plague in their next encounter with Pharaoh: they are to take some ash from an oven and Moses is to scatter it in the air (9. 8: 'Tollite plenas manus cineris de camino, et spargat illum Moyses in caelum coram Pharaone'). In the German version the first of these actions (*tollite*) has been expanded in epic terms to a positive search for an oven with ash in it (vv. 1701 ff.): 'gêt unerchomene | ettewâ zeinem ovene | dâ ir aschen vindet, | iwere hande ir dâ vullet.' In place of the simple command to take some ash the account has now been extended by describing how Moses and Aaron are to go to a place where they are to take some ash, so that the German version here introduces the idea of spatial movement, just as the preceding example likewise suggested the movements of the Egyptian overseers travelling about to collect the Jews. In that this movement also involves time (so that the one event has in each case become a process in time) it is clear that this method of epic expansion results in emphasis being given to the two categories of space and time which distinguish the German work from its source. We shall come across further cases of this in the examples that follow.

As a final general example we may take the introduction to the scene in which Pharaoh's followers try to persuade him to abandon his obstinacy by drawing to his attention the many plagues to which this obstinacy has already exposed his people. The Bible recounts quite simply, after Moses and Aaron have threatened Pharaoh with an eighth plague, how his followers immediately address the king (10. 7): 'Dixerunt autem servi Pharaonis ad eum.' In other words, no mention is made in the Vulgate of the fact that Moses and Aaron, after concluding their threat (10. 6), must have withdrawn from the king's presence (that they did in fact withdraw is made clear subsequently by

10. 8: 'Revocaveruntque Moysen et Aaron ad Pharaonem'), just as we are left in ignorance whether Pharaoh's followers were present while Moses and Aaron had their audience with Pharaoh or whether they went to join him after the departure of the two Hebrews. In this scene, therefore, the biblical account concentrates on the leading personages so that no time is wasted on telling us whether other people were present in the background or whether even the leading personages left the scene after they had performed their immediate function. The action is here conceived abstractly and without superfluous detail. This is quite different in the German account, for the Millstatt author's technique fills in the details for us. We know that the followers of Pharaoh must have been present while Moses was addressing him (vv. 2005 ff.), for no sooner is this speech concluded than we are told of their frightened reaction to this news of another impending catastrophe (vv. 2035 f.). The innovation that concerns us here comes in the following lines, for whereas the Bible had suddenly produced these followers out of empty space when once their presence was required by the needs of the action, the German author, even after indicating their presence in the first place, now describes how these followers, in the urgency of their fears for the future, come closer to Pharaoh in order to plead with him (vv. 2037 f.): 'die in dem hove wâren | ze ir hêrren sî chômen.' These followers are not merely given a location in space (v. 2037), they are also shown as moving in that space (v. 2038), so that some of the abstraction of the biblical account has been broken down—again by inserting a further minor stage in the gradual unfolding of the action which is also at the same time a movement in space.

As I have already suggested, it is the two categories of time and space which the Millstatt author repeatedly employs whenever he expands a scene in his action by introducing a reference, however fleetingly, to the various stages which make up that scene. I propose to look at the remaining examples of this type of scene expansion with regard to these two categories and also with regard to the three positions in any scene where expansion

The expansion of scenes from within

(in time or in space) can take place: at the start of a scene (i.e. a movement in space to the next scene *or* an indication of the time when the next scene started), in the course of the scene itself (i.e. the sequence of events, rather than one isolated event, which constitute that scene), and at the conclusion of a scene (i.e. a movement in space away from the scene which is coming to an end *or* a suggestion of the time when the scene was concluded). Here an interesting anomaly arises from the fact that, with one exception, no examples are known to me where the author of the *Millstätter Exodus* has expanded his source by inserting a reference under the last of these five headings: he nowhere introduces a remark, not found in his source, suggesting the time when a particular scene came to an end. We cannot tell what the explanation of this discrepancy may be (the more striking in view of the examples to be found under the other headings), but it is possible that such a reference was unacceptable to him because of its tendency, by emphasising the conclusion of one scene in time, to cut up the action into separate scenes and thus to weaken that epic continuity which he was so concerned to maintain.

Our first group concerns those passages in which the Millstatt author expands his source by inserting a reference to movement in space towards the site where the next stage of the action is to take place. By such insertions he avoids the more desultory technique of his source with its sudden unmentioned transitions, and substitutes for it a narrative where continuity is better preserved as well as an incipient awareness that the events described take place not *in vacuo*, but against a particular background, however vaguely defined this may still be. In the biblical description of the way in which the infant Moses is hidden amongst the bulrushes it is said that the child was placed in a basket which was then concealed in the reeds (2. 3: 'posuitque intus infantulum, et exposuit eum in carecto ripae fluminis'). Two actions (*posuit* and *exposuit*) are here juxtaposed in a manner which suggests that one may have followed on the other without any interval of time or any change of scene. The German author, however, introduces a tension into this scene where the sorrowing mother is about to lose her child (cf. the significant addition of v. 219: *mit grôʒʒem ungemache*) by separating these two events, for he now depicts them as happening at two distinct places (vv. 218 ff.): 'daz chint si dar in legete | mit grôzzem ungemache, | si verstal sich zeinem bache | an die drâte si daz chint verlie.' The addition of v. 220 transfers the action to the site of the following scene, but also, in transforming two events which follow one upon the other in the Bible into two events separated by a change of location, introduces an element of tension which does justice to the situation. A similar emphasis on change of location is revealed by the treatment of the scene in which Moses first catches sight of the burning bush. In the Bible Moses presumably first notices this from a distance, but we are given no direct view of Moses drawing nearer to look more closely at the bush. Instead, this movement is only implied: in the first place, since Moses in his astonishment says that he will approach and look at this miraculous sight from close up (3. 3: 'Dixit ergo Moyses: Vadam, et videbo visionem hanc magnam, quare non comburatur rubus'), and secondly, in that the following verse describes how God saw Moses approaching the bush (3. 4: 'Cernens autem Dominus quod pergeret ad videndum'). In other words, Moses' movement from where he had been guarding the sheep (3. 1) to the bush where he first encounters God is not described explicitly in the Vulgate, but only indirectly as part of what Moses thinks to himself and of what God sees him do. In the German work this indirectness has been abandoned. Moses' amazement is of course retained (vv. 469–71), as well as his curiosity (vv. 475 f.), but now the idea of approaching the bush is extracted from the context of what Moses says to himself and is depicted as a separate action (vv. 473 f.): 'er begunde dare gâhen | daz er iz besâhe.' With that a bridge has been created between the place where Moses had been looking after Jethro's cattle (vv. 459 ff.) and the site of the next scene (vv. 477 ff.), so that continuity of action is retained by explicitly indicating the moment when the action changes from one site to another.

A similar replacement of oblique implications by explicit

description occurs in the second plague of Egypt. The Vulgate starts this scene by having God tell Moses that he is to go to Pharaoh and what he is to say to him (8. 1: 'Dixit quoque Dominus ad Moysen: Ingredere ad Pharaonem, et dices ad eum...'). These detailed instructions then occupy from 8. 1 to 8. 4. In 8. 5, however, the Lord again addresses Moses, telling him to order Aaron to stretch out his hand and to call forth the plague of frogs. This is performed successfully in 8. 6, but from the fact that the following verse recounts the way in which Pharaoh's sorcerers performed the same miracle we may conclude that between 8. 4 and 8. 5 Moses must have obeyed God's command and gone to Pharaoh's court, but that this detail was passed over in silence. This is again quite different in the Millstatt epic: not merely are God's instructions to Moses converted into an independent action of Moses, but the act of going to Pharaoh's court in order to utter the threat and summon the plague has no longer to be read out of the context, for it now emphatically opens this new scene (vv. 1313 f.): 'die boten aue chômen | ze dem chunige Pharaône.' By this addition the passage of events to a new scene is made quite clear, an innovation which must have been welcome as a means of articulating the repetitiveness of the general pattern of the plague scenes. The same applies to the description of the start of the fifth plague. The Bible recounts how God instructs Moses to go to Pharaoh again and to threaten him with a plague to strike his cattle (9. 1–5), but in 9. 6 the plague itself is briefly reported, so that on this occasion, too, we are told nothing of Moses' appearance before Pharaoh in obedience to God's commands. In other words, although the Bible retains here its habitual twofold rhythm, it is a sequence made up of divine prophecy + divine fulfilment (rather than divine command + human execution), so that on this occasion human activity (even though it had been imposed on Moses by God's command) has been omitted from the explicit narrative. The German author, anxious to retain something of Moses' activity, employs the twofold rhythm of God's command (vv. 1625–8) and Moses' execution (vv. 1629 ff.), but gives added force to this introduction of the human element by another reversal of what he found in his source. Where the Bible typically gives more weight to the description of the plague in God's prophecy (9. 3 f.) than in its realisation as an event (9. 6), the German author's narrative interests lead him to weaken the force of God's remarks (cf. v. 1628: 'ez gienge dem vehe an daz leben') and to concentrate all the weight of his anticipatory description on what Moses says in his address to Pharaoh (vv. 1637 ff.). The role attributed to Moses in the German version (without any real counterpart in the Vulgate since this role is not described there as part of the action recounted) now allows the Millstatt author to show his going from the one scene (his encounter with God) to the next (his appearance before Pharaoh): 'er chêrte hine widere | ze dem heidinisken chunege' (vv. 1631 f.). With that continuity between the two scenes is ensured.

The next group of insertions by the German author concerns his references to the time when the next stage of the action commenced, a temporal counterpart to the continuity and articulation ensured by the references to a change of location. Two examples are provided by the passage in which the birth of two sons to Moses is described. The Vulgate narrates both of these events in one verse, giving also the name (with its interpretation) of each child (2. 22: 'Quae peperit ei filium, quem vocavit Gersam, dicens: Advena fui in terra aliena. Alterum vero peperit, quem vocavit Eliezer, dicens: Deus enim patris mei adjutor meus eripuit me de manu Pharaonis'). From this it is clear that the biblical author is more interested in the names and their significance, by comparison with which the fact of birth is of minor importance and is hence relegated to being no more than an event which took place on two occasions (*peperit*). Although the Millstatt author is normally not interested in such interpretations he here follows his source in explaining these names (vv. 415 f. and vv. 430 ff.). He departs from it substantially, however, by the manner in which he adds to the isolated fact that Moses' wife twice gave birth to a son a reference to the duration of her pregnancy. Thus, the birth of the first child is reported in v. 413, but before this the new scene is introduced by the words (vv. 411 f.): 'Uber unmanige tage | Sêphôrâ begunde tragen', so that emphasis now falls on what led up to the event and not merely on the fact of birth itself. The same is true in the case of the second child. Its birth is reported in v. 424 (this alone corresponds to the biblical *peperit*), but this again is prepared for by another temporal addition which illustrates the sequence of events (vv. 419 f.): 'Dânâh uber gewonelich zît | wart swanger daz selbe wîb', an addition which is further strengthened by the subjective description of the father's rejoicing (vv. 421 f.) and also by the way in which the verse reporting the actual birth of the child (v. 424) is introduced by another temporal phrase (v. 423: 'dô der tach dô bechom'). What the biblical source had therefore depicted as two isolated events, with no mention of the interval separating them, has now been converted into a depiction of two processes (pregnancy + birth, rather than birth alone), explicitly separated by the lapse of a period of time. In each case the new event is introduced by a clearcut time-reference.

After the conclusion of the seventh plague with Moses' success in requesting God to put an end to the thunder and hailstorm the Vulgate passes over without any transition to its account of God's instructions to Moses for the eighth plague (10. 1): 'Et dixit Dominus ad Moysen....' In place of such a harsh juxtaposition the German author introduces his new scene by saying that God gave His command after the plague just described (vv. 1979 ff: 'Nâch susgetânem sêre | himilchunech hêre | der hiez den sînen man...'), so that this temporal phrase clarifies the structure of his action by marking this new turning-point in the narrative. Much the same is true of Moses' summoning of the eighth plague itself. The Bible reports, as three events which are not explicitly described in any temporal relationship with one another, the conclusion of Pharaoh's speech refusing to release the Hebrews (10. 11), the way in which Moses and Aaron were driven from his presence (10. 11) and God's instructions to Moses (10. 12). The second of these events is expanded in the German work from *Statim ejecti sunt de conspectu Pharaonis* to a passage of eight lines in which, by the addition of subjective details, this one event is seen more as a series of events (the anger of Pharaoh's followers—they drive out Moses and Aaron—the latters' reaction: *mit trûrigeme muote*). Only after this expansion of the second event do we reach the third, which is typical in that it depicts Moses' activity rather than God's command how he is to act and which is again introduced by a temporal reference (v. 2151: 'Nâch der rede ende | ûf huop Moŷses die hende'), although it is true that this reference would have been more effective if it had connected what follows with the action of Pharaoh's servants, rather than with the close of Pharaoh's speech in v. 2142.

With the conclusion of the eighth plague the Millstatt author again attempts to provide a temporal reference as a transition to the events which follow. The biblical account characteristically finishes what it has to say about the preceding plague by recounting that the Lord, in answer to Moses' prayer, cast the locusts into the Red Sea (10. 19). Pharaoh's change of heart (the indispensable condition for any further plague) is next described but, as is the regular case, this is attributed to God's intervention (10. 20) so that He may now instruct Moses what he has to do in order to inflict a further plague on the Egyptian ruler (10. 21). In short, there is a continuity of the action in this biblical narrative, but only if we judge it on the divine plane, for it is God who expels the locusts, God who hardens Pharaoh's heart and God who gives His advice and the promise of His support to Moses. This continuity of action was likely to be unacceptable to the German author because it was achieved by transposing events on to the divine plane exclusively and by taking responsibility for their actions out of the hands of the human actors. In the case of the miraculous termination of the eighth plague this was of course inevitable, a fact recognised by the German author and used by him to illustrate the power of the God who protects the Hebrews (vv. 2231 ff.). The German author also retains the fact that it is God who this time tells Moses what to do, but there is likely to be a special explanation of what is an exceptional procedure with him.[1] Instead, he introduces the human element by omitting the suggestion that God caused Pharaoh's hardness of heart. Pharaoh is now described as independently revoking his earlier decision to let the Hebrews go free and tyrannously repeating his wish to keep them enslaved (vv. 2250 ff.), a change of mind which, given his obstinacy, follows quite naturally when once he sees that the locusts have all disappeared (vv. 2247 ff.): 'alsô sciere sô er gesach | daz daz grôze ungemach | sô gare was zegangen. . . .' Even though the Millstatt author is inevitably confronted with the problem of a division of the action between the divine plane (the disappearance of the locusts) and the human (Pharaoh's reaction to this), it is the temporal phrase of v. 2247 which now guarantees the continuity between these two scenes. The miraculous termination of the plague could only belong to the divine plane, but by transferring the results of this to the human plane and by stressing the temporal transition he has brought back his narrative to the plane on which he wishes to depict it and which, in this episode, is missing from the biblical account.

Our last example of a reference inserted to indicate the time when a new episode started concerns the detail that the Jews, on the first stage of their march from Egypt, baked unleavened bread. This is reported quite baldly in the Bible (12. 39: 'Coxeruntque farinam. . . et fecerunt subcinericios panes azymos'), even though it is also explained why this should be so. All this is rendered by the German author, but he takes care to add an introductory remark which, by including a place-reference, makes it clear at what stage of their journey the Israelites did this (v. 2769). 'Dô si chômen ze Sôchôt.' Whereas in the Bible this event takes place *in vacuo*, at some unnamed place and at some unspecified time on the exodus, the German author pinpoints it more clearly. Admittedly, he may have had this particular place-name suggested to him by his earlier reference (v. 2753; cf. 12. 37), but his novelty lies in his decision to take up this suggestion and

[1] See p. 175: v. 2264 brings God's request to Moses to do what He commands him, whilst v. 2268 stresses that in exchange God will do what Moses asks of Him. Together these two lines describe in theoretical terms the reciprocal nature of the compact sworn between God and Moses.

5-2

to introduce this new episode by indicating both the locality and the time (relatively, if not absolutely) at which it took place.

With the third group of insertions by the German author we must now consider those cases, similar to the introductory examples, where a scene is expanded from within by the elaboration of various episodes which, whilst they may well be logically self-explanatory, had at least not been explicitly mentioned in the Vulgate. The elaboration of these episodes is a further sign that the Millstatt author had the epic narrator's wish to illustrate the details and stages of his action, rather than leave them to be filled in by the imagination of his audience, and thus to guarantee as nearly unbroken a continuity of action as possible.

A representative example occurs at the conclusion of the second plague, when it is described how all the frogs that had infested the land suddenly died. The Bible recounts how they were disposed of, but in such a way that it is clear that what interests the author is simply the result, not the actual process (8. 14): 'Congregaveruntque eas in immensos aggeres, et computruit terra.' The second part of this statement undergoes no alteration in the German version (vv. 1447 f.), but with the first we are now also shown the process leading up to this result (vv. 1441 ff.): 'die lantliute ersâhen | die grôzzen gotes genâde, | si roumeten ir selede | mit tragen jouch mit menede | und wurffen zesamine | houffen vile manege.' Here the first stage is the recognition that the plague had ended (and the attribution of this to God) and the second the work of clearing the houses, so that only the third stage, the heaping of the frogs into piles, brings us eventually to the only action which the Bible had seen fit to mention. This one action has therefore been depicted as a sequence of three different actions. A similar expansion by the insertion of a stage in the action with which the Bible was able to dispense characterises the fifth plague of Egypt. The Vulgate describes at some length God's words to Moses (9. 1–5) and then the plague itself in only one verse (9. 6), so that our strongest impression is the indirect one conveyed by God's prophecy. Pharaoh's reaction is then described (9. 7): 'Et misit Pharao ad videndum; nec erat quidquam mortuum de his quae possidebat Israel', which is then followed by the hardening of his heart. This action of Pharaoh (sending to find out whether the Israelites' cattle were also afflicted by this plague) is rendered faithfully in the Millstatt work (vv. 1680 ff.), but is extended backwards and forwards in time in a way which now produces three separate episodes, however brief, where the Bible had only reported one. The backwards extension is provided by the detail that the author describes how the news of this plague is brought to Pharaoh (vv. 1677 ff.: 'Der chunech hôrte sagen | daz dirre selbe scade | den sînen wâre gescehen'), so that the action described in the Bible is provided with a preliminary stage. It is also equipped with another scene as a consequence. Whereas the Bible, in saying that Pharaoh sent to find out about the plague and that none of the Israelites' cattle had died, leaves it in doubt whether this second remark may not be an objective description of the conditions which his messengers found and nowhere describes them reporting back to the ruler, the German work introduces this detail as an additional episode (vv. 1685 ff.): 'man sagete ime gewisse, | ir neheiner hête misse | niehtes des er solte leben | neweder in chorne noh in vehe.' There follows a description of Pharaoh's anger (vv. 1689 ff.) so that, in place of the highlights mentioned by the Bible (Pharaoh's mission—condition of the Israelites' cattle—Pharaoh's anger), the German work is characterised by an almost complete continuity of the action (Pharaoh hears of the plague—Pharaoh's mission—the messengers report back—Pharaoh's anger) resulting from the elaboration of episodes on which the Bible had kept silent.

The scene in which the child Moses is concealed in the bulrushes contains another example of this expansionary technique. The Vulgate describes how the child's mother took a wicker basket made of rushes and then made it waterproof (2. 3: 'sumpsit fiscellam scirpeam, et linivit eam bitumine ac pice'), but in the German epic the simple action *sumpsit* is replaced by a process in which the mother now makes the basket herself (vv. 213 f.): 'ûzzer binezze si worhte | eine zeinen der si bedorfte.' The one process of the Bible (the waterproofing of the basket) has thus been expanded to two consecutive processes. In the biblical description of the conclusion of the plague of flies their final disappearance in answer to Moses' prayer to God (8. 31) is followed by a reference to Pharaoh's hardening of heart (8. 32). This latter event is described at greater length by the German author (vv. 1610–20) and with an effective combination of indirect with direct speech, but this expansion is embedded in the context to which it belongs by an introductory remark which connects it with the conclusion of the plague just reported: 'Der chunich sâ bevant | daz erroumet was daz lant | von der vliegen menige | die dâ wâren mit herige' (vv. 1605 ff.). Again it is the function of such a remark not merely to place what follows somewhere on a temporal scale, but also to provide for continuity in the action and the articulation of a work which has expanded to such proportions that the absence of such indications would be detrimental to its intelligibility.

When the Israelites begin their journey from Egypt the Vulgate, referring back to Gen. 50. 24, describes how they took the bones of Joseph with them (13. 19): 'Tulit quoque Moyses ossa Joseph secum.' This simple statement of fact is expanded in the German work into a short scene consisting of three consecutive actions: first, the arrival of the Israelites at the place of Joseph's burial, secondly their opening of his grave and lastly the fact that they took his bones with them (vv. 2943 ff.): 'also si dô chomen dare | dâ Joseb was begraben | ûf tâten sî daz grap | dâ der guote inne lach, | si nâmen sîn gebeine | daz was heilich unde reine | mit in selben an den sint.' With this last stage the German account reaches the action with which the biblical source had contented itself, so that what has been added is again the preliminary stages leading up to this result and the introduction of these stages by means of a temporal reference which embeds this episode in the framework of the Israelites' exodus as a whole (cf. the general remark in vv. 2939–42). Where the Bible narrative proceeds in its bare, but impressive account from one major event to the next, ignoring what may come in between, the German author has slowed down the pace of his narrative and, by filling in these details and stressing the process of each episode, has strengthened the continuity of his narrative and made the course of its development clear to his audience.

With that we come to the last group of insertions: those references in which the German author indicated the movement of the action away from the scene where it had previously taken place. An illuminating example of this is to be found in the passage where the child Moses is left among the bulrushes. Here the biblical account says simply that the mother placed the child amongst the rushes (2. 3: 'et exposuit eum in carecto ripae fluminis') and then passes over immediately to say that his sister was watching all this (2. 4). The German text translates both of these details (v. 221 and vv. 223 f.), but between them it inserts a remark about Moses' mother after she had placed her child amongst the rushes (v. 222): 'heim si trûrende gie.' With that the mother's departure from the scene is explicitly mentioned (she is no longer allowed simply to disappear into the void when once she has played her role), but hardly for its own sake or because of the author's undisciplined loquacity. Instead, this brief mention of her feelings (like the similar addition of v. 219) provides a subjective comment on the whole scene and is an economical but telling illustration of the sufferings to which the Jews in bondage are exposed by Pharaoh's tyranny. That this expansion of the scene by the insertion of a new episode mentioning the mother's sorrowful return home is not fortuitous, but the result of the author's conscious intentions is made clear by the fact that he has also expanded this scene by inserting two other episodes which we have already had to take into account: the scene in which the mother actually makes the wicker basket for the child Moses (vv. 213 f.) and the scene in which she goes with it to the river (vv. 219 f.). For such repeated expansion to have suggested itself to the German author this biblical episode must have recommended itself to his imagination with some force.

In 9. 12 the Bible describes how Pharaoh's heart was hardened after the plague of ulcers and adds that he refused to pay any attention to the request of Moses and Aaron (*et non audivit eos*). In the German epic this remark is expanded (vv. 1773–86) and made more effective by means of indirect and direct speech in which he reaffirms his refusal to grant freedom to the Israelites. The biblical account therefore passes directly from 9. 12 and Pharaoh's refusal to grant an audience to the instructions given to Moses by God (9. 13), so that no mention is made of Moses' departure from Pharaoh's court after his failure to be given a hearing (although it is implied that such a departure must have taken place, since God now says to Moses: *Mane consurge, et sta coram Pharaone*). The German version fills in this detail by mentioning Moses' departure from the court where this scene had been located (vv. 1787 ff.): 'Moŷses der guote man | als er disiu wort vernam, | er chêrte aue dannan | mit grôzem unwillen.' A comparable elaboration occurs with 12. 27 f. The first of these biblical verses concludes with the Israelites' grateful worship of God after His promise to redeem them from Egypt by means of the tenth plague ('Incurvatusque populus adoravit'), whereas the second briefly mentions their setting out to do as God had instructed them in preparation for the Passover ('Et egressi filii Israel fecerunt sicut praeceperat Dominus Moysi et Aaron'). The German author seizes upon the word *egressi* as the link between these two episodes and expands it by adding a subjective comment and a further place-reference (v. 2643: 'si scieden sich danne | mit micheler mandunge, | iegelîch ze sîner selide | mit michelen vroweden'). Moreover, since he has also extended the brief indication of the Jews' worship of God to a hymn of praise in direct speech (vv. 2629–40) this dislocation of the narrative makes it the more necessary for him to manufacture a means of resuming the narrative. This he does by elaborating on the biblical *egressi* and by providing a similar time-reference to suggest that their worship was concluded (v. 2641: 'Dô si got gelobten | als vile sô si wolten'). This is, as far as I know, the only time-reference added by the author to suggest the time when a particular scene had ended: it occurs significantly in close conjunction with a place-reference with a similar function and obviously has the formal role of providing a bridge between the expanded hymn of praise and the narrative which this hymn had interrupted. Finally, a formal function is also to be detected, as we have seen,[1] when the Millstatt author concludes his description of the preparations of the Egyptian warriors to set out in pursuit of the Israelites by twice referring to the fact that their imminent departure is about to transfer the action to a new scene (v. 3072: 'unde huoben sich an die vart' and v. 3074: 'si huoben sich mit chrafte'). These references conclude the description just given, but also provide a bridge to their departure which the author is about to depict.

The expansion of scenes from within serves therefore to embed the action in the context of time and space, thus confirming what we saw in the preceding chapter of the author's preoccupation with these two categories when expanding his work by the addition of no more than one verse. It is true that we are nonetheless given no detailed description of space as a natural background to events or any *absolute* indication of the time when these events took place (instead of the merely relative fact that one event preceded or followed another). Measured against the skill with which, say, Gottfried or Wolfram organise their epic material by reference to the two categories of time and place, the Millstatt author's technique is undoubtedly quite primitive. Yet this is hardly the proper yardstick to apply to him since, however undeveloped his technique may be by comparison with his successors, it remains true that, in addition to being one of the first German authors of this period to compose a work of epic proportions, he has at least realised that these new proportions demand a new technique and that the categories of time and space, by the sense of continuity which they provide, are well suited to articulating a work of this scope and to bringing clarity into the ramifications of his narrative. To praise the Millstatt author for his perspicacity in seeing what were the demands of his new form and how best to meet them is more equitable than to condemn him for what he has failed to achieve.

[1] See p. 41.

We may conclude this chapter by briefly considering one other minor innovation which the author employs in order to organise his material in some kind of chronological sequence. It concerns the simple word *aue* (=*abir*), admittedly a primitive device for arranging events in accordance with a time-pattern, but certainly one whose frequent employment (by contrast with the Vulgate) shows that the German author is at least aware of the necessity, in a work of these proportions, to group his material in some form of recognisable pattern. In one sense, his subject-matter must have suggested this necessity to him since the frequency with which God addresses Moses, or Moses makes a request to God, or God hardens Pharaoh's heart, or Moses seeks an audience with Pharaoh, demands that some attempt be made to keep one occasion distinct from the other and thus avoid the danger of confusion or of monotony. Where the Vulgate says that God spoke to Moses or told him to do something, the German author, by inserting *aue* in such cases, gives some emphasis to the temporal sequence of events. 'Locutusque est Dominus ad Moysen' (6. 10) becomes 'Got in aue lêrte | wie er gebârôte' (vv. 1167 f.) so as to stress the inexhaustible constancy of God's advice to His spokesman. 'Dixit autem Dominus ad Moysen: Ingredere ad Pharaonem' (9. 1) is rendered by 'got hiez in aue hin gân | ze deme heidinisken man' (vv. 1625 f.) for similar reasons. Conversely, when 'Vade ad eum mane' (7. 15) becomes 'Des anderen morgenes vruo | die boten chômen ime aue zuo' (vv. 1259 f.) or when 'Videns autem Pharao quod data esset requies, ingravavit cor suum' (8. 15) is translated by 'Also ditze dinch ergiench | der chunech aue wider viench | ze sînes herzen herte' (vv. 1449 ff.), this is to reveal the obstinacy of Pharaoh in refusing to acknowledge the omnipotence of the God who has promised His people their liberty. The consistent use of *aue* betrays an awareness by the author of the temporal connections between the events he is depicting. As a thread on which to link these events with one another this use of *aue* may be tenuous and reveal little aesthetic sophistication, yet it is at least a thread and a means of organising the rich material of the exodus story. Furthermore, the chronological framework into which this material is placed is not always characterised so exclusively by the idea of mere repetition as these examples of the use of *aue* might have implied. Here an important suggestion of a more skilled technique is made by the author in describing Pharaoh's hardening of heart before the eighth plague. Whereas the Bible says characteristically: 'Et ingravatum est cor ejus, et servorum illius, et induratum nimis' (9. 35), the German text reduces this to a remark about Pharaoh alone, omits any reference to what God had ordered ('sicut praeceperat Dominus per manum Moysi') and renders it more compelling by attributing it as a direct speech to Pharaoh alone. He concludes his speech, addressed to Moses and Aaron, with the revealing words (vv. 1974 ff.): 'ir muozzet tuon same ê, | in mînem dieneste wesen, | obe ir welt genesen, | ich wil iu wirs mite varn | danne ich her habe getân.' These words stress the continuity of past events with the present (*same ê*), as the Millstatt author is constantly at pains to show, but also suggest that Pharaoh's treatment of the Hebrews is not to be a simple repetition of past treatment, but is indeed to surpass it in severity (*wirs...danne...her*). The author therefore considers the events of Exodus as forming a progression and as leading up to the climax of the passage of the Red Sea itself, a climax which is indicated as such by a number of other means. The author's awareness of the category of time is not confined to the simple comprehension that one event repeats another, for even where this appears to be the case (as with the undifferentiated use of *aue*) he is not content with viewing each separate event in isolation and depicting it impressionistically as a self-contained unit, but is instead concerned to link it with what went before and thus to reinforce the narrative continuity of his work.

IV

THE CREATION OF NEW SCENES

OUR analysis of the methods employed by the German author to expand the material of his biblical source has so far only shown us the results of his inserting one or two lines or of his elaboration of a biblical scene by stressing the sequence of episodes which make it up. These two methods may well slow down the pace of the narrative to a more leisurely tempo and the details with which they allow the author to enrich his account may also tell us much about his aesthetic intentions, but neither of these methods contributes to any large-scale expansion of the author's material. To see how this was achieved we must now consider those lengthier passages for which he is responsible: either complete innovations or so expanded from the allusive brevity of the biblical passage that the result is a new scene which has no counterpart in the original. By this I do not mean to suggest that any insertion, provided it is of sufficient length, of itself qualifies for consideration as part of the aesthetic technique of an epic author. More important than the mere fact of quantitative expansion is the manner in which the author makes use of the opportunity for self-expression which such a temporary liberation from the demands of his source grants him, the manner in which he turns this interval of independence to good advantage by drawing attention to certain aspects of his subject-matter which, although latent in the material itself, need to be elaborated if his interpretation of this subject-matter is to be quite free from ambiguity. We shall see that in each of his ten newly created scenes the Millstatt author has successfully exploited his opportunity by making the new scene subordinate to one of his overall purposes in composing the epic. Expansion is therefore far from being a goal in itself: its purpose is rather to allow the author that amount of latitude which he regards as necessary for his reading of the subject-matter to be made clear to his audience.

The first example of what is virtually a new scene concerns the episode in which the Vulgate briefly reports the slavery and oppression of the Hebrews in Egypt (1. 13 f.: 'Oderantque filios Israel Aegyptii, et affligebant illudentes eis; Atque ad amaritudinem perducebant vitam eorum operibus duris luti et lateris, omnique famulatu, quo in terrae operibus premebantur'). These two verses are expanded by the German author so as to create a new scene in itself—an expansion which, although it may still be very much on a minor scale, successfully attracts more attention than the two verses of the Vulgate. Yet this expansion to twenty-two verses (vv. 119–40) brings with it a particular danger, for the epic author has to ensure that any such scene, acquiring a relative independence of its own, shall still remain firmly embedded in his narrative and shall not, because of the expansion of one detail which it represents, disturb the continuity of his narrative. This danger is avoided in the present case by the care with which the oppression of the Hebrews is depicted as a process in which their Egyptian taskmasters, in obedience to Pharaoh's commands, first scour the land in search of the Jews whom they then gather together and force to their menial labours. The simple *affligebant* of the source has been replaced by a process in time[1] which, although it represents an insertion into the narrative, contributes towards the sequence of events in this narrative and thus avoids disrupting it. The same is true of the passage in this scene which represents the German author's most significant reinterpretation of his source, for, in stressing in vv. 127 ff. the disgrace that it was Hebrews of noble birth who were enslaved by the Egyptians, he adduces each of his important points not as static details of a picture, but as separate stages in a process. Thus, the fact of noble birth (v. 127) is illustrated in the action of tempering clay (v. 128), the social rank of the Israelites (v. 129) is conveyed as part of a similar stage in their labours (v. 130), whereas their courtly

[1] This process in time is further emphasised by vv. 137 f.: 'wande si verscelchet wâren | ze vil manigen jâren.'

77

breeding, exemplified in the striking detail of their well kept hands (v. 131), is effectively underlined by its contrast with the drudgery of their manual labour (vv. 132 ff.). Three descriptive details of what could have been presented as a stationary picture of the noble Israelites have therefore been illustrated as a sequence of events which ensures that this passage, however descriptive, forms an integral part of a continuous narrative and does not stand out in static isolation.

The Millstatt author has also taken steps to show that this descriptive passage has not been inserted for its own sake and that its function is therefore as clearly subordinated to the meaning of the whole work as its descriptive technique is to the overall need for narrative continuity. In the first place, the religious implications of the behaviour of the Egyptian taskmasters in rounding up the Hebrew noblemen are briefly suggested in the words *gotes si vergâ{1}en* (v. 123), so that the audience is not allowed to forget that behind this scene of taskmasters and slaves there lies a conflict between God and those who oppose His purposes. Furthermore, the conclusion of this scene by a description of the Israelites' complaints about their prolonged slavery (vv. 135 ff.—with no counterpart in the Bible), although it acts as a summing-up of what has just been narrated, accentuates the impression of slavery and suffering by revealing the subjective state of the victims. That it should be *hêrren* (v. 135) who are the victims of such treatment heightens the sense of outrage already implicit in this description of tyranny; this is also the reason why the tasks which the Israelites are forced to do are emphatically described as menial and degrading: 'scalklîcher vorhte, | dielîcher werche' (vv. 125 f.). The author therefore uses every opportunity to magnify the contrast between the gentle birth and breeding of the Israelites and the unremitting toil to which they are enslaved by Pharaoh and his representatives. The purpose behind this is twofold. On the one hand, since it was the traditional interpretation of Exodus to see in these events an illustration of man's bondage to sin, a yoke imposed upon him by the Devil as a result of the Fall, the Millstatt author here depicts the gulf between the original nobility of man, as he was first created by God, and the degradation which his enslavement to the Devil signifies for him. On the other hand, by depicting this fate of the Israelites whom he describes by the same aristocratic title (*hêrren*: v. 135) which he later uses in addressing his knightly audience (v. 2907), the author hopes not merely to appeal to the sympathy of this audience for the sufferings of those who are depicted as fellow aristocrats, but more essentially to bring it home to them that his theme (the loss of nobility as a result of bondage to sin) is particularly relevant to the nobleman himself. This suggestion of *tua res agitur* is therefore not just a formal device to arouse the interest of the audience, but instead a means of revealing to them the disturbingly personal implications of the subject-matter chosen by the author.

The next passage for consideration (Moses' flight from Egypt and his encounter with Jethro: vv. 323 ff.) provides quite a different example of expansion, since the scene itself is present in the Vulgate and recognisable as an independent scene (2. 15–21), but has been expanded in the German version with regard only to certain aspects to which the Millstatt author attributed importance. One expansion concerns Moses' flight from Egypt after his killing of the overseer has come to light. In the Vulgate this detail is confined to one verse only (2. 15: 'Audivitque Pharao sermonem hunc, et quaerebat occidere Moysen; qui fugiens de conspectu ejus, moratus est in terra Madian, et sedit juxta puteum'), whereas in the vernacular work it now occupies twenty-two verses (vv. 323–44). What has received more detailed treatment is the fact of Moses' banishment and its meaning for him personally. The biblical remark that Pharaoh sought to kill Moses is therefore translated (vv. 329 f.), but extended by the addition that he tried to prevent his escape (vv. 326 f.: 'dô hiez er behuoten, | daz er dan nesunne | noh ime intrunne'). Equally, the fact that Moses fled from Pharaoh is translated (v. 331), but is reinforced by the addition of Moses' motive (v. 332: 'wand er vorhte den tôt') and by a twofold repetition (v. 333: 'Uz deme lande er entran' and v. 335: 'dar er was entrunnen'). Furthermore, whereas the Bible says baldly that Moses sat down by the well in Madian the German account enriches this by a passage (vv. 337–44) of attempted psychological introspection in which Moses, formerly described as the *hêrre* (v. 331) but now as *ellende* (v. 340), muses upon what he is to do, his complete isolation and lack of companions who might offer him advice. These additions to the biblical version all point in the same direction, and by elaborating various facets of Moses' banishment convey a more detailed impression of a nobleman who, like so many *recken* of heroic tradition (e.g. Herzog Ernst), is forced into banishment by a tyrant.

Whilst such a parallel with a common traditional theme in heroic literature must have been welcome to the German author as a means of stressing the relevance of what he had to say to his knightly audience, we must also ask what it was he hoped to achieve by drawing their attention to this point in particular. There is the possibility that he expanded the detail of Moses at the well because of its general similarity with the scene in which Christ encounters the woman of Samaria at the well and because of the overall typological relationship between Moses and Christ.[1] Yet this would only explain the scene at the well (vv. 336 ff.), not the references to banishment which precede it. Here the important point is that all these supplementary details lay stress on the one fact that Moses was *gewisse ellende* (v. 340) and that when at the conclusion of his work he at last gives an explicit allegorical interpretation of the events he has described the Millstatt author interprets the exodus as a journey *von disem ellende* (v. 3299) to the Heavenly Jerusalem. In other words, Moses' banishment and his fate as an outcast symbolise the fate of the Jews in their banishment during the years of their bondage. Since this fate of the Jews is finally equated with the Christian's banishment from the Heavenly Jerusalem as a result of his bondage to sin, it is clear that the whole episode of Moses' banishment was invested with a representative value which encouraged the author to give it greater weight than in his source. The situa-

[1] See pp. 310 f.

tion in which Moses finds himself is that he has no *râtêre* (v. 342) to assist him, just as the Christian in his bondage is without any help, but the *rât* which comes to Moses eventually from God (vv. 463 ff.) is likewise paralleled by the *rât* which Christ has given to every Christian. In expanding the detail of Moses' banishment the German author has therefore selected a theme well known to heroic literature and likely to appeal to his audience, but he has chosen to elaborate this particular theme for reasons which go beyond this: because it sums up, in one detail, the essence of his story as he wished it to be understood.

Further expansionary passages in the same scene confirm this conclusion. When Moses assists Jethro's daughters at the well against the shepherds the Vulgate quickly dismisses the violent implications of this scene (2. 17): 'Supervenere pastores, et ejecerunt eas; surrexitque Moyses, et defensis puellis adaquavit oves earum.' In the German version there is added to this the reason why Moses gave assistance to the women (vv. 359 f.: 'wande der wîbe chrefte | wider die man netohte') and although the fact of violence is still only implied obliquely the military implications are more clearly revealed by the reference to gaining victory (vv. 361 f.): 'Moŷses half den magiden, | daz sî den sige erwurben.' Furthermore, although the author refers to Moses' opponents as *hirte* (v. 353), in agreement with the biblical *pastores*, when he comes to describe the actual encounter he employs the ambiguous term *chneht* (v. 357) which, in addition to its meaning 'servant', could also designate the warrior (as in v. 95) and therefore suggest that this was a heroic encounter in which Moses was engaged. From these additions we may infer that, although he hesitates to depict fighting directly, the German author is not averse to underlining the military or heroic implications of his subject-matter—a conclusion which will be confirmed when we come to analyse his interpretation of this.[1]

Another expansion in this scene concerns the role of *triuwe*, as exemplified by Jethro. What the significance of this is for the work will occupy us later,[2] but it is certainly also a motif which

[1] See pp. 154 ff.   [2] See pp. 171 ff.

explains one insertion in this scene. By this I mean not just the remark in v. 399 (*Jêtrô triuwen san*) as an introduction to Jethro giving his daughter to Moses in marriage (although the Vulgate, 2. 21, has no suggestion of this: 'Accepitque Sephoram filiam ejus uxorem'), but more especially the conscious way in which Jethro, addressing his daughters on their return from the well, gives an almost theoretical definition of *triuwe* (vv. 379 ff.: 'daz ist ein vil rehter site: | der dem anderm wole vert mite, | daz er ettelîche êre | dâr ingegene chêre'). His behaviour in treating the outcast Moses as his equal (vv. 407 f.) and in thereby exemplifying the essential reciprocity of *triuwe* agrees with his theoretical definition. As we shall see,[1] it is significant in this context of *triuwe* that the author should also employ in this scene an *epische Vorausdeutung* of Jethro's conduct (v. 364). This is the only occasion when he uses this device of an action which is not dictated by God's direct intervention and which is instead the result of a conscious human choice. Since its use of divinely determined actions emphasises the unfailing loyalty of God in supporting His people against their foes, we may be sure that its exceptional employment here to denote human activity, in a scene where the author introduces the idea of *triuwe*, is meant to show the morally binding force of this quality. Lastly, in this same episode and as an expression of this gratitude felt by Jethro, the German author also introduces a passage in which he describes (vv. 389–98) the generous reception given to Moses by the priest and the mutual ties of affection which soon bind them together. If we are justified in seeing in this reception a sign of Jethro's breeding and therefore in regarding it as a courtly feature similar to what Beyschlag has established for the *Wiener Genesis*[2] and to what is also characteristic of later, courtly literature,[3] then we must recognise in this courtly innovation, as well as in the novel stress on *triuwe* and on the military implications of the scene, the work of an author who is consciously depicting this whole

---

[1] See pp. 181 f. [2] *Die Wiener Genesis*, pp. 39 f.

[3] On the courtly nature of such scenes in the *Nibelungenlied* and in courtly literature see N. Dürrenmatt, *Das Nibelungenlied im Kreis der höfischen Dichtung*, pp. 25 ff.

encounter between Moses and Jethro in terms well calculated to appeal to a feudal audience.

The remaining examples of new scenes created by the German author are all concerned with the military aspects of his narrative —no matter whether this theme was suggested briefly by his source or whether it was imposed upon his material by the author himself. In either case, these military implications possess an obvious importance and may help to confirm what we saw of the treatment of Moses' encounter with the shepherds at the well. In the scenes which we now have to consider the military theme is more immediately apparent and dominates the entire scene, as it does not in the scene we have just discussed. The theme of warfare is one to which we shall later have to return when we analyse the author's attitude towards his subject-matter;[1] what concerns us more at the moment is the manner in which he utilised this theme in expanding certain passages and what formal results he achieved by devoting these expansions to this particular theme.

As our first example we may take the passage in which the Hebrew midwives ignore Pharaoh's command to kill all the male children of the Jews, for this is described in negative terms with reference to the slaughter which was avoided and to the opportunity of which the beasts of prey of the battlefield were deprived (vv. 157–70), an expansion which is in marked contrast to the factual brevity of the source (1. 17: 'Timuerunt autem obstetrices Deum, et non fecerunt juxta praeceptum regis Aegypti; sed conservabant mares'). We shall later have to concern ourselves with the purpose behind this marked innovation of the Millstatt author, but we can be quite certain that it represented something of considerable importance to him: not merely because it is an innovation, but in particular because it is introduced in negative terms, so that the impression is gained that the author is contriving a situation which will permit his employment of the heroic imagery of the battlefield. Precisely the fact that the beasts of the battlefield are *not* relevant to this scene in which slaughter is avoided provides the author with a means of introducing a

[1] See pp. 154 ff.

stylistic tension which prevents the scene from becoming a static disruption of the narrative flow. His description proceeds from four negative statements: on this occasion there was no prey for the raven (vv. 157 f.), no opportunity for the vulture (vv. 159 f.), no need for the grey wolf to hasten there (vv. 161 f.) or for the wild dogs to look for corpses (vv. 163 f.). This sequence of four aspects of a negative description leaves the audience in ignorance of what did happen long enough to create a tension which finds release only in vv. 165 f. with the eventual introduction of a positive statement: 'wande der chindelîne bluot | wart vile wole behuot'. This statement is then followed by an indication of the religious motive of the midwives' behaviour (vv. 167 f.: 'von der wîbe vorhten | die si ze gote habeten') and by a brief mention of God's reward to them for their *triuwe* (vv. 169 f.). The negative facets of this description, dictated to the author because the terms of his description have no immediate bearing on the situation, have therefore been used by him to create a tension of uncertainty and impatience for the outcome which helps to strengthen the emotional impact of this scene. Furthermore, the negative aspects of the situation are not described statically, but instead with reference to a series of actions by various beasts of prey which, though they may be strictly simultaneous as events, are depicted as a sequence of successive actions (further emphasised by the strict parallelism of each of the four couplets, vv. 157–64). This technique, comparable with what we saw of the description of the Israelite noblemen's slavery, converts what might have been a static description into an integral part of the narrative itself.

The wild beasts chosen by the German author to give life and tension to this scene (the raven, the vulture, the wolf, the wild dog) are the conventional beasts of prey of the battlefield in heroic literature.[1] Their mention here must therefore have struck

[1] Examples are provided by the *Battle of Maldon* 106 (*hremmas*); *Beowulf* 3024 (*hrefn*); OE *Exodus* 162 (*herefugolas*); *ibid.* 164 (*wulfas*); *Beowulf* 3027 (*wulf*); *Annolied* 696 (*den grawin walthundin*). Germanic heroic literature makes little distinction, of course, between the raven and the vulture.

a familiar note to an audience whose taste in non-religious literature was largely governed by the themes of heroic literature. At the same time, these wild beasts were conventional imagery in such a situation in other literary traditions, amongst which we must include the Old Testament itself.[1] In other words, it is possible that they are quoted here as part of the clerical author's biblical erudition and not simply as an appeal to the secular tastes of his audience. The assimilation of Old Testament events to conditions familiar to a German audience of the twelfth century is therefore made possible by the way in which they share certain things in common; it is this, assisted by the changes introduced by the German author, which allows him to demonstrate the relevance to them of these past events. We must therefore be careful not to assume that the introduction of military themes is due to no more than the author's wish to make his subject-matter palatable to a knightly audience. This may well be part of his intention, but it would be rash to assume that it cannot also have been because the author's own interpretation of his biblical subject-matter made it necessary for him to introduce these military themes. This is particularly true in the case of this scene with the midwives since, as we shall see later,[2] Pharaoh's slaughter of the Israelite children stands in a typological relationship with the slaughter of the innocents by Herod and this event in its turn is related, as the first martyrdom on behalf of Christ, to the latest example of such martyrdom in the twelfth century: that of the crusaders. In introducing these heroic and military references the Millstatt author is far from inserting them just for their own sake or because he may hope thereby to hold his audience's attention. On the contrary, they also serve to make his interpretation of these biblical events and their timeless importance more readily intelligible.

Our next example of the elaboration of military themes concerns the way in which three of the plagues of Egypt (the frogs, the flies and the locusts) are described at far greater length than

[1] E.g. Is. 34. 11 (cf. v. 6 for the context) and 34. 15; Gen. 49. 27; Jer. 5. 6; III Reg. 14. 11.   [2] See pp. 307 ff.

in the Vulgate and in emphatically military terms. These expansions are therefore more sustained than the fourteen lines of the scene with the midwives and, although one of these plagues is described in negative terms similar to those in the shorter expansion, the two remaining descriptions are fully positive. Nonetheless, whether the descriptions are negative or positive, it is obvious that the equation of frogs and insects with human warriors is drastic enough to suggest that the author, as in our last example, was going out of his way to introduce these military associations. This does not mean that we must go as far as de Boor, who sees in this drastic incongruity a sign of the author's irony and detachment from the idea of warriors fighting on behalf of God,[1] for there is ample biblical testimony and evidence from the crusading chronicles to suggest that this equation between insects and human warriors did no violence to the medieval imagination.[2] All we are entitled to conclude from the Millstatt author's comparison of insects with warriors is that he attributed such importance to the military implications of his subject-matter that he was not willing to forgo any opportunity to illustrate them more explicitly than in his source.

The description of the frogs in military terms (vv. 1339 ff.) is negative, like the scene with the midwives, and is characterised by a similar tension, but of increased force because of the greater length of the negative description. The author begins by using an apparently unambiguous term for 'army' (vv. 1339 f.: 'got suohte sî heime | mit herige vile chleinime'), but the audience's doubts, and thereby the tension of the whole description, are raised by the succession of negative statements which follows. For as many as seventeen verses (vv. 1343–59) we are told precisely what this army was *not*. We are informed that it had neither shield nor sword, neither huts nor tents, neither helmet nor armour; that it was not composed of knights with their steeds, their mules and their equipment; that it possessed no spears or bows, no packhorses or horns, no banners or esquires. When at

---

[1] For the passage in which de Boor employs this argument see pp. 305 f.
[2] See pp. 325 ff.

the end of this catalogue of negatives we are given one positive statement (vv. 1360 ff.: 'swie iz wolte vehten | wider den rîchen Pharaônem | vur den himelchunich vrônen') the intention behind this is not to dispel doubts but, by delaying the final explanation, to heighten the tension still further. This delay is increased by the following description (vv. 1363–70) of the manner in which Aaron summoned forth the plague (this alone has any direct counterpart in the Vulgate: 8. 6), so that it is not until vv. 1371 ff. that the final positive statement, dispelling all the doubts that have been raised and putting an end to the tension, is made: 'dannen chômen ziwâre | chroten vile mâre, | ein here grôz unde breit.' Only at this stage, thirty-three verses after the commencement of this description, does the audience learn that it was frogs who attacked Pharaoh and that it is they who constitute the army (v. 1373) which had been referred to at the outset (v. 1340).

What weight the author attaches to this military description (which, although it is explicitly in negative terms, still inevitably associates the frogs with the knightly army which they are not) may be seen in the wealth of details he employs. The introductory point about their numbers (v. 1342: 'iz was vile harte manikvalt') is emphasised by the use he makes of doublets in the following description to convey the impression of the numbers, movement and confusion of a vast army on the attack. Thus most of the pieces of equipment mentioned occur in pairs (v. 1343: schilt and swert, v. 1344: hutten and geʒelt, v. 1345: helm and brunne, v. 1349: scaft and bogen, vv. 1356 f.: ʒeichen and vanen). Where this is not the case, the single item is usually subdivided into two aspects, expressed either by nouns (vv. 1346 f.: riterscephte wunne is divided into: in rossen noh in mülen) or by adjectives (vv. 1351 f.: the soumâre are described as snelle oder trâge; vv. 1353 f.: the horn is seen as grôʒeʒ noh chleineʒ). A later reference to this plague uses the same technique briefly (v. 1413: âne sarwât unde sahs). The result of this flood of doublets, accompanied by a frequency of purely descriptive adjectives[1] which is higher than in other

[1] E.g. tiure (v. 1348), snel (1352), trâge (1352), grôʒ (1354), chlein (1354), wîʒ (1356), rôt (1357).

sections of the epic,[1] is that this military description, although negative, is highlighted by the emphasis placed on the wealth of detail and the visual appearance of the whole scene. This is sufficient to indicate the importance which the author attached to it as a military scene, but it also means that the rapid changes of focus with which the description flits from one detail to another reinforce the carefully constructed tension which proceeds through this sequence of negative statements to its final release in v. 1371 and ensure that this descriptive passage, however prolonged an interruption of the action it may otherwise have been, does not hold up the sequence of events. Even where, as in vv. 1360 ff., an apparently concluding observation is made, underlining the *militia Dei* which this army was to wage against Pharaoh, this still does not interrupt the action since, although it concludes the actual description, it still does not release the tension created by the lengthy negative description and still looks forward to the final explanation of vv. 1371 f.

Finally, as an indication of the Millstatt author's wish to elaborate the military features of this scene, even where the actual nature of the plague seemed to offer him the least opportunity, we may stress the fact that although he indulges in this negative description the frogs do constitute for him an army (*here*) and that he uses this term at two emphatic positions in this passage: first, at the start (v. 1340) so as to create the tension of doubt and expectancy in his audience and, secondly, at the conclusion (v. 1373) when these doubts are finally dispelled. Equally emphatic is the manner in which he uses a conventional heroic term to describe the way in which the Egyptians found it impossible to escape from *susgetanen heleden* (v. 1384). These are positive details used to describe the plague as a military phenomenon and they suggest that the author's intention in introducing his negative description was not a pedantic wish to exclude any possible misunderstanding, but instead a desire to invest this scene with military features at all costs, even if this

---

[1] Except in other passages similarly devoted to a description of military splendour (see below, p. 166).

was only possible by such an indirect method. Why he should have chosen to do this with such apparently unpromising material will engage our attention later.[1]

The next expanded description of a plague in military terms occurs soon after the plague of frogs, for in his conflation of the third and fourth plagues of the Bible the German author inserts a military description of the flies (vv. 1482–98) which has no parallel in his source (8. 24: 'Et venit musca gravissima in domos Pharaonis et servorum ejus, et in omnem terram Aegypti; corruptaque est terra ab hujuscemodi muscis). Here he employs a different technique from his method with the second plague, probably because the same method promised little chance of success if repeated so soon after the first occasion. In describing this plague of flies, therefore, he makes no use of the tension which informed the earlier scene and instead does not hesitate to tell his audience at the start what was the nature of this divine attack on the Egyptians (v. 1470: 'hundesfliegen suln iz werden'; cf. also v. 1478: 'iz wurden hundesfliegen'). But, as we saw with the second plague, the formal device of tension was inseparable from that of negative description since the expectancy of the audience could only be sustained if they could be kept in suspense with a sequence of negative statements. If this next plague in the German version shows no trace of tension we need not be surprised that its technique should now be one of positive description in military terms. This description starts with the emphatic observation (v. 1482): 'gotes rîtere wâren si wilde', a remark which is in striking contrast with the way in which it had been said of the plague of frogs that they were no mounted knights (vv. 1346 f.: '. . .neheiner riterscephte wunne, | in rossen noh in mûlen'). Yet it is unlikely that this difference in descriptive technique is to be explained solely by the employment or rejection of tension as a formal device, since it is conceivable that the swift, darting movements of winged insects suggested the image of mounted knights, careering and swerving in battle, whereas the same image was unusable in the case of the frogs. This

[1] See below, pp. 325 ff.

suggests that the Millstatt author, prepared to accept the knightly image for the one plague but unable to make use of it for the other, was master enough of his material to devise a different technique for each case. In the plague of frogs, where a negative description was unavoidable, he converts this into a formal advantage by employing the device of tension, whereas with the plague of flies, where a positive description in knightly terms proved feasible, he refrains from using the same technique so soon again.

Yet his description of the plague of flies has its own kind of tension, since this is provided by the manner in which the author opens this description by saying, not simply that they were knights, but that they were *gotes rîtere* (v. 1482). This, as we shall see, is important as a crusading term and the same will also prove to be true of the phrase with which his account of their attacks on Pharaoh is concluded (v. 1494): *gotes anden si râchen.*[1] The occurrence of two such typical crusading ideas in quick succession imparts to this description its own significance by suggesting not simply (as with the plague of frogs) the association of their attacks with knightly warfare, but more explicitly that their attacks on the heathen were a form of crusading warfare. With this suggestion the Millstatt author has now conveyed to his audience more clearly than anywhere before an idea of how they are to interpret the events of Exodus and of their relevance to their own day. Yet in saying now of the plague of flies what he had previously said of the plague of frogs (namely, that they were summoned by God and were invincible)[2] he has really succeeded in saying something new and of decisive importance for his interpretation of Exodus. Whereas, in the case of the frogs, this can only mean that an army (*here*) of warriors (*heleden*) whose connection with knightly warfare is only indirect has been called forth by God and promised victory, in the case of the flies it is now said that it is an army of *gotes rîtere* whom God has

---

[1] See pp. 278 ff.

[2] God summons the frogs: vv. 1339 ff., 1394 ff., 1408 ff.; and also the flies: vv. 1484, 1498, 1603 f. Because of this the frogs are invincible: vv. 1385 f.; as are the flies: vv. 1485 f., 1495 ff., 1553 f.

summoned to gain victory on His behalf. With that a direct link with contemporary crusading beliefs is established for the first time, so that the realisation of this by a contemporary audience must have conferred a unique significance upon this scene.

The last example of a plague scene incorporating a military expansion need not detain us long. It concerns the plague of locusts which, in contrast to the biblical description (10. 13 f.: 'locustas, quae ascenderunt super universam terram Aegypti, et sederunt in cunctis finibus Aegyptiorum innumerabiles'), is likewise viewed as a military attack. Here the start of this description brings a slight tension as in the plague of frogs in that the first reference indefinitely mentions *vile manegen vîant* (v. 2164), but since this tension is removed in the very next verse (v. 2165: 'si hiezzen houscrechen') it is clear that the descriptive method employed here has more in common with what we saw of the plague of flies than with the technique used in the plague of frogs. This is confirmed by the manner in which these locusts are compared positively with warriors. They are, as the opening line of the passage says, seen as the *vîant* of Pharaoh and of the Egyptians, they occupy his land by force (vv. 2169 f.: 'mite micheler gewalt | si besâzen daz lant') and they make up an army (v. 2171: *her*) of individual warriors (vv. 2175 ff.: 'si wâren in dem lande | vile guote wîgande | vile snelle helede'). Like the other plagues they are shown as having been summoned forth by God Himself,[1] whom they therefore presumably serve by their warfare. Again it is doubtful whether these references have been introduced merely because of their military nature and their ability to appeal to the taste of a knightly audience. In this case the parallels of locusts sent by God as a punishment in the Old Testament[2] as well as the evidence for similar imagery in crusading chronicles[3] suggest that the author is once again endeavouring to establish a point of immediate contact between events in the Old Testament and the world of the twelfth century

[1] Cf. vv. 2164 f., 2210 f., 2235 ff.
[2] See p. 329, n. 3, p. 331, n. 3 and p. 332, n. 2.
[3] See pp. 328 ff.

and that it is this theme of warfare on behalf of God which proves most useful to him in this.

There remain for consideration four expanded passages of a military nature. These passages concern the departure of the Israelite army from Egypt and the comparable description of the Egyptian warriors setting out in pursuit, as well as two scenes in which both armies give way to despair and fear when confronted by impending disaster. Whether in the form of a brilliant description of knightly trappings and military *élan* or in the contrasting mood of a collapse in morale, all these scenes are therefore military in inspiration. The fact that they form a self-contained and symmetrical group (both armies set out in all their martial glory and both are depicted on the brink of cowardice as disaster threatens) suggests that the Millstatt author was consciously at work in expanding these scenes in this particular manner.

Our first passage describes the departure of the Israelites from Egypt in the form of a knightly army setting out in full panoply (vv. 2877–2942). This is a vast expansion of what had been no more than a fleeting hint in the Bible (13. 18: 'et armati ascenderunt filii Israel de terra Aegypti') and allows us to see in this emphasis on military details a characteristic of the German author. With a description of this length the author cannot avoid having some of his details as static elements of pure description with no contribution to the development of the action. This is true of the fact that helmets and armour shone like gems and like stars (vv. 2883 ff.), for although the essential point of this descriptive detail is conveyed by the verb *scinen* it is a verb which cannot contribute to the action, but only to the elaboration of a new detail in what remains an essentially static impression of military splendour. The same is true of the parallelism of vv. 2895 ff.: 'si hêten umbe ir bein | vil manegen stâlîn zein, | si hêten in den handen | breite spiezze lange, | si hêten ze ir sîten | scilte vile wîte', for the characteristic of this verb *hêten* is that in each case it tells us something new about the impressive situation without showing its development from one action to another. To this extent this prolonged description has certain static elements which extract it partially from the narrative action, which is therefore in some measure disrupted and slowed down. On the other hand, the author has obviously taken trouble to change some aspects of this description into actions which convert an otherwise static description into a sequence of events. In the first place, an impression of activity is conveyed whenever a piece of equipment is not described as it is, but is instead shown (however briefly) in the process of being made. This is the case with the chainmail (vv. 2887 ff.: 'sarwât diu wîze | geworht was si mit vlîze | mit rôteme golde. | si hêten smide holde') or with the enamelling on the Israelites' helmets(vv. 2916 f.: 'gemachet habeten si dar ane | daz tiure gesmelze'). These are only minor details and cannot do much of themselves to create the impression of uninterrupted activity. More important is the manner in which the Jewish knights are not described as simply carrying their equipment with them (an essentially static detail, adding only a further touch to the total impression), but rather as collecting items of their gear as they prepare for the departure (vv. 2929 f.: 'Sumelîche hêten genomen | manegen guoten hornbogen'). This is in turn followed by an *epische Vorausdeutung* which, by informing the audience that these weapons later stood them in good stead (vv. 2931 f.: 'daz edile gescuzze | daz wart in sît nuzze'), is a clear sign that the author was so engrossed in the details of this descriptive passage that he neglected to point out its connections with events which have still to take place. By such an insertion the static isolation of this passage is largely diminished. The same is true of the manner in which the author also introduces and rounds off this lengthy description with two details which stress the movement of the Hebrew army and thus remind the audience that, however static the picture described may be in its details, it is a picture of an army on the move and that this departure, in a work concerned with the theme of exodus, must after all be considered as one of the decisive events of the whole work. Having said that the Hebrews obeyed Moses and set forth (vv. 2871 ff.) the German author commences his description by stressing the splendour of this army, but also the fact that it was an army on the move (vv. 2877 f.: 'daz selbe her vile breit | daz fuor mit grôzir scônheit'). A similar stress falls at the conclusion of the passage, for the author adds to his description of the mounts used by the Israelites the clause (v. 2938): 'dô si rûmeten daz lant', which enables him to pass smoothly from this descriptive interlude to the events which still remain to be narrated (vv. 2939 ff.): 'Mit susgetânen êren | sô vuoren dô die hêrren | von dem ellende | uzzir deme lande.' With that the whole of this description is embedded in the sequence of events now rapidly approaching its climax and at the same time, because of the critical importance of this departure for the meaning of Exodus, sufficient justification is given for the length in which this particular event is described in all its splendid details of well-wrought equipment[1] and military implications.

As in other expansionary passages the Millstatt author is not concerned simply to give a military description for its own sake. He finishes the first half of his description by mentioning that the Israelites' shields had 'manich tier wunderlich' (v. 2905) depicted on them, but then goes on to conclude by emphasising one animal in particular (v. 2906): 'der lewe vreislich'.[2] This is a reference to the symbolism of the lion of Juda[3] and its typological associations with Christ, so that this apparently unimportant and decorative detail has the function of suggesting that this Hebrew army, setting out on the command of God and promised His support, is no less than a prefiguration of a Christian army engaging in battle with divine sanction. This makes it all the more significant that the author should interrupt the flow of his description at this stage (with no obvious formal reason for such a break) to address his audience directly for the only time in the whole work (vv. 2907 f.: 'Nû vernement, mîne hêrren, | ich wil iu sagen

---

[1] For the emphatic manner in which physical details are described in all their splendour see below, p. 166.

[2] He also mentions the eagle (v. 2904), but it is on the lion, mentioned just before the decisive break of v. 2907 and as the conclusion of a description which had begun in v. 2877, that the main emphasis falls.

[3] See p. 108, n. 1.

mêre') and thus make sure that they are alerted to the importance of what he is here describing. This direct appeal is partly justified on the grounds that the author can best hope to hold the attention of his knightly audience when describing heroic splendour, but to see in this the sole explanation would be to make him too dependent on their literary interests and would make it difficult to see how he could hope to gain a hearing for his whole work. A further explanation is provided by the manner in which this appeal to the knights comes just after the reference to the pre-figurative nature of the Israelite army, for this juxtaposition implies that the fulfilment of this prefiguration is somehow con-nected with the knights themselves, which is why the author, at this stage alone, addresses them directly. The *hêrren* in his audience are meant to regard themselves as the knightly peers of the Israelite *hêrren* (v. 2940) whose knightly splendour and equipment (v. 2939: 'Mit susgetânen êren') show how close they stand to the social and knightly ideals of the present. The pre-figurative function of the Jewish army, reinforced by this simi-larity between them and the knights of the present, is meant to draw the attention of these knights to the implicit responsibility which has now fallen to them of continuing religious knighthood in the name of Christ. It is with this in mind, as well as to provide an effective contrast with what is later said of the Egyptians, that the perfect humility of these Israelite knights is underlined (vv. 2927 f.: 'si vuoren iedoch weiz got | âne allerslahte ubirmuot'), for *ubirmuot* is also the traditional vice of the medieval knights in the eyes of the clergy[1] and the sin which they must avoid if they are to be worthy of fulfilling the task for which they have been chosen. The heroic elation which also fills the Hebrew knights (v. 2924: 'wol vrouwet in daz ir muot') is another quality fit to recommend them to a knightly audience, but a quality which, in view of what later happens when danger threatens them, has its ironic overtones as well as its implications for any twelfth-century audience.

This important and lengthy description of the Israelite knights

---

[1] See below, p. 359, n. 2 and p. 392, n. 1.

is soon followed by one of similar length, showing the departure of the Egyptian warriors in pursuit (vv. 3024–78) and likewise an expansion of what had been described in the Bible in slightly more detail than with the Hebrews, but still with remarkable brevity (14. 6 f.: 'Junxit ergo currum, et omnem populum suum assumpsit secum. Tulitque sexcentos currus electos, et quidquid in Aegypto curruum fuit, et duces totius exercitus'). Such a repetition, after so short an interval and rendered apparent by the length of each of these military descriptions, might contradict what we have seen of the author's wish to avoid mere repetitiveness and to stress the economy of his narrative. Yet these two passages do not constitute a simple repetition and, coming towards the climax of his work, they enable the author to make his message quite clear, for, although the two armies give every appearance of being similarly knightly and equally adorned with the finest equipment,[1] they are impelled by very different ideals. It is this difference in outlook which accounts for their different fates and which justifies the author in repeating his description of military splendour as a means of showing the true contrast between these outwardly similar knightly armies.

As with the preceding description, the Millstatt author is concerned in this passage to avoid a description so static that it will impede the flow of events—especially at a time when these are rapidly approaching their climax. He does this again, in part, by briefly describing the manufacture of equipment instead of its appearance, as with the banners of the Egyptians (vv. 3047 f.: '...manegir gruone unde wîz, | geworht wâren si in allem vlîz') or their javelins (vv. 3053 f.: 'den wâren die gêren | geworht nâch den êren'). More significant is the manner in which the whole description starts with a passage (vv. 3024 ff.) in which Pharaoh chose the best from amongst his many warriors, ordered the preparation of his chariots and summoned his dukes and counts, for, although this description of a process renders 14. 6 f. of the Vulgate, it does this at greater length and prepares the way

---

[1] On the way in which the German author emphasises the magnificent appearance of the Egyptian warriors in his description see p. 166.

for what follows. What comes next is a more static description, dwelling with greater leisure on the details of equipment, but it is introduced by a remark which, similar to vv. 2877 f. in the case of the Jews, suggests the splendour of this army as it began to assemble in battle-order (vv. 3039 f.: 'Si fuoren vile scône, | dô si zesamene chômen'). With v. 3058 this more static description is concluded and what follows is another passage in which the various stages in the Egyptian preparations are elaborated (vv. 3059 ff.): the pagan warriors take down their shields and spears from the walls, put on their helmets and ask for their chainmail to be brought. With that the process of preparing for battle is completed and the army now sets out, moving rapidly towards the scene of the climax (v. 3072: 'unde huoben sich an die vart'; 3074: 'si huoben sich mit chrafte') and following in the tracks of the Israelites (vv. 3079 ff.).

We saw that in the description of the Israelite army the employment of an *epische Vorausdeutung* (v. 2932) served to embed the passage in the total sequence of events and to prevent its isolation from the rest of the narrative.[1] The same is true of this complementary picture of the Egyptian warriors, except that on this occasion this device is used very much more frequently, in every case to draw attention to the destruction which is so soon to overtake them (v. 3042: 'in nâhet der bane'; v. 3046: 'in nâhet der tôt'; v. 3064: 'in nâhet allez leit'; v. 3066: 'daz wart in enblanden'; cf. also v. 3088: 'daz fuor ze sîneme leide'). The frequency of these references in this passage far exceeds the employment of this same device in other parts of the epic, so that it is reasonably certain that these anticipations of future disaster are employed not merely to heighten the tension of this scene just before the final climax, but also, as a background of impending destruction, to provide a telling comment on the scene of knightly splendour into which they are inserted. These references therefore pass judgement on the scene which the author has illustrated with such a wealth of detail: they reveal the useless folly of the pagans' military splendour and expose

[1] See p. 93.

the impotence of knightly pomp when confronted by the power of the God who has sworn to uphold the Israelites. Furthermore, as *epische Vorausdeutungen* these references possess an objective quality in that they are not opinions held by any of the actors in the story, but represent the judgement of the author on what he is narrating: they are to be understood as an objective commentary on these events the truth of which is undoubted and soon to be confirmed in the scene by the Red Sea.

As yet the frequency of these references has only shown that the military pomp of the Egyptians, although apparently identical with that of their foes, was radically different from it. We still know nothing of the reasons why it should be condemned. For this we must turn to two remarks inserted at the beginning and the end of the purely descriptive passage. In the first of these the Millstatt author concludes his description of the way in which Pharaoh summons his warriors, chariots and generals by inserting the reply of these generals to his request for their assistance in defeating the Israelites (vv. 3037 f.): 'si sprâchen "daz sculen wir gerne tuon | unsir muoz nû wesen der ruom".' With this emphasis on heroic renown the author has created a contrast to what he had earlier reported of the Israelites' humility in a similar situation (vv. 2927 f.). Whereas, however, this first remark was an objective commentary by the author (since to put a claim for humility into the mouths of the Israelites would defeat its own ends), the later, boastful remark is imputed to the Egyptians who are thus shown to be passing judgement on themselves by these very words. This is confirmed by the author himself in a second remark, for when the Egyptians have completed their preparations and now set out he uses the equally critical terms *sich ver-meʒʒen* (v. 3075) and *gelf* (v. 3077) to make clear what is involved, by contrast with the earlier scene, in this display of knightly heroism. What is condemned in this scene is not knightly magnificence in itself (for the Israelites had been described in similar terms), but rather the false ends which it is here made to serve. The arrogance of the Egyptians lies not just in their preoccupation with military renown, but above all in the blind obstinacy with which they oppose God's will and refuse to acknowledge all the signs of His omnipotence.

It was suggested above that the brief allusion to the heroic elation of the Hebrew warriors as they set out (v. 2924) had ironic implications in view of their loss of confidence when later faced with imminent danger. This is a problem which we shall later have to analyse with regard to the theme of *ʒwîvel* in the *Millstätter Exodus*,[1] but for the moment, when we are concerned only with the formal problem of expansion, it is sufficient to recognise that the author's wish to reveal the ambiguous nature of the Hebrews' position has led him to expand the passage in which these doubts of the Hebrews are vividly expressed (vv. 3105–44). These forty lines correspond to 14. 10–12 in the Vulgate, where all but one of the points made by the German author are at least implied, but his drastic expansion suggests that he attached a novel importance to this scene. This is confirmed by another factor, for an earlier biblical reference to the possibility that the Hebrews might take fright on encountering opposition to their flight from Egypt (13. 17) was omitted by the German author, probably because he felt that this anticipation of later events might detract from the unique importance which he attributed to this scene when the Hebrews catch sight of the approaching Egyptians. Although the word *ʒwîvel* is nowhere used in this passage, it is clear from the fears expressed by the Hebrews in their reproaches to Moses that it is this failing which dominates this scene, which therefore, even if only indirectly, gives additional importance to the role of *ʒwîvel* in the work as a whole. The fault of the Jews lies *not* in the fact that in their danger they make an appeal to God for help (vv. 3109–14; cf. 14. 10), for this could be interpreted as a demonstration of their humility and of their readiness to place their fate in the hands of God, but rather in the manner in which this attitude is soon replaced by a mood of recrimination and pusillanimity in which, by making reproaches to Moses (vv. 3115–44; cf. 14. 11 f.), they indirectly criticise the God in whose name Moses

[1] See pp. 336 ff.

had acted. What is revealed in this criticism is not simply a fear
of the suffering and death which they feel sure awaits them
(vv. 3119 ff.), but more particularly a cowardly and lethargic
wish to cling to the degrading bondage of Egypt (vv. 3133 ff.: 'uns
wâre zewâre | michil bezzôre | daz wir iemer dienôten | danne
susgetâne nôte'), an indolence which appears all the more blame-
worthy if one recalls the traditional interpretation and realises
that it is the bondage of sin which these Hebrews prefer to the
possibility of salvation granted them as a divine gift. How serious
is their reversal of values is shown by the additional detail that
the Hebrews crown their reproaches to Moses with the fear that
they are about to lose the wealth which they had taken with them
on leaving Egypt (vv. 3143 f.): 'disen heiden ist sô zorn, | unsir
guot ist verlorn.' Even though this last point is the only one to
which no hint of a parallel can be found in the author's source,
the very length of this passage amounts to a sustained criticism
of the Jews of some force. Why this criticism of those who had
been described as God's people and as humble in their departure
from Egypt should have been elaborated by the German author
is a problem to which we shall later have to return.

This disturbance of the relationship between the Israelites and
God, clouded by the *zwîvel* which pervades this scene, even if it
is not mentioned by name, is reflected in a formal device employed with some skill. Just as the earlier scene in which the
Egyptian warriors set out for battle was characterised by its
frequent *epische Vorausdeutungen*, so is this scene permeated by
the Israelites' repeated anticipation of the calamity which they
feel is about to strike them. This is indicated on the first occasion
by the author himself when he reports the approach of the
Egyptians in pursuit, for he says of the Jews (vv. 3101 f.): 'si
versâhen sich arbeite | nâch gewonheite.' After this, however, the
expectation of suffering is voiced by the Israelites themselves. In
their cry to God they refer to their *nôt* and request His help 'daz
wir neligen tôt' (vv. 3111 f.), just as they also allude to the *bane*
(v. 3113) which otherwise awaits them. In their reproaches to
Moses these anticipations grow more frequent: the wrath of the

pagans (v. 3121) now confronts them with *nôt* (v. 3120) and means that they are *verlorn* (v. 3122), it is their fate to die (v. 3126: *sturben*) in the desert, to suffer there (vv. 3128 and 3136: *nôte*), to meet death (v. 3139: *tôt*) and to lose their wealth (v. 3144: *verlorn*) as well as their lives. These anticipations of future suffering are therefore as frequent in this scene as they were in the description of the Egyptian warriors' departure. Moreover, they show a certain unity amongst themselves (*nôt(e)* occurs four times, *tôt* and *verlorn* twice), but also in some measure a reflection of what had been said of the Egyptians: *tôt* thus recalls v. 3046 ('in nâhet der tôt'), *bane* takes up v. 3042 ('in nâhet der bane') and, even though there may be no verbal parallel, the fourfold use of *nôt(e)* is at least comparable with the *leit* of vv. 3064 and 3088. Yet this similarity between the two scenes conceals a profound difference. Whereas all the remarks in the scene with the Egyptians were *epische Vorausdeutungen*, i.e. objective comments made by the author in his omniscience about the Egyptians and therefore soon to be confirmed by events, in the scene with the Israelites none of these anticipatory remarks is an *epische Vorausdeutung*; they are all (with the sole exception of vv. 3101 f.) subjective remarks made by the Israelites in their ignorance about themselves and therefore about to be disproved by events. These forecasts of future suffering will be shown to have no foundation in reality (future reality is therefore known only to God, v. 2982, and to Moses, vv. 3145 ff., to whom He has confided this knowledge) and are used by the author—in contrast to his employment of *epische Vorausdeutung*—as a means of showing that the Jews are deluded by their *zwîvel*, by their lack of confidence in God which pervades this scene.[1]

[1] I use the term *epische Vorausdeutung* in the sense which B. Wachinger, *Studien zum Nibelungenlied*, attributes to the term *Erzählervorausdeutung*. On the significant contrast between this and the purely subjective anticipations of personages in the work (in Wachinger's terminology: *Vorausdeutung in der dargestellten Handlung*) see his remark, p. 5: 'Wir haben damit zugleich eine für die ganze Arbeit grundlegende Unterscheidung getroffen: Es gibt eine Ebene der dargestellten Welt und der dargestellten Gestalten, eine Ebene der in sich geschlossenen Handlung, in der wir psychologische Wahrscheinlichkeit erwarten. Hierher gehören — zunächst wenigstens — die Warnungen, Prophe-

The Millstätter Exodus

Our last example of expansion is provided by the scene, complementary to the one we have just considered, in which it is the turn of the Egyptians, as they catch sight of the waters of the Red Sea moving in on them, to express their fear and doubts. The passage (vv. 3213–34) again has a parallel in the Vulgate (14. 25: 'Dixerunt ergo Aegyptii: Fugiamus Israelem; Dominus enim pugnat pro eis contra nos'), but one which is significantly shorter and less detailed than the vernacular version. In this version the Egyptians, like the Israelites in the preceding scene, anticipate the disaster which is about to destroy them (vv. 3219 ff.: 'mit micheler chrefte | vur si wil hiute vehten | ein gewaltiger hêrre'), but in this case it is made clear that this is not, as with the Hebrews, simply a subjective foreboding because of the addition of an objective confirmation by the author in the form of an *epische Vorausdeutung*, the last in the work and one which, occurring right at the climax, shows that these belated fears of God's enemies have more foundation in fact than had the doubts of the Hebrews (v. 3226): 'der tôt was in nâhen.' From the belatedness of this recognition that God was fighting for His people there results the emphasis on the equipment of the Egyptian knights, illustrating how it was of no avail to them on this occasion (vv. 3227 ff.: 'dâ was unnuzze | der spore wol gespizzet, | noh dei ros snellen | . . . | noh die reitwagene'). It cannot be argued that these essentially knightly details, taken from the equipment of mounted warriors, have simply been borrowed from the biblical reference in 14. 28 ('et operuerunt currus et equites cuncti exercitus Pharaonis'), for these details are later given by the German author, in their proper place, when he comes to translate this passage (vv. 3261 ff.: 'daz wazzir bedachte |

zeiungen usw. Es gibt daneben eine Ebene des Erzählers, der alles weiß, eine Schicht, in der Abstand genommen werden kann von den Gestalten, wo reflektiert wird, wo die Gestalten bewertet, bewundert, verurteilt werden, wo Zusammenhänge erklärt werden, die die Gestalten nicht sehen, usw.' It is only this latter level, in which the author gives voice to his omniscience, that can be called objective. Significantly it is on this level that the forthcoming destruction of the Egyptians is anticipated as a fact which cannot be circumvented, whereas the fears of the Israelites (so soon to be proved groundless by the course of events) are depicted subjectively.

die sîne chuonen chnappen | sîne reitwagene | rîche unde manege '). By introducing this passage at v. 3227 (and thus involving himself, against his usual practice, in a repetition) the Millstatt author has managed to suggest, immediately after his last *epische Vorausdeutung*, that it was not just their military equipment which gave the Egyptian warriors no help, but their *knightly* equipment in particular (*spore, ros, reitwagene*)—a point which could not fail to be taken by an audience of knights. This insertion provides in retrospect a further justification of the long description of the Egyptian warriors' splendour as they set out after the Israelites, for the irony of this picture of proud warriors in all their noble equipment lies precisely in v. 3227: 'dâ was unnuzze', it served no useful purpose on this occasion.

We must be careful how we interpret this point, however. It does *not* mean that the author is here suggesting that all knightly weapons and equipment are useless and irrelevant to both parties in a war in which God Himself takes part and, by His intervention with a natural catastrophe of this kind, renders a fixed military encounter superfluous. The most one can say of this passage, where it is specifically the equipment of the pagan knights which is designated as useless, is that it shows the irrelevance of knightly equipment to those who are arrogant enough to oppose God's ends and who imagine that they can measure themselves against God's omnipotence. In other words, what the German author is here criticising is not knightly warfare and its accoutrements, but only this equipment when it belongs to pagans, to knights who have closed their eyes to God's power or who have recognised it too late. The proof of this lies in the contrast between these words used of the Egyptian knights' equipment (v. 3227: *dâ was unnuzze...*) and the similar term employed earlier of the weapons with which the Hebrew knights arm themselves (vv. 2931 f.): 'daz edile gescuzze | daz wart in sît nuzze.' We may not be shown in the *Millstätter Exodus* the scene of battle in which this remark can be seen to be true,[1] but this does not alter the fact that what the author says of the weapons of the Hebrews

---

[1] On the possible reason for this see pp. 432 ff.

he explicitly denies of the equipment of their enemies. Although in this final encounter between the Hebrews and the Egyptians God's intervention means that battle is avoided, this scene is not meant to demonstrate that *in every case* the service of God by armed knights is superfluous (or, even worse: an affront to His omnipotence), but only that armed opposition to those whom He has chosen as the instruments of His will is destined to failure and defeat.

The ten passages which we have considered, where the German author creates what amounts to a new scene either by expanding brief hints given in his source or by inserting a description which has no parallel in the Vulgate, resemble one another in sharing a certain unity of purpose. The scene describing the slavery of the Hebrew noblemen was calculated to appeal to the sympathies of an aristocratic audience with courtly tastes, yet its insertion was not due to this alone since this emphasis on nobility also served to bring out an important aspect of the author's material (the degrading effects of man's bondage to sin). The new emphasis shown by the vernacular work is therefore as much due to the author's interpretation of his theme as to his wish to appeal to his audience; his intention is to show the relevance of this Old Testament book to the present conditions of an aristocratic audience. The interests of such an audience (heroic literature and the ideal of *triuwe*) are also consulted in the scene of Moses' encounter with Jethro—not in the sense that they alone dictate the expansions of this scene, but because they are the points selected by the author as providing the best opportunity for him to drive home this message of relevance. The remaining scenes, whether they be negative or positive descriptions in military terms or whether they describe the loss of confidence by warriors on the field of battle, form a self-contained group, but one which is also easily reconcilable with the more specifically aristocratic, feudal or courtly slant of the first two scenes. In short, all these scenes presuppose an audience of courtly knights, interested in heroic literature and the feudal ideal of loyalty, as well as an author who interprets his material in similar terms and who hopes thereby to reveal its immediate importance to his knightly hearers. We shall see that the same background of knightly and feudal ideals is revealed by an analysis of the changes in subject-matter effected by the Millstatt author,[1] so that the themes he chooses for formal expansion are in close agreement with what can be inferred about his attitude towards his subject-matter.

Another conclusion may be drawn from the fact that all the concentrated passages of visual description which these scenes provide are restricted to scenes of an explicitly military nature. The description of the Jews' menial labours (with its essentially courtly point about their beautiful hands) and the courtly breeding evinced by Jethro in his generous reception of Moses have an important function of their own, but these passages are quickly dismissed and show none of that elaboration of sumptuous detail and vivid interest which characterise the military passages. Only here does the Millstatt author afford himself the epic luxury of describing physical appearances at some length. In other words, visual description of splendid equipment and dress is not to be regarded as part of the author's courtliness, for it is subordinated to his interest in the military episodes: what description of beautiful attire the work contains is not part of a courtly ideal, but is an enhancement of these heroic scenes. In this the Millstatt work offers a significant contrast to the *Wiener Genesis* where, as Beyschlag has shown,[2] the epic expansions of the earlier work give added weight to the similarities between Old Testament life and the agricultural, feudal and courtly aspects of contemporary society, but leave the possibility of military parallels unexploited.[3] The earlier author was therefore anxious to exclude any positive expansion of military themes (so that when he occasionally retains a military motif, but not in expanded form, it is normally so as to imply a criticism),[4] but

[1] See pp. 153 ff.
[2] *Die Wiener Genesis*, pp. 23 ff.
[3] See also below, p. 185 and p. 443.
[4] Cf. Beyschlag, *op. cit.* p. 59: 'Auch die Kampfschilderungen unterstehen damit der Idee der W. Gen., das Heil und seine Erlangung an der Geschichte des

had no compunction in developing the feudal or courtly elements. The Millstatt author, although perfectly aware of courtly life and occasionally prepared to describe it briefly, is much more concerned to stress the military implications of his theme by means of epic expansion and detailed description. In short, the two themes (courtly appearances and military splendour) which later combine to constitute the subject-matter of so many descriptive passages in courtly literature are both known to the authors of the *Wiener Genesis* and the *Millstätter Exodus*, but each of them has chosen to concentrate more on the one and largely to ignore the positive implications of the other.

With that we have concluded our survey of the different methods employed by the Millstatt author to expand the material of his source: by the insertion of short observations occupying only a verse or two, by the elaboration of the various episodes which make up the sequence of events and movements in the total scene and, lastly, by the creation of new scenes. The discrepancy between the frequency with which he employs these three methods and the relative paucity of examples for the converse technique of compression allows us to maintain a further difference between this work and its predecessor, the *Wiener Genesis*. The earlier author's normal attitude to the form of his biblical source was, as Beyschlag has argued,[1] that he could only make use of it in his version by compressing it to its barest essentials, so that with him, if a particular scene happens to be expanded at all, then this is only as an exception and because there are certain compelling reasons in this particular case. With the *Millstätter Exodus*, as we have seen, precisely the opposite is true. The later author normally expands and enriches his biblical material and only rarely compresses it: if he does this at all it is, as we saw in chapter II, normally for very special reasons. Whereas the *Wiener Genesis* may have reached epic proportions

1. Buches Mosis beispielhaft aufzuzeigen: eigenmächtige Gewalttat — das hohe Thema weltlicher Epik — führt zur Versündigung gegen Gott, Friedfertigkeit ist die heilsgemäße Haltung.'
[1] *Die Wiener Genesis*, p. 108.

primarily because of the wealth of biblical material it incorporated and only very partially because of the epic expansiveness achieved in a few of its scenes, with the *Millstätter Exodus* the tempo and formal treatment of scenes are as much an integral part of the epic as the length of material taken over from the Bible. This is confirmed by another consideration. Beyschlag has established that in those relatively few cases where the author of the *Wiener Genesis* expands his material his choice is dictated by the nature of his subject-matter at this particular stage and by his wish to emphasise its importance at greater length. The same is true of the *Millstätter Exodus* but, in addition to this, the expansiveness of the later work is not brought about simply by the nature of the subject-matter; it is also suggested by a number of formal considerations, such as the need to maintain narrative continuity by introducing time-references or by implying the sequence of events or the desirability, especially in a work of such proportions, to make the course of the action unmistakably clear to the audience. These are considerations which the author of a short-scale *Lied*, passing rapidly from highlight to highlight, can afford to ignore and still achieve an aesthetic effect in his very concision. Yet they are considerations which possess a greater significance for the author of a large-scale epic. That the Millstatt author should have been aware of this suggests convincingly that the proportions of his epic are not caused exclusively by the richness of his subject-matter and that he was adequately aware of the truth that an epic narrative on this scale imposed formal demands on its author which had no counterpart in the case of the shorter *Lied*. In addition to composing a work of epic size, therefore, he had the insight to perceive that this new scale demanded a new formal technique.

V

THE AUTHOR'S ATTITUDE
TO HIS MATERIAL

WE have seen that although our author set himself the task of translating part of a book of the Old Testament into German rhymed verse this dependence on an authoritative source hampered his poetic freedom rather less than has been assumed and that he was largely successful in adapting his material to his own formal demands. Something similar can be shown with regard to the way in which he organises his subject-matter. Although the course of the action and also the characterisation of the personages are laid down for him by his source, he is nonetheless free to extract the maximum of artistic value from his material and to allow his theme to speak for itself. This is so because, unlike many other authors of his period, he is perfectly aware of the aesthetic disadvantages which any epic narrative must suffer from the employment of allegorical interpretation as a perpetual and explicit accompaniment of the action. Whatever the religious gains which this technique may confer, its aesthetic benefits are highly dubious whenever it is used not just to provide a work with an overall significance, but also to interrupt the flow of the narrative by continually interposing comments on a plane different from that on which the epic action unfolds.[1] In medieval works of art of mainly liturgical inspiration

[1] I am far from wishing to minimise the formal potentialities of the allegorical technique, but wish merely to emphasise that these are not best realised in an epic work. These objections do not, of course, apply when the allegorical comments are not used as a perpetual accompaniment to the action or where they are not made pointedly explicit. There are, for example, several passages in the *Millstätter Exodus* where the audience is left to supplement the narrative with allegorical dimensions, but is implicitly prompted to do this by the way in which the author has presented his material. Thus the first section of the description of the Israelites' departure as a warlike host concludes with the emphatic point that on their shields was to be seen 'manich tier wunderlich, | der lewe vreislich'

such a divorce from reality may indeed serve a valid aesthetic purpose,[1] but this is hardly likely to be the case with works of an epic nature whose strength resides in the events of reality which they depict. In so largely excluding passages of allegorical interpretation from his epic our author shows, therefore, considerable aesthetic understanding of what this literary genre demanded.

It might be argued against this view that the author refrained from inserting exegetical comments into his narrative for no better reason than that he was simply unacquainted with this technique. Clearly, if this were so his ignorance could not be attributed to him as an aesthetic virtue. We can however demonstrate that this objection is unjustified, since there is enough evidence to show that the author was acquainted with the allegorical method, so that his choice not to employ it must presumably be the result of a conscious decision. In other words, there are passages to be found in this work where the author fleetingly hints at the possibility of this allegorical technique, but does not avail himself of it. In each case the reference is brief and incapable of interrupting the flow of the epic narrative. In each case our impression is that of an aesthetic temptation which is firmly resisted.

We can for the moment ignore the exegetical import of vv. 3297 ff. at the conclusion of the work, since we shall return to it later[2] and since its position at the very end of the epic may well place a particular interpretation on the events narrated but cannot endanger the aesthetic quality of the work by interrupting the narrative. This consideration does not apply to the other

(vv. 2905 f.): a clear, but extremely tactful allusion to the lion of Juda (e.g. Gen. 49. 9) and to its christological associations (Apoc. 5. 5). It is perhaps for this reason that Roland is described in similar terms in the *Rolandslied* (vv. 3985f.). See also pp. 5 f. and p. 120, n. 2.

[1] Cf. H. de Boor, *ZfdPh*, LI, 244 ff. and LII, 72 ff.; H. Fromm, *Untersuchungen zum Marienleben des Priesters Wernher*, pp. 114 ff.; W. von den Steinen, *Notker der Dichter und seine geistige Welt*, I, 201 f. Something similar has been argued, but in the case of non-liturgical works, by H. J. Bayer, *Untersuchungen zum Sprachstil weltlicher Epen*, pp. 16 ff., although many modifications would need to be made to the historical development which this author suggests.

[2] See pp. 119 f.

passages where an allegorical interpretation is hinted at, but here the danger is avoided by the very brevity of these allusions.

A reference to allegory is provided by vv. 2510 ff.: 'sô habet umbemezzen | mit guotem gedanche | iwer selber lanche.' This is the only passage where the author affords us a glimpse of the possibility of an exegetical treatment of his material, but it remains an isolated example and is in any case brief enough not to impede the flow of the narrative. The position is even clearer with the remaining examples, for the references in v. 602 ('der name hât tiefen sin'), v. 2490 ('diu bezeichnunge ist tiure') and v. 2801 ('der bezeichenlîchen dinge') are accompanied by no trace of exegetical explanation.[1] Only in the case of v. 1140 ('einen gewaltigen namen') do we encounter an apparent exception, for the name in question, Adonai, is interpreted in v. 1143: 'daz chuît ich bin des heres got.' We shall see when we come to consider the author's military treatment of his theme that there is probably a special explanation of this interpretation[2] (which happens to be theologically false, in any case), so that even this exception is more apparent than real. With that the total crop of allegorical passages in the *Exodus* is exhausted. We may regard them as so infrequent, so brief and unexploited that they cannot constitute any aesthetic danger to the author's intention in composing an epic, but at the same time they show us that the author was at least acquainted with the exegetical method and could have used it if he had so chosen.

With that the possible objection that the author did not employ

---

[1] Where the names of Moses' two sons are interpreted in vv. 414 ff. and 424 ff. (cf. especially v. 417: 'daz was ein bezeichenlîcher name') this is more a case of drawing attention to two self-explanatory Hebrew names than of allegorical exegesis proper.

The importance of the references 2490 and 2801 lies in the fact that they both occur in passages which are regarded by the author as obviously possessing allegorical implications for his audience. Both passages stress the typological connections between the Passover rites of the Jews and the Christian celebration of Easter (cf. vv. 2541 and 2544 as well as vv. 2824 and 2826; see also p. 152), but the Millstatt author leaves it to his audience to draw this conclusion for themselves—for him to have expatiated on this would have meant breaking the thread of his narrative.

[2] See pp. 157 f.

this method because he was unacquainted with it is adequately refuted. At the same time, it might alternatively be possible to argue that the author, although familiar with the technique, did not make more extensive use of it simply because his theme excluded any far-reaching allegorical interpretation. Anybody who has read any of the exegetical commentaries on biblical books composed in the Early Christian period or in the Middle Ages will rightly remain sceptical of this objection, for it would be difficult to find any theme, however apparently unyielding, to which exegetical ingenuity could not successfully apply its chosen technique. If it was possible to use this method of interpretation of a subject-matter which was apparently so fraught with danger as was the 'Song of Songs'[1] or if no difficulty was found in providing an allegorical explanation of the monkey or the elephant,[2] to name only two random examples from the *Physiologus*, then we need have few doubts as to the exegete's ability to read a convincing allegorical message out of so important an Old Testament book as Exodus.

Indeed, this is confirmed by the frequency with which precisely this book was interpreted allegorically by Early Christian as well as by medieval theologians.[3] In these commentaries it was the traditional method to interpret Pharaoh as signifying the Devil, Egypt as the world, Moses as the prefiguration of Christ and the exodus itself as the salvation of mankind accomplished by

[1] See F. Ohly, *Hohelied-Studien. Grundzüge einer Geschichte der Hohelied-auslegung des Abendlandes bis um 1200.*

[2] *De simia* (7a): p. 13 (text) and p. 25 (commentary). This chapter is missing from the *Ältere Physiologus*. *De elephante* (8): pp. 1a ff. (text) and pp. 26 f (commentary).

[3] These commentaries include, for example, Origen, *Homiliae in Exodum* (*MPG*, 12, 297 ff.); Procopius Gazaeus, *Commentarii in Exodum* (*MPG*, 87 i, 511 ff.); Isidore of Seville, *Allegoriae quaedam scripturae sacrae* (*MPL*, 83, 108 ff.); Bede, *Explanatio in secundum librum Mosis* (*MPL*, 91, 285 ff.); Bruno Astensis, *Expositio in Exodum* (*MPL*, 164, 233 ff.) and Petrus Comestor, *Historia scholastica: historia libri Exodi* (*MPL* 198, 1141 ff.). The practice of subjecting the book of Exodus to an allegorical interpretation is even older than these examples suggest, however, for it was interpreted typologically both by Old Testament writers and in the New Testament. On the important evidence for this see J. Daniélou, *Sacramentum futuri*, pp. 132 ff.

Christ and granted to each Christian in the act of baptism.[1] In some commentaries the emphasis could indeed be shifted somewhat, just as the interpretation of details (as opposed to the general pattern of events) often differed between one work and another, but what concerns us is not so much the variety of possible approaches as rather the more important fact that a tradition of exegetical interpretation of the Book of Exodus certainly existed from the earliest Christian period. Indeed, it is remarkable that one of the biblical passages giving support for what soon became the regular practice of interpreting Old Testament events and persons typologically, i.e. as prefigurations of the fulfilment recounted in the New Testament, should refer to Exodus itself. This is the force of St Paul's words in I Cor. 10. 6,[2] where the Israelites in the desert, after their departure from Egypt, are seen as the prefiguration (*figura* or τύπος), albeit in a negative sense, of the Christians and with specific reference to that event which most nearly concerns us, the passage of the Red Sea, as is made clear by v. 1: 'Nolo enim vos ignorare, fratres, quoniam patres nostri omnes sub nube fuerunt, et omnes mare transierunt.' The authority of this Pauline example and also the dogmatic importance of the interpretation of the exodus of the Jews as the salvation of mankind in Christ thus fully account for the frequency with which this particular book was subjected to allegorical exegesis.[3]

[1] Examples of this interpretation are numerous. Bede, for example, interprets the *rex Aegypti* as the Devil (*MPL*, 91, 287C), Moses as prefiguring Christ (290B), Egypt as signifying this world to which we are banished (cf. 294C: *in hac peregrinatione* or 310B: *voluntates hujus mundi*) and the Red Sea as the waters of baptism (310A). Cf. also Bruno Astensis (*MPL*, 164, 264D): 'Quid enim Pharao cum omni exercitu Aegyptiorum; nisi diabolus cum omni militia daemoniorum? Quid autem Hebraei, nisi Christianorum populus? Quid vero mare Rubrum nisi baptismatis aqua intelligitur?' We may be quite certain that this kind of interpretation was widely known in the Middle Ages because of the manner in which the Good Friday and Holy Saturday liturgy sees the events of the Israelites' exodus as a prefiguration of the crucifixion (see pp. 15ff.).

[2] 'Haec autem in figura facta sunt nostri, ut non simus concupiscentes malorum, sicut et illi concupierunt.'

[3] Even though they nowhere show the explicitness of the Pauline passage it is possible to find traces of this equation between the exodus and the salvation achieved by Christ in the gospels themselves. The description of the transfigura-

We can go further than this, for we can show that this inter-pretation was known to German literature in the vernacular already in the eleventh century, so that there is no reason to assume, especially in view of the allegorical references to be found in our work, that it was not also known to the author of our *Exodus*. The evidence for this is provided by *Ezzos Gesang*, whose author describes (vv. 323 ff.) the ten plagues of Egypt and the Passover, but sums up their significance by saying:

> 335   Daz was allez geistlîch:
> daz bezeichnôt christinlîchiu dinc.

Furthermore, the actual passage of the Red Sea is also drawn into this interpretation by the traditional equation of Pharaoh with the Devil and of the Red Sea with the water of baptism:

> 345   Den tievel unt allez sîn here
> den verswalh daz rôte toufmere.

Lastly, the equation of the Promised Land with Paradise is clearly conveyed by the way in which access to what is termed *unser alt erbelant* is granted us by the sacrifice of Christ on the cross (vv. 347 ff.), by the revealing phrase: 'dar hab wir geistlîchen ganc' (v. 354) and by the way in which redeemed Christendom, freed from the yoke of Pharaoh, is described as *spiritalis Israel* (vv. 359 ff.). These three stages of the exodus (the plagues of

tion by Luke, for example (9. 30: '... Erant autem Moyses et Elias, | Visi in majestate; et dicebant excessum ejus, quem completurus erat in Jerusalem'), is revealing since the term *excessus* translates ἔξοδος, an unusual word for 'death', but obviously chosen because of its Old Testament associations with divine deliverance. Luke's idea is therefore that Christ was to accomplish a new de-liverance at Jerusalem, leading God's people from a greater slavery than that imposed by the Egyptians.

Similarly, Matthew has many passages equating the life of Christ with the events of the exodus. For example, his description of the flight into Egypt (2. 15: 'Et erat ibi usque ad obitum Herodis, ut adimpleretur quod dictum est a Domino per prophetam dicentem: Ex Aegypto vocavi filium meum') contains a quotation from Hos. 11. 1 ('Quia puer Israel, et dilexi eum; et ex Aegypto vocavi filium meum'). Whereas, however, the Old Testament book sees Israel as the son of God, led out of Egypt in the exodus, Matthew uses this passage to refer to Christ as the Son of God.

The best known literary example of a fourfold interpretation of Exodus is provided by Dante's *Epistle to Can Grande* (*The Letters of Dante*, ed. P. Toynbee, p. 199).

Egypt, the passage of the Red Sea, the arrival in the Promised
Land) all receive an allegorical interpretation (as is made clear by
the use of the adjective *geistlîch* or *spiritalis*). Together they
demonstrate not merely that a detailed exegesis of Exodus was
possible, but also that this method was known in Germany with
reference to this book of the Old Testament and was moreover
used in vernacular literature.[1]

From this it follows that the author of our work was himself
acquainted with the allegorical method and could indeed have
used it in composing his epic, if he had so wished. That he did
not suggests that the employment of this method would have
conflicted with his own intentions, whether we regard these as
consisting in the development of an epic narrative form unim-
peded by the demands of exegesis or as lying in a particular
attitude towards his biblical subject-matter.

Exactly how important the formal consideration may have
been can best be shown by a comparison between our work
(where allegorical exegesis plays no constituent role) and that
part of the *Vorauer Bücher Mosis* which treats of the exodus
story, for in this latter work the allegorical technique is dominant.
Here it is not simply the case that in the Vorau work the general
interpretation of the exodus which is introduced in the Millstatt
epic only at the very end is brought forward to a position[2] where

[1] Cf. A. E. Schönbach, *Altdeutsche Predigten*, II, 67, 30: 'die juden heten ein
hochzeit die si vor allen hochzeiten begiengen, daz warn die oster. ze ostern
so slugen si ein lamp, also in geboten waz in der ê, si begiengen daz daz lamp
erslagen wart. wir begen aver ze den ostern daz daz war lamp, unser herre Jesus
Christ, durich unser hail an dem heren chrûtze erslagen wart. oster daz spricht in
unser zungen "ûbervart". do die ostern nahen begunden, do furt unser herre die
michel menige und zaigt uns da mit, alle die dez gernt, daz si an der sel mit dem
hiligen gotes wort gelabet werden. die schûln die ostern also begen, das si ûbervarn
da von der bozhait und sich hefen hintz den tugenden, von den zergænglichen
dingen hintz den ewigen frôuden und von dem tifel hintz dem hiligen Christo.'

[2] 43. 19:   [N]v sul wir
sehen da bi. waz di tagwæide sin.
so wir di werelte lazen varen. so en-
trinne wir den harmscaren. so var
wir von egypto. daz martert uns
diche. pharao tŷt uns vil nôt. den tie-
vel er bezeichenot.

Cf. also 49. 5 ff.

it interrupts the action and suffers by being applied to only one detail of the narrative action (the first *tagewæide* of the Israelites, cf. 43. 19 f. and 44. 7). More important is the fact that countless other details of the action (which are too particularised for the Millstatt author to want to interpret) are equipped with their allegorical explanation, so that the attention of the audience is continually being switched from the foreground events that dominate both the Bible account and the Millstatt epic to their religious significance. The result is that the epic action loses in intensity by being deprived of its integral importance whenever it is interpreted only with regard to what it stands for, but it also loses in continuity because of the constant interruptions which this technique necessitates.

An example of what this difference in technique means in practice is provided by the way in which both authors treat the scene recounted in Exod. 4. 1 ff. The Millstatt author[1] follows his biblical source (but expands it in details) by narrating this stage of the encounter between Moses and the Lord in vivid epic terms, stressing Moses' anticipation of the Israelites' refractory behaviour and the Lord's reply in the form of a demonstration of His power with the staff. He concludes the episode (as does the Bible) by having the Lord explain to Moses the force of this demonstration as a means of persuading the Hebrews that Moses has had divine power conferred upon him.[2] In the Vorau version this explanation has completely changed its nature, for now it is an allegorical interpretation given by the author to his audience, rather than by the Lord to Moses:

35. 12   Daz welle wir evh
devten. daz bezeichenet daz heilige
cruce. sver daz insigele gût. du het
an sinen mût. wil erz offenlichen tra-
gen. ime mac der slange niht gescaden.
deme wirt daz cruze tivre. ein stap
unde ein stivre.

[1] Vv. 685 ff.
[2] Vv. 719–28.

These words are therefore no longer an explanation given within the framework of the action and forming part of it by contributing to this action (by putting Moses' mind at rest and by meeting the objection he had first raised). Instead, they are an extraneous element, inserted into the narrative by the exegetical author. Furthermore, whereas the Millstatt version devotes thirty-four lines (vv. 685–718) to its description of the encounter and only ten lines (vv. 719–28) to God's explanation to Moses (although this explanation is not just an appendix to the action, but part of it), this proportion is disturbed in the Vorau text, where eight lines of action (35. 7–12) correspond to eight lines of allegorical commentary (35. 12–18), so that exegesis is now felt to equal the narrative in importance. With 35. 18 the narrative begins again, but is allowed to continue for only eight lines since 35. 24 sees the resumption of the allegorical interpretation, this time for eight lines (35. 24–9) as a counterbalance to the eight lines of action that have intervened.

This dilution of the action and the discontinuity of the narrative brought about by a constant exegesis of details are also exemplified by the Vorau treatment of the plagues of Egypt, where all narrative pungency is lost. The Millstatt author, by contrast, describes them at some length[1] and in such epic terms that he is able to employ heroic vocabulary in some of his descriptions.[2] Nowhere do we find any allegorical interpretation. The position is quite different in the Vorau version,[3] for here the description of each of the plagues is immediately followed by the relevant exegesis so that the epic flow is continually interrupted at short intervals. Furthermore, the proportion which we have just observed between narrative and exegesis now changes drastically in favour of the latter. This is not yet the case with the first plague, where four lines of narrative correspond to four lines of interpretation,[4] but already in the second plague the proportion is 4:6.[5] The third plague has only three lines of narrative

---

[1] Vv. 1327 ff.
[2] See pp. 86ff. and 15 6.
[3] 38. 6 ff.
[4] 38. 6–8 and 38. 9–11.
[5] 38. 11–14 and 38. 14–19.

as counterweight to seven lines of interpretation,[1] but even this is weakened by the conventional nature of these three lines.[2] The same is true of the fourth plague, where two lines of narrative (of which one is no more than a standing formula with no epic force)[3] are outweighed by fully six of interpretation.[4] The proportions are similar for the remaining plagues (fifth = 4:10; sixth = 4:8; seventh = 2:8; eighth = 2:6),[5] so that the purely epic description given by the Millstatt author is here replaced by a technique which not merely gives a discontinuous account, but largely subordinates its narrative to the purposes of allegorical interpretation.[6]

Although the author of the *Millstätter Exodus* has clearly gained aesthetic advantages for himself in refusing to interpolate exegetical passages into his epic it would be going too far to maintain that his refusal was dictated solely by formal considerations. This is suggested by the way in which, having concluded his account of the story of Exodus as an epic, he then stresses the allegorical import of his subject-matter.[7] From this it follows that he was certainly aware of a close connection between his subject-matter and the method of allegorical interpretation, so that if he excluded this method from the body of his work and avoided any explicit interpretation of details in the manner of the

[1] 38. 19–21 and 38. 22–7.

[2] 'Ob ich is rehte gehukke' is a conventional formula; 'daz dritte waren mukken' states the nature of the plague but does not describe it as epic action, which is in fact confined to the bald statement of the result in the third line: 'di taten in uil not.'

[3] 38. 27 f.: 'Nu sehet daz ich | ev ni ne lige.'

[4] 38. 27–9 and 38. 29–39. 5.

[5] Fifth plague: 39. 5–8 and 39. 8–14; sixth: 39. 14–17 and 39. 17–23; seventh: 39. 23–4 and 39. 25–40. 6; eighth: 40. 6–7 and 40. 7–12. This fragment of the MS breaks off in the description of the ninth plague so that no comparison with the last two plagues is possible. There is no reason to think, however, that the author should suddenly have changed his technique at this point.

[6] The differences in technique between the *Millstätter Exodus* and the *Vorauer Bücher Mosis* are best explained, at least in part, by the difference in their audience: whereas the former work is addressed to a knightly audience (see p. 124, n. 1), the latter is probably meant for clerical consumption (cf. Ehrismann, *LG*, II, 92 and Schwietering, *LG*, 69) and can therefore afford to go into greater details of exegesis.

[7] See p. 119.

Vorau author this must presumably have been because he considered that the needs of his subject-matter were not best served by this method. Furthermore, it is of course unthinkable that a medieval author in this period should have allowed formal considerations (the development of a clear epic structure) to override the implicit needs of his biblical subject-matter with all the theological authority which this possessed for him. This suggests that our author, by excluding exegetical passages from the body of his work, may well have succeeded thereby in avoiding the aesthetic disadvantages from which the *Vorauer Bücher Mosis* suffer, but that his decision may also have been taken in the light of how he wished to organise his subject-matter, what significance he wished his theme to express for itself. That his wish to allow his subject-matter to speak for itself (or at least to express his attitude towards it more implicitly than was possible with the method adopted by the Vorau author) also brought with it certain marked formal advantages is an indication that our author was well in control of both aspects of his work and that his innovations in formal matters are not divorced from the meaning which the Exodus story had for him. If therefore (with the exception of the exegetical passage at the close of the work) the author's attitude to his material is nowhere made explicit, but is instead implicit in the way in which he recounts it as an epic, then our task must be to see what shifts of emphasis in his material may have been accomplished by him and to hope that an analysis of these changes in his subject-matter may tell us what meaning it possessed for the author and his public.

VI

THE AUTHOR'S INTENTIONS

THE preceding chapter has shown us that the author of the *Millstätter Exodus* differs from that of the *Vorauer Bücher Mosis* in two respects. First, his allegorical perspectives are at the most implicit in his work: he hints at them allusively and briefly, leaving it to his audience to supplement these indications and not dwelling on these points with learned explicitness. Secondly, he concentrates all the sustained and explicit exegesis of his subject-matter on one passage alone and reserves this until the conclusion of the work, so that his commentary may well round off his epic, but cannot in any way weaken its narrative structure. He therefore concludes his work (although in a form shorter than in the Bible)[1] with the song of praise in which Moses and the Israelites give thanks to the Lord for His assistance in rescuing them, so that a natural opportunity is presented for the author to reach a fitting termination by including both himself and his audience in this song of grateful thanks:

> 3297 mit im (i.e. Moses) sô tuo wir same
> daz ouch wir muozen varen
> von disem ellende
> heim ze deme lande
> zuo der himelisken Jerusalem
> ir sprechet alle AMEN.

With these lines of allegorical evocation the same kind of interpretation is placed upon our work as in those stanzas of *Ezzos Gesang* dealing with the theme of Exodus and also in that part of the *Vorauer Bücher Mosis* that corresponds to the first fifteen chapters of Exodus. The Jews are equated with the Christians of the present day, their flight from Egypt is interpreted as the Christian's desire to escape from the trammels of this world and

[1] Vv. 3289–96. Cf. Exod. 15. 1 ff.

their entry into the Promised Land (not actually recounted by our author, but certainly prepared for by the events he has described) is seen in terms comparable with the Christian's admission into the Heavenly Jerusalem. Admittedly, not all the parallels that could have been drawn between the liberation of the Jews from Pharaoh and the salvation of mankind in Christ have in fact been adduced here,[1] but there is after all a limit to the degree of explicitness which we can demand of an author in summing up the total significance of his work in no more than six lines. As it is, enough has been said by him[2] to make it clear that his allegorical interpretation of the events of Exodus is fully comparable with the more explicit remarks of the authors of *Ezzos Gesang* and the *Vorauer Bücher Mosis*.[3]

In other words, these three authors are all in agreement with the traditional exegesis of this biblical book as a prefiguration of the salvation of mankind. Although he avoids the constant explicitness we find in the Vorau work our author similarly wishes the Old Testament events to be understood as foreshadowing the salvation of mankind accomplished by Christ. In this concern to place these particular historical events within the general context of the story of salvation he by no means stands alone.

[1] Significantly, no mention is made of the traditional parallel between Moses (as the liberator of his people) and Christ as the Redeemer. This agrees with the fact that the author interprets the exodus not exclusively with reference to the redemption accomplished by Christ, but more in connection with how this opportunity is to be utilised by Christians in the present. See also pp. 363 f.

[2] We may also take the use of the word *heim* in v. 3300 as providing a parallel to the idea of Paradise as the Christians' inheritance, expressed in *Ezzos Gesang* (v. 352) by the words *unser alt erbelant*. Elsewhere in the work (see p. 137, n. 1) Pharaoh is described as so far acting in conjunction with the Devil that at least the possibility of the traditional allegorical equation of Pharaoh with the Devil is suggested by implication.

[3] This type of religious commendation, coming at the end of the work, is the kind of literary *topos* which Curtius has discussed under the heading *Schlußtopik* (*Europäische Literatur und lateinisches Mittelalter*, pp. 97 ff.). Yet in this case it is also much more than this since it provides an explicit connection with the events narrated in the epic itself, equating Christians with Hebrews and the fate of mankind with the exodus of Israel. In addition to its conventional role, therefore, this *topos* is meant to show the relevance of *Exodus* to the audience and to tell them how the events narrated are accordingly to be understood.

Beyschlag has shown[1] that the author of the *Wiener Genesis* so organises his material that the conclusion of his work reflects the undisturbed and harmonious state of God's creation, just as the story of the Old Testament partriarchs is similarly constructed around the idea of mankind's salvation. Schwietering in particular has stressed a similar background to other works of the period that treat of an Old Testament theme[2] or of an extraneous theme which they have assimilated to the Old Testament, whether in fact or in spirit.[3] The fact, however, that the passage in the *Millstätter Genesis* which allows us to view the whole work against this background of the general history of salvation occurs right at the end of the work does not mean that the events which are narrated long before this point is reached are not meant to be so viewed, for something similar is also true of the OE *Exodus*.[4] Nor does the absence of explicit references in the body of the narrative (as, for example, with the *Vorauer Bücher Mosis*) destroy this impression of a wider background, for the significance of the story narrated, made explicit perhaps only at the conclusion, was felt to be implicit in the theme itself, as is also clear with the OE poem. If this is so, then the author may be expected to have suggested what these implications are by the way in which he groups his material, adding one detail to his biblical source but omitting another, emphasising this point rather than that. In this respect we may be certain that the *Millstätter Exodus*, for all its fidelity to its source, resembles the

[1] *Die Wiener Genesis*, pp. 6 f. and pp. 16 ff.

[2] On this aspect of the *Lob Salomons* see Schwietering, *LG*, 71 (cf. de Boor, *LG*, I, 156 f.); on the *Ältere Judith* see Schwietering, *LG*, 72 and de Boor, *LG*, I, 156; on the *Drei Jünglinge im Feuerofen* see Schwietering, *LG*, 73 and de Boor, *LG*, I, 156.

[3] For a discussion of the assimilation of the *Alexanderlied* to the subject-matter of the Old Testament and the interpretation of its theme as part of the history of salvation see Schwietering, *LG*, 74 ff.; on the historical core of this work see also E. Sitte, *Die Datierung von Lamprechts Alexander*, pp. 107 ff., especially pp. 111 f. On the Old Testament spirit of the *Rolandslied* see Schwietering, *LG*, 102 (see also pp. 103 f. for its metaphysical background).

[4] After the conclusion of the epic at the point where the Egyptians have been drowned in the Red Sea vv. 574 ff. bring an allegorical interpretation; cf. also vv. 583 ff.

The Millstätter Exodus

Wiener Genesis[1] in not being simply a transcription of the Old Testament book into a vernacular verse-form: it omits some details from its source, expands many points only touched upon briefly, but also adds whole passages of its own creation which have no parallel in the Bible. It is from an analysis of these differences that we may best hope to determine what aspects of the work appeared as important to the author and in what way he managed to reveal the implications of the wider theme of the story of salvation which were latent for him in the subject which he had chosen.

One way in which we can establish what aspects of the story narrated were important for the author is to analyse the relationship between the two categories of time which are introduced whenever an epic narrative is meant to convey an allegorical message.[2] We saw in the case of the *Vorauer Bücher Mosis* that the narrative of events was interrupted at short intervals so that exegetical passages could be inserted, thus raising the events of historical reality on to the level of their allegorical significance. This means, in terms of the category of time, that the events which are depicted as part of the epic narrative are events that take place on the level of historical time, but that the insertion of passages which interpret these events in the light of their moral or dogmatic truth, applicable not merely to the context just depicted but true of all men at all times, transposes these events into a sphere which is timeless, because of general validity. The technique employed by the author of the *Vorauer Bücher Mosis* rests, therefore, on a continuous tension between time (in the

---

[1] Cf. Beyschlag, *Die Wiener Genesis*, p. 5.

[2] A similar conjunction of these two categories has been emphasised by J. Spörl for medieval historiography at large in his discussion of the views of E. Troeltsch: 'Im Mittelpunkt der mittelalterlichen Geschichtsschreibung stehe das jeder wirklichen Geschichte, jeder Forschung und Kritik entzogene Wunder außerhalb jeder Zeitlichkeit: der Gottmensch, der geschichtliches und zeitloses Wesen zugleich ist, seine Erlösungstat, die in geschichtlicher Hülle ein kosmisches Ereignis sei. Die Heilsgeschichte bringt jene Vermischung von Ewigem und Zeitlichem, von Göttlichem und Menschlichem, die für das mittelalterliche Geschichtsdenken charakteristisch ist.' See his essay in W. Lammers (ed.), *Geschichtsdenken und Geschichtsbild im Mittelalter*, p. 21, previously published in *HJb*, LIII, 281 ff.

events narrated) and timelessness (in their allegorical interpretation). A similar conjunction of these two categories is to be found in the *Millstätter Exodus*, for, although the events narrated remain on the level of historical time, the presence of six lines of allegory at the conclusion is enough to introduce the further category of timelessness. More important, however, is the difference between these two works concealed by this apparent similarity. The result of the continuous alternation in the Vorau work between fragments of narrative and allegorical interpolations is that the recording of events in time tends to be swamped by the exegesis, to be attenuated and disrupted by an interpretation which repeatedly extracts them from the context of time and views them in their timeless significance. In the Millstatt epic, on the other hand, the explicit suggestion of the category of timelessness is relegated to the conclusion of the work, so that it is thus confined to the background and is not allowed to interfere with the sequence of events unfolding in the foreground.

In short, the Millstatt author grants a far greater importance to events described on the plane of human time, even though their timeless significance is always present in the background. This is confirmed by the way in which, although he introduces an allegorical interpretation at the end of his work, he is much more actively concerned with emphasising the time-context of the events narrated, i.e. their relevance to the present day in particular. In this manner the timeless significance of the story of Exodus is given a special bearing on one point of time, the author's present. A similar relationship between the timeless context of the history of salvation and the author's own day has been shown by Beyschlag in the case of the *Wiener Genesis*[1] where, in addition to the elaboration of this timeless context, the earlier author is also concerned to show repeatedly the relevance of this context to his own day and does this by a variety of methods.[2] We shall now have to

---

[1] *Die Wiener Genesis*, pp. 21 ff.

[2] We shall see below that, although the intentions of the two authors are different, the author of the *Millstätter Exodus* uses much the same methods as the author of the *Wiener Genesis* in stressing the parallels between his subject-matter and the conditions of his own day.

consider the ways in which this same relevance is established by the author of the *Millstätter Exodus*, recognising however that he was by no means alone in this. As Beyschlag has emphasised with reference to the earlier epic, there is no real contradiction between the timeless interpretation at the end of the *Exodus* and the emphasis with which the author establishes close links between the events in Hebrew history and his own day, for the significance of the history of salvation is a truth which must be experienced by each generation afresh and it is the task of the author of a religious work to convince his audience that the religious truths he describes have a direct bearing upon their own condition. His task will be made easier if, by the skilful use of omissions and additions, he can establish persuasive parallels (in this case) between the experiences of the Israelites in departing from Egypt and the life and circumstances of his knightly audience.[1]

That such an emphasis on the connections between Old Testament events and the medieval present served a definite purpose has again been suggested by Beyschlag with reference to the

[1] That our author's audience was a knightly, aristocratic one is best revealed not merely by the fact that he once addresses them as *mîne hêrren* (v. 2907), but especially by the manner in which he chooses to do this in the middle of one of his military descriptions (see pp. 94 f.), thus calling for their attention at a point when he can feel reasonably certain of holding their interest. Furthermore, as we shall see, the changes in his material introduced by our author all point to an audience which is interested in military matters and feudal obligations and to whom the author obviously thinks a special appeal can be made by his description of the Israelites as noblemen. In view of such considerations J. Kelle's more restricted interpretation of this form of address as implying a clerical audience of canons (*LG*, ii, 30) has now been abandoned. See Ehrismann, *LG*, ii, 90 f.; Kossmann, *Die altdeutsche Exodus*, p. 82 (following Scherer); Rupp, *Deutsche religiöse Dichtungen des 11. und 12. Jahrhunderts*, pp. 309 f. For a general discussion of this problem see W. Stammler, *Kleine Schriften zur Literaturgeschichte des Mittelalters*, pp. 17 f.

Ehrismann, *LG*, ii, 90, n. 1, has also used this fact of a knightly audience to explain why the author has avoided using the method of allegorical interpretation, suggesting that such a method would have been beyond the grasp of his audience. This may be in part true, but what Rupp has established about the cultural level and needs of this knightly public in this period suggests that they may well have been already capable of understanding such an interpretation and that other considerations may have influenced our author in his decision.

Wiener Genesis.[1] He demonstrates that the differences between the medieval epic and its biblical source (mainly consisting of additions in the former and omissions from the latter) add up to a unified picture of the life of the Austro-Bavarian rural aristocracy around the year 1100, superimposed upon the story of the biblical Genesis. The unity of this picture lies in the emphasis it places on the life of aristocratic, courtly circles, concerned with agricultural pursuits but also with contemporary feudal obligations, including the relationship between lord and vassal and the acknowledgement of *êre* and riches as integral parts of this society, but implying a criticism (on religious grounds) of the military aspects of this form of contemporary life. Beyschlag's argument is a convincing one and demonstrates a far-reaching equation between the Jews of the Old Testament and the landed aristocracy of eleventh-century Germany, an equation which serves to underline the author's message that the happenings of the Old Testament are directly relevant to the lives of his audience.[2] In our case we must ask whether the changes in his source introduced by the author of the *Millstätter Exodus* also serve the purpose of showing the relevance of the story of Exodus to his knightly audience and whether they too add up to any sort of coherent picture, although there is of course no necessity to assume that the picture of contemporary life which may have inspired these changes in the *Exodus* should be in all details the same as that which provided the pattern for the author of the *Wiener Genesis*.

In analysing the way in which the Millstatt author establishes parallels between the history of the Israelites of Exodus and his early twelfth-century knightly audience we shall see that he employs three distinct methods. Negatively, he omits those historical elements in the biblical story which are so peculiar to the Israelites that it would have been difficult to show their relevance

---

[1] *Die Wiener Genesis*, p. 5: 'Und all dies: Auswahl und Zusatz, ist von dieser Idee des dt. Gedichtes her bedingt, die Heilsbedeutung der alttestamentlichen Genesis für seine Zeit darzustellen.'

[2] That the *Wiener Genesis* was also addressed to a knightly audience has been emphasised by Ehrismann, *LG*, II, 83, and by Stammler, *op. cit.* p. 18. Cf. also Beyschlag, *Die Wiener Genesis*, pp. 62 f.

to the present without having recourse to the allegorical technique with which the author wished to dispense. Conversely, there is the positive method whereby the conditions and ideals of the author's own day are superimposed upon the biblical material in such a way that it is coloured in terms of twelfth-century experience. Lastly, the author can make use of a technique which we may call neutral, involving neither additions nor subtractions, but often unavoidably present in the very act of translating from the Vulgate into the vernacular. It consists in the translation by the author of biblical concepts in terms so generalised that, whilst still true of the Old Testament, they are also applicable to the conditions of the author's own present. By such a translation the events in question can be deprived of all historical particularity and thus be shown, by implication, to be as true of the twelfth century as of the Hebrew past. Since our author uses this third technique to produce the same results as are produced by the other two we are justified in regarding it as a conscious process, rather than simply as the chance result of the mere act of translating from the Vulgate (which is not to deny that it may be the result of chance[1] in the case of many other authors, less skilful in their control over their material).

It might be objected that the equation between the Old Testament past and the medieval present which we are about to investigate in the *Millstätter Exodus* is no more than the result of a lack of historical awareness typical of the Middle Ages. Such an equation would therefore be due to intellectual *naïveté* and would be as true of the author as of his whole period, so that it would be false to regard it as a positive characteristic of his artistry. The best answer to this theoretical objection has been given by Schwietering[2] who rightly sees the artistic achievement of our author in the *extent* to which he has assimilated his Old Testament theme to his medieval present, not just in externals but so as to provide the whole work with a new core of meaning, rather than

[1] Or the result of what may have become a conventional equation of a biblical Latin term with an accepted German rendering, probably assisted by the traditional vocabulary of sermons.   [2] *LG*, 69.

in the mere fact that this assimilation has taken place. The fact of assimilation as such is irrelevant to Schwietering's judgement of the quality of this epic since, as he convincingly argues, any period at all sure of its own taste and capable of evolving its own style would view such an Old Testament action in terms of its own experience and not historically as events that befell a certain Middle Eastern nomadic people at a certain point of historical time. Such an objectively historical standpoint is not to be expected in any work of art before the rise of modern historical consciousness. We are therefore as little justified in reproaching the author of the *Exodus* for this (and therefore in refusing to consider the possibility that, behind the bare fact of assimilation, his artistic skill and attitude towards his subject-matter may reside more in the *manner* in which he has accomplished this) as we should be in criticising Tiepolo or Watteau for depicting past events in the setting of their own present.[1]

Furthermore, it is open to doubt whether the claim of modern historicism to be the sole attitude to its subject worthy of the epithet 'historical' is justified. Such a claim would condemn not merely medieval historiography, but all historical writings up to the eighteenth century as unhistorical and subjective, as guilty of introducing criteria irrelevant or indeed harmful to the objective study of history. In answer to this criticism it has been argued[2] that there are indeed signs of historical awareness in the Middle Ages, that there is more than one type of interpretation of history to be found in medieval historians (humanistic, political, apocalyptic, etc.), that events of the time often made their impact felt on the historical awareness of the Middle Ages themselves (as with the Investiture Contest or the Crusades) and that, for example, the spirit or mood of late medieval historiography is radically different from that of an earlier period. Such arguments suggest that we must be careful not to regard medieval

[1] See the essay by O. Brunner on 'Abendländisches Geschichtsdenken', published in W. Lammers (ed.), *Geschichtsdenken und Geschichtsbild im Mittelalter*, p. 435. Cf also the quotation from E. Köhler, *Ideal und Wirklichkeit in der höfischen Epik*, p. 6, given on pp. 357 f.
[2] By J. Spörl in the essay referred to above (p. 122, n. 2), pp. 28 f.

historiography and the attitude to history that it betrays as too uniform and incapable of change, as therefore lacking in historical awareness in the modern sense. But even if that were not the case, the fact that medieval historiography was so largely engaged in establishing the *ratio temporum* as ordained by God and as realised in the workings of history, in elaborating what is exemplary and therefore of eternal validity in historical events, in demonstrating typological relationships between historical events and the Bible, all this amounts to an awareness of events in time[1] (and also in their timeless significance) which, whilst different from the modern attitude, betrays an intense preoccupation with the problem of history and an attitude rich in historical awareness of a particular kind. In short, the fact that the medieval attitude to history (or indeed the general attitude before the eighteenth century) is so radically different from our own is no convincing argument that we must deny to the Middle Ages any historical awareness at all.[2]

Lastly, we may be reasonably certain that the author of the *Millstätter Exodus*, in establishing close connections between the events of Jewish history and his medieval present, was perfectly aware that he was not dealing simply with a malleable body of dogmatic fact, capable of being shaped into any kind of exegetical pattern, but that instead the material upon which he was working was historical material, recording events that had really taken place in the past. Even in the case of the *Vorauer Bücher Mosis*,

---

[1] Cf. H. Grundmann in W. Stammler (ed.), *Deutsche Philologie im Aufriß*, III, col. 1333.

[2] A similar salutary warning has been uttered by H. de Boor, *Frühmittelhochdeutsche Studien*, pp. 5 f., in the case of the so-called 'lack of form' of early MHG poetry. He reminds us that the extent to which formal considerations are so largely ignored or subordinated to other purposes in this literature is the result of a conscious attitude towards the question of form, an awareness that too great a preoccupation with formal embellishments could distract attention from the importance of the religious truth to be expressed. Just as the fact that this period of literature regarded form differently from the courtly period is no proof that the earlier period was unaware of form, so too must we refrain from interpreting the difference between the medieval attitude to history and our own as an indication of a total lack of historical awareness in the Middle Ages. Cf. also *ZfdPh*, LI, 244.

from which he differs so radically by preserving his narrative intact against the inroads of allegorical interpretation, this awareness of historical events is still just retained since, however brief and typified the references to this or that event may be, they still survive in the Vorau text as indispensable pegs on which to hang the exegetical commentary. This awareness that the raw material on which the commentator worked had a historical reality of its own which could not be watered down by any amount of allegorical interpretation is a constant factor in medieval commentaries after St Augustine. Before him it may have been possible for Origen to recommend the use of the allegorical technique as a welcome means of escaping from the factual contradictions in the Bible which had proved to be a breeding-ground of heresy.[1] For Origen allegorical interpretation leads to eternally valid religious truths and is an escape from the historicity of the events and personages of the Old Testament. For St Augustine, however, it was precisely the historicity of these events and personages which it was essential to rescue, for without such a historical foundation the Scriptures would rest on nothing:

Ante omnia tamen, fratres, hoc in nomine Domini et admonemus, quantum possumus, et praecipimus, ut quando auditis exponi sacramentum Scripturae narrantis quae gesta sunt, prius illud quod lectum est credatis sic gestum, quomodo lectum est; ne subtracto fundamento rei gestae, quasi in aere quaeratis aedificare. Abraham pater noster homo erat illis temporibus fidelis, credens Deo . . . Suscepit filium de Sara uxore, jam in senectute utrisque constitutis, ex magna desperatione, sed secundum hominem . . . Tales ergo illos viros vel illos homines habebat Deus, et illo tempore tales fecerat praecones Filio venturo, ut non solum in his quae dicebant, sed etiam in his quae

---

[1] Cf. *MPG*, 11, 378 A: 'Quis vero ita idiotes invenietur, ut putet velut hominem quemdam agricolam Deum plantasse arbores in paradiso, in Eden contra orientem, et arborem vitae plantasse in eo, id est lignum visibile et palpabile, ita ut corporalibus dentibus manducans quis ex ea arbore, vitam percipiat, et rursus ex alia manducans arbore, boni et mali scientiam capiat? . . . Verum ne nos opus quod habemus in manibus justo amplius dilatemus, perfacile est omni volenti congregare de Scripturis sanctis quae scripta sunt quidem tanquam facta, non tamen secundum historiam competenter et rationabiliter fieri potuisse credenda sunt.'

faciebant, vel in his quae illis accidebant, Christus quaeratur, Christus inveniatur. Quidquid Scriptura dicit de Abraham, et factum est, et prophetia est.[1]

It is this view of allegory propounded by St Augustine rather than that put forward by Origen that dominates the allegorical tradition of the Middle Ages[2] so that every allegorical interpretation concerns both a historical fact and its prophetic significance. In our case this means that the Millstatt author, even though he finally refers explicitly to the allegorical background against which the events must be judged, is perfectly aware that these events are real historical events. In other words, if he assimilates these Old Testament events to the experience of his century this is not because of any lack of historical awareness on his part, but rather because his view of history leads him to accept, with St Augustine, both the historicity of these events and also their prophetic significance.

It is part of the tradition of typological interpretation, going back to the New Testament and even to the Old Testament itself,[3] that this prophetic significance of events or personages to be found in the Old Testament should be related to Christ either directly (in His own person) or indirectly (in connection with a person, thing or event deriving its function and meaning from Christ). Thus St Paul himself exemplifies both possibilities, as when in Rom. 5. 14 he sees Adam as the τύπος of Christ,[4] whereas the typological force of I Cor. 10. 6 is that it relates the Israelites in the desert to the Christians.[5] Our problem with the *Millstätter Exodus* will therefore be to decide whether the allegorical significance of the events recounted refers prophetically to Christ Himself or whether it is by reference to Christians at

---

[1] *MPL*, 38, 30 f. (Sermon II, ch. VI). Cf. E. Auerbach, *Scenes from the Drama of European Literature*, p. 39.

[2] Cf. Auerbach, *Scenes from the Drama of European Literature*, p. 36; H. G. Jantsch, *Studien zum Symbolischen in frühmittelhochdeutscher Literatur*, p. 7.

[3] Cf. J. Daniélou, *Sacramentum futuri*, pp. 132 ff. See also below, p. 189, n. 4.

[4] 'Sed regnavit mors ab Adam usque ad Moysen etiam in eos qui non peccaverunt in similitudinem praevaricationis Adae, qui est forma futuri.'

[5] See p. 112.

large that these events were meant to be understood.[1] Here an analysis of the way in which the author has changed his material or given it a new emphasis may tell us which of these two interpretations he had in mind. In this analysis, however, we may be reasonably confident that the author assimilated these events of Jewish history to his twelfth-century experience not for the negative reason that his lack of a historical dimension made any other approach impossible, but rather for the positive reason that these events, despite their undoubted historicity, were felt also to possess a prophetic meaning. The assimilation of these events to the twelfth century is not a sign of the author's lack of historical awareness, but rather a method used by him to reveal, if only by implication, what precisely was their prophetic significance.[2]

We may begin by considering the author's neutral technique which consists in his translating the particularised concepts, titles or names of his source by vernacular terms so general that they are now also applicable to conditions other than the restricted ones of the biblical Exodus, even though they may still be true of this as well. The import of this technique may best be shown by various examples. One of the protagonists of the biblical account, Pharaoh, is still often referred to by the name *Pharaô*, whether by itself[3] or in conjunction with such descriptive epithets as *chunech*, *der heiden*, *der meintâte*, or simply *rîch* or *ubil*.[4] In these cases the vernacular translation is as particularised as its source, so that the passages in which it occurs can only refer to the historical Pharaoh, the king of the Egyptians whose opposition to Moses is

---

[1] Or, in fact, whether a combination of both views may not do better justice to the German work.

[2] Here it is fitting to recall that for the exegete, as St Augustine saw so clearly, the task was to discover the hidden meanings of the biblical narrative, especially in the case of the implicit Christian truths of the Old Testament: 'Quid est enim quod dicitur Testamentum vetus nisi occultatio novi? et quid est aliud quod dicitur novum nisi veteris revelatio?' (*MPL*, 41, 505). By this I do not wish to suggest that the exegete's task was in all respects identical with that of the poet, but simply that in both fields there was ample opportunity for original contributions to be made. It is of this possibility that the Millstatt author so skilfully avails himself.   [3] E.g. 651, 847, 1045.

[4] *Chunech Pharaôn*: 942, 1588, 2707; *Pharaô der heiden*: 2983; *Pharaô der meintâte*: 1819; *rîcher Pharaô*: 1362; *der ubile Pharaô*: 1708.

recounted in the Old Testament.[1] The position is different, however, when this same ruler is referred to in the German work in connection with the general fact of his rulership (by means of such undefined terms as *der chunich*, without the addition of *Pharaô*, or *rîcher chunich, chunich hêre, ir hêrre*)[2] or with the equally general fact of his paganism (e.g. *der heiden*, without the addition of *Pharaô*, or *der heidiniske man, der heidiniske chunich, der heidiniske hêrre, chunich heiden*; cf. also *chunech unreine, vîant*).[3] These terms are still applied to the historical Pharaoh, but their general and undefined nature means that, unlike the former group, they are also applicable to any other pagan ruler. Such terms no longer possess the historical individuality of those in the first group, they are capable of being understood with as much reference to the author's present as to the historical past. This is not to say that they were necessarily so understood, but merely that this technique created the possibility of this interpretation, a possibility which could only be realised in practice by the employment of a more positive technique.

Other examples of this neutral method are provided by the ways in which the German author renders the concepts *Aegyptii* or *terra Aegypti*. In the former case our author uses no word which means specifically 'the Egyptians'; instead he employs general terms signifying their rank (like *hêrren*)[4] or suggesting that they were inhabitants of the land in question (like *dise liut, lantdiet* or *lantliute*)[5] without the name of the land being given. Much more common, however, is his employment of terms that signify their paganism such as: *die heidene, die heidenscaft, hei-*

---

[1] Although it must be emphasised that by the twelfth century the name Pharaoh had long since acquired its established allegorical overtones as indicative of the Devil and his tyranny. See p. 137, n. 1.

[2] *Der chunich*: 979, 991, 1023, 1065, etc.; *rîcher chunich*: 1105; *chunich hêre*: 1271, 1285, 2004; *ir hêrre*: 2080.

[3] *Der heiden*: 1961; *der heidiniske man*: 1626, 3095; *der heidiniske chunich*: 1632; *der heidiniske hêrre*: 1690; *chunich heiden*: 1860; *chunech unreine*: 2243; *vîant*: 2622 (where the context shows that Pharaoh is here viewed as the enemy of God, not just of the Israelites). Of *vîant* the same is also true as of the name Pharaoh (see n. 1 above).　　　　　[4] V. 2139.

[5] *Dise liut*: 1591; *lantdiet*: 2365; *lantliute*: 1299, 1311, 1441, etc.

diniske diet or *heidiniske man.*[1] A similar tendency can be detected with regard to *terra Aegypti*, for although this is more commonly rendered simply by *Egiptus* or *Egyptinlant*,[2] we also find general terms such as *dîn lant, ditʒe lant*, but especially *heidenlant*.[3] By such renderings the particular historical role of Pharaoh and his kingdom, whilst still retained in part as the historical basis of medieval typology, is also so generalised that it is seen more as the general opposition of any pagan ruler to God's designs, true not merely of the period treated in the Old Testament, but of any period and therefore also of the author's present.

A similar method is employed of Pharaoh's opponents, so that Moses and the Israelites are likewise depicted in terms which partly illustrate their historicity, but which are partly so generalised that their import is much wider. Moses is frequently designated as *Moŷses*, either by itself[4] or with further descriptive terms (*Moŷses der guote, der rehte, der tiure man, der heilige man*).[5] In addition to this he is frequently referred to by general circumlocutions that make no mention of his particular name (*der guote man, der heilige man, der tiurliche man, der heilige bote, sîn (= gotes) trût, sîn (= gotes) man*),[6] especially when Moses and Aaron are described as acting jointly, for, although their names can in fact be mentioned,[7] they are more commonly referred to indirectly (*die boten, die gotes boten, die heiligen boten, die ʒwêne man, die heilige man, die gotes gesinden, die gotes trûten, die gotes scalche, die hêrren, die gebruodere lieben*).[8] The same distinction is true of the Israelites at

---

[1] *Die heidene*: 1530, 2378, 3138, 3143; *die heidenscaft*: 2863; *heidiniske diet*: 1489, 1525, 2721, 2749; *die heidiniske man*: 3171, 3206, 3216.

[2] *Egiptus*: 45, 515, etc.; *Egyptinlant*: 841, 2282, etc.

[3] *Dîn lant*: 2389; *ditʒe lant*: 2631; *heidenlant*: 1712, 2271, 2654.

[4] E.g. 258, 282, 389, etc.

[5] *Moŷses der guote*: 787, 1697; *Moŷses der rehte*: 3288; *Moŷses der tiure man*: 1191; *Moŷses der heilige man*: 909.

[6] *Der guote man*: 1923, 2279; *der heilige man*: 1621, 1667, 2124, 2428; *der tiurliche man*: 470; *der heilige bote*: 1928; *(gotes) trût*: 1132, 2263, 3235; *(gotes) man*: 1981. [7] E.g. 1908, 2788.

[8] *Die boten*: 1260, 1452, 2079, etc.; *die gotes boten*: 1833; *die heiligen boten*: 1778, 2650; *die ʒwêne man*: 1578; *die heilige man*: 2202; *die gotes gesinden*: 1390; *den gotes trûten*: 1611; *die gotes scalche*: 1753; *die hêrren*: 1725; *die gebruodere lieben*: 1423.

large. They can be described historically as the *iudene*[1] or by some such phrase as *isrâheliske diet, israheliske chint* or *des guoten Ysrahelis chint*[2] (although even in this latter case we should recognise that the common equation of Israel with Christendom, as attested by the phrase *spiritalis Israel* in *Eẓẓos Gesang*, means that the concept Israel was not confined to the Jewish people, but could also be understood as signifying Christendom). On the other hand the Israelites can be described by terms with no historical particularity, such as those used to denote their noble rank (*die hêrren*),[3] their exile (*dise ellende liute*),[4] their social organisation (*die lieben hûsgenôẓẓen, die genôẓe*),[5] their constitution as a people (*daẓ liut, dise liute, diet*),[6] especially as God's Chosen People (*die gotes diet, die gotlieben hêrren*),[7] or certain aspects of their present condition (*die armen, die tiurlîchen man*).[8] Again a distinction is made by these two groups of nouns between translations which retain an element of historical particularity and renderings that are so general that they could also be applied to the author's own time.

A final example of the manner in which a neutral translation makes it possible for some terms to be understood at least in part with reference to the twelfth century is provided by the term for Jehovah as Lord. The author frequently uses the word *got*, of course, but in order to designate Him as Lord in particular we find that he only uses the word *hêrre*, never *truhtin*. This is the more significant in that the *Wiener Genesis*, composed as the first biblical epic not so very long before the *Millstätter Exodus*, employed *trehtin* with some frequency, just as works later than our *Exodus* continue to use this term, even if more commonly in the rhyme-position. Here our author is to some considerable extent in advance of his time and we may best explain his replacement of *truhtin* by *hêrre* if we recall that by his day the former word, as a religious term for God as Lord, had become

---

[1] 1460, 1499, 1672, etc.
[2] *Isrâheliske diet*: 9; *israheliske chint*: 2437; *des guoten Ysrahelis chint*: 2478.
[3] 135.
[4] 2422.
[5] 1316, 2303, 2341.
[6] 1215, 1399, 1532, 1792, 2722, 1094.
[7] 51, 3021.
[8] 1087, 2962.

archaic. Even in Notker *truhtin* is already forced on to the defensive, being contested in its religious function by *got*, but also by *hêrre*.[1] *Hêrre* is therefore a more modern term in this period, so that its regular employment enables the author of *Exodus* to suggest, by his mere choice of word, the topicality of the events he is narrating, whereas the occurrence of *truhtin* would have implied that these events were past events, confined to historical time and only to be understood on this plane. Furthermore, *hêrre* also had a secular function to perform in this period as a technical term to designate the feudal lord.[2] Its regular employment in a religious epic will therefore suggest that the relationship between man and God has something in common with the relationship between a vassal and his feudal lord. We shall later[3] see that there are a number of passages indicating that this was how the author wished the relationship between Moses (or the Israelites at large) and God to be viewed, so that his employment of *hêrre* exclusively helps to embed his work in the context of twelfth-century feudalism, to suggest a further parallel between these Old Testament events and his own present.

From this survey of the author's neutral technique two conclusions emerge. In the first place, although he still employs names and titles that place the events he is narrating in their unique historical setting, he also generalises the significance of these events by rendering these names and titles by terms so indefinite that they could equally well be applicable to the author's own time.[4] Here the important qualification has to be made that although this means that such an interpretation was made possible, there is no suggestion that it would have to be made. In other words, this neutral technique only contributes indirectly to the process of equating the Israelite past with the medieval present; it does no more than prepare the ground for a more positive technique which alone can make it clear that this relevance of the past to the present is indeed one of the author's

[1] I have tried to show this development in *The Carolingian Lord*, pp. 482 ff.
[2] *Ibid.* pp. 512 ff.   [3] See pp. 170 ff.
[4] See also p. 132, n. 1.

conscious intentions. Furthermore, even though the author may generalise the particular terms of his source and thus extract them in part from their own historical context, he does not do this exclusively, so that enough references occur to make it clear that these are historical events with which he is dealing, however much he may stress their relevance to the present. In this employment of the particular as well as of the general the Millstatt author differs radically from such an author as Otfrid, for whom his allegorical commentary is so much more important than the historical facts which form its basis[1] that he is noticeably more thorough in converting the place-names and personal names of his source into more general terms or circumlocutions.[2] The result of Otfrid's technique is therefore a considerable degree of abstraction and divorce from reality which, whilst perhaps reconcilable with his more didactic purposes, cannot have proved acceptable to the twelfth-century author who is more concerned with elaborating a style of epic realism. When he expands his biblical source he frequently does this by inserting a reference to the change in location,[3] so that in the light of this we may readily understand why he should have retained geographical terms such as *Egyptinlant*. In addition to this, such names as *Pharaô* and *Moýses* retained some of that historical reality which was essential to the kind of typological interpretation favoured by St Augustine.

A second conclusion can be drawn from the way in which the author elaborates a further dimension in the events recounted in his biblical source. He does this by suggesting that Pharaoh (and thereby the Egyptians at large) act in disobedience to God and in association with the Devil, whereas Moses (together with the Israelites in general) are portrayed as acting on behalf of God or

[1] The relationship between Otfrid's commentary and his narrative technique (more closely concerned with the historical facts reported in the New Testament) has been investigated by D. A. McKenzie, *Otfrid von Weissenburg: narrator or commentator?*.

[2] Cf. O. Erdmann's comment on Otfrid 1, 4, 1 in the notes (p. 351) to his edition of Otfrid: *Otfrids Evangelienbuch*.

[3] See pp. 71 ff.

with His active support.[1] This is confirmed by the choice of such terms as *die gotlieben hêrren* for the Jews or by their description as God's Chosen People, just as Moses in particular is not merely *der heilige man*, but also *(gotes) trût* or *(gotes) man*. The result of applying such religious criteria to the enmity between the Jews and the Egyptians is that a conflict which takes place on the human plane also possesses a metaphysical significance since it is regarded as part of the eternal conflict between God and the Devil. This is a technique which is used with dramatic effect in the *Rolandslied*,[2] but just as the battle of Roncevaux is depicted in this work as no more than an episode in the unending struggle between these two metaphysical powers,[3] so are we meant to

[1] Pharaoh's association with the Devil is suggested by vv. 145 ('der tievel gap den rât') and 1966 f. ('des tiuveles anden | in sîn herze er dô nam'—on the full significance of this phrase see pp. 278 ff.). His disobedience to God is indicated by brief references to his arrogant pride (e.g. vv. 1455 f., 1646, 1776 f.; this is also implied by his mock-humility in vv. 2203 ff., for the point of these lines is that whatever they suggest of sudden self-awareness on his part is quite feigned and of short duration, anyhow). In addition to this, the conflict between Pharaoh and God is made quite explicit by such phrases as vv. 1361 f., 1495 ff., 1992 ff.

Conversely, Israel's association with God is amply revealed by the way in which the people is seen to serve God (vv. 861, 973), just as its representatives, Moses and Aaron, are seen as *gotes trûte, scalche* and Moses as *(gotes) man*. We shall see that the German author lays particular stress on God's promise to His people (see p. 174), and of course the lengthy description of the plagues and of the passage of the Red Sea is an epic demonstration not merely of God's omnipotence, but also of His readiness to assist His Chosen People.

[2] This is suggested at the beginning of the epic by the way in which Charles conquers heathen lands *mit gote* (v. 8), by the author's use of the term *rîch* (cf. F. Ohly, *ZfdA*, LXXVII, 189 ff.) and by his equation of Genelun with Judas (vv. 1924 ff.).

[3] Admittedly, there is nothing so explicit in the *Rolandslied* as the stress on the unending nature of Charles' campaigns against the heathen with which the *Chanson de Roland* concludes (vv. 3993 ff.). On the other hand it is likely that the similar scene with which the German work opens (vv. 31 ff.) and which is missing from the French is meant as a rejoinder to the concluding note of the *Chanson*, for now it is Charles who takes the initiative and there is no suggestion of the human despair with which the Emperor first reacted in the French work to his divine task. Moreover, the German author lays considerable stress on the universal nature of Charles' dominion: his kingship, as a reflection of God's rule, is seen as a continually expanding concept (cf. vv. 86, 1533, 6830 ff., 7654 f.). The connection between the universal and the eternal aspects of these expansionary claims is provided by Turpin's speech (vv. 970 ff.) and by his reference to the parable of the vineyard (vv. 976 ff.; cf. Matt. 20. 1 ff.), for the moral of

realise that the events narrated in the *Exodus* are only one battle in an eternal campaign. It is this which explains the relevance of this episode to the author's present, for the conflict which he describes is still being fought out in his own day. The metaphysical background against which the author depicts these historical events has the evocative power to suggest in the mind of his audience that these events possess a timeless validity which is as relevant to twelfth-century conditions as it was to the history of the Jewish people. Here again the Millstatt epic is dominated by a constant tension between time and timelessness, by an insistence that the events described, whilst undoubtedly historical events, are relevant to the needs of all subsequent ages and have therefore lost none of their importance for the conditions of the twelfth century.

With that we may leave the neutral technique employed by our author and consider next his negative technique, the omissions from his source. Beyschlag has pointed to the employment of the same method by the author of the *Wiener Genesis*, who was similarly led by his wish to emphasise the relevance of the Genesis story to his own time and society to delete those historical details in his source which were so particularly true of the Israelites alone that they would have constituted an awkward obstacle to his assimilation of past to present.[1] The author of the *Wiener Genesis* therefore drops those references from his source that concern the unique details of the tribal history of the Jews, he omits the many personal names in the genealogical lists of the biblical Genesis as well as many of the ethnic names and place-names. In addition, the view of the Jews and others with whom

this is that to leave the task uncompleted would be a betrayal of what God had demanded. The continual expansion of Charles' kingdom is therefore one aspect of the everlasting nature of his struggle against the pagans.

[1] *Die Wiener Genesis*, pp. 45 ff. Cf. especially Beyschlag's words on p. 47: 'Das alles rundet sich zu dem einen Bild, daß die W. Gen. konsequent alles spezifisch Historische: den Blick auf das entstehende jüdische Volk, seinen Gegensatz zu fremden Völkern, und auf sein künftiges Land mit allen Begebenheiten, die als dessen Vorgeschichte bedeutsam sind, ausscheidet und statt dessen die gegenwartsbezogene Heilsbedeutung der Patriarchengeschichte zur Mitte ihrer Darstellung macht.'

they have dealings as peoples in the ethnic sense is replaced by a more restricted view in which they are seen only as a kinship or large-scale family. On the other hand, as Beyschlag demonstrates, precisely such particular details can sometimes be retained (against the author's usual practice), but only when he finds it possible to show that they are practices which still survive into his own present (and can therefore be made to serve his assimilation of past to present) or when the historical events in question bear a sufficient resemblance to the themes of contemporary German non-clerical literature that they can assist him in his topical task of passing judgement on the more dubious aspects of these contemporary themes.[1] Not all these considerations, established by Beyschlag for the author of the *Wiener Genesis*, will prove to be equally true of his successor, but there are enough indications that he likewise omitted details which conflicted with his wish to underline the contemporary relevance of Old Testament events.

In the case of Near Eastern place-names the Millstatt author does not follow the example of his predecessor, for in most cases such names as *Jayrôt*, *Magdalôn* and *Belsephôn* are retained in his work. This is not true in every case (as we have already seen in the occurrence of *lant* or *heidenlant* alongside *Egiptus* or *Egyptin-lant*), but at least such place-names occur with sufficient frequency for us to say that the later author does not exclude them so regularly as the earlier. Nor is the reason for the difference between the two far to seek, for in his epic expansion of his source the Millstatt author pays particular attention to the details of place as part of his epic realism[2] and as serving his wish to indicate that the action he describes has both a historical and an allegorical significance.[3] We have also seen[4] that the earlier author, as Beyschlag has shown, sometimes expands his source on the epic scale, but sometimes contracts it and is forced by this latter technique to omit many such superfluous details as references to place. The Millstatt author, however, rarely contracts his source, so that he thereby obtains sufficient scope to include those

[1] *Ibid.* p. 49.
[2] See pp. 60 ff.
[3] See pp. 132 f.
[4] See pp. 31 f.

references to place which he felt contributed to the epic and historical realism of his work.

On the other hand, the Millstatt author generally agrees with his predecessor in omitting the personal names included in the genealogical lists of the Bible. Thus the biblical list of the Israelites who entered Egypt with Jacob (1. 2 ff.) is omitted by the German author and we are told only of the number of those who accompanied Jacob (vv. 43 ff.). The same is true of the lengthy list given in Exod. 6. 14 ff., for the German author conflates 6. 13 of his source with the similarly phrased 6. 26 and has God refer to the twelve who came with their father Jacob, ordering Moses to recount the kindreds of each of these to Pharaoh.[1] This we are not actually shown as part of the narrative, so that although the framework of the biblical passage has been preserved it has been emptied of all those particular details, namely the Jewish personal names, which showed it as part of Jewish tribal history. An omission of quite a different kind, but similarly intended to remove a detail which was too specifically Jewish, is to be found in the translation of 6. 30 ('En incircumcisus labiis sum; quomodo audiet me Pharao?'), for the purpose of the bald rendering in the German text[2] is clearly to avoid any reference to the too explicit word *incircumcisus*.

There are, however, other cases where the twelfth-century author sometimes omits a reference to Jewish or other Near Eastern personal names, but sometimes retains it. In this latter case it is probable that other considerations dictated his decision to preserve these references. What this consideration may have been it is admittedly difficult to say in the case of the biblical references to God as the God of Abraham, Isaac and Jacob, for these names are omitted when the author translates 2. 24; 3. 15; 6. 3 and 6. 8, being ignored altogether in the last two cases, but being translated in the first two by the general phrase (*got*) *iuwerer vorderône*.[3] Against this we have only two examples where

[1] Vv. 1167 ff.
[2] V. 1193: 'wie solt er mich vernemen? | ich nechan nicht reden.'
[3] Vv. 458, 605 f.

these names are retained in the same context of the covenant sworn by Jehovah to these three patriarchs, for 3. 6 is rendered (like 4. 5)[1] by the words:

> 495 'zewâre phligin ich is mich,
> got dînes vater bin ich,
> got Abrahâmes,
> got Isaâches,
> got Jacôbes
> unte alles dînes chunnes.'

With its solemn introductory line and slow, emphatic metre this passage is meant by the author to carry some weight. That he did not use it on the four other occasions where the Bible employed the same phrase is probably due to a sense of aesthetic economy, for a repeated use of this declamatory passage would have weakened its effect. On the other hand, the reason why the author chose to retain the phrase at all, with its reference to the Jewish patriarchs, is no doubt because it emphasises an aspect of Jehovah's relationship with His people which lay very close to the medieval author's heart, namely the covenant existing between Jehovah and Israel and resting on the conviction that He had sworn to uphold and assist His people.[2] Finally, it is probable that our author chose to retain this phrase on these two particular occasions, rather than on any of the other four, simply because they mark off the first encounter between Moses and God and signify that the covenant that existed in the past between God and these patriarchs still exists in the present in the case of Moses. Once more the author stresses that the historical fact of the past covenant is still relevant to the time of Moses and brings this out effectively by referring to it when God first reveals Himself (vv. 495 ff.) and immediately after He has demonstrated His power to protect by performing the first miracle with the snake (vv. 723 ff.). From its inception the relationship between Moses and Jehovah is felt to be a continuation of the earlier pledge between God and Abraham, Isaac and Jacob. Past and present are related to one another within Jewish history just as much as

---

[1] Vv. 723 ff.   [2] See p. 174.

they are in the relationship between the Jewish past and the medieval present.

A similar problem is posed by the way in which the list of names of countries in 13. 5 is omitted by the German author, but retained (and even expanded by the addition of *Gêrêsêus*) when he renders 3. 8 and 3. 17.[1] We cannot argue that these Near Eastern names are retained by the author as part of his wish to impart some degree of geographical realism to his work, because in these two passages he has made a significant alteration: the names which in the Old Testament are meant as names of countries[2] have been converted into the names of kings who rule over these countries.[3] In the first passage our author simply lists their names, but on the other occasion, although two of the names remain unqualified[4] and two are described by means of the neutral epithets *rîch* and *chunich*,[5] three of these rulers are given negative characteristics: *heiden*, *stolʒ* and *tump*.[6] From this we may conclude that these rulers are meant to be seen collectively as opposing God's designs, as had Pharaoh, and that because of this Moses and the Israelites will be justified in despoiling them of their riches, as they had the Egyptians, and in taking possession of their land, promised them by God Himself. In other words, God's assistance of His Chosen People is true not merely of His past relationship with Abraham[7] or of His present one with Moses, but also of the future when the Israelites eventually reach the Promised Land. The force of these two passages in the MHG work, coming again in this first encounter between Moses and Jehovah, is that they indicate the timelessness of God's compact with His people and its validity for the past, present and future. They

[1] Vv. 525 ff., 631 ff. On this name see Kossmann's edition, p. 25.

[2] Cf. the words *ad loca Chananaei* (3. 8) and *in terram Chananaei* (3. 17).

[3] R. A. Wisbey has drawn my attention to the fact that this conversion of what the biblical Exodus lists as names of countries into names of kings was probably suggested to the German author by Gen. 10. 15 ff. (cf. also I Paral. 1. 13 ff.), where the sons of Chanaan include Hethaeus, Jebusaeus, Amorrhaeus, Gergesaeus and Hevaeus. This again confirms the unity of history which the poet seeks to establish as a demonstration of God's plan for the salvation of mankind.

[4] Vv. 633 and 635.　　　[5] Vv. 638 and 639.　　　[6] Vv. 634, 636, 637.

[7] Cf. v. 643: 'des gewere ich sî zewâre, | ich gehiez iz Abrahâme.'

also suggest that this compact may well be as true of the author's present as of any of these three distinct periods in Hebrew history.

There is yet another consideration suggesting that the retention of these personal names was intended as a means of expressing the topical bearing of these Old Testament events on twelfth-century experience. In the first place, the substitution of hypothetical rulers' names for the names of countries implies a conflict between these rulers and the Jews under their leader which has much in common with the conflict between Pharaoh and Moses. This similarity is strengthened by the faint traces of a warlike encounter between the Israelites and these rulers[1] and is in accord with the military view of things which so distinguishes the medieval epic from its source. It is not this in itself, however, which provides the parallel with twelfth-century experience, but rather the fact that it agrees with another point which is peculiar to the medieval period. By this I mean the way in which the kingdom of Canaan, heading the biblical list of kingdoms making up the Promised Land and transformed into a pagan king by the twelfth-century author, can be used in medieval historical writing with explicit reference to the crusades. According to this view, as we shall later see in greater detail,[2] the exodus of the Jews from Egypt and their entry into the Promised Land are seen as prefigurations of the crusaders' journey to Palestine, just as the kings hitherto in occupation of the territory promised to the Jews are equated with the Saracens with whom the crusaders have to dispute the occupation of the Holy Land. The relevance of this typological view of the crusades to our problem is best illuminated by a passage from the *Historia Iherosolimitana* by Robertus Monachus which, however unreliable in its attribution of certain views to the pagans, at least credibly reflects the possible attitude of a Christian towards the events he reports. The chronicler describes a conversation between Corbanam, the Persian king who in his *superbia*[3] has come to lay siege to the crusaders in Antioch, and his mother. The latter reproaches her

---

[1] Cf. v. 524 ('dere gewinnest dû gewalt') and also 632 ('swenne sî bestôzzent | Chânânêum...').   [2] See pp. 258 ff.   [3] *RHC*, III, 811 E.

son for his folly in thinking that he could be victorious over those for whom the true God fights.[1] She argues that her people has offended God who in His anger has summoned the Europeans to take possession of all the territory occupied until now by the pagans.[2] It is in this context, where the parallel between the crusaders' approach to the Holy Land and that of the Israelites to the Promised Land is clear, that the comparison is made by Corbanam's mother between the present situation and the events of Exodus:

Fili, Pharaonem, regem Aegypti, quis submersit in mari Rubro, cum omni exercitu suo? Quis exhaereditavit Seon, regem Amorreorum, et Og, regem Basan, et omnia regna Chanaam, et dedit suis in haereditatem? Ipse idem Deus ostendit quanto amore diligat populum suum.[3]

Here two of the 'kings' mentioned by the Millstatt author, *Chânânêus* and *Amôrrêus*, are mentioned in a comparison with the crusading present, and the transfer of their territory to the Israelites is indicated as a proof that God will similarly aid His people, the crusaders, in ejecting the heathen from the Holy Land. In the light of this comparison it is possible that the biblical reference to these territories of the Promised Land was twice[4] retained by the German author as a means of indicating a parallel with contemporary crusading experience, but whether in fact this parallel is anything more than merely possible, whether it was indeed intended by the author, is a question which can only be

---

[1] *RHC*, III, 812B: 'Si legisses scripta omnium prophetarum antiquorumque sapientum, profecto non ignorares quia ipse (= Deus Christianorum) est Omnipotens et Deus Deorum omnium. Si pugnas contra Christianos, pugnabis contra ipsum et ipsius angelos.'

[2] *Ibid.* 812 F: 'Genti nostrae iratus est Deus ille, quia nec audimus vocem ejus, nec facimus voluntatem; et idcirco de remotis partibus Occidentis excitavit in nos gentem suam, deditque ei universam terram hanc in possessionem.'

[3] *Ibid.* 812 D. The mention of the kings Seon and Og is a reference to Num. 21. 21–35.

[4] That it was retained twice in chapter 3 of Exodus, but not on the third occasion in 13. 5, is probably due to the fact that the two passages in chapter 3 give added emphasis to Jehovah's solemn promise to assist Moses and Israel. The position here is therefore similar to what we saw about the retention of references to Jehovah as the God of Abraham, Isaac and Jacob.

answered when we have discussed the basic problem of crusading allusions in this epic.

A last example of an apparent exception to the author's practice of not mentioning those personal names which provide too much historical particularity concerns his depiction of the sixth plague, for here he refers by name to the two sorcerers employed by Pharaoh as *Jamnes* and *Zambres*.[1] This is not merely contrary to the author's practice with regard to personal names, it also differs from his technique in depicting action, for he normally concentrates events on two main protagonists (Moses and Pharaoh), allowing all the other personages, even Aaron to a considerable extent, to step into the background.[2] Furthermore, there is no mention of these two sorcerers by name in the corresponding passage in the Bible, which is content with the anonymous term *malefici*.[3] In such a case we must obviously seek for a special explanation of our author's procedure. Our problem lies not so much in the form of the names chosen (for there is biblical authority for this, but significantly not in Exodus,[4] and the names appear to have enjoyed an apocryphal popularity)[5] as rather in determining why the author should have chosen to equip these two sorcerers with names at all. A possible answer is suggested by a passage in the *Kaiserchronik* where this same *Zambrî* occurs in the Silvester episode as one of the Pope's opponents in the disputation scene.[6] He it is who questions the power of the Christian God and it is in answer to this that Silvester adduces

---

[1] V. 1749.   [2] Cf. Kossmann, *Die altdeutsche Exodus*, p. 78.   [3] Exod. 9. 11.
[4] II Tim. 3. 8: 'Quemadmodum autem Jannes et Mambres restiterunt Moysi, ita et hi resistunt veritati.'
[5] See the article on Jannes und Mambres in H J Wetzer and B. Welte, *Kirchenlexikon*, VI, 1214. Even if one were to argue that the Millstatt author (like the author of the *Kaiserchronik* and like Konrad von Würzburg) was here merely using a version of the *Vetus Latina* which does give the names of these sorcerers, one would still have to explain why he chose to retain these names on this occasion—against his usual practice.
[6] Whereas, however, in the *Millstätter Exodus* the conflict is between Israelites and Egyptians (so that Zambres is an Egyptian sorcerer), in the *Kaiserchronik* the disputation is held between the Christian Silvester and the Jews, so that here Zambrî has become a Jew. The common factor is his opposition to God, whether of the old or of the new dispensation.

biblical testimony to the contrary. Significantly, the first of his Old Testament examples is the passage of the Israelites through the Red Sea and the protection which God afforded them against the Egyptian army:

> 10251 er (= got) wîste di juden durch daz rôte mer,
> daz ir widerwärtige her
> besouft er in des meres grunt.
> die sîne behielt er alle wol gesunt,
> er gab in vierzic jâr sîn himelbrôt.

It is this power of the Christian God to assist His believers when they call upon Him which is at the centre of this debate, for when the Pope begins to pronounce his formula recalling the bull to life the poet sums up the action by describing it as a demonstration of God's might,[1] a fact which is also acknowledged by the pagan witnesses of this miracle in the way in which they react.[2] From the manner in which this figure of *Zambrî* is depicted in the *Kaiserchronik* it seems probable that there existed a medieval tradition[3] in which these two sorcerers, sometimes seen as pagan and sometimes as Jewish, were regarded as incorporating not just the resistance to truth implied by II Tim. 3. 8, but more particularly a wilful refusal to acknowledge the power of God. This is confirmed by the *Exodus*, for the author makes it clear that these two are punished for their pride in thinking that their magic was stronger than the power of God:

> 1759 daz wart ouch in verwizzen
> wande si solten wizzen
> daz got stercher wâre
> danne ir goucgelâre.[4]

---

[1] Vv. 10305 f.: 'ûf huob er sîne hant, | er besceinte mînes trehtînes gewalt.'

[2] Vv. 10329 ff.: 'under den haiden wart ein michel lop: | si sprâchen, daz wære ain waltiger got, | der durch sine liute | so grôziu zaichen tæte.' *Zambrî* also occurs in the corresponding episode of the *Silvester* of Konrad von Würzburg (vv. 4547 ff.). He too regards the contest with the Pope as a means of disproving the power of the Christian God (vv. 4770 ff.).

[3] The different forms of this name in the *Exodus* and *Kaiserchronik* also argue against any dependence of the later work on the earlier.

[4] Cf. also vv. 1770 ff.: 'si mohten iz vermîden | daz si wolten sîn gelîch | deme der in dem himel ist vil rîch.'

It is the power of the God whom these sorcerers refuse to recognise which assists Moses and Aaron (as well as Silvester) in the miracles they are called upon to perform, it is this same divine power that afflicts the Egyptian opponents of Moses with the plagues and also (as in the remark of Silvester) guides the Israelites safely through the Red Sea and protects them in the desert. In other words, the confirmatory evidence of the *Kaiserchronik* makes it clear that these two sorcerers were regarded in medieval tradition as typical examples of a stubborn and arrogant refusal to acknowledge the power of God, so that when the Millstatt author refers to them by name he does not do this in order to individualise them, but in order to evoke the suggestive power of these symbolical names.[1] The mention of these names was meant to make it clear to the audience what were the implications of this scene, to show them that these two were punished for their blindness in the face of the divine power which assisted their opponents on this occasion, which later protected the Israelites in crossing the Red Sea and when in the desert and which, as Corbanam's mother realised, was still helping the spiritual successors of the Israelites (*spiritalis Israel*!) on the First Crusade.

A final aspect of this negative technique concerns the manner (similar to that of the *Wiener Genesis*) in which the German author converts the Old Testament picture of the Jewish people into a small-scale view of them as a closely knit kindred. Such a contraction of scale is relevant to our inquiry, but for reasons diametrically opposed to those which underlay the translation of Pharaoh by *der heidiniske chunech* or of Egypt by *heidenlant*. In the earlier cases such names as Pharaoh and Egypt were stripped of historical particularity whenever they were rendered by these general terms, being transposed on to a metaphysical plane which imparted to them a large measure of timelessness. In the case of the view of Israel as a kindred, however, the converse is the truth: here the concept 'people', instead of being expanded to the idea

---

[1] The insertion of vv. 1759–72 (with no parallel in the Bible) as an explanatory conclusion of the scene suggests that the author had some such definite purpose in mind in introducing these pagan opponents of God by name.

10-2

'heathendom' as with the Egyptians, is contracted to the smaller unit of the kindred. Whereas to have referred to the Israelites on every occasion as a 'people' in the ethnic sense would have drawn more attention to their historical individuality, their description merely as a kindred emphasises what they have in common with most other peoples of any historical period and furthermore designates them by reference to the institution of the kindred, which still played a role in the German heroic tradition and must therefore have been capable of making an appeal to our author's twelfth-century audience.[1]

The Israelites of the Old Testament are therefore deprived of their historical individuality and are described only in terms of a social organisation which they share with the German author's present whenever they are depicted as a kindred (however large) rather than a separate people. Our author can therefore differ from his source in referring to the Hebrews as *genôʒe, hûsgenôʒʒen, mâge* or as *vriunde*, as forming a *gesinde* or a *chunne* made up of *chunnelinge*.[2] The employment of such terms introduces a perspective which is absent from the biblical account and compels the audience to view the Israelites in a context which is more restricted and parochial, but which has the advantage of being well known to them from their everyday experience. Nor is this technique so superficial as might appear from the bald listing of the various terms employed, for the author goes beyond this in

[1] How persistent the force of the kindred was in early medieval literature it is difficult to tell in view of the poverty of our direct testimony for heroic literature in this period. However, K. Hauck has demonstrated its importance in one particular respect (see his essay 'Haus- und sippengebundene Literatur mittelalterlicher Adelsgeschlechter, von Adelssatiren des 11. und 12. Jahrhunderts her erläutert', revised version in *Geschichtsdenken und Geschichtsbild im Mittelalter*, ed. W. Lammers, pp. 165 ff.). Moreover, its existence as a powerful ideal can be postulated with some reliability because of the way in which it is referred to in crusading chronicles—either as a secular concern which has to be abandoned (e.g. p. 286, n. 2) or, more revealingly, as one to which an appeal can be made on behalf of showing similar virtues in the crusading context (e.g. p. 281, n. 3). E. R. Curtius also follows Gröber in arguing that the twelfth century saw the transformation of French heroic poetry into what he terms 'Geschlechterdichtung' (*ZRPh*, LXIV, 317).

[2] *Genôʒe*: 2303, 2341; *hûsgenôʒʒen*: 297, 1316; *mâge*: 2956; *vriunde*: 3114; *gesinde*: 1920, 2437, 2575, 2710, 2874; *chunne*: 2567; *chunnelinge*: 1159.

using the idea of the kindred on two occasions to heighten the dramatic appeal of a scene. Both occasions are related to the scene, described in Exod. 2. 11 ff., where Moses kills the Egyptian overseer for beating one of the Jews. Admittedly, the Bible itself refers to the fact that this was a kinsman of Moses who was being ill-treated (2. 11: 'quemdam de Hebraeis fratribus suis'), a fact which the German author does not neglect to make clear in his version,[1] but he goes further than his source when he describes Moses' action as undertaken in order to avenge his kinsman:

> 286 er wolte gerne selbe
> rechen sînen anden
> mit sîn selbes handen.
> Dô er dô nieman nesach,
> den sînen chunden er rach.

The killing of the Egyptian by Moses is here made more intelligible to the twelfth-century knightly audience by this reference to a norm of conduct with which they would have had little difficulty in feeling sympathy, but for this to be possible the kindred, as the home of the blood-feud and the duty of vengeance, must have been an ideal to which the author's audience paid more than lip-service.

The same is revealed by the next episode in the same scene when Moses comes across two Hebrews quarrelling and reproaches one of them with these words:

> 300 'durch waz tuost dû ungemach
> dînem chunnelinge?
> des solt dû erwinden,
> slege unde stôzze
> solt dû in erlâzzen,
> durch die gotes minne
> solt dû is erwinden.'

Quite apart from the Christian appeal in the name of God, it is clear that here too the brief remark of the Bible[2] is expanded and explained by reference to the traditional belief that the Germanic

---

[1] Cf. v. 279: 'der eine was ime von chunne liep.'
[2] Exod. 2. 13: 'Quare percutis proximum tuum?'

and medieval kindred rested on the need for peace to reign among all members of the kindred.[1] In both respects (the inner cohesion of the kindred resting on peace and the exaction of vengeance from those outside the kindred who have offended it) this biblical episode is interpreted with reference to an institution and its ideals well known to the author's audience. Because of this, as well as because the occasional description of the Israelites as kinsmen rather than as a people deprives them of some of their historical uniqueness, it seems probable that this method is employed, as in the *Wiener Genesis*, in order that the Israelites of the Old Testament might be seen in the light of twelfth-century experience as acting in a manner and for reasons which could still appeal to a contemporary audience.[2]

Nothing we have so far seen, however, of the German author's neutral and negative techniques can convince us that this was necessarily how he intended the Israelites of the Exodus to be viewed by his audience. All we have so far established is that it was possible for them to be so regarded, that the omission of certain details and a neutral method of translation had removed obstacles to this possible assimilation of the Hebrew past to the medieval present. That this assimilation was consciously intended can only be shown by an analysis of the positive innovations in subject-matter.

Here we must distinguish between two types of innovation. The first (and less important) consists of a statement that a particular detail of Old Testament life still continues or has its counterpart in medieval life. By such a technique the author suggests a continuity between Hebrew past and Christian present which allows him to depict the story of Exodus in terms so

[1] See J. de Vries, *Die geistige Welt der Germanen*, pp. 58 ff.; R. von Kienle, *Germanische Gemeinschaftsformen*, pp. 30 ff. This again would imply that despite clerical opposition the kinship managed to survive as a powerful factor in social life and in the literary imagination.

[2] The same is true of the reminiscences of heroic literature to be found in the MHG *Exodus*, but these are best discussed not in the present context, as with Beyschlag in the case of the *Wiener Genesis*, but in connection with the positive innovations for which our author is responsible.

intimate that it will strike home to his audience and also give further emphasis to the divinely preordained scheme of things. This practice is not unknown to the author of the *Wiener Genesis*[1] who makes occasional use of it to reinforce his view of the relevance of the events he is describing to the society of his own day, as when he traces the sin of hatred back to Cain or, more concretely, the class of serfs to Ham and the feudal tribute to Joseph. References such as these, connecting past with present, occur occasionally in the *Millstätter Exodus* although it would be wrong to dismiss them, as does Kossmann,[2] as nothing more than anachronisms. We have already seen that our author is quite aware of the historicity of the events he is narrating, but that he is equally convinced of their significance for his own day. When he takes care on the one hand to remove those details which might make it more difficult for him to reveal this topical significance, but on the other hand adds the occasional suggestion that such past practices have their parallels in the present, it is probable that this twofold technique, so consciously employed, serves a definite intention and is not just the result of his ignorance of history. This conscious wish to connect past with present is also suggested, as we shall see, with the second type of innovation for which our author is responsible.

It is not therefore a naïve anachronism when the author, recounting Pharaoh's initial speech on the differences between Jew and Egyptian, has Pharaoh say of the Jews:

> 84 ir chint si besnîdent
> an dem ahtoden tage,
> ze touffe wellent si daz haben.

Here we may agree with what Jantsch says of a comparable passage in the *Vorauer Bücher Mosis*, namely that Christian

---

[1] Some examples are given by Beyschlag, *Die Wiener Genesis*, p. 48; cf. also H. G. Jantsch, *Studien zum Symbolischen in frühmittelhochdeutscher Literatur*, p. 80. Beyschlag includes these examples in his survey of the omissions from the Bible in the *Wiener Genesis* but, since the (generally) explicit reference to contemporary conditions is an actual addition to what is found in the Bible, I prefer to discuss them under the heading of positive innovations.

[2] *Die altdeutsche Exodus*, p. 37.

baptism is not felt to be 'derived' from Jewish circumcision, but rather that the author regards the Jewish rite as a valid prefiguration of the Christian sacrament.[1] Any *naïveté* there might be in this passage is not therefore of a historical nature, but consists in the way in which the author, disregarding the fact that Pharaoh is a heathen and that the Jews prefigure the Christians, has Pharaoh stress the difference between Egyptians and Jews by reference to the rite of baptism of which he has no knowledge, not even prefiguratively. In other words, if in this work it had been one of the Jews who had stressed his people's nature by claiming that their rite of circumcision was a form of baptism, this would have been just as acceptable to the author and just as 'unhistorical' in the modern view, but at least there would have been a gain in consistency, for only a Jew could be deemed to have prefigurative knowledge of this kind. From the point of view of an author wishing to elaborate parallels between Jewish past and Christian present this is therefore no anachronism, even though it must be judged as a fault in characterisation.

Similar parallels are provided between past and present whenever a specifically Christian concept is mentioned in this episode from Old Testament history.[2] This is the case when the Passover lamb is referred to by the adjective *ôsterlîch*, the time of the sacrifice as *ôsteren* and the place of the ceremony as *ȝe vrôn tiske*,[3] for here it is the Christian reinterpretation of these Jewish practices which is imposed upon the author's account of Old Testament events. The use of the word *venie* in the phrase *sî suohten ir venie*[4] as a rendering of 4. 31 (*et proni adoraverunt*) also belongs

---

[1] *Studien zum Symbolischen*, p. 81.

[2] It needs to be emphasised that these parallels do not include any reference to Christ, whose name is not mentioned in this work. This fact will prove to be important when we come to decide whether the typological significance of the epic refers to Christ Himself or only to Christians (see p. 120, n. 1). See also p. 364.

[3] Vv. 2541, 2826, 2824. A revealing commentary on this practice of the Millstatt author is provided by the sermon *In sancto die Pasce* of the *Speculum ecclesiae* (54. 17): 'Hivte ist der tac, an dem div iudischâit ende nam unde div kristenheit angenge gwan. Elliv div ê der iûdin div ist uerwandilot in die hoczit ditzes tâges.'

[4] V. 922.

to this context, as does the interpretation of 12. 15 (*peribit anima illa de Israel*) by the Christian idea suggested by the words: *der dolt den êwigen tôt.*[1] On the other hand, other examples given by Kossmann[2] do not really belong here since the Christian implication is sometimes present (however weakly) in the Vulgate itself. This is true of the author's use of the words *engil, ʒe einer mettinʒît* and *ʒe vespir,*[3] where in each case the corresponding word occurs in the author's biblical source[4] so that it would be impossible to claim them as his innovations. The most we could say is that the biblical use of such typically Christian words did not conflict with the author's wish to demonstrate the relevance of the past to the present and that he therefore found it easy to retain them.

With that we have exhausted the examples of this first type of innovation by means of which the Millstatt author implies a certain parallelism between the religious practices of the Jews and the Christian rites of his own time. We may agree that they are infrequent and cannot do much to force the attention of his audience upon the necessity (rather than the mere possibility) of interpreting these Old Testament events as significant for their present condition. It is only with the second type of innovation that this compulsion is more clearly apparent, for here the changes effected are not merely more frequent, they also concern the author's audience more intimately and inescapably. By this I mean that this second group of innovations consists in the author showing up the secular parallels between the life of the Jewish patriarchs and the life of twelfth-century society (even though these secular parallels may then be made to serve a religious purpose). From the increased frequency of this type of innovation

---

[1] V. 2580.   [2] *Die altdeutsche Exodus*, p. 81.

[3] 2555, 2564, 2655, 2667, 2674, 3161, 3202, 2480.

[4] For *mettinʒît* cf. Exod. 14. 24 (*vigilia matutina*) and for *vespir* 12. 6 (*ad vesperam*). In the case of *engil*, however, the first five usages given in the preceding footnote have no parallel in the Bible, for the German author has attributed to an angel the action which in the Bible is carried out by the Lord Himself (cf. 12. 12 and 23). However, v. 3161 corresponds to *angelus Dei* in the Vulgate (14. 19), so that it is conceivable that the German author's readiness to use this term was in part due to the model of this biblical passage.

we may draw the conclusion that, although the author wished to show the religious significance of these events for his present, he was much more anxious to show the relevance of these events to one social class in particular. We shall see that, just as Beyschlag has demonstrated something similar in the case of the *Wiener Genesis*,[1] the social class to which this appeal is made is the class composing his audience, the knightly aristocracy of the author's day. By consciously depicting the Old Testament patriarchs in terms which would interest and appeal to this audience and in which they could with little difficulty recognise themselves our author makes it clear that it is his intention to relate these past events with his own day and also to show that they concern especially the knighthood of his day. The total picture of this knighthood which he projects back on to the Old Testament narrative and which will emerge from our analysis may not agree in every detail with that established for the *Wiener Genesis* by Beyschlag, but the general similarity is recognisable and there is of course no reason why the two pictures should agree in all respects. Indeed, it is possible that the slightly different pictures of contemporary knighthood that are revealed in these two works may assist us in the more difficult task of determining how the appeal made to the knighthood by the later author differed from the earlier attempt or, in other words, how far his poetic intentions were different from those of his predecessor.[2] The various aspects of this total picture which we have to consider are six in number. They show us the Israelites of the Old Testament in terms of the twelfth-century view of warfare, as noblemen (to whom contemporary courtly features can also be attributed), as concerned with the topical ideals of honour and feudal loyalty, and finally described by means of the conventional ideas of heroic literature known to the twelfth century.

Of these six aspects which make of the Old Testament story something quite new the most important is the way in which a predominantly military atmosphere now informs the whole work. This may be shown by reference to the three longest passages in

[1] *Die Wiener Genesis*, pp. 23 ff. [2] See pp. 185 ff. and pp. 442 ff.

the epic where the author diverges from his source and consults his own intentions, for each of these passages gives a lengthy description of a military detail which either is touched upon only briefly in the Bible or is missing altogether. Thus the passage 1342 ff., where the frogs of the second plague are described with reference to precisely the military accoutrements with which they were able to dispense in their attack on Pharaoh and his followers, has no corresponding military suggestion in the Bible,[1] so that this episode is employed as an excuse for introducing a military description on the epic scale, even if only in negative terms. (A similar excuse is manufactured by the author when he also insinuates in vv. 157 ff. the equally negative description of the battlefield beloved of heroic literature which was avoided when the midwives circumvented Pharaoh's intention to have all the male children of the Jews put to death.) The other two passages (2877 ff. and 3023 ff.) where the author branches off into a military description first of the departure of the Jews from Egypt, seen as an army setting out for war, and then of the Egyptian host in full pursuit, are based on a similar view in the biblical passages,[2] but whereas the Bible references are short the Millstatt author has considerably extended them and has converted them into the very core of his description of this scene. These three prolonged descriptions are something characteristic of our author and impart a wholly new dimension to his narrative.

This is confirmed by points of detail where he likewise differs from his source in introducing a military note. Not merely the second plague, but also some of the other plagues are sketched more dramatically by means of military imagery. Just as the frogs of the second plague are seen collectively as a *here*[3] (even though it may be an army which has no need of the conventional weapons), so does God's promise to Moses to afflict Pharaoh with all

---

[1] Cf. the bald simplicity of Exod. 8. 6 ('et ascenderunt ranae, operueruntque terram Aegypti').

[2] Exod. 13. 18 ('et armati ascenderunt filii Israel de terra Aegypti') and 14. 7 ('Tulitque sexcentos currus electos, et quidquid in Aegypto curruum fuit, et duces totius exercitus').

[3] V. 1373.

manners of plague refer to them as a *here*,[1] a term which is also used of the plagues of flies and locusts.[2] Indeed, the locusts are also referred to by such terms as *vîant*, *wîgant* and *helt*,[3] just as the flies can be described as *gotes rîtere*[4] or the frogs (negatively) as attacking the land *âne sarwât unde sahs*.[5] A short negative reference such as this has the same effect as the two longer negative descriptions already mentioned: by comparing the episode with the military encounter which it is *not* the author succeeds in imposing a military view on his subject-matter even where this appeared to offer him the least scope.

Military implications are also revealed in references to the exodus itself, not merely in the longer description of the two armies. This is suggested whenever the Israelites' departure is equated with the idea of military power, however much this power may reside more in the leadership of God than in themselves. Thus Jehovah promises to Moses on their first encounter that He will free His people from their exile *mit gewalte*,[6] just as later they are said to be freed *gewaltichlîche*[7] by the blows inflicted by God on His enemy Pharaoh or to be liberated *mit chrafte*.[8] The forcible nature of this liberation of the Jews resides in the omnipotence of the God who has sworn to assist them, but when the power of this God is directed against the army of their Egyptian masters[9] this serves indirectly to draw the Jews themselves, however passive they may remain, into a military context. This is made clear by the way in which God swears that He will lead His people from Egypt *mit heres scare*,[10] for the more convincingly He is depicted as a military leader scattering His foes the more frequently will the people He leads come to be equated with His army. We find most examples of this in the scene where

---

[1] V. 571.

[2] Vv. 1486 (the same is implied by vv. 1553 f.), 1608, 2171.

[3] Vv. 2164, 2176, 2177.   [4] V. 1482.   [5] V. 1413.

[6] Vv. 515 f.   [7] V. 2624.

[8] V. 2864. Cf. also Pharaoh's remark, vv. 3002 f.

[9] Cf. vv. 665 f. ('Mîne hant wil ich tenen | unde wil slahen dere heidene here'). It is significant that here the corresponding passage in the Bible makes no reference to an army (3. 20: 'Extendam enim manum meam, et percutiam Aegyptum').

[10] V. 2594. This idea is taken over from 12. 17.

the Israelites are leaving Egypt and Pharaoh sets off in pursuit. The assembled Israelites are referred to, before their detailed description as an army setting out, as a *her* led by God.[1] Immediately after the lengthy description of their military splendour they depart from *Sôchôt* and pitch camp at a further stage in their march,[2] whereby it is twice said that God accompanied them.[3] Coming hard upon the explicitly military description of the Jews, this passage leaves us in no doubt but that we are to imagine this as a military encampment in which Jehovah is present as the leader of His people in arms.[4] Even the Egyptians are finally convinced of the force of this when they recognise that their foes are assisted by so powerful a God,[5] for, although this detail is borrowed from the Bible, it is emphasised by the expanded description that follows,[6] showing how little assistance the Egyptians received from their military might in the face of the Lord God of Hosts. Finally, it is probably in the light of these military overtones introduced by our author (both in points of detail and in the longer descriptions) that we may best understand why he should have provided an exegetical explanation of God's name *Adônây* (vv. 1140 ff.), for he interprets this: *daz chuît ich bin des heres got.*[7] This is theologically false (since Adonai does not mean this) and is perhaps due to confusion with the name Sabaoth, which was generally translated by *Dominus exercituum.*[8] We cannot tell whether this false exegesis is a mistake on the part of the German author or the result of a conscious decision, but we can at least be certain that it was his decision (against his usual practice) to introduce a brief explanation of this name. This is most clearly revealed by a comparison with his source, for the Bible says explicitly at this point: 'Qui apparui Abraham, Isaac et Jacob, in Deo omnipotente; et nomen meum Adonai non indicavi eis.'[9] In other words, the divine name which the Bible

[1] Vv. 2751 and 2754 (taken from 12. 41).   [2] Vv. 2959 f.
[3] Vv. 2958, 2963 (only the second reference has a parallel in 13. 21).
[4] Cf. also vv. 2980 ff. (14. 1 f.).   [5] Vv. 3216 ff. (14. 25).
[6] Vv. 3224–34 thus correspond to the *fugientibusque Aegyptiis* of 14. 27.
[7] V. 1143.   [8] E.g. Zach. 1. 3.
[9] Exod. 6. 3.

says was not mentioned on this occasion is given an explanation in the German work, a deviation from our author's normal practice which is probably due to the way in which, by giving this explanation of God's name, he was able to give greater stress to the military function of this God who leads His people like an army against His foes.

Further light on the way in which the Millstatt author wished these military implications to be understood is shed by an analysis of his employment of the traditional military vocabulary of heroic literature. We have already seen that the Israelites could be described as a *here*, just as they can also be seen as *chreftige diete*[1] on the march. These are, however, collective terms which possess none of the positive heroic overtones of such terms for the individual warrior as *rîter* or *helt*. When we consider individual terms of praise such as these we find a noteworthy distinction made by the author. The noun *rîter(scapht)*[2] is used only of the insects summoned by God in the plagues to fight on His behalf against Pharaoh, whereas the terms *chnappe*, *chneht*, *iungeling* and *reche*[3] are used as military terms only of the Egyptians, whilst *helt* and *wîgant*[4] can be employed both of the insects and of the Egyptians. On the other hand, none of these heroic terms is applied by the author to the Israelites. Admittedly, Pharaoh refers to them as 'guote chnehte | geturren wole vechten',[5] but this is no more than a description attributed by the author to the Jews' pagan opponent and therefore not necessarily the author's own view.[6]

---

[1] V. 550.   [2] Vv. 1346, 1482.

[3] Vv. 3262, 3257, 3069, 3258.

[4] Vv. 1384, 2177 (insects), 3031 (Egyptians), 2176 (insects), 3010, 3024 (Egyptians).

[5] Vv. 95 f. *Chneht* can also be used to indicate the aristocratic birth of the Hebrews (v. 129), just as it is also used in this sense of the Egyptians (v. 140) without any military implication. On this passage see p. 162.

[6] A similar technique is employed by the author of the *Rolandslied* with regard to the heroic adjective *virmezzen* which he normally uses of the Saracens, but also on three occasions of the Christian knights (642, 3996, 8368). On each occasion, however, the word is used of the Christian by his pagan opponent, who is therefore shown as capable of understanding the Christian only from his own point of view. Cf. G. Fliegner, *Geistliches und weltliches Rittertum im Rolandslied des Pfaffen Konrad*, pp. 14 ff.

Furthermore, this respect for the Jews' martial qualities is either the result of Pharaoh's past experience with them or a shrewd assessment of a future possibility—in either case, although they may be seen in a military context and are described by the heroic term *chneht*, we do not actually witness the Israelites engaged in military action. This is a point to which we shall later return. In addition, two other possibly military terms are used of the Jews alone, namely *degen* and *vuozvende*. Both may safely be discounted since *degen*[1] is here used not in its military sense, but with its other meaning of 'child' or 'boy', whereas *vuozvende*[2] is no innovation of the poet's, but simply corresponds to *peditum virorum* in the Bible[3] and has the general sense of 'those who went on foot' as opposed to horsemen (a similar distinction is made in v. 2724).

Much the same can be established by analysing the heroic or military adjectives used by the German author. The conventional adjective *mâre* is applied as a heroic epithet only to the insects whose attack is described in military terms,[4] whereas the epithets *chuone* and *vermezzen* (used, however, as a verb rather than as an adjective) are employed only with reference to the Egyptians.[5] *Snel* is used both of the insects and of the Egyptians.[6] None of these terms occurs as a description of the Israelites and if the adverb *baltlîche*[7] is used once to describe the behaviour of Moses and Aaron before Pharaoh this is only because their outspokenness, however brave, is sufficiently distinct from a purely military courage.

[1] Vv. 151, 175, 191, 425. For other examples of the meaning 'child' cf. the MHG compound *degenkint* or Konrad von Würzburg, *Trojanerkrieg* 520 (*der niuweborne degen*); for the usage 'boy' cf. Reinbot von Durne, *Der heilige Georg* 965 (*mugot* and *degon*) or *Der Jüngere Titurel* 3314 (*degon und dirno*).

[2] V. 2758.   [3] Exod. 12. 37.

[4] V. 1372. I have ignored such cases as vv. 2119, 2386 where the word is not used as a heroic epithet, or v. 1831 where it is used as a noun meaning 'news, report'. The fact, moreover, that in the clearly military situation of the approaching encounter between the two armies Moses should refer to *gotes ére* as *michele unde mâre* (v. 3150) certainly suggests that for him the word still has a markedly positive sense. It is not therefore because of any secular overtones which he may have wished to avoid that the author does not use the word of the Israelites.

[5] Vv. 3027, 3262, 3075.

[6] 2177, 3031, 3069, 3257 (in v. 3229 *snel* refers to the horse, not the rider).

[7] V. 943.

Confirmation of this deliberate technique by means of which the Jews, although conceived as an army under the leadership of Jehovah, are not actually described with the individual laudatory terms of heroic literature may be seen on the rare occasions when they are shown as engaged in military action (as opposed to the longer static descriptions of their martial appearance). On these occasions a special explanation is likely in every case. Moses, for example, is twice shown (in agreement with the Bible) as fighting or even as killing, but on each occasion this is before his encounter with the Lord, so that he must be judged to be acting here only on his own behalf and not in the name of God. On the first occasion[1] this detail has probably been retained because it could be made to serve the author's intention of elaborating the idea of the kinship; on the second occasion[2] (where any fighting is suggested only by implication)[3] the motif of fighting is meant to show how Moses unselfishly assisted the defenceless women and procured them justice, so that it is not just a heroic deed which is here briefly mentioned, but instead heroism in the service of valid principles.[4] The remaining references concern the military activity of the Jews as a people under the guidance of God, yet here the decisive fact is that we are not presented with a description of this activity before our eyes, but instead with an allusion to it as a future (or merely possible) event lying outside the framework of the epic itself. In other words, the author stops short of depicting God's people engaged in warfare. We have seen this in connection with Pharaoh's judgement of their military prowess (vv. 95 f.) and also in the fleeting suggestion that they will have to gain possession of the Promised Land by force,[5] once they have escaped from Egypt. Apart from this the only reference is that added to the mention of *daʒ edile gescuʒʒe* in the long military description of the Israelites setting out, for the author laconically

---

[1] Vv. 289 ff.   [2] Vv. 357 ff.

[3] Cf. the circuitous phrasing of vv. 361 f.: 'Moŷses half den magiden, | daz sî den sige erwurben.'

[4] Something similar has been established in greater detail for *Ruodlieb* by W. Braun, *Studien ʒum Ruodlieb*, pp. 28 ff.

[5] Vv. 523 f. and 632.

remarks: 'daz wart in sît nuzze.'[1] The implication is military, but we are not shown the battle in which this observation could be proved to be true. What the explanation may be of this willingness to describe the military appearance of the Israelites, but also this refusal to depict their military prowess in action, we shall have to establish later, but it is clearly connected with the manner in which the author has also suggested a number of marked military overtones to his material, yet has stopped short of describing the Israelites by means of the conventional heroic terms for the individual warrior. The explanation cannot be that the author is employing a technique which we also find in the *Rolandslied*, where the pagans can be implicitly condemned by being described as *ritter* or by being made to utter heroic, but secular sentiments.[2] This cannot be the case in the *Millstätter Exodus*, for the insects that are summoned by Jehovah to serve His cause by their attacks on Pharaoh are described by heroic terms (such as *helt* or *wîgant*) which are also used of the Egyptians. The fundamental distinction in the employment of this vocabulary is not that between those who fight on behalf of God and those who fight against Him, but rather between the Israelites on the one hand and the insects or Egyptians on the other. We shall later consider the implications of this particular distinction. For the moment we must remain content with the observation, important enough in itself, that although the Millstatt author may not have militarised his subject-matter as much as was theoretically possible he is responsible for introducing a remarkable number of military descriptions and allusions. In this he differs from his biblical source and also from his immediate predecessor in the field of the biblical epic in Germany, namely the *Wiener Genesis*, for Beyschlag has shown[3] that the earlier author often omits the warlike scenes which he found in his source and that, if he retains them, this is only so that he

---

[1] V. 2932.

[2] See G. Fliegner, *Geistliches und weltliches Rittertum im Rolandslied*, pp. 16 ff., and D. Haacke, *Weltfeindliche Strömungen und die Heidenfrage*, pp. 33 ff.

[3] *Die Wiener Genesis*, pp. 54 ff., especially p. 59: 'eigenmächtige Gewalttat — das hohe Thema weltlicher Epik — führt zur Versündigung gegen Gott, Friedfertigkeit ist die heilsgemäße Haltung.'

may subject them and the warlike ethos to a Christian criticism. Of this attitude we find no trace in the *Millstätter Exodus* so that we may regard the military interpretation of his biblical source as a characteristic feature of our author.

In his second innovation our author does not stand alone, for the author of the *Wiener Genesis* had also depicted the patriarchs of the Old Testament as noblemen.[1] In our work the passage most often quoted is the only one to describe the Israelites as noblemen at any length and explicitly. It is introduced towards the start of the narrative when the author is recounting the servitude of the Jews in their Egyptian exile and the degrading tasks that were imposed upon them:

124　sine wolten sî erlâzen
　　　scalklîcher vorhte,
　　　dielîcher werche.
　　　der von adele was geborn
　　　der muose berien daz hore,
　　　die hêrlîchen chnehte,
　　　den laim unt den letten,
　　　mit handen vile wîzzen
　　　sô worhten si ze vlîzze,
　　　mit micheler nôte
　　　die mûre vile stâte.

The force of this passage lies in the outrageous contrast between *adel* and *scalklîch*, *dielîch* and (a little later) *verscelchet*,[2] a contrast which is vividly summed up in the image of white, well-kept hands forced to such menial labour.[3] The occurrence of the word *chneht* in this passage has no military implications, but a social significance, for it designates the aristocratic rank of the Israelites. The sense of outrage in this episode results from the ignominy of the Egyptian *chnehte*[4] forcing other *chnehte* into such servitude;

[1] Beyschlag, *Die Wiener Genesis*, pp. 23 ff. and 28 ff.

[2] V. 137.

[3] A similar contrast is illustrated by the author of *Graf Rudolf* in his description of the hero's hardships in fragment H (vv. 21 ff., ed. Ganz, p. 61): 'der wol geborne vŭrste | her was na tod von dŭrste. | det tou den her inme grase vant, | mit siner linden wizen hant, | des nam her alda zu stŭnt | harte lŭzzel in den munt.'

[4] V. 140.

it is a sense of outrage to which the author could well hope to find a sympathetic response in the hearts of a knightly audience. Just as he addresses this aristocratic audience as *hêrren*, so too does he take care to suggest occasionally that the Israelites were of the same rank: they are therefore called *hêrren* collectively and also individually,[1] and the fact that in two of these latter cases it is Moses and Aaron who are termed *hêrren* by Pharaoh[2] suggests that even he acknowledges their noble birth. It is precisely this aspect of Pharaoh's conduct, his willingness to enslave other men who are as aristocratic by birth as himself, which is used by the author to bring home the enormity of Pharaoh's tyranny. He does this by stating explicitly on two occasions that Pharaoh compelled service from the Israelites *âne (allerslahte) lôn*.[3] We shall see when we consider the feudal elements in our author's picture of the Jewish patriarchs that reciprocity is the hallmark of the relationship between lord and vassal, so that the due reward for services rendered, so far from degrading the relationship by converting it into a material transaction, is felt to enhance it by preserving the element of liberty on the part of the follower.[4] By insisting on services without granting a reward Pharaoh reveals the tyrannous nature of his authority and his wish to degrade the Hebrews, despite his awareness of their noble birth and of the respect which is their due.

With that the examples of our author's depiction of the Israelites as noblemen are exhausted: in their brevity as well as in their infrequency they indicate, by contrast with the innovations suggesting a military background, that the Millstatt author, however

---

[1] Collectively: 135, 2940, 3021; individually: 331, 981, 1391, 1725.
[2] Vv. 981, 1391. [3] Vv. 115, 2254.
[4] Cf. the revealing lines (quoted by H. Kolb, *Der Begriff der Minne*, pp. 187 f.) from Bernart de Ventadorn, XXIII, 37 ff.:

> Servirs c'om no gazardona
> et esperansa bretona
> fai de senhor escuder.

A similar attitude is implied in the *Ludus de Antichristo* (I, 1, p. 198) when the *Imperator* replies to the news that the French king has declined to pay him homage with the words (vv. 37 f.): 'Et qui nunc ut milites nolunt obedire, | Tamquam servi postmodum cogentur servire.'

convinced he may have been of the need to describe the Jews in these terms, did not regard this as so pressing as the militarisation of his subject-matter. Indeed, it is probable that the only passage in which he comments on the nobility of the Jews for as much as seventeen lines owes its exceptional treatment to the fact that it presented the author right at the start of his narrative with an opportunity to stress a point which he could feel sure would enable him to make his appeal to his knightly audience all the more effectively.

In the third innovation of the German author, his suggestion of a courtly way of life among the Israelites, much the same is apparent, for these courtly features, however unmistakable, are secondary to the elaboration of a military background. Unlike the position in the *Wiener Genesis*,[1] these courtly details are neither very frequent and characteristic of the work nor do they reveal a conception of courtliness which is at all profound. Nonetheless they are present and suggest that both author and audience were acquainted with the social forms of courtliness.

One example of the courtly emphasis on beauty or breeding (rather than on exclusively military virtues) we have already encountered, for the passage which underlines the ignominious servitude of the noble Israelites achieves this by referring to their *handen vile wîzzen*[2] as an outward sign of their delicate nurture. In this context the striking use of such a detail, stressing not merely aristocratic birth but also the courtly breeding of the Israelites, achieves its effect more convincingly than would have been the case with a general reference. Elsewhere it is the more general reference which we encounter, especially in the employment of such epithets as *scône* or *lussam* which can be applied either to courtly persons or to objects associated with them.[3] In the former case the Millstatt work differs, for example, from the

---

[1] Discussed by Beyschlag, *Die Wiener Genesis*, pp. 39 ff.

[2] V. 131.

[3] *Scône* is used of an Israelite in v. 207 (as a substantive) and of an Egyptian in vv. 229, 3039 (adverb), 3044 (of the Egyptian army in battle array). *Lussam* is used of an Israelite in v. 425, but of Israelites and Egyptians together in v. 3094. It is applied to an object in v. 2959.

Rolandslied whose author can criticise the pagans precisely by the way in which he restricts the use of courtly (and therefore secular) epithets to them alone.[1] The earlier author, on the other hand, makes no such distinction in the case of these courtly epithets, a fact which agrees with what we have already seen of his use of heroic or military terms, where the distinction was not one between those who fought for God and those who resisted Him. In addition to these two epithets the Millstatt author has recourse to *tiurlich* or *tiure* as a general term of praise, applying it to people (as individuals or the Jews collectively)[2] or to objects belonging to them.[3]

The close association of the word *scône* with the idea of courtliness is exemplified by the manner in which Moses is told to go to Pharaoh's court and to make his appeal to him *geȝogenlîche unde scône*.[4] The fact that Moses is instructed to behave in this manner by God Himself (just as God too addresses Moses and Aaron *scône*)[5] suggests that for our author the ideal of courtliness was reconcilable with his Christianity. Here he agrees with the *Wiener Genesis* and differs radically from the *Rolandslied*. The two biblical epics further agree in the acknowledgement of polite forms of social intercourse, especially in the manner in which a guest is received, as is indicated by the emphasis which the Millstatt author places on the polite and hospitable reception given to Moses by Jethro[6] or by the way in which a meeting between two people who have been separated is more than once described as *minneclîch*.[7] Furthermore, Jethro is conscious that in behaving thus he is living up to the norms of correct conduct, for he explains his attitude by saying: 'daz ist ein vil rehter site.'[8] In these detailed references, however rare they may be by comparison with the *Wiener Genesis*, we are afforded occasional glimpses of what is regarded as the fixed conventions of well-bred behaviour by author and by audience alike.

[1] See Fliegner, *Geistliches und weltliches Rittertum im Rolandslied*, p. 13, and Haacke, *Weltfeindliche Strömungen und die Heidenfrage*, pp. 40 f.
[2] Individually: 470, 696, 1191, 2385; collectively: 2962.
[3] V. 3177.   [4] V. 652.   [5] V. 2787.
[6] Vv. 389 ff.   [7] Vv. 366, 891 f., 901 f.   [8] V. 379.

Rare they may be, but this is only because the author is not primarily concerned to sketch the Old Testament patriarchs as courtly personages, but rather to place them against the military background to which we have given priority in our analysis of his innovations. That he subordinated the needs of courtly characterisation to his wish to elaborate the military aspects of his theme may be shown by a consideration of those passages where the author, instead of just fleetingly hinting at the courtly ideal, describes it at length in all the trappings of ornate clothing and finely fashioned accessories, for these passages are significantly those where he depicts the departure of the Jewish and Egyptian armies. It is in these two passages[1] alone that we find a sustained description of the splendour of equipment and attire, conceived on the epic scale and concerned with painting as brilliant a picture of such well-wrought accoutrements as possible. They contain a higher proportion of adjectives of colour (*wîȥ, rôt, brûn* and *gruone*)[2] than we find elsewhere; the same is true of other descriptive or laudatory adjectives (*berhtil, breit, lang, wît, von golde, guot, tiure, edil, scône, hêrlîch*),[3] of adverbs to denote the quality of the workmanship (*ȥe vlîȥe, vil chleine, vil wol*),[4] of adverbs to denote the magnificence of the scene (*mit grôȥir scônheit, vile scône*)[5] and of similes to heighten the impression (*sam diu gimme, sam diu sterne, sam ein brunne*).[6] These passages are a highlight of the author's descriptive artistry, but it is significant that they are not devoted to the description of courtly adornment in itself, but depict this adornment in a military situation and therefore subordinate courtliness to the description of a military scene. Whereas the author of the *Wiener Genesis* was more preoccupied with sketching in the details of courtly life and largely excluded the military aspects of the contemporary society which he took

---

[1] Vv. 2877 ff. and 3039 ff.

[2] *Wîȥ*: 2879, 2887, 2927, 3047; *rôt*: 2889, 3045, 3056; *brûn*: 2927; *gruone*: 3047.

[3] *Berhtil*: 2894; *breit*: 2898, 3041; *lang*: 2898; *wît*: 2900; *von golde*: 2904, 3056; *guot*: 2911, 2923, 2930; *tiure*: 2917, 2936 f.; *edil*: 2931; *scône*: 3044; *hêrlîch*: 3058.

[4] *Ze vlîȥe*: 2880, 2888, 2925, 3048; *vil chleine*: 2892; *vil wol*: 2910.

[5] *Mit grôȥir scônheit*: 2878; *vile scône*: 3039.

[6] *Sam diu gimme*: 2884; *sam diu sterne*: 2885; *sam ein brunne*: 2913.

as his model, the later author, although still aware of this courtly life, is more concerned with elaborating the military facts which his predecessor had largely ignored. A joint ideal of knightly courtliness may well be common to both authors, but between their depictions of this ideal a significant shift of emphasis has taken place.

The fourth innovation of the twelfth-century author is the role which he has created in his work for the knightly concept of *êre*. Here again he agrees with the author of the *Wiener Genesis* who likewise departs from his source in introducing this concept which he sees closely associated with the wealth and power of the noble patriarchs whose story he is narrating.[1] His successor also depicts *êre* as a positive attribute both of God and of man. In its application to God *êre* can be used as a noun to indicate this essential quality of God's nature[2] or, more commonly, in an adverbial phrase.[3] On the other hand, it can also be used of the relationship of man to God,[4] in which case its meaning is close to 'reverence, awe'. The fact, however, that *êre* is employed to denote an aspect of God or the reverence which is His due does not mean that its occurrence is now restricted to the religious sphere alone, for the Millstatt author has no compunction in showing *êre* as a laudatory quality of his Hebrew noblemen. In this function it can be used, as in the *Wiener Genesis*, in close association with the idea of wealth and power, for when God announces to Moses His intention of leading His people into the Promised Land he says that after they have ousted the pagan occupants of this territory they will be granted all that they desire: 'ir werdet geweret | alles des iuwer muot gert: | rîchtuom und êre | vile bezzêre' (vv. 627 ff.). Since this wealth and *êre* are to be granted to the Jews by God as part of His compact with them there can be no talk of an ascetic rejection of *êre* by our author. For him it is a God-given value.

[1] Beyschlag, *Die Wiener Genesis*, pp. 38 f.
[2] Vv. 5, 3149.
[3] *Durch (gotes) êre*: 16, 2000; *(got) ʒe êren*: 607, 3294; *nâch michelen êren*: 2524.
[4] Vv. 1805, 2600 (although it is possible to interpret the latter passage as meaning 'in a way which will bring man honour').

167

This untroubled affirmation of *êre* is further shown in the way in which the author uses it as a term of praise when describing his Old Testament patriarchs. From the moment of his birth Moses is dignified by being designated as *êrlîch*,[1] an attribute which is mentioned at the same time as his beauty, so that *êre*, the quality of one of noble birth, complements *scône*, the mark of his courtliness. At a later stage it is also shown how great an importance Moses himself attributes to his *êre*, for in one of his encounters with Pharaoh the ruler, recognising that he can appeal to his adversary on this score, advises him, if he sets any store by his *êre*,[2] not to appear before him again—an appeal which is answered by Moses with just as explicit an acknowledgement of his *êre*.[3] In addition to these personal examples *êre* is also depicted as a collective concern of the Jews, whether as a result of their behaviour towards God or in a secular context. An example of the latter usage occurs when the Hebrews, complaining to Moses and Aaron that their intervention with Pharaoh has worsened their position, argue that they have lost the *êre* which was once theirs at the royal court:

> 1101   ir machet unsere êre
> vile bôsôre,
> denne sî wâren,
> ê wir iuch gesâhen.
> in des rîchen chuniges hove
> dâ wâren wir ze lobe
> vor allen sînen chnehten.

Here *êre* is conceived as a quality which has its origin quite literally at the court, but elsewhere it can be shown as part of a military scene. The Millstatt author concludes his long description of the Jewish army setting out by summing it up in the words: 'Mit susgetânen êren | so vuoren dô die hêrren | von dem ellende | uzzir deme lande',[4] where *êre* is regarded as the outstanding quality of the *hêrren* that make up so magnificent a host and as a term for the excellence of their knightly equipment (e.g. v. 2931: 'daz edile gescuzze' or v. 2937: 'tiurlich gewant'). When the

---

[1] V. 206.   [2] Vv. 2350 f.   [3] Vv. 2356 f.   [4] Vv. 2939 ff.

Egyptian host gives pursuit and catches sight of the receding Jewish army this army is referred to briefly as 'manegen êrlîchen man'.[1]

It is precisely in respect of their *êre*, a gift given them by God and nowhere criticised by the author, that the Jewish noblemen differ from their Egyptian opponents. This is revealed by the way in which the apparently lame negative reference in vv. 2927 f. ('si vuoren iedoch weiz got | âne allerslahte ubirmuot') is later shown to be a significant contrast with the attitude of the pagan warriors, for they are taken up with thoughts of arrogant pride in their own renown (vv. 3037 f.: 'si sprâchen "daz sculen wir gerne tuon | unsir muoz nû wesen der ruom" ').[2] This contrast between *êre*, a possibly secular concern with one's knightly reputation which does not offend God by lapsing into pride and which can even be confirmed by God,[3] and *ruom*, an inordinate and un-justifiable pride in one's achievements hardly distinguishable from arrogance, is one that had existed a long time before the twelfth century, as E. Karg-Gasterstädt has shown by her analysis of the OHG material.[4] In rejecting *ruom* by attributing it only to the pagans, our Millstatt author is certainly not so radical as was the author of the *Rolandslied* when he similarly cast doubt on heroic or knightly qualities by depicting them as informing only the Saracens,[5] for the earlier author still leaves room for *êre* as a positive concept, whether this be seen as the result of the He-brews' conduct towards God or as a secular concern. In other words, he shows implicitly in his depiction of the Israelites that it is possible both to serve God, as they do, and also to enjoy *êre*

---

[1] V. 3093.

[2] Cf. also vv. 3075 ff. (*sich vermezzen, gelf*). Significantly it is Pharaoh who in his ignorance attributes his own acknowledgement of *ruom* to the Israelites (v. 3008).

[3] Vv. 2441 f.

[4] *PBB*, LXX, 308 ff. Examples of the two possible Christian approaches to the subject of worldly renown are provided by the words spoken, in an obviously critical sense, of Patavrid by Hagano in *Waltharius* (v. 871: 'Et vili pro laude cupit descendere ad umbras') and, on the other hand, by the manner in which the final praise attributed to the Christian ruler Beowulf is precisely that he was *lofgeornost* (*Beowulf* 3182). On this whole problem see L. L. Schücking, *Helden-stolz und Würde im Angelsächsischen*, Abhandlungen der philologisch-historischen Klasse der sächsischen Akademie der Wissenschaften, XLII, no. 5 (1933).

[5] See Fliegner, *Geistliches und weltliches Rittertum im Rolandslied*, pp. 5 ff.

in this world. In this he anticipates the position in courtly literature around 1200 and even though this motif may not be dealt with by him explicitly as a problem this cannot disprove the fact that he is aware of the possibility of serving both God and the world in the particular manner which he has described in his Old Testament narrative.

In turning now to the next innovation in the twelfth-century work, namely the way in which its author has conceived the action in terms of the categories of contemporary feudalism with its stress on mutual loyalty and on the reciprocity of service and reward, we can ignore the infrequent examples of such feudal terms as *sîn man* or *mîne holden*,[1] since this usage was by now so well established in German feudal vocabulary that we cannot hope to derive from it any insight into the personality of our author himself. Instead we shall do better to consider the way in which he depicts the action and its protagonists as governed by feudal ideals, for this will tell us more of the extent to which he has been able to assimilate his Old Testament narrative to the mentality of his own time and society. Three points stand out as particularly important in his work: the function of *triuwe* (the central concept of feudal thinking), the emphasis he places on the way in which God always keeps His promise to His people and the reciprocity between the Israelites' service of God and His unfailing reward.[2]

---

[1] E.g. 1981, 93, 1023, 2143, 2364.

[2] The difficulties in deciding whether to interpret certain aspects of twelfth-century Christianity as representative of a specifically feudal form of Christianity are considerable, mainly because such a feature as the essential reciprocity of the relationship between man and God is also to be found in the Old Testament (see pp. 196 f.), not least in Exodus itself. Here we are confronted by three theoretical possibilities. The first of these (that evidence for reciprocity in twelfth-century Christianity demonstrates the *exclusive* importance of feudal ideas) we may rapidly dismiss, since it grossly belittles the importance of the Christian material which is feudalised and also since it is as patently one-sided as the interpretation (for an earlier period of medieval literature) of the *Heliand* in terms of nothing but a 'Germanisierung des Christentums'. The second possibility is conversely to interpret the twelfth-century evidence as reflecting the exclusive importance of Old Testament ideas, whereas the third possibility is to regard it as resulting from a fusion of Old Testament ideas with feudal ways of thought. In the light of this third theory such particular Old Testament ideas found a ready acceptance

The author's intentions

The essential reciprocity of *triuwe*[1] is amply revealed in the passage in which it occurs in a secular sense and where it is said of the manner in which Jethro munificently treated Moses after he had come to the rescue of his daughters: 'Jêtrô triuwen san' (v. 399). Not merely does the situation make it clear that *triuwe* denotes the kindness with which Jethro hopes to repay the generosity of Moses, but we are also told that Jethro sees the moral need for some kind of reciprocal action, for when he learns from his daughters of what has happened he says:

378 'ware chom der selbe man dô?
daz ist ein vil rehter site:
der dem anderm wole vert mite,
daz er ettelîche êre
dâr ingegene chêre.'

We have already considered this passage as an example of the courtly reception of a stranger, but here the point is that this courtly behaviour is shown as resulting from a conviction of the need to reciprocate a past kindness, a need which is summed up by the word *triuwe*. The reciprocity which governs this secular use of the word also extends to its use as a religious term, as may be seen when it describes both God's attitude to man and man's relationship with God. It is used of God's relationship with Moses and Aaron when Moses is told that in his future dealings

because they were so easily comprehensible and attractive to Christians living in a feudal society, whereas conversely no hesitation was shown in interpreting Christianity in the light of feudalism because of the apparent precedent of the Old Testament itself. That this third possibility (granting at least a conditional role to feudalism in the development of medieval Christian thought) is likely to be correct is suggested by the course of my argument in *The Carolingian Lord*. There I attempted to show that reciprocity, as a feature of the relationship between man and God, was progressively abandoned in the literature of ninth-century Germany, so that its reappearance in vernacular literature after 1060 must be due to reasons which did not operate at the time of Otfrid. These reasons I see in the fact that religious literature is now addressed to a lay, knightly audience (whether in the context of the crusades or not) and seeks to appeal to their modes of thought, and also that the Church itself is progressively more exposed to the pervasive influence of feudal ideas (cf. W. Ullmann, *The Growth of Papal Government in the Middle Ages*, pp. 331 ff., and K. Jordan, *AfU*, xii, 13 ff.).

[1] I have discussed some of these aspects of *triuwe* in *The Carolingian Lord*, pp. 74 ff. and 117 ff.

with Pharaoh God will speak through his mouth and his brother's: '. . .wil ich selbe redenon | mit michelen triuwon; | ich wil iw wârlîchen | niemmer geswîchen' (vv. 807 ff.). Here *mit michelen triuwon* has not been weakened to the function of a mere affirmative phrase, for the force of the negative phrase *niemmer geswîchen* is that it emphasises the *triuwe* of God's nature and assures Moses that he will never be let down in this compact with God. On the other hand, *triuwe* can be used of man's relationship with God, as is shown by the description of the conduct of the midwives Sephora and Phua in rescuing the Jewish male children: 'mit micheler triuwe' (v. 154). We can be reasonably certain that *triuwe* does not represent the attitude of these women towards the children, for these children are represented as being saved 'von der wîbe vorhten | die sie ze gote habeten' (vv. 167 f.), so that their *triuwe*, even though it finds expression in their relationship with the children, is ultimately the quality of their attitude towards God.[1]

In this twofold usage of *triuwe* in its religious sense, reflecting a reciprocal nexus between man and God, the Millstatt author uses a technique which we find elsewhere in MHG literature (for example, in *Ezzos Gesang* or in Wolfram's *Parzival*),[2] where what is significant is not so much the fact that *triuwe* as a quality of God occurs in each of these works as frequently as *triuwe* denoting the quality of a worshipper, but rather the fact that *triuwe* can be employed in this double manner. In this twofold employment the reciprocity of the feudal relationship is also felt to be true of the relationship between man and God. This is perhaps why we find a passage in the *Millstätter Exodus* which is similar to a passage in *Ezzos Gesang*[3] to which Rupp has drawn attention.[4]

---

[1] We cannot be certain whether the words spoken by Moses to Pharaoh in vv. 1404 ff. ('wenne ich erwerbe disiu dinch | mit getriuwenlîchen muote | umbe unseren got guoten') refer to the reliability of his promise to Pharaoh or to the loyalty with which he serves God.

[2] For *Ezzos Gesang* cf. v. 30 (God's *triuwe*) with vv. 235 ff. (man's *triuwe* to God). These passages are discussed by H. Rupp, *Deutsche religiöse Dichtungen*, pp. 44 and 78. For *Parzival* see P. Wapnewski, *Wolframs Parzival*, pp. 191 ff., especially p. 193.

[3] Vv. 383 ff.   [4] *Deutsche religiöse Dichtungen*, pp. 49 ff. and 79.

The author's intentions

The author of the earlier poem takes what today could only be regarded as the liberty of reminding God that, since the conditions under which He first promised mankind that He would take them to Himself after the crucifixion have been fulfilled, He should keep His word: 'nû lêste, hêrre, dîniu wort' (v. 390). Rupp has shown that this remark goes beyond the passage in the fourth gospel to which it refers[1] and that what has been infused into it is a feudal attitude towards God in which the *dînestman* of God,[2] convinced that God is the essence of *triuwe*,[3] feels as justified in claiming the reward to which his service entitles him as would any feudal vassal. It is precisely this feudal attitude, where man thinks he is entitled to remind God that He too has obligations to fulfil, which we find in one passage in the twelfth-century epic where Moses, to whom the Israelites have complained that their position is now worse than it had been before his intervention in God's name, lodges his own complaint with God:[4]

> 1127   si lîdent ienoh die selben nôt,
> dû ne habest sî geledigôt,
> alsô dû iz mir gehiezze,
> noh iz wâr neliezze.

Here Moses can base his complaint on the promise which God had earlier made, just as the author of *Ezzos Gesang* makes a similar appeal to what Christ had once said. Like the earlier author, however, the author of our epic goes beyond his source at this point in introducing this argument since the Bible only says *et non liberasti eos* (5. 23), without adducing any grounds for the complaint.[5] Furthermore, in the German epic the force of this complaint is tacitly acknowledged even by God when there

---

[1] Joh. 12. 32.   [2] V. 393.   [3] V. 30.
[4] Cf. the use of the verb *chlagen* in v. 1121.
[5] To the possible objection that this complaint is at least implied in the Vulgate the answer must be that the Millstatt author here abandons his usual practice of oblique implication in favour of a quite explicit statement, that he adds to Moses' complaint the grounds on which he bases this (an appeal to God's earlier promise) and that he expands the two biblical verses (5. 22 f.) to a passage of twenty lines (vv. 1111–30). All this suggests that the German author is here adapting the biblical suggestion to his own particular ends.

follows, as in the Bible, God's reply in which He assures Moses that He has not forgotten His part of their compact.[1] The Millstatt author, by strengthening the force of Moses' complaint, has therefore depicted his relationship with God as resting on a mutual compact of *triuwe* which, as in *Ezzos Gesang*, modifies the biblical source by introducing the element of feudal reciprocity and therefore the possibility that Moses may justifiably make complaint if he feels that his rights are not being observed.

Both *Ezzos Gesang* and the *Millstätter Exodus* see the relationship of *triuwe* existing between man and God as a promise binding in different ways on both parties to the agreement.[2] It is this promise of God to the Israelites, repeated explicitly to Moses, which is the very core of the story of Exodus, both in the Bible and in the German account, whose author is therefore free to emphasise this motif as particularly relevant to his conception of God's *triuwe*. He is conscious that he can himself appeal to God's word,[3] just as was Moses, and he frequently uses such verbs as *intheizen* or *geheizen*[4] to make the fact of God's promise more explicit, where the occasional use of the phrase *wâr lâzzen*[5] (as in *Ezzos Gesang*) gives greater force to this idea. Indeed, the words spoken by God about Himself when meeting Moses' complaint serve as a commentary on how the poet conceived the import of his story: 'swaz ich in hân geheizzen, | daz wil ich wâr lâzzen',[6] for it is precisely this that is demonstrated in the *Exodus*. The

---

[1] The importance of this point is revealed by the emphatic manner in which God four times assures Moses that He will keep His promise with the Israelites: this is suggested by the choice of the verb *erwettôn* (v. 1144), by the phrase in v. 1148 ('niene vergizze ich in des'), by the command to Moses to tell the Israelites not to doubt Him (vv. 1151 ff.) and by the standing formula with which God concludes His address: 'swaz ich in hân geheizzen, | daz wil ich wâr lâzzen' (vv. 1155 f.).

[2] In quite a different manner Wulfila had employed the Gothic *triggwa* and the related *trausti* to render the idea of the covenant between God and His people. See my remarks in *The Carolingian Lord*, pp. 233 ff.

[3] Vv. 21 ff.

[4] Vv. 41, 644 (cf. 645), 1155.

[5] V. 22 (corresponds to *sprechen*, instead of *geheizen*), 1156.

[6] Vv. 1155 f.

insertion of the occasional author's comment such as 'als er geredet hête' (v. 938) or 'mit wârlîchen worten' (v. 1196)[1] also serves the same end, as also when the author lays stress on the fact that God's *triuwe* is such that He responds to an appeal made in its name almost as soon as it is uttered.[2] For this reason a biblical reference to the pact between God and Israel can sometimes be replaced by the observation that God paid heed to their appeal for love of their forefathers,[3] a remark which is also important for its suggestion that God's promise is of timeless validity, given to earlier generations of Israelites[4] but still of profit to Moses and to those who, unlike him, will live to experience the entry into the Promised Land. Exactly how reciprocal this promise of God appeared to the author is revealed by God's command to Moses (v. 2264: 'dû tuo sô ich dich lêre'), for this is balanced by a remark which implies that Moses can make a successful appeal for God's assistance: 'ich tuon daz dû wil' (v. 2268). The relationship between God and Moses is not simply one of unilateral obedience, for we are here shown that God remains accessible to requests for assistance made by Moses.

That this quality of *triuwe* in God's promise to Israel is no fortuitous aspect of His divinity is suggested by the significant contrast it represents to Pharaoh's behaviour towards the

---

[1] Cf. also vv. 1174 ff. ('den ich nie verliez | in allem sînem dinge | mit allerslahte minnen') and 1797 ('ich dir nieht geswîche'). There is probably a parallel to the use of 'mit wârlîchen worten' (1196) in v. 463, for although Kossmann has 'dâ erscain ime got zewâre', the MS has the much less lame reading: 'dâ erscain ime got der gewâre.' That this word means something more than simply *verax* is implied by its connection with the OHG noun *wâra* (meaning 'treaty, covenant' and therefore highly relevant to the relationship between God and His people) and also by the parallels adduced by Pniower, *ZfdA*, xxxiii, 91, where *gewâre* is used in apposition with *getriuwe*: *Rolandslied* 9038, *Kaiserchronik* 15765, 16144. In view of this we are justified in regarding vv. 1196 and 463 as further evidence of the way in which the Millstatt author gave particular emphasis to *triuwe* as the essential characteristic of God.

[2] Cf. vv. 1947 ff. ('Alsô er dô gebetete | got in gewerete | alles sînes willen'); 2157 f. ('got ûf den himelen | gedâhte sîn hie nidene'); 2231 f. ('Nâch disen selben worten | ich weiz er in erhôrte'); 2268 ('ich tuon daz dû wil').

[3] Vv. 457 f. (2. 24).

[4] The continuing importance of God's past promise is also implied by vv. 41, 643 f. and 1173 ff.

Hebrews. When Pharaoh requests the plague of frogs to be terminated this is reported to God by Moses and Aaron who say that the Egyptian king has promised to grant them permission to leave Egypt if the plague is called off (vv. 1431 ff.: 'wande er dînen willen | gerne wil ervollen, | daz hât er uns geheizzen, | wil er iz nû wâr lâzzen'). When, shortly after this, Pharaoh breaks his promise, even though the plague has been terminated by God in immediate answer to Moses' request, the same phrase, with its revealing use of the verbs *geheizzen* and *wâr lâzzen* which are characteristic of God's relationship to Israel, is applied to Pharaoh again, but in the negative: 'die boten er entwerte | des er in vor gehiez, | nieht er des ne wâr liez' (vv. 1452 ff.). This not only implies a contrast between Pharaoh and God which confirms our earlier impression of the way in which Pharaoh was depicted more in his metaphysical role than as a merely human opponent of Moses and Aaron, it also makes it clear that Pharaoh's tyranny resides precisely in his lack of *triuwe*, his readiness to break his word. If this is the respect in which he so clearly differs from God, then the God who forthwith grants Moses what he requests emerges as a God whose essential characteristic is *triuwe*: a readiness to assist when called upon by His vassal and also to observe His side of the compact He has sworn with His people.

This distinction between God and Pharaoh is also apparent in another detail: the way in which the German author underlines the feudal idea of a strict reciprocity between service and reward. We have seen the force of this reciprocity in a purely human relationship when considering the generous reception afforded to Moses by Jethro as a conscious return for the assistance which Moses had rendered his daughters. Even though the service which Moses had performed had been one of general kindness and not a feudal service, the scene is informed by the conviction that a service of any kind deserves a reward.[1] This conviction is no weaker in the religious context, for, just as the Israelites are depicted as serving God[2] and Moses as (*gotes*) *man* or even as

---

[1] Cf. also vv. 407 f. ('er machôt in gelîche | ime selbem ebenrîche').
[2] Vv. 861, 973.

gotes scalch,[1] so too is the whole action of the *Exodus*, the departure from Egypt and the ultimate conquest of the Promised Land, seen as God's reward to the Israelites: 'daz sol wesen ir lôn' (v. 640). That this remark (which is not to be found in the Bible) should occur in the scene in which Moses first encounters God and the earlier compact with Israel is renewed can only have made it clear to a contemporary audience that all the subsequent events in which God's unfailing assistance was revealed were meant to demonstrate the reward which God was prepared to give in His *triuwe* to those who loyally served Him. Indeed, the reciprocity of service and reward is so keenly felt by our author that on one occasion, when reporting God's words to Moses as to what the future conduct of the Israelites is to be when they have reached the Promised Land, he even goes so far as to suggest that man can reward God, for he has God say that the continued service of God by the Israelites will be their reward to God for having liberated them from Egypt: 'nû birn wir chomen in unser lant. | sus sculen wir dienôn, | daz sol wesen sîn lôn | hinne vur mêre | ze allen sînen êren' (vv. 2866 ff.). Such mutual interplay between service and reward only reflects the *triuwe* which underlies God's relationship with His Chosen People.[2]

It is precisely here that Pharaoh again stands revealed as a tyrant, for it is twice remarked that he demanded service from the Hebrews without giving them any kind of reward.[3] Such a remark

---

[1] See p. 133. Such vernacular expressions may well owe much to the biblical *servus Dei*, but nonetheless, once *man* had come to be used in this kind of expression as a technical term of feudalism (see *The Carolingian Lord*, pp. 93 ff.), the associations called forth by these vernacular terms were likely to be as much feudal as biblical.

[2] The Millstatt author naturally leaves no suggestion of his source unexploited as regards the reciprocity of service and reward. Cf. vv. 169 f. and Exodus i. 20 f.

[3] Vv. 115, 2254. It is of course true that Pharaoh is here in a very special position, since the Jews are not indigenous vassals of his, but foreign elements in his kingdom. Nonetheless, this addition of the words *âne lôn* by the German author (even when there is no formal feudal obligation for Pharaoh to offer any reward) suggests that he is judging the Egyptian ruler in terms of the ideal of *triuwe*. Furthermore, as the example of Moses' encounter with Jethro makes amply clear, this ideal of a loyal reward for a service rendered retains its ethical force even outside a specifically feudal contract. Here too Pharaoh offends against *triuwe*.

is no mere line-filler, chosen only because it provided an easy rhyme. Instead it shows us the tyranny of Pharaoh in a twofold light: his readiness to degrade and humiliate the Hebrew noblemen by depriving them of the nobility of freely rendered service, but also his complete lack of *triuwe*, his failure to realise the moral obligations which, as Jethro had seen, are placed on the man to whom a service is rendered. Since his refusal to reward service distinguishes Pharaoh from God just as much as his inability to keep his word, this detail also helps to build up the impression that God unfailingly rewards all service and that this is merely a facet of His universal *triuwe*. This is the force of the feudal innovations which we have been considering: they suggest that the reciprocity of this relationship between God and those who serve Him is so unassailable that their own nobility can never be degraded, but only enhanced by such service, that God is perpetually ready to protect those who serve Him and that they need have no fear that their due reward might be withheld from them.

The last method chosen by the Millstatt author to assimilate his Old Testament theme to the conditions of his own day, namely its description in terms already conventional in the heroic literature of his time, need not detain us for long. We have seen that, despite the unique manner in which he refers to the Israelites, he is quite prepared to use the conventional heroic terms for the warrior and his bravery in application to the plagues that serve God as well as to the Egyptians. When, however, it is a matter of describing the warrior's external appearance and his military equipment no distinction between the Hebrews and the Egyptians or the plagues is made: all can equally be depicted in their warlike splendour. Some of these conventional phrases of heroic literature in *Exodus* have been investigated by Pniower,[1] who shows that such typical formulas as 'ein here grôz unde breit' or 'noh die hutten noh gezelt' or 'iz ne vuorte schilt noh daz swert' or 'si wâren um daz ort | vil chleine gewierôt', to name only a few, recur in other works belonging to this same literary tradition, including

[1] *ZfdA*, xxxiii, 81 ff.

therefore the *Annolied,* the *Kaiserchronik,* the *Alexanderlied,* the *Rolandslied, Graf Rudolf,* the *Nibelungenlied, Kudrun* and *Willehalm.* There is little safety in using such parallels as a means of dating the *Exodus*[1] precisely because of the traditional nature of these standing phrases, but we may at any rate agree with Pniower's observation[2] that the author of the *Exodus* draws upon the time-honoured material of this literary tradition and depicts Old Testament events in literary terms well known to his knightly audience.

More revealing than this employment of conventional poetic formulas is the occasional use of a particular technique or motif known to the literature of the author's own time. Two examples deserve comment, of which the use of *epische Vorausdeutung* is the more significant. This technique, well known to the heroic literary tradition[3] and also to be found in specifically courtly works, has been investigated above all in connection with the *Nibelungenlied,*[4] but it is possible to establish a number of similarities between the two works.[5] This type of phrase is generally to be found in the *Nibelungenlied* in the last line of the stanza,[6] whilst its occurrence in the *Millstätter Exodus* is restricted to the *b*-verse of the couplet. Just as it would be mistaken to explain it in the later work as resulting merely from the need to pad out the stanza,[7] so is it clear that this type of phrase in the *Exodus* often serves a purpose other than the simple need to find a rhyme.[8] In addition to this, the phrases are not used haphazardly, but are often bunched into groups so as to give relief to an important episode: in the *Nibelungenlied* the important 25th *Aventiure* is

[1] As is Pniower's intention, *loc. cit.*   [2] *Ibid.* p. 85.

[3] Cf. some of the formulas from the literature of the eleventh and twelfth centuries collected by W. Wachinger in Appendix II (pp. 153 ff.) to his *Studien zum Nibelungenlied.*

[4] E.g. Beyschlag, *PBB* (H) LXXVI, 38 ff.; F. Panzer, *Das Nibelungenlied. Entstehung und Gestalt,* pp. 119 f.; Wachinger, *op. cit.* pp. 4 ff.

[5] The examples of this technique in the *Millstätter Exodus* have been collected by Kossmann in his edition, p. 72. To these must be added, however, vv. 70 and 3226.

[6] Panzer, *op. cit.* p. 119; Wachinger, *op. cit.* p. 7.

[7] Wachinger, *Studien zum Nibelungenlied,* p. 7.   [8] See pp. 43 f.

characterised by the frequency with which this type of phrase occurs here[1]; and in the *Exodus*, although it is used throughout the description of the plagues, it is more frequent towards the end of the work, where the battle array of the Israelites and Egyptians is described at length.[2] By doing this the author of the *Exodus* is able to provide an effective poetic contrast between the splendour of the Egyptian host and the mounting knowledge of their approaching doom, just as, for example, the 5th *Aventiure* of the *Nibelungenlied* opens with the brilliant courtly festival at Worms, but concludes with a fatalistic prophecy of Siegfried's death.[3]

These general parallels in the use of this technique by both authors justify our asking the further question whether, as has been shown to be the case with the *Nibelungenlied*, the earlier author uses it with any particular end in view. Here we may best start with the distinction made by Wachinger[4] between those prophetic remarks made by the author of the *Nibelungenlied* himself and those uttered by the personages of his epic from within the framework of the narrative. In the case of the *Exodus* we find that all these remarks are made by the author alone, with the sole exception that on one occasion God is described, very much as a protagonist, as knowing what was about to happen by the Red Sea.[5] Whereas the *Nibelungenlied* sees one person on one occasion as aware of what the future is to bring, but someone else as ignorant, the author of the *Exodus* shares his narrator's omniscience with God alone.[6] His prophecies as to the outcome of the action serve to contrast the false hopes and unfounded confidence of the present with the reality to be disclosed by future events, an interpretation which is confirmed by the fact that all

[1] Panzer, *Das Nibelungenlied*, p. 120.
[2] From Kossmann's collection of the material it is clear that this technique is used five times with reference to the plagues between vv. 1334 and 1968, but nine times in connection with the military descriptions between vv. 2932 and 3088.　　[3] Wachinger, *op. cit.* p. 25.
[4] *Ibid.* p. 5.　　　　　　　　　[5] V. 2982.
[6] Not even Moses, to whom God has spoken of His intentions, is allowed to give voice to any prophetic knowledge by means of an *epische Vorausdeutung*.

but two of the prophetic remarks in the *Exodus* refer to the fate in store for Pharaoh or for the Egyptians.[1] The actions of these enemies of God are therefore ironically shown up as blind and futile attempts to ignore what God has ordained for them. Whereas, however, the author of the *Nibelungenlied* uses these phrases so as to build up the impression that a certain fate awaits a particular character,[2] in the *Millstätter Exodus* the action is controlled not by an ineluctable fate, but instead by an omnipotent God who has announced His intentions to Moses and has sworn to fulfil His promise to Israel. What the Egyptians vainly struggle against is not fate but God, so that this technique is used by the author not merely to bring into full relief the powerless *ubirmuot* of those who oppose God, but also as a means of further emphasising that what God has promised Israel and Moses He will unfailingly accomplish on their behalf. At bottom these prophetic passages delineate not simply God's power, but also His *triuwe*, the steadfastness of His compact with His people. It is this that explains the exceptional use of this technique on the two occasions when it is not used of the Egyptians. It is used once with reference to the Hebrews' future conquest of the Promised Land, a victory which God had pledged Himself to grant them.[3] The other passage[4] is the only example where the author uses this technique without referring to what God had promised to give His people or to inflict upon their enemies, for it concerns the way in which Jethro was later to thank Moses for the assistance he had rendered his daughters. It is precisely this exceptional secular usage which confirms our interpretation of the author's use of this technique to underline God's *triuwe* to

[1] These two exceptions are vv. 364, 2932, but also 169 if we accept Kossmann's textual emendation, proposed in the notes to his edition, p. 138. Admittedly, v. 70 is also ambiguous, but I take it to refer to the fate in store for the Egyptians (v. 68: 'der heidinisken diete') as a result of Pharaoh's arrogance, rather than to the tribulations to which the Israelites (v. 67: 'sîne liebe trûte') were soon to be exposed. The weight of the remaining evidence confirms this view.

[2] Wachinger, *Studien zum Nibelungenlied*, pp. 22 f.

[3] V. 2932. This prophecy cannot refer to the passage of the Red Sea since the *gescuȥȥe* is not used on this occasion, however military the description of the scene may be.   [4] V. 364.

The Millstätter Exodus

Israel, because the thanks which Jethro gives Moses are soon afterwards described as resting on the conviction of mutual obligation, on the need to repay service with generosity, and are even referred to by the word *triuwe*. The prophetic technique is used here not so as to provide any fatalistic explanation of Jethro's conduct, but rather to show its ethical necessity and the morally binding obligation to render like for like. This solitary secular example reveals that Jethro's behaviour was informed by his *triuwe*, just as all the other examples serve to show that this same attribute is an unchanging quality of the God who has sworn a covenant with His people.[1]

The second example of the Millstatt author's relationship to contemporary German literature concerns his attitude to the motif of *list* or trickery which played so important a part in the so-called 'Spielmannsepen' and in heroic literature in general. Beyschlag has shown[2] that the author of the *Wiener Genesis* often inserts an explicit reference to any practice of deceit where his source merely allows the facts to speak for themselves or that he expands certain scenes of his model which allow him to develop this theme profitably. Beyschlag concludes that this is done to suggest the similarity between this biblical epic and contemporary secular literature in Germany[3] and also (as with the motif of military exploits) so as to subject these motifs so well known to vernacular literature to a Christian judgement.[4] In the case of *list*, however, the author can sometimes pass judgement by his choice of word (e.g. *beswîchen, ubeler list*),[5] but on other occasions an adverse judgement is not expressed and would indeed have been difficult to insert precisely because, as in the case of Jacob and Esau, the deceit is practised by a biblical personage whose action is meant to be beyond criticism. In other

---

[1] V. 169 (if we follow Kossmann's suggestion and read 'lôn inphiengen si sît von ime') would represent a religious counterpart to the secular example of v. 364, for the Millstatt author, following Exod. 1. 20 f., takes care to emphasise that God did not fail to reward the midwives for their service of Him (cf. vv. 167f.) in rescuing the male children of the Hebrews.

[2] *Die Wiener Genesis*, pp. 50 ff.   [3] *Ibid.* pp. 49 f.

[4] *Ibid.* p. 60.   [5] E.g. *Wiener Genesis*, 686, 3750, 2787.

words, although the author of the *Wiener Genesis* may sometimes use the motif of *list*, as he did that of warfare, to introduce a criticism of such conduct, this is certainly not always the case, so that the motif may have been sometimes exploited merely because of the suggested parallel with contemporary literature.

This is quite different with the author of the *Millstätter Exodus*. His biblical source had described repeatedly the deceit practised on Pharaoh by Moses (who is even commanded to act thus by God),[1] for the request for leave to withdraw into the desert in order to offer up sacrifices to God is only a ruse to enable the Israelites to escape from Egypt. Despite this biblical authority the Millstatt author changes the motivation of this scene by having Moses and Aaron address Pharaoh *baltlîche* (v. 943), requesting outright and without any kind of subterfuge that they be permitted to depart from Egypt and return to their homeland.[2] This can hardly be because the author has failed to notice the ruse which is attempted in the Bible, for in every other passage where the Bible mentions the Jews' wish to sacrifice in the desert the Millstatt epic either omits the reference to the sacrifice (because of its patent dishonesty) or explicitly adds the reference to the Israelites' journey to their homeland.[3] The result of these changes is that the element of deceit in the biblical account which the author of the *Wiener Genesis* had sometimes used as a criticism but to which he had had no objection in principle is regularly rejected by the later author, even though he could have used this motif to suggest a further parallel with the knightly literature of his own day.

The reason for this change in attitude is by no means certain. We cannot argue that a God whose characteristic is *triuwe* could not be shown demanding deceit from His followers, since the

[1] E.g. Exod. 5. 1.

[2] Although the medieval author retains the detail of offering sacrifices in the desert (vv. 953 ff.), he describes these sacrifices as being intended to propitiate God and thus guarantee them His protection *an unserer heimverte* (v. 962). This addition explains how it is that Moses and Aaron had addressed Pharaoh *baltlîche* and also removes the element of a *pia fraus* contained in the source.

[3] Further examples of these changes are given by Kossmann in his edition, pp. 36 f.

triuwe which He had sworn only to the Israelites would not impose the need upon Him to show a similar *triuwe* to their enemies. Instead, I think that the likely reason is that the author of the *Wiener Genesis* rejects warfare as a positive motif for Christian reasons, so that he has a correspondingly greater need to show his personages achieving their ends by other means. The later author, on the other hand, does not hesitate to imply that Moses defended the daughters of Jethro by force and to state that he avenged his kinsman in killing the Egyptian overseer, so that with him there is less need for the motif of deceit and therefore the possibility of excluding it altogether. I am aware that from Odysseus down to Rother the epic hero could display both military valour and cunning in stratagems, but here the point is that the Millstatt author, in allowing his Israelites to shed blood in what he regards as a good cause,[1] is now free to concentrate his criticism on the offending motif of deceit and thus to give it up entirely.[2] This implies that he is prepared to consider the necessity of bloodshed in a just cause, a conclusion which confirms what we have seen of the role which he concedes to the military implications of his subject-matter.

If we now attempt to sum up the innovations in subject-matter

[1] It must be stressed that the only Israelite whom the author actually depicts as shedding blood (vv. 289 ff.) or at least as showing physical violence (vv. 361 f.) in a just cause is Moses. Both occasions come before the compact between God and Moses, so that the latter shows violence only as an individual and not in God's name. The Israelites as a people, however, who are definitely depicted as God's people, serving Him as part of the covenant, may well be described as a military host, but they are nowhere described as involved in any military encounter. Their warfare on behalf of God is only hinted at as a future event (vv. 523 f., 632, 2932) or as a possibility with which Pharaoh is prepared to reckon (vv. 95 f.). On the implications of this see pp. 430 ff.

[2] I do not regard the robbing of the Egyptians by the departing Israelites (vv. 673 ff., 2743 ff.) as an example of *list*. However dubious the moral argument may be which the German author here attributes to God in justifying this (v. 684), the fact remains that the Israelites are here given divine permission for this course of action which, although it may be summed up by the drastic verb *beroubôn*, is also described more innocuously as a process where the Israelites actually ask the Egyptians for their vessels of silver and gold (vv. 676–80, 2743–7). Not even Pharaoh, in his final angry reference to this (v. 3000), goes so far as to suggest that the Israelites had robbed him by guile.

for which the twelfth-century author is responsible one fact emerges: it is that the important group of changes is that made up of positive innovations and that the author's employment of what we have called a neutral and negative technique is subordinated to this more decisive group. The result is that the events and personages of the Old Testament story are depicted in a manner intelligible to a knightly audience of the author's own day and moreover capable of appealing to their imagination, suggesting that these events of Hebrew history have a more than superficial resemblance to their own manner of life and to their feudal ideals. At the same time, the picture of contemporary knightly life which results from the author's use of this technique, whilst in general similar to that which we find in the *Wiener Genesis*, is different because of one shift of emphasis. Whereas the earlier author, amongst his positive innovations, had stressed the noble birth of his Jewish patriarchs, their courtliness and their preoccupation with the topical ideas of *ère* and feudal obligations and had also exploited to this end the similarities of his source with themes of contemporary heroic literature, nowhere do we find him showing so open-minded an attitude to the theme of warfare. The earlier author excludes the military implications of his source or retains them only in order to criticise them, but his successor, whilst still not fully militarising the Israelites themselves in the spirit of heroic literature, introduces several lengthy passages of military description which place the action in an explicitly military context. The Israelites are depicted as an army of knights on the move, the God who leads this army is a military God whose ends can also be served by the kind of heroic warfare waged on His behalf in the plagues, and Moses as an individual shows physical violence on two occasions without any hint of criticism from the author. In all this the later author differs not merely from his eleventh-century predecessor, but also largely from his biblical source, so that we must see in this stress on the military implications of his story a characteristic of his own personality. The other positive innovations which he shares with the earlier author are either much less important in his case (as with the courtliness of the Israelites) or are retained as different facets of his composite knightly ideal, but facets to which he himself attached less significance than to the elaboration of these military implications.

These different facets of the Millstatt author's picture of contemporary reality, together with his neutral and negative changes, add up to a coherent attitude towards his Old Testament theme. In details as well as in his overall conception he is concerned to connect the story of the exodus of the Jews with his twelfth-century present, more particularly with the present conditions and way of life of his knightly audience. It would be mistaken to interpret these innovations (especially the militarisation of the subject-matter) as concessions made to his knightly audience and their taste by a clerical author anxious to hold their attention by thus 'sugaring his pill'. This view has been put forward, for example, by E. Sitte,[1] whereas Kossmann is much more cautious,[2] arguing that it is impossible to tell whether the author has made concessions to his audience or whether, on the contrary, it may not be the knightly audience that has made the greater concession in listening to a clerical epic. However, a decision in favour of the latter view is suggested by a number of considerations. In the first place, what Beyschlag has established with regard to the theme of warfare in the *Wiener Genesis* and what we have seen of the Millstatt author's refusal to elaborate the motif of *list* show that these clerical authors remained sufficiently masters of their own material to be free to decide whether to admit or to reject any particular theme. Here they do not make concessions to the tastes and interests of their audience, for they go out of their way either not to appeal to them or actually to criticise them.[3] Secondly, the particular way in which the military overtones

[1] *Die Datierung von Lamprechts Alexander*, p. 101. We need waste no time in discussing the author's remark that the clerical authors of this period were not merely clerics, but also 'deutsche Menschen..., in denen noch das alte Blut floß und schneller wallen konnte, wenn sie einmal die Beschreibung eines Heereszuges oder eines Kampfes bieten konnten'.

[2] *Die altdeutsche Exodus*, p. 82: 'Wer die Concessionen gemacht hat, der Dichter oder das Publikum, lässt sich freilich nicht mehr entscheiden.'

[3] See also the salutary remarks made by Stammler, *Kleine Schriften*, pp. 17 ff.

are emphasised by the Millstatt author is paralleled by what Erdmann has to say of the connections between the clerical legend
and knightly literature.[1] He dwells on the manner in which one
and the same person can be depicted in the same work both as a
legendary saint and as a warrior on behalf of God, stressing that
this fusion of two roles is to be found not merely in knightly
literature (where Sitte's suggestion might have a certain theoretical plausibility), but also in clerical works. He interprets this
persuasively, as part of his much broader thesis, as evidence of
the successful attempts made by the Church to impose its ethical
norms upon the lay world of the knights and to subordinate their
secular profession of arms to its own religious ideal. It is precisely this which the Millstatt author is attempting to do when he
gives voice to no criticism of Moses' use of physical violence in
assisting defenceless women and when he contrasts the humility
of the Israelite army with the *ubirmuot* of their equally knightly
opponents.[2] Moreover, this assimilation of the Hebrew past to
the knightly present is an attempt to convince this audience of
knights that just as the Old Testament God showed *triuwe*, the
quality which lay at the heart of the feudal relationship, just as
this God protected the Israelites from their foes as part of His
covenant with them, so can these knights equally hope to serve
God and in return to be protected and rewarded by Him as
members of what the author of *Ezzos Gesang* calls the *spiritalis
Israel*. It is this which is the burningly topical import of his
biblical theme and which explains why the author goes out of his
way to depict it in contemporary terms. With this conclusion we
return to the starting-point of this chapter: to the author's use of
typology as a means of indicating the timeless validity of what
he had to narrate and of suggesting that what was true of the
Hebrew past may still be just as true of their spiritual successors
in the twelfth century.

[1] *Die Entstehung des Kreuzzugsgedankens*, pp. 261 ff.
[2] This humility of the Israelites does not mean that they cannot be criticised
on other scores. For other failings of theirs see below, pp. 336 ff., and also the
critical words of Moses, vv. 687 ff., themselves an expansion of the Vulgate (4. 1).

VII

THE RELEVANCE OF THE OLD TESTAMENT TO THE MEDIEVAL PRESENT

THE characteristic innovations of the Millstatt author show us that he was persuaded of the relevance of the Old Testament story to the conditions of his own day, in particular to the life of the knights whom he was addressing. In order to understand why he should have been convinced of this topical import or what there was in the Hebrew tradition that he wished to apply to his own time it will be necessary to consider the impact of the Old Testament on medieval life at large, for it is against this general background that the particular relevance of the Old Testament to the twelfth century may best be elaborated. Such a general analysis of what the Old Testament meant for the Middle Ages in religious experience, political life and literature is a task which to my knowledge has nowhere been attempted on the scale which its importance merits.[1] It is certainly not my intention to attempt any such evaluation; instead I shall do no more than offer a few suggestions to illustrate why and how the Middle Ages were prepared to adopt some aspects of the Old Testament into their own manner of life. Even here we must content ourselves with reviewing only two aspects of the Old Testament tradition which seem to have made a particular appeal to our Millstatt author. The first of these is the concept of the Chosen People or *populus Dei* which lies (if only by implication) at the core of the Exodus story, for the assistance given to Moses and exemplified in so many ways during the course of the narrative results only from the fact that God had sworn a compact with

[1] Many useful indications are given by B. Smalley, *The Study of the Bible in the Middle Ages*. For an assessment of the Hebrew tradition in its relation to Christian dogmatics in the Middle Ages see A. L. Williams, *Adversus Judaeos*.

the people of Israel and had renewed this with Moses. The other aspect is the theme of warfare as a form of service of God, a motif which is occasionally to be detected in the biblical version of the first fifteen chapters of Exodus and which is more emphatically developed in other parts of this same book[1] or of the Old Testament as a whole, but which the Millstatt author elaborates with some care. We shall see in this chapter that with regard to both these concepts (the *populus Dei* and warfare on behalf of God) the Old Testament had a contribution to make to medieval thought, whereas in the following chapter we shall have to consider what the particular relevance of these two themes was to the twelfth century.

In one fundamental sense the Middle Ages were inescapably confronted with the potential problem of the Old Testament once it had been incorporated into the Christian Scriptures. This incorporation was the historical result of the claim that Christ was the Messiah, a claim which could best be strengthened by an appeal to the Jewish canon. It was Christ himself who interpreted the Old Testament from Moses and all the prophets with reference to Himself in His encounter with the two disciples at Emmaus,[2] a technique which is continued by St Paul whenever he buttresses his argument by the phrase *secundum Scripturas*.[3] Such an appeal to the Old Testament was an obvious, but effective device at a time when the earliest Christian community was still concerned with gaining new adherents from among the Jews themselves.[4] The typological interpretation of the Old Testament by reference to the New therefore formed the starting-point for Christian missionary activity and it remained the dominant method of the Church long after it had ceased to be a Jewish Christian community and had become the Church of the Gentiles.

---

[1] E.g. Exod. 17. 8 ff.   [2] Luc. 24. 27.   [3] 1 Cor. 15. 3 f.
[4] How effective such an appeal was likely to be has been shown by N. A. Dahl, *Das Volk Gottes*, p. 39, who adduces many Old Testament passages suggesting the eschatological expectancy of the Jews themselves: a hope for a new Moses and the conviction that Israel is about to experience a new exodus and its enemies a new defeat like that of the Egyptians. Particularly telling examples are provided by Isa. 43. 1 f. and 16–19 as well as 51. 9–11. See also J. Daniélou, *Sacramentum futuri*, pp. 132 ff., and *Bible et liturgie*, p. 119.

This fact has an importance which far exceeds the limited historical origins of the typological method and which helps to explain (if only negatively) why and how the books of the Old Testament came to make an appeal to heathen converts once the Church had begun to extend its missionary activity to Northern Europe. Here Auerbach[1] has made the significant point that this method of interpretation had the result of converting the Old Testament from a book of laws and a history of the people of Israel into a series of prefigurations of Christ. He writes: 'In this form and in this context, from which Jewish history and national character had vanished, the Celtic and Germanic peoples, for example, could accept the Old Testament; it was a part of the universal religion of salvation and a necessary component of the equally magnificent and universal vision of history that was conveyed to them along with this religion. In its original form, as law book and history of so foreign and remote a nation, it would have been beyond their reach.' Although, as Auerbach stresses, this was certainly never the intention in using the typological interpretation of the Old Testament, the result is that the Old Testament is now made accessible to the minds of European converts by being regarded in a manner which largely strips it of its historical particularity and its uniquely Jewish nature. In other words, the result of employing typology agrees largely with what was one of the methods consciously employed by the Millstatt author, for his negative and neutral techniques, in leading him to omit so many of the Jewish details of his source, had enabled him to depict the story of Exodus in a manner immediately intelligible to his audience. Admittedly, there is a vast difference between the fact that Auerbach's point concerns the unintended result of using the typological method and the fact that the Millstatt author appears to have decided consciously upon his method, but this parallel at least suggests that he was deliberately following a technique which had become established by his time as a traditional approach to the Old Testament.

This is confirmed by the positive technique of the twelfth-

[1] *Scenes from the Drama of European Literature*, p. 52.

century author which allowed him to suggest similarities between the Old Testament and his own day, for this is paralleled by the fact that the conversion of the Germanic tribes to Christianity was largely assisted by a number of general similarities between the Germanic pagan religion and the religious beliefs of the Hebrews, so that the Old Testament, divested of most of its unintelligible particularities, could now make an appeal to the mentality of the Germanic convert which was often more direct and convincing than with the New Testament. In most cases we have no direct testimony to suggest that the appeal to the Germanic convert drew its strength from the way in which certain aspects of the Old Testament tradition within Christianity could be equated (however mistakenly) with outwardly similar features of the Germanic religion. Yet even where such direct testimony is lacking we may assume that, although the Church may not always have exploited such similarities as part of its missionary programme, they acquired their significance after the conversion by forcing the converts' attention on to that strand within the Christian tradition which was closest to the pagan thought world from which they had so recently been won.[1]

Such a problem is too large for us to treat within the framework of this book, but we may briefly discuss four general similarities between the Germanic religion and the religious spirit of the Old Testament in the hope that they will indicate how it was possible for the law book and history of a Near Eastern people to make such an appeal to the religious imagination of medieval Europe.[2]

[1] J. R. R. Tolkien, *Beowulf. The Monsters and the Critics*, p. 28, has some interesting words to say in this respect on the manner in which the author of *Beowulf* depicted Germanic pre-Christian society: 'It would seem that, in his attempt to depict ancient pre-Christian days, intending to emphasize their nobility, and the desire of the good for the truth, he turned naturally when delineating the great King of Heorot to the Old Testament. In the *folces hyrde* of the Danes we have much of the shepherd patriarchs and kings of Israel, servants of the one God, who attribute to His mercy all the good things that come to them in this life. We have in fact a Christian English conception of the noble chief before Christianity, who could lapse (as could Israel) in times of temptation into idolatry.'

[2] It must be stressed here that the following parallels between the religious worlds of Germania and the Old Testament are only meant to show how it was

The Millstätter Exodus

We may start with the fact that both for the Old Testament and for the Germanic pagan there was an inescapable connection between religion and law.[1] The Jewish Torah is therefore the Law of God, but in the oldest tradition God's justice is often regarded only in connection with the help He affords His people against their foes, so that the military triumphs of Israel are seen as testimony of God's justice.[2] Even where this word may not actually be used, the implication is often present that Jehovah's capacity as a Judge means a decision given against the enemies of Israel.[3] But quite apart from the military context, the laws enacted by Moses, for example, are regarded as commands given by God,[4] and for Hosea the wedding gifts brought by Jehovah to His people, reunited with Him, include justice and law.[5] It is this abiding conviction of God's justice that finds expression in the way in which He is seen to protect the individual, to preserve the sanctity of what He has ordained or to pass on this same quality of justice to the king in his function as lawgiver.[6] For the Germanic tribes, on the other hand, the *þing* or legal assembly is of a sacred nature, opened formally by the priest[7] and fenced off by the *vébǫnd*,[8] the gods' will can be equated with legal decisions,[9] certain pagan gods are regarded as gods of the legal assembly,

possible for Old Testament concepts to make a strong appeal to Germanic converts in the earliest missionary period and thus to become an integral part of the tradition of medieval Christianity. I do not wish to suggest that these parallels were still operative as late as the twelfth century—except indirectly, i.e. since they had earlier provided the means, in the conversion period, of allowing certain Old Testament features to be adopted readily as part of the Christian beliefs of Germanic converts and thus to survive as part of traditional medieval Christianity.

[1] How far this Old Testament connection between religion and law differed from Christianity may best be seen in St Paul's distinction between the law and faith, between servitude and freedom. Cf. Gal. 4. 1 ff.

[2] E.g. Jud. 5. 11.

[3] Jud. 11. 27; II Reg. 18. 31.

[4] Exod. 18. 14 ff.   [5] Hos. 2. 19.

[6] Jer. 11. 20; Jer. 9. 23 f.; Ps. 72. 1.

[7] Tacitus, *Germania*, 11.

[8] See W. Baetke, *Das Heilige im Germanischen*, pp. 103 f.

[9] On the legal implications of this see Kauffmann, *ZfdPh*, XLIX, 48 f. Cf. also *Vǫluspá* 6; *Þrymskviða* 14; *Grímnismál* 29; *Vǫluspá* 60.

presiding over the deliberations of their worshippers,[1] and OHG *êwa* meant originally both 'a body of laws, legal system' and 'religion'.[2] In short, the Germanic view of law as a religious ordering of society in which the will of the gods is expressed corresponds to a conception of the gods as judges equipped with legal authority. Worship of the gods is synonymous with a recognition of the law which they embody, a view which, despite considerable differences from the Hebrew conception,[3] has enough outwardly in common with it to explain how the Old Testament, once it had been stripped of its tribal particularities, could make an appeal to Christians recently converted from the Germanic religion.

Much the same is suggested by the outward similarities of the two religions in a second respect, namely the manner in which they both stress the close association of religion with warfare. The worship of Jehovah started as the cult of a tribal deity, seen primarily as a warrior deity, whose function it was to give battle on behalf of His own people against their enemies and to receive sacrifices, homage and obedience in return. This aspect of the Hebrew God is revealed by His epithet *Sabaoth* or by the manner in which the Ark of the Covenant[4] served for a long time as the palladium of the Israelite armies in battle.[5] It is Jehovah as a god of warfare who emerges as a dominant impression from several of the books of the Old Testament (especially the historical ones). It is He who is praised for having cast down the Egyptian army into the Red Sea,[6] His will is consulted before battle is delivered,[7] booty is dedicated to Him[8] and the forces of nature are at His

---

[1] On the inscription *Deo Marti Thingso* see S. Gutenbrunner, *Die germanischen Götternamen der antiken Inschriften*, pp. 24 ff., on *Fosite* see J. de Vries, *Altgermanische Religionsgeschichte*, II, 281 ff. and K. Helm, *Altgermanische Religionsgeschichte*, II, 2, 271 ff.

[2] See J. Weisweiler's article in the Festschrift for W. Streitberg, pp. 419 ff.

[3] Perhaps the most important difference is that the Germanic gods do not sit in moral judgement upon the deeds of men. Cf. A. Heusler, *Germanentum*, p. 56: 'Gebot und Verbot der Götter sind es nicht, die das sittliche Fühlen und Wollen der alten Germanen lenken.'

[4] I Reg. 4. 3–5. 12.   [5] Num. 10. 35; I Reg. 4. 3 ff.
[6] Exod. 15. 21.   [7] Jud. 1. 1; 20. 18.
[8] Jos. 6. 17 ff.; I Reg. 15. 3.

command to assist Him in the war He wages against the enemies of Israel.[1] Jehovah can therefore be praised in His terrible power as a fighting man or as mighty in battle.[2] That a God conceived in such a manner was likely to make a greater appeal to Germanic converts than many aspects of Christ as depicted in the New Testament is suggested by the way in which the Germanic gods similarly acted as the tutelar deities of their tribes in battle. The oracle is consulted on the eve of battle[3] or the opposing ranks are dedicated to the deity in question as a way of ensuring his support in the forthcoming battle.[4] Religious images are removed from the holy grove and taken into battle,[5] while the gods are felt to preside over battle and to grant victory.[6] Prisoners and equipment are reserved for the god who has afforded the tribe victory by being destroyed and sacrificed to him,[7] whilst Wodan in particular is not merely the war god to whom prisoners are sacrificed by being hanged,[8] he is also the god who chooses who is to be slain in the course of the battle.[9] How deeply seated was this Germanic belief in the military functions of the gods is clear from some of our evidence on the history of the conversion of Germania where, as with Constantine at the Milvian Bridge, the decision to embrace Christianity is made to depend on the Christian God's willingness to grant victory.[10] Moreover, when once the term *truhtin* and its cognates become established in the Christian vocabulary as the standing translation of the Christian

[1] Jos. 10. 11; Jud. 5. 20; I Reg. 7. 10.

[2] Exod. 15. 3 and 11; Ps. 24. 8.

[3] E.g. Caesar, *De bello Gallico*, I, 50; Tacitus, *Germania*, 10; *Reginsmál*, 19.

[4] Cf. Baetke, *Das Heilige im Germanischen*, pp. 61 f.; J. de Vries, *Altgermanische Religionsgeschichte*, II, 49.

[5] E.g. Tacitus, *Germania*, 7 and *Historiae*, IV, 22.

[6] E.g. Tacitus, *Germania*, 7; Adam of Bremen, *Gesta Hammaburgensis ecclesiae pontificum*, IV, 22; Bede, *Historia ecclesiastica*, II, 2.

[7] Cf. Tacitus, *Annals*, I, 61 and XIII, 57; Orosius, *Historia adversus paganos*, v, 16 and VII, 37; Jordanes, *Getica*, v, 41.

[8] E.g. Tacitus, *Germania*, 9. The ON names for this god (*Hangi* and *Hangaguð*) are discussed by de Vries, *Altgermanische Religionsgeschichte*, II, 49 f.

[9] See de Vries, *op. cit.* II, 56 ff.

[10] On Fritigern's conversion see K. D. Schmidt, *Die Bekehrung der Germanen zum Christentum*, I, 240 ff.; on Clovis see W. Baetke, *Vom Geist und Erbe Thules*, p. 112.

dominus, the military origins of this Germanic term mean that, for a time at least, the Old Testament view of the *dominus exercituum* is even more strongly emphasised.[1] This Old Testament conception of Jehovah was therefore an aspect of Christianity with which Germanic converts must have found little difficulty in sympathising.

It is clear that both the preceding points agree in concentrating on power or authority as essential to the conception of the deity. It is this emphasis on divine power that constitutes the third parallel between Germanic religion and the Old Testament. Jehovah's ability to confer victory on His people in battle is the result of His power, and His ability to call upon the forces of nature to assist Him in realising His purposes implies that His authority is universal and not confined to His relationship with Israel, His people. Such a God of universal power can make use of other nations so that they may unwittingly serve His purpose: He not merely leads Israel out of Egypt, but also controls the destiny of such peoples as the Philistines or the Syrians, whom He can use as a scourge with which to punish His people when they have aroused His anger.[2] Jehovah's power is most succinctly embodied in one of the oldest Semitic titles for the divinity (*El*),[3] and His authority, conceived in terms of kingship, in the term *Melek*.[4] A close parallel is again provided by the Germanic religion, where some of the gods' names likewise stress power as their essential characteristic (e.g. *Magni, Nerthus*),[5] whereas others equally revealingly point to the authority they were felt

[1] On the military origins of the word *truhtin* see my argument in *The Carolingian Lord*, pp. 270 ff., and on its subsequent demilitarisation after it had been adopted by the Church see also pp. 322 ff. This process of demilitarisation must have been a protracted one so that, as long as it remained uncompleted, *truhtin* could still lend itself to expressing the conception of the Christian God as an Old Testament *dominus exercituum*.

[2] Amos 9. 7. Cf. also Is. 10. 5 f. or Jer. 25. 8 f.

[3] See W. Eichrodt, *Theologie des Alten Testaments*, I, 86 ff.

[4] See the contribution of A. von Gall to the Festschrift for J. Wellhausen, pp. 145 ff., and O. Eissfeldt, *ZAW*, v (N.F.), 81 ff.

[5] On the meaning of these names see de Vries, *Altgermanische Religionsgeschichte*, II, 123; H. Polomé, *HZMTLG*, v, 99 ff.; W. Lange, *Studien zur christlichen Dichtung der Nordgermanen 1000–1200*, pp. 176 f.

to exercise (e.g. *Baldr, Freyr, Bragi*[1] or those formed by the suffix *-ana/-ina,* amongst which *Wodan* is the most important).[2] The occurrence of theophoric personal names with the equivalent of Gothic *þius* as the second element[3] also suggests that the Germanic worshipper regarded his gods as wielding authority over him, just as the ON evidence often depicts power itself (*máttr, megin*) as a supernatural characteristic of theirs.[4] The gods' power is also revealed by their association with magic (or with runic magic in particular)[5] and by the implication that to consult the gods' will at the oracle is a means of finding out what fate may have in store,[6] so that the gods and fate are tacitly equated. Clearly, as with the parallels with regard to law and warfare, there are many differences in details between the Germanic and Hebrew conceptions of divine power, but they share the view that power is an essential attribute of divinity as well as a disinclination to grant much importance to the New Testament idea of God as love or humility.

A fourth parallel is provided by the way in which both religions consider the tribe's prosperity (whether military or agricultural) as a gift conferred by the godhead, more essentially as the divine reward for the religious service they have rendered to the gods. This conception of a fundamental reciprocity between service and reward finds its most telling expression in the Old Testament in the doctrine of the covenant: Jehovah may well be depicted as acting towards His people in terms of the relationship between father and children, but His relationship with them is no natural one, resting on kinship by blood, but instead the result of a conscious choice on both sides, for Jehovah had chosen the

[1] On *Baldr* and *Freyr* see *The Carolingian Lord,* pp. 3 ff. and pp. 19 ff. *Bragi* is discussed by de Vries, *op. cit.* II, 272 ff.

[2] The formation of the name *Wodan* is discussed by K. Helm, *Wodan. Ausbreitung und Wanderung seines Kultes,* pp. 13 ff.

[3] This is well analysed by E. V. Gordon, *MA,* IV, 169 ff.

[4] See the contribution of E. Mogk to the Festschrift for W. Streitberg, pp. 278 ff.

[5] See de Vries, *Altgermanische Religionsgeschichte,* I, 275 ff.

[6] M. von Kienle, *WuS,* xv, 81 ff.; W. Gehl, *Der germanische Schicksalsglaube;* E. Neumann, *Das Schicksal in der Edda.*

Israelites as His people and they had accepted Jehovah. This covenant relationship, which dominates the earliest history of Israel even where the technical word *berith* may not actually be used, is revealed in a tangible manner either in the form of the military victories granted to His people by Jehovah or as fertility and abundance.[1] This double aspect of God's reward for the obedience of His people is given programmatic expression in such prolonged passages as Lev. 26. 1 ff. or Deut. 11. 13 ff., where those who obey God's commands are promised their rewards in this life in the forms of victory over all their foes[2] and unfailing abundance for their fields, cattle and families.[3] A similar attitude has been shown to underlie Germanic religious experience as a result of Baetke's analysis of the pre-Christian usage of the words *Heil* and *heilig*[4] (even though Germanic religion may not show any counterpart to the way in which the relationship between Jehovah and Israel was formally sealed by the covenant between them). *Heil* in its pre-Christian sense can take the form of the gods granting their worshippers victory in battle or fertility and prosperity,[5] but, as Baetke has also been at pains to establish, this is only the result of the ritual sacrifices to the gods being scrupulously observed by these worshippers. As with the practice of gift-giving, where the acceptance of a gift imposed on the recipient the need to restore the balance of the relationship by making a counter-gift to the original donor, it is felt that sacrifices are to be made to the gods as a means of ensuring that they will bless the tribe with victory and fertility.[6] So deeply is this felt that failure on the part of the gods to provide these gifts can even result in an accusation of the gods, blaming

---

[1] The promise of fertility and abundance is of course tangibly present in the conception of the Promised Land. Cf. also Jacob's blessing on Judah (Gen. 49. 8 ff.) and Ps. 72. 16.

[2] E.g. Lev. 26. 7 f. (contrasted with vv. 17 and 25) or Deut. 11. 23 and 25.

[3] Lev. 26. 3 ff. and 9 (contrasted with vv. 16 and 20) or Deut. 11. 14 f. (by contrast with v. 17) and 21.

[4] *Das Heilige im Germanischen*, pp. 206 ff. and 215.

[5] On fertility see Baetke's analysis of the ON phrase *blóta til árs ok friðar* in *PBB*, LXVI, 38 ff.

[6] See M. Mauss, *The Gift*, and also *The Carolingian Lord*, pp. 390 ff.

them for their omission.[1] Moreover, when once Christianity makes use of terms derived from the reciprocal nexus of the Germanic *comitatus* and applies *triuwa* or *huldi* to the relationship between the Christian God and His believers,[2] it is clear that the initial result of this linguistic choice is to give even greater prominence to the reciprocity of this relationship and thus to make it easier for the Germanic convert to regard the Old Testament covenant between Jehovah and Israel in terms of his own religious experience.[3]

Behind these similarities between the Germanic religion and the Old Testament world to which the Germanic convert was given access there lie, however, profound differences in outlook, of which the most important is the critical fact that, whereas the Germanic gods demanded only ritual observances from their worshippers, Jehovah's relationship with Israel was an ethical one in which He imposed norms of conduct on those who served Him. This can at times be made quite explicit,[4] but elsewhere it is equally clearly implied. Thus Jehovah's function as a Judge concerns not merely the law but also righteousness, and the commandments which He transmits to Moses are ethical precepts. Jehovah confers military victory upon Israel only when they have obeyed His precepts, so that His anger, normally directed against their foes, can sometimes be vented against His people if their behaviour falls short of what He has commanded.[5] Heathen nations are not merely punished for their wrongs against Israel,

---

[1] Cf. the words of Coifi, the high-priest of the Northumbrians, as reported by Bede in the *Historia ecclesiastica*, II, 13, or the sentiments attributed to Clovis, just before his conversion, by Gregory of Tours, *Historiarum libri decem*, II, 30. That an appeal could successfully be made by the Christian missionary to this pagan attitude is also implied by the terms of the argument recommended to Boniface by Bishop Daniel of Winchester in his letter to him (no. 23, *MGH* Epp. III, 271 ff.).

[2] See *The Carolingian Lord*, pp. 117 ff. and 140 ff.

[3] *Triuwa* therefore comes to be used to designate the covenant between God and man, and of *huldi* (as used in the OE *Genesis*) M. Ohly-Steimer has said (*ZfdA*, LXXXVI, 85) that it denotes protection against one's foes and the maintenance of earthly life at large as 'die versprochenen Gegengaben Gottes für die geforderten Leistungen des Bundespartners'.

[4] E.g. Is. 1. 11 ff.; Os. 6. 6; Amos 5. 21 ff.   [5] See p. 195, n. 2.

they can also be used by Jehovah as an instrument for inflicting punishment upon a sinful Israel. Defeat in battle or infertility[1] can be interpreted as a merited punishment; so far from this suggesting that Jehovah has abandoned His people and forgotten His covenant, it demonstrates that it is the Israelites who in their sinfulness have turned away from God.[2] This profoundly ethical interpretation of the relationship between the divinity and man was foreign to the mentality of the Germanic pagan, who was in fact brought to realise the identity of ethics and of religion only as a result of the conversion to Christianity.[3] This realisation was, however, the ultimate result of a long process of learning the full implications of the new religion, so that it remains true that, in the period of the conversion and for long afterwards, the Germanic convert would tend to show a greater response to the Old Testament strand of Christianity than to the New Testament and that he would for long remain unaware of the differences that sheltered behind the more obvious similarities between the Old Testament and the religion which he had given up. The Christianity of such converts represents an uncertain fusion of Germanic modes of religious feeling with those aspects of Christianity (partly derived from the Old Testament) which most nearly corresponded to their own attitude and which they could therefore most easily comprehend. What has too often been invoked as a 'Germanisierung des Christentums' was largely the result of this fusion, for the aspects of this form of Christianity which owe much to Germanic religious experience are retained largely because they came to be identified (even if unjustifiably) with certain facets of the Old Testament strand within the Christian tradition. For us the historical importance of this identification is that, in combination with the way in which the typological interpretation of the Old Testament deprived these books of most

[1] Cf. Os. 9. 1 ff. and 16 f. [2] Os. 14. 1 ff.
[3] This identification of ethics with religion in the case of Christianity was largely accomplished by the adoption of *truhtin* and of other terms from the vocabulary of the *comitatus* for Christian ends (see *The Carolingian Lord*, pp. 302 ff.). It is perhaps no coincidence that the term *truhtin*, so useful for rendering the Hebrew idea of the *dominus exercituum*, should also have lent itself to conveying the other Old Testament conception of the identity of ethics and of religion.

of their historical particularity and made them accessible to people living in quite a different tradition and remote from the world of the Near East, it ensured that the Old Testament should acquire an importance for medieval life which would otherwise have been inconceivable.

With that we may now turn to the two aspects of the Old Testament which concern us in the *Millstätter Exodus* and consider how it was possible for the two concepts of the Chosen People and warfare on behalf of God to exercise an influence on medieval thought because of their occurrence in the Old Testament. Here again nothing like a systematic treatment is remotely possible. Instead we shall have to be content with a few general observations on the way in which these two themes entered medieval Christianity from the Old Testament.

The application of the concept of the Chosen People to the Christian community is already to be found in the New Testament and it is this fact which ensures that it is handed on to the Middle Ages. The name *Israel*, with its implication of the religious vocation of the Jews as God's people, occurs in the New Testament precisely in the sense of the Jewish people as God's people,[1] whereas *Judaei* is frequently employed in a derogatory sense, suggesting enmity to Christ.[2] St Paul refers to himself as an *Israelita* (or *Hebraeus*), but never as a *Judaeus*.[3] But if *Israel* is employed as a technical term for the *populus Dei* then the problem arose as to how far it could still be employed of the Jews who had rejected Christ. It is this problem which St Paul discusses in Rom. 9–11, where we find the observation that not all those who are born of Israel are in fact Israelites,[4] so that a distinction is made here in favour of what is by implication the true Israel. In Gal. 6. 16 the term *Israel Dei* is explicitly used of the Christian Church, whereas the reference in I Cor. 10. 18 to *Israel secundum carnem* implies the converse term *Israel secundum spiritum* as a title for the Christian community. The argument for this is provided by St Paul in Gal. 4. 21 ff. where, appealing

---

[1] See G. Kittel (ed.), *Theologisches Wörterbuch zum Neuen Testament*, III, 386 f.
[2] *Ibid.* pp. 380 f.   [3] *Ibid.* p. 383.   [4] Rom. 9. 6.

to the Old Testament authority recognised by his Jewish opponents, he interprets the fact that Abraham had two sons, one born to him by a slave and the other by a free woman, as signifying allegorically the existence of two covenants: Ismael, Abraham's son by the slave *secundum carnem*, is the type of *Israel secundum carnem*, whereas Isaac, his son by the free woman *secundum spiritum*, prefigures the Christian community as *Israel secundum spiritum*, the Israel to whom the promise is made and to whom the inheritance is due. Accordingly, although St Paul only employs the term *populus Dei* in quotations from the Old Testament,[1] he uses it both of the Jewish people and of the Church.[2] Similarly, in referring to the Christian communion as a *novum testamentum*,[3] he is really arguing that the new Israel, the Israel of the spirit, enjoys the new covenant which replaces the earlier one *secundum carnem*. In all this the former rights of the Jews as God's people are shown to have been rendered void by their failure to acknowledge Christ, so that it is now the Christian community that, as partakers of the new covenant of the spirit, is entitled to be regarded as God's people, as the *Israel secundum spiritum*.[4] Once again it is made clear that the extension of the term *Israel* and therewith the application of such Hebrew terms and institutions as *Israel, testamentum* or *populus Dei* to the emergent community of the Christian Church were only made possible by St Paul's use of the typological method.[5] For him Abraham is important not so much as the historical founder of the Jewish people, but as the recipient of God's promise,[6] a promise which is fulfilled only in Christ. Our earliest examples for the application of Hebrew concepts to the Christian Church therefore reveal the same tension between a past historical event and its timeless, metaphysical significance which underlies the

[1] See Dahl, *Das Volk Gottes*, p. 210.

[2] Of the Jews: Rom. 11. 1 f.; 15. 10; of the Church: Rom. 9. 25 f.; II Cor. 6. 16; Tit. 2. 14; Act. 18. 10.   [3] I Cor. 11. 25; II Cor. 3. 6.

[4] This is why he argues elsewhere (Gal. 3. 7) that faith alone entitles one to be numbered among the children of Abraham.

[5] Gal. 4. 24: 'Quae sunt per allegoriam dicta.'

[6] Cf. Dahl, *op. cit.* p. 213.

The Millstätter Exodus

Millstätter Exodus, so that the technique of the twelfth-century author is a fully traditional one, even though the purposes for which he employs it may be quite new in the Germany of his day. A further contribution to the now established equation of the *populus Dei* concept with Christendom is provided by the Augustinian theory of the *civitas Dei*. It would take us too far from our restricted problem to analyse the genesis of this theory of such far-reaching importance for the political and religious thought of the Middle Ages, but a point stressed recently by Ratzinger[1] needs to be equally emphasised in the present context. He draws our attention to the fact that whenever the concept of the πόλις τοῦ θεοῦ is used in the East or that of the *civitas Dei* in the West it arises in connection with the Christian exegesis of the Old Testament, especially with reference to the cities of Jerusalem and Babylon. The pre-Augustinian history of this concept is therefore inseparable from the Old Testament and its role in Christian thought and has its origins in the Pauline use of typology in the passage Gal. 4. 21 ff.[2] which we have just considered. Ratzinger stresses the importance of this same Old Testament background for St Augustine himself, pointing out that he more frequently connects this concept with parallel passages in the Psalms than in the New Testament[3] and that his use of this term is an example of Christian allegorical interpretation of an Old Testament image.[4]

Yet however important the Augustinian concept may have been for medieval thought and however many other examples we may find of the application of the *populus Dei* idea to Christendom in other sources,[5] it is more relevant to our problem to

[1] In his contribution to the proceedings of the Congrès International Augustinien (Paris, 1954), II, 965 ff. and reprinted in *Geschichtsdenken und Geschichtsbild im Mittelalter* (ed. W. Lammers), pp. 62 ff. I quote from this latter source.

[2] See Ratzinger, *op. cit.* p. 63. The use of this particular passage was made possible by St Paul's reference to the city of Jerusalem in Gal. 4. 25 f.

[3] *Ibid.* p. 63, n. 26.　　　　[4] *Ibid.* p. 64.

[5] Cf., for example, H. Zimmermann, *Ecclesia als Objekt der Historiographie*, and his remarks on Eusebius: 'Für Eusebius sind christliche Kirche und Christenvolk identische Begriffe. Da die Kirche aber zugleich das Gottesvolk darstellt, reichen seine Anfänge weit in die Vergangenheit zurück' (p. 23).

consider the possible ways in which this idea entered the German world in particular and thus contributed to the tradition to which our twelfth-century author still belongs. A few examples must suffice for this. The first has been adduced by B. Smalley in her work on the Bible in the Middle Ages,[1] for she indicates that in a group of Frisian chronicles the order of events in the history of the Frisians is deliberately altered so that a closer correspondence between these events and those related in the Old Testament may result. The intention is clearly a wish to compare the Frisians with the Chosen People and thus to depict them as a new people chosen by God.

Even more revealing is the evidence suggesting that the Franks regarded themselves after their conversion as the *populus Dei*. A first example is provided by the prologue to the *Lex Salica*[2] where the Franks are described as founded by God the Creator[3] and as inspired by Him (even before their conversion) in the formulation of their laws.[4] It is God who shows His favour in the conversion of Clovis[5] and the prologue concludes with another praise of the Franks, showing them as superior to the Romans, in which Christ is addressed in the words: 'Vivat qui Francus diligit, Christus eorum regnum costodiat, rectores eorundem lumen suae graciae repleat.'[6] Christ is here seen as showing particular love for the Franks and as guarding their realm with the same kind of care as Jehovah had bestowed upon the Israelites. Furthermore, when Christ is also asked to protect the Frankish army and to give their realm the blessings of peace and prosperity[7] we may recognise in this request a reflection of the same double award which Jehovah had granted His people in the Old Testament. Admittedly, success in warfare and fertility had also constituted the blessings which the Germanic gods had conferred upon their worshippers, so that this passage in the *Lex Salica*

---

[1] *The Study of the Bible in the Middle Ages*, p. xi.
[2] Ed. K. A. Eckhardt, *Lex Salica: 100 Titel-Text*, pp. 82 ff. The importance of this passage has been stressed by Schmidt, *Die Bekehrung der Germanen zum Christentum*, II, 52.
[3] 82. 3 f.
[4] 84. 1 ff.
[5] 86. 4 f.
[6] 88. 3 f.
[7] 88. 4 ff.

represents the fusion of the Germanic with the Old Testament tradition, a transition from the Germanic view of the tribal function of the god worshipped to an equally tribal view of the Christian God which derives from the Old Testament.

Something similar is implied by Otfrid in his praise of the Franks. In his preface *Ad Ludowicum* the ruler is depicted in terms reminiscent of those used in the prologue to the *Lex Salica*: he is protected from his enemies by God who grants him assistance,[1] his health and the peace of his realm are likewise divine gifts which profit both the ruler and his people.[2] Here again the ideas expressed by Otfrid are common both to the Germanic tradition and to the Old Testament, but we may be confident that it is from the latter source that Otfrid is mainly drawing in this eulogy of the ruler because of his explicit comparison of Lewis with David. In contemplating the Frankish ruler Otfrid states that he is reminded of the deeds of David;[3] both kings show the same exemplary patience in face of the afflictions which God has imposed upon them as a trial[4] and Otfrid is even persuaded that, because of this similarity, the Frankish ruler must be of the same descent as David.[5] Yet the more Lewis is equated with the Hebrew king, the more obvious must be the similarity between the two peoples over whom they rule, between the Franks and the Israelites:

> 59   Rihta gener scono   thie gotes liuti in frono:
>   so duit ouh therer ubar jar,   so iz gote zimit, thaz ist war.

In this comparison between *gener* (= David) and *therer* (= Lewis) the term *thie gotes liuti* is common to both, but whereas in the one case it is the Israelites who are this people, in the other case the Christian Franks of Otfrid's day have tacitly replaced them.

The same implicit replacement of the Jews by the Franks recurs in another programmatic passage where Otfrid discusses

[1] Cf. vv. 19 f., 23 f., 32, 51 f.
[2] Cf. vv. 5 ff., 27 ff., 71 ff., 79 f.   [3] V. 37.
[4] This is implied by the way in which the phrase *gilicha theganheiti* (v. 45) compares the Frankish ruler with David who has just been praised for surmounting the trials imposed upon him *so gotes thegane giȥam* (v. 42). Cf. also vv. 47 f.   [5] Vv. 55 f.

his intentions in writing his work. Leonard Forster has shown[1] that the terms in which Otfrid describes the territory of the Franks and its abundance of natural riches[2] owe much to Moses' description of the Promised Land in Deut. 8. 7 ff. and to his warning to the Israelites not to forget God on account of the prosperity which they are to enjoy. We should not press the fact of direct imitation too far, but the general parallel is a striking one. It may have been expressed only in general terms not so much because it was a 'halbbewußte Reminiszenz'[3] as because Otfrid wished only to imply the parallel, leaving it to his audience to draw the obvious conclusion, rather than to state it outright. This is suggested not simply by the similar allusiveness of vv. 59 f. in the preface *Ad Ludowicum*, but also by another implied parallel in the opening chapter of Book I, where in v. 53 Otfrid refers to the singing of God's praise in the *edilzungun*. These languages were understood traditionally as the three used in the inscription on the Cross (Hebrew, Greek and Latin),[4] but in this same chapter Otfrid discusses explicitly only the literary achievements of two of these languages (Greek and Latin).[5] When Otfrid therefore devotes most of this chapter to arguing why God's praise should also be sung in his Frankish tongue[6] the implication is that for him Frankish has replaced Hebrew, just as the Franks were also tacitly regarded as the *populus Dei* of the present. The pride in the Franks which pervades this whole chapter therefore derives not merely from the fact that their achievements may be compared with those of classical antiquity, but also from the religious conviction that God's guiding hand has been transferred from the Israelites to the Franks.

The linguistic evidence of other OHG texts suggests that this extension of the concept *populus Dei* from the Jews to Christendom was well known in Carolingian times. G. Herold has shown that the OHG terms *folk* and *liut* (or *liuti* as a plural) are used in a biblical sense to render the idea of the Israelites not simply as a

---

[1] *PBB* (H) LXXVIII, 316 ff.   [2] I, 1, 65 ff.
[3] *PBB* (H) LXXVIII, 317.
[4] Cf. Erdmann's note on this verse in his edition, p. 340.
[5] I, 1, 13.   [6] I, 1, 33 f. and 113 f.

political entity, but more particularly in their religious function as the people chosen by God.[1] In addition, these same words are employed in a Christian sense to indicate Christendom as the new *populus Dei*.[2] Here again this concept can on one occasion be narrowed down so as to suggest that it is the Franks in particular who are to be regarded in this manner. This occurs as one of the many Old Testament allusions in the *Ludwigslied* where God addresses the Frankish ruler, asking him to return and assist His people against the pagan incursions of the Vikings (v. 23: '*Hluduîg, kuning mîn, Hilph mînan liutin!*'). Indeed, it is significant that in this work which represents a fusion of Germanic with Christian ideas it should be so largely the Old Testament tradition within Christianity that provides one of the constituents. God intervenes in human activity and addresses the ruler, much as in the Old Testament, as His chosen instrument;[3] the Viking attack is seen as a trial imposed by God upon the ruler[4] and the sufferings the pagans cause serve the moral chastisement of the Franks.[5] It is God finally who granted Lewis authority over His Chosen People,[6] who commanded him to give battle to the invaders[7] and who is the guarantor of victory.[8] The conception of the Christian Franks as the new people of God is therefore only one of many Old Testament elements in this work and an indication of how it was possible for the Old Testament tradition to live on with renewed force in the Middle Ages.

It is precisely the *Ludwigslied*, however, that exemplifies the medieval adaptation of the second Old Testament conception we have to consider, the idea of a specifically military service of God,[9] for it shows us God's people doing battle on His behalf.[10]

---

[1] *Der Volksbegriff im Sprachschatz des Althochdeutschen und Altniederdeutschen*, pp. 202 f. and 218 f.

[2] *Ibid.* pp. 203 (*Murbacher Hymnen*) and 220 (*Isidor, Monseer Fragmente, Murbacher Hymnen*, Np, Ngl, Npw).

[3] Vv. 23 ff.   [4] Vv. 9 f.

[5] Vv. 11 ff.   [6] Vv. 5 f.

[7] Vv. 23 f. (cf. vv. 33 f.).   [8] V. 55.

[9] Once more it must be stressed that, as far as the *Millstätter Exodus* is concerned, this only means that the Israelites are depicted as knights with all their military equipment, not that they are anywhere actually described as serving God in battle.   [10] See however p. 214.

This is an Old Testament conception which could gain acceptance in medieval Germany with little difficulty, for the close relationship between religion and warfare in the Hebrew tradition was paralleled by a similar outlook in the pagan Germanic world. In another sense the acceptance of this idea of serving God in battle was rendered difficult precisely because of the New Testament rejection of warfare (and therefore because of a similar rejection by the early Church at large),[1] so that the development of this idea in the Middle Ages may be the result, at least in part, of an increased importance attached to this Old Testament outlook.

Here a point emphasised by R. H. Bainton[2] is of considerable importance, for he traces the development of the idea of warfare on behalf of God within the Old Testament itself. He argues that whereas the original conquest of the Promised Land by the Israelites may well have been little more than 'a gradual infiltration punctuated by conflict' undertaken by pastoral nomads, the later period of controversy concerning the idolatrous effects of fraternising with the Canaanites who still remained in the land sees the traditionalist party amongst the Hebrews advocating a religious war of extermination against these Canaanites, as an act of purification and as a means of safeguarding the faith of Israel. Authority was even given to this policy by a reinterpretation of past events, i.e. of the original occupation of the Promised Land by the Israelites, so that in Deut. 7. 1 f. and 13. 15 f., for example, the later policy of a religious war against the Canaanites is anachronistically attributed to Moses, who is now described as if he were instructing the people of Israel to slaughter the inhabitants of Canaan when once they gained possession of the land which God had promised them. This reinterpretation of Israel's past is continued in the accounts given in Numbers, Joshua and Judges, where Israel fights not merely with the

---

[1] See A. Harnack, *Militia Christi, passim.* On the linguistic and literary evidence for a similar attitude adopted by the Church towards the military and heroic ideals of the Germanic tribes see F. Willems, *Heldenwörter in germanischer und christlicher Literatur.*

[2] *Christian Attitudes Toward War and Peace*, pp. 44 ff.

assistance of Jehovah, but at His command. Where Exodus had merely stressed that there should be no fraternisation with the Canaanites and no worship of their gods,[1] the later books go far beyond this in depicting an aggressive war of extermination against the Canaanites, waged by the Israelites in obedience to God.[2] Bainton has also argued that this development was accompanied by a corresponding change in the character ascribed to Jehovah.[3] In origin the God of the Israelites appears to have been a deity of natural catastrophe, fighting by means of natural elements such as hail, the sea or the stars—an outlook which pervades the Book of Exodus itself. Later, however, Jehovah acquired the characteristics of a warrior. He is therefore described as mighty in battle,[4] as personally wielding the bow and the sword,[5] as scattering His enemies either by the victory which He grants to the Israelite army as a whole or by the power with which He equips the weak instruments of His will such as David before Goliath or Judith before Holofernes. From this last example it is clear that even though the Hebrew idea of a holy war may have suffered an eclipse during the Babylonian period,[6] it was strong enough to undergo a resurgence when conditions were more favourable, as was the case in the period of the Maccabees with the militant reaction to the dangers represented by the Hellenisation of Jewish life.

For centuries, therefore, the Christian Church did not and

[1] E.g. Exod. 23. 23 and 32; 33. 2; 34. 15 f.

[2] We now see that it is probably from this reinterpretation by the Deuteronomists of events recounted in Exodus that the author of the *Millstätter Exodus* obtained the idea of at least suggesting that the Israelites' future occupation of the Promised Land was to be the result of a military conquest (see pp. 142 and 160). That he should agree with another book of the Bible on this point does not detract in the least from his originality in introducing this hint of a military motif, for it was he who chose to follow Deuteronomy at this point rather than Exodus itself.

[3] *Op. cit.* p. 47.

[4] Ps. 24. 8.   [5] Deut. 32. 41 f.

[6] It needs to be emphasised that, even in the apparent defeat of Israel in the Babylonian period, belief in the holy war did not die out, even though it may have undergone a weakening. This is primarily because of the typically ethical interpretation of the Israelites' defeat as a divine retribution for their sins (see pp. 198 f.).

could not realise that the concept of a holy war waged on behalf of God was not an unchanging characteristic of the Old Testament, but that instead it had undergone a historical development, arising at the time of the Deuteronomists, declining in the Babylonian period and enjoying a revival in the days of the Maccabees. From the time when the books that incorporate this concept were adopted as part of the Christian Scriptures the Church was therefore confronted with the problem of these religious wars commanded and sanctioned by God. No matter whether they ignored the problem (or attempted to minimise its significance) or whether they used this testimony as a justification of Christian warfare, the concept of a holy war was now one from which Christian writers could not escape. Its re-emergence in medieval thought clearly owes much to the authority of the Hebrew example.

A few examples may suffice to show the truth of this even in the case of the converted Germanic tribes, whose military ardour might otherwise have been regarded as sufficient explanation of their acceptance of any Christian doctrine of the holy war. That this is not the full explanation, that the Church would attempt to impose its New Testament ideal of peace even upon these newly converted and still warlike tribes, can best be shown in the case of Wulfila.[1] In one of the few direct testimonies on the Gothic bishop which we possess Philostorgius[2] reports in his ecclesiastical history that Wulfila, in translating the Bible into Gothic, omitted the Books of the Kings because of his fear that their numerous warlike scenes would heighten the military passions of his fellow Goths, whereas the need was for this ardour to be subdued. Furthermore, it seems probable that the same motive explains Wulfila's refusal to use the term *drauhtins* (originally meaning the lord of a warrior-band) of Christ as Lord[3], whereas all the

---

[1] I have discussed his attitude to this problem at some length in *The Carolingian Lord*, pp. 278 ff.

[2] The passage in question is reprinted in W. Streitberg's edition of Wulfila's translation, pp. xix f.

[3] The argument that Wulfila consciously rejected *drauhtins* as a Christian term because of its false associations depends on the demonstration that this

The Millstätter Exodus

other Germanic dialects regularly employ *truhtin* and its cognates with no compunction. In just the same way Wulfila employs other terms applicable to the Germanic warrior-band (which in other dialects are simply extended from this military context to the Christian sphere), but in such a way that in the Gothic text their Christian use is instead an extension from their legal function. In Wulfila's Gothic *triggwa* can be used to render the idea of God's covenant with man because of the word's originally legal function.[1] In other Germanic dialects, however, although this association may still be present, the corresponding word is also used of the relationship between God and man because it had previously designated the ties between the warrior-leader and his followers[2] and because the term for the warrior-leader himself, *truhtin*, had now come to be applied to the Christian deity. Wulfila is prepared to use these terms derived from the technical vocabulary of the warrior-band only where he can restrict their function as Christian terms to their legal meaning. Where this is impossible (where, in other words, the military implications of these terms would have remained intact) he excludes them from his Christian vocabulary, so that his linguistic usage represents a close parallel to his decision not to translate some of the books of the Old Testament because of their overtly military subject-matter.[3]

word, although it does not occur in Wulfila's Bible, nonetheless existed in Gothic. I have attempted to show this in *The Carolingian Lord*, pp. 265 f. Baetke's obervations on Wulfila's similar refusal to use **hailags* as a Christian term (*Das Heilige im Germanischen*, pp. 220 f.) likewise rest on the assumption that, although this adjective is not attested with Wulfila, it did exist in Gothic. In this case, however, the assumption is converted into a certainty because of the testimony of the runic inscription on the ring of Pietroassa.

[1] See *The Carolingian Lord*, pp. 233 ff.
[2] This point has been well made by U. Pretzel in his article on 'Treue' in the *Deutsches Wörterbuch* (s.v., col. 286).
[3] R. H. Bainton (*HTR*, xxxix, 189 ff.) has drawn attention to other criticisms of this particular aspect of the Old Testament voiced by the early Church. He cites the example of Marcion (p. 210) who, although a heretic, rejects the Old Testament for reasons which were at least partially acceptable to the orthodox. His criticism is that David killed blind men, whereas Christ healed the blind, or that Moses stretched out his hands towards God on the mountain top so as to bring about the destruction of his foes, whilst Christ stretched out his hands on

On the other hand, wherever the newly converted Germanic tribes succeed in placing a Christian interpretation upon warfare it is significant that the Old Testament conception of the holy war is accepted with little difficulty, but especially with regard to one point where the Hebrew conception could offer an explanation which was unknown to the Germanic view of warfare as a religious undertaking: namely, the problem of defeat. For the Hebrews the fact of defeat was an indication, not that God had deserted His people, but rather that they had offended Him by not remaining true to their compact with Him.[1] For the Germanic tribes, on the other hand, whose gods were served by ritual sacrifice and not by obedience to a moral code of divine origin, the experience of military defeat could at times occasion a religious crisis, casting doubt on the power of the gods to assist and sometimes leading to a change of allegiance, either in favour of another pagan god or in favour of the Christian God.[2] Our evidence suggests that the Church, when engaged in the conversion of Germania, used at least three methods to explain the problem of military defeat suffered by a Christian people, each of which was derived from the Old Testament attitude to the problem. In the first place, it could stress the inscrutability of the Christian God and hence the possibility that He was using the enemy as His instrument, that they were in fact the scourge of God.[3] Secondly, if the Church succeeded in so transforming

the Cross in order to save men. Origen, on the other hand, sought to remove the stumbling block by allegorising the Old Testament military episodes and by imposing a spiritual interpretation upon them (see the quotation from him in *The Carolingian Lord*, p. 279, n. 3). This spiritual interpretation of Origen, allowing him to escape from the unwelcome military implications of the Old Testament, thus fully agrees with what we saw above (p. 129) of his allegorical interpretation and the similar escape it provided from the historicity of the events and personages of the Old Testament.

[1] See pp. 198 f.

[2] The importance of this in the history of the conversion of Germania has been emphasised by W. Baetke, *Religion und Politik in der Germanenbekehrung*, p. 17 (see also p. 41, n. 18).

[3] This attitude is expressed, for example, in the *Ludwigslied* vv. 11 f. at a stage in the poem when, because of the king's absence, the Franks' victory is anything but assured (cf. v. 19). A similar view is to be found with Lebwin, an Anglo-

The Millstätter Exodus

Germanic mentality that it could now conceive of God as a universal deity[1] and not merely as a tribal god in the pagan sense, then it could argue that God, since He was universal, was not necessarily tied to granting victory only to one tribe in particular.[2] Lastly, military disaster can be attributed not to the impotence of God, but instead to the human shortcomings of the defeated Christians:[3] in other words, the Christian God applies an ethical yardstick which had been unknown to the pagan religion. In each of these explanations of the problem of defeat we may see that the Church had already succeeded in transforming the converts' conception of divinity (for they are now ready to believe that God is inscrutable, a universal deity and judge of man's moral conduct), but on the other hand it is significant that none of these explanations goes so far as to deny that victory is still a divine gift. This latter attitude is in keeping with both the Ger-

Saxon missionary amongst the Continental Saxons, who regarded the Franks under Charles the Great as a scourge sent by God to punish the Saxons for their stubbornly held paganism (cf. Schmidt, *Germanischer Glaube und Christentum*, pp. 31 f.). As examples of this conception in the Old Testament see Is. 10. 5 f. or Jer. 25. 8 f.

[1] That the origins of this Christian universalism are to be sought at least in part in the Hebrew tradition (despite the particularism of the doctrine of the Chosen People) should be clear from the fact that the God of Israel had chosen the natural forces of the whole universe and even nations other than Israel to assist Him in His purposes. This wider view is expressed above all in exilic and post-exilic prophecy (cf. Is. 19. 18 ff. and 60. 3). The song of Simeon as recorded in Luc. 2. 29 ff. is also evidence that there were among the Jews some who cherished the hope of a universal message (v. 32: 'Lumen ad revelationem gentium, et gloriam plebis tuae Israel').

[2] Among the Christian Goths, for example, Totila argues that God stands above the nations and does not usually offer His assistance to one particular tribe or people, but to those who treasure justice, for it causes Him no trouble to show His favours elsewhere (Procopius, *De bello Gothico*, III, 21). Similarly, in a final desperate battle the Ostrogothic army sues for peace since, although remaining Christian, it had come to recognise that God was against them (*ibid.* IV, 35). Cf. Schmidt, *Bekehrung der Germanen zum Christentum*, I, 347.

[3] This idea of human shortcomings calling forth divine retribution is often implicit in the first explanation mentioned above ('the scourge of God')— cf. *Ludwigslied* vv. 14 and 20. It also lies behind Bede's readiness to ascribe defeat to the moral faults of the person or army defeated so that, for example, both the sons of Edwin (*Historia ecclesiastica*, III, 1) and King Coinwalch (*ibid.* III, 7) are said to have suffered defeat because of their paganism and obstinate refusal to accept the Christian faith.

manic and the Hebrew traditions, but it differs from the position adopted by Wulfila in his anxiety not to inflame the military ardour of Gothic Christians by giving it a divine sanction from the Old Testament. Each of these three explanations is also derived from the Old Testament, so that we may conclude that the (implicitly) positive Christian attitude to war they represent (seeking the cause of defeat either in the Christian himself or in his inability to comprehend the ways of God, but leaving intact the conception that it is God who grants victory in battle) derives a large measure of support from the Hebrew tradition. Both the more pacific Wulfila and also those who are prepared to countenance a war waged by Christians assisted by God are aware of the crucial relevance of the Old Testament to this problem.

We can go much further than this, however, in assessing the contribution of the Hebrew tradition to the medieval idea of the holy war, for the Old Testament was repeatedly used as a model and as a justification in the various developments which together explain the emergence of the crusading idea, that particular form of holy war which is so characteristic of the Middle Ages. Here again nothing like a systematic survey of this problem is possible within the limits of the present chapter, so that I shall do no more than base myself mainly on C. Erdmann's work on the crusades[1] and show how several of the strands which in his view contribute to the rise of the crusading idea are closely connected with the Old Testament example of the holy war conducted by the *populus Dei* on His behalf.

One of Erdmann's starting-points is the fact that in Carolingian society it is the office of the ruler which is first and most thoroughly christianised,[2] above all by means of the idea of the priest-king[3] and in such a way that one of the ruler's major duties is to defend and even extend the confines of Christendom. Erdmann suggests no more than general parallels between the war of conversion waged by Charles the Great against the Saxons

---

[1] *Die Entstehung des Kreuzzugsgedankens.*   [2] *Op. cit.* p. 19.
[3] On the Old Testament origins of this idea see F. Kern, *Gottesgnadentum und Widerstandsrecht im früheren Mittelalter* (ed. R. Buchner), pp. 64 ff.

and Old Testament precedents,[1] but he also stresses that such a war differs from a crusade by the way in which the religious aim is connected only with the state as a whole (in other words, with the ruler), not with each individual warrior taking part. He adduces the *Ludwigslied* in support of this, pointing out that only Lewis is personally commanded by God to give battle to the pagan invaders and that he receives his victory as a gift from God,[2] whereas his vassals (although they may be referred to as *godes holdon*)[3] are not ordered to give battle by God and are only promised a secular reward by their ruler after the battle.[4] It is only indirectly, *via* the office of the king, that this poem subjects warfare to the needs of Christian ethics. Much the same is true of Otfrid who, however strongly opposed he may have been to the idea that a Christian could serve God directly by taking up arms against His foes,[5] is yet prepared to countenance warfare as a service rendered to a Christian king by his subjects. It is significant that with him a positive attitude to warfare emerges only when he is talking of the Frankish state as a whole and of its ruler in the preface *Ad Ludowicum* and in the section I, I, although even here he stresses that the military virtues of his Franks are revealed in *defensive* warfare so that there can be no talk with him of a war of conversion.[6] The Franks give battle out of duty to their king, whereas victory comes to them because of the relationship between their ruler and God, so that the position is essentially the same as with the *Ludwigslied*.

Our next example comes from the early eleventh century, from the description of a war conducted so as to enforce the *pax Dei*. Erdmann has stressed the importance of this movement for the emergence of the idea of a holy war waged on behalf of God,[7]

---

[1] *Op. cit.* p. 20.   [2] Vv. 23 f. (cf. vv. 33 f.) and v. 55.
[3] V. 36.   [4] Vv. 39 ff.
[5] I have discussed this attitude of Otfrid's in *The Carolingian Lord*, pp. 333 ff.
[6] Cf. *Ad Ludowicum* vv. 21 f., 49 ff., 71 ff. and 79 f.; I, I, 75 ff. In this latter section the references in vv. 59 f. and 63 f. are neutral from our point of view, but obviously are meant to form part of the total picture of a defensive war conducted by the Frankish king.
[7] *Die Entstehung des Kreuzzugsgedankens*, pp. 53 ff.

but what concerns us particularly in the account of Andreas of Fleury[1] is the way in which Old Testament models impose themselves upon the events he is narrating. The people summoned by Archbishop Aimo of Bourges in 1038 to enforce their will upon those who break the *pax Dei* are regarded as a new people of Israel putting their enemies to flight with the assistance of God, but (again in the Old Testament tradition) as being punished by defeat when once they succumb to temptation and themselves become aggressors. In the case of Bishop Waso of Liège[2] we are told that he took part in the defence of his city, conducting operations but without bearing arms personally and without neglecting his spiritual duties. He is therefore praised by his biographer as being a Gregory the Great in his episcopal function, but a Judas Maccabaeus in his warlike exploits. Pope Gregory VII, whose contribution to the crusading idea is rated highly by Erdmann,[3] likewise makes appeal to Old Testament authority when he writes to Rudolf von Rheinfelden and the Saxons, requesting them to offer their bodies in the defence of the Church and of their freedom against Henry IV as a wall in the house of Israel.[4] The same reference to Ezech. 13. 5 occurs with Bernhard von Konstanz,[5] who defends the necessity of a holy war by a variety of arguments, including the suggestion that all members of the Church, laymen as well as clergy, should be prepared to defend the law of the Church, the ones with a physical and the others with a spiritual sword, like a wall before the house of Israel.

Amongst the polemical authors stimulated by the policy of Pope Gregory VII Manegold von Lautenbach justified warfare against Henry IV on the grounds that he and his followers are so manifestly more detestable than the pagans that as little blame

[1] *Miracles de St Benoît* (ed. E. de Certain), v, 192 ff. Discussed by Erdmann, *op. cit.* p. 57.

[2] See *Anselmi Gesta episcoporum Leodiensium*, c. 54–6 (*MGH* SS vii, 221 ff.). Discussed by Erdmann, *op. cit.* pp. 65 f.

[3] *Op. cit.* pp. 134 ff.

[4] See Erdmann, *op. cit.* p. 156.

[5] *MGH* Libelli i, 483, 10 f.; Erdmann, *op. cit.* pp. 221 f.

The Millstätter Exodus

attaches to the Christian who kills one of them as to the believer who kills a pagan, a declared enemy of the Church.[1] He justifies this need for war by reference to known Old Testament examples, including the Maccabees.[2] Anselm of Lucca, another supporter of the Gregorian claims against the Emperor, earned by his organisation of warfare against the imperial party the title of a David doing battle with Goliath,[3] just as he is also said to have encouraged Italian warriors to emulate the deeds of Judas Maccabaeus.[4] Another supporter of Hildebrandine policy, the knight Erlembald who took part in the *pataria*, is also described by Bonizo of Sutri as having led the army of God in these battles as another Judas Maccabaeus.[5] Such Old Testament examples are more easily acceptable whenever (as was the case with the *Ludwigslied*) the opponents are not simply sinful Christians, but pagans, for here the contrast between the Chosen People and the Gentiles will be more obvious. Erdmann refers to a poem celebrating the campaign conducted in 1087 by the city of Pisa against the pagans in North Africa.[6] The campaign was executed in the same manner as a crusade proper and we accordingly find, amongst other elements in the poem, numerous comparisons with events and personages of the Old Testament: for example, Gideon and Judas Maccabaeus, David and Goliath or the liberation of Israel from Egypt. This expedition, conceived as a battle fought by Christ against the enemies of God, derives justification from the force of the Israelite model, from the fact that God is felt to preside over this war in just the same way as He had directed the wars of Israel.

We may conclude this brief survey of some of the ways in which the emergent crusading idea was given a religious sanction

[1] *MGH* Libelli I, 381, 33 ff.
[2] *MGH* Libelli I, 399, 7 ff.; Erdmann, *op. cit.* p. 218.
[3] Rangerius of Lucca, vv. 37 ff. (*MGH* SS xxx, II, 1157 f.); Erdmann, *Die Entstehung des Kreuzzugsgedankens*, p. 223.
[4] *Ibid.* vv. 3659 ff. (p. 1234).
[5] *Liber ad amicum* VII (*MGH* Libelli I, 604, 40 f.). See Erdmann, *op. cit.* p. 231.
[6] The poem is edited by F. Schneider in *Fünfundzwanzig lateinische weltliche Rhythmen aus der Frühzeit*, pp. 34 ff. See Erdmann, *op. cit.* p. 273.

by the force of the Old Testament example by considering two benedictions quoted by Erdmann,[1] the one used with reference to a military banner and the other for the army itself. The first text[2] requests that Christ's assistance be granted through the intermediacy of the archangel Michael and all the heavenly powers, quoting as precedents the blessings granted to Abraham when he triumphed over the five kings and to David in the victorious battles he delivered in Christ's name. The banner which is to be blessed is seen as being used in the defence of the Church *contra hostilem rabiem* and the warriors who follow it are described as *fideles et defensores populi Dei*. In other words, the Church is here equated with the *populus Dei* so that the military assistance afforded to Abraham and David (who is even described as fighting on behalf of Christ, not of God) is now requested as a blessing to be conferred upon their spiritual successors. A similar conjunction of the two themes of the holy war and the *populus Dei* is to be encountered in the second blessing.[3] Here it is God who is addressed, but it is said that the army which is to be blessed by the gift of victory will not attribute its success to its own strength, but will recognise that it owes it to Christ who triumphed

[1] *Op. cit.* Appendix I, p. 333 and p. 334.

[2] 'Inclina, domine Jesu, salvator omnium et redemptor, aures tuae pietatis ad praeces nostrae humilitatis et per interventum beati Michaelis archangeli tui omniumque caelestium virtutum praesta nobis auxilium dexterae tuae, ut sicut benedixisti Abraham adversus quinque reges triumphantem atque David regem in tui nominis laude triumphales congressus exercentem, ita benedicere et sanctificare digneris vexillum hoc, quod ob defensionem sanctae ecclesiae contra hostilem rabiem defertur, quatinus in nomine tuo fideles et defensores populi Dei illud sequentes per virtutem sanctae crucis triumphum et victoriam se ex hostibus adquisisse laetentur. Qui cum patre et spiritu sancto.'

[3] 'Prebe, Domine, misericordiae tuae opem exercitui nostro et sub aeris claritate presta eis optatum proficiscendi auxilium, et sicut Israheli properanti ex Egypto securitatis tribuisti munimen, ita populo tuo in prelium pergenti lucis auctorem dirige angelum, qui eos die noctuque ab omni adversitate defendat. Sit eis itinerandi sine labore profectus, ubique providus eventus, meatus sine formidine, conversatio sine fastidio, moderata fragilitas sine metu, fortitudo sine terrore, copia rerum et preliandi recta voluntas, et cum tuo angelo duce victor extiterit, non suis tribuat viribus, sed ipsi victori Christo, filio tuo, gratias referat de triumpho, qui humilitate suae passionis de morte mortisque principe in cruce triumphavit.'

on the Cross.[1] The Old Testament parallel is provided by the way in which it is requested that, just as God gave His protection to Israel when they set forth from Egypt, He should also give it to His people setting forth for battle ('populo tuo in prelium pergenti'). Here the concept of the *populus Dei* has been narrowed down to the particular meaning of 'the Christian army', rather than 'Christendom' at large, but what concerns us is the fact that the employment of this term in a Christian context presupposes the conviction that the God who stood guard over the exodus of Israel from Egypt will grant a similar protection to His new Chosen People as they set forth for battle. These two benediction formulas show us that both the Old Testament concepts with which we have been concerned, the idea of the holy war and the *populus Dei*, form one unified concept in their medieval continuation, for God grants victory to the Christian army only because they defend (or are equated with) His Chosen People and this people addresses its prayers for victory to the God who assisted Israel only because of the conviction of its election by God.

In his investigation of the origins of the crusading idea Erdmann paid attention to the testimony of vernacular literature only peripherally.[2] Much work still remains to be done in this field, but for our present purposes it is sufficient to point out some of the ways in which the heroic mentality of early twelfth-century knightly literature[3] could be justified by reference to the example of the Jews of the Old Testament. It is this well-established precedent that largely contributes towards making the theme of warfare, as long as it is waged with a Christian end in view, *literaturfähig* as it had not been before. This point was first made by J. Bédier, who was led by general as well as detailed similarities between the Old Testament and the *chansons de geste* to include

[1] This point constitutes a close parallel to the distinction we saw above in the *Millstätter Exodus* (p. 169) between the Israelites' *ére* and the *ubirmuot* or *ruom* of their pagan enemies.

[2] *Entstehung des Kreuzzugsgedankens*, pp. 263 ff. See also P. Rousset, *Les origines et les caractères de la première croisade*, pp. 110 ff.

[3] By 'knightly literature' in the present context I mean literature intended for a knightly audience, not necessarily written by a knightly author.

the example of Jewish history amongst the formative elements of French heroic literature. As a general similarity, for example, he comments on the fact that the story of Judas Maccabaeus contains all the essential themes that recur in the Guillaume cycle.[1] As examples of more detailed parallels[2] he emphasises that Charles the Great in the *Chanson de Roland* is depicted not so much as a baron or even as a saint, but primarily as the leader of God's Chosen People, reigning over France like Saul over Israel, but also as a priest, like David[3] or Moses. His legendary old age confers upon him the majesty of a biblical king, God speaks directly to him in his dreams, and in battle he is assisted by an angel of God or by the way in which the sun stands still in answer to his prayers. That this equation of French heroic literature with Old Testament examples is not the result of chance or merely the subjective impression of the modern critic is revealed by the way in which these Old Testament allusions become even more frequent in the German version of the *Chanson de Roland*[4] and by the way in which Dante, when describing the warrior-saints in Paradise, refers to Joshua and Judas Maccabaeus in the same context as Charles the Great and Roland or Guillaume and Rainouart.[5]

Something similar can be shown for early twelfth-century German literature, for many of the works which deal with an Old Testament theme transpose the events narrated so clearly into the twelfth-century present that the warfare waged by the Hebrews acquires an immediate significance for the knightly audience.[6] We have seen that this technique, which is identical

---

[1] J. Bédier, *Les légendes épiques*, IV, 463.   [2] *Ibid.* pp. 458 ff.

[3] This particular comparison is all the more telling in view of the fact that the historical Charles the Great had been given the title of David by his court circle. Bédier, *Les légendes épiques*, p. 439, n. 2, quotes G. Paris, *Histoire poétique de Charlemagne*, p. 34, on this point: 'N'est-ce pas déjà un trait de l'histoire poétique de Charlemagne que ce déguisement où lui et les siens cachaient leur personnalité barbare sous le masque des plus illustres anciens? Le roi qui tuait mille Philistins et qui chantait le Seigneur sur la harpe, tel était l'idéal qu'avouait l'empereur en prenant le nom de David, et l'image qu'il laissa de lui dans le souvenir de la postérité ressemble en plus d'un trait à celle que le peuple hébreu s'était faite du fils d'Isaïe.'   [4] See pp. 225 f.   [5] *Par.* XVIII, 37 ff.

[6] The relevance of these poems to the crusading experience of the twelfth century has been particularly emphasised by Schwietering, *LG*, 71 ff.

with that employed by the author of the *Millstätter Exodus*, is ignored by the earlier author of the *Wiener Genesis* in its military aspect because he rejected warfare as a welcome Christian theme. It is also largely absent from the *Vorauer Bücher Mosis*,[1] yet this is due not simply to the markedly New Testament conception of a loving God that pervades this work, but also to the technique of allegorical interpretation adopted by the author, for this means that he has as little interest in any military encounters depicted in his source as in the other events of historical reality whose main significance for the author lies in the material they provide for his allegorical method.[2] The close conjunction which we find in this work of an allegorical technique together with a failure to exploit the military implications of the theme corresponds with what we saw of Origen, for whom the historical events of the Bible were likewise so much material for his allegorical technique and who saw in this method of interpretation the only acceptable way of coping with the unwelcome military implications of the Old Testament.[3] A similiar employment of the typological method accounts for the absence of military allusions from the poem *Babylonische Gefangenschaft*.

Apart from these cases the twelfth-century poems dealing with the Old Testament all transpose their themes into the medieval present and emphasise their military implications. Admittedly, the *Lob Salomons* constitutes at once an apparent exception, for, even though the Jewish king is interpreted as God or Christ and is thus equipped with a relevance to the present which would otherwise have been missing,[4] it is his wisdom, wealth and his love of peace[5] that are particularly emphasised. This emphasis

[1] Largely, but not entirely absent. See 62. 16 ff. for an example of the way in which a military description was unavoidable once the author had chosen to follow the biblical Exodus beyond the point where the Millstatt author had decided to break off.

[2] It is of some relevance here that the author probably composed this work not for a knightly, but for a clerical audience. See Ehrismann, *LG*, II, 92 and Schwietering, *LG*, 69.   [3] See pp. 129 and 210, n. 3.

[4] Vv. 209 ff. Some of the motifs selected for inclusion by the author must also have appealed to a contemporary lay audience (see Ehrismann, *LG*, II, 101).

[5] Vv. 239 ff.

on his love of peace is derived from the biblical example of I Paral. 22. 7 ff., but a short reference to Solomon's military power[1] rests on II Paral. 9. 25. Nor is the contradiction between these two aspects of Solomon's authority an insoluble one, for Erdmann has shown the intimate connection between the medieval institution of the *pax Dei* and the crusades,[2] whereby on the one hand the need to enforce this peace (by means of arms, if necessary) led the Church into closer touch with warfare and, on the other hand, the proclamation of a crusade presupposed (in theory and also to a considerable extent in practice)[3] internal peace in Western Europe. In other words, the stress in this poem on Solomon's love of peace need not contradict his military power. Precisely the same is true of the account by Andreas of Fleury of the battles fought on behalf of the *pax Dei* instituted by Archbishop Aimo of Bourges[4] (where, as we have seen,[5] the clerical army is regarded as a new Israel) or of the apparent contradiction, within the *Millstätter Exodus* itself, between Moses' command to maintain peace amongst the Israelites (vv. 300 ff.) and his readiness to show violence to the Egyptian overseer (vv. 275 ff.).

The justification of Christian warfare suggested by an Old Testament precedent is provided most strikingly by those poems that deal with the themes of Judith and of the Maccabees, themes which, as Erdmann's material makes clear, were frequently adduced for precisely this purpose. The *Ältere Judith* sees the

[1] Vv. 173 ff. and 190.

[2] *Die Entstehung des Kreuzzugsgedankens*, pp. 53 ff.

[3] As examples of the theoretical awareness of the close relationship between internal peace and the crusades we may quote some of the remarks attributed to Pope Urban II in connection with the First Crusade: cf. Baldricus, *Historia Ierosolimitana*, I, 4 (*RHC*, IV, 15: 'Haec ideo, fratres, dicimus, ut et manus homicidas a fraterna nece contineatis; et pro fidei domesticis vos exteris nationibus opponatis; et pro vestra Hierusalem decertetis') or Robertus Monachus, *Historia Iherosolimitana*, I, I (*RHC*, III, 728: 'Cessent igitur inter vos odia, conticescant jurgia, bella quiescant et totius controversiae dissensiones sopiantur. Viam sancti Sepulchri incipite, terram illam nefariae genti auferte'). As an example of the situation in practice see what A. Waas, *Geschichte der Kreuzzüge*, I, 186 f., says on the preparations for the Third Crusade.

[4] Erdmann, *op. cit.* p. 57.   [5] See above, p. 215.

conflict between the Israelites and Holofernes as one between those who place their trust in God and those who fight against Him,[1] so that it can be regarded more in its timeless significance as a war between those who acknowledge Christ and the pagans.[2] This parallel between an event taken from Jewish history and the medieval present is further strengthened by lexical and stylistic means,[3] as a result of which the central theme of the poem (the liberation of those who believe in God from the heathen)[4] acquires a topical relevance to the age of the crusades,[5] especially welcome because of its suggestion that, with God's assistance, even a weak woman can defeat the pagan leader. The same conviction of the reliability of God's protection of those who obey Him pervades the *Jüngere Judith*. Again it is the pagans against whom these believers must be protected, but although the term *heidenisk*[6] occurs frequently the conflict is not sketched so explicitly in terms of Christendom and heathendom as was the case in the earlier version. Nevertheless, such a conflict is certainly implied: not merely by the use of specifically knightly terms or of words taken from the traditional heroic vocabulary,[7] but also by the introductory observation that Christ has given us many examples in the case of the Hebrews of the way in which He protects those who obey Him against all their foes, but inflicts punishment on them for their disobedience in the form of defeat.[8] The force of

---

[1] Judith is therefore characterised by the standing phrase 'dû zi gote wol digiti' (vv. 144, 168, 182 and 204) and of Holofernes it is said: 'der streit widir goti gerni' (v. 86), a general characterisation which reveals the similarity of his function to that of Pharaoh in the *Millstätter Exodus*, to whom Moses says: 'wande ir wider got strebet | al die wîle die ir lebet' (vv. 1659 f.).

[2] The term *heidin* is used of the Jews' opponents (vv. 104, 152 and 198), whilst the Jews' confession of Christ (vv. 127 ff.) is taken over bodily from the *Drei Jünglinge im Feuerofen*, 51 ff.

[3] Cf. the use of such terms as *biscof* and *burcgrâvi* and the details of style and motif enumerated by Ehrismann, *LG*, II, 105 and 107.

[4] Vv. 218 f.

[5] See Ehrismann, *LG*, II, 106.

[6] E.g. 128. 25; 129. 4, 24, 26.

[7] Ehrismann, *LG*, II, 109 f., gives some references for the use of feudal terms (e.g. *uûrsten, herzogen unde grâuen; rîter; holden*) and of heroic vocabulary (e.g. *helde; manigen chŷnen man; walblût; uolchwîch*) in this work.

[8] 127. 16 ff.

these examples is clearly that what was true of the Hebrews (even in the case of a *blodeʒ wibelin*)[1] is still true of Christians, so that the employment of contemporary knightly or heroic terms, like the expansion of battle-scenes,[2] demonstrates that knightly warfare against the pagans is not merely as justified as it was in the case of this Old Testament example, but that it will likewise be crowned with victory because of God's protection, as long as it is conducted in the right spirit of Christian obedience.

In the *Makkabäer* fragment there is no suggestion (at least in what is preserved) of a conflict between Jews and pagans, but the very choice of subject-matter reveals an awareness that this Old Testament theme closely resembled German heroic tradition in several particulars:[3] Tryphon is the disloyal vassal,[4] Simon is another Hagen who has foreseen the tragic outcome,[5] and the lament for the dead,[6] coupled with the wish for vengeance,[7] is a typical motif of heroic literature. The result is that, although this fragment shows no trace of the idea of the holy war, the Hebrew and native heroic traditions are felt to have so much in common that an episode from the Old Testament can be readily depicted in terms of heroic literature. The parallel with the technique employed by our Millstatt author is an obvious one. On the other hand, *Die drei Jünglinge im Feuerofen* is pervaded by a sense of the antithesis between pagans and Christians, but does not see this in terms of a military conflict. The biblical story has been modified so as to imply not merely that the Israelites were the only ones to acknowledge God before the coming of Christ,[8] but more particularly that it was for Christ that the three heroes suffered martyrdom[9] and that they wished to convert the pagan king Nebuchadnezzar.[10] Moreover, it is the God whom they confess that saves them in His omnipotence, a fact which deeply

---

[1] 128. 3.
[2] See, for example, Ehrismann, *LG*, II, 109, on the expansion of the biblical phrase in Judith 1. 5 ('pugnavit contra Arphaxad, et obtinuit eum') to the epic description of a battle in thirteen lines (130. 15 ff.).
[3] Ehrismann, *LG*, II, 116.
[4] Vv. 99 ff. (cf. 110 f.).
[5] V. 67.
[6] Vv. 33 ff.
[7] Vv. 51 ff.
[8] Vv. 1 ff.
[9] Vv. 49 ff.
[10] Vv. 38 ff.

impresses the pagan witnesses of the miracle.[1] What results is a Christian martyrs' legend, but one which derives its appeal from the contemporary experience of the crusades[2] (a fact which is revealed externally by the way in which the MS conflates this poem with the *Ältere Judith*). The battle between pagans and Israelites (seen as Christians) and the martyrdom of three Jews (depicted as Christians) who seek to convert these pagans are different facets of the same contemporary experience. In either case the protection which God had once afforded the Jews is the guarantee that He will save the Christians.

In one other Old Testament work of twelfth-century German literature, the *Tobias* of the Pfaffe Lambrecht, we find no traces of the utilisation of Old Testament material to provide a precedent for Christian warfare. Nonetheless, the work possesses an indirect importance for us, since it shows that the author who later composed the *Alexanderlied* was also interested in Old Testament themes. This is also revealed by the Old Testament allusions in the Vorau version of the *Alexanderlied* itself, often inserted where the original offered no obvious opportunity.[3] That this Old Testament background was evident to the twelfth century is best shown by the way in which this work is included in the Vorau MS as part of a cycle of Old Testament works extending from the *Vorauer Bücher Mosis* to the story of Alexander's empire, important in this context because it provides the historical background to the latest events recorded in the Old Testament, the battles of the Maccabees.[4] The role which Alexan-

[1] Vv. 63 ff. and 73 ff.

[2] Schwietering, *LG*, 73. Cf. also the manner in which Charles the Great in the *Rolandslied* appeals to the precedent of the divine help offered to these three martyrs (vv. 7913 f.) in his prayer for assistance and victory in his holy war against the pagans.

[3] This point has been elaborated by Schwietering, *LG*, 74 f. Examples are vv. 695 f., 797 ff., 1461 f. and 1470 ff., where the Near Eastern places involved in Alexander's wars of conquest are used as the occasion to refer to well-known Old Testament events. Elsewhere the example of Old Testament personages is imposed upon the events narrated as a criterion by which the author may judge his hero: 61 ff., 1261 ff.

[4] That this was known to the author is confirmed by his remark in vv. 11 f.

der has to play in this biblical view of history is laid down by the sequence of world-empires prophesied in Daniel's dream,[1] so that his defeat of Darius signifies the transition from the empire of the Persians to that of the Greeks. Alexander is therefore, although quite unwittingly, just as much an instrument of God, helping forward the fulfilment of His plans, as were the Assyrian or Babylonian conquerors of Israel. The military virtues of Alexander and even the harsh vengeance he exacts from those whom he defeats (no matter whether the author regards them positively or negatively)[2] are qualities where the Old Testament ethos and the heroic ideal agree with one another, so that the biblical role attributed to Alexander is the occasion for the author to employ the traditional heroic vocabulary and occasionally to display his acquaintance with heroic literature.[3] That the interpretation of Alexander's function as a biblical one, so that he acts as the scourge of God, is correct has also been made likely by a recent analysis of his role in the *Alexanderlied* of Rudolf von Ems, where his military exploits are explained by the fact that he acts as *gotes geisel*.[4]

A last twelfth-century example of the fusion of Old Testament and native heroic ideals as contributions to the new conception of crusading warfare on behalf of God is provided by the *Rolandslied* which in this respect continues the work of the author of the

[1] Vv. 473 ff. On this see Sitte, *Die Datierung von Lamprechts Alexander*, pp. 93 f. See also *ZfdPh*, xv, 222 ff.

[2] The positive aspects of Alexander's military role are stressed by Schwietering, *LG*, 76, whereas Sitte, *op. cit.* pp. 109 ff., pays more attention to the possibility that Lamprecht was critical of his hero.

[3] A general discussion of Lamprecht's use of heroic terminology is given by Sitte, *op. cit.* pp. 79 ff. The author's acquaintance with native heroic literature is also shown by the comparison in vv. 1321 ff. and also (if we follow Droege, *ZfdA*, LI, 199 f.) by the passage vv. 934 ff.

[4] R. Wisbey, *Das Alexanderbild Rudolfs von Ems*, Frankfurt dissertation, 1956. See especially vv. 10051 ff. in Rudolf's work, where Alexander's function as an instrument of God is described with reference to the Samaritans as a punishment for their secession from the Jews. This whole problem is discussed by Wisbey, pp. 31 ff. That Rudolf should have depicted Alexander as acting wittingly on behalf of God (even if for the wrong motives) distinguishes his work from the Vorau epic, but both at least agree in seeing him as the scourge of God.

Chanson de Roland. Whereas the relationship between the Hebrew and heroic traditions had been so close in the twelfth-century works dealing with an Old Testament theme that heroic motifs and terms could be incorporated into biblical works, the position is reversed in the *Rolandslied*, for now it is the case that Old Testament motifs are imposed upon a heroic subject-matter. Some of these biblical allusions may derive from the French source, but this is not true of all of them, so that this conception of his Christian warriors in terms of their Hebrew predecessors is not one which Konrad has simply taken over mechanically from his source. Archbishop Turpin prays for assistance against the pagan hosts to the God who destroyed Pharaoh's army in the Red Sea[1] and Gideon is invoked as testimony of the reality of God's protection, even against all odds.[2] Like Jehovah the God of the *Rolandslied* performs miracles so that nature may come to the assistance of the Christian warriors[3] (some of these miracles corresponding to Old Testament counterparts).[4] He maintains contact with Charles as His chosen instrument by means of an angel as intermediary or by appearing to him in a dream.[5] The Christian God is now essentially a warlike deity, as was the God of the Old Testament, and He is felt to be engaged in the battle which He conducts himself.[6] Similarly, the vengeful nature of the Old Testament God is reflected in the emperor's prayer to God to assist him in exacting vengeance from the heathen,[7] and the spirit of unbending harshness in the face of one's foes is not simply a warrior attribute native to the heroic tradition, but a quality which is raised to the status of a Christian virtue because of the Old Testament precedent and because the wrathful inflexibility of such a God imposes the need for corresponding qualities

[1] Vv. 5744 ff.
[2] Vv. 5012 ff., 8416 ff. Cf. also the appeals to the example of Daniel (vv. 8180 ff.) and of David (vv. 8847 ff.).
[3] E.g. vv. 4452 ff., 5625 ff., 8563 ff.
[4] E.g. vv. 7017 ff. (cf. Jos. 10. 12 f.).
[5] E.g. vv. 52 ff., 7000 ff., 3030 ff., 7084 ff.
[6] E.g. vv. 55 ff., 1797 ff., 4797 f., 4846 f.
[7] Vv. 6990 ff. (cf. also the angel's reply, vv. 7014 ff., and its counterpart in Ps. 110. 1).

upon those who serve Him. In details as well as in its general attitude this work represents within the specific context of the crusades a close association of heroic ideals with the military outlook of the Old Testament. In this it demonstrates how the Hebrew conception of the holy war persisted in the Middle Ages certainly through to the twelfth century as one of the most important precedents used in justification of Christian warfare.

VIII

THE RELEVANCE OF THE BOOK OF EXODUS TO THE CRUSADES

IN the preceding chapter we saw that medieval authors, up to the twelfth century, regarded a Christian army fighting in defence of Christendom as justified because of Old Testament precedents and because of the conviction that Christendom was a new Israel, so that what God had done to assist the wars of the Jews in His name He would assuredly also do in the case of His people of the New Covenant. This general conclusion as to the way in which the Old Testament could be utilised to justify military undertakings of the medieval present is in close agreement with the more detailed results of our investigation of the positive innovations in the Millstatt epic in chapter VI, where we saw that our author placed particular emphasis on the military implications of the Exodus story and took care to depict his Old Testament personages in feudal or knightly terms. This agreement invites us to inquire what the Millstatt author's precise intention was in giving such prominence to the theme of warfare (which, however recurrent it may be in the Old Testament, is certainly no more than faintly implicit in the first fifteen chapters of the biblical Exodus) and in treating it with topical reference to the knightly warfare of his own day. What purpose did he conceive this form of warfare as serving? Why did he choose to illustrate it in the story of *Exodus* in particular?

To answer these questions we must narrow down the field of our inquiry and concern ourselves no longer with the general relevance of the Old Testament tradition at large to medieval warfare, but instead with the relevance of the Book of Exodus to crusading warfare in particular.[1] This means that we must restrict

[1] The reasons why it is crusading warfare in particular that concerns us will emerge in the course of the argument of the present chapter.

228

our inquiry in two respects. On the one hand we must ask why it was the Book of Exodus, rather than any other biblical book, that appealed to the Millstatt author as an opportunity to illustrate his conception of Christian warfare. That such an appeal could be exercised by this book was apparent in the preceding chapter, where we saw that an *oratio pro exercitu* compared the Christian army with Israel setting forth from Egypt[1] or that a poem celebrating a campaign against the pagans of North Africa should cite, amongst such obvious Hebrew precedents as David, Gideon and Judas Maccabaeus, the example of Israel's liberation from Egypt.[2] Now our task will be not merely to determine that this biblical book was quoted as a model, but rather to establish why it should have been used for this purpose instead of the more obviously military examples provided elsewhere in the Old Testament.

On the other hand, we shall also have to establish how the concept of the *populus Dei* could itself be progressively narrowed down so that it denoted not merely Christendom (or one Christian people) as the new Israel (this was clearly its earliest function), but also the Christian army fighting in defence of Christendom and, more particularly, the crusading army. Again, we have already encountered examples of each of these three usages. Thus, the equation between *populus Dei* and Christendom is present in the cases where Ezech. 13. 5 is adduced as a justification of Christian warfare,[3] for here the Christian warriors are expressly seen as a *murus pro domo Israel,* so that Israel denotes the Christendom they protect by force of arms. The same is true when the benediction formula for a military banner sees the banner as being used in defence of the Church and the warriors as *fideles et defensores populi Dei*[4] or when the *Ludwigslied* depicts Lewis's Frankish warriors as fighting on behalf of God's Chosen People, the Franks.[5] Here admittedly the wider term (Christendom) has been replaced by a narrower (the Franks), but we can be sure that in practice even the passages which equate the *populus Dei*

[1] The passage is quoted above, p. 217, n. 3.   [2] See p. 216.
[3] Cf. p. 215, nn. 4 and 5.   [4] See p. 217, n. 2.   [5] Vv. 23 f.

with Christendom could be employed, if necessary, to justify warfare by one part of Christendom against another. In any case, what is important is the fact that in none of these examples is the concept *populus Dei* used of the army itself, but only of the Christian community it is to defend. The change in the use of this idea, whereby it comes to refer to the Christian army, is present in the account of Archbishop Aimo's campaign against breakers of the peace and oppressors of the Church, for it is the people in arms whom he summons to impose his will upon his adversaries that is described as a new Israel putting its foes to flight with God's assistance.[1] Another example is furnished by Erdmann's *oratio pro exercitu*,[2] for here it is the army itself (*exercitu nostro*) which is seen as God's people setting out for battle (*populo tuo in prelium pergenti*) and therefore compared with Israel departing from Egypt.

More important is the third stage in the restriction of scope undergone by the concept *populus Dei*: its application to the crusading army in particular. This can best be shown in the case of those works, dealing with a crusading theme or at least placed in a crusading context, in which the Old Testament precedent of Israel provides the justification of Christian warfare because of the (often unvoiced) conviction that Christendom is the continuation of Israel. The earliest and most significant example of this is the *Chanson de Roland*, where the Old Testament references serve as a background to military scenes which owe as much to the crusading experience of the present as they do to the historical events of the reign of Charles the Great himself. It is therefore possible, even without accepting Bédier's views on the genesis of the epic, to agree with his observation: 'Dans la mesure où les croisades sont explicables, la *Chanson de Roland* l'est aussi; elle reste mystérieuse dans la mesure où les croisades restent mystérieuses'[3] or with his remark: 'pour expliquer la naissance de la *Chanson*, il faut évoquer. . .toutes les concordances et toutes les harmonies. . .entre l'esprit du poème et l'esprit des croisades,

---

[1] See p. 215. [2] See p. 217, n. 3.
[3] *Les légendes épiques*, IV, 462.

croisades d'Espagne, croisades de Terre Sainte.'[1] Yet if this fusion of Old Testament ideas with the Christian concept of a holy war takes place in the French epic within the context of the crusades, then this is even more clearly the case with the German *Rolandslied.* The German author emphasises at the outset of his work (and repeats subsequently at intervals) that his Christian warriors took the cross and fought under this sign,[2] a detail which is missing from the French work. The conflict which he depicts is not therefore, as in the *Chanson,* at least in part a secular encounter, but is seen metaphysically as part of the struggle between two religions, so that the Christian warriors are shown as dying as martyrs.[3] Just how far these and other details contribute to a picture of Christian warfare which is essentially that of the crusades and which also has much in common with the ideal of the *nova militia* praised by St Bernard of Clairvaux for its realisation in the crusading order of the Knights Templar has been shown recently by Wentzlaff-Eggebert.[4] Although there may be many points where Konrad's ideal differs in some respect from that of the crusading knights it is clear that his thought owes much to this contemporary experience and that his description of those chosen by God for the privilege of serving Him confines them to

[1] *Chanson de Roland. Commentaires,* p. 62. See also H. W. Klein in *NS* (1956), pp. 265 ff. Against this view of Bédier's, see the argument conducted by R. Menéndez Pidal, *La Chanson de Roland et la tradition épique des Francs,* especially p. 243: 'On entend par croisade, à partir du XIe siècle, une guerre provoquée sous l'impulsion de sentiments essentiellement religieux, et proclamée par le Pape avec des indulgences ou la rémission des péchés pour les guerriers qui, animés par ces sentiments, trouvent la mort au combat. Rien de tout cela n'existe dans la *Chanson de Roland.*' For a restatement of the rival view, however, see P. Rousset, *Les origines et les caractères de la première croisade,* pp. 110 ff. I am not persuaded of the impossibility of combining these two viewpoints, since crusading elements (in however attenuated a form) could well have been added to the theme of Roland as a last accretion to material handed down from the ninth century. On this reconciliation of the 'traditionalist' with the 'individualist' view see p. 368, n. 4. Cf. also the remarks of P. Le Gentil, *La Chanson de Roland,* pp. 82 ff., and in *Chanson de Geste und höfischer Roman,* pp. 9 ff.

[2] Vv. 167, 248 (cf. 3332 f., 4979 f., 7475 f.).

[3] E.g. 3252 ff., 3407 ff.

[4] *Kreuzzugsdichtung des Mittelalters,* pp. 82 ff.

the military role of *milites Dei*, a term which, in addition to its traditional metaphorical meaning, is used here in the concrete sense of those who take up arms on behalf of God against the Saracens.

We saw in the last chapter that the experience of the crusades had also probably left its imprint on the *Ältere Judith* and accounted for the manner in which the historical event in question had been transposed into terms intelligible to the twelfth-century present.[1] Similarly, the crusading elements in the *Kaiserchronik* (the crusade of Heraclius with its reference to the example of the Israelites, the crusade of Godfrey of Bouillon and the abrupt conclusion of the whole work in connection with the ill-fated Second Crusade) suggest that here too the elaboration of the theme of Christian warfare (with its significant appeal to an Old Testament example)[2] owes much to the Second Crusade and its impact on Germany.[3] It has also been argued that the *Alexanderlied*, with its Near Eastern setting and allusions to Old Testament events, is the result of French literary influence on Germany, particularly in the area of Regensburg, at the time of the Second Crusade.[4] The manner in which Christian warfare can be justified by the Old Testament example and the ideals of heroic literature be exploited for a Christian purpose as part of the crusading movement is best confirmed by the passage from Dante which we considered earlier.[5] In addition to his mention of Israelite warriors (Joshua and Judas Maccabaeus) and of those from heroic tradition (Charles the Great, Roland, Guillaume and Rainouart) Dante also includes amongst his warrior saints Godfrey of Bouillon and Robert Guiscard:[6] the one a leader on the First Crusade and later ruler of Jerusalem, the other a Norman conqueror of Sicily who happens to have received his lands as a

---

[1] See p. 222. [2] Vv. 11208 ff. See also pp. 344 ff.

[3] Cf. Wentzlaff-Eggebert, *op. cit.* pp. 60 ff.

[4] Sitte, *Die Datierung von Lamprechts Alexander*, pp. 122 ff., although I disagree with what this author has to say here (and also pp. 29 f.) on the absence of any crusading traces in German literature of the early twelfth century. On this problem see below, pp. 296 ff.

[5] See p. 219, n. 5. [6] *Par.* XVIII, 47 f.

fief from the Pope as a guarantee of divine protection in his wars with the Saracens.[1] Dante's threefold grouping of the saints he mentions in this passage reflects the way in which the medieval Church sought to justify warfare by an appeal to three types of war waged on God's behalf: those of the Israelites, the warriors of heroic literature (in so far as these could be depicted as giving battle to the pagans)[2] and the crusaders themselves.

There is, however, another type of evidence to suggest an intimate connection between the wars of Israel as the Chosen People of God and the crusades. It is provided by the way in which an Old Testament book can be rendered into the vernacular (whether French or German) in knightly style, but in either case intended for the consumption of one of the knightly orders that emerged during the crusades. The French example concerns the Book of Judges,[3] narrated in the manner of a knightly epic, but equipped with a prologue which makes it clear that this translation was intended for the order of the Templars. The knightly heroism which informs the work (vv. 40 ff.: 'Ou molt porront grant bien trover | de cens et de bele voudie | Qu'afiert a lor chevalerie') is therefore the point where the Israelites of the Old Testament could be made intelligible not just to medieval knighthood, but particularly to that knightly order of the crusades which had constituted the ideal of the *nova militia* for St Bernard.[4] The German example is the fourteenth-century verse translation, the *Makkabäer*, which Helm[5] has shown to be a work written for the order of Teutonic Knights. This theme had aroused interest

[1] Cf. Erdmann, *Die Entstehung des Kreuzzugsgedankens*, p. 120.

[2] Rousset, *Les origines et les caractères de la première croisade*, p. 133, aptly concludes his chapter on the connections between the *chansons de geste* and the crusade by distinguishing the epics adduced by him in support of these connections from the *épopée féodale* in which the secular exploits of a non-crusading knighthood, attacked as sinful by Urban II, are celebrated.

[3] See M. Melville, *La vie des Templiers*, pp. 81 ff. and P. Mayer, *R*, XVII, 133 ff.

[4] Significantly, the Hebrew idea of election is used of the Templars in this prologue (vv. 46 f.: 'Qui ses eslis chevaliers sont | Et de sa privée maisnée') as it is also in the Rule of the Order (see the edition of H. de Curzon, para. 1, p. 12).

[5] See his edition of the work, p. lxxxii, and also K. Helm and W. Ziesemer, *Die Literatur des Deutschen Ritterordens*, pp. 96 ff.

in twelfth-century Germany, probably because of its topicality in the first century of the crusades, but was almost entirely ignored in the poetry of the late Middle Ages. Here it is treated again as part of the literature composed for this knightly order, mainly because the Teutonic Knights regarded themselves as akin to the Maccabees, an attitude which, as Helm and Ziesemer have stressed, is expressed almost officially in the order's statutes[1] and is given papal sanction in the bull of Honorius III in which the knights of this order are designated as 'novi sub tempore gratiae Machabei'.[2] The fact that both the French and the German works (however late they may be) owe their existence to the literary needs of two crusading orders lends[3] point to Schwietering's argument[3] that most of the twelfth-century German poems treating an Old Testament theme were prompted by the crusading experience and also to the suggestion of Olschki[4] that the twelfth-century French versions of the more warlike books of the Old Testament were likewise called into being by the overwhelming experience of the conquest of Jerusalem.

From such evidence it is clear that for this period of the Middle Ages the treatment of an Old Testament theme could serve as a justification of Christian warfare at large, but also of the particular type represented by the crusades. If we now seek to establish whether the military innovations of the *Millstätter Exodus* concern warfare at large or whether they are connected with crusading warfare, we are confronted by the difficulty of dating, a problem which has led some to reject out of hand the

[1] The relevant passage is quoted by Helm and Ziesemer (p. 97) from M. Perlbach, *Die Statuten des Deutschen Ordens*, p. 25, 4 ff., where after a reference to Moses, Joshua and David as *die Gotes rittere* the prologue to the statutes continues: 'Wir gedenken ouch des lobelichen strîtes, der wert vor Gote was, der rittere, die dâ heizent Machâbei, wie sterclîche die durch ir ê unde umme den gelouben strîten mit den heiden, die sie twingen wolden, daz sie Gotes verlougenten, unde mit sîner helfe sie sô gar uberwunden unde vertiligeten, daz sie die heiligen stete wider gereinegeten, die sie hêten geunreint, unde den vride macheten wider in dem lande. Disen strîten hat nachgevolget herteclîche dirre heilige ritterlîche orden des spitales sente Marien von dem dûtschen hûse.'

[2] See Helm and Ziesemer, *op. cit.* p. 97.

[3] *LG*, 72 ff.

[4] *LG*, 149.

latter possibility.[1] Of the German works we have mentioned, where Old Testament themes or allusions are exploited in a crusading context, none can be reliably dated before the middle of the twelfth century, whereas the *Millstätter Exodus* falls about 1120.[2] The *Rolandslied*, it is true, is thought by some to have been written about the year 1130, but as long as arguments for the later dating of 1170 continue to be advanced it would be unwise to base any defence of the crusading purpose of the Millstatt author on the still contested evidence of Konrad's work.[3] On the other hand, whilst there is no cause to doubt that the *Ältere Judith* was composed some time in the first third of the century, the crusading atmosphere in this poem is sketched only in general terms and with none of that explicitness which we need if it is to provide any support for the Millstatt epic. The other German works all come after the middle of the twelfth century, so that the *Millstätter Exodus*, if it does contain crusading allusions, would remain isolated in the first half of this century. It is for this reason that Sitte rejects the early dating of the *Rolandslied*, arguing that the crusading idea was so little developed in the Germany of 1130 that it is impossible to conceive of this work being written so early, and that Fliegner dismisses the suggestion that Konrad's ideal of the *miles Dei* may have had forerunners in Germany, particularly in the biblical epics. In other words, if we are to argue that the innovations in the *Millstätter Exodus* and also the author's choice of subject-matter are related not just to the theme of warfare, but to the particular theme of crusading warfare, we must be able to show this without reference to these other twelfth-century works for, although they

[1] E.g. Fliegner, *Geistliches und weltliches Rittertum im Rolandslied*, pp. 32 f., and (following him) Sitte, *Die Datierung von Lamprechts Alexander*, pp. 29 f. We shall return to this objection later (see pp. 296 ff.).

[2] See Pniower, *ZfdA*, xxxiii, 73 ff., and Ehrismann, *LG*, 88. See, however, p. 297, n. 3.

[3] The later dating has been supported recently by A. Hämel, *Sitzungsberichte der bayrischen Akademie der Wissenschaften*, 1950 (1), and by L. Wolff, *PBB* (T), lxxviii, 185 ff. On the other hand new early datings have been proposed by P. Wapnewski, *Euphorion*, xlix, 261 ff. (1145 instead of 1130), and by F. Neumann, *ZfdA*, xci, 295 ff. (1150).

may provide a parallel in the way in which they combine Old Testament themes with the idea of the crusades, they come too late to explain the isolation of the Millstatt work.

We may best approach this problem if we recall a significant fact about those works which combine Old Testament subject-matter with the crusading theme. Whereas some treat an Old Testament theme, but transpose it into the sphere of the crusading present by lexical and stylistic means or by references to native heroic literature (here the *Ältere Judith* is a typical example), with others the converse is the case. The *Rolandslied*, for example, treats a native heroic theme adapted to the idea of the crusades, but imposes upon this medieval material Old Testament references and a religious interpretation which is markedly Old Testament in outlook. The fusion of the two themes of the Old Testament and the crusades can therefore be accomplished either with a biblical subject-matter or with a heroic, crusading theme as the starting-point, so that the two possible approaches complement one another. Much the same can be shown in the case of the *Millstätter Exodus*. We saw that this work treated an Old Testament theme, but described the Israelites in feudal, knightly terms and gave greater emphasis to the military implications of the narrative. The converse to this would be a work in which feudal, knightly warfare of the present (or, more exactly, crusading warfare) was treated in Old Testament terms, as events comparable to those recounted of Israel in the Bible and deriving their significance from this parallel. We do in fact possess many such works, namely in the form of the Latin chronicles of the crusades where the crusaders of the medieval present are depicted in terms of the Israelite wars with the Gentiles. Whereas the Millstatt author transposed Old Testament events into the twelfth century, describing them in terms of knightly warfare, the authors of the various chronicles of the crusades appeal constantly to the examples of the Old Testament when treating their topical theme. The one process complements the other, so that the idea common to both is an attitude which either regards the events of the Old Testament as

The Book of Exodus and the crusades

a precedent for the crusades or conversely interprets the crusades as a continuation of the holy wars of Israel. In discussing this evidence from the chronicles we shall have to limit ourselves to those which record the events of the First Crusade alone. Since the *Millstätter Exodus* was written at a date falling between the First and the Second Crusade, only the evidence of the chronicles dealing with the events following on the year 1096 can be used for our purpose, even though many of the same ideas recur in the accounts of the Second Crusade. For the same reason the evidence of St Bernard's *De laude novae militiae*, although written in the early thirties of the twelfth century, has had to be ignored.[1]

This practice of enhancing the events of the present by relating them to the Old Testament and the history of Israel, which was regularly followed by the chroniclers of the First Crusade, is of course only part of their wish to provide a divine justification for this undertaking[2] and belongs to the wider problem of their seeking authority for the events they narrate from the Bible at large, a problem illuminatingly studied by P. Alphandéry. Nonetheless, it is significant that, although the New Testament can be

---

[1] The problem of the relationship between the Old Testament and the crusading chronicles has been investigated in a stimulating article by P. Alphandéry in *RHR*, xcix, 139 ff., and in greater detail by Rousset, *Les origines et les caractères de la première croisade, passim*. To both of these works I owe a large proportion of the passages from the chronicles which are quoted below. Nonetheless, I have thought fit to quote these passages again, together with others, because of what seems to me to be their extreme relevance to problems of vernacular literature in the twelfth century and because of the way in which most works of literary scholarship appear to ignore the important evidence of these chronicles. Thus, although A. Waas is quite aware of the importance of Rousset's book and the problem with which it deals (see his *Geschichte der Kreuzzüge*, 1, 22, n. 74), Wentzlaff-Eggebert appears to make no reference to it in his survey of German crusading literature. Furthermore, Rousset's work gives such an abundance of references to the chronicles (not always grouped in a manner which is logical or which makes it easy to survey the total problem) that it is necessary to isolate and emphasise those passages in particular which refer to the Old Testament or, more explicitly, to Exodus alone. On the criteria I have applied in grouping this material see pp. 241 f.

[2] Ekkehardus accordingly begins his *Hierosolymita* by stressing the divine origin of the First Crusade (*RHC*, v, 11 A: 'De militiae vel expeditionis causa, quae temporibus nostris non tam humanitus quam divinitus ordinata est...').

237

cited as well as the Old, this happens less often;[1] in just the same way the Gospels are sparingly used by the chroniclers of the First Crusade.[2] This argues a certain preference for the Old Testament when the chroniclers sought biblical authority, a preference which is in no way surprising. From all we have seen in the preceding chapter it is clear that a military campaign waged in the name of God could be most easily justified, on the basis of the concept of the *populus Dei*, by reference to the frequent precedents of the Old Testament, but that, although a similar justification could be extracted from some passages of the New Testament, the difficulties here were much more formidable. Furthermore, although the New Testament itself contains a number of prophetic passages which could be utilised by twelfth-century chroniclers to imply that the events of their day were the fulfilment of these prophecies,[3] this prophetic role is not so characteristic of the New Testament as it is of the Old. Since the New Testament was regarded primarily as the fulfilment of the Old, it is clear that it provided fewer opportunities for this kind of interpretation, whereas the Old Testament was exposed by its very nature to this approach.

We therefore find evidence, as Alphandéry has demonstrated, of a general conviction that the events narrated by the chroniclers derive their significance from their relationship to Old Testament prophecies. Robertus Monachus concludes his account of the First Crusade by twice quoting from Isaiah, on the first occasion to show that the crusaders are the *gens justa* of whom it was said that they were to enter Jerusalem[4] and on the second (where the events of the present are felt to have been foreseen by the prophet: 'Hoc a longe per Isaiam prophetam praedixerat') to demonstrate

---

[1] Alphandéry (*RHR*, xcix, 147) has established that Raimundus de Aguilers, for example, draws all his biblical quotations from the Psalms (with the exception of no more than three references to the New Testament).

[2] *Ibid.* p. 149.

[3] Cf. Alphandéry's observation (*ibid.* p. 155, n. 4) that when the chroniclers refer to the Gospels it is commonly the eschatological passages in Matthew and Luke which are employed.

[4] *RHC*, III, 882B (= Is. 26. 1 f.).

that the Christian warriors have been brought to Jerusalem by God and are to build its walls and rule over it.[1] After these two quotations the chronicler finishes by saying: 'Haec et multa alia invenimus in propheticis libris, quae congruunt huic liberationi factae aetatibus nostris.'[2] In a similar vein Fulcherius Carnotensis, reporting on the separate contingents of crusaders from different countries assembling at Nicea, sees this as the contemporary fulfilment of two passages in the Psalms[3] and adds, with a brevity that suggests that this interpretation is central to his outlook: 'De hoc itinere plurima etiam in prophetiis legimus quae revolvendi taedium est.'[4] The same pride in the fact that God has fulfilled His former promises in the deeds which they have been allowed to perform pervades the crusaders' letter to the Pope after their conquest of Jerusalem ('Deus magnificavit misericordiam suam, complendo in nobis ea quae antiquis temporibus promiserat')[5] and Ekkehardus informs us that this belief of the crusaders that their deeds of arms represented the God-ordained fulfilment of biblical prophecies was widespread in his day.[6]

Alphandéry has also drawn attention to the way in which some chroniclers show a predilection for certain books of the Old Testament, as when Fulcherius quotes frequently from the Psalms, but never from Isaiah, who is the main source for Robertus Monachus.[7] Equally revealing is his demonstration that certain books appear to have been quoted with particular reference to certain events: the Psalms are used in connection with the three highlights of the First Crusade (departure, Antioch and Jerusalem), whereas Isaiah comes into his own when he gives authority to the crusaders' rejoicing after the capture of the Holy City.[8] In this context the whole of Is. 40, with its lyrical praise of the future greatness of Jerusalem, provided a wealth of prophetic details which could be used by the chroniclers to suggest that it was in their own day and as a result of the crusade that this

---

[1] *RHC*, III, 882 c (= Is. 60. 9 f.).   [2] *RHC*, III, 882 c and D.
[3] *RHC*, III, 328 c (= Ps. 85. 9 and 131, 7).   [4] *RHC*, III, 328 D.
[5] H. Hagenmeyer, *Epistulae et chartae ad historiam primi belli sacri spectantes,* p. 167.   [6] *RHC*, V, 38 D.
[7] *RHR*, XCIX, 148 f.   [8] *Ibid.* p. 149.

prophecy had been accomplished. Another approach to this problem suggested by Alphandéry[1] is to determine the emotional significance of the various Old Testament quotations made by one chronicler at various stages in his account. He takes Raimundus de Aguilers as an example and shows that many of his quotations from the Psalms are little more than pious interjections (e.g. Ps. 43. 26: 'Exsurge et adjuva nos, Domine, propter nomen tuum';[2] Ps. 23. 8: 'Dominus fortis et potens in praelio'),[3] but even here the fact that these interjections are taken from the same biblical source gives them a certain coherence and stylistic value. Elsewhere his quotations acquire significance by their intimate connection with the particular episode to which they are applied. This is true, for example, of the manner in which the lyricism of Ps. 32. 12 ('O quam beata gens cujus est Dominus Deus ejus! O quam beatus populus quem Deus elegit!') is inserted[4] into the narrative of a battle at a time when the Christian priests are described as standing on the walls of Antioch, beseeching God to protect His people and to give proof of His covenant with them by granting victory to the French,[5] so that the quotation from the psalm in praise of the people chosen by God occurs precisely at the time when events prove the reality of their covenant with God. Similarly, after the capture of the Holy City Raimundus does not simply quote Ps. 117. 24 ('Haec dies quam fecit Dominus, exsultemus et laetemur in ea'), but describes the *canticum novum* sung to the Lord by the victorious Christians, commenting: 'Nova dies, novum gaudium, nova et perpetua laetitia, laboris atque devotionis consummatio, nova verba, nova cantica ab universis exigebat.'[6] Here it is the expansion of the idea of novelty which suggests that, behind the affiliation of contemporary events with those recorded of the Israelites, there lies an awareness of the unique nature of the crusading achievement, a conviction that, whereas prophetic knowledge of these events had long ago been granted to the prophets of Israel, it was to the

[1] *Ibid.* pp. 147 f.   [2] *RHC*, III, 248 F.
[3] *RHC*, III, 256 D.   [4] *RHC*, III, 259 G.
[5] Cf. *RHC*, III, 260 H. See also p. 246.   [6] *RHC*, III, 300 F.

crusaders that the opportunity had been given of realising these promises of God to His people.

These introductory examples, based on the important work of Alphandéry, have shown us the importance of the Old Testament background for the general experience of those who took part in and recorded the events of the First Crusade, strengthening their conviction that they were God's Chosen People and that God would assist them as He had protected the Israelites, and also inducing a feeling of elation because of the belief that they were living in the fullness of time and that it was through them that God had seen fit to carry out the promises which He had long ago made to the prophets of Israel. In turning now to consider the evidence for the ways in which the events of crusading history are given a timeless significance by being so closely connected with the biblical history of Israel, we shall see that this evidence falls into two groups, for the crusaders can be depicted simply as repeating these events from the history of Israel or they can be shown as transcending them through their Christian fulfilment of what had been communicated to the Hebrews only as a promise for the future. In addition to this distinction between repetition and enhancement we shall also have to make another distinction, separating the evidence which connects the crusaders with the Book of Exodus in particular from that which reveals their affiliation with the Old Testament at large. In this latter category, which I propose to discuss first because of its general importance, I shall treat evidence which concerns any book of the Old Testament other than Exodus, but also all those references (such as the description of the crusading army as the *populus Dei*) which cannot be tied to any one book of the Old Testament. These latter references will therefore be as applicable to the idea of the crusaders re-enacting the events of Exodus as to the affiliation of the crusades with any other book of the Old Testament (such as the Maccabees, for example). Our approach will be to discuss first those passages in the chronicles which connect the crusaders with the Old Testament at large or with any book other than Exodus, dividing the material into those cases where the crusaders are depicted as simply repeating the deeds of the Hebrews and those where they are felt to transcend them, and then to repeat this twofold process with the passages which refer the events of the crusades to the Book of Exodus. From this it should emerge that the Millstatt author's technique in depicting the events of Exodus in terms of the knightly, feudal warfare of his own day accurately complements the chroniclers' method of placing crusading exploits against an Old Testament background or against the background of the Exodus story in particular.

The equation of the crusaders with Israel which we have seen exemplified with regard to the ideas of the *populus Dei* and of Christian warfare had also long been suggested by another medieval institution (the pilgrimage to Jerusalem) which Erdmann considers another contributory factor in the emergence of the crusades.[1] That the crusader was a particular type of pilgrim is not simply a fact recognised by modern scholarship, but one which was apparent in the eleventh and twelfth centuries. This equation is suggested by the goal which is common to both, by the route which is frequently identical, and also by the fact that the words *iter Hierosolimitanum* are used as a technical term to denote either the pilgrimage (this is the earlier function) or the crusade.[2] The fact that the crusader is a pilgrim who is also a warrior and is prepared to fight his way to his destination is important for us, since it means that the crusading movement inherits what Alphandéry has called the Hebrew tradition of the pilgrimages.[3] This Hebrew aspect of the pilgrimage can best be explained by the way in which, as soon as it is organised at all regularly (from as early as the fourth century), the itinerary of the pilgrimage to Jerusalem is arranged with as much regard to the journey of the Israelites to the Promised Land as to the sites mentioned in the Gospels. It is understandable that in view of

[1] *Die Entstehung des Kreuzzugsgedankens*, pp. 280 ff.
[2] Cf. Alphandéry, *RHR*, xcix, 154, and *La chrétienté et l'idée de croisade*, I, 9 ff.; see also Rousset, *Les origines et les caractères de la première croisade*, pp. 134 ff.
[3] *Op. cit.* I, 20 f.

this double interest in the Holy Land some pilgrims should journey as far as Sinai or to the land where Abraham was blessed,[1] whilst the pilgrim who travels to the Holy City can be compared with Abraham leaving Chaldea, and the dangers of his journey with the trials undergone by Job.[2] The author of a saint's life reports that his hero wished to see Jerusalem with his own eyes, the city which was hitherto known to him only by the eyes of faith, because of what he had learnt from the patriarchs and the prophets.[3] Furthermore, this interest of pilgrims to Jerusalem in the traces of the Old Testament which they could hope to find in the Holy Land can be concentrated on the Book of Exodus in particular when, as the occasional individual pilgrim gives way to collective undertakings organised on a large scale, the memory of the journey of the Israelites to the Promised Land evokes the image of a new exodus.[4] How the influence of this image was transferred from the pilgrimage to the crusade we shall consider later, but for the moment it may suffice to point out that the crusading chronicles similarly regard the crusaders' conflict with the Saracens in the Holy Land in the light of a biblical war conducted by Israel against the inhabitants of Canaan. We have already considered one example in the chronicle of Robertus Monachus in connection with the way in which the Millstatt author lists the names of the kings whom the Israelites will have to defeat when they claim possession of the Promised Land.[5] The same idea is also present whenever the passage from Deut. 32. 30 ('Quomodo persequatur unus mille, et duo fugent decem millia?') is employed to account for the miraculous victory of the

[1] *Ibid.* p. 21.
[2] *Ibid.* p. 22.
[3] *Ibid.* pp. 22 f.
[4] *Ibid.* p. 22. This interest of the pilgrim in the exodus of the Israelites is not confined, of course, to the large-scale pilgrimage. As an example of this general appeal of the exodus to the pilgrim, see the *Itinerarium Egeriae* (*Peregrinatio Aetheriae*). Here (II, 1 ff.; ed. O. Prinz, pp. 1 ff.) it is described at length how the pilgrim passes through places traversed by the Israelites on their exodus. Some of the pilgrims even manage to penetrate as far as the Red Sea, to the place where the Israelites crossed in escaping from the Egyptians (*ibid.* VII, 2 f.; pp. 9 f.).
[5] See pp. 143 f.

crusaders against all odds,[1] for this passage significantly occurs in the Old Testament in the context of the Israelites' approach to the Promised Land. When this passage is quoted in a crusading chronicle the effect is to equate the present situation of the Christian warriors with the position of Israel as they forced their way into Canaan and to imply that the journey of the crusaders, like that of the pilgrims whose tradition they continue in a new form, is another exodus.

It is from the pilgrimage tradition as well as from the persistent habit of justifying Christian warfare by reference to the precedent of the Israelites that the practice derives of equating the crusades with the events of the Old Testament and of seeing the crusaders as repeating the deeds of the Hebrews. The basis of this equation is the conviction that the crusaders are another Israel, chosen by God to be the means of accomplishing what had been promised to the prophets of Israel. This conception is already present in its wider form (applied to the nation from which the crusaders come, but not yet applied to the crusaders themselves) in the address of Urban II at Clermont, at least if we can accept the account given by Robertus Monachus,[2] who has the Pope open his speech with these words: 'Gens Francorum, gens transmontana, gens, sicuti in pluribus vestris elucet operibus, a Deo electa et dilecta, tam situ terrarum quam fide catholica, quam honore sanctae Ecclesiae, ab universis nationibus segregata: ad vos sermo noster dirigitur vobisque nostra exhortatio protenditur.' Elsewhere, when once the army is under way or engaged in battle, the concept of the *populus Dei* is normally restricted to the crusaders themselves. This term can be varied by the alternatives *gens Dei*, *gens sancta* or *exercitus Dei*,[3] so that the concept of the Chosen People, originally transferred from Israel to Christendom (or at the most to one Christian nation in particular, as in the speech of Urban II), is here employed to describe the crusading army as chosen by

[1] E.g., in the chronicle of Guibertus: *RHC*, IV, 162 F and 216 A. See also below, p. 255.

[2] *RHC*, III, 727 B and C. The words used here catch a faint echo of the prologue to the *Lex Salica* which we discussed above (pp. 203 f.).

[3] E.g. *RHC*, III, 746 C; IV, 41 E; IV, 16 A.

God. The sense of election conveyed by the Pope with regard to France at large is felt by the crusaders with regard to themselves, as when Raimundus de Aguilers describes the words spoken in a vision by St Andrew on the occasion of the discovery of the Holy Lance at Antioch ('Nescisne cur Deus huc vos adduxit, et quantum vos diligit, et quomodo vos praecipue elegit?...Elegit vos Deus ex omnibus gentibus')[1] or when those who fall in battle are described as *jamdudum a Domino praeelecti*.[2] Acknowledgement of this election is even imputed by Raimundus to a Saracen king: 'Video quia Deus hanc gentem elegit: propterea quodlibet faciant, non eis nocebo,'[3] a truth which eventually dawns upon the Egyptians in the *Millstätter Exodus* (vv. 3217 ff.) and which, in the account of Robertus Monachus, Corbanam's mother had tried to impress upon her son.[4] It is the feeling of elation that God has chosen them to be His instruments in such a glorious task that speaks out of the description of the capture of Jerusalem given by Fulcherius Carnotensis ('Et quod idem Dominus per hunc populum suum tam, ut opinor, dilectum et alumnum familiaremque, ad hoc negotium praeelectum, expleri voluit')[5] and which accounts for the relative frequency with which Ps. 32.12 ('Beata gens cujus est Dominus Deus ejus; populus quem elegit in hereditatem sibi!') is applied to the crusaders.[6]

If the crusaders are seen in terms of the Hebrews, as *filii Israel*,[7] it follows that the God who has chosen them will appear in much the same light as Jehovah. Ordericus Vitalis even refers to the God who assists the crusaders as the God of Israel: 'Ibi tunc nongenti milites Christiani contra trecenta millia paganorum pugnaverunt, fortissimoque Deo Israel suos potenter juvante, vicerunt.'[8] Robertus Monachus reports Urban II as saying at Clermont that God had chosen the Franks to accomplish His task because it was they whom he had especially blessed with the military virtues and on whom He had conferred the ability to

---

[1] *RHC*, III, 254 H.
[2] *RHC*, III, 341 D.
[3] *RHC*, III, 273 A.
[4] See above, pp. 144.
[5] *RHC*, III, 360 F.
[6] E.g. *RHC*, III, 259 G, 320, 453 D, 723.
[7] *RHC*, III, 554 A.
[8] *Historia ecclesiastica*, IV, 260.

defeat their foes ('. . . vobis, quibus prae ceteris gentibus contulit Deus insigne decus armorum, magnitudinem animorum, agilitatem corporum, virtutem humiliandi verticem capilli vobis resistentium?').[1] Here the fact that these words include a quotation from Ps. 67. 22 suggests that it is the Old Testament God who is invoked as a guarantor of the victory of His people. The assistance which God gives the crusaders is felt to be a renewal of the miracles He once performed for Abraham ('Antiqua nempe miracula Deus Abraham nuper iteravit')[2] and His relationship with them is regarded, as by Raimundus de Aguilers, as a new covenant, as a *testamentum* which is revealed in the fact of a Christian victory.[3] Guibertus, when he quotes the phrase from Deut. 32. 30 which we have considered, implies that its relevance to the present situation is an indication that it is not the Jews, but the crusaders, with whom God has renewed His covenant. He accordingly, on one occasion, brackets this quotation with the phrase: 'Si enim de his qui nondum a Deo desciverant Judaeis dicitur in veteri pagina. . ., non minus de hac mihi videbitur sentiendum victoria,'[4] whereas elsewhere, when he again quotes the phrase as a concluding commentary on a Christian victory, he prefaces the quotation by saying of the crusaders: 'Qui sponsionis Dominicae ipsis executores effectibus',[5] thereby implying that God's *sponsio* has now been given to the Christian army.

In details, too, a constant equation between the crusaders and the Israelites is carefully maintained. Guibertus, although perfectly aware of the failings of the Israelites, makes an exception of Joshua, David and Samuel as examples of the way in which God conferred victories upon His people,[6] as He continues to do down to the present. For Ordericus Vitalis, Godfrey of Bouillon, as ruler of Jerusalem, is chosen 'in solium regni David regis'.[7] William of Malmesbury compares the appearance of the warrior

[1] *RHC*, III, 728 B.
[2] Ordericus Vitalis, *op. cit.* III, 458.
[3] *RHC*, III, 260 H. See above, p. 240.
[4] *RHC*, IV, 162 E and F.
[5] *RHC*, IV, 216 A.
[6] *RHC*, IV, 203 A ff.
[7] *Op. cit.* III, 612.

saints George and Demetrius during the crusade with the presence of the angels in the wars of the Maccabees ('non diffitendum
est affuisse martyres Christianis, sicut quondam angelos Macha-
baeis simili duntaxat causa pugnantibus'),[1] where the words
simili...causa underline the continuity between the two wars.
In the eyes of another chronicler, Cafarus Genuensis, those crusaders who fall in battle are given the same crown of martyrdom
as was the reward of the Maccabees: 'qui antequam alii qui viam
Sepulcri inceperant prius coronam martirii susceperunt, et uti
martires Dei in coelesti sede illos angeli Machabaeorum socios
posuerunt.'[2] Here it is the word *socii* which underlines the similarity between the events of the Old Testament and those of the
year 1097. For Fulcherius, too, despite his hesitancy in expressing
the thought, the only comparison worthy of the *gesta Dei per
Francos* is the reference to the deeds of Israel and of the Maccabees: 'Licet autem nec Israeliticae plebis nec Machabaeorum aut
aliorum plurium praerogativae, quos Deus tam crebris et magni-
ficis miraculis illustravit, hoc opus praelibatum aequiparare non
audeam, tamen haut longe ab illis gestis inferius aestimatum,
quoniam Dei miracula in eo noscuntur multipliciter perpetrata.'[3]

The prayers with which the crusaders request divine assistance
are frequently those used by the Hebrews. Raimundus de Aguilers
quotes from Ps. 43. 26 ('Exsurge et adjuva nos, propter nomen
tuum') when describing the dangers in which the crusaders find
themselves on one occasion.[4] Robertus Monachus makes use of
Ps. 27. 9 and of Ps. 60. 4, but also of other psalms 'praecipue qui
tribulationi conveniebant' when he describes the prayers and
hymns sung by the clergy to invoke God's assistance at the battle
for Antioch.[5] When confronted later by a similar situation he has
recourse to Isaiah and to two other psalms: 'Stabant autem juxta
ligneam turrim sacerdotes et levitae, ministri Domini, invocantes
propugnatorem gentis Christianae Jesum Christum, Filium Dei,
et dicebant: Domine, miserere nostri. Esto brachium nostrum

[1] *MPL*, 179, 1316 A.   [2] *RHC*, v, 50 F.
[3] *RHC*, iii, 319.   [4] *RHC*, iii, 248 F.
[5] *RHC*, iii, 828 A and B.

in mane, et salus nostra in tempore tribulationis. Effunde iram tuam in gentes quae te non noverunt, et in regna quae nomen tuum non invocaverunt. Disperge illos in virtute tua, et depone eos, protector noster, Domine.'[1] Here it is not merely the use of these Old Testament prayers that constitutes the parallel with the wars of Israel, but the reference to the Christian priests as *levitae* and the way in which Christ, as the *propugnator gentis Christianae*, has taken over the function of Jehovah as *dominus exercituum*.

Fulcherius describes the power of the Holy Cross to confer victory on the Christians ('alioquin sine illa nec ipse nec alii audent ad bellum proficisci'),[2] but adds, when describing how the crusaders were in two minds as to whether to send it to Antioch for safe keeping or to retain it at Jerusalem, their comment: 'Heu miseri! quid faciemus, si permittente Deo perdiderimus in bello Crucem, sicut perdiderunt Israelitae olim foederis archam?'[3] In this episode the Cross has acquired the same function of a palladium as was exercised by the Ark of the Covenant for the Hebrews in battle,[4] but the mere possibility that the Cross might be lost in battle is sufficient to remind the Christian warriors of the similar misfortune which befell the Israelites. This readiness to understand their present situation (and even to decide on a particular course of action) by reference to a comparable episode in the Old Testament is revealed by the preparations made by the crusaders for the assault on Jerusalem. Guibertus, when he has to comment on the siege of the city by the crusaders, is less successful in finding apposite Old Testament material than when actually describing the operation, for in the former case he reveals the way in which he consciously sought for Hebrew parallels, parallels which are not always entirely convincing: 'Sed quoniam in hujus voluminis exordio quaedam exempla praebuimus Scripturarum quae huic tanto quod explicuimus negotio convenire putavimus, attendendum nunc etiam an Iherosolimitanae obsidioni aliquid consonum apud Zachariam

---

[1] *RHC*, III, 847 D and E. The biblical references are to Is. 33. 2 and to Ps. 58. 12 and 78. 6.   [2] *RHC*, III, 445 E.
[3] *RHC*, III, 446 A.   [4] See above, p. 193.

prophetam repperire possimus.'[1] It is the crusaders, at least in so far as Guibertus describes their military preparations, who find a more persuasive parallel, for the chronicler tells us that they took steps to procure divine assistance by fasting and singing litanies before the attack and by processing in bare feet around the walls of the city with banners flying and trumpets blowing. The parallel with the procession around Jericho (Jos. 6. 2 ff.) is an obvious one and is in fact cited by the chronicler: 'Memores igitur idem praesules Ihericontini quondam casus, et quod Israelitae tubis aliquando clangentibus, circuitu septeno et sacrae archae circumlatione, diruerant perfidae moenia civitatis, cum multa spirituum et corporum contritione processiones agendo, Sanctorum nomina flebiliter inclamando, nudipedalia exercendo, Iherusalem circumeunt.'[2]

The chroniclers of the crusades also adduce Old Testament examples when it is a question of providing an explanation for a defeat suffered by the crusading army. It is the Old Testament explanation that is employed, which sees the cause in the offence rendered to God by the sinful behaviour of the crusaders. This is a line of argument which is later used with particular effect and with some considerable sense of urgency by St Bernard in his *De consideratione*, where one of his tasks is to defend himself against the accusations which hold him responsible for the military failure of the Second Crusade. If the need for such a general explanation hardly arose for the First Crusade with its victorious outcome in the capture of Jerusalem, it is nonetheless necessary whenever a local setback gives rise to self-questioning amongst the Christians. Like the Hebrews, the crusaders have often given offence to God: 'in quo Deum mirabiliter, sicut et Israheliticus populus quondam, offenderunt.'[3] For Ordericus Vitalis and for Fulcherius this is sufficient to explain their military setbacks whenever they occur. The former author says that this was a divine punishment for their arrogance, adding significantly: 'Sic nimirum filios Israel in sacris codicibus frequenter afflictos legimus, et in bello victos a

[1] *RHC*, IV, 237E ff. [2] *RHC*, IV, 226 C and D.
[3] Cf. *MGH* SS V, 464, 30 f. (*Bernoldi Chronicon*, a. 1096).

Philistiim et Edom atque Madian,'[1] whilst the latter quotes from
Ps. 72. 7 in explaining the reverses around Antioch in the year
1119 as the direct result of the sinful behaviour of Roger, prince
of that city.[2] In such details, as also in the general course of the
action, the crusading armies conceive themselves as repeating the
events of the history of Israel and interpret their actions, their
successes and their failures in the light of what God had allowed
the Israelites to achieve.

It would be mistaken, however, to attribute to the knights of
the First Crusade and to those who recorded their expedition
simply the belief that in this war against the pagan occupiers of
the Holy Land they were doing no more than repeat, at an interval
of time, the wars previously waged by the Israelites. Undoubtedly
this conviction is present and does much to justify in their eyes
the very idea of a crusade, to impress upon them the belief that
this task has been allotted to them by God Himself and that, as
in the case of the Hebrews, He will guarantee them victory if
only they remain morally worthy of it. These are certainly
powerful enough incentives, so powerful that we may readily
understand why the attempt should be repeatedly made, even
where the situation seems to be quite unpromising, to establish
some kind of parallel between the crusade and the Old Testament.
Nonetheless, we shall fail to understand the mainsprings of
crusading enthusiasm and the sense of fulfilment which not merely
resulted from the capture of Jerusalem but—however para-
doxically—actually made that achievement possible if we ignore
the fact that the Christian army regarded itself as more than just
repeating the deeds of Israel and, instead, as transcending this
earlier achievement, fulfilling those prophecies whose realisation
had not been granted to the Hebrews. Such a conviction of
superiority lies at the heart of the relationship between Christianity and Israel and explains the use of such contrasts as *secundum
carnem* and *secundum spiritum* or *ancilla* and *libera*, which we find
already in the Pauline letters,[3] as well as the conviction of an

[1] *Historia ecclesiastica*, III, 574.
[2] *RHC*, III, 442 A ff.   [3] See above, pp. 200 f.

innovation, of a new relationship between man and God, implied by the words *novum testamentum*.[1] The crusaders, like Christendom at large, were persuaded that they continued to enjoy the privileges of the Hebrews, the people chosen by God under the old dispensation, but that, in addition to this, they possessed the advantage of being Christians, members of the new *populus Dei* under the New Covenant. What had been denied to the Hebrews because of their sinfulness (as their own books made amply clear) and because of their supreme deficiency in failing to acknowledge Christ had now been granted to the new Israel: the privilege of the New Covenant and the recognition that God was now using them to accomplish what the Hebrews had proved incapable of realising. It is this sense of living in an age of fulfilment, of performing the deeds of God in the fullness of time, that pervades the crusading chronicles. It is at the same time the reason why so many of the biblical references are drawn from the Old Testament (for it was in these books that the prophetic message demanded a future fulfilment) and why the chroniclers regard the events they record so often as the fulfilment of Old Testament prophecies which had been accomplished only in their days and in which God had allowed His new people to play their part.[2]

This conviction of a prophecy realised only in the present day is expressed in the sermon preached by Urban II at Clermont, as reported by Baldricus. In his account of the papal appeal for the First Crusade the chronicler attributes to the Pope a number of Old Testament quotations (Ps. 78. 1 ff.; Ps. 78. 4; Ps. 21. 7) which he uses to bring home to his congregation the plight of their fellow Christians in the Holy Land, but which he introduces with the remark: 'Ploremus, fratres, eia ploremus et cum Psalmista medullitus plorantes ingemiscamus. Nos miseri, nos infelices

---

[1] E.g. Matt. 26. 28.

[2] Daniélou, *Sacramentum futuri*, pp. 133 f., has shown that typological references to Exodus in later books of the Old Testament are likewise characterised by a conviction of surpassing the earlier exodus. This conviction is therefore inseparable not so much from Christianity as from the typological method inherited by Christianity from the Old Testament.

quorum prophetia ista completa est.'[1] The mood of this remark may seem to be the very opposite of elation or of a sense of achievement and to stress instead the suffering and humiliation to which Christendom is subjected, but it was by evoking such a mood that Urban was enabled to bring the latent crusading enthusiasm of France into movement and to direct it to Jerusalem.[2] If the state of affairs which necessitated the First Crusade was the fulfilment of an Old Testament prophecy then it was possible to suggest that the crusade was likewise an answer to a prophecy, a suggestion which is taken up by the chroniclers and also, we must assume, by the crusaders themselves. This attitude is expressed by Robertus Monachus, who in the prologue to his work[3] first mentions the *historiographi* of the Old and New Testaments in whose writings the faithful are to learn what wonders God has decided to allow to occur *praefixis temporibus*, but who then leaves his particular Old Testament examples (Moses, Jesu Nave, Samuel and David) and says of his own time: 'Sed post creationem mundi quid mirabilius factum est praeter salutiferae crucis mysterium, quam quod modernis temporibus actum est in hoc itinere nostrorum Iherosolimitanorum?' The way in which the only other events to which he makes reference are those of Hebrew history makes it clear that his comparison is between the crusaders and the Israelites (also confirmed by his later quotation of the phrase 'beata gens, cujus est Dominus Deus ejus, populus quem elegit in hereditatem sibi' from Ps. 32. 12).[4] The same kind of comparison between Christian knights and Hebrews, implying the greater achievements of the former, is also to be found with Guibertus. He too is convinced that nothing in past history can be measured against the exploits of the crusaders ('Diximus non semel, sed forte multotiens, nec repetere piget, tale quid nusquam a saeculo factum'),[5] but then he deals explicitly with the objection that the deeds of the present cannot be held to surpass those of the Israelites. He admits the parallel between the

[1] *RHC*, IV, 14B.
[2] See Erdmann, *Die Entstehung des Kreuzzugsgedankens*, pp. 301 ff.
[3] *RHC*, III, 723.   [4] *Ibid.*   [5] *RHC*, IV, 241A.

two cases, but suggests the superiority of the ways in which the Christian army faces up to its responsibilities: 'Si filii Israel miraculis quae ante eos egerit Dominus mihi referuntur objectis, his ego multo mirabilius astruam mare confertissimae Gentilitatis apertum; his interdiu ex columna nubem divini timoris; noctu lumen divinae spei perhibebo praebitum, quibus Christus ipse columna rectitudinis ac fortitudinis inspiravit exempla; quos verbi Dei, ac si manna coeleste, absque ullius terrenae spei, solum confortavit edulium. Illi pabula coelitus ministrata fastidiunt, Aegyptum derelictam crebro mentibus et voce revisunt; isti sicut nihil unquam retrogradum moliuntur, ita quicquid penuriae ac necessitatis ingruerit, vivacibus animis amplectuntur.'[1] It is because of this conviction that Guibertus, when he finds it possible to apply an Old Testament passage to an event in his narrative, calls his crusaders *pii Scripturae illius impletores*,[2] just as Raimundus de Aguilers regards the capture of Jerusalem as the fulfilment of the prophecy in Ps. 117. 24.[3]

Once the conviction had been established that the crusaders surpassed the Israelites since their deeds were the fulfilment of prophecies whose realisation had not been granted to the Hebrews, the same interpretation came to be applied not merely to the undertaking as a whole, but to any apparently unimportant episodes which had the advantage of suggesting a parallel in the Old Testament. Conversely, certain passages in the Old Testament of considerable prophetic force and personages whose example cannot be allowed to remain unchallenged find their way into the crusading chronicles and are confronted with their medieval fulfilment or with a medieval parallel that transcends them. Thus the prophecy of Isaiah (43. 5) is used when Robertus Monachus describes Raimond de St Gilles as one of the first knights to take the cross: 'Ecce nunc praesentialiter videmus in re, quod olim promisit Dominus per os Isaiae prophetae. Ait enim: Noli timere quia ego tecum sum; ab Aquilone adducam semen tuum, et ab Occidente congregabo te. Dicam Aquiloni:

[1] *RHC*, IV, 241A and B.   [2] *RHC*, IV, 216D.
[3] *RHC*, III, 300F.

253

"Da"; et Austro: "Noli prohibere: affer filios meos de longinquo et filias meas ab extremis terrae." Nunc, ut videmus, filii Dei et filiae, Iherosolimam tendunt ab extremis terrae.'[1] The goal of the crusade recalls Zach. 12. 6 to the mind of Guibertus,[2] so that the final capture of the Holy City is anticipated for him in the prophet's word which he then interprets with reference to the events of his own day, adding, however: 'Proculdubio enim scimus Deum ista nequaquam pro unius civitatis liberatione coepisse, sed contra venturi rabiem Antichristi haec semina, longe lateque fructificatura, jecisse.'[3] The authority of David is invoked by the quotation of two psalms (85. 9 and 131. 7) by Fulcherius when he describes the way in which the crusading armies assemble from different parts and meet at Nicea: 'Quid ego dicam? Insulae marium, et omnia regna terrarum a Deo concussa sunt, ut sit credendum adimpletam prophetiam Davidis, qui dixit in psalmo: Omnes gentes quascumque fecisti venient, et adorabunt coram te, Domine, et illud quod postea illuc usque pervenientes, merito dixerunt: Adorabimus in loco ubi steterunt pedes ejus.'[4] The setting out of the crusaders reminds Guibertus of another biblical passage (Prov. 30. 27) which proves for him that the crusade represents the fulfilment of a saying of Solomon: 'Videres dictum Salomonis evidenter illud impleri: Regem locusta non habet, et egreditur universa per turmas suas. Haec locusta nullum bonae operationis saltum dederat, quandiu longae iniquitatis congelatione torpuerat; at ubi solis justitiae fervor excanduit, geminae ilico transmigrationis evolatione prosiliit.'[5] In battle-descriptions it is frequently the Maccabees who are invoked, not just as a parallel to the present situation, but as a precedent which is surpassed by the present achievement. Raimundus de Aguilers, for example, comes close to extolling a Christian victory of 1097 at the expense of the Maccabees, with whose exploits (II Mach. 8. 1 ff.) he compares it, but reminds himself finally that it is God who acts through His human agents in both cases, although even

[1] *RHC*, III, 739 c ff.
[2] *RHC*, IV, 238 A.
[3] *RHC*, IV, 239 c and D.
[4] *RHC*, III, 328 c.
[5] *RHC*, IV, 124 H.

254

here he adds that the miracle performed by God was greater with the Christians than with the Israelites: 'Auderem, inquam, nisi arrogans judicarer, bellum hoc Machabaeorum bellis praeferre. Quoniam, si Machabaeus, in tribus millibus, hostium quadraginta et octo millia prostravit; hic plus quam sexaginta millia hostium, ope quadringentorum militum, in fugam versa sunt. Sed nos neque Machabaeorum contemnimus, nec virtutem militum nostrorum praedicamus; sed Deum, tunc in Machabaeo mirabilem, in nostris mirabiliorem annuntiamus.'[1] For Guibertus the authority of the Holy City is promoted more by the crusaders than by Judas Maccabaeus:

> Non Ezras olim, vel Machabaeus Judas,
> Post damna, tanto provehunt opes tuas.[2]

In similar terms Baldricus reports Urban II as having compared the crusaders with the Jacobites and the Turks with the Jebuseans, but in such a way that the present struggle is shown to surpass that of the past. After having ordered the knights to cease their fratricidal conflicts, the Pope is reported to have continued at Clermont: 'Et sub Jesu Christo, duce nostro, acies Christiana, acies invictissima, melius quam ipsi veteres Jacobitae, pro vestra Jerusalem decertetis; et Turcos qui in ea sunt, nefandiores quam Jebuseos, impugnetis et expugnetis.'[3] This conviction, implanted in the crusaders by the Pope, that their superiority to the Israelites is a result of their ethically sounder relationship to God (a criterion which is itself of Old Testament origin) can best be shown with reference to the passage in Deut. 32. 30 (or the similar sentiment in Lev. 26. 8) which we considered earlier.[4] We saw that Guibertus regarded the victorious crusaders as fulfilling God's promise to Israel by defeating their Saracen opponents, as being therefore *sponsionis Dominicae executores*, whereas he says elsewhere that the same biblical text is no less true of the Christian warriors than it is of the Jews who turned away from God. The implication behind these two remarks

---

[1] *RHC*, III, 245 A.
[3] *RHC*, IV, 15 A.
[2] *RHC*, IV, 232 C.
[4] See p. 246.

is that the crusaders are allowed to enjoy the honour of contributing to the realisation of God's promise because, unlike the Jews on whom this privilege had once been conferred, they remain steadfastly faithful to Him. This moral judgement of the military situation is reflected in two other chronicles where the same biblical passage is adduced as testimony that it is the Christian warriors who accomplish the fulfilment of a divine prophecy of which the Jews had shown themselves unworthy. The first example comes from Fulcherius, who praises a Christian victory in these terms: 'Quod si Deus pro nobis, quis contra nos? Vere pro nobis et nobiscum fuit, complens in nobis quod Israeliticis per prophetam dixit: "Si praecepta mea servaveritis, hoc dono vos ditabo, ut persequantur quinque de vobis centum alienos, et centum ex vobis decem millia." Et quia in Dei servitio laborem multimodum die ac nocte tolerabamus, et in nullo alio confidebamus, superbiam eorum magnifice cassavit. Et quia devote et in tribulato corde Domino famulabamur, humilitatem nostram respexit.'[1] Here it is the fact that the crusaders, unlike the Hebrews when they suffered defeat as a divine punishment and especially when they turned away from Christ, kept God's commandments and placed their trust in Him alone, thus avoiding the pagans' sin of *superbia*,[2] which is the cause of their victory and the explanation of the way in which the promise made to the Jews is fulfilled only now in the First Crusade. The other example comes from the *Secunda pars historiae Hierosolimitanae*, where the chronicler explains a victory in a similar manner: 'Quare hoc? nisi ut Christiani et vere filii Israel, suum et terra et mari pro se pugnantem videntes Deum, gratulabundo concentu clamarent: Si Deus pro nobis, quis contra nos? Ecce etenim complere sibi etiam visibiliter cernebant divinum illud promissum: Persequentur quinque centum alienos; et centum e vobis decem millia.'[3] Again it is the crusaders' readiness to acknowledge that it is God who is

---

[1] *RHC*, III, 376 D ff.

[2] This attribution of *superbia* to the crusaders' pagan opponents provides a close parallel to the Millstatt author's description of the Israelites' Egyptian foes (see above, p. 169).

[3] *RHC*, III, 554 A.

fighting on their behalf which allows them to avoid the pride of their Saracen foes ('Ecce quo modo victi sunt, qui jam se vicisse gloriabantur!')[1] and to be the instruments of God's fulfilment of His promise, granted not to the Jews but to those who are in truth (*vere*) the children of Israel.

These examples where the victories of the crusaders transcend the episodes with which they are compared in the Old Testament or where they fulfil a prophecy or promise made under the Old Covenant show a certain unity in the frequency with which they stress the fact that this fulfilment is being accomplished now, at the present moment, in the chronicler's own day. This can be suggested by the temporal contrast between contemporary events and *antiqua miracula*[2] relegated to a period qualified as *nondum*, *quondam* or *olim*,[3] it can be implied by the way in which the exploits of the crusaders are praised as being unique in the history of the world[4] and it can be explicitly emphasised by the introduction of such terms as *nunc, praesentialiter, aetatibus nostris* or *modernis temporibus*.[5] The fact of novelty is also brought into relief by the use of words like *novus* and *iterare*,[6] not just in the sense of bald repetition, but more profoundly, so as to suggest that the relationship between the Christian warriors and God rests upon a *novum testamentum* in which features of the old survive in conjunction with others that had previously been unknown. It is this sense of the fullness of time, transcending the old but not denying it, which is finally conveyed by the significant use of such a verb as *complere, implere* or *adimplere*[7] and of a phrase like *sponsionis Dominicae executores*.[8] In all this we may detect an awareness of a time relationship between the events

[1] *RHC*, III, 554 B.   [2] Cf. the reference given on p. 246, n. 2.
[3] The references to the above quotations where the relevant terms can be found are as follows: *nondum* (p. 246, n. 4); *quondam* (p. 247, n. 1; p. 249, n. 2; p. 249, n. 3; *olim* (p. 248, n. 3; p. 254, n. 1; p. 255, n. 2).
[4] Cf. p. 252, n. 3 and n. 5.
[5] *Nunc* (p. 254, n. 1); *praesentialiter* (p. 254, n. 1); *aetatibus nostris* (p. 239, n. 2); *modernis temporibus* (p. 252, n. 3).
[6] *Novus* (p. 240, n. 6); *iterare* (p. 246, n. 2).
[7] *Complere* (p. 239, n. 5; p. 256, n. 1 and n. 3); *implere* (p. 253, n. 2); *adimplere* (p. 254, n. 4).   [8] Cf. p. 246, n. 5.

narrated or prophecies uttered in the days of the Old Testament and the Christian warfare of the present in which the latter is interpreted either as surpassing the wars of Israel or as fulfilling the ancient prophecies. Such a tension between past and present, amounting to a conviction that what was done or said by the Israelites is still relevant to the present because it is only in the present that it is due to be transcended or finally realised, is reminiscent of what we saw was the position in the *Millstätter Exodus*. The German author took care to stress the timeless nature of God's compact with the Hebrews and to make it clear that what had been true of His relationship with Abraham was still true of His relationship with Moses and would lose none of its force after Moses' death. At the same time, the author's introduction of a contemporary view of things and of twelfth-century details had the effect of extending this timeless view of God's covenant with Israel down to the medieval present. The fact that the Old Testament God is now described in terms of a feudal relationship with His people, who themselves are seen as knights of the twelfth century, means that the Millstatt author is convinced, like the crusading chroniclers, that medieval Christendom as the new Israel enjoys a New Covenant with the God of the Hebrews.

We have so far only regarded the way in which the chroniclers of the First Crusade, using a method which complements that of the Millstatt author, placed crusading exploits against the background of the Old Testament at large. Many of the points we have considered (e.g. the crusaders as Israelites or as a *populus Dei*) are as applicable to the Book of Exodus as to any other book of the Old Testament, but we still have to consider the particular relationship between the First Crusade and Exodus if we are to account for the way in which the German author chose to transpose the story of this book into the twelfth-century present. We have already had occasion to comment in passing on the way in which a special relationship could be postulated between Exodus and the crusading present. We saw that an early eleventh-century *oratio pro exercitu* compared the Christian army setting forth for battle with the departure of Israel from Egypt[1] and that the pilgrimage to the Holy Land, once its individual character began to give way more to collectively organised journeys, also conjured up the idea of the march of the Hebrews to the Promised Land.[2] These two examples belong more to the pre-history of the crusades than to the crusades themselves, but they show how the later movement could acquire some of its imagery from its predecessors. That this equation between Exodus and the First Crusade was soon appreciated can be shown from what we are told of the content of Urban's sermon at Clermont. Baldricus quotes him as making use of this comparison immediately after citing a number of Old Testament passages and praising the Holy Land as the land of martyrs: 'Filii Israel ab Aegyptiis educti, qui, Rubro Mari transito, vos praefiguraverunt, terram illam armis suis, Jesu duce, sibi vindicaverunt; Jebuseos et alios convenas inde expulerunt; et instar Jerusalem coelestis, Jerusalem terrenam incoluerunt.'[3] The same idea is also present in the account of this same speech given by Robertus Monachus, with whom the Pope says: 'Viam sancti Sepulcri incipite, terram illam nefariae genti auferte, eamque vobis subjicite, terra illa filiis Israel a Deo in possessionem data fuit, sicut Scriptura dicit, quae lacte et melle fluit.'[4] Here the force of the quotation from Exod. 3. 8 is to underline the fact that the land once promised to Israel on their departure from Egypt is promised to the new Israel on *their* departure.

From the fact that the crusaders, regarded as the new Israel,

---

[1] See p. 217, n. 3. [2] See pp. 243 f.

[3] *RHC*, IV, 14E. At a later period Peter the Venerable writes in similar terms to Louis VII on his departure for the Holy Land: 'Renovantur jam nostro tempore antique saecula, et in diebus novae gratiae vetusti populi miracula reparantur. Processit de Aegypto Moyses, regesque Amorrhaeorum cum subjectis populis delevit. Successit ei Josue, regesque Chananaeorum cum infinitis gentibus Dei jussu prostravit, terramque illam, extinctis impiis, illi tunc Dei populo sorte divisit. Egrediens ab ultimis occiduae plagae finibus, immo ab ipso solis occasu, Rex christianus Orienti minatur, et nefandam Arabum vel Persarum gentem, sanctam Terram rursum sibi subjugare conantem, cruce Christi armatus aggreditur' (*Recueil des historiens des Gaules et de la France*, XV, 641). Quoted by A. Katzenellenbogen, *The Sculptural Programs of Chartres Cathedral*, p. 29.

[4] *RHC*, III, 728 F.

17-2

set out for the same goal as the Hebrews on their departure from Egypt there results a whole pattern of similarities between the two events. We have seen how the concept of the Chosen People was given a particular application in being narrowed down from Christendom at large (or one Christian nation) to the crusading army, so that there was no difficulty for the chroniclers in regarding the Hebrews as prefiguring the crusaders. Both peoples were commanded by God to set out for their distant goal and both are assisted by Him or by an angel on their way. This is quite apparent, of course, in the biblical and Millstatt accounts of the exodus, but the same is also true of what is reported of the First Crusade. We shall see below some examples for the belief that God commanded the institution of the crusade, but it is already expressed in that phrase with which Urban's speech was greeted at Clermont and which soon became the crusaders' battle-cry: 'Deus vult! Deus vult!'[1] That God accompanied the crusaders on their journey, leading them and fighting with them, is made equally clear in the chronicles. Baldricus had had Urban II refer to *Jesus dux* in the case of the Hebrews' conquest of Canaan,[2] but

[1] *RHC*, III, 729 E.

[2] *RHC*, IV, 14 E. It is of course possible that *Jesus* refers here to Joshua rather than to Jesus Christ, since the two names are identical in Hebrew. Yet it is precisely this identity of names and similarity of functions that explain the ease with which Joshua, leading the Chosen People into the Promised Land, is interpreted as prefiguring the redemption accomplished by Christ. This connection is clear in the *Vorauer Bücher Mosis*, 67. 18:

> iesus was
> er geheizen. der aller chûniste helt.
> got hete in irwelt. er was ein also
> gut man. so er gote zeineme genan-
> nen wole zam. In deme selben ia-
> re. daz sagent uns dev bûch ze warc.
> iesus der gute wigant. der furte si
> in daz lant. daz in got der gute. da-
> uore hete intheizen.

On the typological relationship between Joshua and Christ see Daniélou, *Sacramentum futuri*, pp. 205 ff. Cf. also A. E. Schönbach, *Altdeutsche Predigten*, II, 74, 16: 'Josue der unsers herren lûte laitt, der bezaichent den hiligen Christ der in diz werlt chom, das er sinen lûten die im getriu sint und siniu bot behaltent, das er der veint zerstôrt und si von allen irn nôten erledigot und si zû den ewigen genaden belaitt.'

elsewhere he uses the phrase *Christo duce* with reference to the crusaders' victories.[1] God is referred to as *ductor*, as *conductor ac dominus* or as *rex*.[2] How persuasive was this conviction that Christ was the true leader of the expedition to Jerusalem is made clear by Guibertus, who explains that the rulers of Western Europe were excluded from partaking in this first crusade because God wished to lead it Himself and to defer to no other leader: 'Honorem itaque sui nominis Deus, qui facit mirabilia, nolens deferre alteri, ipse solus dux ejus fuit, ipse rexit, ipse correxit, ipse ad efficientiam coepta direxit, ipse hucusque regna porrexit.'[3] Elsewhere this chronicler interprets his quotation from Prov.30.27 (*Regem locusta non habet*), which we considered above,[4] in the same sense: 'Ipsa regem non habuit: quia quaeque fidelis anima omni ducatu, praeter solius Dei caruit, dum illius se contubernalem aestimat, eumque praevium sibi esse non dubitat.'[5]

The comparison between the First Crusade and the exodus derives its strength not just from the fact that in both cases God's people is commanded to embark on this journey by God and assisted on its course by Him, but above all from their common goal. This is why Urban II, in the account given by Robertus Monachus, refers explicitly to Jerusalem as the land *quae lacte et melle fluit*[6] and why, in the version handed down by Baldricus, he should mention the *Jebusaei* and others who were expelled by the Hebrews and whose modern counterparts, the Saracens, have to be driven out by the people of the New Covenant.[7] God's assistance in this war of conquest will be a repetition of the help He afforded the Hebrews in the face of Pharaoh's tyranny:

iv, 382   Mittet in auxilium Deus angelicam legionem;
Opprimet hunc populum, velut oppressit Pharaonem.[8]

Pharaoh is here regarded as a prefiguration of the heathens' present activity in the Holy Land. In this capacity he has lost all

---

[1] E.g. *RHC*, iv, 79 D or 110 F.
[2] E.g. *RHC*, iii, 772 A; iii, 285 B; *MGH* SS vi, 213, 97.
[3] *RHC*, iv, 250 E and F. Cf. also 123 G f.   [4] See p. 254.
[5] *RHC*, iv, 125 A.   [6] *RHC*, iii, 728 F.
[7] *RHC*, iv, 14 E.   [8] *RHC*, v, 773.

historical reality and has become little more than a symbol of pagan persecution of Christianity, so that the chroniclers see no inconsistency in arguing that the Pharaoh with whom the crusaders are to do battle when they reach the Holy Land is also the Pharaoh from whose bondage they have escaped in setting out from Egypt. We have already seen that the exodus from Egypt and the crossing of the Red Sea were adduced by Baldricus as a prefiguration of the crusaders' departure from Europe and their journey across the sea to reach the Holy Land, but the same is true of a speech by Bohemond to his warriors, as recorded by Robertus Monachus: 'O bellatores Dei et indeficientes peregrini Sancti Sepulcri, quis ad haec peregrina loca vos adduxit, nisi ille qui filios Israel ex Aegypto per mare Rubrum sicco vestigio transduxit?'[1] Ordericus Vitalis similarly regards the crusade as a parallel to the departure of Israel under Moses: 'Antiqua nempe miracula Deus Abraham nuper iteravit, dum solo ardore visendi sepulcrum Messiae occiduos fideles illexit, et sine rege saecularique exactione per Urbanum Papam commonuit, de finibus terrae et insulis maris velut Hebraeos de Aegypto per Moysen extraxit.'[2] The Egypt which the crusaders leave behind them in setting out on their exodus, like the Pharaoh who had enslaved them there, is obviously not meant to be understood literally, but in its allegorical sense. By this reading Egypt would signify the bondage of sin from which the crusaders, as the Chosen People, were granted an escape by God in the opportunity to reach Jerusalem either literally (as crusading pilgrims) or allegorically (in that, if they fell in battle, they would gain access to the Heavenly Jerusalem as martyrs). In this view the Pharaoh from whom the crusaders had been delivered would therefore be the Devil, as the prince of this world, who shares with the Pharaoh of the Hebrews the fact of his tyranny and the fact that he is in conflict with God.

Once this general pattern of similarities between the First Crusade and the exodus had been established (with a general correspondence between the two in regard to the Chosen People, the

[1] *RHC*, III, 747 D.   [2] *Historia ecclesiastica*, III, 458.

assistance God gives them, their departure from Egypt, their crossing of the sea, their arrival in the Holy Land and their expulsion of the pagans), it was possible to go further and look for correspondences in points of detail. In this the model of Moses provided one obvious point of departure. This is already clear in the words attributed to the Pope at Clermont by Baldricus, who has him close his sermon by addressing the knights who are to depart for Jerusalem: 'Vos autem qui ituri estis, habebitis nos pro vobis oratores; nos habeamus vos pro populo Dei pugnatores. Nostrum est orare, vestrum sit contra Amalechitas pugnare. Nos extendemus cum Moyse manus indefessas, orantes in coelum; vos exerite et vibrate intrepidi praeliatores in Amalech gladium.'[1] By this reference to Exod. 17. 11 the crusading knights take over the function of Joshua, whilst Urban II is shown in the role of Moses.[2] Elsewhere it is the clergy who, by making themselves *duces exercitus*, repeat the example of Moses and of Joshua,[3] but it is more frequently the case that one cleric in particular, namely Bishop Adhémar of Puy as the papal legate entrusted with the conduct of the expedition, is depicted in terms of his similarity to Moses. For Raimundus de Aguilers he was *Moyses alter*,[4] procuring divine support for the crusading army as had Moses for Israel, and the same phrase is employed by Robertus Monachus to describe how he was put in charge of the undertaking, although unwilling, like Moses, to accept this authority at first.[5] This similarity of function and details (even down to the fact that Adhémar, who died on the way to Jerusalem, resembled Moses

---

[1] *RHC*, IV, 15 F.

[2] Just as Moses acts only on behalf of God and not for himself, so does Fulcherius make this equally clear with regard to the Pope: 'Qua de re supplici prece hortor, non ego, sed Dominus' (*RHC*, III, 324A). Cf. also: 'Praesentibus dico, absentibus mando, Christus autem imperat' (*ibid.* B).

[3] Rousset quotes the *Vita B. Gaufridi* (p. 93), where the following command is attributed to Urban II: 'Religiosis praecipimus auctoritate apostolica ut ipsi fiant duces exercitus, Moysen et Josue imitantes qui populum Israel per multa discrimina fidelissime regebant.'

[4] *RHC*, III, 301 B: 'Moyses alter, exercitum nostrum rebus et colloquiis divinis confovens.'

[5] *RHC*, III, 731A: 'Ille itaque, licet invitus, suscepit, quasi alter Moyses, ducatum ac regimen dominici populi.'

in being allowed only to catch a glimpse of Canaan, but not actually to enter it) is worked out at greater length by Radulfus Cadomensis in his *epitaphium* to the Bishop of Puy:

> Conditus est Moysis clarissimus hic imitator
> Doctrina, studio, moribus, officio.
> Dux populi Moyses, et dux populi fuit iste:
> Ambo duces Christi, coelitus ambo sati,
> Ambo justitiae, doctrinae ambo studiosi,
> Ambo fuere Dei vox media et populi.
> Causa viae Moysi tellus Canaam memoratur:
> Huic quoque causa viae terra fuit Canaam.
> Cernere, non uti, Moysi conceditur illa:
> Huic quoque non uti, cernere ferme datum est.
> Longa Deo Moysen jejunia conciliarunt:
> Hunc quoque longa Deo consecrat esuries.
> Ipse Deus Moysen, hunc papa Urbanus, et ipse
> Praeco Dei sequitur: misit utrumque Deus.[1]

The fact that this comparison should be elaborated in such detail even with regard to points which we today should only regard as fortuitous, is a result of the overall similarity which was felt to exist between the crusade and the exodus and of the conviction that God's plan for mankind is being revealed and accomplished in these events. It is the chronicler's task to recognise and point out these correspondences.

The authority of Exodus is also invoked on the occasion of a Christian victory or of a crusading defeat. As an example of the former we may quote the emphatic manner in which Robertus Monachus describes a hymn of thanksgiving sung by the priests after the crusaders' victory, for the hymn is composed of five extracts (Exod. 15. 11, 6, 7, 9, 13) from the hymn sung by Moses and the Hebrews after their delivery from the Egyptians and the destruction of their foes in the Red Sea.[2] The converse procedure, whereby the example of the exodus of Israel is invoked as an explanation of a temporary setback, is not employed much in the chronicles of the First Crusade, but it dominates the argument of St Bernard in his *De consideratione*, where he is called upon to

---

[1] *RHC*, III, 673 F ff. [2] *RHC*, III, 763 c ff.

explain the disastrous outcome of the Second Crusade. That he should stress the similarity between the sins of the crusaders and the Hebrews' lack of faith,[1] emphasising that Moses, too, was prevented from touching the soil of the Promised Land himself because of the shortcomings of his people,[2] is a measure of the extent to which the crusades of the present could be interpreted by reference to the Book of Exodus and also of the need that must have existed for believing in such a close parallel.

As with the Old Testament, so too with the Book of Exodus it is insufficient to regard the chroniclers as believing that the events they witnessed were merely a repetition of events in the history of Israel, however much this alone must have encouraged confidence in the final outcome and provided an explanation of events which seemed to conflict with the view that God had ordained this crusade and would ensure the victory of those fighting in His name. Behind this view of a parallel between two sets of events there lies the more significant conception that the events of the crusade represent the fulfilment on a higher level of those depicted in Exodus. This is implied by the remark attributed to Urban II when Baldricus writes of him addressing the knights at Clermont with the words: 'Filii Israel ab Aegyptiis educti, qui, Rubro Mari transito, vos praefiguraverunt',[3] for the use of the verb *praefigurare*, as a technical term of typological exegesis, suggests that the antitype transcends the type (by virtue of the fulfilment it represents) instead of merely repeating it.[4] Admittedly,

---

[1] *De consideratione*, II, I: 'Bene, illi increduli et rebelles; hi autem quid?' (*MPL*, 182, 743 c).

[2] *Ibid.*   [3] *RHC*, IV, 14 E.

[4] Here I may quote the views of two authors who have recently discussed the particular importance of typology in medieval literature. Jantsch, *Studien zum Symbolischen*, p. 17, writes: 'Eine typologische Deutung dieser Objekte liegt vor, wenn sie als von Gott gesetzte, vorbildliche Darstellungen, d. h. "Typen" kommender, und zwar vollkommener und größerer Fakten aufgefaßt werden. Fehlt zwischen Typus und Antitypus die Steigerung, stellt also letzterer nur eine Wiederholung des ersten Falles dar, so kann von Fall zu Fall nur bedingt von Typologie geredet werden.' This is in agreement with Auerbach, *Scenes from the Drama of European Literature*, p. 53: 'Figural interpretation establishes a connection between two events or persons, the first of which signifies not only itself but also the second, while the second encompasses or fulfills the first.'

the antitype can also imply a new promise, awaiting a new fulfilment,[1] but the essential point is that this new promise is one which is made by God only to His new people, the Christians, and not to the Hebrews who have turned from Him, so that the antitype still transcends its type.

This may best be shown in the case of the crusading fulfilment of what is recounted in Exodus by stressing the fact that, historically, the exodus of the Hebrews culminated in their occupation of a land which had been promised to them by God, whereas in the Christian interpretation this historical event also prefigures the salvation of Christendom accomplished by Christ. Clearly, in the view of any Christian, this antitype (salvation) transcends its type and represents its fulfilment, but at the same time it still implies a new promise which has yet to be fulfilled, for Christ's act of sacrifice has only created the means or possibility of salvation and it is still open to any Christian to tread this path to salvation or, like the Hebrews, to deny himself the realisation of what Christ has made possible by offending against those commandments of Christ which are the conditions of His promise of salvation under the New Covenant. It is here that the importance of the crusades in medieval religious history is revealed, for

---

[1] This important point is stressed by Jantsch, *loc. cit.*: 'So handelt es sich bei Typologie nicht um religionsgeschichtliche Parallelen, sondern um heilsgeschichtliche Aufeinanderbezogenheit, um die Kontinuität zwischen atl. Geschichte und Jesus Christus im Sinne von Vorbereitung und Erfüllung, *die ihrerseits wieder neue Verheißung ist*' (my italics). See also Auerbach, *op. cit.* p. 58: 'Both (*scil.* type and antitype) remain historical events; yet both, looked at in this way, have something provisional and incomplete about them; they point to one another and both point to something in the future, something still to come, which will be the actual, real, and definitive event. This is true not only of Old Testament prefiguration, which points forward to the incarnation and the proclamation of the gospel, but also of these latter events, for they too are not the ultimate fulfillment, but themselves a promise of the end of time and the true kingdom of God.' Cf. also the words by K. Löwith, *Weltgeschichte und Heilsgeschehen*, p. 172: '...das Königreich Gottes ist bereits erschienen, und dennoch steht es noch aus als ein *eschaton*. Diese Zweideutigkeit ist wesentlich für alle Geschichte seit Christus: die Zeit ist schon erfüllt, aber noch nicht vollendet.' The same point has also been well made by P. Zumthor, *Merlin le prophète*, pp. 128 f. (especially: 'on peut dire en un certain sens qu'elle (*scil.* la Rédemption) est inachevée, puisqu'elle doit se réaliser dans les âmes au fur et à mesure que se succèdent les générations').

participation in them is preached as a new and additional way of attaining to salvation, moreover a way which, unlike monasticism, is better calculated to appeal to the knight as more adequate to his calling in life. This is most forcibly expressed by Guibertus at the start of his work where, after discussing some of the wars of classical antiquity, he argues: '...instituit nostro tempore praelia sancta Deus, ut ordo equestris et vulgus oberrans, qui vetustae paganitatis exemplo in mutuas versabantur caedes, novum repperirent salutis promerendae genus; ut nec funditus electa (uti fieri assolet) monastica conversatione, seu religiosa qualibet professione, saeculum relinquere cogerentur, sed sub consueta licentia et habitu, ex suo ipsorum officio, Dei aliquatenus gratiam consequerentur.'[1] This important passage sets up crusading warfare as superior to the internecine warfare of classical antiquity because it is a means of attaining to God's grace, but it is also implicitly superior to the warfare involved in the exodus of the Hebrews, for their goal was the land of Canaan, whereas that of the crusaders is not simply the geographical region in which Jerusalem is situated, but primarily the gift of God's grace which had remained inaccessible to the Hebrews. The exodus of the new Israel therefore transcends that of the old precisely because it is, as the author of *Ezzos Gesang* makes clear, *spiritalis Israel.*

The superiority of the goal of the crusaders' exodus to that of the Israelites is implicit in the fact that the Jerusalem towards which the medieval knights march is felt to be not simply the physical city which they succeed in capturing, but also the prefiguration of the Heavenly Jerusalem as the true goal of every Christian.[2] Baldricus describes how this double aspect of the city is stressed in a speech before the assault in 1099: 'Certe, si bene et recte considerare volueritis, ista Jerusalem, quam videtis, cui advenistis, cui adestis, illam civitatem coelestem et

---

[1] *RHC*, IV, 124D and E.

[2] On the various possibilities of interpreting the concept of Jerusalem allegorically see the quotation from Guibertus of Nogent on p. 7. See also the article by S. Mähl, 'Jerusalem in mittelalterlicher Sicht', *WaG*, XXII, 11 ff.

praefigurat et praetendit; hanc nobis hostes ecce contradicunt visibiles; porro semitas ad illam pertendentes invisibiles obsident inimici, adversus quos spiritualis constat conflictus. Et gravius est nobis obluctari contra spiritualia nequitiae in coelestibus, quam adversus carnem et sanguinem quos videmus. Hi qui in civitatula ista ganniunt, illorum membra sunt, et suis magistris inferiores et imbecilliores sunt.'[1] Like the Hebrews on the march to Canaan the crusader has to fight his way to the same destination by force of arms, but unlike the Hebrews he recognises that his goal is also a spiritual one and that his conflict is therefore both physical and spiritual. This conviction of a twofold battle is also expressed by Gilo:

> VI, 281 Pugnat pro duplici regno, quia quaerit utramque
> Hierusalem, decertat in hac ut vivat in illa.[2]

Again it is in this respect that the crusaders' expedition surpasses the exodus of the Israelites, for whom Jerusalem was the *terra repromissionis* literally and physically, but not also, as it was for the Christians, *mater nostrae redemptionis ac fidei Hierusalem*.[3] It is in this sense that St Bernard was later to draw a contrast between the land *quae olim fluens lac et mel* and the land which is now the source of salvation for the whole world.[4]

Nor was this conception of Jerusalem as a spiritual goal of the crusades confined to the theological outlook of the clergy, for the chronicles show how this picture of Jerusalem as *mater nostrae redemptionis* impinged upon the experience of the individual crusader in two inescapable ways. On the one hand, the chosen knights of the crusade are assured of the remission of their sins, as is made clear by Urban's words reported by Baldricus, words addressed to the clergy but referring to the knights: 'Confessis peccatorum suorum ignominiam, securi de Christo paciscimini veniam.'[5] The same idea, where the remission of sins given to the

---

[1] *RHC*, IV, 101 A and B. [2] *RHC*, V, 798.
[3] *MGH* SS VI, 212, 42 f.
[4] *De laude novae militiae, MPL*, 182, 929: 'Salve, terra promissionis, quae olim fluens lac et mel tuis duntaxat habitatoribus, nunc universo orbi remedia salutis, vitae porrigis alimenta.' [5] *RHC*, IV, 15 F.

crusader is the guarantee that he will be granted access to the glory of the Heavenly Jerusalem, is attributed to the Pope in the description of the same occasion by Robertus Monachus: 'Arripite igitur viam hanc in remissionem peccatorum vestrorum, securi de immarcescibili gloria regni coelorum.'[1] With the anonymous chronicler of Schaffhausen the identical idea recurs ('...praedicavit et ubique praedicare jussit, ut quicumque christianus vellet se ultro Domino offerre, hoc poenitentiam et remissionem peccatorum susciperet, quo armatus ad expugnandam Hierosolymam pergeret')[2], so that there can be little doubt that the possibility of attaining to the Heavenly Jerusalem by the remission of sins in joining the armed expedition to the earthly city was one of the compelling ideas of the First Crusade. It is also made clear that the crusader who is prevented from reaching the earthly goal of the expedition will nonetheless be assured of access to the Heavenly Jerusalem which is his true destination. Fulcherius indicates this in his report of the papal address at Clermont, for he has the Pope say that the remission of sins granted to the knight setting out would remain valid even if he were to die on the journey: 'Cunctis autem illuc euntibus, is aut gradiendo aut transfretando, sive contra paganos dimicando, vitam morte praepeditam finierint, remissio peccatorum praesens aderit.'[3] Because of this, emphasis is placed on the contrast between the eternal reward awaiting the crusader and the miserable pittance which is the secular warrior's lot: 'Nunc aeterna praemia nanciscantur, qui dudum pro solidis paucis mercenarii fuerunt.'[4] The eternal reward of the crusader who fails to reach Jerusalem is that he dies as a martyr and is therefore to be judged fortunate in being allowed so speedy an access to the Heavenly City. Bohemond, in a harangue reported by Robertus Monachus, argues: 'O felices qui in tali opere deficient; qui ante visuri sunt Paradisum quam patriam suam! O ordo militum, nunc terque quaterque beatus! Qui huc usque fuisti homicidii sanguine deturpatus, nunc sanctorum sudoribus compar martyrum coelesti es

[1] *RHC*, III, 729 B.
[2] *RHC*, III, 324 B.
[3] *RHC*, V, 336 E.
[4] *RHC*, III, 324 D.

diademate laureatus. Huc usque exstitisti incitamentum irae Dei; nunc vero reconciliatio gratiae ipsius, et propugnaculum fidei suae.'[1] Those who die in the course of the journey, whether in battle or not, are felt to have attained to immediate martyrdom, so that it is said of those who died in the siege of Nicea: 'et multi ex nostris illic receperunt martirium et letantes gaudentesque reddiderunt felices animas Deo et ex pauperrima gente multi mortui sunt fame pro Christi nomine, qui in celum triumphantes portaverunt stolam recepti martirii.'[2] The alternative for the crusading knight in any particular battle is therefore victory or martyrdom, and as regards the whole undertaking it is to reach the earthly city of Jerusalem or to be admitted to the Heavenly City. In the latter case he will have reached his ultimate goal as a Christian; in the former he will have done much to ensure his success in finally reaching it.

This interpretation by the chroniclers of the double goal of every crusader who reaches Jerusalem (whilst even those who die on the way are assured that they will reach the spiritual Jerusalem) amounts to a conviction that the exodus of the crusaders, by the very fact of its spiritual goal, transcends the physical goal of the Hebrew exodus. As a member of the new people chosen by God to whom this new means of attaining to God's grace has been granted only in his own time, the crusader can therefore feel confident that the God of Israel has transferred His attention to the new Israel and that the promises and prophecies of the Old Covenant refer only to the fulfilment which he is helping to achieve in the present. This does much to explain the mood of elation and of accomplishment, the feeling of being privileged to live in the fullness of time, which we find in the First Crusade and also to some extent amongst the knightly class and in the knightly literature of Western Europe in the twelfth century. But, as we saw, although the crusading exodus was felt to transcend its *praefiguratio* in the exodus of the Hebrews, like many an antitype it still implies a new promise which awaits

[1] *RHC*, III, 748 A.
[2] See *Histoire anonyme de la première croisade*, p. 42.

fulfilment. It is here that the Hebrew example, although it accounts for the crusaders' sense of achievement and conviction of divine assistance, also provides a salutary warning, for if the crusaders repeat the Israelites' sin of lack of faith then it is possible that God will turn aside from the Christian army as He had once abandoned the Hebrews. This we find expressed by Raimundus de Aguilers, who describes at length a vision in which God appears to Petrus Bartholomeus.[1] He is asked by Christ whether he knows what people God had chosen and replies mentioning the Jews. To this Christ answers with a warning to the crusaders taken from the fate of their predecessors: 'Hi quoniam increduli fuerunt, odio eos habui, et inferiores omnibus gentibus stabilivi. Videte itaque ne increduli sitis. Alioquin, vobis remanentibus cum Judaeis, alios populos assumam, et per ipsos complebo quae vobis promiseram.'[2] Implicit in these words is the view that, although the crusader who meets his death on the journey to Jerusalem may have gained certain entry into the Heavenly Jerusalem, all the others who are taking part in the expedition can have no absolute certainty that they too will be granted admittance, but only the certainty that this will be granted to them as long as they keep faith with Christ. If they fail to do this they are guilty of the sin of the Hebrews, but if they retain their faith they can be assured that they will reach their double goal and thereby transcend the exodus of the first Chosen People. The theory that the crusaders are a new people chosen by God is therefore far removed from a mood of (essentially passive) confidence that victory is assured because of God's support; instead it lays great emphasis on the active contribution which the crusaders themselves have to make, the absence of which can indeed cost them their place in the history of salvation as the successors of Israel and its potential surpassers.

With that we have come to the end of our survey of the way in which the chroniclers of the First Crusade gave the events they were narrating a place and a justification in the Christian view of history by means of a constant parallelism between the events

---

[1] *RHC*, iii, 279 f. [2] *RHC*, iii, 280 D.

of the Old Testament and those of the present. We saw that these parallels could be discovered in various books of the Old Testament, especially in those which treated the wars of Israel with the Gentiles and in the prophetic books with the possibility they provided of interpreting the medieval present as the fulfilment to which the prophets had looked forward. Nonetheless, there is some justification for attributing to the Book of Exodus a special importance in this, for, in addition to the theme of warfare, it provided a general framework which could be applied to the crusaders' exodus for the Holy Land and occupation of the territory of Canaan in the face of pagan opposition. This connection between Exodus and the crusade which the chroniclers establish in such a way that the latter is constantly implied as transcending the Hebrew past has its counterpart in the converse technique adopted by the Millstatt author where he repeatedly transposes the events of the Exodus story into the twelfth-century present and emphasises, not the unique particularity of these events of Hebrew history, but instead their topical relevance to the interests of his knightly audience. The correspondence between these two techniques is a striking one and suggests that there might be a causal relationship between them—in other words, that for the Millstatt author the relevance of the Exodus story to the knights of his day lay in its crusading implications, its suggestion that the support given by God to Moses and the Israelites in their departure for the Promised Land was the guarantee that His assistance would be no less in the case of the knightly exodus to the Holy Land. Against this it might be argued that the correspondence we have established between the method adopted by the author of the *Millstätter Exodus* and the converse technique of the crusading chroniclers is so general that it could be fortuitous and therefore fail to demonstrate a causal relationship between the German epic and the crusades. To meet this objection we must now consider a number of detailed points where certain motifs that occur in the German work can be shown to be characteristic of the crusading movement and the religious attitude that inspired it.

The Book of Exodus and the crusades

We may start with the parallel between the use of the term *gotes rîtere* in the Millstatt epic (v. 1482) and the use of the title *miles Dei* in application to the crusader. Here I am not concerned with the fact that the flies of the plague summoned by God are designated by the more modern term *rîter*, rather than by such traditional heroic words as *recke*, *wîgant*, or *helt*. Much more important is the fact, contested by Fliegner,[1] that this phrase, used for the first time in German literature in the *Millstätter Exodus*, originates in this particular function in the experience of the crusades. It may also be true that this term is not applied to Moses and the Israelites, but instead to the flies called upon to attack the Egyptians as a plague. We shall return to this point later, but in the present context we are interested solely in the fact that these flies, described as attacking the pagans (v. 1489) on God's behalf (v. 1494) as a military formation (cf. the use of *here* in vv. 1486 and 1608), are termed *gotes rîtere* in a manner which has more in common with the use of *miles Dei* to designate the crusader than with the more conventional use of this Latin phrase before the rise of the crusading movement.

Once more we must turn to Erdmann for information on the way in which it is the crusading movement that first introduces a significant change in the use of this phrase. He starts[2] with the fact that the application of the military term *miles* to Christianity first occurs with St Paul (II Tim. 2. 3 f.: 'Labora sicut bonus miles Christi Jesu. Nemo militans Deo implicat se negotiis saecularibus'), but stresses that, since the war in question is waged by the Christian against demons or against the vices within his own character, this usage is purely metaphorical. It is this that remains constant in the Early Christian and early medieval employment of this term for, no matter whether it is every Christian who is regarded as a *miles Dei* or, more particularly, the apostles and missionaries (as with St Paul himself) or clerics or martyrs or monks, the battle is in every case to be fought with spiritual weapons against spiritual enemies. This is confirmed by

---

[1] *Geistliches und weltliches Rittertum im Rolandslied*, pp. 32 f.
[2] *Die Entstehung des Kreuzzugsgedankens*, p. 10.

the equation of *militia Dei* with *militia spiritualis* or by the contrast between secular warfare and *militia Dei*.[1] The metaphorical quality of the phrase is complemented by the position in OHG literature, where the vernacular equivalents *gotes thegan* and *gotes man* are employed so as to indicate the primary fact of service or obedience to God and, if a military context is at all suggested, the need for the passive virtues of the martyr.[2] All this is part of the wider problem of the way in which those terms which had been adopted as part of the Christian vocabulary from the heroic vocabulary of Germanic were made more acceptable by being progressively deprived of their military implications.[3] It is only with the eleventh century, as Erdmann has shown, that this gulf between *militia Christi* and *militia saecularis* is successfully bridged in such a way that a religious justification was granted to the profession of arms whenever it was exercised in the service of the Church or of the poor and weak, so that it is now each individual knight (and not just the ruler as in the OHG *Ludwigslied*) who has religious duties to perform within his station in life.

Erdmann follows this process in detail, but it is significant that he regards his examples for the idea that God can now be served by a military form of service as contributing to the growth of the crusading idea in which this form of service of God finds its historically most important expression. It is reported of the knightly Erlembald who served the papal cause in the *pataria* and who met his death as a martyr that, on his return from a

---

[1] *Die Entstehung des Kreuzzugsgedankens*, p. 11.

[2] On the evidence for this see *The Carolingian Lord*, pp. 323 ff. In this development of the concept of the *miles Dei* a special position is occupied by the martyr. Like the Pauline Christian and like the monk, the martyr faces a spiritual adversary and knows that his struggle is with Satan; but unlike these others, the martyr must also undergo a physical combat, whether in the arena or as the victim of the executioner. This twofold nature of the martyr's *militia Christi* (spiritual and physical) might appear to relate him closely to the crusader's double form of combat, yet the two remain quite distinct since in his physical combat the martyr remains essentially passive and does not take up arms against his adversary. In his *active* function as a physical and spiritual warrior the crusader therefore remains unique in this development.

[3] See F. Willems, *Heldenwörter in germanischer und christlicher Literatur*.

pilgrimage to Jerusalem, he was preoccupied with the idea of becoming a monk, but was advised by a cleric that his merit with God would be greater if he were to remain a knight and fight on behalf of the Church, as had formerly Mathathias and his sons.[1] It is in the period of Gregory VII that the linguistic use of the phrase *miles Dei* confirms the change in attitude which these words of Ariald to Erlembald suggest. Erdmann indicates that this period still commonly uses the term in its traditional metaphorical sense of a form of service of God which was irreconcilable with the shedding of blood by the Christian.[2] This is still true in part of Gregory VII himself, but it is also he who is now prepared to apply this term to those who serve the Church by the sword, so that for him the same Erlembald is a *strenuissimus Christi miles*[3] and those who were to have taken part in the crusade he was planning are described as prepared to defend the Christian faith and to do battle on behalf of the Heavenly King.[4] A similar ambiguity between the metaphorical and literal sense of comparable terms is to be found elsewhere with Gregory: the *gladius s. Petri* can therefore denote a papal excommunication or a war conducted on behalf of the papacy against its opponents.[5] With the term *militia s. Petri* the Gregorian reconciliation of warfare with Christianity proceeds a step further, for it is applied only to laymen and knights and thus has none of that ambiguity which still adhered to the use of *militia Dei*.[6]

It is with the First Crusade that this process, whereby an originally military term employed as a Christian metaphor in a non-military sense once more acquires a fully military connotation (this time in the context of feudalism), reaches its conclusion. We have seen how Guibertus is convinced that God has instituted the crusades in his day so as to provide a means for the knights to achieve salvation without having to leave the world.[7]

[1] Cf. Andreas of Strumi, c. 15 (*MGH* SS xxx, ɪɪ, 1059 f.). Quoted by Erdmann, *Die Entstehung des Kreuzzugsgedankens*, p. 128.
[2] *Op. cit.* p. 185.   [3] *Ibid.* p. 187.   [4] *Ibid.*
[5] *Ibid.*   [6] *Ibid.* pp. 188 ff.   [7] See p. 267.

Something similar is reported of Tancred by Radulfus Cadomensis who describes at the start of his *Gesta Tancredi* how his hero's military ardour, weakened by his awareness of the conflict between knighthood and Christianity, was reawakened by Urban's proclamation of the First Crusade: 'At postquam Urbani papae sententia universis Christianorum gentilia expugnaturis peccatorum omnium remissionem ascripsit, tunc demum quasi sopiti prius experrecta est viri strenuitas, vires assumptae, oculi aperti, audacia geminata. Prius namque, ut praescriptum est, animus ejus in bivium secabatur, ambiguus utrius sequeretur vestigia, Evangelii, an mundi? Experientia vero armorum ad Christi obsequium revocata, supra credibile virum accendit militandi duplicata occasio.'[1] It is the First Crusade that supplies the clearest opportunity for the knights of bridging the gap separating the obligations of their rank from the demands of their religion and even makes it possible for them to cease offending God by shedding Christian blood, and actually to gain salvation by using their swords on His behalf. The alternative for the knight is no longer between exercising his military profession and gaining his soul, as Baldricus makes clear in his account of the papal criticism of the knights' past brutality: 'Vos accincti cingulo militiae, magno superbitis supercilio; fratres vestros laniatis, atque inter vos dissecamini. Non est haec militia Christi, quae discerpit ovile Redemptoris. Sancta Ecclesia ad suorum opitulationem sibi reservavit militiam, sed vos eam male depravatis in malitiam....Porro si vultis animabus vestris consuli, aut istiusmodi militiae cingulum quantocius deponite, aut Christi milites audacter procedite, et ad defendendam Orientalem Ecclesiam velocius concurrite.'[2] Now the choice is between the knight losing his soul by keeping to the way of secular warfare and gaining salvation by becoming a *Christi miles*, so that there is no longer an unbridgeable gulf between his religion and the military functions of his class. By the time of the First Crusade the innovation for which Gregory VII was primarily responsible has therefore become general practice: *Christi milites* or *militia*

[1] *RHC*, III, 606 A and B.   [2] *RHC*, IV, 14 F and H.

Christi is employed frequently in the *Gesta Francorum*, for example, as a standing term for the crusaders.[1] From now on it denotes not merely the monks, fighting a spiritual battle on behalf of God against the demons, but also the crusaders, waging a physical battle on behalf of God against the pagans. The change of meaning which the word *miles* had therefore undergone in its adaptation to Christian ends by St Paul (a spiritualisation of a concrete term) may well persist through the Middle Ages, but from the eleventh century onwards the term, even in a Christian function, can also be materialised again in application to the knight who serves God by the sword.[2]

In other words, Erdmann has demonstrated that the use of the phrase *miles Dei* in a material sense to denote the physical act of serving God in combat is an eleventh-century innovation which reflects the concern of the reform movement to impose a Christian code of conduct upon the feudal knighthood and which is at all stages closely connected with the development of the crusading idea. When, therefore, the author of the *Millstätter Exodus* is not merely the first to employ the term *gotes rîtere* in German, but is also the first to apply this phrase to a physical attack, which he stylises in military terms, launched against the pagans on behalf of God, we can be certain that his linguistic usage is a reflection of crusading ideas and terminology without which it would be unthinkable. It may well be the case that it is the plague

---

[1] E.g. 1, 3 (p. 5), II, 6 (p. 11), II, 5 (p. 11), II, 7 (p. 14). When, however, the first of these examples is translated as 'the Christian army' (p. 6) this may well be the conventional equivalent in modern English, yet it destroys the suggestion that these knights were seen as the feudal vassals of Christ.

[2] Bruno Astensis makes it quite clear how easily the exodus could be interpreted allegorically as a form of spiritual warfare: 'Quod autem filii Israel armati ascenderunt de Aegypto, significatio est, quia ex quo mundum relinquimus, semper contra vitia et malignos spiritus a dextris et a sinistris armati pugnare debemus' (*MPL*, 164, 263 D). He even manages to introduce the idea of martyrdom into this context: 'Venit igitur populus de Ethan in Atharoth, quia jam coepta navigatione, quibusdam virtutum gradibus proficiens, venit ad coronam, sperans, si necesse fuerit, mori posse pro nomine Christi' (*ibid.* 264 D). All the Millstatt author has to do to this interpretation is to represent it physically and literally, as well as metaphorically—an attitude which he shares with those authors analysed by Erdmann who likewise begin to understand the ideal of *militia Christi* in literal terms.

of flies and not the Israelites who are described by such a specifically crusading term, but for us the important thing in the present context is that it is a crusading term which is here employed, not the manner in which it may be used by the author. The crusading implications of this particular scene in the Millstatt epic are also present in another phrase employed by the author when describing the flies' attacks on the Egyptians: 'si bizzen unde stâchen, | gotes anden si râchen' (vv. 1493 f.). The conception that the plague, viewed as consisting of *gotes rîtere*, should be concerned with 'avenging the insults to God' is a motif which occurs elsewhere in crusading literature in the vernacular[1] and appears also to be an innovation resulting from the crusades themselves. The novelty of this idea can best be appreciated by a comparison with the position in Carolingian literature, which here gives expression to tendencies already apparent in the society of the Merovingian Franks. The Germanic phenomenon of the blood-feud, with its legal and moral justification of vengeance, was opposed by the Church from the earliest times.[2] The grounds for this opposition are likely to have been practical ones (the dangers of social disintegration as a result of a prolonged blood-feud), but also ones of principle, where the rejection of warfare by the early medieval Church (especially necessary wherever the Church came into contact with the heroic ideals of Germania) forms the wider background to the particular problem of the feud. In one sense the Germanic idea of vengeance could be given a Christian function, for Wallace-Hadrill has indicated the way in which Rom. 12. 19 ('Mihi vindicta, ego retribuam, dicit Dominus'), itself taken from Deut. 32. 35 ('Mea est ultio, et ego retribuam in tempore'), was regarded very much

---

[1] E.g. *Rolandslied*, 8160 ('daz wir den gotes anden | an in sculen rechen'), Albrecht von Johannsdorf, *MF*, 89, 24 (used by critics of the crusade, but certainly reflecting crusading ideas). The same idea is also implicit in Walther, 79, 6, even though he elsewhere expressed the view that God will seek vengeance for Himself (76, 29; 78, 1). For the *Millstätter Exodus* itself we need also to consider the negative possibility: that Pharaoh, as the opponent of God, is precisely concerned with the insults shown to the Devil (vv. 1966 f.).

[2] See *The Carolingian Lord*, pp. 308 ff.

from the point of view of Germanic experience of vengeance, with God striking to kill, to avenge an insult, like any leader of a warrior-band.[1] But here the novelty of the Christian view was precisely that it was God Himself who intervened in human affairs to exact vengeance or at the most a human agent, such as the king, chosen to act on His behalf. The fact that God's vengeance is stressed at all and is seen in terms of the Germanic form of vengeance means that, in theory at least, there is no place for personal vengeance by the individual in the Christian view of things.

Exactly how deeply felt was this attitude can be shown in the case of the OS *Heliand*, the work which has most often been invoked as testimony to the persistence of Germanic ideas. In this work the verb *wrekan* is used once in the Sermon on the Mount to indicate the force of the divine prohibition of all forms of human vengeance.[2] Elsewhere it is used to show the rejection of this need for vengeance even by Christ (for whom a justification of the *ultio divina* of Rom. 12. 19 would have been conceivable), for we are twice shown His passive humility in the face of taunts or the supreme humiliation of the crucifixion and are told that He refused to obtain vengeance for Himself.[3] By contrast with these clearcut examples (one a theoretical injunction by Christ, the others illustrating His rejection of vengeance even for Himself) the occurrence of the verb on one other occasion to suggest the (secular) punishment which Pilate is to inflict on Christ[4] indicates unmistakably the sinful nature of such vengeance. The same is true of the two occasions when the noun *wrâka* is employed in the OS epics, for in the *Genesis* it refers to Cain's

---

[1] *RJRL.*, XLI, 459 ff. This article has been reproduced in the same author's *The Long-haired Kings*, pp. 121 ff.

[2] V. 1533: 'that gi sô ni uurecan uurêða dâdi, | ac that gi thurh ôdmôdi al gethologian | uuities endi uuammes.'

[3] V. 5078: 'He thagoda endi tholoda: ni sprak imu io thiu thiod sô filu, | thea liudi mid luginun, that he it mid lêðun angegin | wordun uurâchi'; 5539: 'Hie ni uuelda thoh thia dâd uurecan | grimma an them Iudeon.' This verb also occurs once in the OS *Genesis* to describe the angel's punishment of Antichrist (v. 146: 'uurikit ina, uuammscaðon uuâpnas eggiun'), but there is certainly no suggestion that any conclusions are to be drawn from this as to how man may behave.

[4] V. 5365.

murder of his brother[1] and in the *Heliand* it is used with reference
to Peter's incomprehension of Christ's commandment of forgive-
ness.[2] Nor can one argue that of these examples from OS literature
some refer to vengeance exacted (or not) on behalf of injuries
to human beings, so that they represent no true contrast to the
phrase in the *Millstätter Exodus* where it is vengeance for the
insults to God which is obtained. The objection to this argument
is that it ignores the express refusal of Christ to seek vengeance
on behalf of Himself, so that when Peter draws the sword in
defence of Him he is rebuked for it in terms that show that the
OS author, like Otfrid, was prepared to make no concessions to
Germanic mentality on this point.[3] For him bloodshed incurred
in exacting vengeance on behalf of Christ is as reprehensible as
violence in a purely human feud.

When the Millstatt author uses the phrase *gotes anden rechen*
in what he conceives as a military context, his attitude therefore
represents a drastic innovation compared with the view expressed
earlier in Carolingian literature. Are there any grounds for
thinking that this innovation owes anything to the crusading
movement? Here again the chronicles provide us with the information we need, for they frequently refer to the crusade as an
expedition undertaken by the knights to avenge the insult shown
to God by the pagans' occupation of a land which is rightly His
and by the contempt they show Him in practising their rites on
such hallowed soil. The act of religious vengeance which had
been regarded earlier as justifiable only in the case of vengeance
exacted by God or by someone appointed by Him is here conceived as the religious duty of the crusader, who now considers
himself as acting in God's name (whereas previously this role had
been restricted to the ruler). Ordericus Vitalis can mention the
preparation for a departure for the crusade in these terms: 'arma

[1] V. 78: 'uuallandi stêt | thînes brôðor uurâca bitter an helli.'
[2] V. 3245: 'scal ik im siðun sîðun iro sundea alâten, | uurêðaro uuerko, êr than
ik is êniga uurâka frummie, | lêðes te lône?'
[3] On the critical attitude of the OS author and Otfrid to warfare see *The
Carolingian Lord*, pp. 331 ff. It is perhaps significant that Otfrid nowhere even
uses words corresponding to OS *wrâka* and *wrekan*.

emebantur, quibus ultio divina super Allophilos exerceretur',[1] where the conviction that God's purposes (here still referred to as God's vengeance) are being achieved through the crusaders as His agents has much in common with the feeling of elation resulting from their belief that they constituted a new Chosen People. Baldricus, in reporting a harangue before the assault on Jerusalem, has his speaker make a comparison between the vengeance which the knight exacts for an injury done to his kindred and the military assistance which it is his duty to bring to his kinsman Christ:[2] 'Patribus et filiis et fratribus et nepotibus dico: numquid si quis externus vestrum aliquem percusserit, sanguinem vestrum non ulciscemini?[3] Multo magis Deum vestrum, patrem vestrum, fratrem vestrum ulcisci debetis: quem exprobrari, quem proscribi, quem crucifigi videtis; quem clamantem et desolatum et auxilium poscentem auditis: Torcular calcavi solus, et de gentibus non est vir mecum.'[4] Whereas the author of the *Heliand* had stressed the gulf between Christ's precepts and the bloodshed to which obedience to the kinship inevitably led and had rejected the latter unconditionally, now it is the case that Baldricus (or the speaker whose argument he reproduces in obvious agreement with it) can appeal to the kinship and its unquestioned acceptance of the need for vengeance as a means of strengthening his religious argument. The behaviour for which Christ had rebuked Peter in the *Heliand* and in Otfrid's account of the scene where

[1] *Historia ecclesiastica*, III, 468.

[2] The very fact that this comparison could be made is sufficient to indicate the difference in outlook between the ninth century and the period around 1100. Baldricus and his contemporaries can make an appeal to the secular example of vengeance on behalf of the kindred as a way of persuading the knights of their similar duty towards God, whereas the opposite situation is to be found in the *Heliand*. Here the earlier author had not hesitated to subject the institution of the kindred and the vengeance exacted in its name to a Christian criticism (e.g. vv. 1492 ff.), so that with him it is rather the case that vengeance on behalf of the kindred and service of God are shown up as irreconcilable.

[3] The unquestioned way in which vengeance on behalf of one's kindred is accepted here without any hint of criticism provides an interesting parallel to the way in which the Millstatt author similarly depicts Moses' encounter with the Egyptian overseer in terms of vengeance for the kindred. See above, p. 149.

[4] *RHC*, IV, 101 F and G.

the apostle draws his sword in defence of his Lord[1] has become by now a Christian virtue for the crusader, if he is to repay the sacrifice which Christ made for him with an adequate form of service (in the words of Baldricus: 'Et pulchrum sit mori vobis pro Christo in ista regione, pro quibus Christus mortuus est in ista civitate.')[2] So central has this conception of avenging God now become that the crusade can be regarded as an undertaking with this end in view: 'totum mundum Christianitatis contra paganos incitatum ad ultionem pro Deo infremuisse',[3] where the possible reference to the *injuriae Dei*[4] forms an even closer parallel to the words used by the Millstatt author.

The knights' belief that they have been granted the privilege by God of avenging the insults offered to Him, that they are the instruments of His will, presupposes a number of contacts with other aspects of the crusading mentality which suggest that this idea of the knights being in a position to obtain vengeance for God is intimately bound up with the emergence of the crusading idea. One such example is provided by the fact that the crusaders' idea of vengeance rests on the conviction that God has chosen them as the *ultores Dei*, for this sense of election is obviously connected with the Hebrew idea of the Chosen People which we have considered in its application to medieval Christendom at large, and more particularly to the crusaders as the new *populus Dei*.[5] That the election of the knights as *ultores Dei* is causally connected with the conception of the crusaders (rather than of all Christians) as the *populus Dei* is best revealed by the second

---

[1] For a discussion of this scene in these two works see *The Carolingian Lord*, pp. 332 f. and 336.

[2] *RHC*, IV, 101 G.

[3] *Cartulaire de Saint-Bertin* (ed. M. Guérard), p. 271. Quoted by Rousset.

[4] E.g. *MGH* SS VI, 367 ('ultum ire parant injurias Dei in hostes christiani nominis') or the letter written by the crusading leaders after the fall of Antioch (Hagenmeyer, *Epistulae et chartae ad historiam primi belli sacri spectantes*, p. 161): 'Turci, qui multa Domino nostro Jesu Christo intulerant opprobria...et nos Hierosolimitani Jesu Christi injuriam summi Dei vindicavimus.'

[5] The role of *ultores Dei* need not be taken over only by God's Chosen People, but may also be taken over by pagans whom He has appointed to serve His purpose as a scourge of God (cf. the *Alexanderlied*). However, in the case of the crusaders the direct equation of *ultores Dei* with *populus Dei* is normally upheld.

point, for this role of *ultores Dei* can only be played by warriors who are convinced that their profession of arms (and the bloodshed it involves) is acceptable to God if subordinated to the needs of the Church. This conviction, as Erdmann has shown, is established only as part of the emergence of the crusading idea, so that we are justified in regarding not merely the acceptance of Christian warfare at large but also the particular idea of exacting vengeance by force on behalf of God as part of the same process. There is, however, yet a third aspect where our evidence for the idea of seeking vengeance for God appears to be connected with the idea of the crusade. This concerns the argument used by Baldricus, for in the speech before the assault on Jerusalem which he reports the point is made that just as Christ, who is described as the Christian knights' *dux* in battle, died for the crusaders in that city, so ought these knights to be prepared to lay down their lives for Him.[1] This argument, which recurs elsewhere,[2] sees the relationship between God and the crusaders in feudal terms and therefore stresses its reciprocity. This aspect of the vengeance exacted by the crusaders for God leads us to the third parallel between the *Millstätter Exodus* and crusading experience, the fact that both see man's relationship with God as a feudal nexus.[3]

[1] See p. 282, n. 2. This motif therefore expresses both a feudal form of Christianity and a particular manner of knightly *imitatio Christi*.

[2] It is attributed by Baldricus himself to Urban II at Clermont (*RHC*, IV, 15 B): 'Pulchrum sit vobis mori in illa civitate pro Christo, in qua Christus pro vobis mortuus est.' For later examples of the same argument employed by the Church see G. Wolfram, *ZfdA*, XXX, 98 (Popes Alexander, 1181, and Innocent, 1198) and 101.

[3] I do not, of course, wish to suggest in what follows that a feudal conception of Christianity must necessarily belong to the crusading movement—against this it is sufficient to point to the feudal aspects of Carolingian religious literature (see *The Carolingian Lord, passim*) or to the presence of feudal features in a work like the *Wiener Genesis* whose Christianity is so essentially pacific. Instead, my argument is simply that, in a work which conceives *militia Dei* in tangibly physical terms as the military service rendered to God by knights on the field of battle, feudal motifs and symbolism will necessarily be attracted to this concept of warfare waged on behalf of God and come to be closely associated with it. Since this physical understanding of *militia Dei* is something new in the crusading movement (cf. Erdmann, *Die Entstehung des Kreuzzugsgedankens*, pp. 188 ff.), we must expect the feudal terminology of twelfth-century religious literature to have quite different implications from the feudal vocabulary of the ninth century.

The Millstätter Exodus

The adaptation of feudal terminology to Christian purposes was no novelty at the time of the First Crusade, for the evidence of OHG suggests that much of the Christian vocabulary of this period was borrowed from feudalism or from certain aspects of the Germanic *comitatus* which had survived as constituents of emergent feudalism.[1] How far this linguistic evidence of OHG reflects a mental attitude which regarded Christianity in a feudal light we cannot say with any certainty, but at least ninth-century German tells us that in this period the Church made successful attempts to separate its Christian vocabulary from the context of feudalism from which it originally derived and to stress instead the Christian truth that the relationship between God and man was not reciprocal (like the feudal nexus), but that God had unilateral rights over man and that man could not claim any corresponding rights from God.[2] When German literature in the vernacular starts again from about 1060 and implies that the relationship between man and God is a feudal one (Rupp has shown this for *Ezzos Gesang*[3] and we have seen something similar in the *Millstätter Exodus*)[4] we can be sure that this attitude is no direct continuation of the position reached in the latest Carolingian period, for here the achievement of Otfrid had been to break down the reciprocity of Christian vocabulary and to suggest that the relationship between man and God was strictly unilateral. The religious conception of German literature in the period after 1060 (including the Millstatt epic) is therefore as novel as was the development, at about the same time, of the idea that a knight could serve God by taking up arms in His service. In other words, we have to ask whether the feudal elements in the *Millstätter Exodus*, like the use of the term *gotes rîtere* and the idea of gaining vengeance on behalf of God, may not owe their importance to the crusading idea.[5]

[1] *The Carolingian Lord*, pp. 115 ff. [2] *Ibid.* pp. 358 ff.
[3] *Deutsche religiöse Dichtungen*, pp. 27 ff.
[4] See above, pp. 170 ff.
[5] See above (p. 283, n. 3) for the qualification that the feudal elements in such a work as the *Millstätter Exodus*, where they occur alongside crusading concepts such as *gotes rîtere* and *gotes anden rechen*, form part of a crusading ideal

The Book of Exodus and the crusades

Some of our evidence has already suggested the possibility of this. Erdmann, when discussing the Gregorian use of the term *militia s. Petri*, makes the observation that by this time the word *miles* no longer simply designated a warrior, but had also come to be employed as a technical term for the feudal vassal.[1] Something similar is possibly true of the vernacular *rîtere* employed by the Millstatt author[2] (together with such terms as *man* or *trût*), so that its function is likely to have been as much feudal as military. Furthermore, if there is a connection between the idea of *gotes rîtere* and vengeance on behalf of God (which is made likely by the way in which our author introduces both these new ideas in the same episode, separated by only eleven lines), then it is

in which God is served in battle by feudal knights. The same is manifestly not true of such a work as the *Wiener Genesis* where, because of its non-military spirit, these feudal elements cannot be attracted to the crusading theme. These two works therefore agree in both seeing Christianity in a feudal light, but differ radically in that it is only the later work which associates its feudal elements with the ideal of crusading warfare.

[1] *Die Entstehung des Kreuzzugsgedankens*, p. 188.

[2] This cannot be strictly proved for the *Millstätter Exodus*, although I regard it as highly probable. Admittedly, E. Schröder (*ZfdA*, LXV, 289 ff.) argued in favour of a late dating for the *Rolandslied* by claiming that the word *rîter* shows the meaning 'knight' (from which the sense of 'feudal vassal' must be derived), rather than simply 'horseman', only from about 1150 onwards. Against this view L. Wolff (*AfdA*, LXVI, 56) has adduced telling material in favour of an earlier development of the knightly meaning ('Aber seit etwa 1130 ist das Wort in der Bedeutung "Ritter" doch reichlich und klar bezeugt'). He admits the possible ambiguity of *Wiener Genesis* 5060 and concedes that the same is true of *Die Hochzeit* 263 and 303. In the Millstatt epic the word *rîterscephte* (v. 1346) still clearly means 'horsemen' (cf. 1347: *in rossen noh in mûlen*), and the same may perhaps be true of the description of the flies as *rîtere* (v. 1482) since their quick, darting movements may have suggested the image of swerving horsemen. On the other hand, the way in which the *Millstätter Genesis* 77, 7 substitutes *rîter* (in the sense of 'knight') for *herre* of the *Wiener Genesis* (v. 3676) shows that this new meaning was known by about 1130. This brings us to a date very close to that of the *Millstätter Exodus*, so that it is equally likely that the *rîtere* of v. 1482 (where no mention is made of horses as in v. 1347) describes the flies as knights rather than as horsemen. A decision in favour of this interpretation is suggested by the dependence of the phrase *gotes rîtere* on its model *milites Dei*, a term which designated the crusaders not as 'the horsemen of God', but instead as knightly warriors who served God as their feudal Lord.

It is regrettable that J. Bumke, in his invaluable *Studien zum Ritterbegriff im 12. und 13. Jahrhundert*, should have decided not to discuss the evidence for *gotes rîter* (p. 84, n. 107).

probable that the vengeance exacted by these 'knights' for the injury done to God was conceived in terms of a feudal obligation in which the vassal is called upon to put right an affront done to his lord. This would be confirmed by the manner in which Baldricus emphasises the reciprocity of the relationship between the crusaders dying for their *dux* and God who had died for them. It is this typically feudal conception of the reciprocal relationship between man and God (a conception which Otfrid had been largely successful in removing from his Christian vocabulary) which provides such a close parallel between the *Millstätter Exodus* and the evidence of the crusading chronicles. We saw that one of the innovations of our author was to emphasise the reciprocity between man's service of God and God's unfailing reward to man and also to suggest, by his use of the feudal concept of *triuwe*, that man and God were so much bound to one another by mutual obligations that Moses could even reproachfully remind God that He had failed to keep His part of the compact.[1] Such views are also to be found in the chronicles where, as in the Millstatt work, they contrast with the unilateralism established for OHG by Otfrid. The idea of God's reward to the crusaders lies at the heart of such concepts as the remission of sins for those who take part, the promise of admission to the Heavenly Jerusalem, and the honour of martyrs' crowns for those who die on the expedition. It is also given programmatic importance (especially, for us, by its close association with the idea of *militia Christi*) in the words attributed by Fulcherius to Urban II: 'Nunc fiant Christi milites, qui dudum exstiterunt raptores. Nunc jure contra barbaros pugnent, qui olim adversus fratres et consanguineos dimicabant. Nunc aeterna praemia nanciscantur, qui dudum pro solidis paucis mercenarii fuerunt.'[2] Such a promise of divine reward for man's service of God differs obviously from Otfrid's conception because of the fact that the service rendered is explicitly military.[3] In addition to this, the promise of God's

---

[1] See pp. 173 f.   [2] *RHC*, III, 324 D.
[3] On the non-military nature of man's service of God, as conceived by Otfrid, see *The Carolingian Lord*, pp. 333 ff.

reward as the counterpart to service, although not necessarily present in Urban's words, certainly encouraged the growth of the idea amongst the crusaders that by their military service they had a right to expect constant rewards from God. This idea is particularly obvious in the case of battles, for God's apparent failure to reward His knights with victory can sometimes be explained, in accord with the Old Testament example, by reference to their sinfulness, but at times in such a way as to suggest a connection between service and victory that leaves little room for any ethical subtlety. Thus the way in which Christ is described by an English chronicler as appearing to the crusaders, downhearted because of a recent defeat, and promising them victory as soon as they decide to keep their contract with Him ('Dic populo meo: "Revertimini ad me, et ego ad vos; et infra v dies vobis ipse propugnator adero"')[1] complements what we saw in the *Millstätter Exodus* where on more than one occasion the request of the Israelites for protection is immediately followed by God's intervention on their behalf.[2] The close reciprocity between the crusaders' service of God and their expectation that in return God, as their feudal leader, is committed to rewarding them with victory goes even further, for, just as the Millstatt author did not hesitate to show Moses making reproaches to God for His failure to keep His promise, so do the crusading sources show us signs of a comparable attitude amongst the crusaders. In the *Gesta Francorum* the knightly author describes the feudal reaction of a detachment of crusaders upon hearing the rumour that the bulk of the Christian army has been destroyed at Antioch. He relates the words addressed to God by the knight Wido: '"O Deus verus, trinus et unus, quamobrem haec fieri permisisti? Cur populum sequentem te in manibus inimicorum incidere permisisti et viam tui itineris tuique Sepulchri liberare volentes tam cito dimisisti? Certe si verum est hoc verbum quod ab istis nequissimis audivimus, nos et alii Christiani derelinquemus te; nec te amplius rememorabimus, et unus ex nobis non audebit ulterius invocare nomen tuum." Et fuit hic sermo valde mestissimus

---

[1] *RHC*, v, 378 B.   [2] See p. 175.

in tota militia, ita ut nullus illorum sive episcopus sive abbas, seu clericus seu laicus, auderet invocare Christi nomen per plures dies.'[1] In this passage the knight's threat to God that he and the others will abandon their service of Him goes beyond what we find in the *Exodus*, but at least the two works have the reproaches made to God for His apparent omissions in common, so that they share an attitude which stresses God's obligation to reward and protect those whom He has accepted into His service. On other occasions the force of this direct threat made to God in accordance with a feudal conception of Him as lord of His crusading vassals is toned down by being uttered not to God, but to someone to whom He has delegated authority. In the *Couronnement de Louis* the Pope pronounces the following threat to St Peter if assistance is not granted to his champion Guillaume:

> Sainz Pere, Sire, secor ton champion,
> Se il muert, male iert la retraçon:
> En ton mostier, por tant que nos vivons,
> N'avra mais dite ne messe ne leçon.[2]

A similar attitude is expressed in the anger with which Walther von der Vogelweide criticises the dilatoriness which the angels have shown in coming to the assistance of the crusaders.[3] Indirectly this is a reproach to God, but one which is justified, as in the case of Moses, in the eyes of a Christian who conceives his relationship with God in terms of the feudal nexus and therefore as granting him the same kind of rights and duties.

Although this view of the Christian's relationship with God (practically, and not simply as a metaphor)[4] as a feudal bond may

---

[1] IX, 27 (p. 64). Quoted by Waas, *Geschichte der Kreuzzüge*, I, 10 f.

[2] Vv. 1062 ff. (ed. E. Langlois, Paris, 1925). [3] 79, 1 ff.

[4] On the passage from the *Gesta Francorum* just quoted, Waas (I, 11) says: 'Hier haben Worte wie Christus als König gar nichts von symbolhafter, übertragener Bedeutung, sondern sie meinen ganz real, was sie sagen' (although Waas is wrong in directly associating this symptom of the influence of feudal thought on Christianity with 'germanisches Heerkönigtum'). Something comparable has been demonstrated for the Fifth Crusade by J. Greven (*HJb*, XLIII, 24 ff.). He quotes from a crusading sermon testimony for the view that the crusader's relationship with Christ was conceived on the model of the vassal's to his feudal lord (p. 24, n. 30: 'Dominus quidem in patrimonii sui amissione et vult amicos

well have arisen independently of crusading ideas and gained importance as a result of the new concern of vernacular literature to address a lay aristocratic audience,[1] it probably received a strong impetus from the crusading movement at large. We saw that we cannot trace this idea of feudal reciprocity back to OHG since it was precisely the achievement of ninth-century literature to have emphasised the unilateralism of man's relationship with God. When our vernacular sources begin again in the latter half of the eleventh century we already find that feudal ideas have imposed themselves upon Christian thought in *Ezzos Gesang*, and the same is true, in 1120, of the *Millstätter Exodus*. We shall see later that there are grounds for regarding *Ezzos Gesang* as connected with the slow emergence of the crusading idea, but there are also more general considerations that suggest some connection between this feudalisation of Christian thought and the crusades. As the chronicles inform us repeatedly, it is only at the time of the First Crusade that the feudal knight acquires an acknowledged Christian role to play, not merely as the subject of a Christian ruler engaged in a just war, but in his own capacity as an individual knight. The knightly viewpoint has now acquired a direct relevance to Christian thought which it had not enjoyed before and this is reflected in the way in which the Church, attempting to persuade the knight of this role which it wishes him to play, addresses itself more and more to the knighthood as a class, whether in its directly proselytising mission or in the

suos probare, et experiri, si fideles eius vassali estis. Qui enim a domino ligo tenet feodum,—si desit illi, dum impugnatur et hereditas sua illi aufertur, merito feudo privatur'; p. 25, n. 32: 'Consuetudo quidem est nobilium et potentum quod per cyrothecam vel per aliam rem vili precii vassalos suos investiunt de feudis preciosis: sic Dominus per crucem ex modico filo vel panno vassalos suos investit de celesti regno'). Greven's assessment of these passages agrees with that of Waas on the *Gesta Francorum*. He writes (*op. cit.* p. 25): 'Für Innocenz III. wird es sicher mehr als ein bloßes Bild gewesen sein: der Papst als Stellvertreter Christi der Lehnsherr der Christenheit, — ließen sich seine kirchenpolitischen Ziele treffender umschreiben?'

[1] This is again suggested emphatically by the *Wiener Genesis*. On further attempts of vernacular literature in this period to preach a pacific ideal to an aristocratic audience, see R. Schützeichel, *Das alemannische Memento mori*, pp. 123 f.

composition of vernacular works of literature for a knightly audience.[1] At the same time as the knighthood as a class is more thoroughly Christianised we also witness the converse process whereby the Church itself is exposed progressively to the dominant influence of feudal institutions and even to an attitude to Christianity which is knightly in its origins. The result is that, whereas the Church succeeded in winning the knights for its ideal of the *militia Dei* (thus gaining some measure of internal peace for western Europe), it could only do so at the price of becoming associated with warfare in the form of the crusades; whereas it managed to harness the idea of vengeance to the crusading movement as a motive for serving God, it could not avoid the suggestion that vengeance was not *absolutely* wrong (contrary to the uncompromising view of the author of the *Heliand* and Otfrid); and whereas it made progress by acquiring for its own purposes the legal and moral sanctions of the feudal relationship (as it had earlier adapted the idealism of the *comitatus* relationship to its own ends), this was only possible at the risk of implying that the relationship between man and God was a reciprocal one, imposing obligations upon both, and not a unilateral one, as Otfrid had managed to make clear. The gain to the Church was that it managed to impose upon the knights its ethical norms and its view of the role they had to play in Christian society, thus achieving a theoretical Christianisation of the feudal nobility, just as the period of the conversion had previously witnessed the Christianisation of the ruler and his function within the state. The price for this gain, however, was the fact that the two characteristics of the *comitatus* which it shared with feudalism (its reciprocal nature and its military function) and which the Carolingian Church had largely excluded from its form of Christianity now acquired renewed importance in the twelfth century, so that the Church was confronted with the task of slowly modifying these feudal misconceptions of knightly Christianity, just as it had earlier had to refashion a Christian vocabulary largely

[1] See Rupp, *Deutsche religiöse Dichtungen*, pp. 280 ff.; W. Stammler, *ZfdPh*, LXX, 10 ff.

based on the terminology of the *comitatus* so as to make it agree more closely with its own conception of its mission.[1]

There remains for brief consideration one last detail where an aspect of the Millstatt epic forms a close parallel to what we find in crusading sources. This concerns the manner (which we discussed in connection with the knightly ideal of *êre*)[2] in which the author of the German work manages to suggest a truth which later became unacceptable to the author of the *Rolandslied*,[3] namely that it was possible for the Israelites to serve God and at the same time to enjoy *êre* in this life. This is a view which later comes to play an important part in courtly literature and which gives rise to the crucial problem of how man may serve both God and the world. I am far from wishing to argue that there is only one source for this central *topos* of courtly literature, but it seems probable that the occurrence of this theme (in however subdued a tone) in a work which has other connections with the crusading movement may also be related to the occasional presence of the same idea in crusading chronicles.[4] In one sense the crusader is

[1] One result of this feudalisation of Christianity (with the novel importance it granted to serving God as a knight in warfare and the renewed emphasis it placed on a reciprocal relationship between man and God) is that certain outwardly similar aspects of the Old Testament tradition (the conception that the Jewish wars were waged on behalf of Jehovah—see above, pp. 193 f.—and the conviction of a reciprocity between service and reward—pp. 196 f.) were now made more accessible than they had been, for example, in Carolingian literature with its successful exclusion of precisely these ideas of warfare and reciprocity from its view of Christianity.

I hope to treat later of the process whereby this feudal conception of Christianity in medieval German literature was in its turn demilitarised and unilateralised, as had previously happened in the ninth century with Christian terms deriving, directly or indirectly, from the Germanic *comitatus*.

[2] See pp. 169 f.

[3] The much quoted passage vv. 4719 ff. is sufficient evidence of this.

[4] G. Meissburger, *Deutschunterricht*, XIV, (6), 21 ff., has recently evaluated the evidence for the concept of serving both God and the world before its occurrence in courtly literature. His earliest vernacular example is taken from the *Annolied*, but he also lays particular emphasis on the *Liber de vita Christiana* of Bonizo of Sutri as a contemporary confirmation. Although Meissburger nowhere makes any reference to Erdmann, it is worthy of mention that it was this scholar who first appreciated the full historical importance of Bonizo's work (*Die Entstehung des Kreuzzugsgedankens*, pp. 229 ff.). He sees this above all in the way in which Bonizo was the first to establish a code of moral behaviour for the knight *qua*

the epitome of the man who serves both God and the world because, as Guibertus makes clear, it was only at the time of the First Crusade that God instituted the means for the knight to attain to God's grace whilst still remaining in his knightly station and without having to take monastic vows and thus abandon the world.[1] As we have seen, the novelty of this possibility is clearly felt, so that we are justified in attributing some of the impetus which this ideal of the knight's double service rapidly acquires in the twelfth century to the example of the crusades and to the new possibility which only they provided.[2] It is for this reason that Fulcherius, in the passage where he praises the eternal rewards which await the crusader, says of the knight who serves God (by contrast with the secular—and therefore, in his eyes, sinful—knight): 'Pro honore duplici laborent, qui ad detrimentum corporis et animae se fatigabant.'[3] This also explains why Gilo should see the crusaders as equipped with two sorts of arms, physical and spiritual (I, 7: 'Christicolae gentes, gladioque fideque nitentes')[4] or why the pagans should be referred to as *inimici Dei et nostri*.[5] Furthermore, the crusaders' goal is a double

knight and thus make possible the Christian conception of the knight's duties upon which the crusading movement rests. Meissburger's own line of argument would therefore be reconcilable with the suggestion that the knightly ideal of serving both God and the world owes more than just a little to the impetus given to this ideal by the peculiar nature of the role which the crusading knight was called upon to play.

It is possible, however, to find an earlier example than Bonizo of the conjunction of religious function with secular status: in the *Vita sancti Geraldi Auriliacensis* of Odo of Cluny, of which W. Braun has written (*Studien zum Ruodlieb*, p. 35): 'Die militia Christi des Adels erfülle sich in ritterlichem Dienst an der Christenheit, nicht aber im Kloster. An die Stelle des Legendentypus von der conversio militis tritt die Vita des ritterlichen Heiligen.' Even this earlier example, however, still forms part of the rise of the crusading idea, as has been argued convincingly by Erdmann, *op. cit.* pp. 78 ff.

[1] *RHC*, IV, 124 D ff.

[2] In a similar vein St Bernard praises the Templars in his *De laude novae militiae* as a new class of knights: 'Novum, inquam, militiae genus...qua gemino pariter conflictu infatigabiliter decertatur, tum adversus carnem et sanguinem, tum contra spiritualia nequitiae in caelestibus' (*MPL*, 182, 921).

[3] *RHC*, III, 324 E. Compare the use of the phrase *militandi duplicata occasio* in the *Gesta Tancredi* (*RHC*, III, 606 B). [4] *RHC*, V, 728.

[5] See Hagenmeyer, *Epistulae et chartae ad historiam primi belli sacri spectantes*, p. 151.

The Book of Exodus and the crusades

one for, in conquering the earthly Jerusalem on behalf of the Lord, they hope to gain admittance to the Heavenly Jerusalem, as is made clear again by Gilo:

VI, 281   Pugnat pro duplici regno, quia quaerit utramque
            Hierusalem, decertat in hac ut vivat in illa.[1]

It is this conception of a twofold ideal of knighthood which later informs St Bernard's eulogy of the Templars as warriors and as monks, armed with two kinds of weapon and in combat with spiritual as well as human enemies. With him the term *miles Christi* combines its new sense (to designate the crusader) with its old connotation, which in his case (because the Templars form a monastic order) still retains its full spiritual sense. The ability of the crusader to serve both human and divine ends (which is not confined to the Templars, even though they may represent this joint ideal in its purity) thus closely parallels the description of the Israelites in the Millstatt work whose author sees them as serving God (like the crusaders, against the pagans and in terms that reveal them as knightly warriors), but at the same time as preserving their worldly honour intact.[2]

---

[1] *RHC*, v, 798.

[2] Another connection between the *Millstätter Exodus* and the crusades is suggested by the designation of the Egyptians, significantly only in the final scenes where their pursuit of the Israelites is sketched in military terms, as *die selben môre* (3060) or more commonly, with the addition of an adjective for emphasis, as *die al swarȝe môre* (3043), *die vil swarȝen môre* (3198) or *die heidenisken môre* (3256). These are phrases which were used conventionally of the Saracen opponents of Christendom, so that they serve to depict the events of Exodus in terms of the crusading experience of the medieval present.

This connection would be destroyed, however, if we were to accept Beyschlag's suggestion (*WW*, v, 9 f.) that the Millstatt author is here simply following the description of the same biblical scene by Alcimus Avitus, who refers in his epic to Pharaoh as *niger tyrannus* and to the Egyptians as *nigrum agmen*. Although Beyschlag has convincingly established Avitus as one of the sources of the *Wiener Genesis* (*Die Wiener Genesis*, pp. 113 ff.; cf. also Ehrismann, *LG*, II, 80) I am not persuaded that this Latin author also influenced the work of the Millstatt author. When Beyschlag adduces the parallel between the detailed military description of the exodus in the German work and the similar technique employed in the corresponding scene by Avitus, then the objection must be made that what these two have in common is simply their epic expansiveness, for the details of these descriptions on which Beyschlag sets such great store are no

The Millstätter Exodus

In conclusion we may stress the fact that all the points where a close parallel is to be detected between an innovation of the Millstatt author and crusading ideas represent a process in which religious or spiritual concepts are materialised. This process can take one of two forms: either the military or the feudal implications of the situation acquire a literal and concrete importance. Thus *gotes rîtere* represents 'knights' who serve God in battle rather than monks engaged in a spiritual war, the avenging of the injuries done to God can only be conceived in the realistic sense of battle, the feudal conception of God requires tangible signs of God's protection and rewards in the immediate present, and even more than the traditional military details which we should expect in any epic. Only the particular parallel of *die al swarʒe môre* and *nigrum agmen* can be used to suggest a causal connection, but even here another explanation is more likely. We have seen that Pharaoh is equated with the Devil both in the Millstatt epic and in the traditional exegesis of Exodus (see pp. 111 and 136 f.). In this capacity he can be described as 'black' and his realm as 'the shades' to symbolise his wickedness (cf. Origen, *MPG*, 12, 325 c: 'ut et nos eripiat de terra Aegypti, de potestate tenebrarum'; *ibid.* 329 D: 'et discessit a rectoribus tenebrarum, et de potestate Satanae'; Bruno Astensis, *MPL*, 164, 234 A: 'Rex enim iste diabolus est, rex utique tenebrarum, quoniam Aegyptus tenebrae interpretatur'; *ibid.* B: 'Hujus autem populum rex niger, et tenebrarum ideo persequitur'); just as the Devil himself can be referred to in MHG as the *hellemôre* (e.g. Walther 33, 7). In view of this it is more probable that the twelfth-century author used this traditional feature as yet another method of suggesting the parallel between the events of the biblical Exodus and the encounter with the Saracens of his own day, conceived as serving the Devil. The spiritual blackness of exegetical tradition thus comes to be regarded also as a physical blackness.

Nor could one argue in favour of a causal connection between the Latin and the German epic by reference to the way in which both versions break off their account with chapter 15 of the biblical book. That this decision was independently made by both authors is suggested by the obvious artistic climax which the successful passage of the Red Sea provided and by the non-exemplary conduct of the Israelites in the following years in the wilderness. It is probably for just such reasons that the author of the OE *Exodus* likewise decided to take his poem no further than this same point. In this case, although Alcimus Avitus has in fact been suggested as a possible source (e.g. by G. Mürkens, 'Untersuchungen über das altenglische Exoduslied' in the *Bonner Beihefte ʒur Anglistik*, II, 68 ff.), this is no longer accepted (see E. B. Irving, *The Old English Exodus*, p. 13; S. Moore, *MPh*, IX, 83 ff.; J. W. Bright, *MLN*, XXVII, 97; C. W. Kennedy, *The Earliest English Poetry*, p. 177). Furthermore, as we shall see later (pp. 432 ff.), there is yet another reason, peculiar to the Millstatt author's own artistic intentions and not to be explained by reference to Avitus, why the German author wished to terminate his epic at this stage.

the ideal of the crusader's double service represents a concession to the fact of physical warfare, granting it a place alongside its spiritual equivalent. These are some of the results of what I have called the feudalisation of Christianity which took place when the attempt was made to impose religious duties upon the knighthood and to preach these new obligations to them in crusading sermons and in vernacular literature. Yet it can hardly be fortuitous that these changes, amounting to a specifically feudal conception of Christianity, make the appeal of certain Old Testament ideas much more intelligible, for they involve a renewed stress on the concept of divine warfare (which could therefore draw support from the Hebrew example) and on the idea of feudal reciprocity (for which similar precedents could also be found in the Old Testament).[1] This feudal form of Christianity could therefore regard the Old Testament as in many ways akin to itself. It is this fact, together with the way in which the events of Hebrew history were commonly regarded as prefigurations of the crusading experience of the present, which accounts for the Millstatt author's choice of an Old Testament theme as a vehicle for his ideas on the crusades.

[1] Especially in the all-important idea of a mutual compact sworn between God and His Chosen People and the emphasis placed on the reciprocity between service and reward. See above, pp. 196 f.

IX

PROBLEMS OF DETAIL

OUR argument has brought us to the point where it seems likely that the *Millstätter Exodus* was conceived as a translation of part of the biblical book, but also as an adaptation to the ideas which informed the early crusading movement. It is this close connection between his epic and the crusades which accounts for the way in which the author changes the biblical narrative, giving greater prominence to the theme of warfare and assimilating other aspects of his source to contemporary feudalism. It also explains the complementary relationship between the Millstatt author's assimilation of Old Testament material to the contemporary present and the converse technique employed by crusading chroniclers in placing medieval events firmly in the context of the Old Testament, relating them especially to Exodus. Finally, particular terms or motifs, such as the mention of *gotes rîtere* or the conception of vengeance executed on behalf of God, can be causally connected with the crusades and with the revaluation of Christian ideas which they brought about. Against all this, however, certain objections have from time to time been raised, so that only a careful discussion of these criticisms can finally confirm the thesis that the composition of the Millstatt epic took place in the climate of thought created by Urban's proclamation of the First Crusade and by subsequent events. The objections which I propose to consider are four in number and are concerned with two major problems: first, with the question of dating and, secondly, with what is regarded as an incongruity between the alleged crusading theme and its poetic treatment in this work.

The first objection is raised by E. Sitte[1] as part of his discussion of the dating of Lamprecht's *Alexanderlied*. Here he expands

[1] *Die Datierung von Lamprechts Alexander*, pp. 29 f.

Problems of detail

upon a point made by Fliegner[1] with reference to the *Rolandslied*, who maintains that the concept of the *miles Dei* is missing from German literature before the *Rolandslied*. We shall later have to return to Fliegner's dismissal of the evidence of the phrase *gotes rîtere* in the *Exodus*,[2] but for the moment what concerns us is Sitte's adaptation of Fliegner's point. For Sitte only the late dating of the *Rolandslied* can be seriously entertained since, as he argues, very few Germans took part in the First Crusade, so that crusading ideas were so little developed in Germany by 1130 that it is difficult to conceive the composition of such a markedly crusading work as the *Rolandslied* by this date. What Sitte maintains with regard to the suggested dating of the *Rolandslied* in 1130 he must also argue, *a fortiori*, of the *Millstätter Exodus* in about 1120.[3] It is true that he does not mention the *Exodus* in this context, but his approving reference to Fliegner's argument[4] (who does explicitly concern himself with the *Exodus*) implies that he too would deny that the *Exodus*, written so early, could be inspired by crusading ideas. Fliegner therefore contests the existence of crusading literature in Germany before the *Rolandslied* because of the absence of the *miles Dei* idea, whereas Sitte denies the existence of such literature before the year 1130 on the general grounds of dating. At a later stage in his book Sitte develops this argument with regard to the *Alexanderlied*.[5] He considers this work an example of crusading influence on literature and accounts for this by referring to the numerous

[1] *Geistliches und weltliches Rittertum im Rolandslied*, pp. 32 f.
[2] See below, pp. 338 ff.
[3] Despite H. Menhardt's recently proposed dating of the *Exodus* at about 1170–4 (*ZfdA*, LXXXIX, 257 ff.) we may still best operate with the earlier dating —for two reasons. In the first place, Menhardt's suggestion has not yet found anything like general acceptance (cf. L. Wolff, *PBB* (T) LXXXI, 122 on Menhardt's related suggestion that the *Wiener Genesis* and the *Millstätter Genesis* originated in Regensburg between 1175 and 1180). Secondly, if we accept Menhardt's proposal there is obviously no problem in accounting for crusading references in a work written as late as 1170–4. Since the difficulty lies precisely with the early dating it is prudent to ignore Menhardt's proposal (precisely because of its tempting offer of an easy solution) and to attempt to show that, even if the Millstatt work was composed in 1120, it is still possible to account for these crusading allusions. [4] *Op. cit.* p. 30. [5] *Ibid.* pp. 122 ff.

297

The Millstätter Exodus

contingents of German participants on the Second Crusade, won for this undertaking by crusading propaganda in Germany (with St Bernard playing a prominent part). Sitte therefore places great emphasis on the contrast between the First Crusade, with relatively weak German participation,[1] and the Second, which affected Germany as much as it did other countries of western Europe. From this contrast he draws the conclusion that whereas the occurrence of a German work with crusading allusions in the years 1155–60 (the dating which he eventually proposes for the *Alexanderlied*)[2] is readily understandable, the dating of any other work of crusading literature before the Second Crusade is impossible. With that Sitte denies the dating of the *Rolandslied* in 1130 and also, by implication, the possibility that the author of the *Millstätter Exodus*, composed in about 1120, can have regarded his subject-matter as a crusading theme. Sitte's argumentation, although nowhere explicitly developed with the *Exodus* in mind, therefore constitutes a weighty objection to the interpretation given in the preceding chapters.

A discussion of Sitte's argument is all too likely to degenerate into a controversy in which each side imputes reliance on negative evidence to its opponent. Sitte has maintained the absence of crusading enthusiasm in Germany at a date so early as 1130 and has concluded that it would be rash to postulate crusading literature in German before the Second Crusade. On the other hand, our argument has shown us that a German epic was written in about 1120 with crusading intentions, so that we must now inquire whether Sitte's claim that crusading enthusiasm was absent from Germany until 1130 at the earliest may not, in its turn, rest on negative evidence. In the first place, the discrepancy between the date of the First Crusade (1096) and 1130, the year

[1] Sitte could have strengthened his case at this point by a reference to Erdmann, *Die Entstehung des Kreuzzugsgedankens*, pp. 270 ff. Some of the reasons adduced by Erdmann for this reaction to the First Crusade in Germany are of a suspiciously vague and general nature (e.g. p. 270: 'Volkscharaktere', p. 271: 'eine typisch deutsche Haltung'), although there can be little doubt that his reference to the Investiture Contest (confirmed by Ekkehardus, *RHC*, v, 17 E) touches on a primary cause.
[2] *Op. cit.* p. 128.

rejected by Sitte as a possible dating for the *Rolandslied*, is so large that we are forced to ask whether it is certain that conditions true of the year 1096 (namely, lack of crusading enthusiasm in Germany) would remain unchanged until 1130. To argue that the *Rolandslied* could not have been written in 1130 because of conditions which are attested for Germany in the year 1096 is to ignore the possibility that these conditions may have changed in the meanwhile. Sitte nowhere undertakes to investigate this possibility, so that his denial that the crusading idea was well known in Germany before 1130 is strictly unproven. If this weakens the force of his argument against 1130 as the date for the *Rolandslied*, then it also casts doubt on the implication of his contention that the *Exodus*, since it was written even earlier than 1130, cannot be regarded as a crusading work. Furthermore, it is quite unjustified to proceed from the assumption that crusading ideas were not widespread in Germany by 1130 to the conclusion that it was therefore impossible for any author to accept such ideas before this date and to give them poetic expression. For this to be regarded as impossible it would have to be shown, not simply that crusading ideas were not widespread in Germany, but also that they were quite unknown, for only this would provide the required certainty that literary allusions to the crusades cannot fall before 1130. In short, I regard both the premise and the conclusion of Sitte's argument as uncertain and unproven. Indeed, the fact that crusading ideas were known at all in Germany between 1096 and 1130, even if they were not very widespread, should enjoin caution with regard to any argument based on the assumption that crusading literature was impossible in Germany before the Second Crusade. It is quite conceivable that the restricted circulation of crusading ideas (argued by Sitte for the period before 1130) may have acted as a stimulus to a clerical writer who, himself a member of the narrow circle of those to whom these ideas were known and whose allegiance they claimed, wished to propagate them in German society, especially amongst the knights as the class involved in any practical realisation of these ideas. I do not claim that this was necessarily the case with the Millstatt author or that any proof is possible, but merely note that this is at least a theoretical possibility which weakens Sitte's argument by suggesting that in the first third of the twelfth century a crusading epic could have been composed precisely because crusading ideas had met with only a limited response in Germany, as an attempt to recommend them to wider circles of knightly society.

So far the argument against Sitte has concentrated on the weaknesses of his case and has been entirely negative. These objections to his thesis can only be reinforced if it is possible to adduce positive evidence, if it can be shown that crusading ideas were known to Germany and acknowledged by some Germans in the period from 1096 to 1130, however restricted their scope may have been by comparison either with the position in France or with the situation in Germany at the time of the Second Crusade. We may well agree with Erdmann that Germany remained largely aloof from the First Crusade (and his explanation of this attitude as due to the conflict between empire and papacy at this time obviously accounts for this to a large extent), but it nonetheless remains true that only a total failure on the part of Germany to take part in the Crusade could provide a sufficiently firm basis for Sitte's argument. Such evidence is not to be found, and Erdmann himself concedes that crusading ideas subsequently found acceptance in Germany,[1] largely as a result of the successful conclusion of the First Crusade. He does not commit himself to any date by which these ideas succeeded in penetrating Germany, but Sitte's argument rests on the assumption that this revision of ideas could not have taken place in Germany immediately after the conclusion of the First Crusade and that it must have begun only after 1130. For this assumption there is no conclusive evidence.

Indeed, what contemporary evidence we possess suggests that

---

[1] *Die Entstehung des Kruzzugsgedankens*, p. 271 ('Gewiß ist in der Folgezeit der Kreuzzugsgedanke auch in Deutschland durchgedrungen...') and p. 272 ('Erst der tatsächliche Erfolg des ersten Kreuzzugs, der die Pläne Gregors vergessen machte, hat über diese Lage hinweggeführt').

Germany was acquainted with crusading ideas and to some extent shared them at a date far earlier than is implied by Sitte. Here the important point is not that the acceptance of these ideas in Germany was far less widespread than in France (of this there can be little doubt), but that these ideas were certainly known in Germany, in however restricted a circle, and that therefore the composition of a crusading work in the period before 1130 is not rendered historically impossible. Our earliest evidence concerns the repercussions of the People's Crusade in Germany, an undertaking which largely arose out of the crusade preached by evangelicals or itinerant monks, rather than by the bishops whom Urban II had requested to preach the crusade.[1] We learn from Ordericus Vitalis that Peter the Hermit, the leader of this popular expedition, recruited German participants at Cologne,[2] even though it is also reported that many Germans ridiculed these pilgrims for the folly of their intentions.[3] The mention elsewhere of Swabians and Bavarians in Peter's retinue[4] suggests that he gained further adherents on his march through southern Germany. Other groups followed his example: a Rhenish priest Gottschalk imitated Peter by preaching the crusade and gained support in eastern France and southern Germany,[5] whereas Folkmar and his retinue are mentioned briefly as having passed through Saxony and Bohemia[6] and are probably connected with persecutions of the Jews at Magdeburg and at Prague in the same period.[7] It might be objected that although the People's Crusade theoretically forms part of the First Crusade, it was nonetheless largely an affair of popular enthusiasm for the new ideal aroused

---

[1] S. Runciman, *A History of the Crusades*, I, 113.

[2] *Historia ecclesiastica*, IX, 4 (III, 478).

[3] Cf. Ekkehardus, *RHC*, V, 18A. On this, however, see K. M. Setton (ed.), *A History of the Crusades*, I, 259: 'But the Germans, who knew little about the movement at first, changed their attitude as they saw the crowds, who seem to have been very orderly, cross through their country.'

[4] Cf. Albertus, *RHC*, IV, 276A.

[5] *RHC*, IV, 289E and F.

[6] *RHC*, V, 12D.

[7] See Setton, *op. cit.* I, 262. On the close connection between recruitment for the First Crusade and the outbreak of anti-Jewish riots see Runciman, *op. cit.* pp. 134 ff.

amongst peasants and town-dwellers and therefore quite distinct from the knightly contingents recruited in France and unlikely to make an appeal to the German knighthood. The answer to this objection is provided by the evidence that the lesser nobility in Germany was in many cases by no means ill-disposed to the message preached by Peter and his followers. Runciman[1] suggests that, since the knights of France and Flanders chose to join a purely feudal contingent, Peter was concerned to win some of the lesser German nobles for his cause. That he was partly successful in this is confirmed by the mention of German knights who took part in this popular crusade. They include Count Hugh of Tübingen, Count Heinrich of Schwarzenberg, Walter of Teck, the sons of the Count of Zimmern.[2] Some of the anti-Jewish riots that have been associated with these first stirrings of the crusading idea have been attributed to the followers of Count Emicho of Leiningen,[3] from the area between Mainz and Worms, who was joined on his journey through Germany by knightly contingents from other parts of the country. That these German adherents of the People's Crusade were a force to be reckoned with may be concluded from the fact that Peter's following, when he arrived at Constantinople, is said to have included by now thousands of Germans,[4] that some of the German nobles were active in the deliberations which followed the news that a German party of six thousand men had captured Xerigordon in the vicinity of Nicea[5] and that many German knights are listed amongst those who fell at the battle of Civetot (Cibotus).[6] From such evidence we can draw the conclusion that in the particular form of the People's Crusade Germany was to some extent affected by the disturbed currents of the First Crusade and that this influence was felt by members of the lesser nobility in Germany.

[1] Runciman, *A History of the Crusades*, I, 122.
[2] *Ibid*. See also the reference given there in n. 1 to the testimony assembled by H. Hagenmeyer on the German lords who decided to follow Peter.
[3] Runciman, *op. cit.* pp. 137 ff.   [4] Setton, *A History of the Crusades*, I, 281.
[5] Runciman, *op. cit.* pp. 129 f.
[6] *Op. cit.* p. 132. The chronicle of Zimmern (ed. H. Hagenmeyer, p. 29) gives details of the Germans killed in this encounter.

Problems of detail

Many of the features of this People's Crusade must have been disconcerting to anyone convinced of the need to encourage knightly crusaders, but there were two possible reactions to these inauspicious beginnings. On the one hand it could be argued that the disasters that overtook the bands led by Gottschalk, Folkmar and Emicho were a divine condemnation of the whole idea,[1] whereas others saw in this initial failure the need to avoid these errors in any subsequent crusade.[2] Clearly, it is the second reaction which accounts for the way in which the crusading idea could come to find greater acceptance in Germany. That this is what commonly happened can be shown with regard to the crusade of 1101, an expedition which has failed to be designated as a separate undertaking in the conventional numbering of the crusades.[3] Recruitment for this second expedition can be explained by a number of reasons, one of which is the reinforcement of success ensured once the news of the victorious outcome of the First Crusade reached Europe.[4] Recruits for the Holy Land were drawn once more from France, but also from regions whose involvement in the First Crusade had been less profound, amongst them Germany.[5] That Germany should now react more favourably to the crusading idea is not due solely to the capture of Jerusalem

[1] This possible reaction is reported by Albertus (*RHC*, IV, 295 B and C). 'Hic manus Domini contra Peregrinos esse creditur, qui nimiis immunditiis et fornicario concubitu in conspectu ejus peccaverant, et exules Judaeos, licet Christo contrarios, pecuniae avaritia magis quam pro justitia Dei gravi caede mactaverant, cum justus judex Deus sit, et neminem invitum aut coactum ad jugum fidei catholicae jubeat venire.'

[2] Cf. Ekkehardus (*RHC*, V, 21 A and B): 'Sic nimirum, sic nostrae gentis homines zelum Dei, sed non secundum scientiam Dei habentes; quippe qui, in militia quam in liberandis christianis Christus praeviderat, alios vicissim christianos persequi coeperunt, miseratione divina fraterno sanguine repressi, Hungarii quoque liberati sunt. Haecque est causa qua quidem simpliciores fratres, utpote rem ignorantes, scandalizati, totum hujus profectionis conatum vanum atque frivolum ipsi nimis praeproperi judices interpretati sunt.' Cf. also his *Chronicon universale* (*MGH* SS VI, 208, 25): 'quamvis et amplissima utriusque multitudo a quodam Emichone viro militari seducta, vel potius ut Israeliticus quondam exercitus spiritu fornicationis decepta, paucis sibi Pannoniae ingressum in presidio Miesenburg obstantibus, fuga nemine persequente repatriaverit.'

[3] See Waas, *Geschichte der Kreuzzüge*, I, 119, n. 1.

[4] Setton, *op. cit.* p. 346.   [5] *Ibid.*

in 1099, but also to the changed relationship between the empire and the papacy.[1] Whereas the conflict between the two had meant that the First Crusade, as a papal undertaking, had not been preached in Germany, now in 1101 Germany was enjoying a respite from this conflict. Henry IV therefore offered no resistance to the recruitment of German participants, who now include even some of his supporters. Although the chronicles mention recruits from the various regions of Germany, most of those who are mentioned by name come from Bavaria, including Welf IV of Bavaria, Count Friedrich of Bogen, Burggraf Heinrich of Regensburg, Archbishop Thiemo of Salzburg and Bishop Ulrich of Passau.[2] The figures cited in two chronicles for the combined forces of the Aquitanians and Bavarians on this second expedition are 160,000:[3] however exaggerated they may be,[4] there is no reason to think them more inflated than the grand total of 300,000 given by Ekkehardus,[5] so that the German contingent now represented a high proportion of the total strength (whatever this may have been). In addition, it is evident from the high status, secular or ecclesiastic, of some of those recruited for this expedition in Bavaria that the crusading idea is now capable of appealing not merely to the lesser nobility who had been drawn into the wake of the People's Crusade, but also to the higher ranks of the knightly aristocracy.

One other fact suggests that German interest in the crusades, already visible in the People's Crusade and on the increase by the time of the expedition of 1101, continued for some time after this date and did not die away again until its re-emergence on the eve of the Second Crusade. This is the fact that two of the chronicles of the First Crusade, upon whose reports we are largely dependent for any reconstruction of these events, were written by Germans. One of these is the *Hierosolymita*, written by Ekkehardus, abbot of Aura, near Nürnberg.[6] The chronicler

[1] Setton, *A History of the Crusades*, I, 350. [2] *Ibid.* [3] *Op. cit.* p. 351, n. 14.
[4] On the unreliability of the figures quoted in contemporary sources see Runciman, *A History of the Crusades*, Appendix II (I, 336 ff.).
[5] *RHC*, v, 28 E. This same figure is also given by Albertus (*RHC*, IV, 559 C).
[6] See Runciman, *op. cit.* p. 330, and Setton, *op. cit.* p. 220.

had personal knowledge of Palestine since he had gone there on the crusade of 1101, and in about 1115, on his return to Germany, he wrote this chronicle of the First Crusade, intending it to be part of a world chronicle which he also composed.[1] The second German chronicle is the *Historia Hierosolymitana* by Albertus Aquensis (i.e. of Aachen) who did not go on a crusade himself and who appears to have written his work, a compilation of legendary material together with indispensable eye-witness accounts culled from returning crusaders, some time after 1119.[2] Between them these two German chronicles show that interest in the crusades persisted well after the expedition of 1101 and was sustained in precisely that period which saw the composition of the *Millstätter Exodus*. We cannot therefore accept the explicit point of Sitte's argument (that the *Rolandslied* cannot have been written as early as 1130 because of the ignorance of crusading ideas in Germany before that date), nor can we agree with what is the implication of his thesis (that a work like the *Exodus*, written as early as 1120, cannot for the same reason contain any crusading allusions). This dating of the Millstatt work does nothing to invalidate the suggestion that it was written with the contemporary crusading experience in mind.

This interpretation of the work, even if not contradicted by the date of composition, has been criticised by de Boor on three other counts,[3] each of which concerns what he claims to be the inadequacy of the subject-matter as a vehicle for crusading sentiments. From the disparity between subject-matter and this interpretation of its theme de Boor concludes that the interpretation must therefore be mistaken. He writes:

Wenn bei der Schonung der jüdischen Kinder durch die Hebammen das ganze Pathos einer Schlachtschilderung eingesetzt aber negiert

[1] *Chronicon universale* (*MGH* SS vi, 33 ff.).

[2] See Runciman, *op. cit.* i, 331, and Setton, *op. cit.* i, 253. F. Duncalf (responsible for the relevant chapter in Setton) dates Albertus' chronicle between 1119 and the middle of the century, whereas Runciman suggests some time about the year 1130. In either case we can accept the composition of this chronicle as evidence that interest in the crusades persisted in Germany in the period between the First and Second Crusades.   [3] See de Boor, *LG*, i, 151.

wird (*da nedorft der rabe bluotigen snabel haben* usw. 121, 15 ff.) oder wenn das Ungeziefer der Plagen im Stil streitbarer Ritter geschildert wird, so wirkt der Gegensatz von Ding und Stil eher ironisch, eine bewußte Herabsetzung des weltlichen Stils. Doch auch die breite Schilderung der prächtigen Streitrüstung der Juden bei ihrem Auszug aus Ägypten durchdringt die Szene nicht mit einem neuen heroischen Ethos. Vor den nachfolgenden Ägyptern beben und jammern diese ritterlich ausstaffierten Juden wie in der Genesis.[1]

These are criticisms which must be taken seriously, for if they were accepted it would be impossible to maintain that the Millstatt author had intended to adapt this biblical material to crusading ideas. If de Boor is correct the contrast between the intention and the means employed in sketching the rescue of the Jewish children and the attacks of the plague in heroic, knightly terms would be too harsh. Similarly, the contrast between the prolonged knightly description of the Israelites on the march and their unknightly behaviour when they catch sight of the Egyptian army in pursuit would make it difficult to believe that the author seriously intended this account of the Exodus story as a model for knights of the crusading period. In seeking a reply to these three points raised by de Boor we may in turn inquire whether the discrepancy between intention and means on which he places such emphasis is not perhaps something which appears as a discrepancy to modern taste, but which would not necessarily have been felt as such by a twelfth-century audience. We may also ask whether the irony which de Boor attributes to the author is not a characteristic too sophisticated to be reconciled with what else we have learned of his skilful, but essentially straightforward artistic personality. Finally, it is legitimate to inquire whether the fact that the Israelites show cowardice, but are nonetheless granted victory by God, necessarily disqualifies them from serving as models (albeit negatively) to crusaders who are felt not simply to repeat the deeds of Israel, but actually to transcend them by

---

[1] This third point raised by de Boor (the cowardice of the Israelites) also forms the basis of Fliegner's objection to the interpretation of the *Millstätter Exodus* as a crusading work (*Geistliches und weltliches Rittertum im Rolandslied*, pp. 32 f.).

virtue of their ability to keep trust with God, a quality which distinguishes them radically from the Israel of past history. In the light of these general observations we may now consider the three points raised by de Boor and determine how far each of them may still be reconciled with the general crusading interpretation which we have so far maintained for this work.

The first objection concerns the scene in which the midwives avoid the slaughter of the male children of the Israelites. De Boor sees in the contrast between what actually happens (or rather, does not happen) and the wealth of heroic formulas[1] invoked for what amounts to no more than a negative description a sign that the heroic style is being employed here only so that it shall be subjected to the author's ironical criticism.[2] If this were correct the attitude of the Millstatt author towards the heroic style and ethos would correspond closely to the equally critical position adopted by the author of the *Wiener Genesis*,[3] so that this would seriously weaken the argument that the Millstatt author modified his biblical material in the light of the crusading experience.

To meet this objection we may recall that medieval literature frequently describes the martyrdom of another group of children, the innocents of Bethlehem put to the sword by Herod, in terms that suggest that they are regarded as the soldiers of Christ despite their tender years. Otfrid, for example, says that the

[1] It is possible, of course, that behind these formulas of the Millstatt author there stands not merely the conventional vocabulary of heroic literature in Germany, but also the imagery of such biblical passages as Jer. 15. 1 ff. (with a reference to Moses, cf. Exod. 32. 11). I am grateful to R. A. Wisbey for drawing my attention to this possibility.

[2] We may mention at the outset the interesting parallel provided by the OE *Exodus*. The poet gives a description (vv. 154–69) of the battlefield, using the conventional imagery of heroic poetry. But in this passage the reference to the birds of battle circling above corpses (v. 163: *ofer drihtnēum*) has no appropriate function since there has been no military encounter between the Israelites and their foes. Similarly, when the Egyptian army perishes, the drastic image of blood spreading through the water (v. 463) is equally out of place in what is meant to be a description of death by drowning, not in battle. The English poet, like his Millstatt colleague, is keen to use every opportunity to introduce military allusions despite the inconsistencies in which this involves him.

[3] See Beyschlag, *Die Wiener Genesis*, pp. 54 ff.

soldiers of Herod accomplished a great slaughter without having to fight,[1] but he is nonetheless convinced, because the innocents are martyrs and therefore *milites Christi*, that this is really a battle:

I, 20, 21   Wig was ofto manegaz   joh filu managfaltaz,
ni sah man io, ih sagen thir thaz,   thesemo gilichaz.

This battle is unique in one sense because of the extreme youth of those who apparently suffer defeat,[2] but in another sense because the child Christ, who is described as the *kuning*[3] of those who fall in battle on His behalf, is later to shed His own blood for His followers, a fact which in Otfrid's eyes sets Him apart from the kings of this world.[4] Any criticism of the heroic style which is present in this passage attaches only to the secular king, not to his followers (to whom no reference is here made).[5] Like these followers of the secular king the innocents are engaged in a battle (*wig*), but unlike them their *militia* is a passive form of martyrdom (*ana fehta*). It is this passive *militia Christi* which commends the innocents to Otfrid's poetic attention[6] and which allows him to apply to their Christian form of warfare some of the vocabulary of heroic literature,[7] even though (as the phrase *ana fehta* shows) the battle he describes is as negative as that narrated in the *Millstätter Exodus*.

Equally remote from modern taste is the way in which Notker Balbulus describes the innocents in the sequence *Laus tibi Christe*

[1] I, 20, 3: 'Er santa man manage   mit wafanon garawe,
joh datun se ana fehta   mihila slahta.'
[2] Vv. 23 f.
[3] V. 31.
[4] V. 34: 'tho goz er bi unsih sinaz bluat,   thaz kuning ander ni duat.'
[5] I do not wish to deny that Otfrid is elsewhere prepared to criticise the followers of a secular king (see, for example, III, 26, 39 ff., and my discussion of this passage in *The Carolingian Lord*, pp. 333 f.). This is not the case, however, in Otfrid's description of the slaughter of the innocents, so that we cannot argue, in de Boor's words, that this too is meant as 'eine bewußte Herabsetzung des weltlichen Stils'. On the contrary, Otfrid is enhancing the secular style here by using heroic terminology in its metaphorical application to the *militia Christi*.
[6] On Otfrid's essentially passive conception of the *militia Christi* see *The Carolingian Lord*, pp. 338 ff.
[7] Cf. also *githigini* (v. 35).

cui sapit.[1] He too sings of them as *teneri milites*[2] and is convinced of the unique victory which Christ, seen as a warrior (*athleta*), conferred upon His warrior-bands:

7	Quis athletarum	8	Quantam vagiens
	fortissimus umquam		coaevulis tuis
	Exercitibus		Tu praestitisti,
	tantam, Christe, suis		mittens eos caelum
	contulit victoriam,		regnaturos perpetim?

Military vocabulary is therefore justified in the case of this first historical example of *militia Christi*,[3] but it does not conceal the fact, apparent also with Otfrid, that the military heroism of the innocents is as passive and as metaphorical as any which could be attributed to the Israelite children whom Pharaoh had ordered to be slaughtered.

There is of course a striking difference between the two slaughters instigated by Pharaoh and by Herod: whereas that commanded by Herod is shown as being brutally carried out in the description of Otfrid and of Notker, the Millstatt author evokes his picture of the battlefield only when describing how this slaughter was avoided by the midwives. By contrast with this, when Pharaoh repeats his command to his own followers and they do not hesitate to carry it out, the action itself is quickly dismissed in no more than six lines (vv. 189–94) without the heroic imagery used in the earlier scene with its entirely negative description. Why this should be so we shall have to consider.[4]

---

[1] See the edition by W. von den Steinen, Editionsband, p. 18. He comments on the remoteness of this imagery (Darstellungsband, pp. 346 f.) in the following terms: 'Daß die Kleinen von Bethlehem als Streiter oder Ritter im Heere erscheinen, daß ihr Tod mit kühnen Heldentaten verglichen wird, klingt heute fremd. Aber es entspricht unsern Vorstellungen vom frühmittelalterlichen Christentum und wird uns in Notkers Märtyrerhymnen noch auf vielerlei Weise begegnen.' It is my contention that what is true of Notker's description of the innocents applies equally to the Millstatt author's description of the Exodus scene and that the discrepancy claimed by de Boor between the author's intention and the means he employs is really a discrepancy between the medieval and the modern imagination.

[2] Stanza 3.

[3] Cf. stanza 10: 'Et confessorum | insignes gemmulae sanctorum.'

[4] See below, p. 362.

What concerns us now is the difference between the heroic description in the Millstatt work (applied negatively to a battle which is avoided) and the military terminology used by Otfrid and Notker of a battle which is drastically real, since it is this use of a negative description in the Millstatt epic which has called forth de Boor's criticism. This difficulty is more apparent than real, as can be shown by the readiness with which Christian exegesis equated the two events and placed them in a typological relationship with one another, thus showing that for the exegetical tradition what both these events had in common was more important than what distinguished them. That such a relationship should have come to be established between the Israelite victims of Pharaoh and the innocents of Bethlehem is intelligible not simply because of the outward similarity of the two episodes, but more significantly because they are episodes from the lives of Moses and Christ, two figures who are regularly related to one another as type and antitype, as prefiguration and fulfilment.[1] In terms similar to what is said of Christ, Moses can be regarded as the leader of his people, sent by God to redeem them from servitude and to guide them towards the Promised Land. As with the similar creation of an overall pattern of equations between the crusades and Exodus,[2] once this general typological relationship was established it brought with it numerous parallels in detail, which served to enrich the basic pattern. It is probably as a part of this process of filling in the details that the killing of the Israelite children from which Moses is rescued came to be seen as a prefiguration of the slaughter of the innocents from which Christ is safely delivered,[3] even though there may be minor discrepancies between the two (such as the fact that, whereas

---

[1] The commentaries quoted on p. 111, n. 3, give ample testimony of this.

[2] See above, pp. 262 ff.

[3] Cf. the words of Réau, *Iconographie de l'art chrétien*, II, 181, on the rescue of Moses from the Nile: 'C'est la préfigure de l'Enfant Jésus échappant au massacre des Innocents.' In the same manner Pharaoh is the precursor of Herod (p. 180). The antiquity of this association of the events surrounding the birth and early history of Moses with those at the birth of Christ, as a new Moses, is attested by St Matthew's description of the flight into Egypt (2. 13 ff.).

the intention of Herod was to remove the threat which Christ alone presented, with Pharaoh there is no wish to kill Moses in particular).

Two examples of this typological connection between the two events may suffice, one from Prudentius towards the beginning of the Christian literary tradition in Western Europe and the other from St Bernard as a representative of the twelfth century. Prudentius, in the twelfth poem of his *Cathemerinon*,[1] refers to the slaughter of the innocents (vv. 101 ff.) and stresses that Herod derived little profit from this crime since Christ was enabled to escape (vv. 133 ff.). It is at this stage that Prudentius quotes the similar scene from the life of Moses:

> 141   Sic stulta Pharaonis mali
> Edicta quondam fugerat,
> Christi figuram praeferens
> Moses, receptor civium.

We can be quite certain that this comparison is meant as more than just a stylistic embellishment, not merely because Moses is here described as the *figura* of Christ (a term which places these two events in a typological relationship), but also in view of the sustained typological comparison between Moses and Christ which is introduced in vv. 157 f. by the words: 'Licetne Christum noscere | Tanti per exemplum viri?' For Prudentius the slaughter from which Moses escaped is a valid prefiguration of the slaughter of the innocents. In other words, if Otfrid and Notker Balbulus are justified in describing the innocents as *milites Christi* and their slaughter as a battle in which they fall as passive martyrs in the service of their leader there seems to be no valid reason to deny the adequacy of the same technique when used, as in the *Mill-stätter Exodus*, with reference to the typological *figura* of these *milites Christi*, to the Israelite children.

A similar parallel is provided by St Bernard in his Sermon 1 *In octava paschae*. He writes:

Recolant quibus nota est historia Veteris Testamenti, quemadmodum in Aegypto dum parvuli omnes Israelitici germinis necarentur,

[1] *MPL*, 59, 901 ff.

The Millstätter Exodus

expositum in aquis Moysen tulerit filia Pharaonis. Et vide si non manifeste Christi et in hoc ipso videtur praecessisse figura. Simile nempe cum Pharaone etiam Herodes suspicione laborans, ad eadem conversus est crudelitatis argumenta, sed eodem modo est et ipse delusus. Utrobique pro unius suspecta persona trucidatur numerositas puerorum: utrobique qui quaerebatur, evadit. Et quomodo Moysen filia Pharaonis, ita Christum quoque Aegyptus (quae non immerito Pharaonis intelligitur filia) suscepit conservandum.[1]

Here the similarity between the two events is stressed by such terms as *eadem... argumenta, eodem modo, quomodo... ita* and the double use of *utrobique*, but at the same time the words *videtur praecessisse figura* make it clear that what is here established is no mere comparison, but a strictly typological relationship in which Moses and this event in his life are prefigurations of Christ and the corresponding aspect of His childhood.

So far we have seen that the Millstatt author's description of the scene with the Israelite children in military terms (even if only negatively) is connected with the slaughter of the innocents by virtue of an external similarity between these two events, but above all because the one is a typological prefiguration of the other. This still tells us nothing of any possible connection (typological or not) between the Israelite children and the crusades, to which, as our argument has suggested, the events of the biblical exodus have been assimilated by the German author. Furthermore, the parallel between Pharaoh's slaughter of the Israelites and Herod's killing of the innocents rested partly on the fact that any warfare in which the victims could be shown as engaged was of a passive and therefore metaphorical nature. If we are to connect this scene in Exodus with the events of the crusades we shall have to account for this transition to an active and literal form of warfare waged by the crusaders. In short, only if it is possible to show how the scene described by the Millstatt author in negative military terms could be regarded as relevant to the crusading present can one be reasonably certain that this military description was meant to perform an exemplary function,

[1] *MPL*, 183, 294B f.

312

providing the knights with a model for their military behaviour rather than subjecting it to the kind of criticism we encounter in the *Wiener Genesis*.

Our argument will be that the fate of the Israelite children was regarded as prefiguring not merely the martyrdom of the innocents, but also the martyrdom of the crusaders. To this extent the fulfilment which the innocents represent (transcending their Old Testament type in that they die for Christ Himself) is only potential, deriving part of its force from the way in which it provides later generations of Christians with an *exemplum* which they in their turn may emulate. We have already remarked on this partly potential nature of typological fulfilment.[1] The central example is given by Christ Himself, for in His life and sacrifice He fulfilled the prefiguration of His office given in the Old Testament, but still provided an *exemplum* which His followers were free to accept or reject and which therefore looked forward to a possible fulfilment on the part of every Christian. The same is true of the innocents of Bethlehem: their martyrdom could be interpreted as a typological fulfilment of the slaughter of the Israelites (belonging to the wider pattern of relationships between Moses and Christ), but at the same time their service of Christ also constituted an *exemplum* which every Christian was henceforth potentially capable of realising in his own life. The typological relationship between the Israelite children and the innocents can therefore be extended and applied also to those who convert the potential into the actual by being themselves prepared, like the innocents, to serve Christ to the extent of laying down their lives for Him. How this extension of the typological relationship between these two episodes from the Old and the New Testament came to be used of the crusading movement in particular we must now consider.

One crusading phenomenon shows this relevance of the *exemplum* of the innocents in all clarity: the Children's Crusade of the year 1212, where the very youth of the participants would

---

[1] See p. 266 and pp. 270 f.

evoke this New Testament image.[1] A version of the song chanted by these child crusaders on their march under the leadership of one Nicolaus has been preserved in an Austrian source, the *Anonymi Chronicon Rhythmicum*, where it is said of this crusade:

Nicolaus famulus Christi transfretabit,
Et cum innocentibus Ierusalem intrabit.[2]

We can be certain that the use of the word *innocentes* in this context was intended not simply to designate the youthful purity of these crusaders, but rather to establish a definite parallel between their readiness to serve Christ and the martyrdom of the innocents at Bethlehem. This is suggested by the manner in which the chronicler, when he comes to report on the fate of these crusaders (some were drowned on the way to the Holy Land and many others were sold into slavery in North Africa), explicitly refers to Matt. 2. 18 where, after the slaughter at Bethlehem, Rachel weeps for her children. It is with this scene that the chronicler establishes his parallel when he writes of the fate of the child crusaders:

Plorant matres ut Rachel, nati morti dantur.[3]

That this view of these crusaders was not a conception restricted to one chronicler or to the children themselves is shown by another account of the departure of the children from Marseilles and of the storm which cost so many of them their lives: 'Expeditio infantium... facta est hoc anno... Cumque venissent ad duas dietas in mari ad insulam Sancti-Petri, ad rupem quae dicitur Reclusi, orta tempestate, duae naves perierunt et omnes infantes de illis navibus submersi sunt, et, ut dicitur, post aliquot annos Papa Gregorius IX ecclesiam novorum Innocentium in eadem insula fecit.'[4] Those bodies which were recovered from the sea were placed in the church and, so this account concludes, are still shown today to pilgrims. From this we may conclude that

[1] The most helpful recent discussion of this phenomenon has been given by Alphandéry, *La chrétienté et l'idée de croisade*, II, 115 ff. I follow him in all essential respects.

[2] *MGH* SS xxv, 356, 5 f. [3] *Ibid.* l. 28.

[4] *Recueil des historiens des Gaules et de la France*, XVIII, 778 C f.

the equation of these particular crusaders with the innocents of Bethlehem was not a view shared only by the children themselves and by one chronicler, but appears to have enjoyed papal sanction and may therefore be presumed to have been considerably widespread.

There is also another respect in which the evidence of the Children's Crusade is relevant to our inquiry. This concerns the manner in which the child crusaders regard their undertaking as a new exodus in which they too are to cross the Red Sea in order to reach Jerusalem. In holding this conviction the children share it with other, knightly, crusaders who, as we have seen,[1] likewise saw their expedition as a renewed exodus. The song of the child crusaders preserved in the Austrian chronicle makes it clear that these children were convinced that under divine leadership they would cross the sea miraculously and with dry feet, thereby being granted the same assistance as God had shown His Chosen People in leading them through the Red Sea. Nicolaus, accompanied by his *innocentes*, is described as about to cross the sea and reach Jerusalem:

Mare siccis pedibus securus calcabit.[2]

The same belief is imputed to these children in the *Annales Scheftlarienses Maiores*, whose author describes the manner in which the children assembled for their expedition, convinced that divine election was the guarantee that the miracle granted to the Hebrews in crossing the Red Sea would not be denied to them on their journey to the Near East: 'Eodem anno quidam puer nomine Nicolaus surrexit, qui multitudinem puerorum et mulierum sibi aggregavit, cum quibus Ierusalem, crucem dominicam liberaturus, iussu angelico adire debere, mare sicut quondam populo Israelitico siccum iter prebere, asserebat.'[3] Elsewhere it is suggested that the miraculous crossing of the sea, repeating that of the Red Sea, was felt by the children to be so tangible a proof of divine election and a guarantee of their entry into Jerusalem

[1] See above, pp. 259 ff.   [2] *MGH* SS xxv, 356, 7.
[3] *MGH* SS xvii, 338, 4 ff.

315

that this one event comes to predominate over anything else and to be proclaimed as their goal. In the *Hermanni Altahensis Annales* we read under the year 1212, after the laconic entry *Derisoria expedicio puerorum*, the words:

> Anno milleno ducenteno duodeno
> Ad mare stultorum tendebat iter puerorum.[1]

That the sea which is here conceived almost as the goal of their journey must be regarded as the equivalent of the Red Sea in the journey of the Hebrews and therefore as tantamount to religious redemption is made evident by the words of the Austrian chronicler after he has given the theme of the crusading song of these children, for he describes their assembly prior to departure in these terms:

> Aures cunctis pruriunt, virgines ornantur,
> Annos infra sedecim euangelizantur.
> Concurrentes pueri certant, ut sequantur
> Et rubrum mare videant...[2]

From this evidence we learn that the Children's Crusade of 1212 was no different from other, feudal crusades in its interpretation, by participants or by contemporaries, as a renewal of the liberation of Israel from Egypt. For us the important thing is that this evidence suggests that these child crusaders, who see themselves explicitly as new innocents of Bethlehem, could also apply to themselves imagery taken from Exodus. This makes it conversely quite possible that the Millstatt author, whose intention it is to depict the Hebrew exodus as a prefiguration of the crusades, should have interpreted the slaughtered children of the Israelites as foreshadowing not merely the children of Bethlehem, but also the crusaders who reveal a similar readiness for service of Christ and for martyrdom.

The objection to this last point[3] is that, although the child

---

[1] *MGH* SS xvii, 386, 49 ff.   [2] *MGH* SS xxv, 356, 16 ff.

[3] I attach relatively little importance to the possible objection that the Children's Crusade occurs so late as 1212. In his discussion of this feature Waas (*Geschichte der Kreuzzüge*, I, 253 ff.) has drawn attention to the important testimony of the *Kaiserchronik*, 14933 ff., as an indication of the existence of this idea long before 1212 (although not necessarily so early as Waas appears to believe

crusaders could be regarded as *novi innocentes* because of their youth, there is no very obvious manner in which the slaughter of the innocents (the typological fulfilment of the killing of the Israelite children) could be regarded as related to the condition of ordinary feudal crusaders, as opposed to the particular case of the child crusaders. To meet this objection we shall have to discuss the way in which the position of all crusaders at large, and not just of the children, could be illuminated by the example of the innocents of Bethlehem.

Here two considerations are of importance. The first concerns the fact of martyrdom which we may regard as one of the motives impelling the crusader to undertake the journey to the Holy Land[1] and which was capable of making a particular appeal to the knight because it suggested the reciprocal reward which God would confer upon him for the feudal service which the knight rendered Him as his Lord. The knightly crusader to whom the assurance of admittance to the Heavenly Jerusalem was held out as the reward of a Christian martyr would consequently come to regard himself as standing in an intimate relationship with other Christian martyrs. This is one of the reasons why, with the development of a Christian sanction of warfare and of the individual warrior investigated by Erdmann, particular importance comes to be attached to those saints and martyrs who had also been soldiers, such as Mauritius, Sebastian or George.[2] This rise of the cult of saints who came to be regarded as knightly saints

with his dating of the *Kaiserchronik* between 1106 and 1139!). The passage concerns an episode in which Charles the Great, after the pagans have inflicted a defeat upon him, is advised by an angel to turn to an army of young maidens for assistance. Their youth is explicitly stressed (14946: 'manich maget junge'), as is also the fact that they act as the agents of God (14936: 'got wil sîne tugent dar an rescainen. | wil dû got vurhten unt minnen, | die megede suln dir dîn êre wider gewinnen'). Equally important is the way in which the pagans are thereupon won over to Christianity, so that an actual military encounter is avoided (14985: 'alse tet in got sigehaft | âne stich unt âne slach. | wol rechanten dô die mägede daz, | daz got von himele mit in was'). These are details which agree with what we know of the later Children's Crusade, so that we may assume the existence of such ideas in Germany by the middle of the twelfth century or even earlier.

[1] See pp. 269 f.
[2] Erdmann, *Die Entstehung des Kreuzzugsgedankens*, pp. 253 ff.

ensures that the crusading knights can now rely on the patronage of saints who were both warriors and martyrs.[1] It is this double function which the crusading knights have now taken over for themselves so that, because of the development of the cult of these saints in particular, the crusader who is prepared to embrace martyrdom in his feudal service of God is now brought into close connection with all Christian martyrs (warriors or not). From the contemporary Christian point of view, what is of primary importance is the fact of martyrdom (whether actually realised by the death of a crusader or only accepted as a possibility by the knight who is prepared to embark on the crusade), rather than the particular way in which martyrdom is achieved (whether by a warrior who falls in the service of God or in a non-military manner).[2] At the same time, the crusader who achieves martyrdom in the medieval present is seen as the latest recruit to the heavenly legions of Christian martyrs, so that inevitably he will also come to be seen in relation to the first martyrs in Christ.[3] Together they form the first and the latest, together they ensure that the

[1] On the manner in which the military aspects of these martyrs are reinterpreted so as to provide a closer parallel to the military role of the crusaders see below, p. 325.

[2] The distinction between the martyr who met a warlike death in the service of Christ and the martyr whose sacrifice was a pacific one was weakened by the manner in which the Church early came to regard martyrdom metaphorically as a struggle with the Devil. On this see F. J. Dölger, *AuCh*, III, 177 ff. The crusading revaluation of this tradition, like the reinterpretation of the *militia Dei*, has only to see this conflict both as a physical one and as a spiritual one for a close connection to be established between the martyrs of the Church and those who die as crusaders. Furthermore, we have already seen (p. 274, n. 2) that, despite the difference between passive and active combat, the *militia Christi* of the martyr agrees with that of the crusader (and differs from that of all other *milites Dei*) in that both have to engage in a physical combat.

[3] The exemplary importance of the innocents is well brought out by von den Steinen in his discussion of Notker's sequence for 28 December (*Notker der Dichter und seine geistige Welt*, Darstellungsband, pp. 344 f.): 'Durch treue Gefolgschaft Christi den Tod überwindend, stellt der Mensch im Himmel die vollkommene Schöpfungszahl der Unsterblichen wieder her. Die ersten nun, die diese Gefolgschaft leisteten — das waren eben jene Kinder von Bethlehem: selber nichts davon ahnend und dergestalt, daß erst dreißig Jahre später, nach dem Tode und der Höllenfahrt Christi, ihr Aufstieg wirklich und deutlich und den Gläubigen glaubhaft werden konnte. Seit dem Tage von Christi Himmelfahrt nämlich steigen die Seelen der Märtyrer unmittelbar von der Todesstätte ins

crusading martyrdom of the present belongs to a continuous Christian tradition and that these military expeditions against the pagans are justified in the eyes of God.

It cannot be fortuitous that in the account given by Baldricus of the speech of Urban II an *exemplum* is held up to the knights about to go on the First Crusade in the form of the first Christian martyr. The Pope refers to the Holy Land and explains its sanctity by the hallowing presence of Christ, Mary and the apostles as well as by the blood of the martyrs shed there: 'Quam Terram merito Sanctam dixerimus, in qua non est etiam passus pedis quem non illustraverit et sanctificaverit vel corpus vel umbra Salvatoris, vel gloriosa praesentia sanctae Dei genitricis, vel amplectendus apostolorum conventus, vel martyrum ebibendus sanguis effusus.'[1] It is to the first martyr, St Stephen, that Urban draws particular attention because it is his service of Christ which is the model for the present: 'Quam beati, o Stephane protomartyr, qui te laureaverunt lapides?'[2] This special interest in St Stephen as the first of the martyrs to whose ranks the fallen crusaders are added as the latest recruits is borne out by the frequency with which the crusading chronicles, when describing the physical details of Jerusalem, refer to the church erected on the site of his martyrdom, and add explicitly the word *protomartyr*.[3] This is also confirmed by a passage in the *Chançun de Guillelme*:

547	Car sainz Estiévenes	ni li altre martir
	ne furent mieldre,	que serunt tuit icil
	ki en l'Archamp	serunt pur Deu ocis.[4]

In such a reference to the example of past martyrs it is felt necessary to mention by name only St Stephen because of his preeminence as protomartyr. He is the *exemplum* which the Christian knight seeks to emulate.

Paradies, und nur die Körper warten noch bis zum Jüngsten Tage. Die Unschuldigen Kinder hingegen samt Johannes dem Täufer haben als die letzten des alten und zugleich als die ersten des neuen Bundes noch hinter dem Höllentore auf den Auferstehenden warten müssen.'

[1] *RHC*, IV, 14 D.   [2] *Ibid.*
[3] E.g. *RHC*, III, 102, 159, 217 and 686 G.
[4] Quoted by Rousset, *Les origines et les caractères de la première croisade*, p. 123.

There are other cases where it is clear that the innocents of Bethlehem are regarded as the first to meet death in the service of Christ and therefore as the earliest Christian martyrs. This conception of the role of the innocents is in part explicable by their liturgical celebration on a day (28 December) close to that of St Stephen (26 December), and also by the manner in which the Church was prepared, as in the case of Notker Balbulus, to take the deed for the wish and to view the fact of the slaughter of the innocents as more decisive than any willingness on their part to undergo martyrdom. St Bernard therefore treats of the innocents in the same liturgical context as St Stephen and also St John (27 December) and argues that, whereas only St Stephen demonstrates the martyrdom of longing and of deed, St John shows that of the wish alone, but the innocents that of the deed alone.[1] If it is insisted that the combination of wish and deed is necessary for the fact of martyrdom, then St Stephen's priority remains unaffected, but if the deed is taken for the wish then priority will now pass to the innocents who died before Christ had even begun His ministry. That this view could also be held in the Middle Ages is shown by the sermon of St Bernard, and also by the manner in which Prudentius refers to the innocents collectively as *vos prima Christi victima*[2] or Notker Balbulus calls them *floresque martyrum*.[3]

This brings us to our second consideration: the fact that a typological fulfilment can also point forward to the possibility that each individual Christian has to realise it in practice for himself[4] so that, in this sense, the supreme typological fulfilment of Christ's death remains only a potential fact, providing an *exemplum* which every Christian is free to accept or to ignore. In the same way, the innocents of Bethlehem are the typological

---

[1] Sermo in nativitate SS. Innocentium (*MPL*, 183, 129 D): 'Habemus in beato Stephano martyrii simul et opus et voluntatem; habemus solam voluntatem in beato Joanne; solum in beatis Innocentibus opus. Biberunt omnes hi calicem salutaris, aut corpore simul et spiritu, aut solo spiritu, aut corpore solo.'

[2] *Cathemerinon*, XII, 129 (*MPL*, 59, 909).

[3] Stanza 9 (Editionsband, p. 18). This same phrase was also used by Prudentius (v. 125). [4] See pp. 266, 270f. and 313.

fulfilment of the prefiguration given in the slaughter of the Israelite children by Pharaoh, but at the same time an *exemplum* of martyrdom in the service of Christ which every Christian is at liberty to follow in his own life or not.[1] The First Crusade is regarded by Church and participants alike as a novel means of serving Christ and as the latest occasion for achieving martyrdom. The crusading knights who fall during the expedition and are assured of martyrs' crowns are Christians who have not hesitated to seize the opportunity presented to them of emulating the self-sacrifice in the service of Christ shown for the first time by the innocents. The prefiguration given by the slaughter of the Israelite children, which was fulfilled potentially by the children of Bethlehem, is realised in practice and enabled to bear fruit in the present by the readiness of the crusaders to follow the example of these innocents. Indirectly, but in a manner characteristic of typological interpretation, the crusaders resemble the innocents in that both achieve martyrdom in the service of Christ, so that both represent the fulfilment of the prefiguration given in Exodus with the slaughter of the Israelite children.

Our argument has brought us to the point at which it seems likely that a typological connection could be established between the slaughter of the Israelite children in the *Millstätter Exodus* and the crusading movement of the twelfth century only to the extent that the martyrdom of the crusaders was connected with the slaughter of the innocents, itself the conventional typological fulfilment of the scene from Exodus. That this equation between the crusaders and the innocents was known to German literature can be shown in the case of the *Rolandslied*. Here the author describes how Turpin announces to Roland the approach of the

[1] Although he introduces no specific reference to martyrdom it is significant that Otfrid closes his chapter on the slaughter of the innocents (1, 20) by stressing that their service of Christ as their king is still continued down to the present day:

35 Nu folget imo thuruh thaz   githigini so managaz,
    thaz ther nist hiar in libe,   ther thia zala irscribe.

As with the equation between the crusaders and the innocents (or St Stephen), the important thing is the direct relationship between the first martyrs and the last, between their example and the present in which every Christian has to decide whether to emulate it or not.

pagan hosts for a renewed attack just before the scene in which Roland finally blows his horn. Turpin's announcement is followed by a description of the speed with which the Christian warriors prepare for battle and martyrdom. They are described as *manc heiliger marteraere* (v. 5793), about to occupy the thrones prepared for them as martyrs from the beginning of time:

> 5759 Si sûchten die stôle,
> si îlten ze dem trône,
> dâ in got mit wolte gelten,
> dem von angenge der werlte
> den heiligen marterêren gehaizen was.

They achieve martyrdom by fulfilling the promises which they had made to God at baptism,[1] so that their heavenly crown is a reward for their loyalty in serving God. In this they resemble the innocents of Bethlehem, as Konrad now adds:

> 5767 Sie wâren liuter unt raine
> âne rost unt âne mailen,
> sam diu heiligen chindelîn,
> di durch selben mînen trechtîn
> Herodes hiez erslahen.

When in the following lines[2] a brief reference is made to the heavenly choir which the crusading martyrs are to occupy, it is clear that these crusaders are directly linked with the innocents since they are the first and the latest of those Christians recruited to make good the celestial ranks because of the loyal service which both alike have rendered their heavenly Lord.[3]

---

[1] The evidence interpreted by Harnack, *Militia Christi*, pp. 33 ff., and by F. J. Dölger in his article on the 'Sacramentum militiae', *AuCh*, II, 268 ff., makes it clear that the baptismal formula was understood by the early Church as the military oath sworn by the Christian who thereby joined the ranks of Christ's army. Cf. also *Annolied* 73: 'in der doufe wurde wir Cristis man.'

[2] Vv. 5772 f.

[3] Cf. the remarks of von den Steinen, quoted above, p. 318, n. 3. For a French example of the manner in which crusading martyrs are felt to be following the example of the innocents see the *Chanson de Roland*, vv. 1521 ff.:

> Mais d'une chose vos soi jo ben guarant:
> Seint pareïs vos est abandunant;
> As Innocenz vos en serez seant.

Equally significant for the course of our argument is the fact that the author of the *Rolandslied* should have chosen this episode as the occasion for providing an explicit link between his crusading martyrs and the events with which the book of Exodus is concerned. When announcing the approach of the pagan warriors Turpin adduces the typological example of the Israelites' passage of the Red Sea and deliverance from Pharaoh, an example whose significance lies in the fact that it was interpreted typologically both as a prefiguration of the redemption of mankind accomplished by Christ[1] and also with reference to the particular means of redemption employed by the crusaders of the medieval present.[2] Turpin's words make this connection between the Old Testament event and what is regarded as the crusading present quite clear:

> 5744 Der flûch mûze uber si werde,
> dâ got mit sînem gewalte
> Pharaonem mit ervalte:
> den verswalch daz mer
> unt al sîn wôtigez her;
> den sîn half er ûzer nôt:
> in der wûste gap er in daz himilprôt.

As He did with the Israelites, God will guide the crusaders to their homeland (5753: *haimverte*), to Paradise. The fact that Konrad adduces this prefiguration of redemption on the same occasion as when he refers to the coming martyrdom of the crusaders in terms of their similarity with the innocents of Bethlehem implies that for him this contemporary form of martyrdom illustrated one particular means of gaining redemption. The evidence of the *Rolandslied* shows us that in the twelfth century the salvation achieved by the crusading martyr could be seen in terms both of the exodus from Egypt (as a prefiguration of salvation at large or of the crusades in particular) and of the innocents of Bethlehem (the typological fulfilment of the slaughter of the Israelite children). That the crusaders could be seen in this double context of Christian martyrdom and the exodus from Egypt is also revealed by the words attributed to Urban II by

---

[1] See pp. 111 f.   [2] See pp. 259 ff.

Baldricus who reports, after his reference to St Stephen as the protomartyr quoted above, that the Pope went on to an explicit comparison between the crusaders and the Israelites' deliverance from Egypt: 'Filii Israel ab Aegyptiis educti, qui, Rubro Mari transito, vos praefiguraverunt, terram illam armis suis, Jesu duce, sibi vindicaverunt.'[1] Here again the equation of the crusaders as the latest martyrs with the protomartyr takes place in the context of the exodus which, as a prefiguration of salvation or of the crusades, provides the general setting in which this martyrdom will be achieved. The argument used by the Pope differs from that which we encountered in the *Rolandslied* only in the way in which St Stephen is referred to as the protomartyr, rather than the innocents; apart from this both agree in connecting the crusading martyrs with what they regard as the earliest Christian martyrs and in stressing the general parallel of Exodus.

The technique of the Millstatt author in describing the scene of the provisional escape of the Israelite children from the slaughter intended by Pharaoh therefore resembles the method used by Otfrid in sketching the similar scene with the innocents: both authors regard the episode as a battle which they sketch in negative terms. The twelfth-century author refers to the beasts of prey of the battlefield which were not present on this occasion, whereas Otfrid describes a battle (*wig*) which took place without any fighting (*ana fehta*). Furthermore, we saw that both these biblical episodes were related typologically as prefiguration and fulfilment, but that this fulfilment could be provided by the Christian martyrdom of the innocents, and also by that of the crusaders, who likewise die in the service of God. There is therefore little difficulty in accepting the view that, just as the *Millstätter Exodus* in its entirety was related to the contemporary experience of the crusades, so was this particular episode dignified with the heroic associations evoked by these conventional formulas because of its prefigurative ability to suggest the heroic martyrdom of the crusading knights. The possible objection that, whereas the martyrdom of the Israelite children and of the inno-

[1] *RHC*, IV, 14E.

cents of Bethlehem was passive (and the military imagery applied to them therefore strictly metaphorical), that of the crusaders is entirely active (so that in their case the heroic vocabulary is to be understood literally) is irrelevant. Here the important point is that the crusades, while still employing the military imagery inherited from the early Church, now for the first time use it in a literal, physical sense as well as in its traditional metaphorical sense.[1] The suggestion that the crusader achieves martyrdom (and thereby follows the example of the innocents), but with his sword in his hand, fully agrees with the way in which *miles Christi* now no longer designates only the monk engaged in a spiritual battle with demonic adversaries, but also the knight who serves God as a crusader. It also agrees with Erdmann's observation that, in the period which he regards as critical for the final emergence of the crusading idea, Christian saints who had achieved martyrdom *after* relinquishing their military status now begin to be celebrated as saints who achieve martyrdom *while* still remaining soldiers.[2] Such saints become the patron saints of crusading knighthood. Whereas their martyrdom had earlier been regarded (like that of the Israelite children or the innocents) as passive and non-military, now with the rise of the crusades it is felt to resemble that of the crusaders in its active, military nature. This equation of a passive form of martyrdom (suffering violence inflicted by warriors, but in the service of God) with a more active form (serving God by inflicting violence on the pagans, as well as suffering it in martyrdom) is another example of the manner in which Christianity, now seen in its bearing on the functions of knighthood and therefore in part feudalised, undergoes a process of materialisation on which we commented at the conclusion of the preceding chapter.[3]

The second objection advanced by de Boor concerns the manner in which the insects of the plagues of Egypt are described as knightly warriors. Here too he sees a discrepancy between the

[1] See pp. 273 ff.
[2] Erdmann, *Die Entstehung des Kreuzzugsgedankens*, pp. 253 ff. and 261 ff. For St Sebastian see p. 254, for St George pp. 257 f.
[3] See pp. 294 f.

scene described and the imagery employed which is so drastic that he feels it necessary to conclude that this must imply a negative criticism of knightly warfare. If we were to accept this conclusion, then it would be difficult to maintain that the Millstatt author intended to convert knightly warfare to positive ends in the context of the crusades. I am not convinced, however, that this conclusion is a compelling one or that the incongruity which we may feel to exist between a crusading intention and this use of knightly imagery would have been regarded in the same light by a medieval audience.[1] We have seen how careful we must be not to attribute our own aesthetic reactions to a twelfth-century audience in the case of the description of child martyrs as warriors who die fighting on behalf of Christ. A similar caution is enjoined upon us in the case of the insects, especially if we recall the manner in which the author of the *Vorauer Bücher Mosis* even interprets the worms which developed from the remnants of the manna with which God had fed the Israelites as signifying Christ Himself:

svaz sin wart ze leibe.　daz wur-
den wurme chleine.　daz bezeichenet
dich crist herre got.　du uon diner

[1] Our problem, in other words, is to decide whether the author's use of crusading terminology (v. 1482: *gotes rîtere* and v. 1494: *gotes anden si râchen*), but in application to these insects, would have been likely to recommend itself to his knightly audience. One may meet this objection not so much by simply pointing out that these insects were after all summoned to this task by God Himself (v. 1484: *von gote chômen si dare*), but more tellingly by the following argument. The appeal which the author hopes to make to his audience of professional warriors at this stage is that, if even the insect world has been enrolled in this universal conflict with the pagans, how much more incumbent is it on the Christian knight, whose *raison d'être* is the profession of arms, to serve God by obeying His call to fight the heathen. The Millstatt author's appeal to the example of the insect world as a means of rousing his audience to an awareness of their duties is comparable with the method adopted by Walther in his second *Reichstonsspruch* (8, 28) where all branches of the animal and insect worlds (9, 10: *daʒ nû diu mugge ir künec hât*) are adduced as an example which the world of man should learn to follow. If Walther could hope to make a successful appeal in terms of the *mugge*, I see no reason to deny the same intention to the Millstatt author in terms of the *hundesfliege*.

R. A. Wisbey has also drawn my attention to the equally drastic example of Is. 41. 13 f.

Problems of detail

mûter name fleisk unde blût.   uon
ir suzeme lutereme wizzeme lichna-
men.   ane alle werltlichen man.[1]

If the exegetical tradition allows such a drastic (and, to modern
sensibility, tasteless) comparison to be made even in the case of
Christ, the comparison of the insects of the plagues with crusaders
certainly falls within the limits of what this tradition regarded as
permissible.

Quite apart from this general criticism of de Boor's approach
to this problem, it is possible to show that there is a number of
other medieval examples where insects are described in the context of Christian warfare or especially crusading warfare. In other
words, the Millstatt author by no means stands alone and it is
probably owing to this general possibility of referring to insects
in such a context that he was enabled to refer the insects of his
biblical source to the crusading experience of the present. That
this possibility (however ludicrous it may seem to us) existed
from an early date and with regard to Christian warfare in general
is made clear by the account given by Theodoretus of the manner
in which Bishop Jacobus of Nisibis undertook, in the fourth
century, the defence of this city against the Persians, for he is
described as invoking the name of the Lord to send clouds of
gnats and mosquitoes to irritate the trunks of the enemies'
elephants and the nostrils of their horses: 'Paruit vir divinus,
et turrim quamdam conscendit, et innumerabilem cernens multitudinem, exsecratione alia non est usus, sed siniphes et culices in
eos immitti postulavit, ut ex minutis bestiolis auxiliatoris poten-
tiam agnoscerent. Orantis votum secutae sunt siniphum et culi-
cum nubes, quae cavas proboscides elephantum, equorumque, et
reliquorum jumentorum aures naresque compleverunt. Qui cum
animalculorum impressionem ferre non possent, ruptis loris,
excussisque sessoribus, ordines turbarunt.'[2] We cannot tell for
certain whether Jacobus actually conceived himself in the light of
Moses' experience before Pharaoh and whether it was necessarily

[1] 79. 11 ff. Cf. Jantsch, *Studien zum Symbolischen*, p. 95.
[2] *MPG*, 82, 1079 A f.

the scene from Exodus which provided the *exemplum* for this episode, but at least it informs us that from the fourth century Christians could be thought of as receiving the same kind of divine assistance in the form of insects attacking their foes as was granted earlier to the Israelites.

More important for us is the recognition that this possibility also existed for the crusades in particular. Here the assistance rendered to the crusaders by swarms of insects forms only a part of the wider view in which God is seen as impelling not only human beings, but also various parts of the animal kingdom, to fulfil His purpose in the war against the pagans. Raimundus de Aguilers describes the miraculous dew which God allows to fall on the crusaders as they commence battle, and adds that it was not only the knights who were refreshed by this, but also their horses for whom little fodder had been available for the last week ('Non minus hoc idem mirabile equis nostris etiam contigit').[1] God therefore performs His miracles through these animals as well as through the knights themselves: 'Operabatur ibi mirabiliter Dominus tam in viris quam in equis nostris.'[2] For Ekkehardus it is a miracle that herds of animals, captured from Arabs, should constitute themselves into military formation and accompany the ranks of the crusaders: 'Pridie autem quam bellum fieret, multa millia camelorum et boum et ovium cepit exercitus; cumque jussu principum populus haec dimississet, pugnam progrediens, mirabile dictu, multiplices turmas eadem fecerunt animalia, et comitabantur exercitum, ita ut cum currentibus currerent et cum stantibus starent.'[3] Clouds again bring divine solace to the crusaders so that Ekkehardus can report that the whole of nature fought on behalf of the Christian knights: 'Pugnabat certe orbis terrarum pro christianis.'[4]

If the crusade is therefore envisaged as a universal conflict in which the whole of creation is involved, there is little cause to wonder at the way in which, alongside the various animals miraculously conscripted in the service of God, insects of various kinds should also be described as summoning their own crusades

[1] *RHC*, III, 261 C.   [2] *RHC*, III, 261 D.   [3] *RHC*, V, 25 C.   [4] *RHC*, V 25 B.

and migrating in the same way as large bodies of knights were put into motion by the same compelling need to serve God against the pagans. It is immaterial whether we see in these references, with Alphandéry,[1] an attempt to find parallels in the animal kingdom for the events of the human sphere or to account for prodigies of nature recorded for this period, or whether we lay greater stress on the need of the twelfth century to feel convinced that the miraculous assistance given to the Israelites (the plagues of insects, dew from heaven) was being repeated in the present. What is significant is the fact that contemporary chronicles record the conviction that animals and insects as well as men were assembling in their swarms in order to set out in the service of God. Amongst these reports we may include that contained in the *Annales S. Medardi Suessionensibus* for the year 1209 in connection with the Children's Crusade, for here the belief is chronicled that at regular intervals various animals (including the *ranae* of the second plague of Egypt) assembled and set forth: 'Dicunt quidam et pro certo affirmant, quod de decennio in decennium quod antequam illud mirabile accidisset, quod pisces, rane, papiliones et aves simili modo secundum genus suum et tempus proficiscebantur... Quidam vero senes et decrepiti istud pro certo affirmant, quod de diversis Galliarum partibus innumera multitudo canum apud castrum Campanie quod vocatur Monshymer congregata est. Ipsi vero canes in duas partes divisi, ad invicem fortiter et acriter pugnantes, fere omnes sese mutuo cede interfecerunt, et paucissimi reversi sunt.'[2] The *Annales Brixienses* (under the year 1147) record that in this year there was a general departure for the Second Crusade and that there were also many caterpillars (!): 'cruce fuerunt, et magna gens ultra mare iverunt.'[3]

[1] *La chrétienté et l'idée de croisade*, II, 129 ff.
[2] *MGH* SS xxvi, 521, 14 ff.
[3] *MGH* SS xviii, 812, 47 (A). For biblical examples of these same insects as an army sent by God see Joel 1. 4 ('Residuum erucae comedit locusta, et residuum locustae comedit bruchus, et residuum bruchi comedit rubigo') in connection with Joel 1. 6 ('Gens enim ascendit super terram meam, fortis et innumerabilis: dentes ejus ut dentes leonis; et molares ejus ut catuli leonis'), but especially Joel 2. 25 ('Et reddam vobis annos quos comedit locusta, bruchus, et rubigo, et eruca, fortitudo mea magna quam misi in vos').

For the Crusade of 1101 we have the evidence of Ekkehardus, who reports the migration of swarms of what may well have been locusts[1] in this year: 'Sequenti anno, qui est Domini MCI, visus est a nostro quodam familiari, ab Occidente in Orientem volans, ignis ad instar non modicae civitatis; vermiculorum quoque, quos papiliones a similitudine tabernaculorum vocant, exercitus incredibilis, per tres continuos dies, quasi a Saxoniae finibus in Bajoariam volabat. Mox profectio populosa, ut quae paene priori posset numero dumtaxat aequari, subsequitur, quae, post auditas ultra spem res Hierosolimae prospere gestas, a residuis totius Occidentis gentibus...denuo parabatur.'[2] The juxtaposition of the swarm of insects and the hordes of crusaders, as in the *Annales Brixienses*, presupposes that the chronicler saw these two phenomena in some kind of causal connection and that, as Alphandéry suggests,[3] the one event was regarded as a *prefiguratio* of the other.

As a complement to this credulous view of events which sees insects and animals engaged in the same activity as the feudal knights, we find, rather less frequently, the occasional comparison of the crusaders themselves with insects such as locusts. One example we have already briefly considered.[4] It is provided by the description which Guibertus gives of the manner in which the knights to whom the *novum salutis genus* had just been offered by the Pope's proclamation of a crusade eagerly made their preparations for the departure. It is at this stage[5] that Guibertus quotes Prov. 30. 27 ('Regem locusta non habet, et egreditur universa per turmas suas') which he then interprets in two respects. One of these we discussed above,[6] for the fact that these locusts have no king is interpreted with reference to the absence of any king from the First Crusade, so that this undertaking, shared between the papacy and the knighthood, is subject to the leader-

---

[1] For this interpretation see the editorial footnote *g* to the word *vermiculorum* in *RHC*: 'Forte locustae, quarum meminit Anna Comn. (*Hist. gr. des cr.*, I, II, p. 5; éd. P., p. 284).' See also Runciman, *A History of the Crusades*, I, 116 f.

[2] *RHC*, V, 28 B ff.   [3] *Op. cit.* II, 130 f.

[4] See p. 254.   [5] *RHC*, IV, 124H.

[6] See p. 261.

ship of Christ alone.[1] The other detail which Guibertus interprets concerns the fact that it was the locust of whom this was said in the biblical proverb. For him the locust designates the crusading knight who had for long remained static in the lethargy of sinfulness, but who now at last moves or leaps in the act of taking the cross, thereby departing from his home and changing the nature of his life: 'Haec locusta nullum bonae operationis saltum dederat, quandiu longae iniquitatis congelatione torpuerat; at ubi solis justitiae fervor excanduit, geminae ilico transmigrationis evolatione prosiliit; dum de patris domo ac cognatione digreditur, et per sanctae intentionis assumptionem moribus immutatur.'[2] That this comparison is not simply the result of the author's need to interpret this proverb with reference to the crusade, but instead reflects a more general attitude (which may therefore have been the reason why Guibertus should have chosen to quote this particular proverb) can best be shown by the fact that elsewhere chroniclers describe crusading warfare by comparing it with the attacks of a swarm of locusts.

In one sense, the introduction of the image of a swarm of locusts need be no more than a stylistic device to convey some idea of the enormous numbers involved on both sides. We find the image of the locusts employed with reference to the numbers of the Saracens who confront the crusading armies, as when Fulcherius wonders why the superior forces of the heathen did not attack the territory of Baldwin: 'Tot populi, tot regna, quare regnulum nostrum et popellum invadere metuebant? Cur de Egypto, de Persida, de Mesopotamia, vel de Syria, non coadunabant saltem centies centum millia pugnatorum, ut nos hostes eorum viriliter aggrederentur; et ut solent locustae innumerae messem in agello, nos omnino consumerent et destruerent, ut nec mentio de nobis in terra ab olim sua ulterius fieret?'[3] We may be reasonably certain that the locusts are not always adduced as a means of conjuring up an idea of the numbers involved, but that they were also intended as a divine portent (and therefore com-

---

[1] *RHC*, IV, 125 A.   [2] *RHC*, IV, 1241 f.
[3] *RHC*, III, 383 D. This same image occurs frequently in the Bible, e.g. Jud. 6. 5.

parable with the swarms of insects reported by some chroniclers in connection with the departure for the crusades)[1] if we consider the manner in which locusts are used not just as an image for the pagan numbers, but actually as a substitute for these enemies of the crusaders. The *Secunda pars historiae Hierosolimitanae* reports for the year 1117: 'Anno .M.C.XVII., hostium vice, Jerosolimitanum totum fere territorium infinitae multitudines occupavere locustarum, ita catervatim continuatimque de pessundatis jam locis ad alia procedentes pessundanda, ut ex devoratis cunctis virentibus terrae perpendere evidenter liceret Dominum praecepisse locustae indisciplinatorum devorare terras incolarum; si forte, revertentes ad cor, animadverterent perversi quam non locustis vastandi, sed ipsis Sarracenis tradi mererentur trucidandi.'[2] Here the locusts, who are not equated with the Saracens but act *hostium vice*, act on behalf of God and are the means He employs to recall the crusaders to obedience and penitence for their sins.[3] In other words, the locusts are employed by God and

[1] That swarms of locusts can appear to the crusaders in the Holy Land as divine portents to which attention must be paid is suggested by the way in which two chronicles report on such a phenomenon in Jerusalem for the year 1114 and attach to it as much importance as they do to an earthquake occurring at the same time. Cf. Fulcherius, *RHC*, III, 428 D, and the *Secunda pars historiae Hierosolimitanae*, *RHC*, III, 572 A.

[2] *RHC*, III, 574 C f. The same event is reported by Fulcherius, *RHC*, III, 434 A ff., in a manner which shows that he too conceives of the insects as a divine admonition to the crusaders. In addition to this, Fulcherius describes the attacks of the locusts with reference to the assaults of human warriors, so that his technique closely resembles that of the Millstatt author's description of the insects of the plagues of Egypt in knightly terms: 'Deinde, Maio mense, advolaverunt in terram Iherosolymitanam locustarum infinita multitudo, amplius solito devorantes tam vineas quam segetes, necnon arbores omnigenas, quas videretis accurate ad morem exercitus hominum per vias, tanquam consilio provido prolocutas, ordinate progredi. Et facta expeditione sua diurna, aliae pedites, aliae vero volantes, hospitium sibi communiter eligebant. Consumptis itaque herbis viridibus et arborum corrosis corticibus, tam bruci quam locustae catervatim abierunt. O improbitas hominum perverse incessabiliter malignantium! Tot et tantis nos Conditor noster increpationibus tangit et praemunit, signis territat, minis concitat, documentis edocet, flagellis coercet!' A biblical parallel for this equation of the attacks of locusts with an army of human warriors is provided by Apoc. 9. 7 and 9. 9.

[3] Of the earthquake which follows the plague of locusts in 1117 and which is regarded as a similar kind of portent it is said (*RHC*, III, 574 G): 'iram Dei

act in His service in place of human foes in just the same manner
as the locusts of the eighth plague in the biblical Exodus are
summoned by God to inflict His wrath upon the sinful Egyptians.
Here they are called into action against the crusaders because of
their sinfulness, but elsewhere, so long as the feudal knights continue by their conduct to act on behalf of God, it is the crusaders
who are compared with locusts. An example of this, with reference to the numbers of the crusaders, occurs in the description
by Baldricus of the departure of 1096 in which he writes how
some went by sea and others by land. Of the latter he says: 'et
qui terra ibant, universae terrae faciem, sicut locustae, occu-
luerunt.'[1] The fact that this phrase includes a quotation from
Judith 2. 11 is significant, for, whereas the biblical phrase refers
to the numbers of the pagan enemies of the Hebrews, Baldricus
reverses the usage and applies it to the new Israel, enemies of the
pagans of the present. Elsewhere Baldricus attributes this same
comparison of the crusaders with locusts to the Saracen ruler
Corbarannus in what appears to be a contemptuous usage. Corbarannus, after having been shown a weapon of the Franks, says
boastfully: 'Haec sunt arma bellica, arma nimis pretiosa, quae
attulerunt locustae illae de mendica Gallia; his nos expugnare
minantur, his contra nos obluctantur.'[2] This self-confident
attitude of the Saracen ruler corresponds closely to that revealed
by Pharaoh in Exodus, not merely in face of the threat of the
locusts, but also with regard to the other plagues. Even more
revealing are the words used by Corbarannus in a letter which
he sends to the Caliph, for here Baldricus attributes to him a view
why the crusaders are to be regarded as locusts which is in fact
the Christian conception of the crusader's task which we encountered earlier with Guibertus. The letter of Corbarannus
begins: 'Caliphae, nostro papae, et Solimano, regi magno, perpes
salus et honor immensus. Noveritis quoniam locustae illae,
quae propriam non habent mansionem, qui Christiani dicuntur,

praemonens citius debere placari', and also: 'ut dura hominum stolidorum ad
poenitentiam concuterentur corda'. As a biblical example of locusts sent by God
as a punishment cf. II Paral. 7. 13.

[1] *RHC*, IV, 18 B.   [2] *RHC*, IV, 61 F.

latibula sua irreverenter exierunt.'[1] Here the crusaders are called locusts because they have given up their own dwelling-place, because they have undertaken a pilgrimage—or, to use the phrase of Guibertus, because they have accomplished the leap out of the lethargy of sin. The way in which Corbarannus uses the image of the locust in the first of these passages may well express his contempt, but the second quotation makes it likely that the origin of this image was Christian and that it served to show the religious function of the crusaders to whom it was applied.

From this evidence it is clear that in the early crusading period two attitudes were possible: either the various parts of the animal kingdom (including insects) were felt to be engaged in crusading warfare like the feudal knights or, conversely, the crusading knights could be compared with the swarms of insects who were likewise serving God—whether in a crusading function or as a divine admonition sent to recall the sinful knights to the path they had forsaken. So profound was this experience of the earliest crusading generations that it was apparently impossible for them not to believe that the whole natural order of the universe was engaged in the conflict which summoned them to the Holy Land, that their struggle was one of cosmic dimensions. For them the whole of nature is interpreted in the light of their crusading experience, just as, in quite another context, Walther's preoccupation with imperial politics leads him to see the same problems reflected in the various subdivisions of the animal kingdom.[2] What was possible for Walther's attitude to feudal society was

[1] *RHC*, IV, 62 c. This naïve attribution of Christian sentiments to a pagan opponent is also revealed by the way in which the Caliph to whom the letter is written is addressed as *noster papa*. We may see in this a parallel to the manner in which the Millstatt author attributes to Pharaoh, when he is talking of the Hebrew rite of circumcision, knowledge of Christian baptism (see pp. 151 f.).

[2] See Walther 8, 28 ff. As in the feudal realm, so in the animal kingdom the presence of warfare is an acknowledged fact (8, 35 ff.), but the animal kingdom differs from mankind in at least maintaining the proper social order in regard to justice (9, 5), kingship (9, 6), and the distinction between lord and serf (9, 7). Wolfram, too, conceives the universe in essentially knightly terms: for telling examples of this see W. Deinert, *Ritter und Kosmos im Parzival*, p. 131 (concerning *Willehalm* 309, 20 ff.) and p. 136.

equally possible for those who were more concerned with the problems raised by the crusades—both saw their themes as extending far beyond the human realm and as reflected in other aspects of nature. In view of this we need feel little astonishment that the author of the *Millstätter Exodus*, in agreement with contemporary chroniclers of the First Crusade, should have suggested that the insects of the plagues of Egypt were warriors in the service of God. Since for him the Hebrew exodus was a prefiguration of the crusades, the insects sent by God to assist in the liberation of the Israelites are consequentially related to the swarms of insects which the twelfth century interpreted as sent by God to assist in the recovery of the Holy Land by the new Israel—either directly by their departure from Europe (as a parallel to that of the knights) or indirectly by being the agents of God's admonition to the crusaders when they grow unworthy of their task. The only discrepancy in this respect between the Millstatt work and the evidence of the chronicles is that in the German work it is the insects alone, and not the knights as well, who are referred to as *gotes rîtere*. This is not a unique case in the *Exodus*, for we have also seen that it is the insects alone who are described as avenging the insults to God[1] and to whom the laudatory terms of heroic vocabulary are applied.[2] Why this should be the case we shall later consider,[3] but it is clear that, apart from this, the role of the insects in the biblical epic is remarkably similar to their function in the chronicles. An equation of insects with crusaders which may appear to us as quite incongruous had no such necessary implications in the twelfth century, so that there is no compelling reason to accept de Boor's conclusion that this equation was meant by the Millstatt author to suggest an ironical criticism. On the contrary, the employment of heroic terms and concepts in the crusading context (whether of knights or of insects conceived as knights) can only imply that the heroic ideal, by being thus harnessed to a religious purpose, was given a sanction which had previously been lacking.

This brings us to the third and final objection raised by de

[1] See pp. 278 ff.   [2] See pp. 158 ff.   [3] See pp. 430 ff.

Boor to any interpretation of the *Millstätter Exodus* which regards the military description of the Hebrews in a positive light, as representing an ideal worthy of emulation. His objection is based on the contradiction between the lengthy description of the Jews in military terms as they depart from Egypt and the cowardice they show once they catch sight of the Egyptian army in pursuit, so that for him this discrepancy only makes sense as a criticism of the heroic ideal. We have just seen, however, that de Boor's similar appeal to the presence of a discrepancy in the case of the slaughter of the Hebrew children and in that of the plagues of insects ignores the difference between the modern and the medieval reactions to such scenes and that his conclusions are not therefore necessarily indicative of what the twelfth-century author might have had in mind. Are there any grounds for thinking that de Boor's third objection has as little validity as his others?

The first point which needs to be made about the Millstatt author's description of the Hebrew knights' loss of courage and of Moses' attempt to restore their confidence (vv. 3105 ff.) is that it is no innovation of his, since it derives from a corresponding passage in Exodus (14. 10–13). What is new about this passage in the German work is not its mere presence, but rather the manner in which it has been expanded by comparison with the source. We have seen that this process of expansion is typical of the author's epic technique, but also that he did not hesitate to omit a detail if it conflicted with his poetic purposes. In view of this it seems likely that the author attached some importance to this passage and that he regarded it as fully reconcilable with his intentions. At the same time, it is significant that the Egyptian warriors, too, when they see the waters of the Red Sea about to close on them, are depicted at some length (vv. 3213 ff.) as losing heart and as militarily powerless despite all their equipment.[1] This second detail, not mentioned by de Boor, would appear to confirm his thesis, for this final scene could be interpreted as revealing the vanity of knightly splendour: the knightly trappings

---

[1] This again is an expansion of the succinct brevity of the biblical source, Exod. 14. 25 and 28.

of the Hebrew army (vv. 2877 ff.) would be shown up as no more than a cloak for their pusillanimity, whereas the heroic description of the Egyptian warriors (vv. 3024 ff.) only heightens their impotence in the face of God's intervention. Both armies, it could therefore be argued, are criticised for their military pretensions, so that there would be little likelihood that the Hebrews were intended as a model to be emulated by the twelfth century.

In answer to this two details must be stressed. The first concerns the difficulty of reconciling this argument (by which both the opposing armies are criticised for their military arrogance) with what we have seen of the author's different attitude towards the Hebrews and the Egyptians.[1] If it is said of the Hebrew knights that they were without any trace of *ubirmuot* (v. 2928), whereas precisely this sin is attributed to their opponents (vv. 3038 and 3075 ff.), it is difficult to believe that in reality both groups of warriors are to be subjected to the same criticism, that both are shown as exponents of the overweening arrogance of the warrior class and of its utter futility. Clearly, some kind of criticism of the Hebrews must be intended because their angry reproaches to Moses for having brought things to such a pass amount to a criticism of the God in whose name Moses had acted, but what must be questioned is the assumption that the Hebrews are criticised for the same reason as the Egyptians. The heroic qualities of the Egyptian warriors are subjected to criticism because they are displayed against the Chosen People and are opposed to God, whereas the Hebrews, whilst still under God's guidance and never actually forfeiting His assistance, are criticised precisely at the moment when their service of God demands heroic qualities and when they fail to live up to this demand. The two related scenes in which the impotence of the Egyptians and the cowardice of the Hebrews are revealed illustrate, therefore, two distinct features: the vanity of even the greatest military might when pitted against God and the need for those who serve God never to lose confidence and at all times to display the heroic virtues when these are called for in their service of God.

[1] See pp. 158 f. and p. 169.

Nonetheless, those who feel the force of de Boor's argument could still maintain that there was something incongruous in a description, meant as the climax to the Millstatt epic, in which the Hebrews who are elsewhere shown as models for knightly behaviour in the crusading present are revealed in a negative light, as the antithesis of what the crusaders should try to achieve. Indeed, there seems little doubt that it is this apparent inconsistency which has led some scholars to reject the possibility that the *Millstätter Exodus* is a work of crusading literature.[1] Such a rejection is unjustified, not least because it rests on the assumption that the conduct of medieval crusaders could be influenced by a positive *exemplum*, but not by a negative model. That this assumption is groundless can be shown with reference to the typological method which is employed by the Millstatt author to show the relevance of his biblical theme to the needs of his day. In the first place, the typological relationship between two events or persons in the Old and the New Testament can be either positive (in which case more stress will fall on the fact that the Old Testament prefigures the New) or antithetical (where greater importance will attach to the manner in which the New Testament represents the fulfilment of prophecies which had been denied to the Old). As a general example of positive typology we may quote Heb. 9. 11 ff., where the sacrifice represented by the blood of Christ is the fulfilment of the sacrifice performed by the high priest in the Old Testament;[2] as a particular example of the same attitude towards the interpretation of Exodus we may cite the common exegesis of Moses as the prefiguration of Christ, likewise the liberator of His people.[3] Antithetical typology, on

[1] Fliegner, for example, when dealing with this episode in his *Geistliches und weltliches Rittertum im Rolandslied*, says that it cannot be interpreted as part of a crusading work: 'Denn das von Gott geleitete Volk zeigt wahrlich keine heldenhaften Regungen' (p. 32). Cf. also p. 33: 'Hier spüren wir noch garnichts von dem opferwilligen Geist einer "nova militas", die in den Kreuzzügen auf den Plan gerufen wurde.'

[2] For the connection with the Old Testament cf. the use of *tabernaculum* in v. 11 and the parallel between v. 12 and Lev. 16. 15.

[3] E.g. Isidore of Seville (*MPL*, 83, 109 A = Na 59): 'Moyses typum Christi gestavit, qui populum Dei a jugo servitutis eripuit, et ipsum diabolum in aeterna poena damnavit.'

the other hand, implies that what had been denied under the old dispensation has now been achieved under Christ. Obvious examples of this form of typology are provided by the relationship between Adam and Christ[1] or between Eve and Mary,[2] where clearly the connection between type and antitype is now also informed by a degree of tension or contradiction which is lacking between, say, Moses and Christ. That this kind of antithetical typology was also seen in Exodus from a very early date can be shown with reference to the passage in I Cor. 10. 6 which has already been mentioned[3] ('Haec autem in figura facta sunt nostri, ut non simus concupiscentes malorum sicut et illi concupierunt'), for here it is the function of the *exemplum* provided by the story of the Hebrews in Exodus to demonstrate to Christians the way in which divine assistance can be forfeited by behaviour which amounts to a betrayal of the mission imposed upon His followers by God.[4]

This brings us to the second respect in which the use of this exegetical method involves the employment of antithetical typology. Typology implies that the antitype transcends its type by virtue of the way in which it fulfils or realises a promise latent in the type, but even this fulfilment remains only potential in its bearing on each individual Christian as long as he has the freedom to accept or to reject the gift of redemption which Christ has achieved for him.[5] In other words, typology presupposes a fulfilment of what was promised to the type only in the case of those Christians who affirm Christ for themselves and who shape their lives accordingly, whereas on those who reject Christ by living without regard for what He implies this potential fulfilment is lost as surely as it was on the Jews when they failed to acknowledge

---

[1] Der arme Hartmann, *Rede vom Glauben*, 793 ff.
[2] Cf. Frau Ava, *Das Leben Jesu*, 11 ff.   [3] See p. 112.
[4] Origen places a similar interpretation on the passage selected by the Millstatt author to demonstrate the negative *exemplum* of the Jews: 'Et tu ergo si ab Aegyptiis recedas, et de potestate daemonum fugias, vide quanta divinitus tibi praeparantur auxilia, vide quantis adjutoribus uteris. Tantum est ut permaneas fortis in fide, nec te Aegyptiorum equitatus et quadrigarum formido perterreat, nec reclames contra legem Dei et Moysen' (*MPG*, 12, 329 c).
[5] See above, pp. 266, 270 f. and 313.

Christ. The negative example of the Jews, together with its suggestion that their fate will be shared by the Christian who neglects to realise for himself the potential fulfilment offered by Christ, is an integral part of the typological method, so that we should not be surprised to find an author for whom the exodus of the Israelites prefigures that of the crusaders also stressing the failings of these Israelites in their present implications. Nor need we doubt that these shortcomings of the Israelites were felt to be relevant to the crusading present, for we have already seen[1] that, in the account of a vision given by Raimundus, Christ compares the shortcomings of the Jews with those of the crusaders and threatens the latter that, just as He abandoned the Jews because of their lack of belief, so might He also transfer His support from the crusaders to another Chosen People: 'Videte itaque ne increduli sitis. Alioquin, vobis remanentibus cum Judaeis, alios populos assumam, et per ipsos complebo quae vobis promiseram.'[2] Admittedly, this particular argument could only be applied to certain episodes of the First Crusade, not to the whole undertaking because of its successful outcome with the capture of Jerusalem. With the failure of the Second Crusade the position is radically altered, so that we now find St Bernard explaining this disaster by an explicit comparison between the sinfulness of the Hebrews in the wilderness and that of the crusaders.[3] The fact that Moses was able to lead his people out of Egyptian captivity and through the Red Sea but was unable to lead them himself into the Promised Land cannot be attributed to him as a personal fault, since in all he did he acted only on behalf of God. The implication is clear: the same cannot be imputed to St Bernard himself as a fault since, as with the Hebrews, the error lies rather with the lack of faith and the rebelliousness of those whom he led: 'Bene, illi increduli et rebelles; hi autem quid?'[4] Success in the crusade and the ability to assist in the fulfilment of divine promises originally made to the Hebrews, but of which they had proved themelves unworthy, are assured to the crusader only so

[1] See p. 271.　　　　　　　　　　　　　　　　[2] *RHC*, III, 280 D.
[3] *De consideratione*, II, 1 (*MPL*, 182, 743 C).　　[4] *Ibid.*

340

Problems of detail

far as he takes their negative example to heart and thus avoids the risk of being abandoned by God in his turn. The Hebrews therefore provide the crusaders with a double incentive: their successes are a guarantee that God cannot grant less to the new Israel, and their failures are an indication how the crusaders, the typological fulfilment of the Hebrew exodus, may actually achieve that fulfilment which had been denied to their spiritual predecessors.

Before we can be certain, however, that the Millstatt author's expansion of a biblical passage in which a criticism of the Jews is implied must be regarded as an example of antithetical typology, we must consider whether this interpretation of Exodus was known not simply to the chroniclers of the First and Second Crusades (as we have just seen), but also to vernacular literature in Germany in the first half of the twelfth century. We find evidence of this in an exegetical translation of the Exodus story into MHG (the *Vorauer Bücher Mosis*), and also in a crusading episode in the *Kaiserchronik*, where the negative *exemplum* of this episode from Jewish history is adduced just before battle with the heathen is commenced. An analysis of these two examples will show us that the Millstatt author, in using an episode from Exodus in the spirit of antithetical typology, by no means stands alone in his period and can also suggest to us why he may have chosen precisely this episode for this purpose.

The author of the *Vorauer Bücher Mosis* bases his example of antithetical typology on the episode in Exodus to which St Paul had also referred in I Cor. 10. 6. The German author writes on this episode, adducing it immediately after his recapitulation of the Hebrews' escape through the Red Sea:

> So si wir durch daz mere geua-
> rn. so scule wir dar nach bewaren.
> daz wir niht unrehte geraten. so
> di iuden taten. di mit murmele
> unde mit lugen. sich von der go-
> tes helfe zugen. unde si got den
> gûten. in der einoten irgremeten.[1]

[1] 49. 28 ff.

341

This passage, as is made clear by the exegetical explanation of *gotes helfe* as *daʒ heilige himelbrot*,[1] refers to the episode described in Exod. 16. 2 ff. where the Jews complain (*murmurare*) about the shortage of food in the desert. Moreover, the fact that these complaints are associated with the sin of arrogance (*mit murmel unde mit hoh uerte*),[2] by contrast with the humility of others,[3] makes it clear that the shortcoming of the Jews in this episode is seen as an unjustified rebellion against divine authority, resulting from too weak a trust in God and in the assistance He has shown them. It is the function of this *exemplum*, with its explicit contrast between *wir* und *di iuden*, to stress the need for Christian humility by illustrating the opposite quality in the case of the Jews.

This episode from Exodus in the *Vorauer Bücher Mosis* can also assist us in deciding what the Millstatt author's intentions may have been in similarly showing his Jews in a critical light, but in connection with a different episode. Two reasons suggest themselves as to why he should not also have made use of this episode of the Jews in the wilderness to illustrate his point, even though the long treatment of this theme in the biblical Exodus as well as the fact that St Paul singles it out for special mention would have provided his illustration with greater biblical authority than in the episode of the Jews' panic when they catch sight of the Egyptian army. One reason why this course was not open to him is the fact that he wished to terminate his epic with chapter 15 of his biblical source—not merely because of the aesthetic advantages of concluding at such a climax, but also, as we shall see later,[4] for a reason which tells us much about his attitude to the theme which he had chosen to treat. Another reason must be because this episode of the Jews in the wilderness could not be utilised to illustrate precisely that negative quality against which he wished to warn an audience of potential crusaders. Although the attitude of the Jews in this scene is fundamentally one of distrust or lack of confidence in God, the way in

[1] 50. 6 f.
[3] 50. 7 ff.
[2] 50. 14 f.
[4] See pp. 432 ff.

which this finds expression is more suggestive of an overweening rebellion against God's authority, as is demonstrated by the equation with *hohvart* and the contrast with *devmût* in the *Vorauer Bücher Mosis*. In other words, the Jews in this episode more nearly resemble the Egyptians in the earlier scene in the Millstatt work, who are explicitly described in terms of arrogance and are contrasted with the Jews on this score.[1] What the Millstatt author wished to illustrate in the negative example of the Jews was therefore not the sin of arrogance, as shown by the Egyptians and also by the Jews in this later episode, but instead a lack of confidence which, although it may ultimately underlie the Jews' attitude even in the scene in the wilderness, is not so readily apparent. What appears to have happened is that the Millstatt author was struck by the force of Exod 16. 2 ff. as a traditional example of antithetical typology and wished to make use of the method for his own purposes (even though he could find little use for the illustration of the sin of arrogance which this episode most obviously provided). Wishing to find an episode in the first fifteen chapters of Exodus in which the method of antithetical typology could be used, he chose the scene where the Hebrews lose confidence in the face of the advancing Egyptian army, since the biblical treatment of this scene already provided him to some extent with a precedent[2] and since it had the further advantage of allowing him to illustrate this non-exemplary quality of the Hebrews in close connection with one of those military descriptions which characterise his work so profoundly. In short, it seems likely that the Millstatt author derived the idea of making use of antithetical typology from that chapter in the Bible which followed immediately on the chapter at which he had decided to terminate his German adaptation. This does not mean that the negative qualities illustrated by the Hebrews of the Millstatt author are the same as those apparent in chapter 16 of the biblical account or in the *Vorauer Bücher Mosis*. What these negative qualities are is determined by the new context into which the Millstatt author has transposed them and by what his intentions

[1] See p. 169.   [2] Exod. 14. 10 ff.

were in deciding that he wished to employ the method of antithetical typology at all.

It is to the *Kaiserchronik*, and in particular to the episode dealing with the campaign of the Emperor Heraclius against the pagan Cosdras, that we must turn for confirmation that the history of the Hebrews after their passage of the Red Sea could be used to provide an example of antithetical typology in the context of the crusades. We have seen something similar in the case of St Bernard's justification of his policy after the Second Crusade and, of course, this problem is only part of the wider one of the general parallelism between the events of Exodus and those of the crusades which we considered earlier in chapter VIII, whilst even this general parallelism is subsumed under the larger question of the relationship between crusading ideas and the Old Testament at large.[1]

We can hardly regard it as fortuitous that it is in the Heraclius episode that the *Kaiserchronik* provides us with an instance of the application of antithetical typology to the crusades. The significance of this lies in the fact that the historical Heraclius, who in 622 conducted a holy war against the Persians for the reconquest of Jerusalem and the recovery of the Holy Cross, came to be regarded centuries later, once the crusades had redirected Christian energies towards the same goal and had prompted men to begin a search for precedents, as the first crusader. It is for this reason that William of Tyre includes the history of this cam-

[1] It is significant that crusading literature can appeal to the testimony of the Old Testament not merely when it is a case (as with this scene in the *Kaiserchronik* or in the *Millstätter Exodus*) of warning crusaders against succumbing to the doubts which overcame the Israelites, but also when it is required to find an *exemplum* which will allay doubts amongst the crusaders. We find appeals being made to Old Testament examples in the *Rolandslied* whenever the risk of doubts afflicting the Christian warriors seems to be particularly great. Thus, the encounter between 1,500 Christian warriors (v. 5005) and 12,000 pagans (vv. 4993 f.) is related to the victory of Gideon (vv. 5012 ff.) as a *gût urchunde* of the fact that God will grant His servants victory over their more numerous enemies. Similarly, on the occasion when Charles, regarding it as impossible to pursue the pagans, comes closest to despair (cf. vv. 6965 ff. and especially 7000 ff.) the miraculous victory of Joshua is repeated (vv. 7017 ff.) when God prolongs daylight to enable the emperor to execute his vengeance.

paign by Heraclius in his history of the crusades,[1] with such effect that the title of his history (*Historia rerum in partibus transmarinis gestarum*) is changed in its Old French translation so as to give pride of place to Heraclius: *L'Estoire de Eracles, empereur, et la conqueste de la Terre d'Outremer*.[2] The decision of William of Tyre has been repeated more recently by Runciman in his *History of the Crusades*.[3]

In view of this medieval conception of Heraclius as the first crusader it is not surprising that the episode dealing with him in the *Kaiserchronik* should be informed, as Ohly and Wentzlaff-Eggebert have shown,[4] with typical crusading motifs. The words with which the author introduces Heraclius,[5] stressing his religious salvation and the way in which he extended the *êre* of Rome, touch upon the motif of serving both God and the world which owes much of its growth in the twelfth century to the new means of achieving this goal which had been made available to the knighthood by the crusading movement.[6] His pagan opponent, Cosdras, is consequentially seen as possessed by the sin of *superbia*,[7] as incited by the Devil himself[8] and as not hesitating to lay waste Jerusalem and seize the Holy Cross as booty.[9] Heraclius, like Charles the Great in the *Rolandslied*, is prompted by a heavenly voice to win back the Cross[10] and he transmits this command issued by God[11] to his followers to whom he makes it clear that the God who has instituted this campaign will not fail the Christian knights[12] since the pagan ranks are destined to join the Devil in Hell.[13] These are traditional crusading motifs and provide the setting for the harangue which Heraclius

[1] *RHC*, I (part I), 9 ff.
[2] *Ibid.*   [3] See i, 3 ff.
[4] *Sage und Legende in der Kaiserchronik*, pp. 180 ff.; *Kreuzzugsdichtung des Mittelalters*, pp. 68 ff.
[5] Vv. 11140 f.   [6] See pp. 291 ff.
[7] V. 11147: 'vil gerne wolt er got sîn.'
[8] V. 11144: 'dem geriet der vâlant...'
[9] Vv. 11156 ff.   [10] Vv. 11177 ff.
[11] V. 11185: 'daz gebiutet dir von himele der waltinde got.'
[12] V. 11204: 'der uns dise hervart gebôt, | ich wæne, er uns iht geswîchôt.'
[13] V. 11199: 'ich wæne, der tievel ain michel here | hiute samt im welle | vuoren zuo der helle.'

addresses to his warriors on the eve of battle. He begins with an explicit reference to the Hebrews as a model for his own warriors:

> 11208 owol ir helde snelle,
> ich sage iu ze aim bîspelle:
> ain liut haizet Hebrêî,
> dâ sult it nemen pilde bî.

The following passage, in which the example of the Hebrews is elaborated, makes it clear that their model is to be understood as a negative one, since it is concerned with the events of the Hebrew exodus which are recounted in Num. 13. 2 ff. Heraclius describes how Moses, following the order given him by God,[1] sends spies into the land of Canaan to report back on its fertility and on the military strength of its inhabitants and how the Israelites (with the exception of Joshua and Caleb), on hearing what they have to report, lose heart, give up all hope of occupying Canaan and are therefore abandoned by God.[2] The author of the *Kaiserchronik* makes it clear that, by contrast with the similar episode of the rebelliousness of the Jews referred to in the *Vorauer Bücher Mosis*, it is now the Jews' lack of confidence, rather than rebellion against God,[3] which constitutes their true sin:

> 11236 alse di boten daz mære vollesageten,
> die liute gar verzageten,
> daz lant si verliezen.
> mîn trehtîn gehiez in,
> nû si an sînen guoten
> sô harte gezwîvelt hêten,
> daz si in sîne râwe
> niemer mêre chômen zewâre.

The verbs *verʒagen* and *ʒwîvelen* are taken up again in the following lines with the word *ʒagehait*[4] where the conclusion is drawn from the Hebrews' failure of belief and applied to the present position in which the Roman 'crusaders' find themselves. The author is now employing the general typological method

---

[1] Cf. Num. 13. 2 and 4.　　　　　　　　[2] Cf. Num. 14. 11 ff.
[3] Even though the biblical source stresses more the aspect of rebellion in Num. 14. 9.　　　　　　　　[4] V. 11245.

(hinted at in the words *bîspel* and *pilde* at the beginning of Heraclius' speech) of relating the Israelite past to the 'crusading' present, but in this case he is assisted by the way in which this is suggested as a possibility in Num. 14. 11, where God, in His anger with the Hebrews for their lack of belief, announces that He will strike them with a pestilence and will make Moses the leader of a greater and more powerful nation: 'te autem faciam principem super gentem magnam, et fortiorem quam haec est.' The fact that God turns away from the Hebrews (thereby allowing them to suffer defeat)[1] and even reveals His decision to confer His favours upon a new Chosen People is enough to suggest to the author of the *Kaiserchronik* that this new *populus Dei* can only be the Christians to whom the opportunity has now been granted of achieving what the Hebrews had forfeited by their pusillanimity:

> 11244   Nu si gotes gebot ubergiengen,
> durch ir zagehait gevielen,
> nû in sô harte missescæhe,
> nu gedenchet, helede Rômære,
> daz got selbe des geruochte,
> daz er sîn dienest an iu suochte.
> dienet ir im hiute flîzeclîche,
> er lônct es iu mit sînem rîche.

In other words, the past failure of the Hebrews is the reason why the crusaders of the present are offered the means of salvation in their stead (the opportunity to gain entrance to the Heavenly Jerusalem, *sîn rîche*, whereas the Hebrews had lost the chance of entering the Promised Land), but it is also the reason why the crusaders should avoid a repetition of the Hebrews' fault and should themselves not lose faith in God. It is the duty of the crusaders, representing the new Chosen People, to learn from the mistakes of the first Israel, since failure to do so could likewise lead to their being abandoned by God.[2] This is the same

---

[1] Num. 14. 40 ff.

[2] Without wishing to join the argument conducted by Jantsch, *Studien zum Symbolischen*, pp. 202 ff., against Ohly's typological interpretation of the

argument as that which was used by Raimundus in explaining an episode of the First Crusade and by St Bernard to account for the failure of the Second, so that it seems reasonably established that the crusaders' conviction that they were a new Israel brought with it not merely a feeling of confidence that the military successes of the Israelites would be repeated in their own case, but also an awareness that any loss of confidence in God or fear that His assistance might not be effective entailed the greater risk that God would turn from them as He had once done from the Israelites. Both the victories and the failures of the Israelites are of immediate concern to their crusading successors.

The Heraclius episode in the *Kaiserchronik* shows us that the employment of antithetical typology in referring an event from the exodus of the Israelites to the twelfth century was not unknown in the crusading literature of this period, so that the corresponding example in the *Millstätter Exodus* is not so isolated as to arouse invincible doubts. At the same time, another facet of this same episode in the *Kaiserchronik* reveals that the author was concerned to warn his audience not merely of the sin of *ʒwîvel* or *ʒagehait* which we have so far considered, but also of the opposing fault of *ubermuot*, the fault which the author of the *Vorauer Bücher Mosis* had chosen to attack by his employment of antithetical typology. It is true that in this second facet of the Heraclius episode the author does not employ this technique in order to make his point, as he had done in the case of *ʒwîvel/ʒagehait* or as the author of the *Vorauer Bücher Mosis* had done in the case of *hohvart*. Instead, he describes how Heraclius and his followers, after recovering the Holy Cross, incur the guilt of *ubermuot* by the manner of their return to Jerusalem and are rebuked for this by an angel.[1] Nonetheless, this detail is meant

Kaiserchronik and of this episode in particular (he sees the typological relationship as one between the pagan 'crusade' conducted by Titus and its Christian fulfilment under Heraclius, *Sage und Legende in der Kaiserchronik*, pp. 184 ff.), I think that Jantsch is at least more likely to be correct in the emphasis he places (*op. cit.* pp. 223 ff.) on the typological relationship between the Hebrews and Heraclius.

[1] Cf. especially vv. 11310 ff. (*mit grôʒer ubermote*), 11328 ff., and the stress on humility in v. 11343.

to provide a lesson for the present, as is suggested by an explicit reference (v. 11339: 'daz ist uns armen gesaget ad exemplum') and by the general moralising note on which the whole episode is concluded.[1] Even though this negative *exemplum* of the need to avoid falling into the sin of *superbia* (whether as a Christian or more particularly as a crusader) may not make use of the typological technique or refer to a negative *exemplum* from Jewish history, as is the case with the similar condemnation of *superbia* in the *Vorauer Bücher Mosis*, it shows us that both faults, *ubermuot* as well as *zwîvel*, were dangers which threatened the crusader and against which he could be effectively warned by reference to the exodus of the Israelites.[2] The two faults complement each other since *ubermuot* can result from an excessive reliance by the knight on his own qualities as a warrior, whereas *zwîvel* implies too weak a sense of confidence (either in himself or in the power of God to assist). *Ubermuot* and *zwîvel* therefore belong together as related faults of which the Christian warrior might prove guilty, in much the same way as do *praesumptio* and *desperatio* as complementary concepts in the moral theology of the twelfth century.[3] It is against both *ubermuot* and *zwîvel* in a crusading context that the author of the *Kaiserchronik* warns his audience (even though he only employs antithetical typology in the latter case), and against *hohvart* that the author of the *Vorauer Bücher Mosis* warns his audience by reference to the example of the Jews (even though he does this without any crusading suggestion), whereas it is the sin of *zwîvel* which the Millstatt author criticises in potential crusaders by illustrating this typologically in the case of the Hebrews and by restricting the sin of *ubermuot* entirely to their Egyptian opponents.

---

[1] V. 11344: 'ubermuot ist sô getân: | diu gescendet ie den man.'

[2] Cf. also the way in which St Bernard refers to the Hebrews as an example of lack of faith as well as of rebelliousness: 'Bene, illi increduli et rebelles; hi autem quid?' (see p. 340).

[3] On the presence of *vürgedanc* and *zwîvel* in Hartmann's prologue to *Gregorius* see H. Nobel, *ZfdPh*, LXXVI, 42 ff., and also W. Ohly, *Die heilsgeschichtliche Struktur der Epen Hartmanns von Aue*, pp. 10 ff. The latter quotes (pp. 12 f.) from Petrus Lombardus, for whom *obstinatio* (= *praesumptio*) and *desperatio* are complementary sins.

That *zwîvel* was a concept which played an important part in the Millstatt author's thinking can be shown by an analysis of the cases where he refers to this quality explicitly, for these make it clear that the concluding episode in which the Hebrew knights show *zwîvel* in face of the Egyptian army is not just added mechanically, but is instead a theme for which careful preparation has been made. One of these earlier cases concerns the relationship between Moses and God, the other that between the Israelites and God.

The temporary occurrence of *zwîvel* as a quality clouding Moses' attitude to God is significantly to be found in the scene in which God first establishes His covenant with him and reveals His intention to liberate His people. After God has proclaimed Himself and revealed His power by performing two miracles[1] Moses still attempts to evade his responsibility by putting forward his lack of eloquence as an excuse. God's reaction is to stress that, as the creator of all things, it is as much in His power to speak through Moses as it was for Him to perform the miracles, but the author begins this rebuke by referring to Moses' doubts:

> 769 Got frâgen began
> den selben man
> dô er zwîvelôte
> an sîneme worte...

When Moses is still dubious even after this rebuke the same verb is repeated (vv. 787 f.: 'Moŷses der guote | ienoh zwîvelôte'), but this time the reaction of God is not merely to impart a rebuke, but to display His anger (vv. 793 f.: 'ze verre habet er geredet, | got wart sîn beweget').[2] Despite the anger with which God reacts to these two displays of *zwîvel* His willingness to assist is shown as stronger and more lasting than His annoyance. His response to Moses' first *zwîvel* is therefore his statement: 'ich wil dich pewaren' (v. 782), whereas His reply to Moses' repeated doubt, although it starts on an angry note, soon comes round to a

---

[1] Cf. vv. 695 ff. and 729 ff.
[2] Although this also represents a clear toning-down of Exod. 4. 14: 'Iratus Dominus in Moysen.'

solemn declaration of loyalty which includes the significant words: 'ich wil iw wârlîchen | niemmer geswîchen' (vv. 809 f.). In both cases Moses' doubt, however much annoyance it may cause, is the occasion for God to reaffirm His unchanging loyalty towards His people. The nature of this reaction is such as to suggest that Moses' offence had been more than just intellectual doubt (since the words spoken by God in vv. 809 ff. would be an incongruously excessive reaction to this alone). The further quality present in Moses' attitude is revealed by the way in which the words used to describe Moses' doubt (v. 771: 'dô er zwîvelôte') take up the depiction of his mental state in v. 760: 'mit erchomenlîchem muote', so that his attitude is shown to be compounded of intellectual doubt and of lack of confidence or courage. Admittedly, the adverb *erchomenlîcho* had also been applied to Moses at an earlier stage (v. 544) without calling forth the word *zwîvel*, but the implication here is that, although Moses may be excused for showing lack of confidence or courage when God first revealed His intentions and before He demonstrated His miraculous power, he was wrong to persist in his attitude after this demonstration. In this passage *zwîvel* denotes not merely intellectual doubt, but also lack of confidence or bravery, together with a stubborn refusal to recognise the power and the *triuwe* of God.[1]

The second episode in which *zwîvel* is illustrated as an attitude of man towards God concerns the scene in which the Hebrews, groaning under the increased burden placed upon them by Pharaoh after the interview between him and Moses and Aaron, complain that their position is now worse than it had been before and that the *êre* which they had once enjoyed at the royal court is destroyed. This complaint is couched in general terms of lamentation (vv. 1095 ff.: 'diu dâ was in sorgen | den abent unde den morgen. | si hêten weinôt unde wuoft, | chlagennes alzoges genuoch'), but when they direct their complaint towards Moses and Aaron it is

---

[1] That the *MHG* word *zwîvel* can often cover several shades of meaning on one and the same occasion has been rightly emphasised by H. Hempel in his contribution to the Festschrift for K. Helm, p. 163.

clear that indirectly it is meant for the God in whose name these two had acted.[1] Accordingly, Moses transmits this complaint to God in a feudal manner,[2] thereby associating himself with the complaint of the Hebrews. On this occasion God does not react by showing anger, but instead by reaffirming His willingness to help. In other words, just as Moses was not rebuked on the first occasion when he revealed insufficient determination in his encounter with the Lord (vv. 543 ff.), but roused God's anger when he repeated his hesitations (vv. 769 ff. and 787 ff.), so the Hebrews are not rebuked when they, on first encountering resistance from Pharaoh, fail to show sufficient confidence. That it is lack of confidence on their part which is involved here, and not just a complaint which they are justified in making in the spirit of a feudal relationship, is shown by the way in which God's reply to Moses describes the Hebrews' attitude as *zwîvel* (vv. 1151 f.: 'dû heiz si nieht zwîvelôn, | wande ich wil si ledigôn') and concludes with another reaffirmation of His unfailing loyalty.[3] Even when the Hebrews again express their unwillingness to run further risks (vv. 1163 ff.) God still does not show His anger and the same is true in the final scene of the passage of the Red Sea, for God's response to this prolonged description of their lack of confidence is to intervene and deliver them from the Egyptians. In this God shows His loyalty and observance of the covenant He had established with His people, even though their repeated *zwîvel* means that they have fallen short of keeping their part of the covenant. The fact that *zwîvel* injures the covenant and renders it invalid would have justified God in showing the Hebrews His anger (as He had briefly to Moses) by allowing them to suffer the results of their lack of confidence. This is the danger which

[1] That the Hebrews were fully aware of this origin of the authority claimed by Moses and Aaron is made quite clear by the author in vv. 917 ff.

[2] See pp. 173 f.

[3] The Millstatt author gives no indication that he was at all aware of the potential problem which this episode constituted, for he nowhere suggests where the legitimate feudal complaint and reminder to the Lord cease and pass over into *zwîvel*. This is, of course, a problem inseparable from the feudalised form of Christianity to which he gave such firm expression. It is also one of the problems underlying Parzival's estrangement from God.

the Hebrews had incurred by their *ʒwîvel* and from which they had been rescued only because God's *triuwe* exceeded the legal terms of His covenant.

Two conclusions follow from the way in which this final episode of the Hebrews' pusillanimity is prepared earlier in the work by a twofold anticipation of the theme of *ʒwîvel*. In the first place, the repeated occurrence of this theme makes it clear that *ʒwîvel* was a problem to which the author attached considerable importance. Although the word itself does not occur explicitly in the final episode (as it does in the two earlier scenes), there can be little doubt but that it was this episode on which the author concentrated his attention: this is revealed by the prolonged and vivid description he gives of the Hebrews' fear and by the position it occupies at the climax of the work. Moreover, the fact that the Hebrews' lack of confidence should be so clearly emphasised here (by contrast with the rapid dismissal of the same motif, suggested in Exod. 5. 21 ff., in vv. 1095 ff.) shows that the Millstatt author is exploiting this scene as an example of antithetical typology and that he is applying to it the same interpretation as other authors gave to the later scene in the wilderness where the Hebrews voice their complaints against God or reveal their lack of confidence (e.g. Exod. 16. 2 f.; 17. 2 f.; 32. 1 ff. and also Num. 14. 1 ff.). It is from these later scenes in the history of the exodus that our author has transferred the motif of the Hebrews' lack of confidence as an offence against God, but the way in which he applies this motif to the final episode shows just how important he felt it to interpret this episode in this manner. Nor is it difficult to see why he should have regarded this as so important, since it is at this stage, with the Egyptian army in pursuit, that the Israelites are guilty of lack of courage, not in the abstract but instead in an explicitly military context whose warlike nature has been firmly underlined by the preceding detailed descriptions of the Israelite and Egyptian warriors. What is demonstrated to the German author's audience by means of this negative *exemplum* from the history of Israel is the need for the Christian warriors to show unswerving trust in God's ability to assist them in battle with the pagans and to avoid the danger to which the Israelites exposed themselves. The second conclusion that may be drawn from this final episode and from the author's preoccupation with *ʒwîvel* concerns the actual nature of this offence. We have seen that the function of this word is to express intellectual doubt as to God's willingness to assist, and also the emotional quality of fear or lack of confidence, a quality which is particularly apposite in this scene where the military shortcomings of the Israelites are criticised. That this second function of *ʒwîvel* is by no means peculiar to the *Millstätter Exodus* has been shown by recent discussions of the semantic role of this word in OHG and MHG.[1] Thus, in translating the scene where Peter attempts to walk on the water, but begins to sink when he loses courage, Otfrid uses the word *ʒuival* in close connection with *forahta*,[2] whereas the author of the *Heliand* uses the cognate and synonymous verb *tuehon* in apposition with *andrâden*.[3] The same association of *ʒwîvel* with fear is attested for Notker when he employs the word in conjunction with *angist* or with *furhten*.[4] These are examples of what Hempel has defined as 'Gefühlszweifel',[5] which he sees as implying 'Angst, Besorgnis, Sorge, Verzagtheit'[6] as well as 'Ängstlichkeit, Kleinmut, Tadelsucht'[7] and for which he adduces ample testimony from MHG. His remark ('Der Kleinmut bekommt im höfischen Bereich als Gegenteil des *hôhen muotes*, der geradezu unter die Tugenden zählt, ein stark negatives Vorzeichen')[8] is particularly relevant to our inquiry since the Millstatt

[1] Cf. L. Pauly, *Das Begriffsfeld des Zweifels in der ahd., as. und kluniaʒensischen Literatur* (Freiburg dissertation, 1944); E. Düring, *Zwivel* (Tübingen dissertation, 1944); the contribution of H. Hempel to the Festschrift for K. Helm, pp. 157 ff.; D. Ruprecht, *Tristitia*, pp. 69 f. and 140 ff.

[2] III, 8, 40 (cf. vv. 38 and 46).

[3] V. 2945 (cf. v. 2943). The author of the *Heliand* also uses the verb *twîflian* of the Jews in their characteristic function of doubting the divinity of Christ (3003: 'thea liudi sind farlorane,   farlâten habbiad | uualdandes uuord,   that uuerod is getuîflid').

[4] Nc 693, 29: 'in angisten unde in zuiuelheiten'; 724, 10 'in zuuiueligero unbaldi furhtender'; 772, 26: 'taz si angestlîcho zuuîuelota'.

[5] Festschrift for K. Helm, p. 162.   [6] *Op. cit.* p. 165.

[7] *Op. cit.* p. 166.   [8] *Ibid.*

author, using not *hôher muot* but *ubirmuot* in an entirely negative meaning, likewise contrasts *zwîvel* with *ubirmuot* in this final episode. This does not mean that *zwîvel* has now become a positive quality, but, instead, that *zwîvel* and *ubirmuot* signify contrasting faults. *Ubirmuot*, applied to the Egyptians, suggests their arrogance and excessive confidence in themselves, whereas the Israelites, because of their lack of arrogance, are particularly exposed to the danger of *zwîvel* or lack of confidence amounting to fear. Hempel has shown a further function of *zwîvel* when used in the context of actions: namely, 'Untreue, Verrat, auch Feigheit, auch Abfall von der eigenen Bestimmung'.[1] Something close to this range of meaning is also implied by *zwîvel* in the Millstatt epic and by the final episode in particular, although here we have to make the important reservation that this interpretation is only possible if we define 'Untreue' not simply as a positive action which conflicts with the spirit of an oath of loyalty (of this the Hebrews cannot be called guilty in this episode), but also as a sin of omission, as a failure to live up to the obligations which the oath of loyalty imposes.[2] In this latter sense the Hebrews are indeed guilty of *zwîvel* in a meaning which lies close to *untriuwe*, but they are saved from the consequences of their action only by the fact that God's *triuwe* far exceeds the precise terms of His covenant. That God should nonetheless keep faith with His people even after they have failed to keep faith with Him can only be ascribed to the supererogatory nature of His *triuwe*, but for anyone to rely on this in repeating the sin of the Hebrews would be tantamount to the 'tempting of the Lord'

---

[1] *Ibid.* pp. 166 f.

[2] On the manner in which the oath of loyalty implies the need to live up to the obligations which loyalty imposes see V. Ehrenberg, *Commendation und Huldigung nach fränkischem Recht*, p. 112: 'Durchaus dominirt also in dem Begriffe der Treue das subjective Moment, das Gewissen des Verpflichteten, und dadurch unterscheidet sich die Treue eben von dem Gehorsam. Der Gehorsam thut das, was befohlen ist, ohne Rücksicht auf das Interesse dessen, der befiehlt; die Treue dagegen handelt lediglich im Interesse des Herrn, mag das zu Thuende befohlen sein oder nicht.' This sin of omission has been discussed with particular reference to the neutral angels by B. Nardi, *Gli angeli che non furon ribelli ne' fur fedeli a Dio*. I am indebted to E.P.M. Dronke for drawing my attention to this essay.

which it is called in Exod. 17. 2. This is why the Millstatt author attaches such importance to this episode and why he is prepared to close the action of his epic on an apparently jarring note: emulation of the Hebrew example must not blind his knightly audience to the dangers of doing this uncritically, they must realise that the Christian virtue of humility brings with it the danger of succumbing to the corresponding sin of *ʒwîvel*. *Zwîvel* for him is a failing which he depicts at length only in this final military episode and which he conceives primarily as cowardice resulting from a failure of trust in God. It is an offence against the ideal of the crusader's military and feudal obligation towards God on which the author has concentrated such attention and which, as a conclusion to his work, serves to round off from the negative side this total picture of the crusader's relationship with God.

One final conclusion about this closing episode to which both de Boor and Fliegner have taken objection may be reached if we ask why the Millstatt author was concerned to depict the theme of *ʒwîvel* in his work. We have seen that in this episode he greatly expands the short reference to be found in his source and that he transfers to it from later episodes in the Bible the idea of using it as an occasion to describe the Hebrews as falling short of their obligation towards God. These are, however, only details that tell us *how* the author made use of the theme of *ʒwîvel*, not *why* he chose to incorporate it into his work. The same is true of the manner in which he exploits this theme to give further emphasis to the Christian warrior's military and feudal duties towards God, both of which had already been so clearly stressed that there was no pressing need to add this final example. Clearly, the fact that the author exemplifies these duties in this closing episode by making use of antithetical typology stands in some sort of relationship with the manner in which other authors employ the same method: for example, the author of the *Vorauer Bücher Mosis* in a non-crusading context, and also the author of the *Kaiserchronik*, Raimundus and St Bernard in close connection with the crusades. In this latter respect the use of antithetical typology is no more than a particular example of the application of the typological method to the crusading experience. One of the reasons for the application of this method to the crusades was that, by providing a connection between the religious wars of Israel and those of the present, it helped to justify the whole conception of the crusade—a conception which, by its very novelty, was in need of justification, as may be seen from some of the statements in criticism of the idea of a religious war in the period leading up to the First Crusade or from the reaction in Germany to the First Crusade.[1] In addition to justifying the crusades, the employment of the typological method strengthened the conviction that what the crusaders were engaged upon was no less than part of God's plan of salvation for the world, that they were now God's Chosen People and that, since they acted on His behalf, they were assured of His support just as much as the Israelites of the Old Testament had been. The result is that the crusaders were sustained by a feeling that it had been given to them to help realise the age-old prophecies of the Hebrews, that God had granted to them what their predecessors had forfeited and that they were living in the fullness of time. From this there emerge a sense of achievement, an elation and a pride in being the elect of God which do much to explain the growth of an independent knightly ideal of life in the twelfth century. What Köhler says of the relationship of knightly literature to the classical past is equally true of the crusader's attitude to his spiritual predecessors in Israel: 'Die souveräne Unbekümmertheit, mit

[1] On the critical attitude of Petrus Damiani, for example, see Erdmann, *Die Entstehung des Kreuzzugsgedankens*, pp. 131 f. The reaction in Germany is described by Ekkehardus, *RHC*, v, 18 A f. (see also below, p. 360) and it is more than likely that what he reports about the ignominious fate that overtook the followers of Folkmar and Gottschalk may show how this initial reaction could be confirmed by subsequent events: 'Haecque est causa qua quidam simpliciores fratres, utpote rem ignorantes, scandalizati, totum hujus profectionis conatum vanum atque frivolum ipsi nimis praeproperi judices interpretati sunt' (*ibid.* 21 A f.). Cf. also Albertus Aquensis in the same context: 'Hic manus Domini contra Peregrinos esse creditur' (*RHC*, iv, 295 B).

Köhler, *Ideal und Wirklichkeit in der höfischen Epik*, p. 5, has some important words to say on the medieval tendency to justify the present by reference to a past which is interpreted in the light of the needs of the present.

der das Mittelalter die Vergangenheit travestiert, ist nur zu einem geringen Teil Naivität, zum größten Teil ist sie Selbstinterpretation mit Hilfe einer Geschichtsauslegung, die hinter den bloßen Fakten eine zwar meist mehrdeutige, aber immer auf eine Erfüllung hin, d.h. letztlich heilsgeschichtlich verstandene Bedeutung sucht...'[1] The example of the Israelites is the precedent by which the crusader is able to justify himself, but which also, because of the conviction that he transcends them, provides him with his sense of achievement and confidence.

Yet how far can the same be said of antithetical typology, where the characteristic point is that the Hebrews are not to be emulated in every respect? In so far as a typological fulfilment can be only potential and still need to be realised by each individual Christian, the negative example of the Hebrews remains permanently relevant to every generation of Christians, so that antithetical typology is inseparable from typology itself. Furthermore, the sense of fulfilment that informs the use of typology in the crusading chronicles rests on the fact that the crusaders constitute a new Chosen People to whom God's favours have been transferred as a result of the Hebrews' failure to keep faith with Him. In other words, the crusaders' sense of election (which alone made the use of typology possible in their case and which explains their sense of achievement) is a result of the fact that in the past the Hebrews had forfeited their original role as God's people. The negative example of the Hebrews is the necessary condition for the crusaders to be able to regard themselves in a typological light at all, so that they are called upon to keep this fact in mind if they are to maintain their role as the new Israel and to continue their contributions to the fulfilment of God's plans for mankind. It is significant that *zwîvel*, the fault which the Millstatt author regards as endangering this role of the crusaders as it had once that of the Israelites, should have as one of its meanings, so defined by Hempel, 'Abfall von der eigenen Bestimmung'.[2] This is precisely what befell the Israelites when they forfeited their role as God's people and it is against a repetition

---

[1] *Op. cit.* p. 6.   [2] In the Festschrift for K. Helm, p. 167.

358

of this danger that the Millstatt author, like Raimundus,[1] utters his warning.

We still have to explain why it should be *zwîvel* in particular which the Millstatt author (followed also by the author of the *Kaiserchronik* in the Heraclius episode) regards as constituting the real danger for the potential crusader, rather than the sin of *ubermuot* which is more commonly attributed to the knighthood as their primary sin.[2] Indeed, this problem is increased when we recall that the crusader who falls short of his obligations by losing confidence is guilty of a form of rebellion against God. This interpretation we found in the *Vorauer Bücher Mosis*, where the loss of heart by the Jews is actually equated with *hohvart*, and it is significant that *zwîvel*, the term used to denote such a loss of heart, can also express such ideas as 'Auftrotzen gegen Gott' and 'Auflehnung und trotziges Widerstreben'.[3] If both ideas (loss of confidence and rebellion) are implicit in the situation described by the Millstatt author and can be conveyed by the word *zwîvel* itself, why should he have chosen to concentrate the weight of his criticism on the meaning 'loss of confidence'?

The answer to this question lies in the conditions in Germany in which the author composed his work, in the fact that, since acceptance of the crusading idea was still by no means so widespread in Germany as in France, it needed a persuasive advocate to recommend an idea for which the time was not yet so ripe as it had been in France as early as 1095. Here we must remember that, although we have seen the falsity of the view which denies that any German knights took part in the crusades before the proclamation of the Second,[4] nonetheless their participation was a very sporadic affair and the First Crusade was not preached

---

[1] *RHC*, III, 280D.

[2] Cf. der arme Hartmann, *Rede vom Glauben*, vv. 2370 ff. Cf. also Urban's words addressed to the (still secular) knights at Clermont, as reported by Baldricus: 'Vos accincti cingulo militiae, magno superbitis supercilio; fratres vestros laniatis, atque inter vos dissecamini.'

[3] Hempel, Festschrift for K. Helm, pp. 167 and 174. See also Ruprecht, *Tristitia*, p. 69, on OS *tuuifli/tuiflan* in the sense of 'auf begehrend, zornig'. We have already seen (p. 349, n. 2) how St Bernard regarded the Hebrews in the wilderness as being not merely *increduli*, but also *rebelles*.   [4] See pp. 300 ff.

systematically in Germany.[1] Furthermore, some of those crusaders who crossed Germany from the west met with a degree of scorn and incomprehension[2] which suggests that there was work to be done if the mass of the German knighthood was to be won over to the new ideal—work which was taken in hand only on the eve of the Second Crusade and which even then encountered difficulties.[3] If in this period before the Second Crusade and in these conditions a German author who was himself won for the crusading idea wished to gain adherents in his own country, his primary task was to convince his compatriots of the desirability and feasibility of such an undertaking. His task was to persuade them that this was what God demanded of them and that if they placed their full trust in Him His assistance was a sure guarantee of their eventual success. If his problem was to instil in the knighthood of Germany that degree of trust which alone would make it possible for them to take the cross, then the attitude which he had to attack was precisely lack of confidence, an unwillingness to believe that this was what God intended, doubts as to the possibility of the whole idea. The frame of mind to which the Millstatt author was primarily opposed is that which Ekkehardus reports as shown by the German population to the crusaders passing through their territory, for they jeer at them for their folly in leaving their home and abandoning the certain for the uncertain: '... quasi inaudita stultitia delirantes subsanabant, utpote qui, pro certis incerta captantes, terram nativitatis vane relinquerunt.'[4] His object was therefore to show that what these German doubters had termed the *terra nativitatis* was in reality an *ellende* (v. 3299) and that in journeying to Jerusalem the crusaders, like the Israelites, were returning to their true home (v. 3300: 'heim ze deme lande'). What to these mockers appeared to be *incerta* (by comparison with what the crusaders were leaving behind) he wished to show to be even more certain than the goods of this life and that they were to be won by the man who placed his trust in God.

[1] Cf. Ekkehardus, *RHC*, v, 17 E.
[2] See p. 357, n. 1.
[3] Cf. Waas, *Geschichte der Kreuzzüge*, I, 167 f.
[4] *RHC*, v, 18 A.

Problems of detail

The stress which the Millstatt author places on the need to overcome *zwîvel* results therefore from the position in which he found himself as the writer of a crusading epic in German in about the year 1120. This does not mean that the opposing sin of *hohvart* or *ubermuot* was not an insidious danger for the knight in particular: whether for the secular knight who did not take the cross or for the crusader himself. It does mean, though, that for the potential crusader, for the man who is to be persuaded to set out for Jerusalem, the first obstacle is *zwîvel* and it is accordingly on this that the Millstatt author concentrates most of his attention. *Ubermuot* may later become a temptation for the crusader once he has acknowledged the need to set out for the Holy Land (as it did for Heraclius and his followers after their recovery of the Holy Cross), but at this initial stage it is the possible objections of *zwîvel* which the German author must overcome. In depicting the Israelites in a negative light in this final episode our author draws the attention of his audience to this failing of theirs, their repeated unwillingness to show complete trust in the God whose essential nature is omnipotence and loyalty. The implication of this scene as the climax of a crusading epic is therefore twofold. On the one hand the audience is shown that God rescued the Israelites, despite their *zwîvel*, because of the immensity of His *triuwe*, but that, as the ultimate fate of the Hebrews in losing their role as *populus Dei* shows, it would be unwise for the new Israel to tempt God by similarly relying on the strength of His *triuwe*, to repeat the offence of their predecessors by failing to show complete trust. On the other hand, the implication is clear: if God granted victory to the Israelites on this occasion, when they had lost heart and succumbed to unheroic cowardice, how much more assured of victory must those be who follow their God into battle against the Saracens and do not allow such base fears to get the better of them. The encouragement which such an episode was meant to offer the feudal knight whose pride was in his *manheit* is similar to that conveyed by the story of Judith as part of crusading literature: if God can grant victory to His people through the hands of one whom the author of the *Jüngere Judith* calls *ein blode͜z wibelin*,[1] then how much more certain must victory be when God is served by such redoubted warriors as those who obey His call to the Holy Land. *Zwîvel* is the quality to be shunned by the crusader if he is to avoid the fate of the Hebrews and it is *z͜wîvel* in potential crusaders which the Millstatt author hopes to overcome by appealing to the most undoubted quality of a knightly audience, the bravery which is the hallmark of the knight's profession. It is at this stage that we may return to a point referred to above[2] with the hope of understanding it in a new light: the passage in which the heroic imagery of the beasts of prey on the battlefield is evoked negatively in the episode of the slaughter of the Israelite children. We saw that this scene was meant as a prefiguration of the contemporary martyrdom achieved by crusaders, but it was also clear that there was a certain incongruity between the evocation of this negative imagery on the occasion when the midwives succeed in avoiding the slaughter and the fact that this imagery is not employed when the situation would apparently have demanded it, namely when Pharaoh implements his order and has the Israelite children put to death. If we apply to this episode the conclusion we have reached in considering the role of *z͜wîvel* in the Millstatt epic (the author's need to remove all doubts and fears from the hearts of potential crusaders), then it appears likely that he had no hesitation in appealing to the heroic vocabulary of the beasts of prey on the battlefield precisely when no martyrs are put to death, but that, when the slaughter actually takes place, he judged it more prudent to avoid emphasising it by the employment of heroic images. This does not mean that the German author was not as fully convinced as were the chroniclers that martyrdom was the reward of any crusader who fell in battle, but simply that he thought it more judicious to stress the unfailing support given by God even to the Israelites when they showed *z͜wîvel* and therefore to adduce the heroic imagery of military martyrdom only at that stage of the work where the need for such martyrdom is successfully avoided.

To remove *z͜wîvel*, therefore, the author of the *Millstätter*

[1] 128. 3.   [2] See p. 309.

Exodus had to do everything in his power to strengthen the confidence and optimism of potential crusaders, both by implying that the victories once afforded to the Hebrews must be granted to their spiritual successors and also by suggesting that the Christian knights, as a typological fulfilment which surpassed its Old Testament model, were enabled by their Christian and military virtues of loyalty and bravery to avoid the defeats which the Israelites had suffered because of their corresponding shortcomings. In his task of strengthening the confidence of potential crusaders the Millstatt author comes close to what we find in other sources for the crusading movement at large, where the means used to justify the holy war against the pagans can also be utilised to strengthen the confidence and sense of election of those who take part in this enterprise. In other words, whenever the function of the crusaders is legitimised by earlier precedents the result will be that the knightly class from whose ranks they are drawn and whose supreme task it is to provide recruits for this God-ordained expedition is itself legitimised and given a role in society and in history which it had been denied before this new, knightly way of attaining to salvation was made accessible to it as part of the crusading movement. The historical precedents for crusading knighthood which are commonly adduced in the chronicles are three in number and it is in emulation of them that medieval knighthood is enabled to establish its own independence and function within society.

With the first of these precedents, the Hebrew warriors of the Old Testament, we have been concerned throughout the course of this work and there is little that has to be added at this stage. Two points need to be emphasised, however. The first is that the typological relationship between the Hebrews and the crusaders is not merely a frequent comparison, occurring in most of the chronicles of the First Crusade, but one which is attributed independently by a number of chroniclers to Urban II himself at Clermont.[1] In other words, the Pope responsible for the First

[1] E.g. Robertus Monachus (*RHC*, III, 728 B and F), Baldricus (*RHC*, IV, 14 B ff. and E; 15 F; 16 D), and Guibertus (*RHC*, IV, 138 D and F; 139 G).

Crusade legitimises the undertaking by appealing to the hallowed precedent of the Old Testament, but is also responsible for heightening the knights' self-esteem by stressing that it is to them in particular that God has granted this new manner of gaining salvation[1] and that it is on them that He has conferred the honour of surpassing the exploits of His former Chosen People. Secondly, as Alphandéry has pointed out,[2] the use of the typological method with reference to the crusaders (*not* merely in the tropological interpretation) represents an innovation of considerable importance in the history of medieval exegesis, for although the method itself may remain unchanged, the principle which it is meant to serve is now quite different. No longer is Christ the object of the Old Testament prophecy and the object of the allegory, but instead Christians or a special class of Christians, the crusaders. They still derive their importance only from the fact that they serve Christ, but the crucial point is that the fulfilment of the Old Testament prophecies which are quoted is to be found in the medieval present and is accomplished by the crusading knights. This confers an importance on the events of the present and on those who take part in them which it would be difficult to exaggerate and which does much to explain the new-found independence and sense of achievement revealed by knightly civilisation in the twelfth century.[3]

A second historical precedent by means of which crusading knighthood is allowed to find its function in history is provided by classical antiquity. Guibertus opens Book I of his chronicle of the First Crusade by recording the various wars of classical antiquity which were conducted, he argues, for no better reason than the love of power.[4] For him it is clear that these wars under the leadership of kings and consuls must be inferior to the crusading expeditions whose warriors are assembled not under the

---

[1] Cf. *RHC*, IV, 124 E.   [2] *RHR*, XCIX, 141 f.

[3] It is probably not by chance that the explicit interpretation given by the Millstatt author at the end of his work (vv. 3297 ff.) should stress the role of Christian believers and that no reference is made to the traditional interpretation of Moses as the prefiguration of Christ. See also p. 120, n. 1.

[4] *RHC*, IV, 123 D: 'sine ulla ratione, pro sola dominandi libidine.'

command of a secular ruler, but under the sole authority of God. Significantly, the passage in which this contrast between the classical past and the present is made to the advantage of the latter also opens with a similar parallel between the deeds of the Hebrews and those of contemporary Christians: 'Si Deum in Judaico populo magnificatum audivimus, Jesum Christum, sicut heri apud antiquos, ita et hodie apud modernos, esse et valere certis experimentis agnovimus. Reges, duces, dictatores ac consules uspiam pugnaturi populorum examina conflaverunt, et ex dictis potentibus undecumque gentium numerosos exercitus contraxerunt. Hi tamen, hi coeunt hominum terroribus acti. Quid de illis dicam, qui sine domino, sine principe, solo videlicet Deo impulsore, non modo extra natalem provinciam, extra etiam originale regnum, verum quoque extra multitudinem inter-jacentium nationum progressi...castrorum suorum acies pro-duxere?'[1] It is by contrast with what Guibertus calls the *vetustae paganitatis exemplum*[2] that the modern crusading knight is afforded the *novum salutis genus*.[3] He shares with his classical predecessors the function of warfare, but surpasses them by virtue of the religious goal and motives to which this warfare is subordinated.[4] Another example of the way in which the warfare of classical antiquity could be regarded as a precedent for the medieval present (whether to be surpassed or not is this time left

[1] *RHC*, IV, 123 F f.   [2] *RHC*, IV, 124 E.
[3] *Ibid.*

[4] A similar (potential) superiority felt by the Christian present to the classical past in matters of warfare is shown quite unambiguously in the Prologue to the *Historia de preliis* (44, 1 ff.): 'Certamina vel victorias excellentium virorum infidelium ante adventum Christi, quamvis exstitissent pagani, bonum et utile est omnibus Christianis ad audiendum et intelligendum tum praelatis quam subditis, videlicet saecularibus et spiritualibus viris, quia cunctos ad meliorem provocat actionem. Nam prelati, id est rectores, legendo et considerando, quem-admodum praedicti pagani idolis servientes agebant se caste et fideliter atque in omnibus se inreprehensibiliter ostendebant, per eorum exempla bonorum operum ita acuant mentes suas, eo quod fideles et membra Christi esse videntur, et multo magis meliores se illis demonstrent in castitate et justicia atque pietate. Subiecti vero, id est milites sub milicia constituti, legendo vel audiendo talia certamina et operationes commilitum suorum, qui magis daemonibus quam deo militabant, certent se prudentiores ostendere illis in omni opere bono, sicut decet militibus Christi.'

uncertain) is provided by a poem entitled *Adelae Comitissae*[1] written by that Baldricus to whose crusading chronicle, *Historia Hierosolimitana*, we have often had to refer. Baldricus describes his memory of a visit to the court of Adela, his astonishment at the enormous size of the hall and his admiration of the splendid quality of the tapestries that covered the walls. He describes the themes of these tapestries in detail, indicating how one was concerned with the events of the Old Testament from Noah down to the kings of Judah[2] and how another reproduced scenes from Greek mythology, the siege of Troy and Roman history.[3] Both these tapestries, however, are surpassed in quality by one which decorated the recess in which the bed of the countess was placed and which depicted the battle of Hastings.[4] Whether the superior quality of this tapestry is meant to indicate that the kind of warfare waged at Hastings was superior to that waged by the Hebrews or at Troy is left in obscurity, but it is clear, since Erdmann's emphasis on the role which papal support for the Norman Conquest played in the development of the crusading idea,[5] that here a modern quasi-crusading war is related to its precedents in classical and Hebrew antiquity.[6] Much the same is true of the

---

[1] Edited by P. Abrahams, *Les œuvres poétiques de Baudri de Bourgueil*, pp. 196 ff. I am indebted to C. R. Dodwell for drawing my attention to this testimony. There is little reason to doubt that Baudri de Bourgueil is identical with the author of the *Historia Hierosolimitana* whose name is attested as 'Baldricus, episcopus Dolensis', since he became Archbishop of Dol in 1107 (see Abrahams, *op. cit.* p. xxi). [2] Vv. 141 ff. [3] Vv. 169 ff.

[4] The description of the scene depicted begins at v. 235. The passage vv. 207 ff. stresses the superior quality of this particular tapestry.

[5] *Die Entstehung des Kreuzzugsgedankens*, pp. 172 f. and 181 ff.

[6] A similar relationship between the deeds of William the Conqueror and the exploits of the heroes of classical antiquity is repeatedly established by William of Poitiers in his *Gesta Guillelmi*. He is compared to Agamemnon and Xerxes, for example, but it is stressed that he excelled the former in ships and the latter in courage (II, 7; p. 162 in the edition by R. Foreville); Marius and Pompey were honoured with triumphs, but William was more worthy because he courageously did his own reconnoitring (II, 9; p. 168); Agamemnon with the help of numerous kings only succeeded in destroying the one city of Priam after ten years of siege and Rome at the height of its power took several years to reduce a few cities, one by one, but William subdued all the cities of England in a single day (II, 26; p. 208). At the same time, it is made quite clear that William excelled these classical models, at least in part, by virtue of his Christian piety and the

scenes in one of the rooms of the castle of Lochstedt, belonging to the Order of Teutonic Knights.[1] Here St George is depicted because of his role as the patron saint of knighthood, but also those warriors of the past whose prowess is to be emulated by the knights of the Order. They include Joshua, David and Judas Maccabaeus from the Old Testament, but also Hector, Alexander and Caesar as heroes of antiquity. In addition, as medieval models, Charles the Great, Arthur and Godfrey of Bouillon are depicted, so that the crusading knight is here felt to be the heir to a variegated and age-old tradition which passes on to him its aura of historical and mythical renown. That something similar was also attempted in the case of secular knighthood by tracing its ancestry back to Troy is clear from the prologue to *Moriz von Craûn*[2] or to the *Ritterfahrt des Johann von Michelsperg* by Heinrich von Freiberg.[3]

The mention of the picture of Charles the Great at Lochstedt brings us to the third historical tradition in which the crusading knight was found a place: that of Charles the Great himself. If we are to believe Robertus, it was Urban II who appealed to this potent example as a means of rousing the warrior pride of those who listened to him at Clermont: 'Moveant vos et incitent animos vestros ad virilitatem gesta praedecessorum vestrorum, probitas

divine assistance which this secured for him. The counsellors of Normandy are compared to the Roman senate, to whom they are shown as superior since they bowed to the wisdom of their prince, knowing that God gave wisdom to the pious (II, 1; pp. 148 f.). William himself is compared to Aeneas and Achilles, but the author adds that, whereas Virgil and Statius would have placed William amongst the gods, he will note his piety towards the true God (II, 22; pp. 198 f.), a virtue which is confirmed later by the manner in which it is stressed that William, although he served both God and the world, concentrated more on the former since he recognised that it was to God that he owed his success. I am indebted to C. R. Dodwell for drawing my attention to these passages.

[1] See Helm and Ziesemer, *Die Literatur des deutschen Ritterordens*, p. 25, and also the work to which they refer by C. Steinbrecht, *Schloß Lochstedt und seine Malereien*.

[2] Vv. 1 ff. On this theme see J. Schwietering's contribution to the Festschrift for G. Ehrismann, especially pp. 49 f., and also R. Harvey, *Moriz von Craûn and the Chivalric World*, pp. 62 ff.

[3] Cf. the significant relationship between vv. 30 f. ('Mit ritterschaft die lant erstreit | der künec Alexander') and v. 40 ('Nu blüet ein helt in Bêheimlant').

367

et magnitudo Karoli Magni regis, et Ludovici filii ejus aliorumque regum vestrorum, qui regna paganorum destruxerunt et in eis fines sanctae Ecclesiae dilataverunt.'[1] In a different tone, but citing the same model, Guibertus reports that Urban II had said that, in appealing to the Franks to come to the aid of Christians, he was continuing a practice of some antiquity, for predecessors of his, such as Popes Stephen and Zacharias, had also turned to Pippin and Charles for assistance.[2] It is in the light of this attachment of the relatively young crusading movement to the older Carolingian tradition that we can best explain other allusions to Charles the Great in crusading works. The crusading leader Baldwin of Flanders is proclaimed as a descendant of Charles, but in a manner which reveals just how many other strands of historical tradition come together to create the impression of elevated ancestry which is now attributed to the crusader: 'A magno illo rege Carolo genus trahens, super solium David sessurus divinitus habebatur. Jure igitur ac merito Alexandrum vincebat, cujus illustrabant Carolus ortum, David occasum.'[3] Conversely, Charles the Great is seen as a crusader himself in much the same way as this role was also imposed retrospectively upon Heraclius. The expeditions conducted by Charles now take on the character of a crusade: this is most obviously true of his Spanish campaign in its crusading reflection in the *Chanson de Roland*,[4] but it also means that the Emperor is now seen as having conducted an armed pil-

---

[1] *RHC*, III, 728 B f. Cf. also the similar testimony adduced by Bédier, *Les légendes épiques*, IV, 454 f.

[2] *RHC*, IV, 135 D: 'Apostolicae nempe sedis pontificibus ab antiquo consuetudinarium fuit, si quam sunt passi a finitima gente molestiam, auxilia expetere semper a Francis. Stephanus et Zacharias pontifices, uterque sub Pipino et Karolo regibus, confugium fecit ad ipsos.'

[3] *Gesta Tancredi*, c. XXXVII (*RHC*, III, 633 B).

[4] This does not mean that Bédier's views have to be accepted in their totality (on this see the stimulating remarks of Menéndez Pidal, *La Chanson de Roland et la tradition épique des Francs*, pp. 241 ff., under the heading 'Le Charlemagne du "Roland" est-il un croisé?'), but rather that there is no reason why the theme of Roland, which may well have developed along the 'traditionalist' lines postulated by Menéndez Pidal, should not have been later informed with some of the crusading themes of a later period. (The example of the courtly elements in the *Nibelungenlied* is an obvious parallel.) See the remarks of H.-W. Klein, *NS* (1956), pp. 284 f.

grimage to Jerusalem. This is treated at length in the *Chanson du pèlerinage de Charlemagne*, and we catch a glimpse of the same idea when Robertus, describing the overland journey to the East, reports that the route followed was that originally taken by Charles: 'per viam scilicet quam Karolus Magnus, incomparabilis rex Francorum, olim suo exercitui fieri usque Constantinopolim praecepit.'[1] A similar reference occurs in the *Gesta Francorum*.[2] Elsewhere, however, the belief is attested that Charlemagne has come to life again and is to lead the crusaders against the Saracens, as when Ekkehardus reports: 'Inde fabulosum illud confictum est de Karolo Magno quasi de mortuis in id ipsum resuscitato, et alio nescio quo nihilominus redivivo.'[3] This belief can take the form that certain leaders of the crusade are regarded as being themselves *Carolus redivivus*, the Last Emperor who had risen again to fulfil the Sibylline prophecies: we find this in the case of Godfrey of Bouillon himself,[4] and also with the Emicho whom we have already considered as testimony to the fact that Germany was not totally unaffected by the First Crusade.[5] In other cases, individual crusaders can be compared with one or other of the paladins of Charles the Great, as when the author of the *Gesta Tancredi* says of the prowess of Robert, Duke of Flanders, and Hugh the Great:

> Rollandum dicas Oliveriumque renatos.[6]

By such means as these, some sanctioned by the Church but others belonging to the realm of popular superstition, the crusaders were given a place in an already established tradition of native origin, in addition to those deriving from classical and Hebrew antiquity. The result is similar in all cases, for the force of these three models which the crusaders emulate is to provide a justification and a precedent for an undertaking so novel and also to equip the crusaders with the confidence and buoyancy of

[1] *RHC*, III, 732 A.
[2] I (ii), p. 2: '...per uiam quam iamdudum Karolus Magnus mirificus rex Franciae aptari fecit usque Constantinopolim.'   [3] *RHC*, V, 19D f.
[4] See Alphandéry, *La chrétienté et l'idée de croisade*, I, 131 f.
[5] *Ibid*. p. 131.   [6] *RHC*, III, 627D.

spirit which come from the knowledge of being carried forward by the tradition to which they ascribe themselves. It is also significant that the three traditions from which the crusaders derive a legitimation and the conviction of their new-found role in history (Hebrew, classical and Carolingian) should also be the traditions on which the institution of sacral kingship depends so much in the early Middle Ages. This is in full agreement with the important observation made by Erdmann[1] that the Christianisation of feudal knighthood, coming historically later than that of the royal office, largely reveals that the knights were equipped with a Christian role in society by having transferred to them as individuals duties which had earlier been demanded of the royal office alone. In our case, the establishment of an independent function of the crusading knight likewise reflects the similar (and earlier) process in the case of the medieval sovereign.

When Walther in the context of the crusades can affirm the sense of personal value which he feels as the result of possibly imaginary pilgrimage to the Holy Land (14, 38: 'Allerêrst lebe ich mir werde') or stress the honour which has accrued to the knightly class from the privilege which has been granted to it alone of gaining redemption by wielding the sword and thereby meeting the obligations of its social status (125, 1: 'dar an gedenkent, ritter: ez ist iuwer dinc'), he stands at the peak of a development at whose beginning the author of the *Millstätter Exodus* is to be found. Whether we regard this powerful and creative sense of achievement and election shared by the knights as confined only to those who went on a crusade or as spreading beyond this sphere to inform the knightly ideal at large, in its secular expression as well as in its religious, it is clear that the Millstatt author's endeavours to infuse a sense of religious purpose and confidence into those who he thought might be won for the crusading ideal indicate the development which the knightly class of Germany was to undergo in the twelfth century. They are a reliable measure of his perspicacity in seeing what was needful in the conditions of his own time.

[1] *Die Entstehung des Kreuzzugsgedankens*, pp. 74, 232, 236 f., 309 f.

X

GENERAL CONCLUSIONS

W^E have considered the *Millstätter Exodus* as an example of epic expansion of biblical material and also with regard to the author's reinterpretation of his source in the light of the crusades. Our survey has shown us that the formal changes for which the Millstatt author was responsible are closely connected with the way in which he refashioned his material so as to make his interpretation obvious to his audience. A brief recapitulation of these parallels will show us that these two aspects form a close unity at many points and that there can be little talk of the epic form of this work being no more than the result of an undisciplined loquacity or a fumbling inability to cope with the problem of rhyme. Instead, as these parallels show us, it is the author's interpretation of the events of Exodus and his need to suggest this reading to his audience which have recommended to him a work of epic proportions, together with all the other stylistic features which this involves.[1]

We saw that the Millstatt author, unlike his predecessor with the *Wiener Genesis*, contracted his material much less frequently than he expanded it. In some cases this contraction was for a formal reason (the wish to avoid repetitiveness or to achieve an

---

[1] This corresponds closely to what Beyschlag has written of the expansionary elements in the *Wiener Genesis* (*Die Wiener Genesis*, p. 108): 'Die inneren und äußeren Ausmaße der Vorlage, der alttestamentlichen Genesis, und vor allem die gedankliche Ausrichtung, die das dt. Gedicht erfahren hat, drängen dann dazu, diese gegebene kurze Form der erzählenden Teile immer mehr zu überschreiten, gerade dort, wo der dt. Dichter sein Werk in besonders greifbarer Weise in den Lebenszusammenhang mit seiner Zeit stellt. Hier verläßt er auch die Art der nur umrißhaft zeichnenden Darstellung und wächst im ganzen an seiner Aufgabe in das Maß buchepischen Stils hinein.' The *Millstätter Exodus* differs from the earlier work, however, by concentrating more regularly on expansion (and therefore contracting only very infrequently) and by stressing more the military (rather than courtly) implications of its theme.

economy of action), but in the remaining cases, as with the omission of details which are too patently Jewish, we can be sure that this procedure is followed by the author as a negative condition for any successful equation between these events from the history of Israel and the medieval present. Since his crusading interpretation of Exodus rests entirely on such an equation we can be sure that it is the manner in which he understands his biblical theme which accounts for these omissions. The same also applies to those cases where the author's decision partly to exclude God from his foreground narrative by granting a greater independence to the human actors has led to a similar contraction of the Bible version. The result of this kind of change is that a greater responsibility now rests with man and with his moral decisions (as is made clear in the case of *zwîvel*)—a change of emphasis which can only have been welcome to an author convinced of man's duty to render knightly assistance to God in the crusades and of the need to bring this home to his knightly audience.

What is true of some of the author's infrequent contractions is even more relevant to our understanding of his expansions, a feature which is much more characteristic of him. It is probable that it was by the creation of new scenes that he was best able to suggest the manner in which he understood the events he was narrating. Of the ten scenes which the Millstatt author has introduced where the Bible had none, or has expanded where his source had no more than a brief reference, the first (describing the enslaved Jews in Egypt in courtly and knightly terms) served to stress the relevance of these events to the author's aristocratic audience,[1] whilst in the second (the encounter between Moses and Jethro) the emphasis on Moses' banishment was a graphic means of illustrating the plight of the Hebrews at large in their exile and of suggesting the traditional interpretation that mankind, in bondage to sin, was similarly in banishment from the Heavenly Jerusalem.[2] Both these scenes represent an expansion which has not been undertaken for exclusively formal

[1] See pp. 78 f.   [2] See pp. 80 f.

reasons, but rather to demonstrate certain aspects of the way in which the events of Exodus are meant to be understood.

The remaining eight scenes all contain military implications (whether positively, as an allusion to warlike attacks or heroic splendour, or negatively, when the loss of confidence of the Israelites and of the Egyptians is described). These implications, for which no lengthy parallel was to be found in the Bible, are of obvious importance for an author who interprets Exodus in terms of the military encounter between crusaders and Saracens, but in addition each of these expansionary scenes is meant to contribute further to the understanding of the author's intentions. Thus, the negative description of the battlefield when Pharaoh orders the killing of all the male children was meant as a prefiguration of the slaughter of the innocents by Herod, but this first example of Christian martyrdom, in its turn, had a particular relevance to the crusaders as the latest of those who were prepared to die on behalf of Christ.[1] The military description of the plague of frogs, even though it is necessarily in negative terms only, provides a forceful suggestion that if even these unarmed creatures can gain a victory with God's support, so much more likely is victory if the knights of the author's day, professional warriors whose whole ethos is based on warfare, were to take up arms against the Saracens.[2] In the military description of the plague of flies it is the mention of such phrases as *gotes rîtere* and *gotes anden rechen* which introduces a reference to the crusading present,[3] whilst the similar description of the locusts, because of parallels in the Old Testament and in crusading chronicles, may be interpreted in the same way, at least by implication.[4] The description of the departure of the Israelite army serves the similar function of relating these past events to the knightly present: it is intended as a prefiguration of a Christian army setting out on its exodus to the Holy Land and as an illustration of the paramount need for such Christian knights to show the virtue of humility if they are to enjoy divine assistance.[5] It is not by

[1] See pp. 307 ff.   [2] See pp. 325 ff.   [3] See pp. 273 ff.
[4] See pp. 325 ff.   [5] See pp. 94 f.

chance that in the middle of this description, where a Hebrew army is shown as the forerunner of an army of Christian knights, the author should choose to appeal for the attention of his knightly audience by addressing them directly on the only occasion in the whole work. The complementary description of the setting out of the Egyptian warriors illustrates the futility of their pride in their military strength, for this is not merely revealed later in the description of their annihilation, but is already made quite clear by the employment of *epische Vorausdeutung*.[1] The two remaining scenes (depicting the fear of the Israelite army and then of the Egyptian warriors) have a similar role to play, even though their example is a negative one. The scene with the Israelites illustrates the *zwîvel* to which they have succumbed in terms of a lethargic clinging to the bondage of sin and a hesitancy in accepting the opportunity of escape which they have been offered.[2] With the Egyptians, we are meant to realise the complete uselessness of even the finest knightly equipment and heroic readiness for battle when it is pitted against God's Chosen People,[3] a lesson which derives its relevance to any audience of twelfth-century knights from the fact that these knights, once they had taken a vow to join a crusade, qualified for membership of the new *populus Dei*, the crusading army.[4] Furthermore, the stylistic contrast between the subjective fears attributed to the Israelites and the objective *epische Vorausdeutung* which is once employed in this corresponding scene with the Egyptians is a skilful means of showing that the Jews' *zwîvel* was quite unfounded, whereas the fears of their enemies are confirmed by a defeat made inevitable because they have taken up arms against God's people. All these eight scenes not merely bring into relief the military implications of the subject-matter, as the Millstatt author sees it, they also depict in different ways the relevance of this military interpretation to an audience of knights in the period between the First and Second Crusades. If, by contrast, expansionary matter of a non-military nature is introduced into no more than

[1] See pp. 97 f.   [2] See p. 100.
[3] See pp. 102 f.   [4] See pp. 229 ff.

374

two scenes, this is a clear indication that, however much the author was prepared to see his Hebrews in courtly terms, it is the military aspect which lies at the heart of the epic expansion which these new scenes represent.

It is also evident, quite apart from these scenes where formal expansion has taken place, that there are other stylistic features of the *Millstätter Exodus* which the author has introduced because he judged them to be best fitted to conveying the sense of his interpretation of his subject-matter. We saw that the reduction of the frequency with which, in the biblical account, God intervened by means of prophecies, commands or a strict control exercised over Pharaoh's freedom of action meant that the German epic revealed a greater continuity of the narrative on the plane of human activity.[1] To this alteration, brought about by formal means, there corresponds the fact that the Millstatt work differs radically from such a work as the *Vorauer Bücher Mosis* by almost entirely excluding allegorical exegesis.[2] Whereas the events of the exodus, as recounted in the Vorau text, are only very haltingly allowed to develop on the plane of human time because they are constantly subjected to exegetical interruptions which interpret these events in the light of their timeless importance, these events retain their narrative independence in the Millstatt version. This exclusion of exegetical interpolations with their timeless associations thus constitutes a parallel to the manner in which God's interventions are considerably reduced—the reason for both features is that an author concerned to demonstrate the task which befalls the knights as crusaders called upon by God to assist in the liberation of the Holy Land must necessarily grant a role to human activity and to the contribution which it is privileged to make towards the realisation of God's plans for salvation.

We also saw that this increased emphasis on human activity nowhere amounted to a total exclusion of God, but instead implied that, whilst God stayed more in the background in ultimate control of events, it was the human actors in the foreground

[1] See pp. 34 f.   [2] See pp. 114 ff.

on whom our attention was largely focused. If this position is changed towards the end of the work in the description of the exodus and passage of the Red Sea, so that God now steps more evidently into the foreground, this is because events now rapidly approach the climax in which God's loyalty and omnipotence are to be given their final demonstration. The approach towards this climax entails an increased tension which means that, however important the human role had been, it is now God who is to intervene to bring events to their preordained conclusion. This is a formal device which agrees with the other methods (such as *epische Vorausdeutung* or the depiction of several preparatory stages to usher in the decisive event) employed by the author to equip his work with a constant tension[1]—a tension which is latent in the subject-matter as he has chosen to treat it, for his restriction of his theme to the first fifteen chapters of Exodus makes of the passage of the Red Sea a climax to which all the other events are necessarily subordinated. By using various formal devices to convey a sense of tension the German author has shown that he is fully aware that this restriction of subject-matter has brought with it its own formal demands.

This emphasis on the scene by the Red Sea in which the exodus is accomplished is fully reconcilable with what we have learnt of the author's crusading interpretation of the biblical narrative since the actual crossing of the sea on the way to the Holy Land was one of the details which allowed the medieval crusaders to see in the biblical Exodus a prefiguration of their own undertaking.[2] At the same time, we saw in chapter I that it is this same feature of crossing water which explains the equation between Exodus and the Christian rite of baptism[3] and furthermore that it is this identical scene, in which the exodus is finally achieved, to which repeated references are made in the Easter liturgy.[4] We are confronted, therefore, with three rival interpretations of the historical events of Exodus (with reference to

---

[1] See also p. 44, n. 2 for further references to the employment of tension as a formal device.   [2] See pp. 260 ff.
[3] See pp. 8 ff.   [4] See pp. 15 ff.

baptism, to the Easter liturgy and to the crusades), so that our problem is to determine the relationship between these three possibilities. In other words, if the Millstatt author's formal expansion of his narrative to epic proportions as well as other facets of his style are determined by the way in which he interprets his subject-matter, our concluding task must be to adjudicate between these three interpretations, each of which has left traces in his work.

We may approach this problem by recalling the traditional acknowledgement of a fourfold meaning in the Bible which in chapter I we saw illustrated in the example given by Guibertus of Nogent with his interpretation of the term Jerusalem. The example of this definition does no more, however, than suggest that it is also possible to accept a manifold reading of *Exodus*. To demonstrate that this is probable we have to go further and show what the various readings have in common which made it possible for the Millstatt author to combine them in the one work. I propose therefore to discuss the features which are shared by the two interpretations which we considered in chapter I (the baptismal and the paschal interpretations) and then to consider what the connections are between each of these interpretations and the reading of the German *Exodus* in terms of the crusades.

We need not be surprised that the *Millstätter Exodus* should contain traces of the baptismal and paschal interpretations of Exodus, for these two readings have certain features in common which could account for their being incorporated in the same work. In the first place, they share a common type and are indirectly linked with one another by this alone: the exodus of the Israelites and their passage of the Red Sea are a prefiguration not merely of Christian baptism, but also of the redemption achieved by Christ and celebrated in the Easter liturgy.[1] More important than this formal link is the common meaning shared by the

---

[1] G. Mathew, *Byzantine Aesthetics*, pp. 79 f., gives some interesting examples of this multiple relevance of Old Testament prefigurations from the mosaic scenes in the sanctuary of San Vitale at Ravenna.

baptismal and paschal interpretations by virtue of the common type to which they both refer. The rite of baptism is the means whereby the convert is granted an escape from the trammels of sin and access to a new life, whereas what the Easter liturgy celebrates is precisely the same divine gift presented to mankind at large by the sacrifice of Christ. Baptism and the Easter liturgy differ from one another in the scope of their operation, since baptism offers redemption to the individual convert whereas the theme of the Easter liturgy is the gift of universal redemption. On the other hand, what they both have in common, Christ's gift of salvation, is of greater importance than any difference in scope, and it is this common function, rather than any arbitrary result of typological interpretation, which explains why it is that these two themes of salvation should refer to the exodus as the type which they both share.

It is this common function which also accounts for the manner in which the rite of baptism should also play a central role in the liturgy of Holy Saturday: the offer of salvation for the individual is fittingly given its liturgical setting in the celebration of the salvation given by Christ to the whole of mankind. We have seen that it was in the Easter vigil that neophytes were baptised and that Easter was accordingly a favoured time for the reception of new converts.[1] This is amply reflected in the liturgy of Holy Saturday itself. Thus, the lessons with which the vigil is opened were originally intended as a final preparation of the catechumens for baptism and the eucharist, and it is immediately after the last lesson that the baptismal water is consecrated, a ceremony which lays particular stress on the rebirth and the new life won for all men by Christ,[2] but here tangibly given to the neophytes in the sacrament of baptism. Significantly, the fourth of these lessons is taken from Exod. 14. 24 ff. and contains the account of the annihilation of the Egyptians and the safe passage of the Israelites

[1] See p. 10.
[2] On this see such words spoken by the priest as: 'fontemque baptismatis aperis toto orbe terrarum gentibus innovandis' or: '...in novam renata creaturam, progenies caelestis emergat' or: 'Totamque hujus aquae substantiam regenerandi fecundet effectu.'

out of bondage: in this extract Christ is understood typologically as prefigured in Moses and the water of baptism in that of the Red Sea in which the tyrant Pharaoh (the Devil) and the Egyptians (our sins) are finally destroyed.

Confirmation of this threefold equation between the exodus, the celebration of Easter and the rite of baptism is not difficult to find. Daniélou has categorically emphasised the intimate connection between these three: 'L'initiation chrétienne avait lieu dans la nuit du samedi saint au dimanche de Pâque. Cette circonstance la mettait directement en relation avec la mort et la résurrection du Christ. Mais la résurrection du Christ s'était déjà inscrite dans le cadre de la fête juive de la Pâque. On comprend dès lors que la liturgie de l'initiation soit toute chargée de réminiscences de la Sortie d'Égypte.'[1] This is borne out by the instruction which St Augustine recommends to candidates for baptism: for him the passion of Christ was prefigured by the blood with which the Israelites were to mark their doors on the night of the Passover and it is also commemorated in the sign of the cross made on the neophyte's forehead at baptism.[2] In this St Augustine is doing no more than follow the example given by Justin.[3] For Justin there is a clear parallel between the Jews saved by the Blood of the Passover lamb and Christians redeemed by the blood of Christ, so that when he refers to the sign (σημεῖον) on the door of the Jewish household he implies that it is the sign on the forehead of the Christian, the *sphragis* which he received at baptism, which is the mark of his salvation. A similar juxtaposition of Exodus, Easter and baptism occurs in the vernacular—in the passage of his *Weltchronik* where Rudolf von Ems gives

---

[1] *Bible et liturgie*, p. 220.

[2] *De catechizandis rudibus*, I, 20 (*MPL*, 40, 335): 'Apertius autem Christi passio in illo populo figurata est, cum jussi sunt ovem occidere et manducare, et de sanguine ejus postes suos signare, et hoc celebrare omni anno, et appellare Pascha Domini. Manifestissime quippe prophetia de Domino Jesu Christo dicit, quia tanquam ovis ad immolandum ductus est (Isa. 53. 7). Cujus passionis et crucis signo in fronte hodie tanquam in poste signandus es, omnesque Christiani signantur.' Cf. Daniélou, *op. cit.* p. 227.

[3] *Dialogus* iii (*MPG*, 6, 732 c f.); Daniélou, *op. cit.* p. 223.

The Millstätter Exodus

a typological interpretation of the hymn of thanksgiving sung by the Israelites after their delivery:

> 11007   nach cristenlicher e gebote
> begat noch dú christenheit
> die gewonheit nah der underschiet,
> alse nu bi dirre frist
> elich und gewonlich ist
> inden ostrlichen tagen:
> so wir getŏfet unde getwagen
> werden von unsirn súnden
> in dez heiligen tuofis undin.[1]

Such evidence, as well as the role of baptism in the liturgy of Holy Saturday, suggests that the Millstatt author's allusions to baptism and to the Easter liturgy in his interpretation of Exodus do not constitute a contradiction and that he was following a typological tradition in introducing both kinds of allusion into his work. Yet the German author does not attribute equal importance to both these interpretations: on the contrary, the baptismal references are of less importance for him than the paschal allusions. This is made clear by the passage in which he describes God's instructions to Moses on the future celebration of the Passover, for, although both Christian baptism (as the antitype of circumcision) and the celebration of Easter (as the antitype of the Passover) are alluded to in his text, baptism is regarded as the condition upon which attendance at the celebration of Easter is to be permitted.[2] If baptism is thus subordinated

---

[1] Quoted by R. A. Wisbey, *ZfdA*, LXXXVI, 297. The connection between the biblical hymn of thanksgiving and the practice at Easter (*inden ostrlichen tagen*) is best explained by the way in which the fourth lesson of the liturgy of Holy Saturday is followed by a tractus made up of Exod. 15. 1–3, i.e. the commencement of the Israelites' song of praise.

[2] This is shown by the way in which the references to circumcision in the passage dealing with the celebration of Passover are all phrased as a condition which has to be fulfilled if attendance at the Passover feast is to be at all possible. Vv. 2805 f. thus begin with an emphatically conditional *ob* and say that the lamb may only be consumed by the circumcised ('. . . ob er sich besnîde | daz er daz lamp nemîde'); vv. 2820 ff., again, make of circumcision a condition for access to the sacrificial table ('welle er sich besnîden, | den nesolt dû nieht vermîden, | sô

to the Easter liturgy in the Millstatt work, this is no more than we should expect from what we have seen of the relationship between the two: the potential redemption of one convert, represented by his baptism, is after all on quite a different level from the universal redemption of mankind celebrated at Easter, and the liturgy of Holy Saturday makes this difference clear by celebrating the baptism of neophytes only as a part of its celebration of the Easter events. Nonetheless, even though the Millstatt author's references to the baptismal interpretation may be less important than his allusions to the paschal reading, this does not mean that the two cannot be reconciled with each other, for their unity is guaranteed by the way in which the one (baptism) forms part of the other (Easter liturgy). Our problem is to decide how these two interpretations, both reconcilable with one another, can in their turn be reconciled with the crusading reading of the *Millstätter Exodus*.

Before considering the similarities of detail between baptism or the Easter liturgy and crusading thought we may best review the general possibilities of a connection between them. In what follows I shall base myself mainly on the evidence collected by J. Daniélou,[1] even though I make a selective use of his material, ignoring numerous strands in the complex history of liturgical symbolism and concentrating only on those which suggest how it is that the liturgical rites of baptism and Easter could have made an appeal to an author concerned with interpreting his material in the light of crusading experience.

A first explanation is provided by the frequency with which both the baptismal rite and the celebration of Easter were interpreted in terms of their military symbolism. This is already clear

mage er gewisse | gên ze vrôn tiske'); and vv. 2829 f. similarly stress that the Israelites may only associate (for the purposes of the sacrificial ceremony or for any other reason) with one who has been circumcised ('swer aue sich nelât besnîden | den solt dû gar vermîden'). However vital this condition may be, it clearly derives its importance from the ceremony to which it provides access, so that it is the Passover, in its typological reference to Easter, which lies at the centre of this passage.

[1] *Bible et liturgie.*

in the period of Lent when the candidate for baptism is prepared for his admission into the Church. Daniélou comments on an early interpretation of the initial interrogation to which the would-be candidate must submit[1] by saying that this shows right at the start one of the themes of baptismal theology: the escape of the baptizand from his servitude to the Devil in the form of a conflict with Satan.[2] This is also true of the daily exorcisms which the catechumen is to undergo during Lent, for these can be interpreted as stages in the conflict whereby the soul of the candidate is finally freed from the clutches of the Devil.[3] This attitude is expressed with symbolic force in the ceremony of baptism itself. The ceremonial anointing of the neophyte's body with oil is interpreted, in the light of the athlete's[4] oiling of his body before a contest, as a preparation for the struggle which he is about to undertake under the guidance of Christ[5]—a struggle which refers not merely to the future course of his life as a Christian, but particularly to his descent into the water of the baptistery, conceived as the waters where dwells the dragon of death over whom Christ first gained victory in His baptism in the Jordan.[6] Military implications are also present in the *sphragis*, a word meaning literally seal or sign and used of the sign of the cross made on the forehead of the baptizand, but of such symbolic importance that it could designate the whole baptismal ceremony.[7] Amongst the numerous interpretations which such a rite suggests we may single out, first, the fact that the *sphragis*, as the proprietary mark used by shepherds to brand their flock, was regarded as a mark of ownership,[8] and also as a guarantee and

---

[1] Theodore of Mopsuestia, *Catechetical Homilies* (ed. R. Tonneau, *Studi e Testi*, CXLV, 1949), XII, 18 (p. 351), 19 (p. 353) and 24 (p. 361). Cf. Daniélou, *op. cit.* p. 31.

[2] *Op. cit.* p. 32.

[3] Cf. Cyrillus of Jerusalem, *MPG*, 33, 359 A ff.; Daniélou, *op. cit.* p. 35.

[4] The Latin *athleta* was of course used not merely of the athlete but also, in the Christian context, of the warrior of God.

[5] Dionysius Areopagita, *MPG*, 3, 402 c f.; Daniélou, *op. cit.* p. 58.

[6] Cyrillus of Jerusalem, *MPG*, 33, 441 A ff.; Daniélou, *op. cit.* p. 59.

[7] Daniélou, *Bible et liturgie*, p. 77, n. 1.

[8] Cyrillus of Jerusalem, *MPG*, 33, 371 B; Daniélou, *op. cit.* p. 79.

protection against thieves.[1] This suggestion of protection against
the dangers which await the Christian is part of the general interpretation of baptism as a conflict with the Devil, but this is even
more evident with the second reading of the *sphragis*, for it was
also taken as representing the enrolment of the new Christian
in the army of Christ,[2] just as the *signaculum* was employed in
the Roman army as a form of tattoo to mark the recruit's enrolment under a particular general. In the light of this symbolism
the inscription of the candidate's name in the registers of the
Church at the beginning of Lent can also be read as his first
step in joining the campaign conducted by Christ.[3] Similarly,
the baptismal oath can be associated with the *sacramentum* as a
military term[4] and thus come to denote the neophyte's military
service of Christ. It is because of this that the *sphragis*, the mark
of the cross which defeated Satan, renders the Christian an object
of fear to the Devil[5] and assures the neophyte that he will emerge
victorious from his conflict. His marking with the cross in the
vigil of Holy Saturday is a guarantee of his final victory in the
conflict which awaits him and a direct reference to the victory
over Satan gained by Christ in the Easter period to which the
baptismal rite so significantly belongs. We may also adduce the
fact stressed by Daniélou that some details of the baptismal ceremony are best explained by reference to the martyrs of the Church
(e.g. the need for the baptizand to engage in conflict with Satan
if he is to attain to Christ[6] or the clothing of the freshly baptised
convert in white tunics.[7]) This is in full agreement with the fact
that the last *lectio* of the twelve in the Holy Saturday service
should come from Dan. 3. 1 ff. and be devoted to the victorious
martyrdom of the three young men in the fiery furnace. In this,
the last lesson before their baptism, the catechumens are instructed

[1] Gregory of Nazianzen, *MPG*, 36, 364 A (σφραγῖδα δὲ, ὡς συντήρησιν, καὶ
τῆς δεσποτείας σημείωσιν) and 378 A; Daniélou, *op. cit.* pp. 79 f.
[2] Cyrillus of Jerusalem, *MPG*, 33, 427 B; Daniélou, *op. cit.* p. 82.
[3] Cyrillus of Jerusalem, *MPG*, 33, 333 A ('Ονοματογραφία τέως ὑμῖν γέγονε,
καὶ στρατείας κλῆσις); Daniélou, *op. cit.* p. 81.
[4] F. J. Dölger, *Die Sonne der Gerechtigkeit und der Schwarze*, pp. 110 ff.
[5] Daniélou, *op. cit.* pp. 83 f.   [6] Daniélou, *op. cit.* pp. 35 f.
[7] Daniélou, *op. cit.* pp. 73 f.

on the heroism of the martyrs and on what is expected of them as *milites Christi*.[1]

A second thread in the interpretation of baptism and Easter is of equal importance for us, for it shows how closely these two ceremonies were associated with the rejection of idolatry and hence with the defeat of paganism. Daniélou has pointed out that the baptismal formula in which Satan is renounced is connected with the rejection of idolatry[2] (so that *pompa diaboli* is meant as the worship of idols)[3] and could therefore only have appeared in the context of a Gentile Christianity. The reference in some liturgies to Satan and his angels is interpreted by Theodore of Mopsuestia as referring to those men, followers of Satan, who by their secular pursuits spread the error of paganism and increase idolatry.[4] The same is true of the exodus, for when Isaiah (51. 9 f.) refers to the crossing of the Red Sea he sees this as a victory of God over Rahab, the dragon of the sea that signifies Egypt[5] or more particularly, if we associate this with Exod. 12. 12,[6] Egyptian idolatry and worship of false gods. In similar terms, the column of fire which accompanied the Israelites can be interpreted as Christ in His role as *lux mundi*,[7] dissipating the shadows of paganism, a detail which recurs both in the use of a word meaning 'illumination' (φωτίσμος) to designate baptism and in the ritual with the candles in the Easter vigil. This light symbolism can also be applied to the fact that Easter falls on the spring equinox and

[1] The convincing suggestion has been made by J. W. Bright ('The relation of the Caedmonian *Exodus* to the liturgy', *MLN*, xxvii, 101) that it is this same liturgical fact which explains why the OE *Exodus* should be followed immediately in its MS by the OE *Daniel*.   [2] Daniélou, *Bible et liturgie*, p. 39.

[3] Cf. Tertullian, *De corona* 13 (*MPL*, 2, 97 A): 'Haec enim erant pompae diaboli... : et in omnibus istis idolatria.'

[4] Theodore of Mopsuestia, *Catechetical Homilies*, xiii, 8 (pp. 379 and 381).

[5] Daniélou, *op. cit.* p. 121.

[6] The fact that the Millstatt author translates this passage of his source (vv. 2537 ff.) without placing any undue emphasis on it need not contradict the suggestion that he found support for his crusading interpretation in the liturgy of baptism and Easter. We have seen repeatedly how tactful he is in allowing his interpretation to be no more than implicit in his material.

[7] Cf. Ambrose, *De sacramentis* I, 22 (*MPL*, 16, 424 A): 'Columna lucis quid est, nisi Christus Dominus, qui tenebras infidelitatis depulit, lucem veritatis et gratiae spiritalis affectibus infudit humanis?'; Daniélou, *Bible et liturgie*, p. 128.

coincides with a full moon, since this suggests the triumph of light over the darkness of idolatry.[1] The recurrence of Easter as a spring festival can be used to give force to a cosmic symbolism, as when Gaudentius of Brescia argues that Christ established Easter as a spring festival so that, as the *sol justitiae*, He might dissipate the darkness of Judaism and the ice of paganism (these he associates with autumn and with winter) before the summer heat of the Last Judgement.[2] Finally, the fact that the paschal lamb was slaughtered towards evening is interpreted as suggesting that Christ had chosen, even at a late hour when the present age was approaching its end, to recruit followers from the Gentiles, from those nations which had not yet heard His message.[3] Exodus symbolism, informing both the baptismal rite and the ceremony of Holy Saturday, is therefore capable of demonstrating both the extension of the Christian revelation to peoples who have not yet heard of it and also, as a complement to this, the defeat of paganism and of the false gods. It is this which has led one modern commentator on liturgical symbolism to say: 'Encore un peu de temps, et les autels des faux dieux seront renversés de toutes parts; encore un peu de temps et l'homme, régénéré par la prédication évangélique, reconnaîtra son créateur et abjurera les infâmes idoles.'[4]

If we combine these two strands in the liturgy of baptism and of Easter which we have considered only separately it is clear that together they suggest that service of Christ is to be regarded by the neophyte as a form of spiritual warfare which he is to wage against the Devil and his followers and that he is to be engaged in this warfare not merely throughout the course of his life as a Christian, but also in the decisive action which he is soon to

[1] Gregory of Nyssa, *MPG*, 46, 1027 c f.; Daniélou, *op. cit.* p. 403.
[2] *MPL*, 20, 843 c f.: 'Opportuno tempore Dominus Jesus beatissimus festivitatem Pascha voluit celebrari, post autumni nebulam, post horrorem hiemis, ante aestatis ardorem. Oportebat enim Solem Justitiae Christum, et Judaeorum caliginem, et rigorem Gentilium, ante ardorem futuri judicii, placido Resurrectionis suae lumine dimovere, cunctaque in statum tranquilli primordii revocare, quae fuerant velamine tetro confusa ab illo principe tenebrarum.'
[3] Cyrillus of Alexandria, *MPG*, 69, 423 A f.; Daniélou, *op. cit.* pp. 397 f.
[4] P. Guéranger, 'Le temps pascal' (in *L'année liturgique*, vol. VII), I, 262.

accomplish: in descending into and passing through the waters of the baptistery as did Israel through those of the Red Sea. It is important to stress that this warfare against the Devil, suggesting the possible need for martyrdom and the connection between this warfare and paganism, is essentially spiritual and hence metaphorical. What is involved is a psychomachia against the army of Satan, a readiness for passive martyrdom in the service of Christ and an extension of the gospel message to the Gentiles without any hint of physical force. The implications of the baptismal and Easter liturgies are therefore quite distinct from the idea of crusading warfare with its employment of the physical sword against human opponents to compel them to adopt Christianity. Yet it only needs the addition of a literal, physical reading to this spiritual warfare to make these implications of the liturgy of baptism and Easter immediately relevant to crusading needs. Service of Christ will now be seen both as a psychomachia waged against the Devil and as a physical war conducted against the human followers of Satan, martyrdom will be understood as death in the service of Christ both peacefully and on the battlefield, whilst the propagation of Christianity will be equated both with the missionary preaching of the word of God and with the attempt to extend the frontiers of Christendom with the sword. Since we have repeatedly seen that precisely this literal interpretation of what had been earlier understood only as a spiritual metaphor is an essential characteristic of the crusading ideal, we need not be surprised to find an author of the twelfth century able to reconcile the theme of Exodus (with its baptismal and paschal implications) with his crusading preoccupations. Once the ideal of *militia Christi* came to be conceived physically as well as spiritually the implications of the liturgy of baptism and Easter would acquire a wholly new significance.

After this joint survey of the manner in which baptism and Easter could both come to be relevant to the author of a crusading work we must now consider separately the bearing of each of these liturgical rites on an epic concerned to illustrate Exodus in this manner. In turning first to the connection between baptism

General conclusions

and the crusading theme of the *Millstätter Exodus* we may best commence with the particular theme of the psychomachia. We saw in chapter I that this theme was commonly treated with reference to the book of Exodus[1] and that it was this interpretation which allowed the association of baptism with the passage of the Red Sea.[2] In addition to this, the theme of psychomachia is also fundamental to the crusading interpretation of Exodus—not in the sense that the Millstatt author may have conceived the clash between the Israelites and the Egyptians exclusively as a spiritual warfare between good and evil, but in the sense that he depicts this encounter in military terms which are meant to be both spiritual and physical. In other words, although there may be traces in his work of a psychomachia, he goes beyond this by also making it clear that the struggle is physical as well as spiritual. This depiction of a psychomachia in physical terms represents a close parallel to what Erdmann has shown to be a physical reinterpretation of spiritual warfare as a result of the crusading movement.[3] Whereas the term *miles Dei* had earlier designated a Christian engaged in spiritual conflict with evil and had been used in an exclusively metaphorical sense, it acquired under the impetus of the crusades a further sense as a term for the crusader engaged in conflict with the pagans. This by no means implies that a spiritual meaning has now been replaced by a physical one, for the term *miles Dei* can still continue to be employed as a metaphor (applied, for example, to the spiritual warfare of the monk) and, in any case, the crusader is felt to be waging a double kind of warfare (physically against his Saracen opponents and spiritually against the evil of unbelief which they represent),[4] so that even in the crusading context the term *miles Dei* still retains its spiritual function, but has enriched it by adding to it a physical connotation. This is also the position with the theme of psychomachia in the Millstatt work for, in addition to the suggestion of spiritual conflict between the Israelites and the Egyptians, the author

[1] See pp. 11 ff.   [2] See pp. 8f.
[3] *Die Entstehung des Kreuzzugsgedankens*, pp. 185 ff. See also above, pp. 294 f.
[4] See below, pp. 393 ff.

makes it clear that their encounter was also a physical one. It is this double nature of warfare, spiritual as well as physical, which makes of the *Millstätter Exodus* a work profoundly influenced by crusading thought.

There can be little doubt that the encounter between the Israelites and Egyptians, frequently depicted in military terms, was meant to be understood in a physical sense. This can best be shown by two considerations. In the first place, if our typological interpretation is correct this must mean that the author was persuaded of the literal and historical reality of the events he described (whatever further meanings his typological method may then have added to these events), for typology means the understanding of past events, objects or persons as prefigurations of other, future phenomena. Typology depends, as St Augustine maintained,[1] on the fact that the past event, object or person is believed to be a historical reality and not just an abstract truth.[2] If this is so, then the fact that the Millstatt author, using the typological method in application to the events of Exodus, described these events in military terms can only mean that these military events possessed a historical reality for him. The military implications of his narrative are part of the historical truth which he is concerned to convey, so that we are not justified in reading his epic, as we are the work of Prudentius, *exclusively* as a psychomachia. Whatever further significance the Millstatt work may possess, we cannot question that the events it sketches in military terms were meant to be regarded as real historical events and their military implications as equally real.

[1] See above, p. 129.

[2] Cf. the distinction made by J. Chydenius, *The Typological Problem in Dante*, p. 24, between the allegorical method of Philo of Alexandria and Christian typology: 'To the Platonic view, earthly existence is only a likeness and the historical truth of Scripture a matter of indifference, as it only serves to express the real truth that exists in the world of ideas. To the Christian view, earthly existence is an incontestable reality, and what Scripture gives as history is historically true, even if it is also a type of the higher reality that exists in the world of eternity.' For a different formulation of the same idea see C. S. Lewis, *The Allegory of Love*, p. 225: 'When you accepted the exodus of Israel from Egypt as a type of the soul's escape from sin, you did not on that account abolish the exodus as a historical event.'

General conclusions

This argument as to the physical nature of the warfare which the German author introduces can be confirmed by taking our earlier analysis of the military and heroic expressions used in the epic one stage further. We saw that such an explicitly crusading term as *gotes rîtere* (unmistakably employed to describe a physical attack) was used only of insects,[1] not of the Hebrews, and that in other scenes where military attacks are described (without any particular reference to the crusades) it is again only the insects which are so depicted. As regards some of the conventional military terms of heroic vocabulary we noticed a contrast between their application to the insects or to the Egyptians and the marked manner in which the author refrained from using them of the Israelites.[2] Furthermore, although the Israelites are described as warriors this remains only an illustration of martial splendour and we are not shown them engaged in military action.[3] Where this is hinted at, it is confined to a reference to a past event or to a future encounter which is not described in the present as taking place before us. Such a deliberate restriction, whereby a work with military implications yet stops short of explicitly describing the Hebrews as waging war, means that the Millstatt author has hesitated to illustrate in his narrative all the implications of the positive role which he is prepared to concede to the idea of warfare waged on behalf of God. Whereas in *Ruodlieb* or in the *Wiener Genesis* the theme of warfare was introduced only so that it might be subjected to a Christian criticism,[4] with the *Millstätter Exodus* a much less negative attitude towards this theme[5] is revealed, even though the author hesitated to exploit every possibility which this innovation offered him.

[1] See pp. 273 ff.   [2] See pp. 158 ff.

[3] See pp. 92 ff. The possible objection that Exod. 1–15 nowhere depicts an armed encounter between Israelites and Egyptians can best be answered when we come to discuss the probable reasons why the German author chose to take his version of Exodus no further than chapter 15. See below, pp. 432 ff.

[4] On *Ruodlieb* see Braun, *Studien zum Ruodlieb*, pp. 28 ff.; on the *Wiener Genesis* see Beyschlag, *Die Wiener Genesis*, pp. 54 ff. (especially p. 59).

[5] Thus, the Millstatt author nowhere introduces any of the explicit criticisms of warfare which characterise *Ruodlieb* and the *Wiener Genesis* and if he criticises the Egyptian army this is not because of their martial qualities, but because of

It is precisely the hesitancy of the Millstatt author on this point which tells us something about the way in which he wished his military innovations to be understood. If he is responsible for these innovations, but stops short of exploiting every opportunity they offered to show the Israelites engaged in warfare this can only mean that the passages of Exodus which contain warlike scenes (for example, chapter 17 with the battle against the Amalechites or even such brief references as 13. 18 or 14. 6 f.) were understood by the German author in terms of physical conflict. If he had regarded these passages in any other way, as illustrating no more than a spiritual warfare between good and evil, then he would have had as little objection as Prudentius to attributing heroic deeds to *both* parties of the conflict and to describing them *both* with conventional heroic terms, since these deeds and terms would have been meant only metaphorically. Instead, the Millstatt author conceives warfare in literal terms as a physical form of conflict waged with visible and tangible weapons. Since we saw that it was he who introduced and emphasised the role of warfare in his treatment of Exodus we must conclude that it was his conviction that the events of Exodus were to be interpreted in terms of physical warfare which impelled him to grant such importance to the military theme. This is a conclusion which confirms our crusading interpretation of the Millstatt work and which makes it improbable that the author meant his account to be interpreted exclusively as a psychomachia.

This does not mean that his work contains no trace of a psychomachia, but only that it is characterised by the double function it attributes to warfare, physical as well as spiritual. The spiritual aspect of this conflict is admittedly not revealed by the use of personifications, as with Prudentius, but instead by the suggestion that the physical encounter between the Israelites and the Egyptians is part of a metaphysical conflict between God and the

their arrogant confidence in their military strength. Finally, when the Israelite warriors are criticised for their *zwîvel* it is significantly in a military setting that this happens, so that their shortcoming is shown to be, at least in part, a military deficiency.

390

Devil. We have seen how the author emphasises the manner in which Moses and, through him, the Hebrews act as the agents of God,[1] helping to fulfil His plan of salvation by their obedience to His commands, whereas Pharaoh is shown in his stubborn resistance to God as acting in concert with the Devil.[2] This metaphysical perspective revealed by the German author is in full accord with the conventional typological interpretation of Moses as a type of Christ and Pharaoh as signifying Satan, but the fact that the author makes use of the typological method is important in another respect. The presence of typology in this work means that the encounter between the Israelites and the Egyptians possesses, in addition to its historical reality, a metahistorical significance as a prefiguration of such future antitypes as the redemption achieved by Christ, the rite of baptism and the medieval crusades. Typology sees in a historical fact a timeless significance, not just in the simple sense of an *exemplum* of lasting validity, but more profoundly in the sense that the historical fact is part of God's process of salvation and is destined later to find fulfilment. It is the author's use of the typological method and not any deficiency in historical awareness which explains the conjunction of time with timelessness throughout this work[3] and which also suggests that the events he narrates possess, in addition to their physical and historical reality, a spiritual and timeless reality. This also explains another detail by means of which the German author stresses the spiritual nature of the encounter between the Israelites and the Egyptians: the fact that God's people are shown in their humility and are contrasted with the arrogant self-confidence of their enemies.[4] The significance of this for any spiritual interpretation is that the pride of the Egyptians in pitting themselves against God's people is the same sin as that shown by Satan in his first rebellion against God. In addition, if we are to believe what is reported of the attempts made by Urban II to wean the knights of his day from secular

[1] See pp. 133 f.   [2] See p. 137, n. 1.
[3] On these two features of the work see pp. 122 ff.
[4] See p. 169.

391

knighthood to the crusading ideal,[1] we must recognise that this same sin of pride was regarded by the Church as the characteristic sin of secular knighthood. What this means is not simply that the sin of pride converts the Egyptians into liegemen of Satan, but more significantly that the medieval knight, as long as he remains wedded to a secular ideal and has not embraced the crusading ideal, is similarly to be found in the ranks of the Egyptians and of Satan. The import of the spiritual aspect of this warfare as delineated by the Millstatt author is that the knighthood of his day has been granted the opportunity, by taking the crusader's vow, of escaping from the ranks of an army destined to destruction through its service of Satan and of joining an army which, like that of the Israelites, is assured of victory through the loyalty of the God who leads it.[2] Even when he has become a member of this army led by God, however, the knight is still confronted with the duty of avoiding such other sins as the *zwível* of the Israelites, so that what this depiction of the Exodus events as a spiritual war illustrates is the *bellum intestinum* of the knighthood whom the author is addressing: the crucial struggle to avoid the sin of arrogance and the perdition this entails by abandoning secular warfare in favour of the crusading ideal, and also the constant fight to escape from the *zwível* which overcame the Israelites and the rejection by God which this occasioned.

[1] Cf. the words of Baldricus in his *Historia Hierosolimitana* (*RHC*, IV, 14F), reputedly used by the Pope in his address to the knights assembled at Clermont: 'Vos accincti cingulo militiae, magno superbitis supercilio; fratres vestros laniatis, atque inter vos dissecamini. Non est haec militia Christi, quae discerpit ovile Redemptoris.' St Bernard talks in similar terms of the secular knighthood in his *De laude novae militiae*: 'Et ira tibi aut superbia dominante, frustra gloriaris de homine superato' (*MPL*, 182, 923 A). Cf. also *ibid.* 923 D: 'Non sane inter vos aliud bella movet, litesque suscitat, nisi aut irrationabilis iracundiae motus, aut inanis gloriae appetitus, aut terrenae qualiscunque possessionis cupiditas.'

[2] Cf. Baldricus (*RHC*, IV, 14G): 'Certe via ista pessima est, quoniam omnino a Deo remota est. Porro si vultis animabus vestris consuli, aut istiusmodi militiae cingulum quantocius deponite, aut Christi milites audacter procedite, et ad defendendam Orientalem Ecclesiam velocius concurrite.' On the secular knight's service of the Devil see the words with which St Bernard introduces his description of the virtues of the *milites Christi*: 'Sed jam ad imitationem seu ad confusionem nostrorum militum, non plane Deo, sed diabolo militantium...' (*MPL*, 182, 925 D).

General conclusions

The spiritual warfare of the *Millstätter Exodus* is thus a struggle within the hearts of the knights to whom the author makes his appeal, a struggle to win them for a new ideal of knighthood which will assure them of salvation rather than perdition.

The role attributed to warfare by the Millstatt author is therefore a double one: he sees it in its physical sense, but also interprets it as a spiritual encounter. It is precisely here that his conception comes close to that of crusading thought since the crusaders were commonly seen as engaged in a double form of warfare which set them apart from the purely spiritual warfare of the monastic way of life and from the exclusively physical warfare of the secular knighthood. Although this double function is characteristic of the crusading movement at large, it is to St Bernard that we owe the most explicit formulation of this situation, so that in this case it will be more helpful to turn to him as testimony that the crusades, like the encounter between Jews and Egyptians in the *Exodus*, were imagined as a double form of warfare. St Bernard sees the crusading ideal best illustrated in the order of the Knights Templar because they demonstrate the double role assigned to the crusading knight. It is for the Templars that he writes the *De laude novae militiae*[1] and dwells at length on the unheard-of novelty of this particular type of knighthood. Its novelty lies in this double function of its warfare, so that the knights of this order are regularly engaged in a conflict against their human, pagan enemies and also against spiritual foes: 'Novum, inquam, militiae genus, et saeculis inexpertum: qua gemino pariter conflictu infatigabiliter decertatur, tum adversus carnem et sanguinem, tum contra spiritualia nequitiae in coelestibus.'[2] Such a knight is afforded a double protection against his enemies, for his body is protected by iron and his soul by the breastplate of faith: 'Impavidus profecto miles, et omni ex parte securus, qui ut corpus ferri, sic animum fidei lorica induitur.'[3] This double breastplate is the reason why he need fear none of his enemies, neither man nor the Devil: 'Utrisque

[1] *MPL*, 182, 921 ff. [2] *MPL*, 182, 921 c.
[3] *Ibid.* 922 A.

393

nimirum munitus armis, nec daemonem timet, nec hominem.'[1] It is this double warfare, separating not only the Templars but all crusaders from the onesided type of warfare waged by the monk or by the secular knight,[2] which causes St Bernard to wonder which name, that of monk or that of knight, he may more fittingly apply to this new phenomenon which, by combining what had previously been regarded as separate, appears to have no parallel to which he might turn in his search for an adequate term to describe it: 'Ita denique miro quodam ac singulari modo cernuntur et agnis mitiores, et leonibus ferociores, ut pene dubitem quid potius censeam appellandos, monachos videlicet, an milites: nisi quod utrumque forsan congruentius nominarim, quibus neutrum deesse cognoscitur, nec monachi mansuetudo, nec militis fortitudo.'[3] That this profound conviction of a double military function is not confined to St Bernard (or to the Templars alone) may best be shown by the way in which, as Wentzlaff-Eggebert has demonstrated, the author of the *Rolandslied* characterises his crusading knights in monastic terms, applying to them the various virtues enjoined upon the monk by the Benedictine Rule.[4] Similarly, Gilo can write of the crusader that he *pugnat pro duplici regno* because he seeks to attain to both Jerusalems, to the earthly as well as to the heavenly city,[5] just as he also

[1] *MPL*, 182, 922 A.

[2] That St Bernard conceived the crusader in general, and not just the Templar, as gaining spiritual salvation by wielding a physical sword (and therefore as engaged in a double warfare) is clear from his crusading letter (no. 363) to the clergy and laity of Germany. After attacking the ideal of secular knighthood (*MPL*, 182, 566 C: 'Cesset pristina illa non militia, sed plane malitia') he addresses the knights in these terms (*ibid.*): 'Habes nunc, fortis miles, habes, vir bellicose, ubi dimices absque periculo; ubi et vincere gloria, et mori lucrum. Si prudens mercator es, si conquisitor hujus saeculi, magnas quasdam tibi nundinas indico; vide ne pereant.'

[3] *MPL*, 182, 927 B.

[4] *Kreuzzugsdichtung des Mittelalters*, pp. 87 ff. Braun (*Studien zum Ruodlieb*, pp. 92 ff.) has shown a similar influence of Benedictine practice on the courtly life described in *Ruodlieb*. Important though this may be, especially in view of the earlier date, for any history of the rise of courtly civilisation, it is only in the *Rolandslied* that the Benedictine ideal is applied to the knight *in his military function*, as a crusader.

[5] Quoted on p. 293.

describes him as advancing with the sword, and also because of his Christian faith.[1]

In all these cases the emphasis finally falls on the crusader's spiritual warfare—not simply because his spiritual function is regarded as more worthy of comment than his physical, but also because it was precisely this novelty (in St Bernard's words: 'novum... et saeculis inexpertum') which attracted attention and had to be explained: that the knightly class whose military exploits had brought suffering and bloodshed to their own society and had been condemned by the clergy were now shown to be waging a spiritual warfare in God's name. We find that some authors go so far as to argue that the warfare of the crusader was purely spiritual and not physical[2]—although this argument is not surprising (in view of the need to emphasise this new aspect of knightly warfare), it is an inadequate description of the crusading phenomenon and must be rejected in favour of that proposed by St Bernard. Yet even he, although fully convinced that the Templars and the crusaders were involved in a double form of warfare, sometimes verges on an exclusively spiritual interpretation, especially where we may suspect embarrassment on his part when confronted with the implications of the physical nature of crusading warfare. This is particularly evident when he has to justify killing in the name of Christ. He argues[3] that the *miles Christi* is the servant of God and that he carries his sword as a punishment for evildoers and as praise for good men (the context of the whole work makes it clear that under malefactors St Bernard included the pagans).[4] He continues by saying: 'Sane cum occidit malefactorem, non homicida, sed, ut ita dixerim, malicida.'[5] It would be impossible to determine from the revealing use of the words *ut ita dixerim* whether St Bernard was himself

---

[1] *RHC*, v, 728: 'Christicolae gentes, gladioque fideque nitentes.'

[2] E.g. *Histoire anonyme de la première croisade* (ed. L. Bréhier), p. 84: '...quia hoc bellum non est carnale, sed spirituale.'   [3] *MPL*, 182, 924 A f.

[4] Cf. the start of chapter I (*ibid.* 921 B): 'Novum militiae genus ortum nuper auditur in terris, et in illa regione, quam olim in carne praesens visitavit Oriens ex alto.' Similarly, the reference to the *malefactores* is followed by the explicit remark (*ibid.* 924 B): 'In morte pagani christianus gloriatur, quia Christus glorificatur.' The *malefactor* is therefore identical with the *paganus*.   [5] *Ibid.* 924 B.

aware how close this passage comes to abandoning, for the sake of this particular argument, his doctrine of a double warfare waged by the Templars. Instead, we must concentrate on the linguistic ambiguity of the word *malicida* (someone who slays an evil man, *malus*, or someone who slays an evil, *malum*) and on the fact that St Bernard, by explicitly denying that the *miles Christi* who wields the sword is a *homicida*, excuses killing in the name of Christ by suggesting that it is an evil, rather than a human being, which has been destroyed. It was probably the difficulty of conducting his argument at this stage which compelled St Bernard to ignore his usual explanation of the warfare waged by the Templars and to place all his emphasis on the spiritual nature of their warfare, implying that their enemies were not flesh and blood, but evil itself.

This equation of the Templars' pagan adversaries with abstract evil is of particular importance for us, because it illustrates St Bernard's conviction that the crusaders were engaged in a spiritual warfare, and also because, as an example of crusading psychomachia employed by one of the leading supporters of the crusading idea, it has a direct relevance to another work in which St Bernard interpreted baptism as a psychomachia. I refer to the passage in his *Sermones in Cantica*, which we considered briefly in chapter 1, in which he interprets the military imagery of Cant. 1. 8.[1] This imagery (whose provenance from the Exodus description of the passage of the Red Sea is made clear by the biblical words *in curribus Pharaonis*) is interpreted spiritually by St Bernard as a psychomachia, so that the safe crossing of the Israelites and the destruction of the Egyptians are to be read as a prefiguration of the double gift of baptism, bringing salvation to men and destruction of their sins ('. . .baptismi gratia evidenter exprimitur, salvantis homines, et crimina submergentis'[2]). Here too, as in the passage from the *De laude novae militiae*, the Jews (as a type of the Christians) are seen in their humanity (*homines*; cf. the personal noun *malicida* applied to the Templar), whereas their pagan adversaries are identified with abstract evil (*crimina*;

[1] See pp. 13f.   [2] *MPL*, 183, 977 C.

General conclusions

cf. the denial that the Templar is a *homicida* and the possibility of deriving *malicida* from *malum*). A further parallel between St Bernard's interpretation of the Templars' conflict with the pagans as a psychomachia and his reading of the passage of the Red Sea as a baptismal psychomachia is provided by the way in which he concludes his reading of this Exodus scene by pointing out that, still in his own day, the tyrant Pharaoh continues to pursue Israel in its departure from Egypt ('...in his etiam his diebus exeuntem Israel de Aegypto insequitur'[1]). This emphatic insistence on the relevance of this scene (in its typological interpretation) to the twelfth century suggests that St Bernard was persuaded of the close connections between the events of Exodus, their interpretation as a baptismal psychomachia and their reading as a crusading psychomachia.[2]

In the light of this evidence from the writings of the most eloquent and influential advocate of crusading ideas in the twelfth century we may now return to the question of the baptismal interpretation of Exodus and its possible connection with the crusading interpretation which I have proposed for the Millstatt epic. Since St Bernard has suggested the general possibility of a relationship between baptismal psychomachia and the spiritual warfare of the crusaders we must attempt to find out whether this relationship can be confirmed by any other considerations. If such confirmation can be found it would mean that the *Millstätter Exodus*, with its conjunction of baptismal allusions with a crusading interpretation, by no means stands alone.

In the first place, there is a close connection in medieval eyes between crusaders and those who have been freshly baptised because both share a common prefiguration in the climax of the

[1] *MPL*, 183, 981 B.
[2] This application of St Bernard's remark on Pharaoh's present persecution of Israel to the psychomachia of the crusaders rests of course on the belief that he agreed with many of his contemporaries in equating the crusades with the events of the exodus. This assumption is amply confirmed by his employment of parallels from Exodus to explain the failure of the Second Crusade in the second book of the *De consideratione* (*MPL*, 182, 743 B f.: 'Moyses educturus populum de terra Aegypti, meliorem illis pollicitus est terram....Eduxit; eductos tamen in terram, quam promiserat, non introduxit').

events of Exodus, the passage of the Red Sea. We saw how this event was traditionally used to shed light on the significance of baptism,[1] but that it was also regarded, from the time of the First Crusade, as a prefiguration of the crusaders' voyage across the water in their exodus from the sins of this world and towards the Promised Land.[2] As we saw, however, when discussing the possible connections between the baptismal and paschal interpretations of the Israelites' exodus, it is not enough to establish a formal parallel on the strength of their both sharing a common prefiguration. We also have to determine what there is about the spiritual significance of these two interpretations which suggests an inner relationship and only because of this allows their common prefiguration to develop its exegetical fertility.

In the case of the crusades and baptism we must see this inner relationship as resting on the fact that both parts of the equation, the military undertaking and the Christian rite, were seen as providing a purification from sin and thereby the possibility of realising the salvation offered to mankind by Christ. With Christian baptism this is so obvious as to need no further discussion, but in the case of the crusades this mode of thinking needs to be illustrated. Indeed, the promise that whoever took the cross in the right spirit of devotion and in order to liberate the Christians of the Near East could count the journey as a penance for the sins which he had confessed seems to have been one of the most powerful motives in persuading the knights to journey to Jerusalem. This is clear from what information we possess on Urban II at Clermont. Of the thirty-two canons of this council only one, the second, is concerned with the crusade, but this makes it certain that such absolution from sins was held out as a promise by the Pope to the knights whom he was specifically addressing: 'Quicumque pro sola devotione, non pro honoris vel pecuniae adeptione, ad liberandam ecclesiam Dei Hierusalem profectus fuerit, iter illud pro omni poenitentia reputetur.'[3] The

---

[1] See pp. 8 ff.   [2] See pp. 258 ff.

[3] J. D. Mansi, *Sacrorum conciliorum nova et amplissima collectio*, xx, 816E. On the Pope's specific appeal to the knights see A. Waas, *Geschichte der Kreuz-*

crusade, undertaken with the right piety, and not for such motives as the vainglory and greed which characterise the secular knighthood from whom the crusaders are to distinguish themselves, is an opportunity from which the knight may profit in order to be absolved from his sins. The same idea is also expressed in a letter which the Pope addressed a year later to Bologna: 'Sciatis autem eis omnibus, qui illuc non terreni commodi cupiditate sed pro sola animae suae salute et ecclesiae liberatione profecti fuerint, poenitentiam totam peccatorum, de quibus veram et perfectam confessionem fecerint',[1] except that here a more personal note of devotion is struck by the emphasis on the need for a total confession. Absolution from sins is also reported by Baldricus as having been ordered by the Pope at Clermont ('Confessis peccatorum suorum ignominiam, securi de Christo celerem paciscimini veniam'[2]) and Robertus underlines the certainty of salvation which this opportunity presents: 'Arripite igitur viam hanc in remissionem peccatorum vestrorum, securi de immarcescibili gloria regni coelorum.'[3]

Elsewhere it is this certainty which is depicted as the reward which awaits the crusader who has availed himself of this new opportunity of gaining salvation. This we find in the chronicles, as also in works of literature. A literary example is provided repeatedly in the *Rolandslied*,[4] especially in the speech with which Turpin exhorts the Christian warriors to embrace martyrdom in face of the heathen attacks (vv. 3922 ff.): 'Wâ macht ir nu gewinnin| also gûten soldât, | sô er selbe geheizen hât?' This comparison, implicit in the rhetorical question, between the generosity shown by God to the crusaders and the rewards (obviously suggested

ʒüge, I, 71 f. The fact that *honor* and *pecunia* are explicitly excluded as possible motives for the departing crusader is of some relevance to our interpretation of the *Millstätter Exodus*, where the Israelites' humility is contrasted with the *ruom* of the Egyptians (v. 3038), but where their subsequent lapse into *ʒwîvel* is condemned by means of the description of their clinging to earthly possessions (v. 3144).

[1] Hagenmeyer, *Epistulae et chartae ad historiam primi belli sacri spectantes*, p. 137.
[2] *RHC*, IV, 15 F.   [3] *RHC*, III, 729 B.
[4] See Wentzlaff-Eggebert, *Kreuʒʒugsdichtung des Mittelalters*, pp. 96 ff.

as smaller) which await the secular knight is a close parallel to the contrast made by Urban II in the account given by Fulcherius: 'Nunc aeterna praemia nanciscantur, qui dudum pro solidis paucis mercenarii fuerunt.'[1] More important for us is the fact that this remark of Turpin in the *Rolandslied* is followed by his absolution of the Christian warriors, for he does this in words which equate these knights, freshly absolved of their sins, with a child freshly baptised in the font:

> 3929   Mit den wortin sprechen wir iu antlâz.
> In der wârheit sage wir iu daz:
> vor gote birt ir inbunten
> von allin werltlichen sunden
> sam ain niuborn westebarn.

With these words an unmistakable connection is established between the crusades and baptism, between the crusader and the newly baptised child: what they share is not merely their common prefiguration in the events of the exodus, but also, more profoundly, the forceful image they present of the state of grace as a condition of salvation. In the *Rolandslied* this state of grace is stressed by Turpin's concluding words,[2] in which he imposes the killing of pagans as a penance on the crusaders,[3] and by the poet's observation that the absolution was pronounced in the presence of God. The description of the crusaders' abandonment of all earthly concerns (vv. 3942 ff.: 'dô hêten si verlâzen | allez ir chunne | durch di gotes minne, | aigen unt burge') further illustrates the fact that, in conformity with the terms of the promise held out to the knights by Urban II, these crusaders are not motivated by any concern for worldly renown or wealth. Their cutting of all earthly ties and their absolution have indeed put them into the situation of newly born children, fresh from baptism.

This is not the only occasion on which Turpin employs the image of baptism when exhorting the Christian warriors, for

---

[1] *RHC*, III, 324D.   [2] Vv. 3934 f.
[3] This *bûʒe* of Turpin is thus Konrad's interpretation of what Urban II had meant by his words: 'iter illud pro omni poenitentia reputetur' (see p. 398, n. 3).

with v. 5260 there begins a speech in which this image occupies a significant part.[1] Turpin begins with an invitation to appeal to Christ and to request 'daz wir raine fur in chomen' (v. 5263). What is implied by this reference to the purity of the crusaders is made clear by the following lines:

> 5264 Wir werden hiute geboren
> zû der êwigen wunne:
> hiute werden wir der engel kunne,
> hiute sculen wir frôlichen varen,
> hiute werden wir liutere westerparn;
> hiute ist unser froudetac,
> want sich sîn frouwen mac
> elliu die heilige cristinhait.

From this it emerges that the reference to purity (*raine, liuter*) is connected with the cleansing force of the water of baptism (*westerparn*) and with the rebirth which awaits the crusaders ('wir werden hiute geboren')—a rebirth not merely into a new life as a state of grace, but into the eternal life which is granted to the crusader as a reward for his martyrdom (v. 5272: 'hiute vergilt man uns di arbeit'). What the further implications of this passage are will occupy us shortly,[2] but it is clear that the redemptive purification of baptism is a conception easily reconcilable for the twelfth century with the idea of crusading martyrdom and that this unity of ideas may help to explain the validity of both a baptismal and a crusading interpretation of the *Millstätter Exodus*.

The *Rolandslied* also presents us with another example of an equation between baptism and crusading martyrdom which, although it may not be so explicit as the two passages in which the term *weste(r)barn* is employed, is nonetheless very relevant to our problem. This last example concerns the author's description of the Christian warriors' eagerness to embrace martyrdom after they have just been warned of a further attack which the

---

[1] The word *westerchint* also occurs in v. 7318, but this usage has no bearing on our problem.

[2] See pp. 407 ff.

pagans are about to launch. Their preparation for battle and readiness for self-sacrifice are summed up in the following words:

> 5765 Swaz si gote in der toufe gehiezen,
> wî wâr si daz allez liezen!
> Sie wâren liuter unt raine
> âne rost unt âne mailen,
> sam diu heiligen chindelîn,
> di durch selben mînen trechtîn
> Herodes hiez erslahen.

We have already considered this passage with regard to the equation between the Hebrew male children put to death by Pharaoh, the slaughter of the innocents by Herod and the present-day martyrdom of the crusaders,[1] but what concerns us here is the light shed by these words on the comparison of the crusader with the newly baptised child. Once more emphasis is placed on the crusaders' purity (*liuter* and *raine* occur again, and are even reinforced by v. 5768), but this purity of heart, which we have hitherto seen directly compared with that of the freshly baptised child, is here conceived as the purity of those who have remained true to the promise to God made on their behalf at baptism (vv. 5765 f.). This loyalty to the baptismal oath (incidentally, expressed by the same rhyme-words *geheiʒʒen* and *wâr laʒʒen* as are used in the Millstatt epic to reveal the loyalty of God or the treachery of Pharaoh)[2] is a reference to the renunciation of the Devil and all his works included in the baptismal formula, but interpreted actively and in physical terms as a readiness to serve God not merely in a psychomachia with the Devil, but also in physical conflict with his followers, the Saracens.[3] The crusaders, by remaining true to their baptismal obligations, have retained the purity which was granted them in the font and can justifiably be indirectly compared with the freshly baptised child. As in the other two passages which mention the *weste(r)barn*, this loyalty of the Christian warriors is rewarded by the salvation which God offers them: with them salvation takes the form of the martyr's throne (vv. 5759 f. and vv. 5763: 'den heiligen mar-

---

[1] See pp. 321 ff.   [2] See pp. 174 ff.   [3] Cf. also p. 322, n. 1.

General conclusions

terêren'), but this honour is still conceived as God's reward (v. 5761: 'dâ in got mit wolte gelten'). The concept of martyrdom is further developed in this richly allusive passage by the manner in which the crusading martyrs are seen in connection with the innocents slaughtered by Herod.[1] The implication behind this parallel is that the crusaders who fall in battle are the latest to join the heavenly ranks of martyrs on behalf of Christ, whereas the innocents were considered as the first to serve Christ in this way: the lacuna created by the fall of Satan and his associates, which had first begun to be filled by the innocents, is now further made good by the crusaders (v. 5772: 'Den chôr sculen si mit rechtir urtaile haben'[2]).

The fact that the author of the *Rolandslied* should adduce the example of the innocents in the very passage where he chooses to hint at the equation of the crusader with the freshly baptised child may throw further light on the Millstatt author's emphasis on the military implications of the scene in which Pharaoh orders the killing of the Israelite male children (the Old Testament prefiguration of the slaughter at Bethlehem). What the innocents and the baptised child have in common is their extreme youth, but also their freedom from sin—in the former case by virtue

[1] See p. 322.

[2] J. Bumke, *Wolframs Willehalm*, p. 30, n. 47, gives evidence for the view that the martyr's soul is cleansed by the blood which he sheds for Christ (*lavacrum sanguinis*), just as the soul of the baptizand is cleansed by the rite which admits him to the Church. Bumke's reference to *Willehalm* 405, 20 ff. suggests that this equation of (crusading) martyrdom with baptism was not unknown to German literature. Equally relevant is the crusading poem in which Marcabru calls the Holy Land a *lavador* (*Poésies*, no. XXXV, ed. Dejeanne, pp. 169 ff.). On this poem see Wentzlaff-Eggebert, *Kreuzzugsdichtung des Mittelalters*, pp. 48 f.

Further evidence is provided by the iconography of the mosaics in the cupolas of the Baptistery of the Arians and the Baptistery of the Orthodox at Ravenna. Here, in buildings dedicated to the rite of baptism and in which the centre-piece of the cupola is taken up by a mosaic depicting the baptism of Christ in the Jordan, this centre-piece is surrounded by a mosaic depicting the apostles in procession and bearing their crowns of martyrdom. Furthermore, in the Baptistery of the Orthodox a lower register of the mosaic depicts, amongst other iconographical details, the vacant thrones in paradise which await the martyrs. Illustrations of these scenes are to be found in G. Bovini, *The Churches of Ravenna*, p. 77 (see also p. 82 for closer detail) and p. 53 (see also pp. 56 and 60) respectively.

of their sacrificial martyrdom and in the latter as a result of the cleansing power of the water of the font. A comparison of the crusaders with the freshly baptised child could therefore lead without difficulty to their further comparison with the innocents —and this quite apart from the already suggestive parallel between the innocents and the crusaders as the first and the latest martyrs. If we apply this to the *Millstätter Exodus*, then the suggestion becomes insistent that the typological link between the Israelite male children (prefiguring the innocents) and the crusaders was strengthened by the author's allusions to baptism, for it is redemptive purification from sin which the crusaders are felt to share with such martyred children. In other words, this passage from the *Rolandslied* helps not merely to explain the function of the baptismal references in the *Millstätter Exodus*, but also to account further for the prominence which the author accorded to the scene in which Pharaoh ordered the killing of the children.

Yet this passage in the *Rolandslied* is relevant to our inquiry in a further respect since it follows immediately upon (and is meant to reveal the reaction to) Turpin's warning speech[1] to the crusaders in which he likens the approaching heathen warriors to Pharaoh's army destroyed by God in the Red Sea. In other words, this scene contains three of those themes which recur together in the Millstatt work and whose possible connections we are attempting to explain: crusading warfare, the passage of the Red Sea as the climax of the exodus, and baptism (with its reference either to the purity of the crusading martyrs or to the redemptive martyrdom of the children). The fact that this one short scene should prompt the author of the *Rolandslied* to combine precisely the same motifs which we have traced in the Millstatt epic is an indication that their conjunction in the *Exodus* is not fortuitous and that a crusading interpretation of Exodus could without difficulty attract to itself such allusions to baptism and to the prefigurative significance of the male children of the Israelites. The various themes which St Bernard had combined

[1] See p. 323.

only in two separate works (in the *Sermones in Cantica*, an interpretation of the exodus as a psychomachia prefiguring baptism, and in his *De laude novae militiae*, a demonstration of the crusades as a psychomachia) are all fused together not merely in the *Millstätter Exodus*, but also in this rich passage in the *Rolandslied*.

If there was therefore a close connection in medieval thought between baptism and the crusades and if the baptismal and the paschal interpretations of *Exodus* can be reconciled with one another[1] then we may conclude that there is not likely to be any objection to the proposition that the references in the Millstatt work to the Easter liturgy are reconcilable with our crusading interpretation of this epic. This is only a theoretical observation, however, and is as little capable of demonstrating our case as the consideration that both the Easter liturgy and the crusading idea are reinforced by their reference to a common type, the events recounted in the biblical Exodus. Something more than a theoretical possibility or a formal parallel is here required—we have to look for the common spiritual function of the Easter liturgy and the crusading idea which may have allowed them to be associated with one another and which may account for the traces of both in the *Millstätter Exodus*.

The most convincing testimony known to me is provided by a witness of no less authority than Innocent III in his formal opening of the Lateran council of 1215. In his sermon opening the assembly[2] the Pope declares that he has been prompted especially by two motives in convening the council: by a desire for a general reform of the Church and by a wish to institute a crusade for the recovery of the Holy Land ('...propter reformationem universalis ecclesiae, ad liberationem potissimum terrae sanctae: propter quae duo principaliter et praecipue hoc sacrum concilium convocavi'[3]). This council, one of whose two major purposes was conceived by Innocent III as being the

[1] See pp. 377 ff.
[2] Mansi, *Sacrorum conciliorum nova et amplissima collectio*, XXII, 968 ff.
[3] *Ibid.* 969 A.

405

institution of a crusade to liberate the Holy Land, is formally opened with a sermon in which the Pope takes as his text the words of Luc. 22. 15: 'Desiderio desideravi hoc pascha manducare vobiscum, antequam patiar.' In other words, we have in this choice of text and in the way in which Innocent develops his argument in support of his two major concerns impressive testimony that the paschal rite was felt by him to be intimately connected with the crusading idea.

The starting-point chosen by the Pope is the traditional interpretation of *pascha* as *transitus*, to which he adds the parallel of the Greek πάσχειν ('Sane pascha Hebraice dicitur phase, quod est transitus, Graece vero πάσχειν, quod est pati: quia per passiones debemus transire ad gloriam, secundum quod Veritas ipsa dicebat: Oportebat pati Christum, et sic intrare in gloriam suam'[1]). Although Innocent later quotes Exod. 12. 11, where the use of *transitus* refers to the passage of the Lord over the houses of the Israelites, he himself employs the word in its subjective sense to designate the passage of Christians, as the new Israel, from one condition to another. In the passage just quoted it is *we* who are to pass over into glory through our suffering, a point which he then reinforces by arguing that our suffering, as a suffering with Christ, is indispensable if we are to reign with Him in glory ('Quia si volumus conregnare, oportet et compati'[2]). In other words, *pascha* is referred not merely to the passion and sacrifice of Christ, but also, in the unvoiced context of an *imitatio Christi*, to the Christian who is prepared to suffer with Christ and to sacrifice himself on His account.

This subjective and moral interpretation of *pascha* provides the basis for the Pope's threefold interpretation of the words which he has taken as his text. This follows the pattern of what he terms a physical, spiritual and eternal sense in which these words must be understood ('Triplex autem pascha sive phase desidero vobiscum celebrare, corporale, spirituale, aeternale'[3]). The third of these is the conventional anagogical sense: the

[1] Mansi, *Sacrorum conciliorum nova et amplissima collectio*, XXII, 969 B. The quotation is from Luc. 24. 26.   [2] *Ibid.* 969 C.   [3] *Ibid.* 969 E.

passage from this life to eternal life ('. . . aeternale, ut fiat transitus de vita in vitam, pro caelesti gloria obtinenda')[1] and, as the general theme of the council's deliberations under which the two particular purposes of the Pope could readily be subsumed, it is dealt with somewhat summarily, but nonetheless as the conclusion of the whole sermon.[2] The other two senses of the evangelist's words are equated by the Pope, however, with his two major concerns in calling the council and are therefore interpreted at greater length. We need pay no attention to the equation of the spiritual sense with the reform of the Church ('. . . spirituale, ut fiat transitus de statu ad statum, pro universali ecclesia reformanda'[3]), for what primarily concerns us is the manner in which the Pope relates what he calls the corporal sense to the need for a crusade: 'corporale, ut fiat transitus ad locum, pro miserabili Jerusalem liberanda'.[4] With that the explicit equation of the crusade with the celebration of the paschal rite is made. What follows is an appeal on behalf of the oppressed city of Jerusalem with conventional references to Old Testament passages. For us the importance of this sermon of Innocent III lies not in the way in which he marshals his arguments in favour of renewing crusading activity, but rather in the decisive fact that he relates these arguments to an interpretation of Luc. 22. 15 which equates the celebration of Easter with the crusade he envisages. Furthermore, by relating the paschal sacrifice and passion of Christ to the readiness for self-sacrifice and suffering which the crusader is meant to show as part of his *imitatio Christi*, the Pope has employed an argument which can also be applied to the interpretation of the *Millstätter Exodus*.[5]

In the light of this evidence we may now return to a passage in the *Rolandslied* (vv. 5260 ff.) which we considered above[6] as an example of the manner in which the crusades could be equated with baptism. Wentzlaff-Eggebert has discussed this same passage[7] and sees in the repetitive emphasis of the word *hiute*

---

[1] *Ibid.*   [2] *Ibid.* 972 D and E.   [3] *Ibid.* 969 E.
[4] *Ibid.*   [5] See pp. 418 ff.   [6] See p. 402 ff.
[7] *Kreuzzugsdichtung des Mittelalters*, pp. 96 ff.

(occurring seven times) and in the refrain *gloria in excelsis deo* (v. 5278) a clear allusion to the Magnificat antiphon of the second vesper before Christmas with its similar refrain and repeated use of *hodie*. The parallel is illuminating, but cannot explain everything about the passage in the *Rolandslied*. The force of the repeated *hodie*, for example, is weakened by Wentzlaff-Eggebert's own observation that it occurs not merely in the Christmas liturgy, but also in six other feasts of the liturgical year.[1] Furthermore, if we extend our inquiry from the verbal parallels to the function of the particular liturgy in which they occur, it is clear that there is a vast discrepancy between the fact that the Christmas liturgy celebrates the birth of Christ (*hodie Christus natus est*) and the passage in the *Rolandslied* the rebirth of crusading martyrs (v. 5264: 'Wir werden hiute geboren'), or between the liturgical emphasis on the appearance of Christ amongst men on earth (*hodie Salvator apparuit*) and the vernacular author's mention of the Christian martyrs' appearance before Christ in heaven (vv. 5273 ff.: 'Wir werden hiute emphangen | ... | zû den himilischen êren. | Hiute gesehe wir unseren herren'). In view of these differences of emphasis, despite the similarity of wording, we must supplement Wentzlaff-Eggebert's interpretation of this passage as a reflection of the Christmas liturgy, and it is to the liturgy of the Easter period that we must turn for this. In the first place, it can hardly be by chance that Turpin should open his address by an appeal to the example of Christ's passion (vv. 5260 f.: 'Nu flêhet alle mînen trechtîn, | want er durch uns dolte den tôt'), for it is this sacrifice which the crusaders are being called upon to imitate. If, according to Wentzlaff-Eggebert's suggestion, it was Christ's birth which provided the model for the crusaders' rebirth then we should not expect a reference to the passion at the start of this speech. Secondly, it is permissible to seek a liturgical parallel for the repeated use of *hiute* not in the Christmas antiphon or in the other yearly festivals mentioned by Wentzlaff-Eggebert, but instead in the recurrent use of the *haec nox* formula in the liturgy of Holy Saturday.[2] The fact

[1] *Kreuzzugsdichtung des Mittelalters*, p. 346, n. 77.   [2] See above, pp. 19 f.

General conclusions

that this service was originally an Easter vigil celebrated in the evening, whereas we have no means of telling whether the *Millstätter Exodus* (if it was intended for an Easter reading) was recited at any particular time of day, is sufficient to account for the difference between the *haec nox* of the Holy Saturday liturgy and the words *an disem tage hiute* of the Millstatt work (v. 3312) or the *hiute* of the *Rolandslied*. In addition, the tone of rejoicing in the passage from the *Rolandslied* (v. 5267: 'hiute sculen wir frôlichen varen'; 5269: 'hiute ist unser froudetac | want sich sîn frouwen mac | elliu die heilige cristinhait') which Wentzlaff-Eggebert has associated with the Christmas liturgy[1] may with equal force, like *die vroude* at the conclusion of the Millstatt work (v. 3311), be derived from the *paschale gaudium* of the Easter period. Finally, Turpin's stress on the rebirth which awaits the crusading martyrs (vv. 5264 f.: 'Wir werden hiute geboren | zû der êwigen wunne') has its close parallel in the references to rebirth and regeneration included in the consecration of the baptismal water in the Holy Saturday liturgy ('fontemque baptismatis aperis toto orbe terrarum gentibus innovandis' or 'in novam renata creaturam, progenies caelestis emergat' or 'totamque hujus aquae substantiam regenerandi fecundet effectu'). That the liturgy should stress rebirth in the context of baptism is in full agreement with the way in which the *Rolandslied* closely associates the rebirth of the crusaders (vv. 5264 f.) with the image of them as children purified at the font of baptism (v. 5268). It also agrees with the central importance of baptism in the liturgy of Holy Saturday. For these reasons we must regard this important passage from the *Rolandslied* not merely as testimony for the close kinship felt to exist between the crusades and baptism, but also as evidence for a similar connection between the crusades and Easter. This passage is a poetic confirmation in the vernacular of the conviction which Innocent III was later to express in his conciliar sermon on behalf of a renewal of the crusading idea.

A third example of the general parallel between the celebration

[1] *Kreuzzugsdichtung des Mittelalters*, p. 97.

409

of Easter and crusading thought is provided by two medieval Latin poems, one by Berter of Orléans and the other an anonymous poem in the *Carmina Burana* (no. 48). The poem by Berter,[1] composed in 1187[2] (the year in which Saladin captured Jerusalem), is an appeal to crusaders to come to the relief of the Holy City. It shows two interesting similarities with the *Millstätter Exodus*. It depicts the Saracens as the new Philistines (v. 32) whose capture of the Holy Cross repeats the Philistines' capture of the Ark of the Covenant, so that the Christian crusaders are depicted implicitly as a new Israel, enjoying a new covenant (v. 35) with God. Secondly, the feudal overtones of the way in which the knight takes his crusading vow[3] (he uses the technical phrase *illi me commendo*, v. 76, and regards this service as reciprocating what Christ had done for him on the cross, vv. 76 ff.) reflect the similar feudal implications of the Millstatt work. More important, however, is the paschal allusion with which the poem commences. The first two lines ('Iuxta Threnos Ieremiae, | vere Syon lugent viae') are an explicit reference to Lam. 1. 4 which derives its significance from the fact that this same Old Testament book provides some of the material for the service of matins on Holy Saturday (the first *lectio* = Lam. 3. 22–30, the second = 4. 1–6 and the third = 5. 1–11). The prophet of Israel's misery thus gives voice to the grief of Christians on the morning of Holy Saturday and also to the sorrow of the poet at the loss of Jerusalem to Saladin (here the use on Holy Saturday of Lam. 5. 2: 'Hereditas nostra versa est ad alienos: domus nostrae ad extraneos' is particularly relevant to the crusading poem). That it is the liturgical employment of the Lamentations of Jeremiah as part of the Easter ceremony which lies behind the poem by Berter is made clear by the way in which he continues stanza 1. Whereas the prophet had said that the ways of Zion mourn because none come to the solemn feasts, the medieval poet (even though these biblical words would have

---

[1] *Oxford Book of Medieval Latin Verse*, no. 201, pp. 297 ff.
[2] *Ibid.* p. 489.
[3] See Waas, *Geschichte der Kreuzzüge*, I, 12.

been adequate to the situation he was describing) continues by incorporating a reference to the Easter situation:

Iuxta Threnos Ieremiae,
vere Syon lugent viae
quod sollempni non sit die
qui sepulcrum visitet
vel casum resuscitet
huius prophetiae.

The visit of the three Maries to the tomb is used as a means of emphasising the shameful fact that Christian crusaders do not visit the Holy Sepulchre, that there are no knights who, by emulating the events of the first Easter and taking the path to the tomb, may reconquer Jerusalem from the Saracens. The Easter context in which this appeal for a new crusade is placed is further emphasised by the words *sollempni. . . die*, a time-reference which has its counterpart in the liturgical use of the phrase *haec nox* and in the Millstatt author's demonstrative employment of the words *an disem tage hiute*. It is the liturgical celebration of Easter which lies behind both the German epic and the Latin poem.

The same fact emerges from *CB* 48,[1] another crusading poem which must be later than the Saracens' capture of Jerusalem in 1187.[2] There is no need to dwell on the characteristic crusading allusions which inform this poem,[3] since what concerns us is the paschal background to this appeal for a renewed crusade. This may be shown by the refrain with which each stanza is equipped (*Exsurgat Deus!*) and by the manner in which this refrain is continued syntactically only in stanza 2 ('. . . Et dissipet hostes'), for these two phrases now combine to form an allusion to Ps. 68. 2 ('Exsurgat Deus, et dissipentur inimici eius'). This reference does much more than suggest that the Old Testament conflict between the Hebrews and their enemies is a prefiguration of the

---

[1] I have used the edition of A. Hilka and O. Schumann, *Carmina Burana*, I, 95 ff. (text) and II, 100 ff. (commentary).

[2] *Ibid.* II, 102.

[3] For these see Wentzlaff-Eggebert, *Kreuzzugsdichtung des Mittelalters*, pp. 165 ff.

present conflict between Christendom and the Saracens. For us
the importance of this refrain lies in the way in which its use at the
end of stanza 4 is taken up and varied by the commencement of
stanza 5 with the forceful statement: *Exsurrexit!* This can best
be interpreted as a reference to the word of the angel at the tomb
(*surrexit*) on the morning of Easter Sunday,[1] and therefore implies
that the optative of the Old Testament quotation has found its
typological fulfilment in Christ's Easter victory.[2] This is of
immediate relevance to the position in which potential crusaders
find themselves, as the poet now makes clear:

> Exsurrexit! et nos assurgere
> ei propere
> iam tenemur atque succurrere.
> Ierusalem voluit perdere,
> ut hoc opere
> sic possemus culpas diluere.

The crusaders are called upon to bring their help to Christ by
liberating Jerusalem (even though God in His omnipotence has
no need of their assistance and has only created this situation so
as to offer the knights the means of their salvation),[3] but the use
of the verb *assurgere* in their case, with its echo of *exsurgere* to
describe Christ's Easter victory, is meant to assure them that the
victory won by Christ is a guarantee of the victory awaiting
those who fight in His name. The opportunity which this crusade
presents is the chance for every crusader, by following Christ's
Easter example, to enjoy the fruits of His victory and resurrection.[4] What was true of the military symbolism of the bap-

[1] Matt. 28. 6; Marc. 16. 6; Luc. 24. 6.
[2] The use of an optative form (implying therefore no more than a request to
God, however urgent) as the Old Testament type which finds its fulfilment (as
interpreted here) in the resurrection, rather than a historical event of Israelite
history, may best be explained as a wish which presupposes knowledge that this
was the manner in which God had acted towards His people at the time of the
exodus and in which He may therefore be presumed to act again.
[3] See 4. 4 ff. and 5. 7 ff. See also below, p. 436, n. 1.
[4] In other words, we have here the same threefold pattern (Old Testament
prefiguration: New Testament fulfilment: imitation of this fulfilment by the individual Christian) which we saw in the case of the scene in the *Millstätter Exodus*

General conclusions

tismal *sphragis* (that it was the guarantee of the neophyte's victory) is equally true of the Easter allusion in this crusading poem. It is perhaps from this point of view that we may best hope to understand the implications of a remark made by Fulcherius in his crusading chronicle when he observes that a crusader can fight in greater safety and with firmer confidence on a Sunday because this was the day on which Christ rose from the dead.[1] The culmination of the Easter cycle in Christ's victory over the Devil and in His opening up of the way to eternal life is thus of immediate relevance to crusading experience.[2]

A last example of the general relevance of Easter symbolism to the crusading experience is provided by a French manuscript illumination of the fourteenth century.[3] The miniature depicts the storming of a city by an army of knights, complete with a siege tower, scaling ladders and a catapult machine, all in the foreground. Such a general description implies no more than the capture of any medieval city and certainly fails to suggest any

where Pharaoh orders the killing of the children of the Israelites (see pp. 320 f.). The same pattern may also be said to pervade the whole of the German epic, see pp. 427 f. Confirmation of the importance of this pattern is provided by Daniélou, *Bible et liturgie*, p. 32: 'Ce parallélisme de la scène du Paradis et de celle du baptême, avec au milieu celle de la vie du Christ, va reparaître tout au long de la catéchèse baptismale.' See also his remarks, pp. 61 f.

[1] *RHC*, III, 412 F: '...quatinus die crastina, quae dies erit Dominica, qua Christus a morte resurrexit, securius praelietur, et adjunctis orationibus vestris et eleemosynis apud Deum roboratus, confidentius pugnet.' On Sunday as the day on which Christ's resurrection is celebrated see J. A. Jungmann, *The Early Liturgy*, pp. 19 ff.

[2] Another possible link between the paschal victory of Christ and the victory of the crusaders who follow in His footsteps is provided by Ps. 117. 24 ('Haec est dies quam fecit Dominus; exsultemus et laetemur'). This verse is used in the gradual for the first six days of the Easter period and is also revealingly quoted by Raimundus in his chronicle on the occasion of the crusaders' capture of Jerusalem (*RHC*, III, 300 F). It is the recognition that Christ's conflict with Satan in the Easter period and the crusaders' with the infidels have much in common which prompts the chronicler to use this psalm on this particular occasion. Cf. *ibid*. H: 'In hac die cantavimus officium de Resurrectione, quia in hac die ille qui sua virtute a mortuis resurrexit, per gratiam suam nos resuscitavit.'

[3] See Pl. 4. The MS in question is Ms. fr. 352 of the Bibliothèque nationale and the miniature occurs on f. 62. I have to thank Mlle M.-Th. d'Alverny, formerly of the Bibliothèque nationale, for her assistance in interpreting this miniature.

connection with the particular themes of crusading warfare and of Easter. The connection with the crusades is provided by the standards carried by the knights storming the city, for the immediately preceding pages in the MS[1] show other miniatures depicting the various lords, secular and spiritual, who took part in the First Crusade, together with their own standards. From this it is clear that this assault is being led by Godfrey of Bouillon and the knights of Lorraine, followed by those of Flanders, Champagne and Catalonia. This crusading context is confirmed by the text of the MS which this miniature decorates, since it is an abridgement of a French translation of the crusading chronicle of William of Tyre, known under the title of *L'Estoire de Eracles, empereur, et la conqueste de la Terre d'Outremer*.[2] This, together with the occurrence of our miniature in that part of the chronicle which is concerned with the First Crusade and the establishment of the Frankish kingdom of Jerusalem, makes it clear that the assault depicted is a scene from the First Crusade.

Indeed, it is likely that the city under attack is Jerusalem itself so that it is nothing less than the climax of this expedition which has been chosen to illustrate the chronicle. That Jerusalem is the object of the crusaders' assault is suggested by the twofold nature of the city as depicted in this miniature, for its base is that of a fortified city, equipped with heavy freestone walls, a portcullis and a series of towers, but this structure is surmounted by what appears to be a church in Gothic style. This church is meant to represent the earthly Jerusalem in terms of the Heavenly Jerusalem (for the latter could be depicted in the Gothic period not merely as a city, but also as a church),[3] just as conversely the mosaic of Santa Pudenziana in Rome represents, as a background to Christ and the apostles, the Heavenly Jerusalem in terms of the earthly city as it appeared in the fifth city.[4] Furthermore, the

[1] From f. 47 v. on.
[2] Published in *RHC*, I and II.
[3] See H. Sedlmayr, *Die Entstehung der Kathedrale*, pp. 132 ff.
[4] The mosaic in question is reproduced as Pl. 130 in W. F. Volbach, *Early Christian Art*. See also the note on this plate on pp. 336 f., as well as E. Mâle, *La fin du paganisme en Gaule et les plus anciennes basiliques chrétiennes*, p. 89.

chroniclers of the First Crusade make it clear that siege towers were used in the capture of Jerusalem in 1099[1] and that Flemish knights under Godfrey of Bouillon were the first to breach the walls of the city.[2]

What is of decisive importance is the paschal background provided for this climax of the First Crusade by the manner in which the five bays of the Gothic church which is the heart of Jerusalem all contain scenes from the passion of Christ: the kiss of Judas and Christ's arrest, His scourging, Christ carrying the cross on the way to Calvary, the crucifixion[3] and the burial of Christ. These scenes depicting the martyrdom of Christ are to be read in their sequence from left to right, just as the crusaders, in redeeming their pledge to follow Christ and undergo martyrdom, also advance from left to right in entering Jerusalem and, in scaling the walls, rise from ground level to a level just below that on which Christ's passion is depicted. We are meant to regard these five closing scenes from Christ's life not simply as an adequate decoration for a church representing Jerusalem, but more profoundly as an *exemplum* which the crusaders under Godfrey of Bouillon visibly follow and to which they draw near in their victorious capture of Jerusalem. What this *imitatio Christi* means in religious terms is made clear by two scenes which, placed on the left of the miniature, comment on the major scene, for the representation (below) of the Dormition of the Virgin and (above) of the Ascension of Christ is meant as a token of the life eternal which the crusaders have won for themselves by their readiness to follow Christ to the extent of embracing martyrdom. It is of the nature of this martyrdom that it should be understood as a voluntary imitation of Christ's passion and it is for this reason

---

[1] See Runciman, *A History of the Crusades*, I, 282 and 284 f.

[2] *Ibid*. pp. 285 f. See also the following footnote.

[3] That this association between the climax of Easter and the climax of the First Crusade did not escape notice is suggested by the terms in which the breaching of the walls of Jerusalem is described in the *Histoire anonyme de la première croisade*, x, 38, p. 202: 'Appropinquante autem hora, scilicet in qua Dominus noster Ihesus Christus dignatus est pro nobis sufferre patibulum crucis, nostri milites fortiter pugnabant in castello, videlicet dux Godefridus et comes Eustachius, frater ejus.'

that the events of the first Easter are depicted as a commentary on the events of the First Crusade.

Yet this association of the crusades with Easter rests on much firmer ground than the detailed, but perhaps fortuitous evidence provided by a papal sermon, by a handful of lines from a vernacular epic, by two Latin poems and by a late medieval illumination. By this I mean that the crusades, as understood by those who took part, shared one vitally important theme with the Easter ceremony: both were concerned with redemption and with the means whereby it might be realised by men in the present. In the case of the Easter commemoration of Christ's redemptive sacrifice this remark is self-evident and needs no elaboration, but in the case of the crusades an appeal to contemporary evidence may help to show that this was a central factor in crusading thought.

In the first place, the redemptive force of the crusade, granting an opportunity to the knights to attain for themselves, by a particular means unknown to other classes of society (except the monks), that salvation which Christ's sacrifice had won potentially for all men, was an experience which left a deep impression on the first crusading generations. Whereas only the monks had hitherto been given the privilege of a special way to salvation, open to them alone (but at the cost of withdrawal from the world), now this was shared by the crusading knights (formerly members of that worldly knighthood which had attracted clerical censure) who could even gain salvation without having to abandon the world. It is the conviction of the novelty of this phenomenon which pervades the words of Guibertus at the beginning of his *Gesta Dei per Francos*: 'Instituit nostro tempore praelia sancta Deus, ut ordo equestris et vulgus oberrans, qui vetustae paganitatis exemplo in mutuas versabantur caedes, novum repperirent salutis promerendae genus; ut nec funditus electa (uti fieri assolet) monastica conversatione, seu religiosa qualibet professione, saeculum relinquere cogerentur, sed sub consueta licentia et habitu, ex suo ipsorum officio, Dei aliquatenus gratiam consequerentur.'[1] Admiration for God's special concern for the

[1] *RHC*, IV, 124D and E.

knights, for the offer of this particular possibility of salvation, without the need to abandon the world, to the class whose violence had hitherto destined them to perdition, is also apparent in the words used by Bohemond, in the account given by Robertus, to encourage his followers to accept martyrdom: 'O ordo militum, nunc terque quaterque beatus! Qui huc usque fuisti homicidii sanguine deturpatus, nunc sanctorum sudoribus compar martyrum coelesti es diademate laureatus!'[1] The knights who leave Europe for the Holy Land are thus granted the opportunity of passing from the status of homicides to that of martyrs. Their exodus is to be understood in the corporal sense which Innocent III read out of Luc. 22. 15 (for they help to liberate Jerusalem), but also in his eternal sense (for they pass from this life to the next for the sake of obtaining heavenly glory). With St Bernard, too, we encounter a recognition of the abundance of grace which God has shown in this period by granting such an opportunity: 'Neque enim simile est tempus istud caeteris, quae hucusque praeteriere, temporibus; nova venit e coelo divinae miserationis ubertas.... Dico vobis, non fecit Dominus taliter omni retro generationi, nec tam copiosum in patres nostros gratiae munus effudit.'[2] For St Bernard it is the very artificiality of the occasion (since God in His omnipotence has no need of human assistance to rescue Jerusalem) which proves the magnitude of God's grace in devising a situation which will prompt men to seek salvation: 'Videte quo artificio utitur ad salvandum vos; considerate pietatis abyssum, et obstupescite, peccatores: necessitatem se habere facit, aut facit, aut simulat, dum vestris necessitatibus subvenire de coelo venit.'[3] When he uses this same argument on another occasion St Bernard, like Bohemond, sees in this crusading opportunity a divine gift offered to sinners as a token of God's grace: 'Non vult mortem vestram, sed ut convertamini, et vivatis; quia sic quaerit occasionem, non adversum vos, sed pro vobis. Quid est enim nisi exquisita prorsus et inventibilis soli Deo occasio salvationis, quod homicidas, raptores, adulteros, perjuros, caeterisque obligatos criminibus, quasi gentem quae

[1] *RHC*, III, 748 A.   [2] Letter 458, *MPL*, 182, 653 A.   [3] *Ibid.*

27   417   G M E

justitiam fecerit, de servitio suo submonere dignatur Omnipotens? Nolite diffidere, peccatores: benignus est Dominus. Si vellet punire vos, servitium vestrum non modo non expeteret, sed nec susciperet quidem oblatum.'[1] The words *Nolite diffidere, peccatores*, addressed to crusaders about to embark upon the exodus to the Promised Land, upon what Innocent III had termed a *transitus* from this life to eternal glory, possess a particular relevance to the *Millstätter Exodus*, for the German author had similarly found it necessary to allay *zwîvel* if he was to succeed in arousing support for the crusading idea. For St Bernard, as for the chroniclers of the First Crusade, the war against the heathen is a particular opportunity for salvation, made available only in this period of history and offered to the knights especially—as such it is related not merely to the salvation of Israel, accomplished in the exodus from Egypt, but also to the salvation of mankind at large, achieved by Christ's self-sacrifice and commemorated in the Easter liturgy.

Yet this by no means exhausts the fund of associations between the crusades and the events at Easter. To penetrate further into this complex body of biblical allusions we must recall the fact, implicit in the argument employed by Innocent III, that the crusader was felt to be involved in a particular form of *imitatio Christi*. This is already demonstrated by Urban II at Clermont in his quotation from Luc. 14. 27 when urging the knights present to take the crusader's cross upon themselves and thus, in this tangible sense, follow in the footsteps of Christ: '. . . complebunt illud Domini praeceptum quod ipse jubet per Evangelium: Qui non bajulat crucem suam et venit post me, non est me dignus.'[2] Christ is to be imitated by those who bear His cross and undertake the journey to Jerusalem so that, although the need to suffer with Him is not expressed so explicitly as it was later by Innocent III, the crusader's readiness to sacrifice himself is seen in connection with Christ's paschal sacrifice. The assistance rendered by the crusader is an imitation of the liberation achieved by Christ, as is made clear by another account of the Clermont speech, when

---

[1] Letter 363, *MPL*, 182, 566A.   [2] *RHC*, III, 730A.

General conclusions

remission of sins is promised: '...eis doctor egregius remissionem omnium condonat peccatorum, si, renuntiatis omnibus quae possidebant, crucem post Christum unanimiter portantes, periclitantibus conchristianis ferrent auxilium.'[1] The same biblical image is employed in an anonymous history of the First Crusade to describe the movement of French knights towards the Holy Sepulchre: 'Cum jam appropinquasset ille terminus quem dominus Ihesus cotidie suis demonstrat fidelibus, specialiter in evangelio dicens: Si quis vult post me venire, abneget semetipsum, et tollat crucem suam et sequatur me.'[2] The crusader, bearing his cross and with the site of the crucifixion as the goal of his journey, is engaged in a direct imitation of Christ's last journey of sacrifice and redemption along the *Via Dolorosa*.

It is permissible to doubt whether the proclamation of this *imitatio Christi* by the crusader would have called forth such an enthusiastic reaction from the knights of Western Europe if it had been based exclusively on the precepts of self-sacrifice and suffering in fellowship with Christ. The knights whose secular exploits are condemned as sinful violence would not have been won for a doctrine of Christian self-abnegation if there had not been some more active aspect to the role allotted to them. It is here that we must attach particular importance to the manner in which they are called upon to render armed assistance to the Church of the Orient and to bring liberation to their fellow Christians. This is a more active knightly task, capable of appealing to contemporary knighthood, but also one which develops the idea of an *imitatio Christi* since the crusaders' liberation of their fellow Christians in need can now be compared with the salvation brought to mankind by Christ and with the liberation which He accomplished. Urban II paints the persecution and misery which the Christians of the Orient are suffering at the hands of the Saracens in the blackest possible colours.[3] This

---

[1] *RHC*, v, 15 c.   [2] *Histoire anonyme de la première croisade*, p. 2.
[3] Cf. Baldricus, *RHC*, iv, 12 G ('Christiani, fratres nostri, membra Christi, flagellantur, opprimuntur, injuriantur') or *ibid.* 13 A ('Effunditur sanguis Christianus, Christi sanguine redemptus; et caro Christiana, carni Christi consanguinea, nefandis ineptiis et servitutibus nefariis mancipatur').

enables him to stress the duty which this imposes upon the
Christian knight. Refusal to give assistance will call forth divine
anger ('O quanta improperia vobis ab ipso Domino imputa-
buntur, si eos non juveritis qui professione Christiana censentur,
sicut et vos'![1]), it is the duty of the Christian to help his brothers
('Necesse est enim, quatinus confratribus vestris in Orientali
plaga conversantibus...accelerato itinere succurratis'[2]) as well
as to defend the Church ('et ad defendendam Orientalem Ecclesiam velocius concurrite'[3]). The Pope gives added point to his
argument by quoting the words of Christ: '...quia et charitas
est, pro fratribus animas ponere.'[4] The point about this particular
injunction is not simply that it derives its authority from what is
reported as Christ's actual words (Joh. 15. 13), but rather that
these words, behind their general formulation, have an immediate
bearing on Christ Himself and that, in foreknowledge of what is
so soon to happen, He addresses them to His disciples at the Last
Supper and hence on the eve of the passover. It is therefore the
paschal aspect of Christ's sacrifice which Urban II, like his successor Innocent III, places before the knights as the example
which they are to imitate in bringing help and release from
suffering to their brethren in the East. The concepts of a paschal
sacrifice, a liberation brought to one's fellow men, a taking up
of the cross and a journey to Jerusalem, to the site of the crucifixion, are all ideas which establish an affinity between Christ's
actions in the Easter period and the knights' military expedition
to the Holy Land. Against the more passive concept of sacrifice
we must set the active aspects of this *imitatio* which are likely to
have appealed to the knighthood: the journey itself to the Holy

[1] *RHC*, III, 324 C. [2] *Ibid.* 323 F.
[3] *RHC*, IV, 14 H. The same ideas are also expressed in the chronicles outside
the context of the papal speech at Clermont. According to Albertus, the inhabitants of Bethlehem implore the crusaders to liberate them from their slavery
(*RHC*, IV, 462 D: 'videlicet vos Christianos confratres ad excussionem jugi servitutis nostrae adesse, et loca sancta Iherusalem restauranda') and Bernold of Konstanz gives the same motive of assisting oppressed fellow Christians (*MGH* SS
V, 464, 13: 'His temporibus maxima multitudo de Italia et omni Gallia et Germania Hierosolimam contra paganos, ut liberarent christianos, ire cepit').
[4] *RHC*, IV, 15 C.

Land, the taking up of the cross in the form of warfare with the sword, and knightly assistance rendered to those in need, a justification of warfare and of the knightly class which had been employed as early as Bonizo of Sutri.[1] The crusading knights' *imitatio* of Christ's redemption therefore passes far beyond the passive ideal of self-sacrifice and contains enough active elements to appeal to the warlike mentality of the secular knighthood from which they were to be recruited.

This argument cannot be decisively weakened by an appeal to the differences which separate the crusader's *imitatio* from the model of his behaviour which is provided in Christ's deeds of the Easter period. We need attach little importance to the fact that, whereas Christ redeemed the souls of men, the most that the crusader's 'redemption' could achieve was the liberation of men's bodies and of the earthly city of Jerusalem. If we were to regard this distinction as so critical as to invalidate any comparison of the crusader with Christ, then we should also be compelled to admit that no man was capable of imitating Christ and that the concept of an *imitatio Christi* was a contradiction in terms.[2] Similarly, we can ignore the discrepancy between the salvation of mankind achieved by Christ and the fact that the crusader, in bringing salvation to the Christians of the Orient, was thereby enabled to gain salvation for himself. Although this constitutes an irreducible difference between Christ's deed and His imitation by the crusader (since Christ cannot be said to have redeemed Himself by His sacrifice), this is a difference which applies to any Christian who takes Christ's life as his model, but which cannot disprove the relevance of the doctrine of *imitatio Christi* to Christian ethics. Although the Christian can only imitate Christ

[1] See Erdmann, *Die Entstehung des Kreuzzugsgedankens*, pp. 229 ff.

[2] Against this possible objection we need only refer to the ample testimony of the New Testament with its repeated asseveration that the true Christian is he who in this life follows in the footsteps of Christ. Cf. Matt. 16. 24 ('Tunc Jesus dixit discipulis suis: Si quis vult post me venire, abneget semetipsum, et tollat crucem suam, et sequatur me'; cf. Luc. 9. 23), Luc. 14. 27 ('Et qui non bajulat crucem suam, et venit post me, non potest meus esse discipulus') or Joh. 8. 12 ('Iterum ergo locutus est eis Jesus, dicens: ego sum lux mundi; qui sequitur me, non ambulat in tenebris, sed habebit lumen vitae').

in His humanity, but cannot extend this to an imitation of His metaphysical nature, this does not invalidate the importance of the realm in which this human imitation is possible. Finally, if we bear in mind the fact that Christ's redemption of mankind was commonly seen in terms of a new exodus,[1] just as the crusaders' expedition to the Holy Land was also regarded as the typological fulfilment of the exodus of the Israelites, it is clear that this common relationship with the same Old Testament type will inevitably bring the crusaders into close association with Christ and suggest that their deeds are not simply an antitype of the Old Testament events, but also an imitation of Christ's redemptive sacrifice in the Easter period.

These parallels are sufficient to suggest that there was an intimate connection, obvious to contemporary observers, between the crusades and the events of Easter. If this is so, then the author of the *Millstätter Exodus* does not stand alone in combining references to Easter with a crusading interpretation of his biblical theme. This must not be taken to mean that he goes as far in this respect as some of the authors whose statements we have regarded as evidence that such a conjunction of two apparently unrelated themes did no violence to twelfth-century ways of thought. All we can maintain is that the Millstatt author agreed with others in being persuaded of the intimate relationship between these two themes; we cannot argue that all the considerations suggesting this were utilised by him in his description of the exodus. Two important possibilities, for example, remain unexploited. Whereas crusading chroniclers, whether reporting the speech of Urban II or commenting on events independently, give prominence to the idea that each individual crusader, in taking up his cross to follow Christ, is engaged in a personal *imitatio* of Christ (involving a readiness to suffer with Him and to sacrifice himself in His name), the German epic is concerned only to illustrate the exodus of the whole Israelite army as a prefiguration of the crusaders' general exodus. In so far as this may imply an *imitatio* of Christ's

[1] See Daniélou, *Sacramentum futuri*, pp. 135 ff., for examples of this conception of Christ's life in the New Testament.

redemption (seen as a new exodus) it is clear that this *imitatio* is a much more collective one, affecting the whole of the crusading army and only indirectly seen as a personal *imitatio Christi* by each individual warrior. The suggestion that in these events *tua res agitur* is thus addressed to the knighthood at large and little attention is paid to elaborating the personal implications for each knight as an individual. The second restriction in the German epic concerns the redemptive theme of crusading warfare. In the evidence of the chronicles this theme is worked out under two headings: active, in that the crusaders bring their form of salvation to the Church of the Orient by removing the Saracen yoke, and passive, since those who contribute towards this liberation of their fellow Christians are thereby assured that salvation is to be granted to them. By his choice and treatment of theme the Millstatt author has concentrated almost entirely on the theme of passive redemption: there is no suggestion in his work that the exodus of the Israelites brings about the liberation of anyone other than themselves and furthermore, whatever role he may have conceded to human activity in the early part of the epic,[1] it is only by God's intervention in the passage of the Red Sea, especially in view of their own loss of confidence, that their deliverance is finally brought about. The active redemptive role which distinguished the crusading knight and which contributed towards the manner of his *imitatio Christi* is absent from the German work, so that its emphasis falls on the opportunity for salvation which is being offered to the knighthood of the twelfth century. If we add to these two observations the equally important fact that the German author obviously hesitated to make full use of the possibilities presented to him by his acknowledgement of a positive function of warfare,[2] that he stopped short of depicting his Israelites engaged in a battle required of them by God, it then becomes clear that the Millstatt author, for all his important innovations, cannot be said to have made use of every possibility which his innovations offered him. He is the first to introduce the theme of crusading warfare into German

---

[1] See pp. 34 ff.　　　　　　　　[2] See p. 389.

literature, but he also stands very much at the beginning of this particular tradition.

Our argument has reached the point where it has become clear that the various interpretations of his theme suggested by the Millstatt author are reconcilable with one another and are hardly likely to be purely fortuitous. We have seen that the equation between an Old Testament theme and the crusading present was a widespread conviction in the period of the crusades and that this belief was well developed in the case of Exodus. We have also seen that the close connections between baptism and the liturgy of the Easter period make it intelligible that our author should have thought fit to include allusions to the two possibilities of a baptismal and a paschal interpretation of the events narrated. Finally, it has become apparent that the crusading period frequently had recourse to the imagery of baptism and of the Easter liturgy as a means of interpreting the crusading experience itself. In other words, the various possibilities of interpretation which are suggested by the German work (the historical events of the exodus, the crusades, baptism and the Easter liturgy) form a coherent whole; they are not the chance result of an undisciplined mind seeking to extract, at all costs, the maximum profit from his chosen theme. In reaching this conclusion about the rich allusiveness of the Millstatt author's attitude to his theme, we have come very close to what we saw of his technique of epic expansion, where it was clear that Kossmann was wrong in attributing this solely to formal clumsiness in matters of rhyme and in denying to him a considerable degree of conscious control over his material.

It is essential to emphasise that, however important the typological method may have been in interpreting this work, the coherence of the work rests on more solid foundations than the formal unity provided by the various exegetical possibilities subsumed under the typological method. What is of decisive importance for the unity of the Millstatt work is not the fact that each of these readings is reconcilable with the others because they all form part of the same exegetical method, but instead the

General conclusions

fact that the exegetical method was able to suggest these readings because they already shared a common function. The function of each of these four readings is its ability to signify the redemption of mankind by Christ. The choice of this Old Testament theme was made by the author not because of any impartial interest in the historical events themselves (although this by no means implies that he was not persuaded of their historicity),[1] but instead because he regarded them traditionally as prefiguring the salvation achieved by Christ. Similarly, the crusading interpretation is significant only because it illustrates how the redemption offered by Christ to all men at all times may be realised by certain men (the knights) at a certain time (the crusading present). The allusions to baptism are likewise explained by the opportunity for redemption which this sacramental rite holds out to the convert, while the references to the Easter liturgy derive their force from that festival in the Church year which commemorates the historical salvation achieved by Christ. Redemption is the theme which binds these four interpretations together and which allows them to be adopted by the typological method. Or in other words: although Christ is nowhere mentioned in the German work and although none of these interpretations explicitly refers to Him and to His sacrificial redemption of mankind, it is He who forms the unifying nucleus of this work. It is to Him that the exodus of the Israelites looks forward and it is from Him that baptism acquires its meaning. Similarly, it is His sacrifice which the Easter liturgy commemorates and it is in His footsteps that the crusaders follow. The *Millstätter Exodus* is therefore a work totally informed by the theme of redemption. In addressing it to a knightly audience its author is attempting to reveal the new means of salvation which has now been offered to them in particular.

How may we best connect this redemptive theme, illustrated in a number of aspects, with the four senses (historical or literal, allegorical, tropological and anagogical) of the typological method which the author has employed? Clearly, there is no

[1] See pp. 128 ff.

425

difficulty in equating the historical or literal sense with the author's narrative of the events which befell the Israelites on their departure from Egypt, for there is nowhere any suggestion that he doubts the historical truth of these events. The allegorical sense, referring to the words and deeds of Christ or to the sacraments of His Church, may with as little difficulty be associated with the allusions to the sacrament of baptism and to the liturgy of the Easter period. Our problem is to determine whether the remaining interpretation (the crusades) may be reconciled with the typological method and also to inquire whether the two remaining senses (the tropological and the anagogical) have any counterpart in the German work. That the anagogical sense is present in the Millstatt epic, even though it may not be developed at any length, is made clear by the author's words when he concludes the hymn of thanksgiving at the end of the work by expressing the wish that we too may attain to the Heavenly Jerusalem.[1] This is the traditional anagogical interpretation, so that this sense is clearly present. That it should be only briefly indicated (and thus not inform any details of the work itself) is reminiscent of the way in which Innocent III in his conciliar sermon dismissed what he called the eternal sense (equivalent to the anagogical) of his text with relative speed at the end of his discourse. With Innocent III this was because he attached more immediate importance to the other two senses he was discussing (the crusade and the reform of the Church), so that we may assume, from the fact that the German author likewise fails to develop his anagogical sense, that he too attached more immediate importance to the other senses. The same is true of the possible presence of the tropological sense in the vernacular epic (the function of *zwîvel* and of *ubirmuot*,[2] the spiritual aspect of the conflict between the Israelites and the Egyptians[3]): only the latter may be said to inform the whole of the narrative, but even this suggestion of a psychomachia does not acquire any inde-

[1] See vv. 3298 ff.
[2] See pp. 336 ff. and pp. 169 f.
[3] See p. 137, n. 1, pp. 169 f. and pp. 390 ff.

pendence since it remains subordinated to the baptismal or to the crusading interpretation.[1]

It is this crusading interpretation which forms the crux of our reading of the *Exodus*. Of its presence in the work there can be little doubt, but our remaining problem is to decide on the typological sense to which it corresponds. We may do this by recalling first the typological truth that the exodus of Israel prefigures the salvation of mankind by Christ and secondly the fact, stressed repeatedly in the chronicles, that the exodus was also regarded as a prefiguration of the crusades. This suggests that the crusading interpretation corresponds to the allegorical sense of traditional typology, since the contemporary crusades were regarded as repeating, but transcending, their Old Testament type. Yet how can we associate the crusading interpretation of the Millstatt epic with the traditional allegorical sense, if this sense is conventionally applied either to Christ Himself or to the sacraments of His Church? The answer to this is provided by the result of our investigations into the parallels between the crusades and the Easter liturgy, for we saw that the redemptive theme common to both implied that the crusaders were engaged in a direct *imitatio Christi*. The crusades stand in a typological relationship to the exodus of the Israelites not by virtue of any characteristic peculiar to them, but only because Christ, by His redemption of mankind, transcended the Old Testament type, so that consequently the crusaders (who imitate Christ in their journey to the Holy Sepulchre) will likewise be seen as transcending the Israelite exodus. Again it is Christ, even though there is no explicit reference to Him in the German work, who forms the indispensable link between the Old Testament event and its typological fulfilment in the present, for without Him these events would fall apart and lose the intense quality of their reciprocal relationship. As we saw from some of the evidence of the chronicles and in our discussion of *zwîvel*,[2] the Christian warriors of the crusades were assured that they would not merely repeat the exploits of the Hebrews, but actually transcend them, only as long as they

[1] See pp. 386 ff.   [2] See p. 271 and pp. 339 ff.

avoided the sin of the Hebrews—i.e. as long as they remained true to Christ and continued to follow His precepts and His example. The theme of such an *imitatio* is therefore central to the typological relationship between the Hebrew exodus and the twelfth-century crusades and allows us to equate the Millstatt author's crusading interpretation with the allegorical sense of traditional typology.[1] All the interpretations of the *Millstätter Exodus* (apart from the literal one) which have occupied our attention (crusades, baptism and Easter liturgy) correspond to the allegorical sense: the last two because they signify the sacramental functions of the Church, and the first because it illustrates a means of imitating Christ's deeds and qualities. None of these interpretations refers to Christ directly, who therefore remains unmentioned, but all are concerned to demonstrate His relevance to the present: the last two because they commemorate Him liturgically, and the first because it reveals the relevance of His example to the present opportunity offered to the knighthood.

This equation between the various interpretations suggested by the Millstatt author and the four senses of the typological method implies a significant distribution of emphasis. Whereas very little weight falls on the anagogical sense (this is implied only at the conclusion of the work) and on the tropological sense (the motif of spiritual warfare is subordinated to the theme of baptism or the crusades), considerable importance attaches to the literal or historical sense (since this provides the factual elements

---

[1] In other words, the pattern which we saw earlier (pp. 320f.) in the author's treatment of the scene in which Pharaoh orders the killing of the male children of the Israelites is the same as the pattern which informs the whole of his crusading interpretation of the events of Exodus. In both cases we encounter a typological relationship between an Old Testament type and its New Testament fulfilment (the killing of the male children: the slaughter of the innocents at Bethlehem *or* the exodus of the Hebrews from Egypt: Christ's redemption of mankind from bondage to sin); in both cases the antitype (the innocents *or* Christ) is not expressly mentioned, but is left to be read out of the work by implication; and in both cases the crusaders are given a typological relationship with the Old Testament type by virtue of their imitation of the antitype (as the latest Christian martyrs they imitate the *exemplum* of the innocents, the first to die on behalf of Christ, and as crusaders their whole undertaking is an *imitatio Christi*, especially of Christ's deeds in the Easter period).

General conclusions

of the author's narrative) as well as to the allegorical sense (since this has attracted to itself the crusading, the baptismal and also the paschal interpretations). The fact that the literal and allegorical senses play a much more important role in the work than the others may possibly be connected with what J. Chydenius has remarked on the use of typology in connection with the crusades. After quoting several chroniclers to the effect that the crusading events of the present constitute a literal or historical fulfilment of Old Testament prophecies (*ad litteram impleri* or *exhiberi historialiter*) he says: 'The examples that have been quoted from the Crusade authors show that the First Crusade meant a recovery of the historical sense of the prophecies of the Old Testament, which had originally possessed such a literal meaning but had till then been interpreted by the Christians in a non-literal way.'[1] Chydenius appears to be confusing the fact of a literal, historical fulfilment of a prophecy with the literal or historical sense of typology, since the implication of his argument is that the literal historicity of an event removes it effectively from the allegorical[2] range of senses (allegorical, tropological and anagogical). That this is not so has been shown effectively by E. Auerbach in his interpretation of a passage from Dante (*Par.* IX, 109 ff.). He argues in favour of the necessary historicity not merely of the prefiguration, but also of its typological fulfilment: '... denn beide Pole einer typologischen Figur bewahren ihre historisch reale Konkretheit; der typologische Sinn zerstört nicht den wörtlich historischen Sinn des prophetischen Ereignisses, und auch die auf diese Weise figurierte Erfüllung ist stets ein als wirklich geschehend erwartetes Ereignis, nicht eine Abstraktion.'[3] In

[1] Chydenius, *The Typological Problem in Dante*, p. 80.
[2] I use the word 'allegorical' here to indicate any one of the non-literal senses.
[3] *Typologische Motive in der mittelalterlichen Literatur*, p. 8. I must confess that I find it difficult to explain a passage in the *Gesta Dei per Francos* of Guibertus (quoted by Chydenius, *op. cit.* p. 78) in which the chronicler, relating the capture of Jerusalem by the crusaders to the prophecy of Zach. 12. 3, says that this prophecy need therefore no longer be interpreted allegorically: 'Sed levata Iherusalem, "omnia regna terrae adversus eam colliguntur"; quod non ut allegoria subintelligendum, sed, ut historia noviter relata, supernis oculis intuendum proponitur' (*RHC*, IV, 238c). I suspect that the

other words, the historical reality of the crusade is no reason why its employment in typology should be confined only to the literal or historical sense; as a fulfilment of an Old Testament prefiguration it can be equated with the allegorical sense. With this modification (conceding literal historicity both to the literal sense and to the allegorical) we may agree with the observation made by Chydenius that the crusading movement placed a greater emphasis on those typological senses in which a historical interpretation was possible (by contrast with the tropological or anagogical sense). What Chydenius says of the influence of the crusades on the typological method agrees with what we have observed of the greater importance which the Millstatt author attaches to the literal and allegorical senses of his poem. In both cases it is the particular nature of the crusading experience (combining spiritual warfare with physical conflict and granting a way to spiritual salvation by means of the sword) which has brought about this shift of emphasis towards the physical and historical, without ever denying the presence of the spiritual or timeless aspects.

Our last question concerns the presence of the theme of warfare in the Millstatt epic. We have seen that, despite the novelty of introducing this theme without any direct criticism, our author is hesitant about describing the Israelites as engaged in battle in God's name. Such reservations suggest not merely that the Millstatt author was a pioneer in this respect and was himself conscious of this fact, but also that the battle which he has in mind is a physical conflict and not simply a spiritual one. This

explanation of this passage is similar to what we saw above (pp. 393 ff.) of the dual nature (spiritual and physical) of crusading warfare and the difficulties this occasioned for those who sought to understand this new phenomenon. St Bernard therefore argues that he is at a loss to know how best to describe the Templars, for they are both knights and monks (*MPL*, 182, 927 B), and it is perhaps because of this uncertainty that he elsewhere in the same work comes close to abandoning this view of the dual nature of the Templars by suggesting that they are not *homicidae* but *malicidae* (*ibid.* 924 B), just as Bohemond is reported as claiming that *hoc bellum non est carnale, sed spirituale* (see p. 395, n. 2). If the complex nature of the new phenomenon leads such authorities to place excessive emphasis on one aspect of the crusades it is equally possible that Guibertus has conversely denied an allegorical sense to the fulfilment of Zach. 12. 3 in his own day for similar reasons.

conclusion is most relevant to the problem of deciding whether he attached equal importance to each of his three major interpretations (crusades, baptism and Easter liturgy). If he had regarded his work as illustrating the psychomachia of baptism or the spiritual conflict of Christ with Satan in the Easter period, then he could have used his military vocabulary in an exclusively metaphorical sense and would have felt no hesitation in applying it to the Hebrews. Since this hesitation is present, it can only imply physical warfare (even though this may also be combined with a psychomachia) and hence a dominant role granted to the theme of crusading warfare. Furthermore, from what we have seen of the contemporary evidence for the conception that the crusader's martyr purity placed him on a par with the newly baptised child, just as his readiness to imitate Christ made the events of Easter relevant to his condition, it is intelligible that a central crusading theme should have attracted to itself the secondary themes of baptism and Easter. The converse is much less probable, since there is little likelihood that an author whose main intention was to interpret the events of Exodus as prefiguring either Christian baptism or the events of Easter would have felt it necessary to strengthen either of these readings by an appeal to the role of the crusaders in the present. On the other hand, an author primarily concerned to illustrate his crusading reading would conceivably find it helpful to appeal to the authoritative examples of baptism and of Easter. This in fact we saw in the sermon of Innocent III and in the *Rolandslied*. From all this we may conclude that it is the crusading interpretation which is our author's chief preoccupation and that the baptismal and paschal readings are meant to contribute to this major purpose. Equally subordinate (if not for the author's total religious personality, then at least in this particular work of his) are his references to a tropological reading (*zwîvel, ubirmuot* and a spiritual conflict) and an anagogical one (the Heavenly Jerusalem). This does not of course mean that the crusades were more important to him than the possibility of attaining to the Heavenly Jerusalem, but rather that the need which he felt urgently in composing this work was to illustrate this particular opportunity of reaching the Heavenly Jerusalem, open to the knights if only they could be won over to taking the cross.

The central importance of the crusading interpretation can also be used to suggest an explanation why the German author should have chosen to treat no more than the first fifteen chapters of Exodus. His attitude towards warfare in the name of God was, we saw, still unresolved. He was not averse to describing such warfare when waged by the insects, but in the case of men he remained content with a description of their military appearance and with no more than an oblique reference to their warlike exploits in the past or in the future. The theme of warfare is undoubtedly present and is the Millstatt author's main contribution to his biblical material, but equally discernible is his uncertainty how far he may make direct use of it. In the end, he settles for a direct exploitation of this theme with the insects, but only an indirect one in the case of human beings. In view of this uncertainty it is of considerable importance that, had he decided to continue his account beyond the stage where he concluded it, he would have been confronted with the necessity of describing the Israelites' battle with the Amalechites, as related in chapter 17 of his biblical source. This is the first of those battles to which God had prophetically referred and in which He had promised to assist His people so that they might gain possession of Canaan.[1] Whereas the German author had retained this earlier reference[2] (because it only indirectly hinted at a future battle), his reluctance to describe the Israelites as warriors directly engaged in battle would have caused considerable difficulties if he had continued his work so as to include the later chapter. That this reluctance is attested in the work itself (and is not simply inferred from the negative fact that he stopped short of chapter 17) is best confirmed by the clear distinction he draws between the Israelites on the one hand and the insects or Egyptians on the other, applying to the latter heroic terms and epithets which he refuses to use of the former.

[1] Cf. Exod. 3. 8 and 17.   [2] Vv. 515 ff.

General conclusions

It is at this stage that we may best halt to consider an alternative explanation of the Millstatt author's reluctance to describe his Israelite warriors as engaged in battle in God's name.[1] We have seen that this reluctance suggests that the warfare he had in mind was of a physical nature.[2] If this is so, then it would be possible to concede the presence of crusading allusions in the *Millstätter Exodus* and yet to argue that they were intended by the author as a criticism of the ideal of Christian warfare which he, in common with the authors of *Ruodlieb* and the *Wiener Genesis*, was not prepared to accept. This is an attitude similar to that of de Boor whose argument we considered earlier. But whereas de Boor's argument was based on no more than three isolated details we must recognise that the present alternative explanation is capable of a sustained interpretation of the whole work. In other words, it would be possible to argue that the Millstatt author's repeated stress on God's omnipotence, His guidance and control of events and His continual interventions leaves little room for any decisive human activity, for any contribution on the part of man such as the crusaders' warfare on behalf of God was felt to be. From this initial point it would be possible to proceed to the view that even the glowing description of the Israelite warriors as they set out from Egypt, combined with references to their humility and their unheroic fears when they realise they are being pursued, and characterised by a total absence of any military contribution by the Jews to their own salvation (achieved by God alone), was meant as an emphatic reminder to the knightly audience that all this knightly splendour of the Hebrews, like that of the Egyptians, was impotent before the might of God. If this reading were to be accepted, then the poet's explicit message would be to attribute the glory of this outcome to God and to argue that man's role was simply to praise God's omnipotence—an attitude which informs Moses' hymn of praise at the conclusion of the epic and

---

[1] I have to thank R. A. Wisbey who, whilst himself not wedded to the alternative explanation discussed in the following pages, has skilfully played the role of an *advocatus diaboli* and forced me to think out my position in greater detail.

[2] See pp. 430f.

which is of course eminently characteristic of the Easter liturgy. Equally important for us would be the further suggestion implicit in this: that knightly reliance on heroic virtues and on physical weapons was totally irrelevant. From this it would be feasible to develop a third argument and to maintain that if the Millstatt author had continued his work beyond the passage of the Red Sea then he would soon have had to depict a scene in which God was shown assisting His people in physical warfare—and this he refused to do because, like earlier authors, he did not approve of warfare waged in the name of God. In short, this argument would accept the presence of crusading elements in the *Millstätter Exodus*, but would maintain that their function is to express the author's rejection of this new ideal. The Millstatt epic would therefore be novel only in its bare acquaintance with the crusading ideal of Christian warfare, since its rejection of this novelty would place it in the company of such older works as *Ruodlieb* and the *Wiener Genesis*.

In attempting to meet this argument we should do well to recognise that a considerable measure of agreement is possible between this rival explanation and the views which I have advanced—primarily because I do not regard the Millstatt author as wholly won over for the new idea of Christian warfare, but instead as still poised between rejection and acceptance and therefore revealing undeniable reservations about the whole problem of crusading warfare. The question therefore is: are these reservations strong enough to explain his total attitude or do they serve, however significant they may be, only to qualify his acceptance of Christian warfare? If I hold that the latter is more likely this is not because I am not conscious of the difficulty of deciding where the Millstatt author's main allegiance lies and it does not mean that his espousal of crusading ideas was not accompanied by doubts on his part.

Two general considerations lead me to question whether these doubts about Christian warfare were strong enough to cancel out the appeal which this new ideal exercised upon him. In the first place, we saw in chapter I that the German epic was informed not merely by crusading allusions, but also by baptismal and paschal references. We have also seen that it is possible to reconcile these three types of reference and to understand why an author primarily engaged in elaborating the crusading implications of his theme should not regard the further incorporation of baptismal and paschal allusions as irrelevant to his purpose.[1] Yet if this is so, if the Millstatt author chose to support and enrich his crusading theme by adding to it these further allusions from the liturgy, then this can only mean that he regarded his basic theme in a positive light and that these additional allusions were meant to enhance an idea which, despite the hesitations of which he is still guilty, already claims his main allegiance. The baptismal and paschal allusions not merely enrich the author's primary crusading theme, they also imply that his attitude towards this theme was more positive than negative. This may be confirmed by a general chronological consideration. If we accept 1120 as the likely date of composition we must regard the work as composed at a time when support for the crusading idea was only very slowly gathering in Germany.[2] In such circumstances, when infinitely fewer German knights had been won for the crusading idea than was the case in France as early as the First Crusade, it is easier to conceive of a clerical author seeking to enlist support for the new idea than to imagine him superfluously devoting his energies to combating and rejecting an idea which had gained so little foothold amongst the knights he was addressing. On the other hand, if we accept the later dating proposed by Menhardt[3] (1170–4), it is equally difficult to explain the archaisms of the Millstatt work.

Despite these general considerations we still have to meet the three particular arguments which could be advanced against the *Millstätter Exodus* as a positive crusading work. The first (that God's omnipotent intervention left little room for any human contribution) has already been dealt with, since we saw that although the Millstatt author left unchanged the final scene in which God rescued His people from Pharaoh he also consistently

[1] See pp. 377 ff.   [2] See pp. 296 ff.   [3] See p. 297, n. 3.

modified the earlier scenes of the Vulgate so as to confer a greater independence on Moses and Aaron, who now act more in their own right than simply as the mouthpiece of God. God's omnipotence may be an important facet of the Millstatt epic, but this does not mean that the human actors (especially Moses) are thereby deprived of any independent contribution which they might make to the course of the action. Nor is there any contradiction between the changes effected by the Millstatt author and crusading testimony, for here too the argument is frequently employed that, although God is omnipotent and could drive the Saracens from the Holy Land by His own power if He so wished, He chooses not to exercise this power, so as to offer mankind, and particularly the knights, a unique opportunity to contribute towards their own salvation.[1] In crusading thought as in the Millstatt work God's omnipotence is unquestioned and of decisive importance, but it does not exclude the possibility of a human contribution—in the crusades as an opportunity for the knighthood to gain salvation and with the *Exodus* in the manner in which Moses, as the leader of the Hebrews, has conferred upon him a greater independence than in the biblical account.

[1] This argument is most clearly employed by St Bernard in his crusading letter (no. 363) to Germany: *MPL*, 182, 565 c ('Nunquid abbreviata manus Domini, aut impotens facta est ad salvandum, quod ad tuendum et restituendum sibi haereditatem suam exiguos vermiculos vocat?...Omnino subest ei, cum voluerit, posse: sed, dico vobis, tentat vos Dominus Deus vester...Miseratur enim Dominus populum suum, et lapsis graviter providet remedium salutare'). This attitude is not unknown to the poets of this period, as is attested by Albrecht von Johannsdorf (*MF*, 89, 25: 'die sprechent alle "wære ez unserm herren ande, | er ræche ez âne ir aller vart." | nu mugen si denken daz er leit den grimmen tôt. | der grôzen marter was im ouch vil gar unnôt, | wan daz in erbarmet unser val') or by *CB* 48, stanza 5, 4 ('Ierusalem voluit perdere, | ut hoc opere | sic possemus culpas diluere, | nam si vellet, hostes destruere | absque nobis et terram solvere | posset propere, | cum sibi nil possit resistere'). A similar argument is employed by Thomasin von Zerclære in his *Welscher Gast*, for he records as a hypothetical objection to the crusades the view that, if this was what He really wanted, God could Himself liberate the Holy Sepulchre and thus dispense men from the need to take the cross (vv. 11499 ff.). Thomasin concedes that man can of course do nothing without God (vv. 11509 ff.), but later argues that the crusades are no less than an opportunity for martyrdom offered to man by God: 'Got hât uns materge geben | daz wir mugen von disem leben | hin zim nâch marteræere wîs' (vv. 11679 ff.). See also vv. 11533 ff.

General conclusions

The second stage in the alternative explanation concerned the impotence of the Israelite warriors before the might of God. This fact is incontestable and would not be questioned by any Christian author, but we must ask whether the Millstatt author's intention in so depicting the Israelites was the same as in his scene describing the military splendour of the Egyptians. I take it that there would be little disagreement with the view that the impotence of the Egyptian warriors is meant as a criticism of their form of knighthood. Their arrogant boasting (*ruom, sich ver-meʒʒen, gelf*) is a quality well known in heroic literature and forms an integral part of their military description, just as the passage describing their destruction achieves some of its effect by the enumeration of the items of knightly equipment which afforded them so little protection in this final crisis.[1] On the other hand, to regard the Israelite warriors as subjected to the author's criticism because of their knighthood is to ignore the moral difference between them and their Egyptian opponents: in the passage describing their military departure it is explicitly said that they were guilty of no *ubirmuot* (a quality traditionally characteristic of the pagans as of secular knighthood) and, throughout the whole work, heroic terms and epithets used of the Egyptians (or the plagues) are not applied to the Hebrews. This differentiation between the Israelites and the Egyptians informs the Millstatt author's work and is the more telling because, at the conclusion when both armies approach the climax of the Red Sea, they are described as being outwardly similar in their knightly trappings. Admittedly, these Israelite warriors are of course criticised in the scene by the Red Sea—however, *not* because they are knights, but rather because, in thus demonstrating their lack of confidence in God, they reveal how deficient is their knighthood in the service of God.[2] The knightly aristocrats whom the Millstatt

[1] See pp. 102 f.

[2] These deficiencies of the Hebrews (they prefer to let things stay as they are when Moses' appeal to Pharaoh produces only an increase of their burden; in the hour of deliverance they are shown as a panic-stricken herd of fugitives and even Moses at first shrinks from the task which God places upon him) are a standing warning to all Christians. This is accentuated by the appearance of

author is addressing are taught to transcend the Hebrews in two ways: their Christianity, i.e. their election as God's new Israel, is to safeguard them against the loss of divine favour which befell the earlier Israel, but at the same time their knightly professionalism, the heroic ethos of chivalry, is a guarantee that, unlike the Israelites of the exodus, they will not tempt God by lack of confidence. It is this twofold negative *exemplum* of the Israelites which is covered by the term *zwîvel* and which accounts for the significant role it plays in the German epic.

The last stage in the rival argument concerns the fact that the German author did not proceed beyond chapter 15 of the Vulgate and sees in this a sign that he did not approve of the physical warfare on behalf of God which he would otherwise have had to depict. Reservations on this score are present, but I doubt whether they are strong enough to explain this decision of the author as an outright disapproval of the principle of Christian warfare, rather than merely an understandable reluctance to depict this warfare in action (for the first time in German literature!). If rejection of the principle itself was the reason why the author chose to break off the biblical account at this point, how are we to explain the presence of vv. 2931 f. ('daz edile gescuzze | daz wart in sît nuzze') where the future battles waged by the Israelites to gain possession of the Promised Land are anticipated? These lines are an addition of the author's and there is no compelling reason why, if he disapproved of the principle of warfare in the service of God, they could not have been omitted. The same is true of the manner in which God's prophecy to Moses of the manner in which His people will enter upon their inheritance in Canaan (vv. 521 ff.) hints at a military encounter between the Hebrews and the Canaanite kings—this again was not forced upon the German author by his source and could have been easily dropped if it had offended his attitude towards warfare in the name of God. In the light of these two passages it is possible that vv. 95 f., where Pharaoh expresses his concern at the military

similar features in the story of Christ's passion: His disciples flee at the moment of crisis, one of them betrays Him and another disowns Him in public.

prowess of the Israelites and the danger which this represents, are meant to be regarded as objectively true and not just as the opinion of a pagan ruler (and therefore conceivably mistaken).[1] In short, these allusions to the military exploits of the Israelites reveal the author's hesitancy in depicting Christian warfare in action, but their presence in the work at all is sufficient to indicate that it was not the idea of divine warfare about which the German author felt scruples, but rather the direct depiction of this idea in action. He concluded his work at chapter 15 not for the extreme reason that he disapproved of the Israelites' warfare against the Amalechites, but for the more half-hearted reason that, whilst not disapproving of this, he still hesitated to draw the logical artistic conclusions from his new conviction and to describe God's people serving God on the field of battle.

Another reason why the German author may have decided not to go beyond chapter 15 is suggested by a theme which his biblical source develops, first, slightly, towards the end of chapter 15 (at a point already beyond the passage where our author broke off), but then more emphatically in chapter 16: the murmuring of the Israelites against Moses or, indirectly, their rebelliousness against God.[2] This is the first of those scenes in which the behaviour of the Israelites in the wilderness shows none of that edifying perfection which an author could wish for who was proposing them as a model for present conduct. Although the Millstatt author is prepared to make use of this theme in passing (he therefore brings the import of these scenes forward by expanding the brief hint of a similar failing which the Bible gives in 14. 11 f.[3]), the incorporation of this theme into his work by

---

[1] See however p. 158. In other words, we should have to distinguish between Pharaoh's recognition of the martial qualities of his enemies (a recognition shared by the author and therefore meant to be objectively true) and his use of the heroic term *guote chnehte* to express this (a usage which tells us more about Pharaoh than it does about the author's attitude towards the Israelites). Fliegner, *Geistliches und weltliches Rittertum im Rolandslied*, pp. 14 ff. has pointed to a similar distinction in the *Rolandslied* on the three occasions when Christian warriors are described by the heroic epithet *virmezzen*.

[2] Cf. Exod. 15. 24 and 16. 2 ff.

[3] See pp. 99 ff.

a continuation beyond chapter 15 would have disturbed the balance of the whole epic as he conceived it. Any detailed development of this theme would have converted a work meant to reveal to the knights a way of salvation which God was graciously offering to them into a work disturbingly full of criticisms of the Hebrews' behaviour after their successful exodus. It is not by chance that St Bernard appeals in particular to the example of the Hebrews in the wilderness after their passage of the Red Sea when, in his *De consideratione*, he has to explain the failure of the Second Crusade.[1] If the Millstatt author had dwelt at any length on those scenes which St Bernard regarded as providing a reason for the defeat of the crusaders, then he would have given excessive prominence to awkward problems and doubts which were foreign to his purpose. An author concerned with persuading his audience of knights of the importance of the crusading idea would regard the passage of the Red Sea as his climax, for this demonstrated that their knightly exodus to the Promised Land would likewise bring them victory and salvation,[2] whereas the scenes in the wilderness would reinforce those doubts which he was anxious to allay. The Millstatt author was prepared to indicate the danger of following the Hebrews' negative example where they are alarmed by the sight of their Egyptian foes, but not to the extent that he was willing to devote more than a short episode to this potentially dangerous theme. Yet the fact that he was prepared to admit this theme into his work at all, however briefly, is enough to dispose of the possible argument that it is the wish to avoid treating the negative behaviour of the Hebrews in his work rather than the need to avoid a description of military action undertaken by God's people which led him to conclude his work at chapter 15. Both reasons may have influenced his decision, but this does not weaken the contention that it was primarily

[1] *MPL*, 182, 743 B ff.

[2] This demonstration of victory and salvation explains why the majority of the Exodus references in the liturgy of Good Friday and Holy Saturday concern the events of Exodus immediately before and including the successful crossing of the Red Sea. It is possible that the force of these liturgical passages also persuaded the Millstatt author to stop at this decisive point.

his interpretation of his subject-matter in terms of physical warfare which caused him to avoid facing the problem of describing his Israelites actually waging such warfare which would have been posed by any treatment of the critical chapter 17.

It is possible that yet another consideration, of a purely formal nature, also played a part in this decision. We have remarked on the obvious climax which the passage of the Red Sea marks as the final demonstration that God has liberated His people[1] and on the German author's employment of a number of formal devices to underline this climax and to make the most effective use of the tension which it introduces into his work.[2] From the point of view of form, a conclusion at this stage had much to recommend it although, from what we have seen of the unity between the author's formal changes and his interpretation of his subject-matter, I doubt whether we would be justified in seeing in this formal consideration the only motive for this restriction of his work to the first fifteen chapters. That he was able to extract formal advantage from his decision to conclude with the passage of the Red Sea is a sign of his skill in finding the style best suited to his conception of his theme; it is not a proof that these formal criteria were the major reason for his decision to go no further. It is here that his interpretation of the work in terms of physical warfare (despite his hesitancy in describing this in action) provides us with the most convincing answer, even if it may also have been confirmed by such other considerations as his wish to avoid depicting any sustained rebelliousness of the Hebrews, his conviction that the knights of his audience were more likely to be won over by the positive force of the salvation represented by the passage of the Red Sea than by the negative example of the Hebrews' shortcomings and, finally, his awareness of the formal advantages in concluding his work at such an obvious

[1] By either typological interpretation (the deliverance of Israel from their bondage or the salvation of mankind by Christ) the crossing of the Red Sea denotes the end of an epoch. It is therefore quite fitting that the Millstatt author, like the author of the OE *Exodus*, should have drawn a formal conclusion from this fact and closed his version at this point.

[2] See p. 44, n. 2.

441

climax. These reasons seem to me to be more telling than any dependence of the author, as yet not convincingly established, on the example of Alcimus Avitus.[1] Repeatedly we have had occasion to emphasise the importance of the Millstatt author's readiness to grant a positive function to warfare waged on behalf of God and to the results which followed from this decision. Our final problem is to determine his position within the development of this theme in German literature—a theme which is of considerable importance not merely in crusading literature, but also in courtly literature where the knightly hero's career is plotted as a series of knightly encounters. In this development we can afford to ignore such a work as the *Memento mori* for, although it is addressed to a lay audience, probably of aristocratic knights,[2] and although its connection with the contemporary *Friedensbewegung* has now become much more clear,[3] there is still no explicit treatment of the theme of warfare which would make it relevant to our inquiry. Instead, I propose to concentrate on a few examples where the theme of warfare, whether conceived positively or negatively, forms an integral part of the work in question. By a comparison with these we may hope to define the position of the Millstatt author more accurately.

The examples of *Ruodlieb* and of the *Wiener Genesis*, whose attitude to warfare has been analysed by Braun and Beyschlag respectively, have been adduced so frequently in the course of our argument that there is little need to dwell on them now. Braun has made it clear that, although the author of *Ruodlieb* is concerned to propagate his ideal of the Christian knight as part of the reform of society envisaged by the Church, this ideal shows close parallels to the *De vita sancti Geraldi Auriliacensis*

---

[1] As Beyschlag has suggested, although very much in passing. See p. 293, n. 2.

[2] Cf. Rupp, *Deutsche religiöse Dichtungen*, pp. 6 and 9. Schützeichel, *Das alemannische Memento mori*, does not deal specifically with the problem of the audience addressed by the poet, but his comments on such fundamental concepts as *Friede* and *Fehde* (pp. 117 ff.) and his suggestion that the poem is to be judged in the context of a 'Reform des laikalen Rittertums' (pp. 121 ff.) are revealing enough.

[3] Cf. Kuhn, *Dichtung und Welt im Mittelalter*, p. 110; Schützeichel, *op. cit.* p. 79 and pp. 116 ff.

General conclusions

of Odo of Cluny[1] and is characterised by a pacific conception of the knight's Christian duties which is remote from the crusading ideal[2] and has much more in common with the negative attitude towards warfare still adopted, for example, by Petrus Damiani.[3] A similar feature has been revealed by Beyschlag in the case of the *Wiener Genesis*. He corrects the oversimplified view of A. Weller[4] that military scenes contained in the Bible are omitted by the German author by a careful analysis of precisely those military episodes which have been retained. He establishes that these episodes have been retained for a particular purpose: implicit in each is a condemnation of violence, which is shown to rest on injustice and to issue either in sin or in God's direct intervention to prevent it.[5] Whether we have regard, like Weller, for those episodes which have been simply omitted or, like Beyschlag, for those which have been retained but subjected to a Christian criticism, the result is, as with *Ruodlieb*, a knightly ideal[6] which in its pacifism reflects, as Braun has suggested, the attempts of the Church to reform the knighthood before the rise of the crusading movement created a place for knightly service of God with the sword.

The next stage in this literary process of assimilating warfare to Christianity is represented by those works where a more positive attitude to Christian warfare may be detected, but whose authors have nonetheless hesitated to describe the results of this revision in direct terms. This is an unresolved attitude, characteristic of a painful transition, which we attributed to the author of the *Millstätter Exodus* but which may also be shown, illus-

---

[1] *Studien zum Ruodlieb*, pp. 28 ff., especially pp. 35 ff.

[2] *Ibid.* p. 31: 'Wo liegen die Wurzeln dieses durch eine tiefe Kluft vom traditionellen Heldenbild antiker oder germanischer Prägung getrennten Ideals eines christlichen Rittertums, das über die härtere Züge tragende Dichtung der frühen Kreuzzugszeit hinweg auf die höfische Welt um 1200 vorauszuweisen scheint?'

[3] See Erdmann, *Die Entstehung des Kreuzzugsgedankens*, pp. 131 f.

[4] *Die frühmittelhochdeutsche Wiener Genesis nach Quellen, Übersetzungsart, Stil und Syntax*, p. 51.

[5] *Die Wiener Genesis*, p. 59.

[6] Beyschlag has demonstrated that it is a contemporary knightly ideal which the German author has projected back upon the Old Testament patriarchs.

trated in different ways, in such works as *Ezzos Gesang* and the *Ältere Judith.*

It has recently been suggested that *Ezzos Gesang* is to be judged not merely in the context of the pilgrimage to the Holy Land (to which our attention is drawn by the information given in the *Vita Altmanni*[1]) but more specifically as poetic evidence for the development of the crusading ideal in Germany, even at so early a date as 1064–5. Mergell[2] has drawn attention to the concentrated use in one passage of heroic terminology as part of an ideal of *militia Christi.* Thus precisely those stanzas which treat the exodus from Egypt in its typological significance[3] are followed by a passage which emphasises the dangers which beset the Christians' exodus in markedly military terms: Christ is our *herzoge* (v. 367) and Satan is *der unser alte viant* (v. 363); it is our task to follow Christ in readiness for battle (v. 366: 'den wec scul wir mit wîge varen'), never to lose confidence (v. 368: 'ub uns ne gezwîvelet daz muot') and to gain possession of the lands which are our inheritance (v. 370: 'mit im besizze wir diu lant'). The military tone of this passage has also been stressed by Rupp, who suggests that Satan's wish to harm us (v. 365) means that our way to God in this world must be a battle against the devil, a 'crusade'.[4] It is probably this general suggestion of what he regards as a crusading background which has led Rupp to interpret the exemplary function of one of the stars that shone between the Fall and the birth of Christ (vv. 123 f.: 'sîn lieht daz gab uns Abel, | daz wir durch reht ersterben') as implying not simply the idea of martyrdom, but possibly the particular idea of crusading martyrdom.[5] Likewise, Wentzlaff-Eggebert points out the similarity between the use of *wîgant* (v. 343) or *unser alt erbelant* (v. 352) and the imagery of crusading texts. He also sees in the devil's opposition to our journey (vv. 363 f.) an indication that the devil, as in the *Rolandslied,* incorporates heathendom.[6]

[1] *MGH* SS xii, 230, 5 ff.
[2] *PBB* lxxvi, 213. Cf. also G. Ehrismann, *LG,* ii, 45.
[3] See above, p. 113.
[4] *Deutsche religiöse Dichtungen,* p. 48.　　　　[5] *Ibid.* p. 36.
[6] *Kreuzzugsdichtung des Mittelalters,* p. 37.

Yet it may be questioned whether these military terms and parallels are enough to establish that this poem is a crusading hymn, rather than a pilgrimage song. The difference between the pilgrimage and the crusade rests on the fact that the former was essentially non-military, whereas the latter was a pilgrimage prepared to fight its way through to the Holy Land with the sword. If we wish to argue that *Ezzos Gesang* belongs to the context of the crusading movement, and not simply to the pilgrimage of 1064 to which the *Vita Altmanni* assigns it, then we should have to establish that the military imagery in this poem is used in a manner which agrees with crusading experience, i.e. that it also refers to the fact of physical warfare and not exclusively to a spiritual conflict. This has not been done by Mergell, Rupp or Wentzlaff-Eggebert and, indeed, their suggestion of a crusading context remains a hypothetical one[1] or alternates with the view that *Ezzos Gesang* was after all a pilgrimage song.[2] But despite all the parallels between a pilgrimage and a crusade, physical warfare constitutes the essential difference[3] and it is here that there is no explicit evidence in the German poem to compel us to regard it as a crusading hymn, rather than as a pilgrimage song. It may perhaps be the case that the author employed his imagery in a deliberately ambiguous way so that it could be understood both in its literal and in its metaphorical sense, but until we know that he deviated from the traditional Christian use of these images as metaphors by definitely also intending a literal sense we cannot appropriate this poem for the crusading movement.

[1] Rupp, *op. cit.* p. 48, accordingly takes care to place the word *Kreuzzug* in inverted commas and on p. 36 he qualifies his suggestion by a double *vielleicht* ('hier spielt vielleicht der Gedanke an die Märtyrer und vielleicht auch der Gedanke an den Kreuzzug herein').

[2] Rupp, *op. cit.* p. 81, expresses his agreement with Kuhn's view that the poem was intended for a *Kreuzfahrt*, whereas Wentzlaff-Eggebert, *op. cit.* p. 36, seeks to bridge the gap between a pilgrimage and a crusade by saying that it was composed 'auf der Kreuzfahrt des Bischofs Gunther von Bamberg, die besser als eine bewaffnete Pilgerfahrt bezeichnet wird'. On this see below, p. 446, n. 3.

[3] On the similarities and differences between the two movements see Erdmann, *Die Entstehung des Kreuzzugsgedankens*, pp. 280 ff., Rousset, *Les origines et les caractères de la première croisade*, pp. 39 ff., and Alphandéry, *La chrétienté et l'idée de croisade*, I, 9 ff. Cf. also Setton (ed.), *A History of the Crusades*, I, 68 ff.

The Millstätter Exodus

There remains one possibility whereby this poem (either a pilgrimage song or a poem deliberately ambiguous about the literal or metaphorical sense of its imagery) could come to be regarded as a crusading hymn. This is suggested by the pilgrimage to the Holy Land under the leadership of Gunther of Bamberg in 1064 and by the events which befell those who took part in it.[1] I do not intend to reopen the question whether *Ezzos Gesang* was composed at Bamberg (as the introductory stanza informs us) or on the pilgrimage to the Holy Land (as the *Vita Altmanni* says), for any doubts which may attach to the Latin biography concern only the date and place of composition of the poem— they do not amount to a denial that the poem was known to these pilgrims and was sung by them on their way. In view of this connection between the German poem and the pilgrimage of 1064 we must pay close attention to the evidence that, at one stage at least, this unarmed pilgrimage came to within an inch of developing into a fully fledged crusade. The pilgrimage consisted mainly of laymen and contained a large number of knights,[2] yet there can be no doubt that, like any pilgrimage, it was an unarmed undertaking—here the evidence of our sources, as E. Joranson has shown, is unimpeachable.[3] When they were attacked by Bedouins in the vicinity of Kafar Sallām most of the pilgrims remembered that they had entrusted their safe keeping to God and refused, on clearly religious grounds, to use force in defending themselves,[4] whilst others, probably making up a

---

[1] Contemporary accounts of this pilgrimage are provided by the *Annales Altahenses maiores* under the year 1065 (ed. E. L. B. von Oefele, Hanover, 1891, pp. 66 ff.), the *Annales* of Lambertus Hersfeldensis under the years 1064 and 1065 (ed. O. Holder-Egger, Hanover, 1894, pp. 92 ff.) and by the *Chronicon* of Marianus Scottus under the same years (*MGH SS* v, 558 f.). For a useful exploitation of these and other sources as well as for a historical assessment of the whole pilgrimage see the article by E. Joranson in *The Crusades and other Historical Essays* (ed. Paetow), pp. 3 ff.

[2] See the references given by Joranson, in Paetow, *The Crusades*, p. 11, n. 24.

[3] *Annales Altahenses maiores*, p. 68: *Nostri...ut inermes*. Cf. Joranson, *op. cit.* pp. 14 f.

[4] See the *Annales* of Lambertus Hersfeldensis, p. 94: 'Plerique christianorum religiosum putantes manu sibi auxilium ferre et salutem suam, quam peregre proficiscentes Deo devoverant, armis corporalibus tueri.' Joranson, *op. cit.* p. 21.

rather large minority,[1] were able to persuade themselves that a pilgrimage did not necessarily exclude the use of force in self-defence. To this substantial minority Gunther of Bamberg and his followers belonged. These pilgrims were initially unarmed since they had set out with pacific intentions, but they managed to defend themselves first with stones, in which the area abounded, and later, after they had withdrawn to an unoccupied *castellum* or *atrium*, with javelins, swords and shields which they had managed to wrest from the hands of the enemy. With these weapons they did more than just defend themselves within the *castellum*, for they were able to make sorties and engage in hand-to-hand fighting and, by a successful stratagem, finally make good their escape.

The importance of this episode for our inquiry is twofold. On the one hand it confirms the view that the eleventh century was a period of transition from the tradition of pacific pilgrimages to the military undertakings of the crusading period.[2] Whilst most of the pilgrims, when attacked, remained true to the pilgrimage ideal of religious pacifism even in the case of self-defence,[3] a considerable minority under the leadership of Gunther was prepared to fight. With them the idea of religious pacifism had already largely lost its hold. This fact appears to have caused the chroniclers some embarrassment: some are at pains to justify the pilgrims for having fought because of the brutal attack upon them,[4] others suggest that they were compelled to fight,[5] and others, whilst mentioning that they were attacked, avoid saying

---

[1] Joranson, *ibid.*, draws attention to the revealing use of the words *plerique christianorum* to describe those who refused to defend themselves in the passage quoted in the preceding footnote.

[2] Joranson, *op. cit.* pp. 39 ff.

[3] It hardly needs to be emphasised that the ideal of religious pacifism was by no means confined to the pilgrimage movement. For an example illustrating the general scope of this ideal see *The Carolingian Lord*, p. 323.

[4] See Joranson, *op. cit.* p. 6 and also n. 12 on the *Annales* of Lambertus and on the *Annales Altahenses maiores*.

[5] Joranson, *op. cit.* p. 41, n. 143, quotes from the *Annales* of Berthold (*MGH SS* v, 272, 36 f.) and from the *Chronicon* of Bernold (*ibid.* 428, 27 f.): 'Nam et bellum cum eis inire sunt coacti.'

expressly that they fought at all.[1] Nonetheless, despite this embarrassment and despite the fact that others refused to defend themselves, it is incontestable that in the action of this large minority under Gunther of Bamberg we have an example of the transition from the pilgrimage ideal to the crusading ideal. The second point concerns *Ezzos Gesang* in particular. It is clear from this episode and from the important role played by Gunther in rallying around him those who were prepared to use force that the German hymn, if it was sung frequently on the pilgrimage, would appear in a very different light to Gunther and his followers *after* the events at Kafar Sallām. Although we know nothing of Ezzo's intentions (was the military imagery metaphorical or literal?) and although before this skirmish with the Bedouins his hymn may have been understood in a purely metaphorical sense by those pilgrims who joined in singing it, it is difficult to believe that the hymn was sung in exactly the same spirit after Kafar Sallām and that this experience with the Bedouins did not lead to a greater prominence being granted to the literal sense of a physical warfare demanded of those who were making the exodus to Jerusalem and whose journey had been opposed by the heathen. This literal reading in terms of physical warfare may or may not have been intended by Ezzo, but the events which occurred on the pilgrimage in which he and his episcopal patron took part helped to convert what he may have conceived only as a pilgrims' song into something close to a crusading hymn, just as surely as they contributed to the transition from the unarmed pilgrimage to something similar to a crusading expedition. *Ezzos Gesang* may therefore have been in conception only potentially a crusading poem, but the circumstances under which it was sung brought the implications into full relief.

Whereas it was only the force of circumstances which made explicit what was implicit in *Ezzos Gesang*, adding the literal meaning of physical warfare to what may have been intended as

---

[1] In the *Chronica* of Sigebert (*MGH* SS vi, 361, 21 f.) it is simply reported that the pilgrims were besieged and that many of them were killed or wounded, but *not* that they actually took up arms themselves.

General conclusions

no more than a metaphor, the similar transitional quality of the *Millstätter Exodus*, whose author introduces the theme of physical warfare in a positive function but fails to exploit it by describing it in action, is due entirely to the author's hesitations in developing this new theme. Something similar is also true of the *Ältere Judith*. Here a contemporary crusading background is suggested by the stylisation of the conflict between the Jews and Holofernes into one between Christians and pagans,[1] an interpretation which is strengthened by such heroic terms as *wîglîchi* or *baltlîchi*.[2] In this poem there can be no doubt that the military encounter is also meant in its physical sense: not only because of the historical reality of the warfare between Holofernes and the Jews, but also because Judith, in slaying him, was conceived as killing a real person with a real sword. Even this does not justify us in seeing in the equation of this historical episode with the crusading present a clear acknowledgement of the Christian function of physical warfare. Reservations are suggested by the fact that the theme chosen by the author, although an episode from a divine war waged by the Israelites, does not illustrate the victory conceded by God to the army of His Chosen People, but instead the fact that it was to a woman that God granted this honour.[3] If it was later possible, in the case of the Children's Crusade, to regard the victory that was to be theirs as an implicit criticism of the unsuccessful crusade waged by the knights with the sword,[4] then we should be wise to see in the *Ältere Judith* evidence that the gap between knightly warfare and Christianity had not yet been completely closed. This suspicion is confirmed

[1] See p. 222. [2] Vv. 211 f.

[3] This is brought out more emphatically in the *Jüngere Judith* (128. 2): 'wie er siv beschirmte | mit einem bloden wibelin.'

[4] See Waas, *Geschichte der Kreuzzüge*, I, 253, and also the two quotations given by N. P. Zacour in Setton (ed.), *A History of the Crusades*, II, 326, n. 4, from the *Annales Reineri Sancti Iacobi Leodiensis* for the year 1212 (*MGH* SS XVI, 665, 23: 'Erat autem eorum intentio mare se velle transire, et quod potentes et reges non fecerant, sepulcrum Christi recuperare') and from the *Chronicae regiae Coloniensis continuatio prima* for the year 1213 (*MGH* SS XXIV, 17, 47 ff.), where the failure of so many others ('reges multi, duces plurimi, populi innumerabiles') is contrasted with the unarmed weakness of the children.

by the fact that the poem, as it has come down to us, closes not with a description of Judith striking off the head of Holofernes, but instead with no more than an indirect narration of the words spoken by the angel, instructing her to do precisely this.[1] The physical violence of this biblical theme is not described explicitly, but instead either indirectly (as in the words of the angel) or as an *epische Vorausdeutung* of what is to happen later (e.g. v. 100: *sît slûg in Jûdith ein wîb*). The parallel between this and the *Millstätter Exodus* is obvious: both authors regard Christian warfare in a positive light, but both hesitate to describe such military action openly and directly.

The position occupied by the *Millstätter Exodus*, as well as by *Eʒʒos Gesang* and the *Ältere Judith*, with regard to the problem of crusading warfare is therefore comparable in general terms with those historical events (such as the so-called 'Byzantine crusade', the *Reconquista* of the Iberian peninsula, the battles between the Normans and the Arabs in the Mediterranean and the pilgrimages[2]) which share some of the features of the crusade proper, but which cannot strictly be said to possess all the necessary characteristics of a crusade. These historical phenomena have accordingly been subsumed by French scholarship under the general term *précroisade* (or, alternatively, *presque-croisade* or *avant-croisade*)[3] and it is in a similar sense that we must interpret the position of these three German works. They possess many of the features that characterise a crusade but, in hesitating to take the final step of describing warfare waged on behalf of God or to make this theme explicit, they stop short of unreservedly acknowledging the new ideal.

The final abandonment of these reservations is illustrated in the *Kaiserchronik* and in the *Rolandslied*. In both works warfare on behalf of God, whether in a crusade proper[4] or in a war which

---

[1] Vv. 203 ff.

[2] These have been briefly discussed in the light of the crusading movement by Rousset, *Les origines et les caractères de la première croisade*, pp. 27 ff., and by Waas, *Geschichte der Kreuzzüge*, I, 96 ff.   [3] See Rousset, *op. cit.* p. 27.

[4] As with the description of the First Crusade in the *Kaiserchronik* or with the *Rolandslied*.

is felt to be identifiable with a crusade,[1] is unquestioningly acknowledged. Nonetheless, I should place the *Kaiserchronik* earlier in the process leading to a complete affirmation of crusading warfare in German literature, if only because the crusading theme, however important it may be for an understanding of the author's position,[2] still only informs a certain number of the episodes he treats, whereas in the *Rolandslied* the crusade waged by Charles the Great in Spain is the central theme of the whole work. By this stage the slow and protracted transition from an ideal of Christian knighthood which rejected the use of arms to the crusading ideal in which the knight serves God by wielding the sword had been accomplished.[3] In this process we must accord the Millstatt author a position of decisive importance, for with him a positive Christian function is for the first time assigned to knightly warfare. It is this revaluation of the role of warfare, its elaboration in terms of the crusading ideal, and not least the novel epic form which he evolves to give sustained expression to these new ideas that constitute his main claim on our attention.

[1] As with the treatment, in the *Kaiserchronik*, of the wars waged by Heraclius and by Charles the Great against the heathen.

[2] See Ohly, *Sage und Legende in der Kaiserchronik*, *passim*, and Wentzlaff-Eggebert, *Kreuzzugsdichtung des Mittelalters*, pp. 60 ff. (especially p. 61: 'Die Vorstellung von der notwendigen Ausbreitung des christlichen Gottesstaates unter dem Kaisertum römisch-germanischer Prägung...läßt Idee und Wert der Kreuzzüge zum Begleitthema der Kaiserchronik werden').

[3] A further development was rendered possible at a later stage by the application of certain features of the crusading ideal to the conception of the secular knight which evolved above all in Arthurian literature. I hope to come back later to this problem of the relationship between the crusades and the courtly romance.

BIBLIOGRAPHY

Sources

Ältere Judith, ed. A. Waag, *Kleinere deutsche Gedichte des XI. und XII. Jahrhunderts* (2nd ed.), pp. 38 ff., Halle, 1916.

Alexanderlied, ed. K. Kinzel, Halle, 1884.

Altdeutsche Predigten, ed. A. E. Schönbach, Graz, 1886 ff.

Annolied, ed. K. Meisen, Bonn, 1946.

Battle of Maldon, ed. E. V. Gordon, London, 1949.

Bede, *Historia ecclesiastica gentis Anglorum*, ed. C. Plummer, Oxford, 1896.

Beowulf, ed. F. Klaeber, New York, 1941.

Carmina Burana, ed. A. Hilka and O. Schumann, Heidelberg, 1930 ff.

Chanson de Roland, ed. J. Bédier, Paris, 1947. See also the same author's volume of commentary (3rd ed.), Paris, 1927.

Dante, *Divina Commedia*, ed. G. Vandelli, Milan, 1958.

—— *Letters*, ed. P. Toynbee, London, 1920.

Drei Jünglinge im Feuerofen, ed. A. Waag, *Kleinere deutsche Gedichte des XI. und XII. Jahrhunderts* (2nd ed.), pp. 36 ff., Halle, 1916.

Edda, ed. G. Neckel, Heidelberg, 1914.

Eusebius of Caesarea, *Historia ecclesiastica*, ed. E. Schwartz, Leipzig, 1903 ff.

—— *Vita Constantini*, ed. I. A. Heikel, Leipzig, 1913.

Ezzos Gesang, ed. A. Waag, *Kleinere deutsche Gedichte des XI. und XII. Jahrhunderts* (2nd ed.), pp. 1 ff., Halle, 1916.

Frau Ava, *Das Leben Jesu*, ed. P. Piper, *ZfdPh*, XIX, 140 ff.

Gesta Francorum, ed. R. Hill, London, 1962.

Graf Rudolf, ed. P. F. Ganz, Berlin, 1964.

Hartmann, der arme, *Rede vom Glauben*, ed. F. von der Leyen, Breslau, 1897.

Heinrich von Freiberg, *Die Ritterfahrt des Johann von Michelsberg*, ed. A. Bernt, *Heinrich von Freiberg*, pp. 239 ff., Halle, 1906.

Heliand, ed. O. Behaghel, Halle, 1933.

Herrera, Fernando de, *Poesías*, ed. Don Vicente García de Diego, Madrid, 1914.

Histoire anonyme de la première croisade, ed. L. Bréhier, Paris, 1924.

Historia de preliis, ed. F. Pfister, *Der Alexanderroman des Archipresbyters Leo*, Heidelberg, 1913.

Bibliography

Hochzeit, Die, ed. A. Waag, *Kleinere deutsche Gedichte des XI. und XII. Jahrhunderts* (2nd ed.), pp. 87 ff., Halle, 1916.

Itinerarium Egeriae (Peregrinatio Aetheriae), ed. O. Prinz (5th ed.), Heidelberg, 1960.

Jüngere Judith, ed. J. Diemer, *Deutsche Gedichte des 11. und 12. Jahrhunderts*, pp. 125 ff., Vienna, 1849.

Jüngerer Titurel, ed. K. A. Hahn, Quedlinburg, 1842.

Kaiserchronik, ed. E. Schröder in MGH Deutsche Chroniken, I, 1.

Konrad von Würzburg, *Silvester*, ed. P. Gereke, *Konrad von Würzburg. Die Legenden*, vol. I, Halle, 1925.

—— *Trojanerkrieg*, ed. A. von Keller, Stuttgart, 1858.

Lex Salica: 100 Titel-Text, ed K. A. Eckhardt, Weimar, 1953.

Lob Salomons, ed. A. Waag, *Kleinere deutsche Gedichte des XI. und XII. Jahrhunderts* (2nd ed.), pp. 27 ff., Halle, 1916.

Ludus de Antichristo, ed. K. Langosch, *Geistliche Spiele*, pp. 179 ff., Darmstadt, 1957.

Ludwigslied, ed. W. Braune and K. Helm, *Althochdeutches Lesebuch* (11th ed.), pp. 118 f., Halle, 1949.

Mansi, J. D., *Sacrorum conciliorum nova et amplissima collectio*, Florence, 1759 ff., Venice, 1769 ff., Paris, 1901 ff.

Makkabäer, ed. C. Kraus, *Deutsche Gedichte des 12. Jahrhunderts*, pp. 25 ff., Halle, 1894.

Makkabäer, ed. K. Helm, Tübingen, 1904.

Millstätter Exodus, ed. E. Kossmann, *Die altdeutsche Exodus*, Strassburg, 1886.

Notker Balbulus, ed. W. von den Steinen, *Notker der Dichter und seine geistige Welt*, Bern, 1948.

Odo of Cluny, *Vita Sancti Geraldi Auriliacensis*, *MPL*, 133, 639 ff.

Oeuvres poétiques de Baudri de Bourgueil, ed. P. Abrahams, Paris, 1926.

Old English Exodus, ed. E. B. Irving, New Haven, 1953.

Ordericus Vitalis, *Historia ecclesiastica*, ed. A. Le Prévost, Paris, 1838 ff.

Otfrids Evangelienbuch, ed. O. Erdmann, Halle, 1882.

Oxford Book of Medieval Latin Verse, ed. F. J. E. Raby, Oxford, 1959.

Physiologus, ed. F. Wilhelm, *Denkmäler deutscher Prosa des 11. und 12. Jahrhunderts*, pp. 4 ff. and 13 ff., Munich, 1960.

Poésies complètes du troubadour Marcabru, ed. J. M. L. Dejeanne, Toulouse, 1909.

Reinbot von Durne, *Der heilige Georg*, ed. C. von Kraus, Heidelberg, 1907.

Rolandslied, ed. F. Maurer, Leipzig, 1940.

453

Bibliography

Rudolf von Ems, *Alexanderlied*, ed. V. Junk, Leipzig, 1928.
—— *Weltchronik*, ed. G. Ehrismann, Berlin, 1915.
Speculum ecclesiae, ed. G. Mellbourn, Lund, 1944.
Tacitus, *Germania*, ed. J. G. C. Anderson, Oxford, 1938.
Thomasin von Zerclære, *Der welsche Gast*, ed. H. Rückert, Quedlinburg, 1852.
Vorauer Bücher Mosis, ed. J. Diemer, *Deutsche Gedichte des 11. und 12. Jahrhunderts*, pp. 1 ff., Vienna, 1849.
Waltharius, ed. K. Strecker, Berlin, 1947.
Walther von der Vogelweide, ed. C. von Kraus, Berlin, 1950.
Wiener Genesis, ed. V. Dollmayr, Halle, 1932.
William of Poitiers, *Gesta Guillelmi*, ed. R. Foreville, Paris, 1952.
Wulfila, ed. W. Streitberg, Heidelberg, 1919.

Secondary literature

Alphandéry, P., *La chrétienté et l'idée de croisade*, Paris, 1954.
Auerbach, E., *Scenes from the Drama of European Literature*, New York, 1959.
—— *Typologische Motive in der mittelalterlichen Literatur* (2nd ed.), Krefeld, 1964.
Baetke, W., *Religion und Politik in der Germanenbekehrung*, Leipzig, 1937.
—— *Das Heilige im Germanischen*, Tübingen, 1942.
—— *Vom Geist und Erbe Thules*, Göttingen, 1944.
Bainton, R. H., *Christian Attitudes towards War and Peace*, London, 1961.
Bayer, H. J., *Untersuchungen zum Sprachstil weltlicher Epen des deutschen Früh- und Hochmittelalters*, Berlin, 1962.
Bédier, *Les légendes épiques*, Paris, 1926 ff.
—— *Chanson de Roland. Commentaires* (3rd ed.), Paris, 1927.
Berron, G., *Studien zum Heliand als Kunstwerk*, Tübingen dissertation, 1939.
Beyschlag, S., *Die Wiener Genesis. Idee, Stoff und Form* (Sitzungsberichte der Akademie der Wissenschaften in Wien, vol. 220, 3), Vienna, 1942.
Boeckler, A., *Die Regensburg-Prüfeninger Buchmalerei des XII. und XIII. Jahrhunderts*, Munich, 1924.
Boor, H. de, *Frühmittelhochdeutsche Studien*, Halle, 1926.
—— *Geschichte der deutschen Literatur von den Anfängen bis zur Gegenwart*, Munich, 1949 ff.

Bibliography

Bovini, G., *The Churches of Ravenna*, Novara, 1960.

Braun, W., *Studien zum Ruodlieb*, Berlin, 1962.

Bulst, W., *Festschrift for*, Heidelberg, 1960.

Bumke, J., *Wolframs Willehalm*, Heidelberg, 1959.

—— *Studien zum Ritterbegriff im 12. und 13. Jahrhundert*, Heidelberg, 1964.

Chanson de Geste und höfischer Roman (*Studia Romanica*, vol. 4), Heidelberg, 1963.

Chydenius, J., *The Typological Problem in Dante*, Helsingfors, 1958.

Curtius, E. R., *Europäische Literatur und lateinisches Mittelalter*, Bern, 1948.

Dahl, N. A., *Das Volk Gottes*, Oslo, 1941.

Daniélou, J., *Sacramentum futuri*, Paris, 1950.

—— *Bible et liturgie*, Paris, 1951.

Deinert, W., *Ritter und Kosmos im Parzival*, Munich, 1960.

Dölger, F. J., *Die Sonne der Gerechtigkeit und der Schwarze*, Münster, 1918.

Dürrenmatt, N., *Das Nibelungenlied im Kreis der höfischen Dichtung*, Bern, 1945.

Ehrismann, G., *Geschichte der deutschen Literatur bis zum Ausgang des Mittelalters*, Munich, 1922 ff.

Ehrismann, G., *Festschrift for*, Berlin, 1925.

Eichrodt, W., *Theologie des Alten Testaments*, Leipzig, 1933 ff.

Eisenhofer, L., *Grundriß der Liturgik des römischen Ritus* (5th ed. by J. Lechner), Freiburg, 1950.

Erdmann, C., *Die Entstehung des Kreuzzugsgedankens*, Stuttgart, 1935.

Fliegner, G., *Geistliches und weltliches Rittertum im Rolandslied des Pfaffen Konrad*, Breslau dissertation, 1937.

Focillon, H., *Peintures romanes des églises de France*, Paris, 1938.

Freudenthal, K. F., *Arnulfingisch-karolingische Rechtswörter*, Tübingen, 1949.

Fromm, H., *Untersuchungen zum Marienleben des Priesters Wernher* (Annales Universitatis Turkuensis, B, LII), Turku, 1955.

Gehl, W., *Der germanische Schicksalsglaube*, Berlin, 1939.

Green, D. H., *The Carolingian Lord*, Cambridge, 1965.

Guéranger, P., *L'année liturgique*, Tours, 1920 ff.

Gutenbrunner, S., *Die germanischen Götternamen der antiken Inschriften*, Halle, 1936.

Haacke, D., *Weltfeindliche Strömungen und die Heidenfrage*, Berlin dissertation (Freie Universität), 1951.

455

Bibliography

Hagenmeyer, H., *Epistulae et chartae ad historiam primi belli sacri spectantes*, Innsbruck, 1901.

Harnack, A., *Militia Christi*, Tübingen, 1905.

Harvey, R., *Moriʒ von Craûn and the Chivalric World*, Oxford, 1961.

Hebert, G., *When Israel came out of Egypt*, London, 1961.

Helm, K., *Altgermanische Religionsgeschichte*, Heidelberg, 1913 ff.

—— *Wodan. Ausbreitung und Wanderung seines Kultes*, Giessen, 1946.

Helm, K. and Ziesemer, W., *Die Literatur des Deutschen Ritterordens*, Giessen, 1951.

Helm, K., *Festschrift for*, Tübingen, 1951.

Herold, G., *Der Volksbegriff im Sprachschatʒ des Althochdeutschen und Altniederdeutschen*, Halle, 1941.

Heusler, A., *Germanentum* (4th ed.), Heidelberg, n.d.

Hortus Deliciarum. Le 'Jardin des Délices' de Herrade de Landsberg, Strasbourg, 1945. (No editor or author given, but the introduction is by E. and J. G. Rott.)

Jantsch, H. G., *Studien ʒum Symbolischen in frühmittelhochdeutscher Literatur*, Tübingen, 1959.

Jungmann, J. A., *The Early Liturgy*, London, 1960.

Katzenellenbogen, A., *Allegories of the Virtues and Vices in Medieval Art*, London, 1939.

—— *The Sculptural Programs of Chartres Cathedral*, Baltimore, 1959.

Kelle, J., *Glossar der Sprache Otfrids*, Regensburg, 1881.

—— *Geschichte der deutschen Literatur von der ältesten Zeit bis ʒur Mitte des elften Jahrhunderts*, Berlin, 1892 ff.

Kennedy, C. W., *The Earliest English Poetry*, London, 1943.

Kern, F., *Gottesgnadentum und Widerstandsrecht im früheren Mittelalter* (ed. R. Buchner), Darmstadt, 1954.

Kienle, R. von, *Germanische Gemeinschaftsformen*, Berlin, 1939.

Kittel, G. (ed.), *Theologisches Wörterbuch ʒum Neuen Testament*, Stuttgart, 1932 ff.

Knab, D., *Das Annolied. Probleme seiner literarischen Einordnung*, Tübingen, 1962.

Köhler, E., *Ideal und Wirklichkeit in der höfischen Epik*, Tübingen, 1956.

—— *Trobadorlyrik und höfischer Roman*, Berlin, 1962.

Kolb, H., *Der Begriff der Minne und das Entstehen der höfischen Lyrik*, Tübingen, 1958.

Kuhn, H., *Dichtung und Welt im Mittelalter*, Stuttgart, 1959.

Lammers, W. (ed.), *Geschichtsdenken und Geschichtsbild im Mittelalter*, Darmstadt, 1961.

Bibliography

Lange, W., *Studien zur christlichen Dichtung der Nordgermanen 1000–1200*, Göttingen, 1958.

Le Gentil, P., *La Chanson de Roland*, Paris, 1955.

Lewis, C. S., *The Allegory of Love*, Oxford, 1946.

Löwith, K., *Weltgeschichte und Heilsgeschehen* (4th ed.), Stuttgart, 1961.

McKenzie, D. A., *Otfrid von Weissenburg: Narrator or Commentator?*, Stanford, 1946.

Mâle, E. *La fin du paganisme en Gaule et les plus anciennes basiliques chrétiennes*, Paris, 1950.

Mathew, G., *Byzantine Aesthetics*, London, 1963.

Maurer, F., *Festschrift for*, Bern, 1963.

Mauss, M., *The Gift* (transl. I. Cunnison), London, 1954.

Melville, M., *La vie des Templiers*, Paris, 1951.

Menéndez Pidal, R., *La Chanson de Roland et la tradition épique des Francs*, Paris, 1960.

Nardi, B., *Gli angeli che non furon ribelli ne' fur fedeli a Dio*, Alcamo, 1959.

Neumann, E., *Das Schicksal in der Edda*, Giessen, 1955.

Ohly, F., *Sage und Legende in der Kaiserchronik*, Münster, 1940.

—— *Hohelied-Studien, Grundzüge einer Geschichte der Hoheliedauslegung des Abendlandes bis um 1200*, Wiesbaden, 1958.

Ohly, W., *Die heilsgeschichtliche Struktur der Epen Hartmanns von Aue*, Berlin dissertation (Freie Universität), 1958.

Olschki, L., *Die romanischen Literaturen des Mittelalters*, Potsdam, 1928.

Paetow, L. J. (ed.), *The Crusades and other Historical Essays*, New York, 1928.

Panzer, F., *Das Nibelungenlied. Entstehung und Gestalt*, Stuttgart, 1955.

Paris, G., *Histoire poétique de Charlemagne*, Paris, 1865.

Perlbach, M., *Die Statuten des Deutschen Ordens*, Halle, 1890.

Rathofer, J., *Der Heliand. Theologischer Sinn als tektonische Form*, Cologne, 1962.

Réau, L., *Iconographie de l'art chrétien*, Paris, 1955 ff.

Rousset, P., *Les origines et les caractères de la première croisade*, Neuchâtel, 1945.

Runciman, S., *A History of the Crusades*, Cambridge, 1951 ff.

Rupp, H., *Deutsche religiöse Dichtungen des 11. und 12. Jahrhunderts*, Freiburg, 1958.

Ruprecht, D., *Tristitia. Wortschatz und Vorstellung in den althochdeutschen Sprachdenkmälern*, Göttingen, 1959.

Schmidt, K. D., *Die Bekehrung der Germanen zum Christentum*, Göttingen, 1936 ff.

Bibliography

Schmidt, K. D., *Germanischer Glaube und Christentum*, Göttingen, 1948.

Schücking, L. L., *Heldenstolz und Würde im Angelsächsischen* (Abhandlungen der philologisch-historischen Klasse der sächsischen Akademie der Wissenschaften, XLII, 5), Leipzig, 1933.

Schützeichel, R., *Das alemannische Memento mori*, Tübingen, 1962.

Schwietering, J., *Deutsche Dichtung des Mittelalters*, Potsdam, n.d.

Sedlmayr, H., *Die Entstehung der Kathedrale*, Zürich, 1950.

Sehrt, E. H. and Legner, W. K., *Notker-Wortschatz*, Halle, 1955.

Setton, K. M. (ed.), *A History of the Crusades*, Philadelphia, 1958 ff.

Sitte, E., *Die Datierung von Lamprechts Alexander*, Halle, 1940.

Smalley, B., *The Study of the Bible in the Middle Ages*, Oxford, 1952.

Stammler, W., *Deutsche Philologie im Aufriß*, Berlin, 1952 ff.

—— *Kleine Schriften zur Literaturgeschichte des Mittelalters*, Berlin, 1953.

Steinen, W. von den, *Notker der Dichter und seine geistige Welt*, Bern, 1948.

Streitberg, W., Festschrift for, Heidelberg, 1924, and Leipzig, 1924.

Tolkien, J. R. R., *Beowulf. The Monsters and the Critics* (Proceedings of the British Academy, XXII), London, 1936.

Tristram, E. W., *English Medieval Wall Painting. The Twelfth Century*, Oxford, 1944.

Trübners Deutsches Wörterbuch, ed. A. Götze, Berlin, 1939 ff.

Tyrer, J. W., *Historical Survey of Holy Week, its Services and Ceremonial*, London, 1932.

Ullmann, W., *The Growth of Papal Government in the Middle Ages* (2nd ed.), London, 1962.

Volbach, W. F., *Early Christian Art*, London, 1961.

de Vries, J., *Die geistige Welt der Germanen*, Halle, 1945.

—— *Altgermanische Religionsgeschichte* (2nd ed.), Berlin, 1956 ff.

Waas, A., *Geschichte der Kreuzzüge*, Freiburg, 1956.

Wachinger, B., *Studien zum Nibelungenlied*, Tübingen, 1960.

Wallace-Hadrill, J. M., *The Long-haired Kings*, London, 1962.

Wapnewski, P., *Wolframs Parzival. Studien zur Religiosität und Form*, Heidelberg, 1955.

Weller, A., *Die frühmittelhochdeutsche Wiener Genesis nach Quellen, Übersetzungsart, Stil und Syntax*, Berlin, 1914.

Wellhausen, J., Festschrift for, Giessen, 1914.

Wentzlaff-Eggebert, F.-W., *Kreuzzugsdichtung des Mittelalters*, Berlin, 1960.

Wetzer, H. J., and Welte, B., *Kirchenlexikon*, Freiburg, 1882 ff.

Bibliography

Willems, F., *Heldenwörter in germanischer und christlicher Literatur*, Cologne dissertation, 1942.

Williams, A. L., *Adversus Judaeos*, Cambridge, 1935.

Wisbey, R., *Das Alexanderbild Rudolfs von Ems*, Frankfurt dissertation, 1956.

Wolff, L., *Das deutsche Schrifttum bis zum Ausgang des Mittelalters* (2nd ed.), Göttingen 1951.

Zimmermann, H., *Ecclesia als Objekt der Historiographie* (Österreichische Akademie der Wissenschaften, 235, 4), Vienna, 1960.

Zumthor, P., *Merlin le prophète*, Lausanne, 1943.

INDEX

Index

Index

Index

Index

Index

Index

Robertus Monachus, 143, 238, 239, 243, 244, 245, 247, 252, 253, 259, 261, 262, 263, 264, 269, 363 n., 367, 369, 399, 417
Roland, 219, 232, 322
Rolandslied, 121 n., 137, 158 n., 161, 165, 169, 219, 224 n., 225–7, 231, 235, 236, 278 n., 285 n., 291, 297–9, 305, 321–4, 344 n., 345, 394, 399–405, 407–9, 431, 439 n., 444, 450–1
Rudolf von Ems, 225, 379–80
Ruodlieb, 389, 394 n., 433, 434, 442, 443

Saladin, 27, 410
Silvester, Pope, 145–7
slavery
of Christians, 16, 18, 28, 33 n., 78–9, 104, 372
of Israel, 8, 9, 18, 20–1, 28, 33 n., 46, 57–8, 71, 77–9, 84, 100, 104, 162–3, 164, 372
sphragis, 379, 382, 383, 413
Stephen, St, 319–20, 321 n., 324
superbia, 24, 95, 98, 143, 146–7, 169, 181, 187, 256, 337, 342, 343, 345, 348–9, 355, 359, 361, 391–2, 426, 431, 437

Tancred, 276
Templars, Order of, 233, 292 n., 293, 393–4, 396, 430 n.
tension,
as a narrative device, 44, 50, 52, 75, 86–7, 88, 89, 90, 97, 376
Thomasin von Zerclære, 436 n.
time, concept of, 122–5, 141–2
time-references, 44–5, 60–1, 64–8, 72, 73, 74–5
trehtin (or *truhtin*), 134–5, 194–5, 199 n., 210
Turpin, Bishop, 137 n., 226, 321, 322, 323, 399, 400, 401, 404, 408
typology, 10, 18, 22, 23, 85, 94, 110 n., 112, 119–20, 128, 130–1, 143, 187, 189–91, 199–200, 201–2, 250–1, 257–8, 260 n., 265 n., 266, 307–12, 313, 317–25, 339–41,

346–8, 356–8, 363–4, 378–9, 380 388, 424–30, 441 n.
antithetical, 338–9, 341, 343, 344, 348, 353, 356, 358

Urban II, Pope, 244, 251, 252, 255, 259, 260, 261, 263, 265, 268, 269, 276, 283 n., 286, 287, 296, 301, 319, 323, 330, 359, 363 n., 367, 368, 391, 392 n., 398–9, 400, 418, 419, 420, 422

vengeance, 149–50, 226, 278–83, 285–6, 290, 294
rejection of, 278–80
verdammôn, 21
Vorauer Bücher Mosis, 56, 114–17, 118, 119, 120, 122, 151, 220, 326, 341–2, 343, 346, 348, 349, 356, 359, 375

Waltharius, 169 n.
Walther von der Vogelweide, 278 n., 288, 294 n., 326 n., 334 n., 335, 370
warfare
allusions to, 81, 83–107, 143, 154–62, 185–6, 228, 307 n., 308–9, 438–9
Christian epics, 218–27
Christianity, 24, 28, 29, 86, 88, 94–5, 189, 203–5, 206–7, 209, 213–18, 228, 234, 244, 258–71, 283, 290, 294–5, 419–20, 430–51
criticism of, 161–2, 184, 185, 207, 209–10, 214, 220, 286 n., 303, 357, 389, 433–4, 443, 446–7
Germanic religion, 193–5, 197–8, 203, 207
Old Testament, 193–5, 196–8, 203, 207–9, 228
religious problem of defeat, 211–13, 222, 249–50, 264–5, 287
Wodan, 194, 196
Wulfila, attitude to warfare, 209–10

Zambres (or Zambri), 145–7
zwîvel, 28, 48, 99–101, 346, 348, 349, 350–63, 372, 374, 390 n., 392, 418, 426, 427, 431, 438

467